Strategic Accounting for Management

Dedicated to opportunists everywhere!

Strategic Accounting for Management

Bob Ryan
Professor of Financial Management
Royal Holloway,
University of London, UK

Australia • Canada • Mexico • Singapore • Spain • United Kingdom • United States

Strategic Accounting for Management

For more information, contact Thomson Learning, High Holborn House, 50-51 Bedford Row, London WC1R 4LR or visit us on the World Wide Web at:
http://www.thomsonlearning.co.uk

British Library Cataloguing-in-Publication Data
A catalogue record for this book is available from the British Library

---

ISBN 1-86152-462-5

First published 1995 by The Dryden Press, Harcourt Brace & Co, Ltd
Reprinted 2001, 2003 and 2005 by Thomson Learning

Printed in the UK by TJI Digital, Padstow, Cornwall

Contents

Preface

This book represents some three years of effort. In it I offer a range of ideas and methods which have proven very useful to student managers, companies and, indeed, to myself over the years. The title of this book represents the last vestige of a debate I have had with my publisher.

I believe the ideas contained in this book have wider implications than the purely strategic. What I have written should be of equal relevance to the operational as well as the strategic manager. The key concept for all levels of management is the idea of the business 'opportunity' and its systematic exploitation. For me, accounting should be about enabling managers to value their opportunities and efficiently control the resources consumed in their exploitation.

Finally, with your help I can engage in a process of continuous improvement on this book. Please feel free to contact me with your criticisms and suggestions for improvements.

Bob Ryan
February 1995

Acknowledgements

In 1984, John Hobson and I wrote *Management Accounting – a contemporary approach* which was a great critical (but modest financial) success. John did not join me on this project but I owe him a great debt for the ideas we worked through together in that earlier book. Many of those ideas have survived the intervening decade and appear in this book.

Over the year I have had the privilege of teaching many able students, some of whom have gone on to eminent positions in commerce and industry. It is a fact of management teaching that the students give back as much as they receive from their tutor. In the best classes the role of the tutor is to sort out the ideas and make sense of them for the whole group. I am indebted to them all.

I would also like to acknowledge intellectual support from an unusual source. During my years as Director of the Southampton University Management School, I enjoyed the support and mentoring of Dr Stanley Crooks, Vice Chairman of University Council and ex Chairman of Pireli General. Stanley contributed many pungent insights into my approach to financial management and into the problems of successfully managing a business enterprise. Many of those insights are reflected in this book.

Finally, many thanks to the team at Thomson Learning and especially Jennifer Pegg for her efforts in bringing this book to fruition.

Chapter 1

Introduction

Level E

Contents

Summary

This chapter will introduce you to the financial problems which beset all types of organisation. I then introduce three important principles or laws of financial management and invite you to consider the role of theory in management and suggest that theoretical reasoning is intrinsic in all thought – what matters is to have simple but effective theories about how the world of management works. Finally, I offer a route map through this book with different chapter sequences dependent upon your preferences and experience.

INTRODUCTION

The only equilibrium position for a business is failure.

This book is dominated by the proposition that there is no sustainable equilibrium for any organisation. If a business does not grow it will fail. This is an empirical proposition which is rarely, if ever, contradicted. However, much of the business literature suffers under the illusion of success. That is, at any point in time, the only organisations we see are those which have survived, some of whom may have survived in the same form for many years. Since the Second World War less than one in a hundred firms which have been started still exist. Of all new start-ups less than one in six remain in existence at the end of five years.

This may seem a rather pessimistic way to start a book on strategic accounting and finance for the management market. But, in my view, much of the business literature fails miserably when it comes to the problem of how to survive. For the manager, there is no 'winning through', there is no 'ultimate success'. All there is, is a persistent attention to detail, the avoidance of damaging decisions, the careful analysis of opportunities and the ruthless balancing of the various forces which impact upon any organisation.

Few firms have the power to deflect market or economic forces. Only the very largest companies can significantly effect markets – and the overwhelming majority of you reading this book do not work in, or own, businesses with that sort of power. The best that can be managed is to learn how to cope with the markets which our businesses face and turn those markets to our best advantage.

Some businesses fail because they cannot withstand the competitive pressures and changing fortunes of the market place. Others fail because of internal contradictions or weaknesses within their management. We know from the physical sciences that closed systems, i.e. systems which have no possibility of interaction with their environment, become progressively more chaotic or disordered as time goes by. Open systems, such as business firms, also become more disordered over time unless positive work is applied to hold back or reverse that process. In the business context, this is the role of management. Management's supreme duty is to seek out opportunities for the business to work, and to coordinate and control that work in the most effective way possible.

The role of the manager is central to the concept of an organisation. Indeed, it is difficult to conceive of a completely unmanaged organisation. Like the perpetual-motion machine, such an entity does not exist. In this book, we focus on the functions of finance, financial management, and financial and management accounting in as far as they support the needs of the general and the operational managers within the firm. In particular we consider the problems of financial management from the coordinator's rather than the specialist's point of view. This is a book, therefore, for the general manager who wishes to understand the implications of finance for the business as a whole, or for other managers who need to understand and direct the efforts of financial specialists.

So this is not a book for those who are training to become producers of financial information but rather for those, who by virtue of their position and their responsibilities need to interpret that information. The title of this book is designed to reflect the orientation of our subject. 'Strategic accounting for management' lays claim to a way of treating the topic and our market. However, our treatment extends the concepts of strategic management to include the systematic search, discovery, evaluation and exploitation of opportunities.

RYAN'S THREE LAWS OF FINANCIAL MANAGEMENT

Law 1: the financial critical success factor

A business will not survive if, by using its core capability and by operating in the most cost-efficient way, it cannot generate sufficient cash to cover the costs of sustaining that core capability.

Law 2: the law of financial events

Costs and revenues only arise when cash flows occur across organisational boundaries.

Law 3: the law of financial dynamics

Short-term changes in corporate liquidity are positively associated with changes in contribution-generating sales under neutral or positive terms of trade. Short-term changes in corporate liquidity are negatively associated with changes in contribution-generating sales under negative terms of trade.

RYAN'S THREE LAWS OF FINANCIAL MANAGEMENT

Laws are very difficult to find in business. Those which have been defined over the years, such as the laws of diminishing returns and demand are derived necessarily from the way economic terms are defined. They are not empirical laws in that they are not derived from observation in the first instance. The three financial laws of business are similar in that they are truths derived from the essential logic of business itself. However, the logic of these three laws lie right at the heart of running a business and they therefore lie at the heart of this book.

The first law says that a business will not survive unless it can generate sufficient cash surplus from its operations to fund the costs of sustaining itself in existence. The second law strips away much of the mystique of accounting and goes to the nub of what is a cost or a revenue to a business. The defining event which yields a cost or a revenue is that point at which cash passes in or out of an organisation's control, i.e., when cash passes over the organisational barrier either coming in or going out of the business. Finally, the third law is the primary governing factor determining the ability of a business to respond financially to changes in its trading fortunes. It is not the case, for example, that a business can necessarily improve its short-term financial position by increasing its volume of trade (how much it sells), even if that trading is deemed to be 'profitable'. It all depends on the speed with which the business can recover cash from its customers compared with the time it is required to take to pay its various suppliers.

Over many years of teaching and practising financial management I have become convinced that understanding these three laws is critical to the success of any business, and that their implications influence general management in quite profound ways. In this book, I define the topic of 'strategic accounting' which is concerned with the implications of these three laws across management. In my view, the conventional distinctions of 'financial' and 'management' accounting are becoming less relevant in business. The professionalisation of accounting over the last 50 years has produced a stratification of the subject and a degree of specialisation which has made the problems of the financial management of organisations much more difficult than it ever needs to be. In this book I strip away the mystique of finance and show how a single, overall view of the financial management of firms can be created.

Over the last 20 years the academic industry has generated a wide range of theories about the effective management of business firms. In addition, Western manufacturing industry has been hit by the combined forces of recession and the impact of sophisticated, and sometimes devastating, competition from the Pacific rim countries. This competition has stimulated, and partly been a product of, a change in values from technologically driven to customer-led manufacturing and services. From cars to telephones, from shipbuilding to financial services, customers have begun to perceive that it is their agenda that counts not that of the technologists and the producers.

In this climate, many of the old ways of thinking about business in the West have crumbled and the old certainties lost. Business managers, who are often under intense pressure, are required to build strategies for coping and planning for future opportunities as well as finding ways to produce their products more efficiently, on time and to the quality standards demanded by their customers. This book is the product of extensive deliberations with my intended customers – practising managers. They have told me that this book should:

- help them understand the major financial issues which their businesses are likely to face;
- be readily understandable and easily translated into their own business context;
- present them with descriptions of good, as well as actual, practice;
- focus on the exploitation of business opportunities in terms of valuing those opportunities and controlling the consequences of the decisions made.

We have discerned an increasing impatience with the finance functions within business partly, we suspect, because of the increased professionalism of other branches of management, and partly because of a slow recognition that accountants and other finance specialists have not upgraded their underlying theories of management. Many accountants talk about management in the terms of the nineteenth rather than the late twentieth century, and the majority of textbooks on the subject appear to be in the philosophical traditions of Kafka rather than Descartes.

Too often strong businesses entered a terminal stage because they did not recognise the dynamic problems of managing their cash flows. They have in many cases been subjected to considerable amounts of accounting advice, and no one is more surprised than the accountant when something goes wrong. The problem is that most accountants and finance specialists are neither experienced nor trained in management. With the best will in the world they lack the vision, and indeed the responsibility, of being a manager. In particular, the manager knows that his or her priorities are cash return, cash flow and cash control. Profit measures are invariably too subjective and imprecise to be useful except as overall measures of corporate performance.

In this book I stress the importance of understanding the cash mechanics of business organisations. This approach capitalises on recent developments in financial and economic modelling, production planning and methodology (including Total Quality Management) and generates a simple and logical framework for the design of financial information systems within all production-oriented organisations.

Accounting is just one part of any organisation's total management function and should be designed to serve the needs of effective managerial decision making. The older emphasis on standardised procedures is giving way to more flexible accounting systems which focus on the analysis of business opportunities. In addition, the problems of measuring and reporting 'profit' and 'income', whilst important, are now being recognised as subordinate, 'presentational' issues, and cash management and optimisation are seen as the key to long-term business success.

This book has some features designed to enhance its utility:

(i) Chapters are restricted to approximately 4000 words. This word count is close to the limit which a careful and thoughtful reader can understand before exhaustion sets in. This book also offers a more balanced approach in the use of graphics, numerical examples and written descriptions than is common in accounting books. In my experience, practising managers find the heavy reliance on numbers in such books somewhat daunting as they do have a marked preference for contextualising and arguing issues. I have attempted to satisfy that general preference within this book.

(ii) Each chapter is, in the modern jargon, 'modular' in that even though cross-chapter references and allusions may be made, each chapter is largely self-contained. The benefit of this is that each chapter can be studied independently of others and 80% or more of the content can be understood at a useful level without cross reference to other material. However, the serial reader will discover that our material has a theme which we discuss later in this chapter. But in order to achieve a reasonable degree of independence between chapters, a degree of repetition of basic material has proved necessary. I apologise to the serial reader, although I hope that the variation in presentation of repeated material will relieve the burden somewhat.

(iii) Each chapter is graded at its head as follows.

E Easy reading – concentrates on the fundamental concepts of accounting and finance and their implication for business.

M Moderate difficulty – some abstract material developed which involves insights from other subject areas not within the scope of general knowledge.

G Graded chapter – the first sections are at the E level but the latter sections move rapidly to the D level.

D Difficult material – explores more advanced conceptual and technical ideas.

(iv) At the end of the book there is a range of questions and cases which the manager should find useful in practising the skills and techniques explored in this book. A workshop manual consisting of more technical information on methods will be made available as a companion text.

(v) Good quality bibliographic references are given at the end of the book with an indication of the relevance of that reading to the material presented. In this way the interruptions in the main body of the text through citations has been kept to a minimum.

THE READERS OF THIS BOOK – OUR MANAGERIAL MARKET

Approximately 10% of the work force in Britain has some form of managerial responsibility in that:

- they plan and decide upon the allocation of physical and/or human resources to meet opportunities presented to them; and/or
- they are involved in leadership, motivation and the control of people; and/or
- they are involved in the control of material and financial resources.

From this description, it is clear that management is a generic activity which applies to all walks of life. Indeed, there are great similarities between the skills required to effectively run a family and those required to run a business. In this book the approach adopted should appeal to anyone involved in management in industry, commerce, or the public sector. Many of the examples in this book are drawn from the area of manufacturing because that sector best exemplifies the issues of production and control which are central to our treatment of strategic accounting. There are some unique issues in service industries and the public sector which we address when they become relevant in the text.

In industry, management is conventionally described in the following terms.

- *Strategic* (concerned with the integrative and directional purpose of the organisation as a whole or in substantial part). This is usually a 'senior management' role within the business.
- *Operational* (concerned with conversion of organisational resources into products and services in accordance with the strategic intent of the business). The operations management role covers all levels of seniority, in that in a large organisation there will almost certainly be a director of operations with senior management support, as well as middle-ranking and junior managers working for them.
- *Functional* (concerned with specialist management tasks in the areas of finance, marketing, procurement, sales, human resources and R&D). Again, each functional area will have managers of different levels of seniority working within it.
- *Administrative* (concerned with the successful procedural execution of the organisation's strategic, operational and functional activities). Prior to the 1930s the term 'management' was not widely used in business and commerce, although the concept of an administrator was

well understood. Administrators were usually depicted as individuals who execute the decisions of others through the application of rules and procedures. Today, there are still some specialist administrative tasks associated with the office of the Company Secretary and with personnel in most large commercial concerns, although the public services are still largely administered as opposed to managed organisations.

In Figure 1.1 we show how these different areas of management interact to deliver the overall performance of the organisation. Within each manager's role he or she will have some decision-making power over the deployment of the firm's available resources. In each of the four quadrants of management described above and shown in Figure 1.1 there will be differing levels of seniority. For junior levels of management, decision making is usually restricted to those areas where the consequences are realised over a short time horizon. Decisions about the operating conditions of plant, or the deployment of medical staff between wards, take their effect and yield their results over very short periods of time. At the middle levels of management, decisions about product pricing, marketing campaigns and volumes of output are likely to generate consequences both in the short and the intermediate term. However, at the senior management level, decisions about mergers and acquisitions, sourcing finance and market positioning may well have profound consequences over many years. This time function, as depicted in Figure 1.2, has implications for the resourcing and cost consequences of decisions. Senior management typically has all of the costs of the organisation under its control, whereas at lower levels, as we shall see in later chapters, the degree of managerial discretion over cost becomes much more restricted.

This characterisation of management indicates a wide range of potential readership for this book, but that the issues which those various levels find most pertinent may well differ. However, there are some eternal truths in the financial management of business of which all managers should be aware. In this book we seek to expose those truths and make their consequences very clear for management decision making.

THE ROLE OF THEORY IN ACCOUNTING AND FINANCE

In this book we deploy many theoretical arguments making assumptions about the ways individuals and firms work, the way the economy works and so on. What we mean by theory is where general assumptions are used, either to allow us to deduce certain

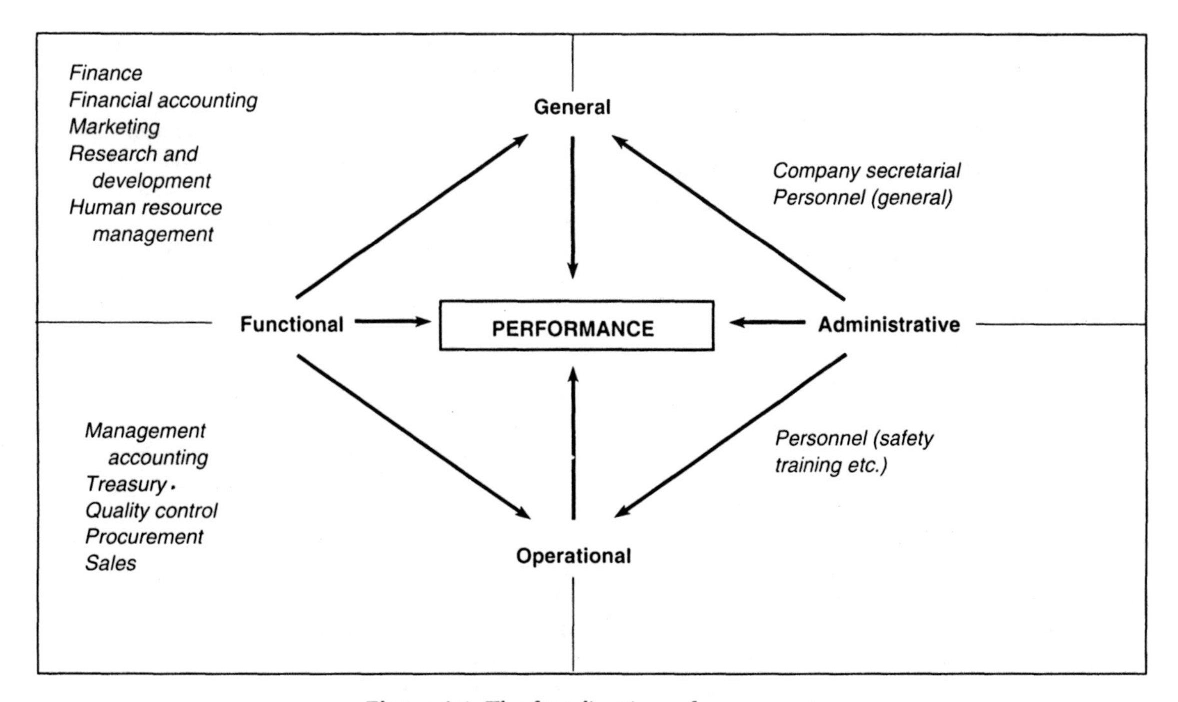

Figure 1.1 The four directions of management.

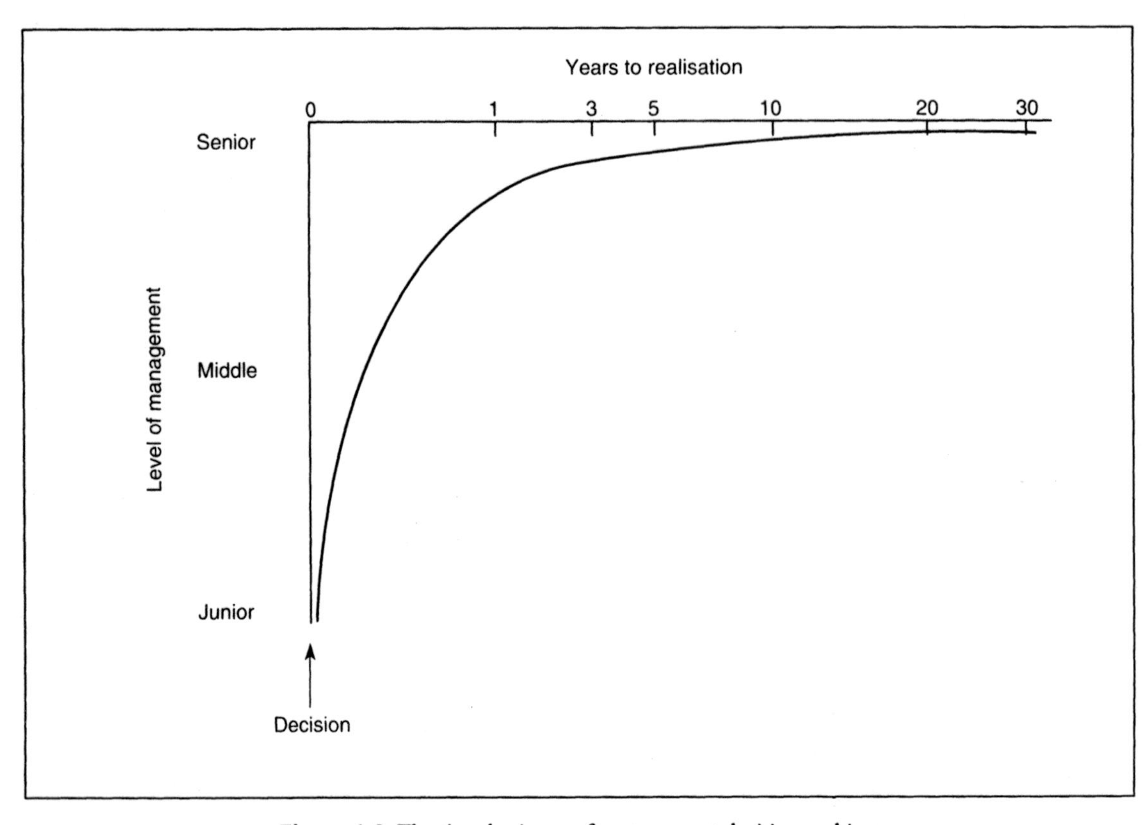

Figure 1.2 The time horizons of management decision making.

specific conclusions about consequences (predictive theories) or to explain certain practical observations (explanatory theories). Managers are often nervous about theories for two reasons:

(i) they may believe that the generalised assumptions upon which a theory is based are realistic but may mistrust the use of the long sequences of logical or mathematical argument required to yield conclusions;
(ii) they may not believe that the generalised assumptions upon which a theory is based are a fair representation of reality and hence they view any conclusions derived therefrom as suspect.

However, theories are a characteristic of all rational thinking whether in business or outside it. If we were to rely on practical experience alone we would have just point impressions of events and incoherent recollections of the past. Whenever, we try to make sense of our experience we need some conceptual framework depicting how the world works. This is what is often referred to as our 'theory in use'.

Unfortunately we rarely test these theories in use. For example, one theory which we all have (and which would be difficult to live without) is that we all mean the same thing by the same words. Occasionally we test this theory by checking our mutual understanding of what has been said, and mostly we are satisfied with the outcome. However, it is surprising the number of different interpretations which different people put on quite ordinary words such as, for example, 'value' and 'cost'. The point is not that we have different interpretations of meaning (this issue is explored in later chapters) but that discourse would fail altogether if we did not have some governing theory about meanings and how they are shared.

The role of theory in management (and in most other walks of life) is not to replace our experiences but to help us reconstruct our experience in more meaningful ways. The simple theory of investment choice developed in Chapter 5, for example, ignores the problem of risk but it does bring into account the concept of the time value of money. That is, the idea that money receipts which are delayed (like the future returns from investment) are worth less than identical sums of money available to a decision maker now. A naive, experience-based approach would be likely to ignore both risk and the time value of money. Theory in this case, although based upon simplistic assumptions, allows the decision maker to bring further variables into consideration when analysing the real problems with which he or she is faced. Even though the theory at issue is based upon simplistic assumptions, they are not simple minded. In theorising, we simplify a complex reality in order to enhance understanding of those elements of that reality which are important.

I believe it is a mistake to think that theory and practice are separate. There is, in reality, no distinction between theoretical and practical reasoning except that in practical reasoning the theoretical presuppositions deployed by the individual concerned may not be made explicit. Often, when the conceptual apparatus of the 'practical' manager is made explicit, its naivety becomes plain to see. As we discuss in the final section of this book, this is no more apparent than in the way many practical managers view financial accounting information.

In this book, theory is deployed in a way designed to make experience more meaningful. I will make explicit the assumptions upon which those theories are built, and will not make the reasoning any more abstract than is necessary to gain useful results from what can be a very messy management reality.

THE THEME OF THIS BOOK

The main text is divided into six parts representing a 'top down' treatment of the subject. In Part I, eight chapters offer an introduction to the concepts of strategic, opportunity-based accounting ('strategic accounting' for short) and its context within the business firm. In Chapter 3, for example, we explore the nature of the firm and examine the 'economic glue' which holds firms together. We try to make clear in that chapter that the economic rationale for a firm is a necessary but not a sufficient condition for its continued existence. In Chapter 4 we offer a series of theorems concerning strategic accounting which are designed to enhance your understanding of strategic accounting and the vocabulary used throughout the book.

These chapters may appear rather deep from a theoretical point of view and although you will find them very useful in gaining an overall understanding of the conceptual problems involved they can be deferred until some of the more practically orientated material has been covered. In Table 1.1 we suggest an alternative sequence for those who are more comfortable with a 'practical then theory' approach.

As Part I develops we argue that the commitments undertaken by a business determine it value and that this value is realised by changes in the cash flows of the organisation. We argue in Chapters 5, 7 and 8 that understanding the cash mechanics of an organisation is critical for its success and that the concept of cost is cash determined. Chapter 6 explores another generic theme of this book namely the 'accruals principle' whereby costs and revenues are removed from their incidence in time and are matched together for decision making or reporting purposes.

In Part II we explore the problems of developing the economic capability of the organisation through choosing and costing sources of finance, effective business planning and understanding the nature of risk. In Chapter 12 we explore the nature of options as financial instruments and through them gain some insights into the ways open to the manager for moderating business risk. In Chapters 14, 15 and 16 we develop techniques for measuring the value of projects to enhance the capability of the firm and, how using the methods described in previous chapters, value the firm itself.

In Part III we examine the financial issues associated with exploiting the capability of the business. This is the traditional area of short-term business decision making. Chapter 17 is concerned with the question of how managers should choose the most appropriate level of output and in Chapters 9 and 20 we discuss the vexed question of product pricing. In Chapter 21 we turn our attention to the issue of quality and how it may be valued and costed. In that chapter we discuss the problematic nature of the concept of quality and how differing perceptions about its meaning produce difficulty in establishing the value which quality adds to a business.

In Part IV we commence with a discussion and a critique of the traditional costing methods employed in business. Then, in Chapter 24, we explore the technique of activity-based costing, developed over the last decade, where accountants attempt to accrue general organisational costs to production according to certain activity variables. We continue that chapter with a discussion of a more radical costing procedure based upon a technique we refer to as 'production flow costing'.

In Part V we examine the problem of control within organisations turning first, in Chapter 25, to budgeting. In this chapter we explore the way that

Table 1.1 Suggested chapter sequences

Chapter	Theory first	Theory last	Accounting aware	Finance aware
1 Introduction	1	1	1	1
Foundations of Strategic Accounting				
2 Strategic accounting and the business enterprise	2	2	2	2
3 The economic basis for organisations	3	28	3	
4 Theorems of strategic accounting	4	29	4	3
5 Cash dynamics of a business	5	3	5	4
6 Measuring business performance	6	30		5
7 Opportunity costs	7	4	6	6
8 Opportunity costs under scarcity	8	5	7	7
Developing Business Capability				
9 Creating a business plan	9	6		8
10 The nature of business risk	10	7	8	
11 Options and risk	11	31	9	
12 The financial markets and the financing decision	12	8	10	
13 Costing the firm's capital resources	13	9	11	
14 The investment decision	14	10	12	
15 Product portfolios and product life cycles	15	11	13	9
16 Valuing the firm and building value	16	12	14	10
Exploiting Business Capability				
17 The output decision	17	13		11
18 The practical estimation of cost–output relationships	18	14		12
19 The economics of the pricing decision	19	15		13
20 The practical evaluation of price	20	16	15	14
21 Quality evaluation and costing	21	17	16	15
Costing Resources and Products				
22 Overhead accruals and standard costing	22	18		16
23 Costing in different production environments	23	19		17
24 Activity-based and product flow costing	24	20	17	18
Controlling Financial Performance				
25 Budgeting	25	21		19
26 Variance analysis and budgetary control	26	22		20
27 The control of short-term working capital	27	23		21
Measuring and Interpreting Financial Performance				
28 Basic financial reporting concepts	28	24		22
29 Commitment accounts	29	25	18	23
30 Accrual accounts	30	26		24
31 Interpreting financial reports	31	27	19	25

budgeting procedures should map onto the value flows within organisations and reflect the real lines of accountability which exist. In Chapter 26 we work through the theory and practice of budgetary variance analysis as an instrument of management control. In Chapter 27 we examine the problems of controlling working capital and valuing stock.

In Part VI we look at the external accountability of the firm and demonstrate how easy traditional financial accounting is in practice. Financial accounting becomes complex because of the regulatory framework of laws and standards which surrounds this area. We would refer you to more specialised texts for a discussion of these regulatory issues. In this book we focus on the structure of financial reports and how changing business decisions affect the published performance in the corporate accounts. In Chapter 31 we complete the text with an examination of the problems of interpreting accounting reports and the problems of the creative use of the accruals principle in manipulating performance measures.

Part I

Foundations of Strategic Accounting

Chapter 2

Strategic Accounting and the Business Enterprise

Level E

Contents

Summary

In this chapter we commence our discussion of the economic purpose of organisations. We then take a rather abstract diversion to consider a philosophical model of the organisation. The purpose of this model is to show the way in which organisational misunderstandings create confusion of intention and action. We then proceed to a discussion of the role of accounting and finance in business and indicate the principal characteristics of strategic accounting. Finally, we discuss the decision-making needs of both owners and managers and how they might differ in practice.

INTRODUCTION TO BUSINESS FIRMS

Business firms are particular types of human organisations which in an economic sense are dedicated to the exploitation of business opportunities. They represent the productive sector of the economy and they need to generate an economic profit to survive. The role of the firm in an economic sense is to convert resources (thus incurring costs) into products and services (thus earning revenue). In this respect, the business firm differs from public sector organisations such as universities, schools, hospitals and so on in that these organisations are dedicated to the conversion of their income into expenditures in order to generate the largest amount of service for those who use or need them. In the next chapter we will discuss, in more detail, the economic motivation of firms and their management.

In recent years in the UK and other western economies, governments have become more committed to the business ethos and have urged it upon public sector bodies as a way of becoming more efficient. There are undoubtedly gains for any organisation in becoming more business-like in the way that it deals with its affairs. However, in understanding the finance of such organisations it is important to remember this fundamental difference in their economic function, outlined and depicted in Figure 2.1.

A PHILOSOPHICAL MODEL OF BUSINESS ORGANISATIONS

In order to understand the organisational role of accounting it is necessary to say something about the philosophy of organisations at what appear, at first sight, to be a very abstract level. As we will discover in the next chapter there are economic, social and cultural motivations for the creation of firms rather than individuals acting on their own as independent traders in free markets. What does, however, characterise the typical business organisation is the degree of specialisation which its participants adopt and this is reflected in the way those individual think and, most importantly, speak, understand and interact with one another. In a mature business firm we can identify four principal ways of thinking: the

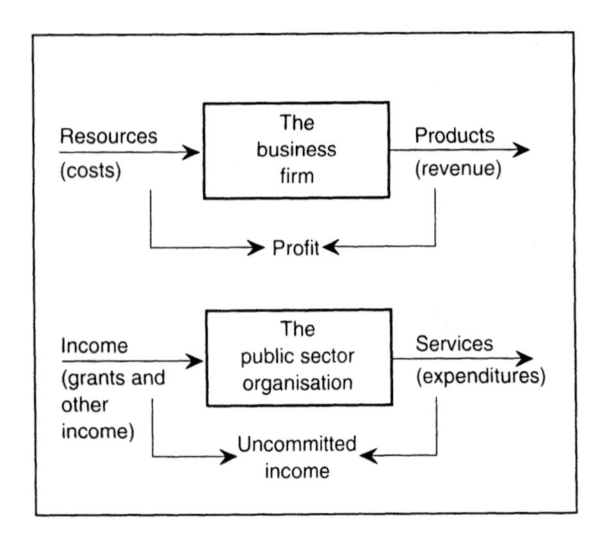

Figure 2.1 Business and public sector organisations as economic inputs and outputs.

ethical, the functional, the formal and the real. Other ways of partitioning an organisation can be proposed. However, our purpose is to create a simple model which can be helpful in understanding complex organisational realities.

This four-fold division of the way people think and the language which is spoken in organisations is what we refer to as the 'four-world model' of the organisation (Figure 2.2). Each of these four ways of thinking we refer to as a 'world of organisational meaning' because in many important ways, even though the same language is spoken, the meanings attached to that language can be quite different.

The 'real' world is the world of production and operations. Note that we are not making any claims about what is 'real' and what is not, but rather that this is a level of discourse of a particular and distinctive type within a business. It is a world where physical attributes, standards, measurements and processes are discussed in language which attempts to be precise and descriptive. It is the language of observation.

The 'formal' world is where ideas for products and services are created and developed. Again, it is typified by a precise language which will have a heavy conceptual and theoretical element. It is this world of discourse which design teams inhabit. Linking the real and formal are certain translational rules which allow the meanings developed in the world of form to be translated into the real world and *vice versa*. The reason for this is that ideas within the formal world are often trapped in certain terms (for example: temperature, tensile strength etc.) which have many different ways of being interpreted observationally.

Above the 'formal world' we have the 'functional world', which relates to the discourse concerning

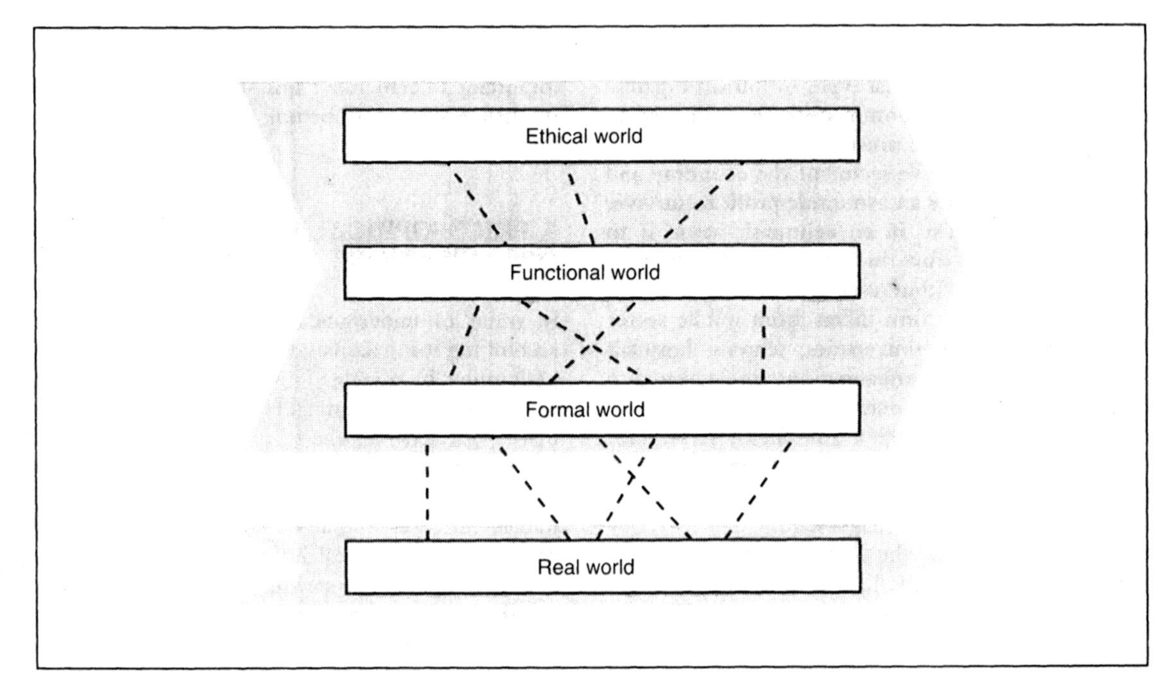

Figure 2.2 The Four-world model of the organisation.

the function to which the products and services of the organisation are put. It is in this world, for example, where the needs of the organisation's customers and the promises of its suppliers are understood and talked about. Again, certain translation rules govern the exchange of meaning at this level with the level below it as, for example, customer needs are translated perhaps through the marketing department into product designs and specifications within the formal world of discourse.

Finally, we can identify a level of discourse which transcends the three levels described above and which we refer to as the 'ethical world' of the organisation. Ethics is concerned with value systems and the value system of any business firm will be discussed by senior management and others in terms of 'missions', 'visions', 'strategies', 'objectives' and many of the other ideas upon which management spend so much time attempting to translate through various levels of the organisation.

The important point about these four worlds of discourse and meanings is that translations between them are only provisional. They are like sliding layers or, as one manager described them, 'shear planes' tentatively linked together by translation rules which can and do change. Many of these translation rules and the terms which are embedded within each layer are to do with financial values, and ideally the role of the accountant is to service the financial information needs of management within each level and to ensure (as far as possible) comprehension and understanding. But, is not all of this hopelessly theoretical?

EXAMPLE

A large electronics manufacturer had a number of organisational problems to do with quality and poor cost competitiveness.

- *Organisationally the business was functionally divided into a manufacturing and a design and development division with little managerial interaction (or mutual comprehension) between the two divisions. Individuals within the two divisions appeared to be using identical terms but meant quite different things. by them. The business also had a serious 'formal' quality problem which was, fundamentally, due to a lack of agreement between the real and formal worlds of the organisation.*
- *The marketing department was uniformly despised. The marketing people talked in a language which made little or no sense to the rest of the business and as a consequence that department had been under considerable pressure and was under-resourced. The business also complained of a decline in customer satisfaction with its products and services and major contracts were being lost or not renewed. This was symptomatic of a failure in 'functional quality' which appeared to be due to a lack of agreement between the functional and formal worlds of the organisation.*
- *Senior corporate management ran the business using a minimal set of financial ratios with a strong emphasis upon maximising return on capital employed and labour productivity. These financial imperatives had generated a climate of alienation and fear between senior corporate management and the manufacturing divisions. There had been a high turnover of divisional management staff and a severe but undisclosed lack of understanding had developed which generated failures in quality throughout the business. This lack of articulation between the ethical and the other worlds of understanding and discourse created represented a failure in the 'ethical quality' of the business.*
- *The accounting function throughout the organisation served the needs of senior corporate management. It was distrusted by management at the other levels who attempted to manipulate the information systems to their own ends. Managers at different levels understood different things by simple terms such as 'cost', 'overheads', 'price' and 'profit'.*

Later in this book we will draw upon this four-world model as a source of inspiration for ideas in accounting and finance. But before leaving it, we use it to discuss two organisational issues and their implications which will be of significance later.

First, the model leads us naturally to think of a utopian state where there is perfect consensus between meanings at all the various levels. At this point the separation of the four worlds would collapse. Clearly such a state is unlikely ever to exist, although it could be seen as a worthwhile strategic goal. It would be a high quality state, and the inherent disorder within the organisation in both meaning and intention would be zero. This is what we describe as a 'zero entropy' organisation. Later we will discuss some strategies for reducing the entropy within an organisation, but two are worth identifying at this point.

- Activities which achieve net simplification across the organisation are preferable to any activities which generate increased complexity. This is an obvious statement, but organisational tendencies towards increased complexity are often difficult to resist.

- Information systems which permit effective communication between and across levels have the potential to reduce entropy by increasing coherence in the way that decision makers within the organisation understand one another.

The accounting system of an organisation forms one part of its total information system. The value which management places upon the accounting system will be governed by a number of factors such as:

- the value they attribute to accounting information as part of the total information available to them for their business decision making;
- the extent to which the rewards offered to management are geared to the financial performance of the business;
- the level of integrity which managers at different levels impute into the accounting information they receive.

ACCOUNTING, FINANCE AND BUSINESS

Accounting and finance are fundamental to effective organisation. The most ancient records of human civilisation reveal that the role of stewardship, and the keeping of financial accounts was a common feature of day-to-day life. The Bible, for example, is replete with tales of stewards (rarely complimentary) in both the Old and New Testaments, with numerous examples of wickedness and perfidy.

Traditionally, financial accounting has been concerned with the provision of information for external users of accounting information and in particular the shareholders. However, a number of different groups use financial accounting information both within and outside the organisation. The word 'stakeholder' is used as a generic term to describe anyone who has an interest in a business firm. The stakeholders of the typical business firm are, therefore:

shareholders	(those who have invested risk capital in the business)
lenders	(those who have lent funds to the business such as banks and other financial institutions)
creditors	(those who supply the firm with goods and services on credit)
customers	(purchasers of the business's goods and services)
employees	(and their agents such as unions and professional bodies)
tax authorities	(Inland Revenue, Customs and Excise, local authorities)
government	(Central Statistical Office, Registrar of Companies and so on)

However, the financial accounting function also serves the needs of management in that it provides them with their most important vehicle of accountability to the shareholders of the firm.

Management accounting is about providing financially based information for the decision-making needs of management (who for this purpose would include the directors who as the agents of the shareholders give direction to the firm's management). However, in most developed businesses, the financial and management accounting functions overlap (Figure 2.3). In large businesses, the financial reporting systems and the management accounting information systems are usually so intertwined that it is difficult to separate them in any meaningful way. In smaller firms, the financial reporting system often doubles as the management accounting system with management relying on periodic statements of profit and loss to control the firm.

As we will discover in later chapters, strategic accounting treats these two areas as one. It does, however, emphasise a 'decision-orientated approach' in that it imposes a usefulness criterion on all information produced by a firm. However, as we will also show in the chapters which follow, there is also a wider dimension to accounting. Because accounting activity imposes rules and procedures upon the organisation, it profoundly influences (and is influenced by) the structure of relationships which exist within the firm. It influences not only the way individuals behave personally, and the way they interrelate and communicate with one another. This 'behaviourial' dimension to management accounting is extremely important.

In recent years, informed management thinking has become increasingly concerned about the effectiveness of traditional accounting procedures. In particular, the formal separation of the management from financial accounting functions has become less relevant, as both are typically driven from common management information systems. In addition, taken as separate functions, neither, in their traditional form, offer an effective basis for the long- and short-term decision-making needs of the organisation. It is the intersection between the various finance functions which is occupied by strategic accounting.

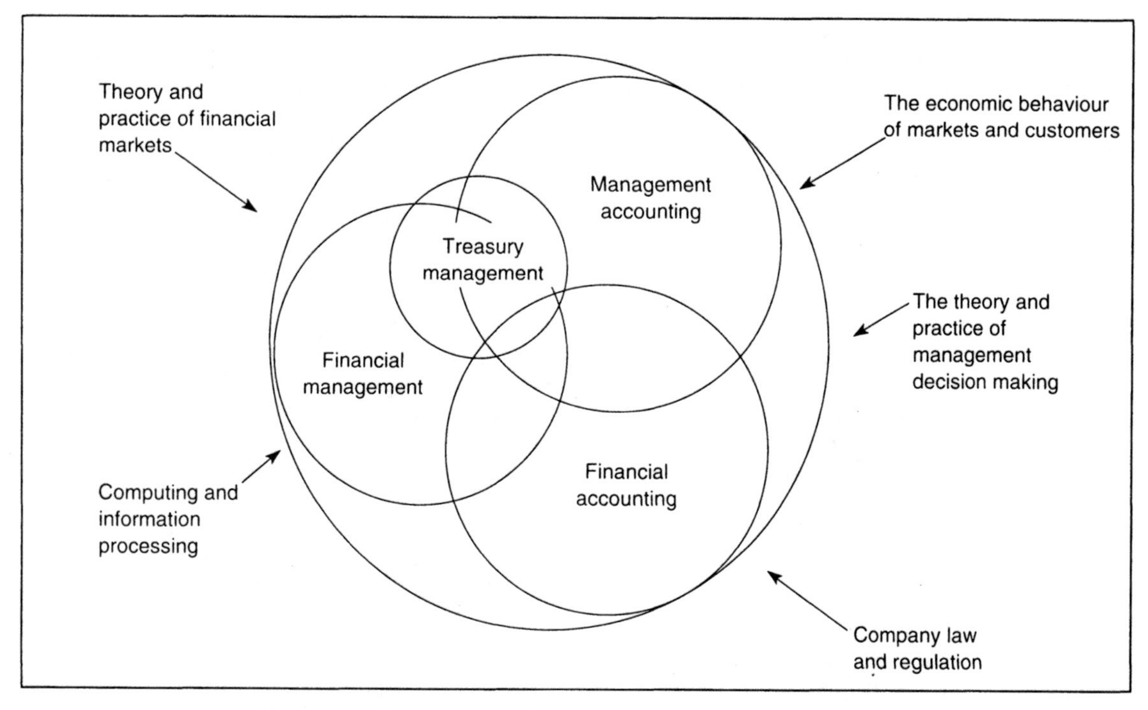

Figure 2.3 The interaction of accounting and finance within the firm.

DECISION-MAKING NEEDS OF OWNERS AND MANAGERS

Individuals start businesses for a variety of reasons. They often fail, but some survive and continue to grow until they become large industrial or commercial concerns quite removed from the interests of their original owners.

In general, the concept of ownership in large organisations is different to that in smaller single-owner businesses or partnerships. In the former, the owner is the manager and is looking to the business to provide him- or herself with a complete livelihood. The large proportion of the owner's real, and often the totality of his or her emotional, capital is absorbed in the business. In this type of business the trade off between risk and return is often not clear. The perception of the owner manager is usually that current risk is being borne in large measure to create the growth required for future returns.

In the large organisation, ownership is a much more abstract concept than in the smaller organisation. Typically, ownership is shared among a large number of individuals who will regard their 'shareholding' as just a financial investment. They will not, for example, hold any rights to manage the company concerned and their ability to control its overall policy will be limited to their voting rights at annual or extraordinary general meetings. Ownership, in this sense, is very much a residual concept in that the shareholder of the large firm is entitled to what is left after all other claims have been met, both on an annual basis (in calculating profit for distribution) and at the end of the company's life when its assets are liquidated.

Within the context of a large, publicly quoted company, the individual shareholder will (typically) hold his or her shares as a small part of their overall wealth. The value of those shares will be measured in terms of the cash dividends expected in the future and the realisable value of the shares at the anticipated point of sale. Indeed, given that it is the case that all an individual shareholder ever receives from a publicly quoted company is a cash dividend, then his or her expectations of eventual sale value will be governed in its terms by the market's expectations of future dividends. In Chapter 16 we will explore in some detail how shares in public companies can be valued using expectations of growth in future dividends.

For the small company with a single, or just a few, owner-managers, the objectives of the owner(s) will be confused by issues such as their own and their family's needs for security, job satisfaction and in many cases the maintenance of family traditions within particular trades or businesses. Clearly, they will be interested in the profit they gain from their effort, but we cannot assume that this will be the single or even the dominant motivation for their activities. In the large organisation, however, the ability of the firm to generate profits for distribution to shareholders (or for retention for future investment) will be an important consideration for them and, therefore, the concept of profit maximisation, either in the long or the short term would appear to be a reasonable objective of the shareholder group.

For the purposes of our discussion we will assume that there is some formal separation of ownership and management within the framework of a limited company. In such an organisation, the owners (or potential owners) will perceive their claim on the business to be in the form of a financial shareholding which they hold (or could hold) for investment purposes. In this situation they are faced with a 'buy or hold' decision:

- to buy if the perceived value of the benefits they will receive from their shareholding is in excess of what they are required to pay for the shares;
- to sell if the perceived value of the benefits they will receive from their shareholding is less than what they are required to pay for the shares.

Now, as we have argued above, the shareholder perceives benefit in terms of a future pattern of cash dividends and capital realisation on the eventual sale of shares which he or she hopes to obtain. *A priori*, therefore, we would argue that to make the buy or hold decision the shareholder needs to be able to create a realistic assessment of:

(i) the future cash dividends he or she can reasonably expect to receive;
(ii) the uncertainty attached to future dividends measured as the range of possible outcomes around those expected dividends.

Given this information, the investor would undertake some personal procedure for valuing the benefit of those future cash sums and the conditionality (or risk) attaching to them. In a situation where no formal market existed for the shares, we would expect the owner shareholder to require or mandate the managers that they employ to run the firm and to act so as to maximise the value of their shareholding. If a formal market exists where the owners can trade their ownership claims (their shares) then the market price (given reasonable degrees of competitive perfection) will represent the owner group's consensus of the value of those shares.

There are a number of difficulties with this approach to understanding the motivation of investors in companies. In the next chapter we will consider different models of the organisation in more detail. At this stage, however, we can at least be satisfied that we have a model of ownership motivation which leads in a simple way to some prescriptions of the likely decision needs of the owners of large firms.

It is an interesting issue, however, whether or how the owners of a large firm can enforce their objective of value maximisation upon the managers who actually operate the business on their behalf. This is an issue to which we will return after we have had a look at the motivation and decision-making needs of management.

THE DECISION-MAKING NEEDS OF MANAGEMENT

As we discussed in the last chapter, one essential characteristic of management as opposed to other human inputs into a business organisation is its decision-making role. The word management conjures up the concepts of controlling, leading and decision-making, and indeed the activities of controlling and leading would have little meaning if the manager was not able to make choices between alternative courses of action. This is the essence of a decision situation where the individual is faced with alternative courses of action and attempts to choose between them with some objective in mind.

In Chapter 1, we outlined the decision time horizons typically associated with different levels of management. Long-run decisions entail the procurement of the fixed resources of the firm and their commitment to a particular process or activity. For example, raising long-term finance, investing in buildings, plant and machinery, undertaking a merger and opening a new product market all entail long-term commitments of effort and resources. In addition, in most cases the making (and reversal) of such decisions will bring major upheaval and disturbance to the firm over a number of years.

Short-run decisions do not normally involve altering the fixed resources of the firm and would not, in most practical situations, influence the firm over longer than a single planning period (usually a year). Of course, short-run decisions entirely presuppose some long-term decision. Time is a crucial factor in decision making. It affects the value of outcomes, as we shall see in Chapter 5, and it also affects the hierarchy of assumptions that we are required to make. In long-run decision making, a feasible set of consequential short-run decisions must be assumed. In short-run decision making a set of preceding long-run decisions are presumed and form the constraints which restrict the choices available to the decision maker.

The decision types identified in Figure 2.4 will be explored in later chapters of this book. However, this traditional classification of business decision making begs certain questions about the objectives which govern the choices that management make. Classical economic theory and the modern theory of the firm assume the profit maximisation objective in line with our discussion in the previous section. Implicitly, that approach assumes that managers will act on behalf of and serve the interests of, the owners of the firm.

This may be a reasonable approximation to reality where the owners themselves are actively engaged in the management of the firm. However, it is unrealistic in a setting where ownership and management are separated. If we assume that like owners, managers are themselves value maximisers, then there is the potential for quite a clear conflict of interests. The situation is exacerbated where there is a difference between the two parties in the access to information about the performance of the firm (and implicitly, therefore, management) and where the two parties may have different perceptions and degrees of aversion to the risks involved.

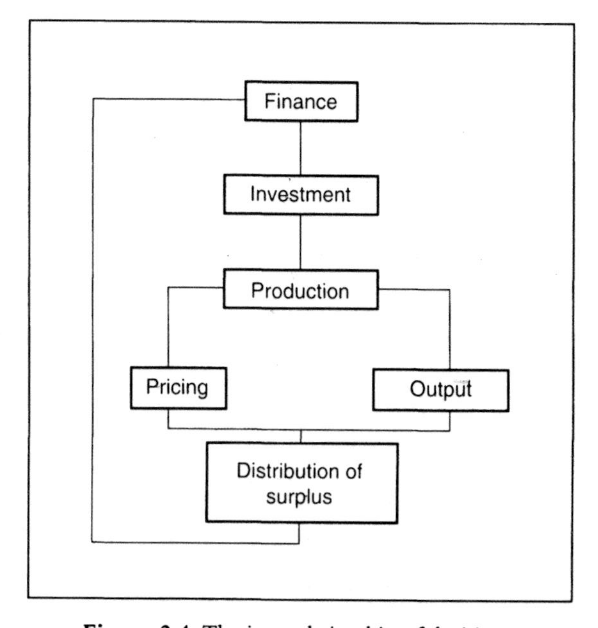

Figure 2.4 The interrelationship of decisions.

We must defer a formal discussion of the issues involved until Chapters 3 and 4 but, to prepare for the issues involved consider the following situation.

EXAMPLE

Three similar firms are involved in the construction business and are engaged in long terms building contracts. The rules of accounting allow them, within wide margins to bring forward or defer revenue and expenditure within any given year. Firm A is controlled by senior managers who are on fixed-term salaried contracts with no performance related element to their pay. On the other hand, firm B is controlled by senior managers who are paid relatively small salaries but who enjoy extensive profit-related perks. Managers in firms A and B are required to produce periodic reports on the revenues and their expenditures associated with their activities and recommend dividends to shareholders at their company's Annual General Meetings. Both sets of managers can make use of expense accounts for 'entertaining' purposes, they can lease company cars and take benefit from free medical insurance. They are not obliged to show details of this expenditure in their annual accounts to the shareholders. Firm C is managed by its owners.

Is there likely to be any difference in the reported profits and dividends of the three businesses?

A few moments reflection may lead to the conclusion that the differences in the employment contracts of the managers concerned is unlikely to effect their decision making and hence their use and management of information. If this proved to be the case then accounting would be a much simpler task than it is. In reality, it would be naive to assume that the profit objectives of management would be pursued unambiguously by management. The decision-making needs of management and owners are likely to be different to a degree at least, and partial disclosure may be the name of the management game.

CONCLUSION

In this chapter we have considered accounting and finance within the context of the management of the firm and the decision-making needs of owners.

This lays a foundation for our next area of study which is concerned with the economic basis of organisations. By the end of this chapter you should have a preliminary idea of the domain of strategic accounting and how it offers a basis for examining financial and accounting problems at the point within a firm that matters most – the exploitation of business opportunities.

Chapter 3

The Economic Basis for Organisations

Level M

Contents

Summary

In this chapter we explore some of the economic reasons why firms exist and take the place of markets for certain types of business transactions. In particular we will explore the idea that firms come into existence in order to undertake activities in more cost-efficient ways to that which could be achieved by people undertaking those same activities in open markets. In this chapter we are not particularly concerned with all the cultural, social or psychological reasons why people should wish to work in organisations rather than as independent free traders. In the first section we will explore the significance of the profit motive for firms and look at some of the reasons why profit maximising may not be the real issue within firms. We then proceed to explore the contractual and cost-minimising aspects of why firms exist.

WHY BUSINESSES EXIST

Business organisations come into existence for a number of reasons.

- They provide individuals with a social context in which to work and they permit individuals to mitigate some of the risk inherent in working as sole traders.
- They permit the drawing together and financing of resources on a scale which would be impossible for individuals to achieve on their own account.
- They allow technologies to be developed through combined action in research and development which would be impossible in an individual context. Indeed, over the last 20 years more and more leading edge research is being undertaken within companies than within the universities – indeed, in areas such as biotechnology (including gene research), superconductors, computing, space systems and software engineering most of the new discoveries and developments are occurring in corporate laboratories rather than in universities.

However, given all of these reasons there is one necessary precondition for the survival of any business which is a necessary condition for all firms to exist. This condition is that the economic value to the stakeholders within a business must be greater through its existence than through conducting exactly the same set of business transactions in an open-market context. No business organisation can survive if there is a better economic solution to the needs that it attempts to fulfil, either through the competitive action of other organisations or simply because its customers realise that it would be cheaper to fabricate the product or service involved themselves.

THE FIRM AND ITS MANAGEMENT

The economic theory of the firm is an attempt to formalise an economic rationale for the existence of firms. The very oldest theories were based on the presupposition that the owners of firms sought to maximise their own wealth and that they operated, or engaged managers to operate, the firm so as to maximise economic profit to themselves. If a firm was unable to achieve profits through the opportunities it took up then it would fail to exist. However, the belief that firms existed simply to make profits for their owners was based on the idea that a firm is simply an extension of the owners and that their rights would always dominate the interests of any other stakeholders.

Many problems developed with this simple theoretical perspective although much of the current theory of market behaviour in economics still relies upon this profit-maximising assumption. Indeed, most modern economics textbooks, although recognising the weaknesses of the profit-maximising motive, still persist with it as a basis for the formal analysis of firm and market behaviour.

The first problem with the profit maximisation concept is that it assumes that owners only have an ownership interest in the firm. However, this is rarely the case. Owners can also be customers, suppliers, employees, management and indeed government, and in those capacities they will have interests which clearly conflict with profit maximising on the firm's behalf.

However, a more difficult problem with profit maximisation is that although the owners of a business may wish profits to be maximised they may not be able to persuade management to act always and solely in their best interests. It has been recognised since the path-breaking study by Berle and Means in 1932 that ownership and control is usually separated in organisations (Figure 3.1) and that managers will have their own agenda which will include a desire to maximise their own wealth at minimum risk. The separation of ownership and control in large business organisations is due to a number of factors.

- Having the wealth to own part of a business does not necessarily imply that the individual concerned has the skill to manage that business.
- For a large firm, ownership has to be diversified over a wide base in order to bring together sufficient capital to fund the business. As we will see in Chapter 12 this generates a need for a secondary market in ownership claims on the business which will act to disconnect the ownership of shares from the management of the businesses concerned.
- The risk held by shareholders in the capital market is most efficiently reduced by financial strategies such as diversification or insurance rather than through intervening in the operation of the business itself. The managers, on the other hand, have usually invested the bulk of their life capital within the business and along with the other employees are fully exposed to business risk which they cannot diversify. For this reason there is likely to be wide discrepancies between the attitudes of shareholders and management to the risk to which the company is exposed and hence how it should be shared between them.

Owners

Maximise their own wealth at minimum risk. They have residual rights to the assets of the company and its earnings.

Directors

Are legally responsible for the governance of the company under the Companies Acts. They take the policy decisions of the business and may be involved in its management.

Managers

Make decisions concerning the functioning of the business and act as the agents of the directors in implementing their policy decisions.

Other Employees

Follow the instructions of management donating their skills and labour to the business in exchange for their wage and security in employment.

Figure 3.1 The classical view of the hierarchy of relationships and responsibilities in business.

In practice, the formal power in large corporations is focused in the board of directors. The shareholders who are usually referred to as the 'owners' have very few rights except to vote at company meetings and receive accounts. They do not have the power to propose and pass management policy and enforce those decisions against the directors. The directors may also be the senior managers of a business but not always so. In small companies, the role of the directors is interwoven with the management of the business, and those directors may also hold a substantial proportion of the company's equity.

AN AGENCY THEORY APPROACH TO THE ECONOMIC MOTIVATION OF FIRMS

Traditionally management has been viewed as agents of the owners in whom legal rights of ownership are invested by tradition and by law. However, in modern company law it makes little sense to view the shareholders as the principal actors in a business with the managers acting as their agents. In modern business organisations of any size the board of directors possess the principal contracting role with other managers as their agents. In this view of the corporation the management is perceived as undertaking its activities within a contractual setting where it exchanges its services for the remuneration and perquisites agreed with the directors. This 'principal–agent' (p–a) framework for understanding managerial action has been refined into a general economic theory of the firm by agency theorists. This approach has led to a number of unique insights into the way in which risk is distributed in business relationships and the problem of 'moral hazard' (where the agent uses the information about the principal's business to his or her advantage without disclosing the fact).

Although agency theorists argue that even though the shareholders, or the directors or the managers may wish to maximise their own wealth that this will not be translated into everyone working to maximise the profit of the business. How the business actually operates will be determined by the nature of the contracts of employment of all the individuals within the firm and how risk is shared between them.

Theoretically, agency theory assumes the following.

- All parties in the contracting relationships are personal utility maximisers (where utility is a term economists use to describe the personal value or benefit which an individual places on any economic good they receive) and that they are rational (in that they know what they are doing and they are consistent).

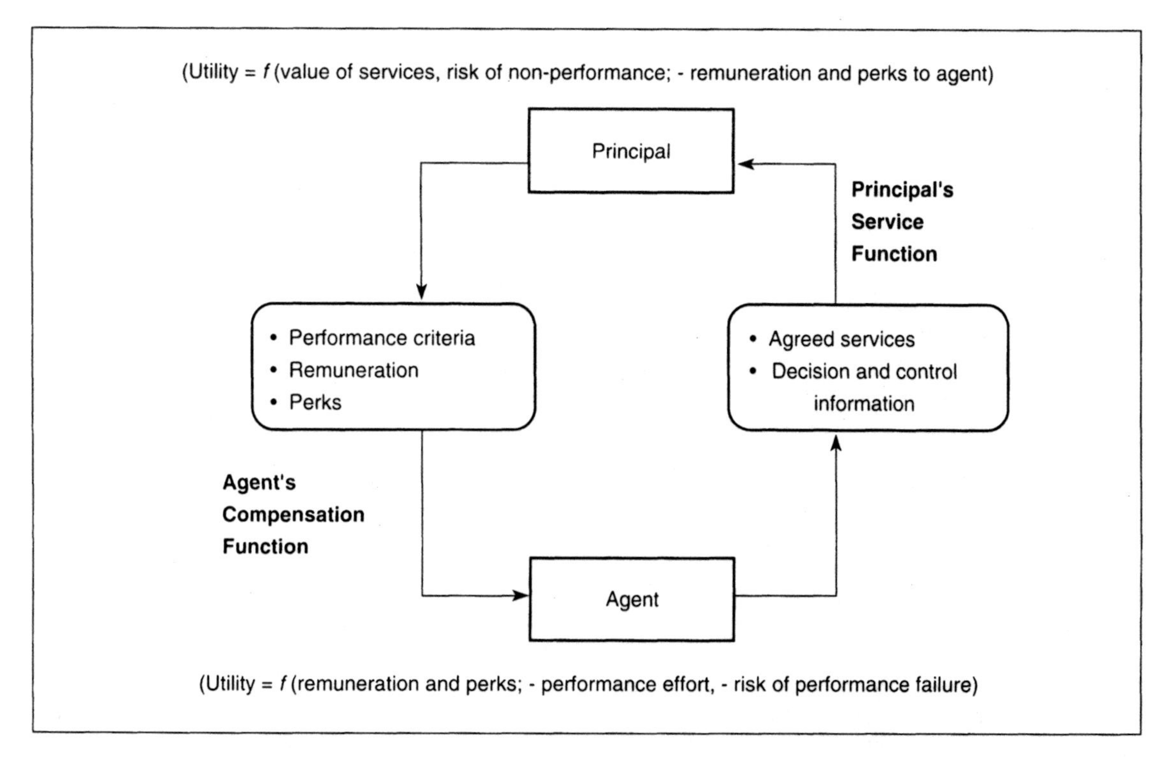

Figure 3.2 The Principal–Agency (P-A) model of managerial behaviour.

- A contract is formed when the utility achieved by the principal from the contract is equal to the utility of the agent. In Figure 3.2 we show the principal contractual flows in the P–A relationship implied by the agency theory view of the firm.
- The firm is simply a 'nexus' of contracts of the 'P–A' type, and firm behaviour can only be analysed in terms of a detailed economic analysis of the components of each contract.

The agency theory approach to understanding the economic motivation of firms offers the following insights.

(i) If both the principal and the agent in a relationship are indifferent to risk, then an optimal risk-sharing contract of employment which maximises both of their interests is possible.
(ii) If either the principal or the agent or both are averse to risk, then such an optimising contract will not be possible.

The agency theory approach offers many insights into the problems associated with running firms: it explores the contractual basis behind business relationships; it explains, in part, some of the problems of business control and monitoring. However, as a theory, it is only a partial explanation of managerial behaviour. It does not, for example explain some important issues such as why organisations structure themselves in the way that they do. To address issues of this type we need a deeper theory of managerial and firm behaviour.

UNDERSTANDING A TRANSACTION

Ronald Coase, the winner of the Nobel Prize in Economics in 1991, proposed, as long ago as 1937, that the fundamental unit of economic activity is a transaction. It is through transactions that economic value is translated from one individual to another, and ultimately it is the stuff of which markets are made and firms created.

A transaction occurs when two individuals enter into a commitment to exchange goods and services for cash or some other reward. In the transaction, the supplier (A) in Figure 3.3 commits to supply goods or services to the customer (B) and incurs transactions costs in so doing. 'A' is the creditor in this transacting relationship. 'B', who is the debtor in the relationship, is committed to the settlement of the agreed price and will also incur a range of transaction costs associated with procurement.

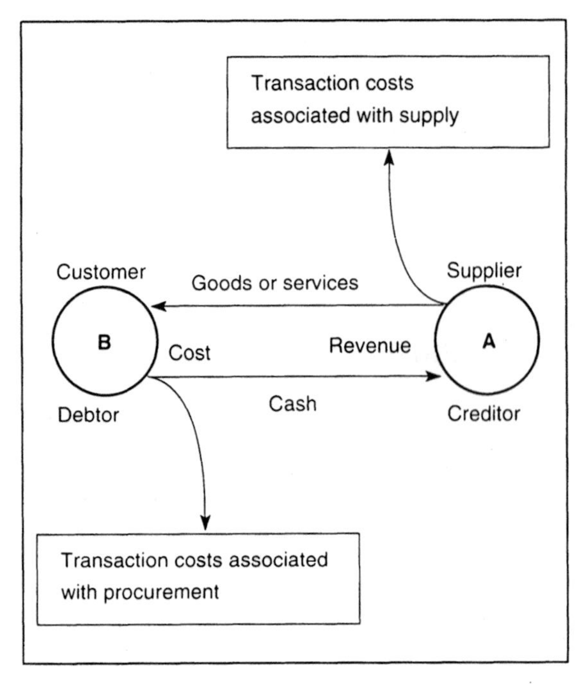

Figure 3.3 Transaction flows.

This line of reasoning has led to an approach to the theory of the firm called 'transaction cost economics' (TCE). Coase proposed that transactions costs will be incurred simply through engaging in certain transactions – perhaps in acquiring information, discovering the price of a product, paying commissions or even in getting to the place where a deal can be struck. In addition, where certain transactions are undertaken repetitively, the long-run cost of those transactions could be substantial, and some other form of transacting, rather than in the context of a free market, could be attractive. Coase proposed the following.

- There are two alternative ways in which individuals can, in principle, transfer or reallocate resources. The first is a market context where individuals freely buy and sell the resources in question, and the second an organisational context where individuals seek cooperative solutions to the transfer problem.
- Individuals are transaction cost minimisers in that they will always seek minimum cost solutions to engaging in the transactions that interest them.

Coase (1937) advanced the important insight:

> A firm has a role to play in the economic system if transactions can be organised within the firm at less cost than if the transactions were carried out through

the market. The limit to the size of the firm is reached when the cost of organising additional transactions within the firm exceed the cost of carrying out the same transactions through the market.

For some transactions, the associated costs are so trivial that a market context is the most appropriate vehicle for undertaking them. For other transactions, the costs of transacting in a free market may be so prohibitive that it becomes worthwhile to organise to achieve the same end. In contracts of employment for example, the contract may be specific for given services to be rendered. Most people engage this type of contract if they hire a solicitor to conveyance their property or an accountant to file their tax return. Other employment contracts are more open in that a wage or salary is paid, but the full nature of the actual services to be delivered is not made specific. These types of employment contract, which many of us enjoy through our salaried employment, entail considerable monitoring and other costs on the part of the employer to ensure that reasonable service is delivered.

EXAMPLE

A small business has used the services of an accountant on an occasional basis to produce its monthly management accounts. This has worked well in the past with the accountant being paid an hourly rate of £15 for the work done, and she has tendered an account, as she does for all her other clients on a regular basis. However, over the last 12 months the business has expanded and has found itself calling upon her services on a much more frequent basis. Given that a full-time accountant could be employed for the equivalent of £10 per hour for a 35-hour week, we can predict when the business would choose to 'internalise' what has become a highly repetitive transaction. It is also easy to see that the economics would favour 'internalising' if, for example, it was impractical to get the part-timer in at less than 48 hours notice or it was clear that she had to go through a period of refreshing herself on the business's position before she could undertake new work.

Transaction cost economics is a rich source of insights into why firms come into existence and indeed take the internal structures that they do. In fact, if transactions costs were not a feature of all economic activity, i.e. all markets were competitively perfect and efficient then there would be no firms, no managers and (possibly) no accountants. Adam Smith's 'invisible hand' would operate, so as to allow all products and services to be produced and purchased by individuals buying and selling their skills in free markets where all prices were equilibrium prices and served to achieve an optimal and efficient movement of resources throughout the economy. No matter how complicated the final product, individual specialist producers would be able to buy and sell their skills at the best price, undertaking work on various aspects of the eventual product, but with none being aware, except for the last producer in the chain, what the overall purpose of their activity was being directed towards.

In Figure 3.4 we show a product logic network (PLN) for a product made from three constituent parts. Each link from raw material to final product represents a transaction with an associated cost. In a pure market setting, each part (A, B and C) would be produced by an individual, as would each intermediate component combination ($A+B$), ($B+C$) or ($A+C$) and the final product ($A+B+C$). The sequence of transactions which will dominate in a market setting are those which generate a minimum final cost of the components to the end producer. We explore the concepts behind PLNs further in Chapter 24, but as can be seen

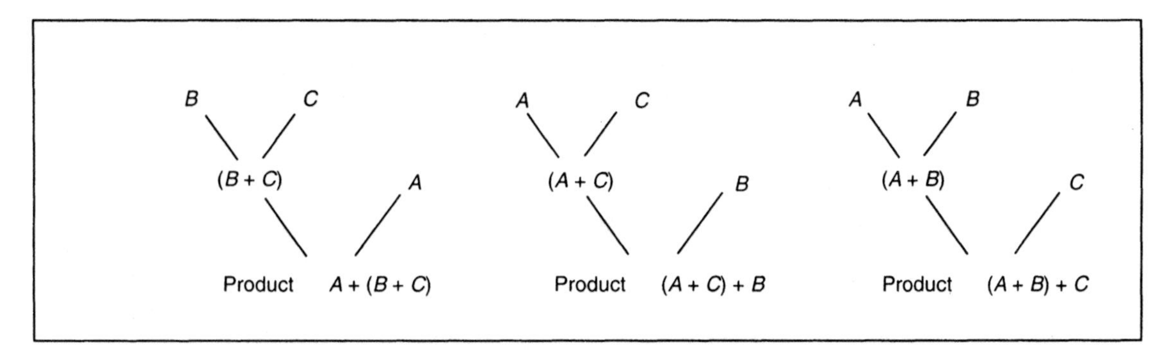

Figure 3.4 Three product logic networks.

from these networks, there are several organisational possibilities even with the three-part product described. What will determine the eventual organisational–market combination is the minimum cost solution to the fabrication of the final product.

TCE is a powerful theory of economic activity in the real world. However, like all theoretical descriptions of reality it has deficiencies. Its most important deficiency is that it does not explore the nature of transactions themselves (it takes the presence of a transaction cost as a given) and it does not illuminate the real fundamental of economic activity namely the concept of a commitment.

THE STRUCTURE OF PRODUCTIVE ORGANISATIONS

A number of theorists have attempted to discover the economic rationale for the structure and size of business firms. Perhaps the most successful of these has been Oliver Williamson who, following the ideas of Ronald Coase, has attempted to construct an economic theory of structure.

Williamson's work is based on the idea that individuals:

- exhibit 'bounded rationality' in that there are limits to the ability of any individual to comprehend all possible options and make the best choices;
- are opportunistic in that given the possibility they will make choices in their own best interests and may make those choices by guile;
- within limits, attempt to act efficiently and to avoid waste, i.e. minimise transactions costs.

Williamson also pointed out that in order to understand why firms exist and make the choices that they do, it is important to realise that assets (human and real) vary to the extent which they can be redeployed from one use to another.

From these propositions, Williamson (1991) proposed the following prescription for successful firms:

> align transactions (which differ in their attributes) with governance structures (the costs and competencies of which differ) in a discriminating (mainly, transaction cost economising) way.

Or, to put it more simply, the way firms are structured and organised should be such that the types of transactions in which they engage (both internally and externally) can be conducted in the most efficient way possible. Williamson's perspective on corporate strategy is that misalignment costs (where there is a poor fit between governance and structure and the contingencies of the market place) can be critical in deciding between success and failure for a firm.

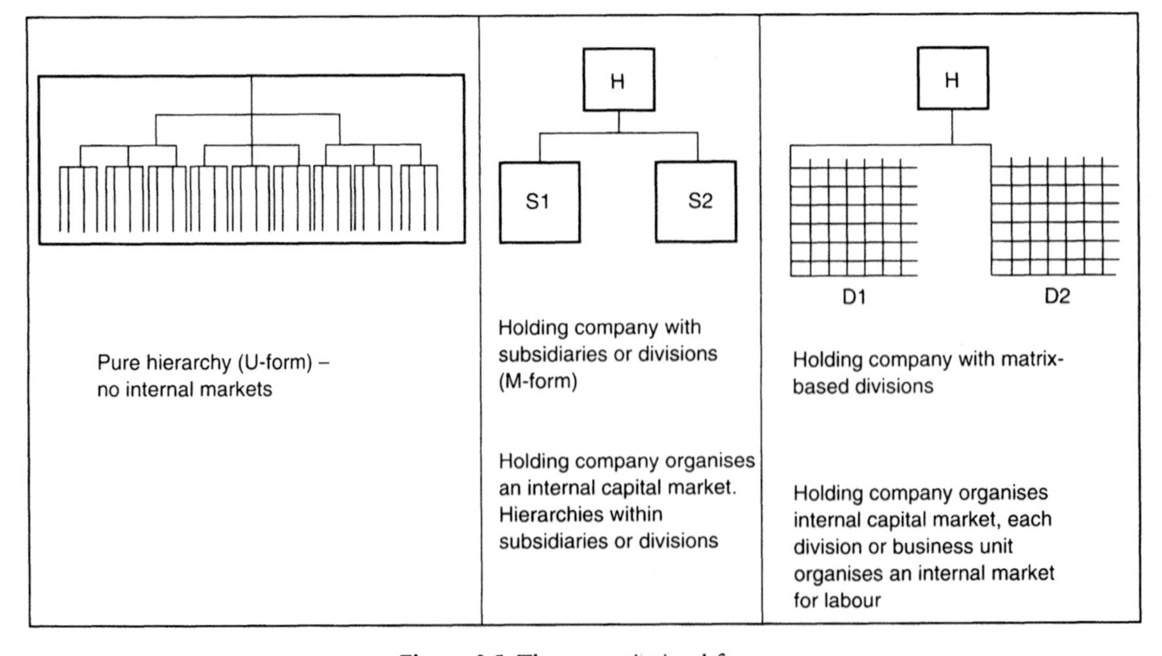

Figure 3.5 Three organisational forms.

In Figure 3.5 we outline three business structure forms:

(i) the unitary structure with a set hierarchy of relationships and accountabilities;
(ii) the holding company form with hierarchical structures in each unit;
(iii) the full internal market form.

In certain types of market situation, where assets are specific to a particular use, then a unitary structure for an organisation may be most appropriate. However, where the assets deployed have low specificity, a more market-based approach to the organisation of the firm may be indicated.

One common type of organisational structure is where a holding company controls two or more subsidiaries or divisions. In this case, the holding company, Williamson argues, can distribute capital more efficiently than would be the case if the divisions were able to compete for funds in the open market. This type of organisational structure is referred to as the M-form organisation and is most appropriate in handling systems where there is low capital asset specificity.

At the business unit level (i.e., the level of the subsidiary or division) the problem the firm may be faced with is how to make the most efficient use of labour across various products and/or projects. The matrix organisational form is a common method for establishing an internal market for labour, although in practice the significance of its quasi-market nature is often not fully appreciated.

THE MATRIX ORGANISATION

We can represent the M-form organisation where the holding company regulates the supply of capital to its subsidiaries and provides strategic management services as a simple matrix (Figure 3.6). In that diagram, the vertical vector shows the two principal functions supplied by the holding company to the various subsidiary operations, s_1, s_2, s_3 and s_4 along the horizontal vector. The chief executive will usually have responsibility for governing the operation of the matrix, with each division or subsidiary having a managing director at its head. The director of finance will usually manage the allocation of capital resource, whilst the chief executive will usually manage the allocation of strategic management services to the users.

Most companies have a transfer price (expressed as an interest rate) for capital to each subsidiary (i_1 to i_n) and will also attempt to price its strategic management services through a central overhead (o_1 to o_n).

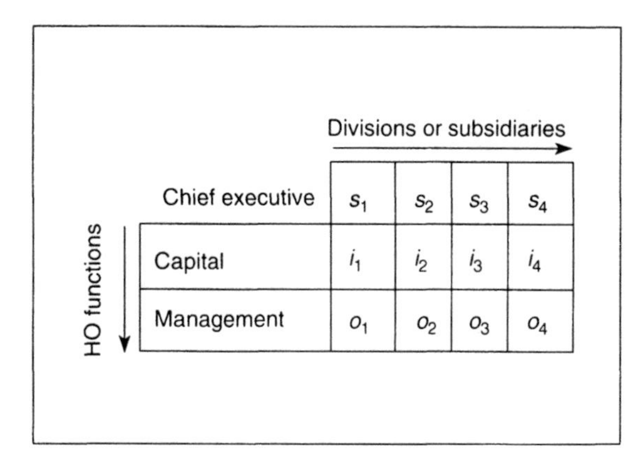

Figure 3.6 Holding company operation as a matrix.

The concept behind the matrix organisation at the business unit level is that suppliers of particular work skills are held within various functional groups (the supply side) and they are contracted, on a temporary basis, to individual projects or products (the consumers). Although they may have a high level of skill, those skills can be redeployed from project to project at low cost. In other words there is a low degree of human asset specificity. The internal market works through the organisational consumers 'buying' resources from the functional groups at the current labour rates.

In Figure 3.7 we show an organisational matrix at the operational level. The vertical vector shows the projects, products or jobs in which the business is engaged. The horizontal vector shows the various functional groups. As personnel are required for a particular activity (say p_2) they are drawn down from their group (say R_3) into their transaction or activity cell. The pseudo-market transactions required to fabricate product p_3 are transactions $t_{1,3}$ to $t_{n,3}$.

EXAMPLE

A space systems manufacturer organises its projects on a matrix basis. At any one point in time there may be six or more large scale projects underway, each of which will have its own business or project manager. He or she is required to negotiate with various departments: technical services, research and development, personnel services, finance, production engineering and so on for the resource needed to complete the contract. The business had

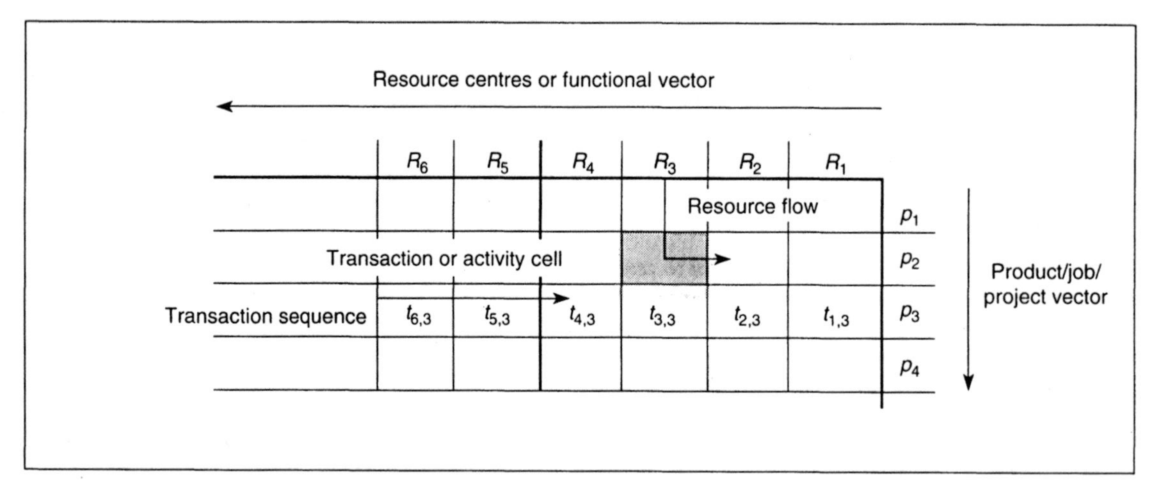

Figure 3.7 The organisational matrix showing resource and transaction flows.

problems in that it did not have any formal regulation in place to govern the negotiations between business and functional managers. Further, the budgeting system placed resource accountability on the functional rather than on the business managers. There was considerable antagonism between managers, which focused in its most extreme form on the Director of Personnel, who was seen as blocking the hiring of new staff to meet the needs of business units. The company did not have in place any mechanisms for regulating the operation of the matrix, and the business and functional managers only met as a group on very infrequent occasions. The matrix was unable to operate effectively as an internal market, and considerable management time and opportunities were lost attempting to 'firefight' on late contracts. There was a large degree of disillusionment amongst the management staff.

The input–output matrix is generic to any production system, although the adoption of such management structures in practice is rarely understood in economic terms as a form of internal market. For a matrix organisation to work in efficiently allocating resources, certain conditions need to be in place.

- Neither business or functional managers dominate in the power relationship and 'contracts' between them for the deployment of staff can be freely made and executed.
- There must be some regulatory mechanism which can override negotiation if the internal market appears likely to act against the strategic interests of the firm or if management cannot agree on resource allocation.
- There must be an effective pricing mechanism for transferring labour and any other resources throughout the matrix. This may not be the direct labour cost, but some 'overhead' charge may be applied in addition to represent the scarcity value of the staff involved.

The structure of a business has profound implications for accounting.

- It shapes management perceptions of how resource flows (and their most effective allocation) are mapped onto the structure.
- It determines organisational accountabilities and limits the range of choice which the business has in its short term management of resources.
- It limits the opportunities which management is able (or willing) to recognise.

From a transaction cost economics perspective, organisations come into existence when the cost of transacting though organisational contracting is less than the cost of transacting in open markets. Further, the economic imperative for business firms is to establish structures which most readily align themselves with the types of transactions which that firm seeks to engage in.

The authority-based line management systems with no internal markets for resource allocation will be favoured in situations where there is a high degree of asset specificity (i.e., assets cannot be switched from one use to another). Where there is low asset specificity, intermediate market-based forms exploiting internal market mechanisms will be favoured. For the accountant or finance specialist it is critical to understand the way in which a business is structured, first, to be able to price and allocate resources internally in the most efficient way possible and, second, to understand how the financial control mechanisms operate throughout the business.

CONCLUSIONS

In this chapter we have considered in some depth the economic rationale for organisations as a precursor to a discussion of the basic theorems of strategic accounting. We have favoured a description of the firm as an economic entity which can only exist providing it offers cheaper solutions to the contracts it undertakes than that offered by direct market mechanisms. This perception that a firm competes not only with other firms, but also with other market-based methods of transacting, pervades this book and teaches us that businesses hold a precarious existence which they can only justify through relative effectiveness and cost.

Chapter 4

Theorems of Strategic Accounting

Level E

Contents

Summary

In this chapter we discuss some of the conceptual background to strategic accounting. Strategic accounting is the name we give to a particular way of looking at the financial and accounting problems of the organisation. The approach we develop in this book transcends the classical distinctions between financial accounting, management accounting and financial management. Those distinctions reflect a theory of organisations and the way they come about which has long been superseded. Our approach to strategic accounting focuses upon certain key elements of the ways businesses generate economic value which we represent as our 'C-cycle'. The 'C-cycle' approach focuses our attention on commitments, capabilities, costs and control. in strategic accounting. The first two Cs are discussed in this chapter.

INTRODUCTION

In the last chapter we examined the role of management in the firm and discussed the contribution of scholars in the area of transactions cost economics in explaining the economic motivation of firms. Transaction cost economics asserts that organisations can only be sustained as economic entities if the cost of engaging in the transactions they represent is less than would be the case if those transactions were conducted in free markets. However, the concept of a transaction is not sufficient for a full understanding of the problems posed by accounting analysis. For this we have to explore the basic commitments upon which transactions are based. Commitments generate the capability within a business to undertake valuable opportunities.

THE FOUR Cs OF STRATEGIC ACCOUNTING

Strategic accounting focuses on commitments and opportunities.

- Organisations through their management make a variety of business commitments which result in exchanges of value through transactions. In understanding these commitments we can understand how the organisation's value has changed during the course of a given period of time and its degree of exposure to risk. The problem is in understanding the financial consequences of commitments and in reporting those consequences to those who are interested in them.

- Managers are the agents of various interest groups within the organisation (most notably the owners in a business firm). They do not always make commitments which are in accordance with the policy of the organisation, or in the most effective way possible. In addition, the ability to make commitments will be distributed throughout the various levels of management and, in some cases delegated to individuals or organisations outside the firm. This generates a problem of control – both between the stakeholders in the organisation and the management and between different levels of management.
- Commitments generate value changes for an organisation which will materialise in tangible form as cash flows. Cash is the 'primary resource' of any organisation and it is the resource upon which all other resources act. Cash is directly measured in terms of the monetary unit of measurement of the currency concerned and it is by definition the most financially liquid asset of them all. Understanding the cash mechanics of a business is the key to handling the problem of managing its prosperity and ensuring its survival.
- Finally, commitments are won and undertaken by management exercising the capability of the organisation. The problem of understanding that capability, maximising its potential and deciding upon its most effective deployment is the primary issue and problem which faces management.

In Figure 4.1 we show our '4C-cycle' of how an organisation sustains and creates capability. First, a given organisational capability defines the opportunities which a business can exploit, although the decision whether to exploit or not will depend on whether the commitments incurred lead to net cash changes in its favour. Once those decisions are taken, their consequences must be controlled and the organisation learn from its successes and failures. This creates the environment in which further capability can be developed.

In summary, strategic accounting is concerned with the financial analysis of the problems associated with the four Cs: commitment, control, cash and capability. In this chapter we will develop an understanding of commitments and capability as a set of propositions or theorems. These theorems generate principles around which we can integrate the financial problems of any organisation – whether it be in the public sector, a charity, a business firm or, indeed, the local sports club! The other two Cs we will develop in our later chapters on cost (Chapters 7 and 8) and control (Chapters 25–27).

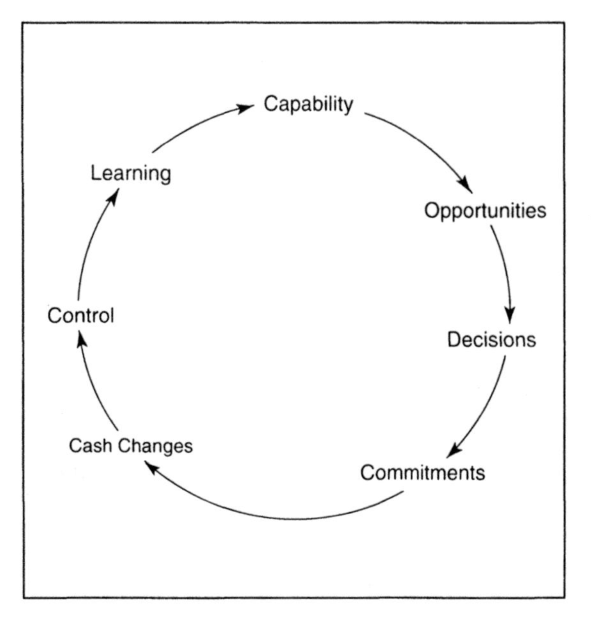

Figure 4.1 The 4C-cycle.

UNDERSTANDING A COMMITMENT

A commitment is a freely negotiated agreement between two or more parties to undertake some activity which has economic significance. Commitments are central to business because they are the point at which economic value is exchanged. They are the unit of activity around which transactions are engaged and, in this section, we will develop a series of theorems and a 'vocabulary' around the concept of a commitment. We will then begin to indicate how the concept of commitment leads to the notion of 'accountability' and discuss the principles of how a system of financial reporting can be constructed upon this key concept.

The question arises as to how a commitment relates to the economic concept of a transaction. The point is rather subtle but nevertheless important. A commitment relates to a contract which is established between two parties; a transaction, on the other hand, relates to the economic activity concerned. It is possible to possess a series of commitments; you cannot possess a transaction, rather you undertake it. The economic value of a transaction is governed by the commitments to which those transactions relate. Later we will explore the concept of undischarged commitments and how they bring together the central ideas of decision making and stewardship in accounting.

Business is created through relationships. These relationships can be very subtle with different power balances and meanings between the parties involved. Relationships are formed through the creation of commitments. When a motorist drives into a petrol station to fill up his or her car, he or she enters into an implicit commitment with the provider to pay the stated price for the petrol taken from the pump. The commitment is discharged as soon as the price is paid.

As soon as the motorist starts to put petrol into the car, the petrol station has a right (which is legally enforceable) to expect the customer to honour the commitment. The purchase or sale is not made at the point at which the cash is transferred and any commitment discharged. Similarly, if a company receives an order for some goods and accepts that order either verbally, in writing or by delivery of the goods in question, then the commitment is engaged and the value flows between the two parties.

A commitment, from a financial point of view, must entail some exchange of resource which can be measured in monetary terms. A friendly exchange of goodwill or a promise of loyalty by a customer to a company's products may represent valuable assets to that company. However, they would not be classed as commitments from a financial point of view. Further, a commitment must be capable of being located in time: i.e., a specific point at which the commitment is engaged and the period of time over which it will operate. Finally, a commitment must possess legal certainty.

THE COMMITMENT THEOREMS

1. *Economic value is transferred at the point a contractually binding commitment is entered into by an individual or organisation.*

What this means is that value flows with commitments. A commitment represents an agreement by one party to transfer an economic resource (i.e., a good or a service) to another party for some reward. Commitments in business are distinguished by their dual nature (there must always be at least two parties), their contractual nature in that if they are freely made they are usually legally enforceable, and finally, once made they serve to preclude other activities (opportunities) with which they conflict.

2. *Commitments can be either simple or compound.*

A 'simple commitment' is one which can be discharged by a single payment or transfer of goods or services at a particular point in time (Figure 4.2). Thus the sale of goods for cash would be a simple commitment, providing there was no residual liability in the form of a service contract or a guarantee on the goods sold. Such a commitment is engaged when the order for the goods is received and is discharged when the goods are paid for in full. A 'compound' commitment consists of a

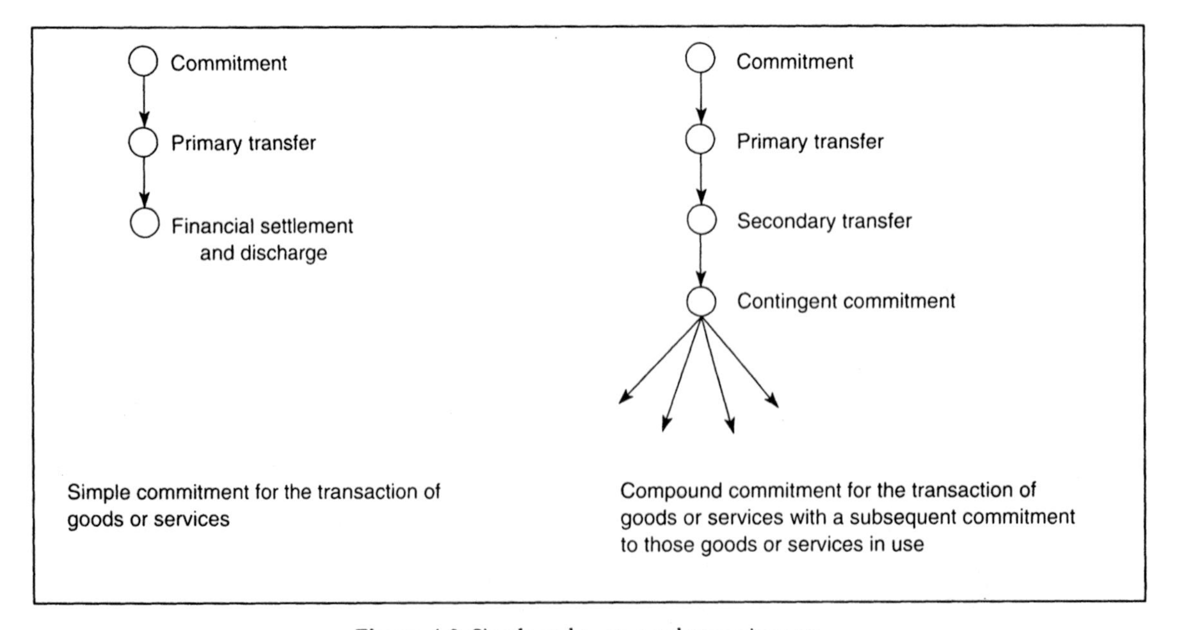

Figure 4.2 Simple and compound commitments.

primary commitment and a series of secondary contingent commitments which are engaged through the discharge of the primary commitment. Our sale of goods would be a compound commitment if they were offered with a guarantee. The primary commitment is for the supply of the goods for the stated price – the secondary commitment is engaged as soon as the goods are delivered.

3. *A commitment is complete when it is discharged without any residual claim remaining between the parties. At any point in time a business will hold a set of undischarged or uncompleted commitments.*

The concept of 'completion' is an important one for management. An incomplete commitment represents a constraint upon the capabilities of the organisation. Such a commitment is completed when it is fully liquidated, either by the receipt or by the payment of cash. For example, if a sale is made on credit the business holds a commitment from the customer which is only completed when full cash settlement is received.

4. *Commitments have discharge value.*

At any point in time a commitment will have a 'discharge' value. Discharge value is the minimum cost to one party which the other will accept to provide a free and complete release to both parties from the commitments. The discharge value represents the economic value to the party concerned of that commitment, and at any point in time a commitment will be either be 'discharged', in that no future claim exists from that commitment for either party, or 'undischarged' where some residual claim may exist.

5. *Commitments can be classified as either resource commitments or income-generating commitments.*

Resource commitments create the capability to engage in and complete income-generating commitments. A resource commitment will generally entail the expenditure of cash to discharge the commitment, an income commitment is discharged when cash is received from another party. Thus the sale of goods upon credit is an income-generating commitment which is created when an order for goods is received and discharged when the cash is finally paid by the customer. It will be an undischarged commitment whilst the goods are awaiting dispatch and the supplier is awaiting settlement of the account.

6. *A commitment which is undischarged by default of one party passes a one-time default option to the other party.*

If an order is placed for some goods and those goods turn out to be defective, I have two options: (i) I can cancel the commitment and reclaim any cash paid or (ii) I can accept the substandard goods. This option can be nullified by agreement in the contract between the two parties. The option element generated by default creates considerable risk for a business and is a source of serious contingent liabilities at any point in time.

7. *Commitments are either determinate or perpetual in time.*

Business commitments are usually determinate although the contingent liability attaching to service agreements can extend for very long periods into the future. However, such contingencies can usually be insured and the premium value is an approximation to the value of the liability. Some commitments, such as those between a company and its shareholders can be perpetual, in that the shareholder has the right to the residue of the business at any time in the future.

8. *An organisation is a complex set of simple and compound commitments.*

A business lies at the 'nexus' of an extensive array of commitments – some of which may be deeply interconnected. These commitments define the reality of the organisations and prescribe what is situationally possible for it to undertake. The network of organisational commitments therefore define its capability. At any point in time a cluster of commitments will relate to the providers of finance to the business, another cluster will be determined by the choices management make about the type of business they are in and yet another will be concerned with the way the organisation undertakes its production. Finally, other commitments will also be engaged which determine the output of the business.

9. *Commitments can be matched either by decision or temporally.*

When a decision is made to engage in an expansion of plant capacity or a contract to produce certain goods, then commitments will flow from that decision. There will be necessary commitments for expenditures and other commitments won for the purchase of goods and/or services by suppliers. When the value of the necessary expenditure commitments is deducted from the value of the income-generating commitments earned as a result of that decision and for no other reason, we have the contribution surplus generated by that decision. Much of the decision analysis which we examine in this book depends upon the concept of commitment matching. Commitment matching allows us to measure the net benefits which flow from given decisions.

Temporal commitment matching occurs when we seek to allocate to given periods of time (in conventional accounting usually a year) the value of the commitments engaged in achieving the income generating commitments claimed. The net value of temporally matched commitments gives a measure of period surplus or deficit.

10. *A commitment is valued in terms of the consequential cash change to the business caused by the decision to undertake that commitment.*

Commitments are generated by the exploitation of opportunities. Decisions about opportunities create a committed gain or loss. An opportunity is valued in terms of the net committed gain or loss it is expected to generate. This equates to the net cash contribution in the business produced by that opportunity.

Opportunity flows are the cash consequences of decisions to the business. An opportunity cost is the cash value flow caused by resource commitments made as the consequence of a given decision. Operationally, opportunity cost may be defined as the net cash change to the decision maker as a result of a decision to engage in and complete a resource commitment.

This is a very important definition which links together the concepts of opportunity, commitment and cost.

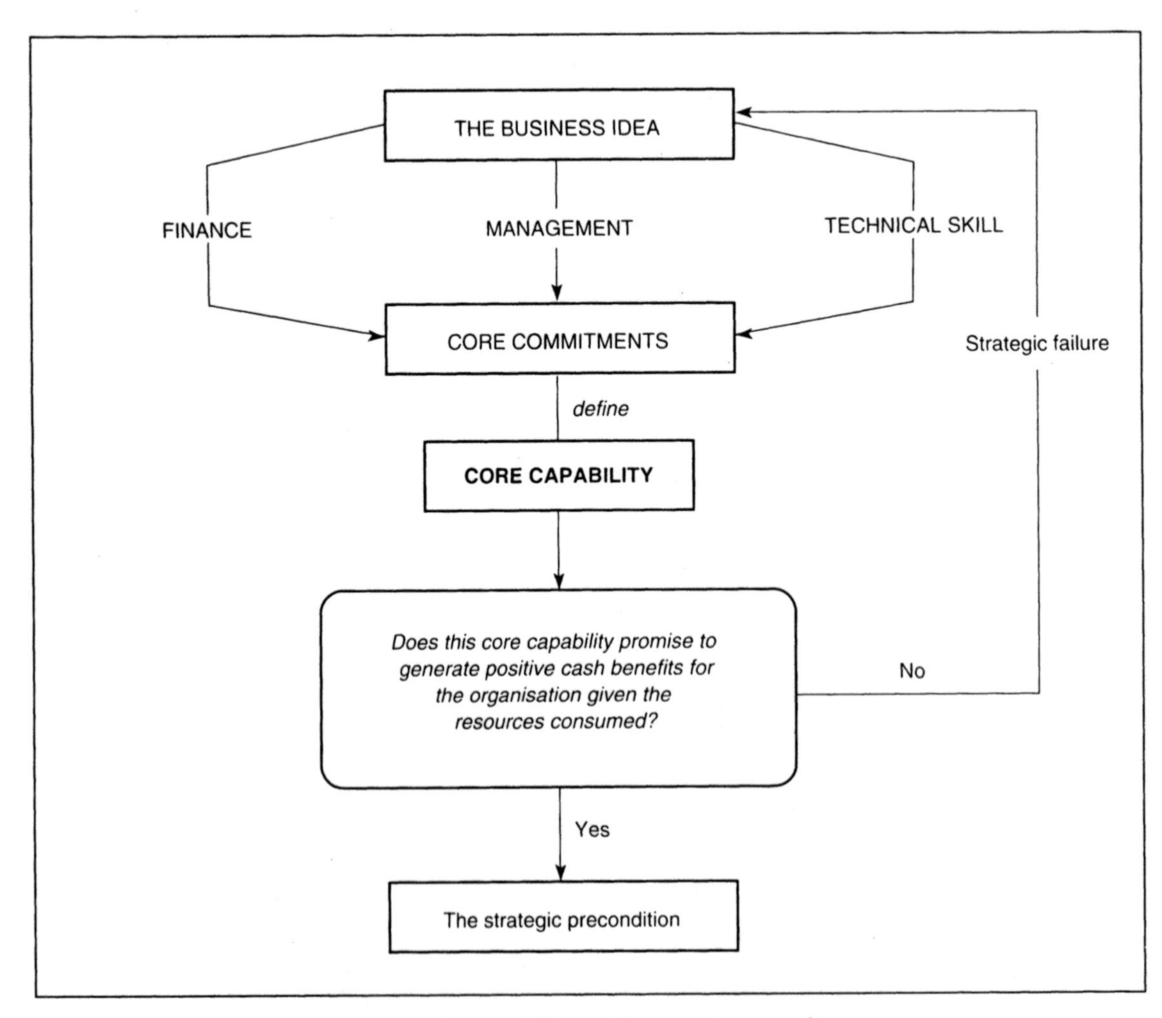

Figure 4.3 Core capability and the strategic precondition.

Opportunity cost can be visualised as follows: at any point in time the organisation will have a total stock of cash (which may, in certain sad situations, be a negative balance). When a decision is made to exploit an opportunity, this will result in certain commitments being made to the consumption of resources such as: capital, stocks, labour etc. The net change to the organisation's cash stock caused as a consequence of those commitments represents their opportunity cost.

UNDERSTANDING BUSINESS CAPABILITY

You may have heard the popular refrain: 'focus on core business'. Indeed, many of the popular management gurus make this a central point of their message. Indeed, it has been so influential in many American and British board rooms that companies have divested subsidiaries, shed product lines and given up training departments. However, it is dangerous nonsense. What a business should focus upon is its core capability (Figure 4.3). The only business which is 'core' to an organisation is that which it can undertake more cheaply or more efficiently or to a higher quality than the competition. In other words, that business in which the organisation has a superior capability.

The problem is that the business in which a company is engaged is the result of a sequence of events, decisions and commitments made over a period of time. A company's capability determines what business it can engage in successfully and what business it should ignore. The issue is *capability* and, in particular, that capability which, if exercised efficiently, can lead it to achieve its purpose most effectively.

THE CAPABILITY THEOREMS

11. *Organisational capability is the actual or potential ability of the organisation to undertake purposeful work.*

Organisational capability is directly analogous to the physical concept of energy – an analogy which we will explore in some detail. All organisations have a finite capacity to undertake work at any point in time. Organisations also have the ability to become more efficient in the work that they do and a 'high capability' organisation is one which can direct its abilities in the most purposeful ways possible. Clearly, however, the concept of high or low capability is predicated upon some notion of organisational purpose and some of these purposes we discussed in Chapter 3 when considering the nature of organisational missions and objectives. Because organisational work can be undertaken in many different ways, it is meaningful to talk about organisational 'capabilities' to represent the plurality of ways in which it can act.

12. *Organisational capability can be generated by its participants contributing their individual efforts in agreed ways or it can be endowed by external agencies.*

The capability of an organisation is created through the commitments an organisation makes and the way that connects together the various resources at its disposal. A manufacturer, for example, will bring together technical expertise, capital equipment, raw materials and financial resources to create products for sale. A service company will not, generally, make such extensive commitments to capital equipment but will invest more in the technical expertise which it is attempting to sell. Sometimes capability is created through some external agency such as government, which has the ability to nominate certain capabilities to particular groups. For example, the ability to conduct an audit of a limited company is restricted to qualified professionals and other approved individuals.

13. *An organisational 'resource' is a store of organisational capability which can be subsequently released.*

All of the resources of an organisation offer the potential of satisfying particular opportunities. For example, finished stocks offer the capability to fulfil customer orders on demand; capital plant offers the capability to produce in that plant and so on. The potential for release defines the life of a particular resource.

14. *Organisational capabilities fall into four conceptual classes: core, latent, intersecting and detrimental.*

Some organisational capabilities will be core to its mission, others latent and yet others detrimental. A fourth class of capability intersect with all of the other capabilities of the organisation (Figure 4.4).

A core capability is one which is central to the primary purpose of an organisation which in a business firm will lead it to exploit profitable or value generating opportunities. Core capability for a business relates to what the strategists refer to as 'competitive advantage'; namely, the ability, in a competitive environment, to undertake profitable

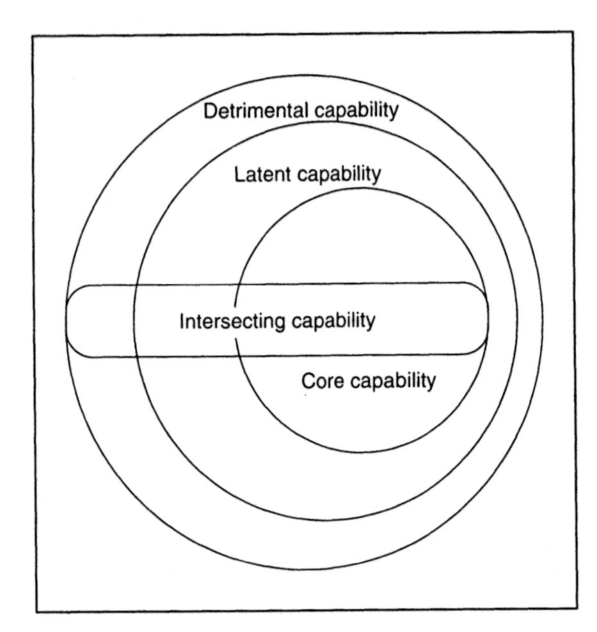

Figure 4.4 Capability levels in business.

commitments. When an organisation has learnt the trick of sustaining and possibly developing a core capability, then it is said to have 'sustainable competitive' advantage.

In addition to core capabilities, an organisation may have a range of other capabilities which are latent to the core. Such capabilities do not offer any particular current advantage to the organisation, although they may be capable of being developed into the core. However, the organisation will have to deploy considerable capability (which will inevitably withdraw short-term capability from the core) in order to achieve the transformation. For example, a firm of graphic designers had developed considerable expertise in the development and representation of corporate stationery. They also had some capability amongst their staff in general marketing although this had not been well developed. The management decided to divert considerable effort towards enhancing this capability through education and training in an attempt to break into the corporate imaging business. They were eventually successful in creating a new core capability for themselves but at considerable short-run expense in terms of missed opportunities and personal effort.

Some capabilities will always exist, in any organisation, which if exercised will lead to the consumption of resource with no net gain to the organisation. These are what we call 'detrimental capabilities'. For example, a major computer manufacturer developed a network-based system which allowed open access to all its employees' diaries and gave anyone the capability to book a colleague's time for a meeting. It was possible for the victim in the process to reject a meeting request, although this required an e-mail message with, in the majority of cases, some excuse being provided. The effect was that no employee had full control over their time without keeping a careful watch on their diaries and by being vigilant in rejecting appointments with all the necessary excuses that entailed. Considerable organisational effort went into (i) unnecessary meetings and (ii) protecting time.

Finally, some capabilities will be intersecting in that, although they are not themselves in the core and they do not generate competitive advantage in their own right, they do permit other capabilities to be more effectively exercised. For example, a company had a reasonable capability in financial management which provided timely and relevant information for a variety of users throughout the organisation. The point about intersecting capabilities is that although they enhance the power of core capabilities in achieving the ends of the organisation, they also exacerbate those capabilities which if exercised would be to the detriment of the organisation.

15. *Capabilities can be enhanced in scope and in power, although a Coulomb barrier exists which inhibits such enhancement.*

The concept of organisational capability allows us to make some sense of some inertial properties of organisations. Like all systems, it is rarely possible to make a change from one organisational level of capability to another without donating some 'transitional energy' to that change (Figure 4.5).

The amount of this organisational energy required for successful change is dependent upon:

- the nature of the energy input and how well it is focused on the change in question; this will to a certain extent be conditioned by
  - (i) the organisation parameters, such as its structure or culture, which can diffuse the energy input, and
  - (ii) the height of the capability barrier being surmounted.

16. *Organisational capability is quantised.*

What this means is that when organisational capability is lost, its decay occurs suddenly and in a particular way defined by the arrangements of capabilities which sustain that capability. This seems an unusual proposition as, on first sight, we would

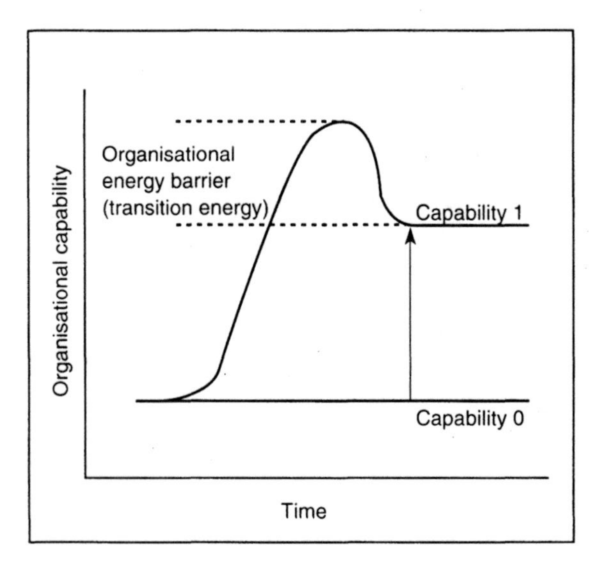

Figure 4.5 The capability barrier.

expect an organisation's capability to fade slowly rather than be lost suddenly. However, in a perfectly competitive world we can see the problem. Suppose, in a world where there are many buyers and sellers, that a single producer loses efficiency and his or her costs rise relative to the market. In that situation, if the producer raises the price of the product concerned, he or she does not lose market share gradually; the loss will be sudden and complete. Dynamically, for any system, where its capability is under the control of a number of different variables, sudden discontinuities will occur in permissable system states.

17. *Organisational capabilities can be enhanced by good organisational design, correspondingly they can be nullified by inappropriate design.*

Organisational structure is formed by the network of formal and informal relationships which exist between individuals, groups or offices within the business. Where those structures are rigidly constrained to accommodate just certain types of commitment, or the exercise of a particular capability, then change will be restricted.

CONCLUSION

In this chapter we have explored the theorems of strategic accounting concentrating on the two Cs of commitments (upon which transactions are based) and capability. The remaining two Cs of the strategic accounting approach – cash and control – will be discussed in later chapters. The language we have developed in this chapter pervades much of our discussion of accounting and finance throughout this book and helps us synthesise issues in those subjects with the strategic problems of the firm. In the next chapter we turn our attention to cash dynamics and the impact of opportunities upon the cash resources of the organisation.

Chapter 5

Cash Dynamics of a Business

Level M

Contents

Summary

In this chapter we distinguish two aspects of a business's ability to generate cash: the static problem, which focuses on how strong a business is as a cash engine, and the dynamic problem, which is concerned with how good the company is at converting its resources into cash. We commence our analysis with a discussion of the nature of cash as a perfect asset and describe how that asset is generated through the operational activity of the business. In our analysis of the dynamic properties of cash, we examine the impact of time-lag effects upon cash holdings and how time effects produce problems across the cash engine of the business.

INTRODUCTION TO THE CASH PROBLEM

From the financial perspective a business organisation can be regarded as an engine for the generation of cash. There is considerable confusion in many managers' minds about the role of cash in a business and how it relates to its profitability. In this chapter we take our first steps in understanding the significance of cash, and in the next chapter we will explore the nature of profit and how it relates to the cash concept.

Cash is economic value temporarily trapped in instantaneously negotiable form. In order to understand cash more fully we should define what we mean by a concept called the 'perfect asset'.

The perfect asset is, like all assets (imperfect or not), an embodiment of economic value to the holder. In other words an asset gives an individual or a business power over current or future consumption. A car gives us the power to 'consume' transport. Consumption is simply economists' jargon for the capability to use or enjoy something – not just the ability to eat it (although it may be that as well). A piece of plant, or a building gives us (or contributes towards) our ability to produce things in the future which will, we hope, increase our economic value.

The perfect asset also has the following characteristics:

- It is capable of instantaneous conversion into consumption which implies that it is perfectly exchangeable into other goods or services.
- It is perfectly stable in value.
- There are no barriers to anyone holding the perfect asset such as transactions costs in buying and selling.
- It is perfectly divisible and perfectly portable.

This is a formidable list, and in a real economy only the national currency is likely to be a close approximation to the perfect asset. In practice, the cash held by a business will be denominated in the local currency, and most of it will be held in the form of bank balances. In Figure 5.1 we have put a range of assets onto a graph showing the two principal characteristics of negotiability and stability in value.

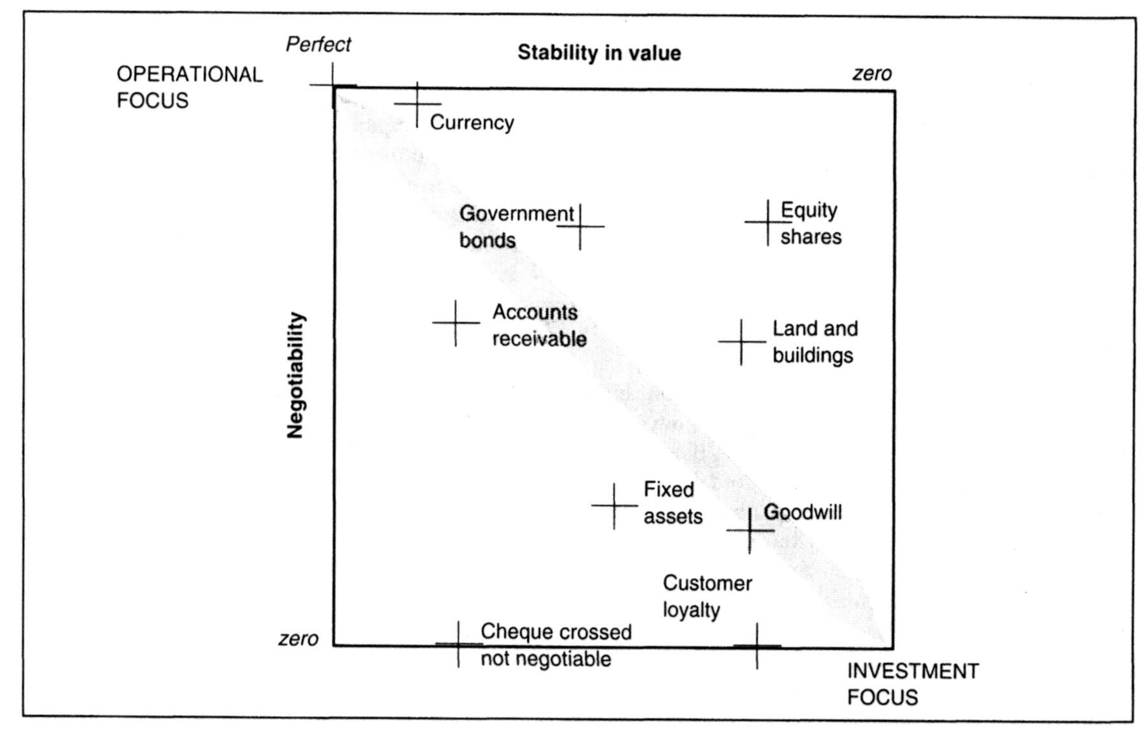

Figure 5.1 The asset spectrum.

When we say an asset is perfectly negotiable we mean that it can be exchanged with someone else, instantaneously and with no loss of value. By definition, therefore, there are no transaction costs in transferring a perfectly negotiable asset, and to achieve this it would need to be perfectly divisible and portable. By stability in value we mean that the asset will not lose value simply by virtue of being held for a period of time.

The perfect asset also has the advantage that it is perfectly additive, i.e. asset values attaching to different sources (say receipts converted from the sale of goods and from the sale of a fixed asset) can be added together to derive a total value if they are converted at the same point in time. Because pure cash has this additive property, it provides a ratio scale for valuing all other assets.

Note also that investment is about yielding up the perfect asset for less perfect assets but which do have a greater ability to generate future return. Clearly, once imperfect assets are held, we then have the operational motive to convert them or exploit them in such a way that cash is generated. Indeed, the long-term investment problem for any business can be defined as the conversion of current cash into the most productive real assets possible. The operational task of the business is, however, just the reverse – to utilise real assets to produce cash again.

The cash problem of a business can be divided into two complementary problems.

(i) The static problem: how strong is the business at generating cash? Cash statics can be subdivided into two further problem areas:
- structural or 'capital' statics which are concerned with the potential of the business to raise large tranches of cash for investment purposes;
- operational or 'revenue' statics which are concerned with the ability of the business to generate cash surplus from its operations.

(ii) The dynamic problem:
- understanding the lags between the operations of the business and the consequential cash changes which occur (the lag problem);
- managing the flow of cash through the business and ensuring that the cash is deployed in the most effective way possible.

The static problem dominates the dynamic problem in that, in the long run, if the company cannot solve its cash problem at the static level, then it will not survive. If a business cannot generate sufficient sustainable cash return on its business, then no matter how adroit it is in managing its cash resources, it will have insufficient in the longer run to fund its commitments. However, even given the solution of the static problem at both the structural and the operational levels the business may still not survive if it cannot maintain the necessary flows of cash through the business.

The business cash engine is shown in Figure 5.2. Cash is brought into the business by either capital or revenue transactions. There are two principal sources of capital funds.

(i) The owners of the business who, in forming the business, put their own resources into the project in the form of equity capital. They may add to that capital subsequently and they may withdraw some of that capital as drawings in an owner-managed business. If the business generates a surplus of cash then they may decide, or their directors decide on their behalf to reward them with a dividend.
(ii) The lenders to the business such as the banks, financial institutions or private individuals who put in cash to the business in the expectation of interest payments and the eventual repayment of their debt.

These two sources of funds should be used to finance the capital equipment which a business needs to exploit the opportunities available to it. The business must make a choice about the proportion of capital funds it should acquire through debt or equity, and its success will be measured in terms of how cheaply it can acquire that funding. In investing that funding it will seek out those opportunities which maximise the cash generating value of the business and, as a general rule, no investment project should be accepted which will deplete its cash stock over the longer run.

Projects should only be accepted which tend to increase a business's stock of cash after taking account of the payments it must make to its owners and lenders in the form of dividends and interest as compensation for their investment of capital. It is a strategic precondition for success that a business should only ever make capital investments in cash-contributing projects.

Revenue cash is generated from customers in payments for goods and services supplied. Note that

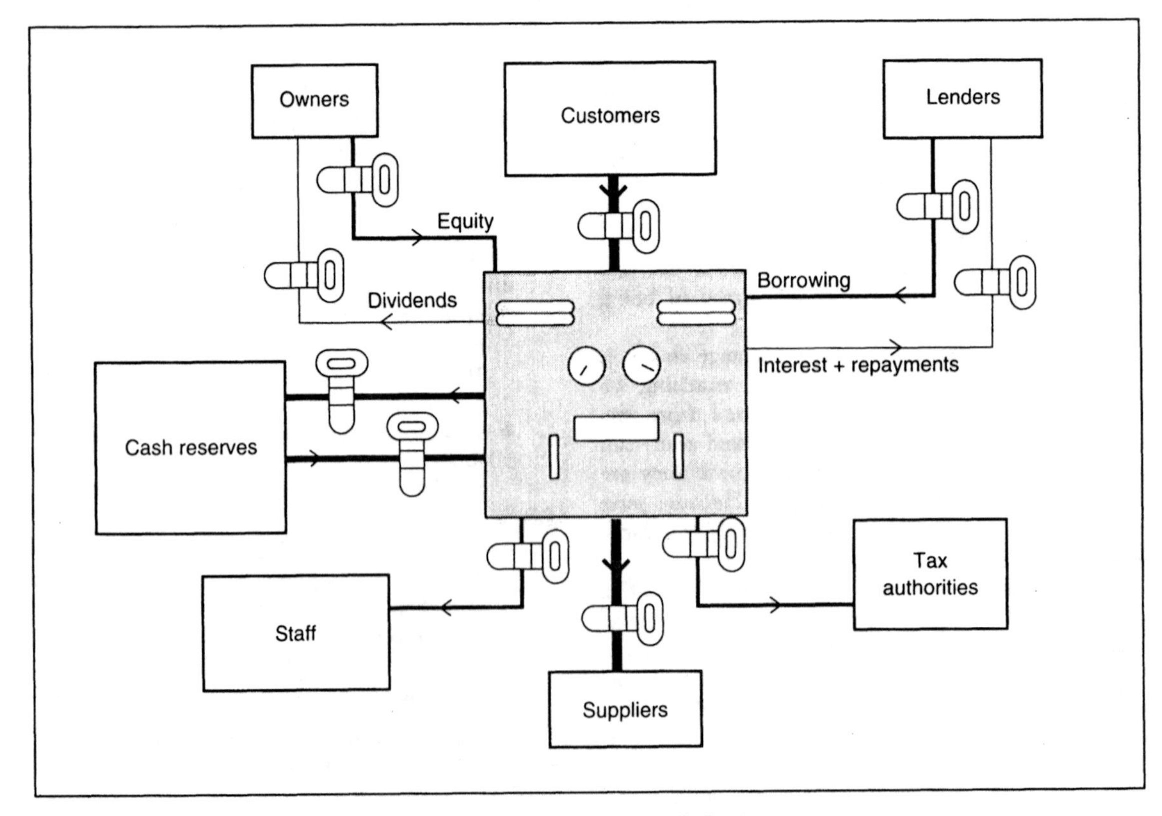

Figure 5.2 The cash engine of a business.

revenue cash tends to lag the actual sale to the customer by some time because in many business sectors customers expect credit. Indeed, in certain situations it may well be that the company has purchased and paid for the resources needed to provide the service or goods concerned some considerable time before the cash is received from the customer.

A company will make expenditures to essentially three groups:

(i) its suppliers for the goods and services they provide (revenue transactions) and for capital equipment, land and buildings (capital transactions); as with customers there may well be some credit period taken by the business against its suppliers;
(ii) its labour force for the work they do;
(iii) the tax authorities for the collection of Value Added Tax, Corporation Tax, Local Tax and Income Tax for its workforce.

Finally, the company will place its surplus cash into its reserves in a form that it can recover for its investment needs.

Figure 5.2 shows in schematic form the cash engine of any business. Part of the art of financial management is to be able to regulate the flows in such a way that the value of the business is maximised and it always has access to the cash that it needs for further investment, funding working capital (stocks and sales of goods ahead of payment by customers).

THE CONDITIONS FOR BUSINESS SUCCESS

In Chapter 4 we introduced the idea that the core capability of a business must offer the potential for undertaking business opportunities which generate a contribution of cash to the business. There is considerable confusion over this issue, largely because of the pervasive notion that a business must be profitable to survive. As we shall see in the next chapter, profit is a highly abstract concept which is difficult to measure in practice. In this chapter we propose a simple financial law of business:

RYAN'S FIRST LAW

A business will not survive if, by using its core capability and by operating in the most cost-efficient way, it cannot generate sufficient cash to cover the costs of sustaining that core capability.

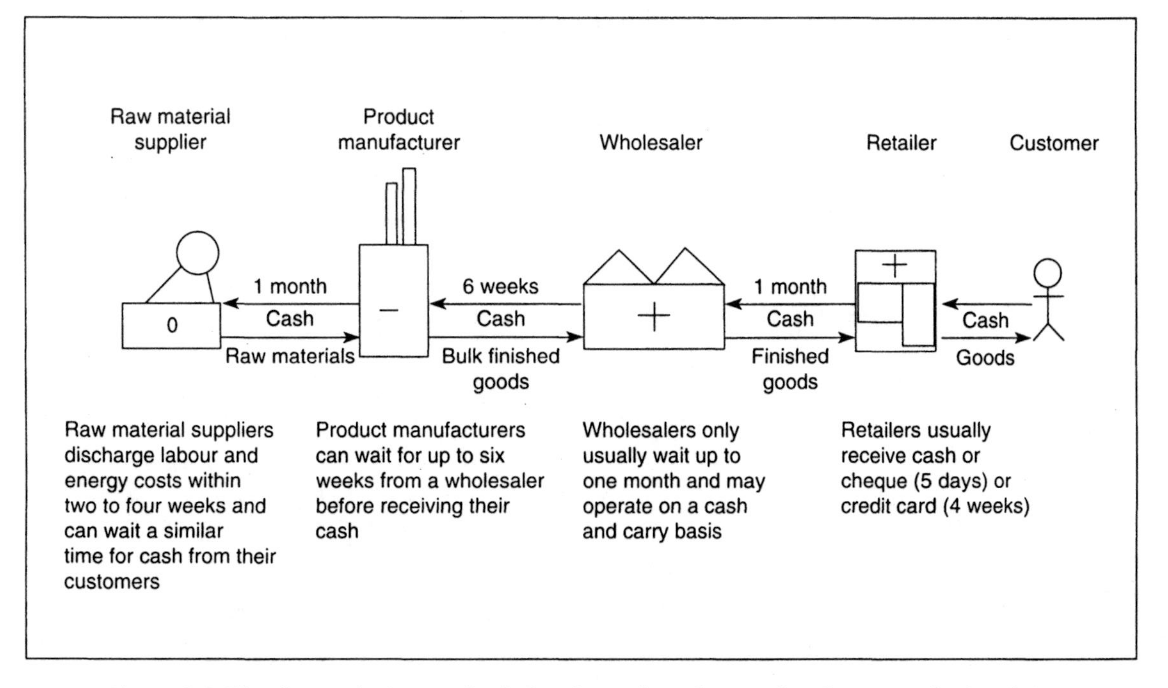

Figure 5.3 The pluses and minuses of cash flow from sales and to suppliers down a production chain.

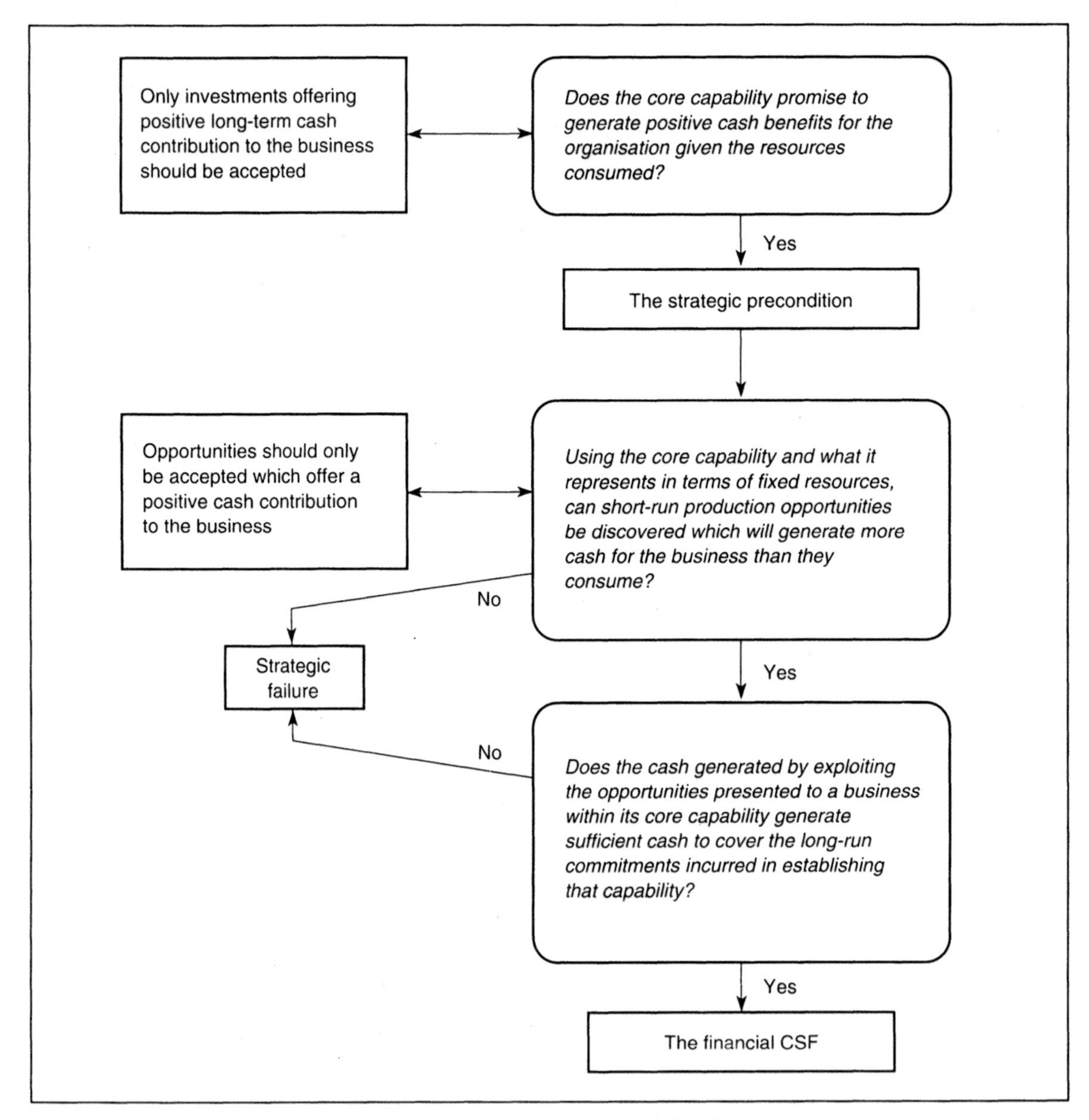

Figure 5.4 The financial critical success factor (CSF) for a business.

In Figure 5.4 we show in schematic form the conditions required to fulfil the financial critical success factor (CSF).

EXAMPLE

Jones & Co. had an established construction business which required £1.5 million annually to sustain its operation. This finance was required to:

- *finance the company's debt;*
- *maintain a modest head office and staff;*
- *maintain and operate a production facility, warehouse and distribution network.*

During the year the company engaged in eight public works projects which generated revenues and incurred direct cash expenditure on each project (Table 5.1).

As this example shows, each of the projects (except project 5) generated a net cash contribution to the business after deducting the direct cash cost incurred in fulfilling each project. Of the eight,

Table 5.1

Project	1	2	3	4	5	6	7	8
Revenue (£'000)	800	200	400	650	1 500	775	985	990
Direct cost (£'000)	700	150	150	500	1 650	650	600	720
Contribution (£'000)	100	50	250	150	(150)	125	385	270

Total contribution on all eight projects	£1 180 000
Less: fixed costs of operation	1 000 000
Surplus cash generated in year	£180 000

incurred in fulfilling each project. Of the eight, only project 5 produced a negative cash contribution but overall the business was able to earn surplus cash of £180 000. This business has satisfied the strategic imperative in the year in question. It has, by using the core capability created by its previous investment decisions in plant, building and know-how, earned more cash than it needed to spend in order to sustain that capability.

HOW TO MEASURE THE STATIC CASH-GENERATING POWER OF A BUSINESS

Our discussion of Jones & Co. above suggests a simple way of determining the power of the cash-generating engine of the business. Our critical success factor in financial terms is to be able to generate sufficient cash from productive operations to fund the fixed committed cost of the business during a given trading period. We can, therefore, devise a simple business ratio which we can apply to the financial figures of a business to determine the power of its cash engine:

$$\text{Static power ratio} = \frac{\text{contribution from all productive activities in a given period}}{\text{total business fixed costs}}$$

In Jones & Co.'s case, in the year in question, this ratio was:

$$\begin{aligned}\text{Static power ratio} &= 1\ 180\ 000/1\ 000\ 000\\ &= 1.18\end{aligned}$$

Any value less than 1.0 indicates that the business has not been able to generate sufficient cash from operations to cover its fixed costs, and it would have to withdraw cash from reserves to survive. Any value in excess of 1.0 indicates a positive position, and the greater the value of the excess over 1.0 the more powerful the business. Over a period of time, if we observed a downward trend in this ratio, it would indicate that the business was running into trouble.

Only two remedies exist for a business whose static power ratio is declining.

(i) Increase the cash contribution generated by opportunities by (a) increasing sales revenue and/or (b) reducing the direct cash costs associated with that opportunity.
(ii) Reduce the fixed cost of operation, searching out cheaper ways of sustaining and developing the business's core capability.

Easy? Well of course any business problem can be solved by either increasing revenue or by reducing costs. However, if you agree with the sense of the analysis above, that is, that a business should only exploit opportunities which yield more cash than they consume, then the implications of that simple step can be enormous. We will start to examine those implications in the next three chapters of this book.

Before we move to a consideration of the dynamic aspects of a business's cash engine, there is one further problem to be considered. The business approach we have discussed above conjures up an image of the business investing to build its capability and then, like some miser, collecting into a pile the benefits of those opportunities which yield more cash than they exploit. The problem with this is what we refer to as the paradox of cash.

THE PARADOX OF CASH

The paradox is that as soon as a business gains cash it

should attempt to do something with it. In other words, our whole emphasis so far is to generate capability and consequential opportunities which are positive cash generators for the business. However, large idle balances of cash are a sign of weak, rather than good, management, and even temporary holdings of cash should be invested until needed. A prudent business has the following three choices in dealing with its idle cash resources.

(i) Reinvest that money into enhanced core or intersecting capability. So, the business could fund further capital expansion, training and education for its workforce or invest in superior financial or management capability.
(ii) Place the money into the best short-term, highest-yielding use outside the business (perhaps through the money markets) in such a way that it can be recovered when the business needs the cash for (i).
(iii) Return the money to its investors as dividends or offer its employees enhanced benefits in the form of pay rises, incentive bonuses, or better work facilities.

CASH DYNAMICS

The dynamic problem of a business is concerned with the efficient conversion of assets into cash and in particular the rapid recovery of accounts due from customers. The crucial element in cash dynamics is time. It is important for any business to recover the cash benefits of its operations as quickly as possible and to exploit the credit opportunities available to it to the full.

In order to understand the cash dynamics of a business it is necessary to understand some simple techniques for valuing cash flows received at different points in time. If cash changes occur at the same point in time, then by the additivity principal for the perfect asset they can be added together, for example:

Cash realised on the sale of fixed assets	£45 000
Cash recovered from customers	£16 000
	£61 000
Cash paid to suppliers	£20 000
Net cash change from these transactions	£41 000

However, if the cash values are receivable at different points in time then they are not additive. For example, a bond returning £100 in one year's time cannot be valued in the same terms as cash of £100 receivable now. In other words cash has 'time value'.

Even if our return of £100 in one year's time was certain (in terms of both its value and our confidence that we would receive it) we would still not equate that future cash value with a present value of £100 held currently. This reflects the fact that individuals have a higher preference for holding current cash rather than a claim on cash in the future, even if they perceive the cash to be the perfect asset. In a perfect world, the market rate of interest would reflect the difference in preference between cash held now and in the future.

EXAMPLE

(i) A £100 bond is due to mature in 1 year's time. At a market rate of interest of (say) 4% per annum the present value of that bond is given by:

$$£100.00/1.04 = £96.15$$

(ii) An investment fund is due to yield £10 000 in each of the next three years. The present value of

Table 5.2

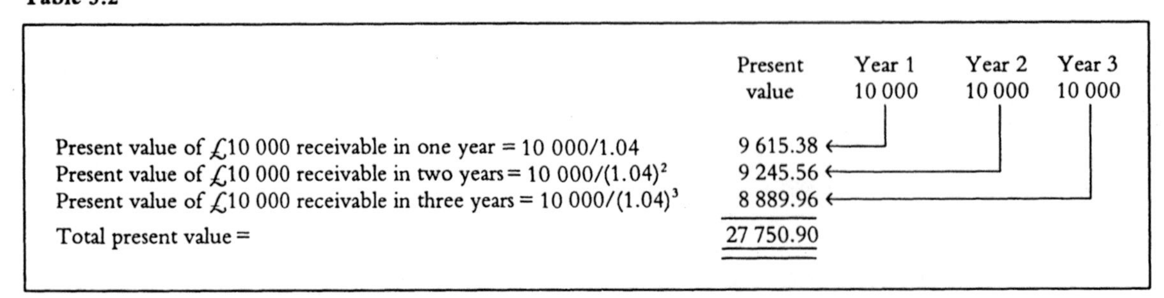

	Present value	Year 1 10 000	Year 2 10 000	Year 3 10 000
Present value of £10 000 receivable in one year = 10 000/1.04	9 615.38 ←	┘		
Present value of £10 000 receivable in two years = 10 000/(1.04)^2	9 245.56 ←		┘	
Present value of £10 000 receivable in three years = 10 000/(1.04)^3	8 889.96 ←			┘
Total present value =	27 750.90			

The general formula for calculating the present value of a future cash sum receivable at period (n) in the future at the period rate of interest (i) is:

$$\text{Present value} = \frac{\text{future value}}{(1+i)^n}$$

We explore the mechanics of this procedure in greater detail in Chapter 14. The problem with this present-value procedure is that it becomes very cumbersome when we are dealing with balances which are being reinvested at short intervals (bank balances, for example, are 'compounded' on a daily basis). It is also cumbersome when we are dealing with fractions of a year. To cope with this we need a formula which allows us to calculate a present-value equivalent for any cash flow using an annual rate of interest, but where the cash arrives at any point in time.

The present value of a continuously discounted cash flow at rate of interest i per annum is given by:

$$\text{Present value} = \text{future value} \times e^{-it}$$

where

t = time in days/365 or weeks/52 or months/12

EXAMPLE (i)

A company has customer accounts outstanding of £90 000 for which it expects to receive payment in 30 days. The annual rate of interest is 12% per annum:

$$\begin{aligned}\textit{Present value} &= 90\,000 \times e^{-(0.12 \times 30/365)}\\ &= 90\,000 \times e^{-(0.009\,863)}\\ &= 90\,000 \times 0.990\,19\\ &= £89\,117\end{aligned}$$

EXAMPLE (ii)

A £100 bond is due to be redeemed in nine months time. It has an interest rate of 10% per annum attached.

$$\begin{aligned}\textit{Bond present value} &= 100 \times e^{-(0.10 \times 9/12)}\\ &= 100 \times e^{-0.075}\\ &= 100 \times 0.927\,74\\ &= £92.77\end{aligned}$$

We now have a method of finding the present value of any cash sum due to an individual or a business and, conversely, the present value of any cash payment which a company may be required to make. We, therefore, have a direct method of valuing the flows of cash incident upon a company to determine their relative impact upon the business.

EXAMPLE (iii)

A company has average accounts receivable from customers of £10 000 which it expects to receive in 90 days. It also has accounts payable to its suppliers of £10 000 which it is required to pay in 30 days. The rate of interest is 10% per annum.

Present value of accounts receivable

$$\begin{aligned}&= 10\,000 \times e^{-(0.1 \times 90/365)}\\ &= £9756\end{aligned}$$

Present value of accounts payable

$$\begin{aligned}&= (10\,000) \times e^{-(0.1 \times 30/365)}\\ &= £(9918)\end{aligned}$$

Loss of present value through time lag

$$\begin{aligned}&= (9918 - 9756)\\ &= £(162)\end{aligned}$$

So, the effect of a lag on the business is a loss of £162 simply through the lost interest in financing outstanding customer balances. This is an important effect about which we will say more in Chapter 31 where we develop a technique called the 'financial μ' for evaluating the cash dynamics of a business from its accounts.

EXAMPLE (iv)

A company has instituted a just-in-time (JIT) policy on production which has had the effect of reducing raw material stock from £100 000 to £85 000. In addition, the average holding period of an item of raw material stock has fallen from 30 to 20 days. The rate of interest is 15% per annum.

Present value of stock held prior to change

$$\begin{aligned}&= £100\,000 \times e^{-(0.15 \times 30/365)}\\ &= £98\,775\end{aligned}$$

Present value of stock held after change

$$\begin{aligned}&= £85\,000 \times e^{-(0.15 \times 20/365)}\\ &= £84\,304\end{aligned}$$

To give a value difference

$$= -£14\,471 \textit{ due to change}$$

of which the value effect was

$$= (85\,000 - 100\,000) \times e^{-(0.15 \times 30/365)}$$
$$= -£14\,816$$

and the timing effect was

$$= [e^{-(0.15 \times 30/365)} - e^{-(0.15 \times 20/365)}] \times 85\,000$$
$$= 0.004\,067 \times 85\,000$$
$$= £345$$

What this calculation reveals is that there has been a reduction in the present stock value of £14 471 due to the JIT policy change. Of this value, £14 816 was due to reduced stock value held which, although shown as negative from the stock point of view, would have yielded this amount of cash for other purposes in the firm. The value of £345 was gained as the positive value of holding the stock for a shorter period.

In this example, we deploy an important technique called 'value partitioning' where an overall value change is split into two or more component parts. We will examine this technique again in our work on variance analysis in Chapter 26. However, the point to note about the example is that we have identified both from a policy change such as a move to JIT manufacturing. In this case the former outweighed the latter by some considerable margin, which indicates to us that the real benefit of the JIT policy change was not that it reduced stock holding times, but that it reduced the average stock value by £14 816 in present-value terms.

Using this technique it is possible to value timing differences across any aspect of an organisation's financial performance; furthermore, we can use the technique to explore the implication of timing differences – leads and lags – in cash flows for the business.

THE TREASURY FUNCTION

The management of the cash balances held by a business at any point is the responsibility of the 'treasury function'. Even in a small business, active treasury management allied with strict credit control can be the difference between competitive success or failure. The treasury manager will be responsible for ensuring that:

- cash flows are matched to the operational needs of the business;
- any unused balances of cash are invested on the money market at favourable rates of interest;
- foreign transactions are financed with foreign exchange at the best rates and minimum risk;
- cash is never left 'lying around' unused within the business.

Treasury management is a skilled business and although only the largest organisations can usually afford professional treasury managers even the smallest business should ensure that its cash resources are rigorously controlled and exploited.

CONCLUSION

In this chapter we have examined a critical issue which lies at the heart of business success, namely sustaining the cash resources of the business. In particular we have considered the necessary conditions for business success and defined a first financial law of business. This financial law states that a business will not survive if it cannot generate sufficient cash through the use of its core capability to sustain that capability in existence. This introduces two problems: (i) ensuring a sufficiency of cash; (ii) managing the dynamics of the resultant cash flows so that financial needs are met as they arise. Both of these problems have been considered in this chapter. We now turn our attention to the measurement of business performance and the importance of the matching principle in accounting.

Chapter 6

Measuring Business Performance

Level E

Contents

Summary

The matching principle is designed to ensure that the costs which gave rise to particular revenues are matched with them. In this way the efficiency with which a particular product's costs are converted into revenue (or the surplus we call profit) can be measured. The matching principle is, therefore, all about measuring business performance which we take to mean the performance in creating profit. After an initial discussion of the matching principle we will examine 'temporal matching' which is concerned with allocating revenues to the time periods in which they are earned and the costs of the resources consumed to those time periods. We then consider decision matching which is the logical analysis of the cost and revenue consequences of any given decision to determine the contribution that decision can make to the business as a whole. Finally we will consider cost matching to individual products by allocation and by activity.

INTRODUCTION

In this chapter we consider the problem of business performance. This is a generic problem which management faces when examining the consequences of its business decisions, whether for internal control purposes or for reporting to external stakeholders. At the heart of the business performance issue is the matching principle which converts raw commitment and cash data into information about how the business is expected to perform, or actually has performed. This chapter is an important precursor to the work we do in the next chapter and in the last section of this book which is concerned with the issues of external reporting.

Business performance can be measured at a number of levels:

- firm level, where certain key aspects of financial performance over an accounting period (usually annually) are reported to external stakeholders;
- divisional or subsidiary level, where the financial performance of a significant part of the business over a given accounting period is reported to group level management;
- business unit level, where the financial performance of substantial components of the business are reported to divisional or group management;
- production level, where the activities of individual production units or projects are assessed and reported to business unit management;
- product level, where the performance of individual products are assessed as contributors to the business's overall performance.

In order to understand the issues within the measurement of financial performance it is important to understand what accountants refer to as the 'matching' principle. The matching principle is what converts the routine analysis of financial data into an art form.

The performance of any system can be thought of in one of two ways:

- how quickly the system achieves the goal or target which has been set for it;

- the efficiency with which the system converts inputs into outputs.

To a certain extent, these two ways of viewing performance may be interlinked, but in most business situations it is the latter which is of most concern. In business firms management is usually interested in the efficiency with which costs are converted into revenues during a set period of time to create what is loosely termed 'profit'. As we shall see later, profit is a tricky concept to measure, and sometimes accountants are accused of 'creatively' measuring profit to give distorted views of performance.

Profit is the surplus of revenue over the cost which can be fairly attributed to the activity of earning that revenue. For a business system,

$$\text{Mark-up ratio} = \frac{\text{profit in period}}{\text{total cost in period}} \times 100$$

is a simple measure of the efficiency of a business in converting the resources consumed in a period into profit. A directly analogous ratio is profit to sales revenue (or the turnover ratio) which is:

$$\text{Turnover ratio} = \frac{\text{profit in period}}{\text{total cost in period}} \times 100$$

$$= \frac{\text{profit in period}}{\text{turnover}} \times 100$$

THE MATCHING PRINCIPLE

To be consistent in measuring performance we must be able to match the inputs to outputs (Figure 6.1), and in financial terms this means matching business costs to business revenues. So in order to measure performance it is necessary to define a 'matching principle', that is we need to create some rule which will allow us to decide which costs can be matched with given revenues and which cannot.

Matching can be achieved in the following ways.

- Temporal matching, where costs incurred in earning revenue in a given period are matched against that revenue. The surplus, as we have stated above, is the 'profit' for the period.
- Decision matching, where the costs necessarily incurred as a result of a given decision are matched with the revenues or other benefits which are expected to flow from that decision. The surplus is referred to as the 'contribution' of the decision.
- Allocation matching where indirect costs are matched to units produced, using either some input measure into the production of the product concerned, or some input activity into the product concerned.
- Operation matching, where the revenues generated by a particular business operation or activity are matched with the costs which are directly attributable to that operation or activity.

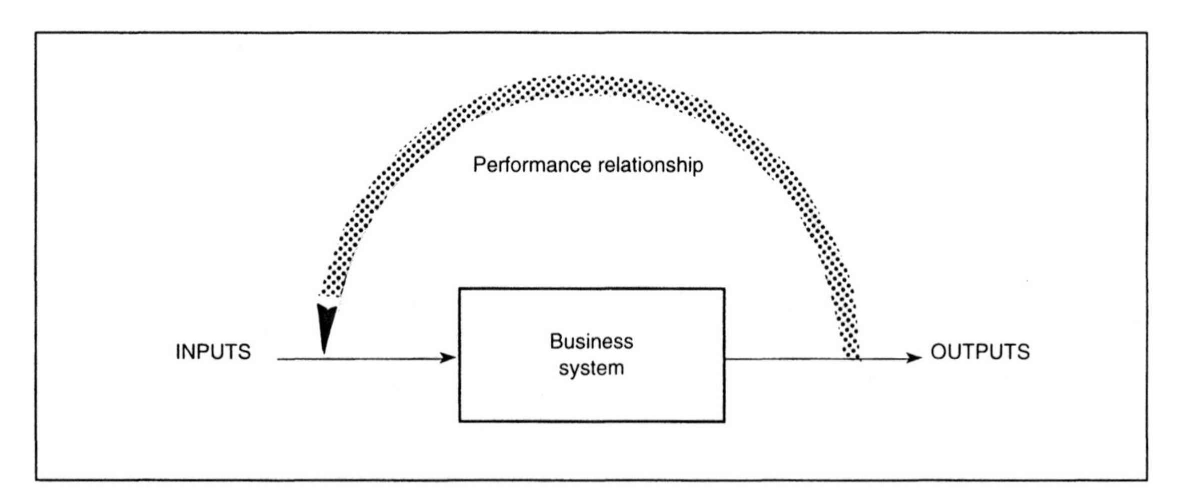

Figure 6.1 The relationship of system outputs to inputs. The ratio of outputs/inputs for any business system is a crude measure of performance providing the inputs are matched with outputs.

TEMPORAL MATCHING

In the preparation of the annual accounts of a business, certain revenues and expenditures will be brought into account and others are ignored. It may be that there has been some significant previous expenditure to establish fixed resources which the business has utilised during the year in question. On the revenue side, cash may have been received in advance in a particular year for work which the business is undertaking beyond the financial year end. In this case the accountants will argue that only part of the cash received should be recognised as revenue in the year in question.

Such temporal matching of expenditures and revenues is a favourite pastime of accountants at the year end when they work to produce the business's statement of profit or loss for the year.

Examples: capital expenditure

When a business spends capital resources on the acquisition of buildings, plant, equipment, vehicles and so on, it expects to use those fixed assets to generate revenue for a number of years. The commitment to purchase the fixed asset, and the discharge of that commitment, usually occurs within one financial period. However, that discharged commitment generates a capability which will be utilised over a number of revenue-generating periods. The problems which management has to solve in determining cost performance are as follows.

- For how many revenue earning periods will that capability be enjoyed by the business?
- Will the capability be exercised uniformly in each period or in some other pattern?

EXAMPLE (i)

A company purchased some specialised plant and equipment for £120 000. The revenue which would be generated by this investment is expected to be £80 000 per annum for five years and the direct period costs are £20 000 per annum (Table 6.1).

In matching the acquisition expenditure to periods we are using a straight line method of 'depreciation' based upon the original purchase price:

Annual depreciation charge = 120 000/5 = £24 000

In interpreting the matching principle in this way we are making a number of assumptions.

- The cost at which the asset was purchased, when allocated to various periods, represents the current value of the capability consumed in a given period. The valuation of existing capability for production and sales is a complex business, but in principle in valuation we can choose:
  - (i) the cost at which the asset was originally acquired (its historical cost) which is the conventional way depreciation is calculated in practice;
  - (ii) the current purchase price of the asset calculating the depreciation charge in each year as though the asset had been originally purchased at the new price (a replacement cost valuation principle);
  - (iii) the difference in the sale value of the asset at the beginning and at the end of the period (realisable value principle).

  There are other ways of estimating the value of capability consumed in production, all of which have their advocates although a detailed consideration of them is beyond the scope of this book.

Table 6.1

	Year 0	Year 1	Year 2	Year 3	Year 4	Year 5
Revenue		80 000	80 000	80 000	80 000	80 000
Direct cost		20 000	20 000	20 000	20 000	20 000
Annual contribution		60 000	60 000	60 000	60 000	60 000
Capital asset	120 000					
Depreciation	└──→	24 000	24 000	24 000	24 000	24 000
Profit for period		36 000	36 000	36 000	36 000	36 000
% profit/cost		82	82	82	82	82

- The depreciation charge matched to periods is based upon some expectation of the life of the asset. Indeed, accountants, when working out the best way to depreciate fixed assets, tend to view the problem from the point of matching the decline in value of the asset to the period in question. The opportunity accountant, on the other hand, views the problem as one of estimating the value of the capability used up in the task of earning revenue. True revenue matching, therefore, would charge to each period's revenue a valuation of the capability consumed in generating the revenue as a proportion of the total capability of the asset.

EXAMPLE (ii)

The asset in example (i) is expected to generate £400 000 of revenue over its life and that revenue would require an expenditure of £100 000 of direct costs. The pattern of revenue follows a typical product life cycle with its direct costs incurred in direct proportion to revenue.

If we follow the conventional accounting procedure of matching the capital expenditure on a straight-line basis we see that the performance of the business is severely distorted. The profit to cost consumed follows a somewhat idiosyncratic pattern (Table 6.2).

However, if we charge depreciation on the basis of the revenue generated compared with the revenue expected from that fixed asset over its life, then we come up again with the intuitively obvious conclusion that the performance of the business in converting cost into profit has not changed (Table 6.3).

This example reveals a particular problem with any matching principle in identifying how matched costs translate into revenue; or, to put it another way, how fixed capability is 'used up' in generating revenue. With some fixed resources such as land and buildings, their use in production has little direct impact on their value. With others, such as plant and equipment, the degree to which they are used will have some impact upon their value. It is always a very subjective judgement about how we value the capability of these resources into revenue generation in a given period, but it is a serious problem for management to solve if they wish to derive a fair measure of their business's performance.

In the example above, it may appear that matching the capital cost to the revenue-earning potential of the asset concerned predetermines the performance to 82%. However, if any of the critical variables in determining performance during the life of the project change, then the performance measure will change as follows.

- If management boosts the potential revenue-earning power of plant during its life, then the mark-up ratio will improve (and *vice versa* if the plant proves to have less capability than originally assumed).
- If management achieves an improvement in the conversion of direct cost into revenue, then the performance will proportionately reflect that improvement.

To summarise, therefore, temporal matching works best when the allocation of costs to periods matches the consumption of the capability purchased by those costs within the period consumed. It is also most appropriate when measuring the performance of a whole business over a fixed period of time, because it draws into the performance measure all of the revenues generated in that period and all of the expenditures incurred as a consequence of the previous decisions made by all levels of management. It loses its potency as a per-

Table 6.2

	Year -0	Year 1	Year 2	Year 3	Year 4	Year 5
Revenue		40 000	80 000	100 000	100 000	80 000
Direct cost		10 000	20 000	25 000	25 000	20 000
Annual contribution		30 000	60 000	75 000	75 000	60 000
Capital asset	120 000					
Depreciation	└→	24 000	24 000	24 000	24 000	24 000
Profit for period		6 000	36 000	51 000	51 000	36 000
% profit/cost		18	82	104	104	82

Table 6.3

	Year 0	Year 1	Year 2	Year 3	Year 4	Year 5
Revenue		40 000	80 000	100 000	100 000	80 000
Direct cost		10 000	20 000	25 000	25 000	20 000
Annual contribution		30 000	60 000	75 000	75 000	60 000
Capital asset	120 000					
Depreciation	→	12 000	24 000	30 000	30 000	24 000
Profit for period		18 000	36 000	45 000	45 000	36 000
% profit/cost		82	82	82	82	82

formance measure when one moves to the operational levels of the business, because it tends to confuse different aspects of performance. In the example above, for instance, are we measuring the operational performance of the business (which is to do with converting direct costs into revenue) or are we measuring the performance of the capital expenditure decision which led to the expenditure of the £120 000 on the plant and equipment? If we are seeking to measure the performance of operational levels of management, then temporal matching would appear to be inappropriate.

We will return to a more comprehensive discussion of the temporal-matching issue when we examine the mechanics of producing period-based accounts in Chapters 28 to 31.

DECISION MATCHING

The function of decision matching is to identify those cash expenditures which are necessarily incurred as a consequence of a decision to pursue an opportunity to gain a business benefit (in terms of increased revenue or some wider cost savings). A decision to exploit an opportunity will bring some change in expenditure (opportunity costs) by the business as a whole and some contingent increase in revenue. In evaluating decisions, it is important to be rigorous in isolating the effects of that decision from all of the other decisions a business may be making, has made or is planning to make.

We have already emphasised in our analysis of the commitment theorems in Chapter 4 how important it is to match anticipated expenditure commitments to anticipated revenues for decision-making purposes. However, the logical extension of this approach is that we should then translate the principle of decision matching into measuring the ex-post performance of that decision when it has been acted upon and its consequences realised.

EXAMPLE

Deltawing Co. undertook a contract to produce some flight wing components for the Navy. The contract revenue had been £280 000 for four units. The project had entailed the purchase of materials and components for £85 000 and the commitment of 3000 labour hours. Some of that labour (1000 hours) had to be hired at a rate of £24.00 per hour from an engineering agency. The balance of the time was absorbed into the current workforce time at the standard rate of £16.00 per hour. No other work was displaced, although 200 hours had to be paid at the overtime rate of £24.00 per hour.

Machinery was deployed on the contract which was under-utilised in the factory, although new tooling costs amounted to £18 000. The depreciation on the machinery was £40 000 for the duration of the contract. This project would not materially affect the expected life of the machine, although the tooling costs would solely relate to this job. Company overheads are charged to production at two times the standard labour rate. Only one-quarter of the overheads is incurred as a necessary consequence of taking on this job.

In measuring the performance of this project we need to match the revenues and the cost incurred to the decision, and to eliminate from our analysis any revenues or costs which are not incurred as a direct consequence of the decision Deltawing management took to proceed with the contract (Table 6.4).

Note that in this analysis we have excluded all costs which were not incurred as a direct consequence of accepting this contract. The labour cost,

Table 6.4

Directly attributable revenue			£280 000
Contingent costs:			
Materials		£85 000	
Labour	1000 hours @ £24	24 000	
	200 hours @ £24	4 800	
Machinery	Tooling costs	18 000	
Variable overhead		24 000	
	Total costs		155 800
Contract contribution			£124 200

Contribution margin $= \frac{\text{contribution}}{\text{revenue}} \times 100$

$= \frac{124\,200}{280\,000} \times 100$

$= 44.36\%$

for example, is made up from the new labour hired at £24 per hour from the agency and the additional overtime payments which the company *would not otherwise have paid*. The depreciation on the machine is a cost which may be attributable in estimating the performance of the division or company during the year, but not in measuring the performance of this contract. The reason for this is that the depreciation is a cost associated with the decision to purchase the machine originally, not the decision in question. Similarly, we have ignored all overheads which are not variable with this decision. Those overheads were incurred as a result of the pre-existing decision to be in business, not the decision we are concerned with here.

Attributable overhead =

$0.25 \times 3000 \times 2 \times £16.00 = £24\,000$

Clearly, the consequence of this job is that the company has won a £124 200 contribution to its pre-existing committed costs which it would not have had if the decision to contract with the Navy had not been taken. Under the conventional matching approach, the 'profit' on the project would have been as in Table 6.5.

In this case the accountant has calculated what is termed 'full cost', that is cost using indirect and temporal matching, which we will discuss more fully below. The interesting point to note, however, is that in conventional terms this contract would appear to be making a loss; but the direct effect of the decision would be to engage in business which contributes £124 200 to the committed costs of the business.

The decision-matching principle allows us to assess whether a project can contribute towards a business's pre-existing commitments, and if

Table 6.5

Directly attributable revenue			£280 000
Contingent costs:			
Materials		£85 000	
Labour	1000 hours @ £24	24 000	
	1800 hours @ £16	28 800	
	200 hours @ £24	4 800	
Machinery	Tooling costs	18 000	
	Depreciation	40 000	
Total overhead		96 000	
	Total costs		296 600
Contract loss			£(16 600)

rigorously applied, it prevents us from confusing the performance of more than one decision at a time.

ALLOCATION MATCHING

Allocation matching is the name we give to the procedures adopted by accountants to match costs to revenues by estimating, on some proportionate basis, the share of the total costs of the business which can be allocated to an aspect of production or to an individual product as part of its total unit cost of production. In order to undertake allocation matching, an 'allocation basis' must be chosen. Traditionally, in manufacturing, this has been labour cost. A product cost would then be constructed as follows:

Direct costs of production
(such as materials and direct labour costs)
+ variable overheads
(such as energy, tooling and variable stockholding costs)
+ fixed overheads
(fixed plant costs, factory costs, administration and central management charges)
= total product cost

The share of fixed overheads which should be borne by a product is given by the following formula:

Fixed overhead allocated =

$$\frac{\text{total firm overhead}}{\text{total allocation units in firm}} \times \text{no. of units of allocation base in product}$$

EXAMPLE

A firm has total overheads of £3 200 000 which include all central management, administration and factory costs which are not directly associated with production. The firm's total labour cost is £800 000. A particular product has a price of £78.00 per unit. The direct materials cost is £15.00 per unit, direct labour is £10 per unit and variable overheads are £5.00 per unit. Fixed overheads are allocated on the basis of labour cost into production. The product's selling price is £100 per unit.

The allocated fixed overhead absorbed into this product cost is calculated on the basis of the share of the firm's total overhead of £3 200 000 which can be attributed to £10.00 of labour cost given that the total labour cost is £800 000 (Table 6.6). Clearly, the allocation rate is £3 200 000/£800 000, i.e., £4.00 of overhead for every £1.00 of labour cost.

The rationale for this type of matching is that every product should bear its 'fair share of overheads' in assessing the value of that product to the firm and the extent to which it will contribute to the annual profits of the business. This is a limited perception of product performance, and the allocation matching principle is dependent upon the allocation basis used for matching costs to production and hence to the revenue or price gained. We will return to a discussion of this issue in Chapter 22 when we consider costing techniques in more detail.

OPERATION OR ACTIVITY MATCHING

This concept of matching relies upon the accountant defining a series of production operations or activities which are deemed to attract cost. Thus the

Table 6.6

Price per unit		£100.00	
Direct materials		£15.00	
Direct labour		£10.00	
Variable overheads		£5.00	
Allocated fixed overhead =	$\frac{3\,200\,000 \times 10}{800\,000}$	£40.00	
Total unit cost			£70.00
Profit per unit			£30.00

cost of a unit of production is determined by the following:

- the direct materials, labour and other variable costs required to produce the product concerned;
- non-direct costs matched to the product in proportion to the number of activities of a particular class that product absorbs.

These non-direct activities which are deemed to attract cost are variously referred to as 'cost drivers' and sometimes, rather misleadingly, as 'indirect cost transactions'. Such cost drivers can be:

- the number of management or other interventions required to ensure final product quality (the quality driver);
- the number of logistical interventions required to bring the product to completion (e.g. procurement orders and change orders to production systems would be deemed to be logistical interventions (the logistic driver));
- other management interventions required to market the product, provide after-sale service etc.

The aim of this type of analysis is to provide a means of ultimately matching all organisational costs to production units, either as a basis for price setting or for determining product profitability. We will discuss the relative advantages of operational over allocation matching in Chapter 23 when we discuss 'activity-based costing' in more detail. At this point, however, simply note that operational matching is a variation on the theme of analysing costs in such a way that some meaningful comparison with revenue or product price can be made. For example, the commitments which a firm undertakes to establish a quality control function are not related in time nor in scope to the activity of creating products on a production line or bench. The accountant takes those costs from the context of the commitment which created them and reassigns them in ways which are designed to create meaningful product costs.

CONCLUSION

In this chapter we have opened up an issue which will become increasingly relevant as the book progresses. The problem of performance measurement is serious issue for any business, and making sure that like is compared with like is central to the matter. In this chapter we have identified the matching principle as the fundamental defining characteristic of the accounting function for both internal and external reporting. Later, we will discuss its relevance for both management and financial accounting. However, in the next chapter we turn to the problem of matching for decision-making purposes and the all-important concept of 'opportunity cost'.

Chapter 7

Opportunity Cost

Level E

Contents

Summary

In this chapter we explore the concept of opportunity cost. This concept of cost is fundamental to the idea of strategic accounting and to the problem of making choices in a business concept. Opportunity cost as applied in strategic accounting is based upon commitment theorem number 11 in Chapter 4. When a resource is consumed as a result of a decision then the net cash change attaching to that resource consumption which arises as a logical consequence of the decision is its opportunity cost. The logic of opportunity cost is straightforward, but few business people like the consequences of it. We explore some of those issues and how, in particular, maximising the cash contribution from operational decisions can lead to an overall situation which is optimal for the business.

INTRODUCTION

Of all the cost concepts we discuss in this book, opportunity cost (OC) is the most fundamental. It is fundamental for some very simple reasons.

- It is derived from the core idea of a business commitment (see commitment theorem no. 11, Chapter 4).
- It arises as a logical consequence of management choice between competing opportunities.
- It is observable in cash terms.
- It represents the minimum which a business must achieve through sales revenue to stay ahead of the game.

Opportunity cost is related to the concept of a decision. When considering one opportunity against another, the *difference* between that opportunity and the other must determine whether we take it or whether we do not. At the heart of the opportunity cost concept lies the notion of difference. Indeed, economists often refer to the opportunity cost of a particular course of action as the cost of the next best alternative forgone. Why next best? The answer is that we assume that the decision maker is acting rationally in that, if he or she does not choose to take a particular course of action, he or she would take the next best alternative.

The next concept we need to understand opportunity cost is the idea that the cost of an opportunity is to do with the cash forgone by the decision maker as a result of that decision and for no other reason. If you go into a bar and buy a glass of beer, the opportunity cost of that beer is the negative cash change the transaction brings about. So, some key ideas here are: negative cash change and transaction incurred by a decision. However, in many situations the cash change is not explicit because, for some reason we have decided not to transact. For example, on my desk I have a book which I have read and which I do not intend to read again. In putting that book on my shelf I am incurring a cost. Why? Because, by deciding to keep that book I have foregone the next best alternative which is to sell it. Its sale price (less any transactions costs) represents the cash benefit I have foregone in keeping the book on my bookshelf.

We can summarise these ideas into a simple definition of opportunity cost:

The opportunity cost of a decision to pursue a given alternative is the negative cash change to the decision maker as a result of that decision and for no other reason.

The financial consequences of a particular opportunity can be analysed as follows:

- *Benefit*: revenue or positive cash change which results from the decision to pursue that opportunity and for no other reason.
- *Cost*: the negative cash change caused by taking that opportunity compared with the next best course of action available.

Benefit − Cost = Net cash contribution

of that opportunity

Thus, it is only worthwhile accepting an opportunity if, and only if, it generates a net cash contribution to the decision maker who, as a result of taking up the opportunity, has more cash than if he or she would have done otherwise. This definition does raise an issue of who is the decision maker in any given situation. For an individual, it is easy enough – it is the person concerned. For a family unit, then, only external cash transactions would fall within the definition. Cash transfers between one partner and another would not be classed as opportunity costs to the family. For corporate decision making, cash transactions between departments would not count as opportunity costs, but cash transactions with external individuals or companies would be.

RYAN'S SECOND LAW

Costs and revenues only arise when cash flows occur across organisational boundaries.

The importance of this second law is profound in that only once the organisational boundary has been defined – at the individual, family, corporate or other organisational level – is it possible to identify financial flows, i.e. costs and revenues. This step of identifying the decision maker and the financial boundary is a necessary precursor to any analysis of the costs and revenues associated with decision making.

Interestingly enough, in our experience of teaching managers over the years at all levels, most accept the idea above as simple and coherent. It wipes away much of the mystique of accounting and costing – all we ever need to know, whenever we are faced with an opportunity which has financial consequences, is whether or not it offers us a positive net cash contribution. If you are in business, consider what your current wealth would be if you had only ever accepted opportunities which had served to add cash to your business!

The problem which comes with this concept of cost is when we follow through its logic and then try to live with the consequences.

FIRST-LEVEL CONSEQUENCES OF THE OPPORTUNITY COST CONCEPT

In evaluating an opportunity, we are concerned with whether the decision to pursue that opportunity will add more cash to our wealth compared with the next best alternative. Cash payments made for whatever reason prior to the decision cannot, in logic, be regarded as part of the opportunity cost of that decision. The reason is that those cash payments will have been made no matter which alternative is chosen. It does not matter whether the opportunity under consideration is adopted or some other course of action chosen, the prior expenditures (often referred to as *sunk* costs) should be ignored.

For example, I am deciding whether or not to purchase house A or house B. House A will cost £180 000 and house B will cost £195 000. The original purchase price of my existing house was £85 000 and I have just paid for a survey on house A at a cost of £500. It is easy to see that the original purchase price of my existing house is completely irrelevant when choosing between House A or House B, but what about the survey cost on house A? If the opportunity cost of purchase is the only consideration in choosing between A and B, then at the decision point (which, remember, is after I have had and paid for the survey), the cost of the survey becomes irrelevant *because it will have been incurred whichever house I choose.*

This idea that pre-decision expenditures or costs are irrelevant to a decision is a hard one for many business people to accept, although, in logic, it is unassailable. The old adage that bygones should be bygones is never truer than when evaluating the net cash contribution from alternative courses of action.

The idea that pre-decision costs are irrelevant is truly profound in decision making. It means, for example, that the cost consequences of some prior business decision to choose one particular means of financing, or set up the head office or factory, or indeed employ particular workers is irrelevant in making a decision about what level of output to choose from production. In principle, therefore, costs which can be regarded as fixed with respect to a given decision should be ignored and should be disregarded when evaluating its financial consequences.

When viewing the total cost of a business over a period of time we can identify four levels of cost:

(i) the cost of financing the business, which will be driven by the particular source and mix of funds chosen;
(ii) the cost of operation as a business, which will be driven by the governance structure chosen, the way head office is established, the provision of corporate wide functions such as marketing, R&D and finance;
(iii) the cost of production which will be driven by the decisions the business makes in terms of how it will produce particular products – its choice of technology, quality level and a wide variety of operational decisions concerned with translating ideas into products;
(iv) the cost associated with the level of activity chosen to meet market demand.

When making business decisions, there will be a point on the spectrum above which costs implications will not arise (Figure 7.1).

So, when choosing whether to produce 5000 or 6000 units of a particular commodity, only activity levels costs such as materials, direct labour and energy costs are likely to be relevant. The costs of plant, pre-existing business costs and the costs of finance have already been incurred. But, if the decision to produce 6000 units in a given period would necessarily entail incurring additional plant costs for new machinery, then the cost of that new machinery would be relevant. Further, if producing at 6000 units would incur the establishment of

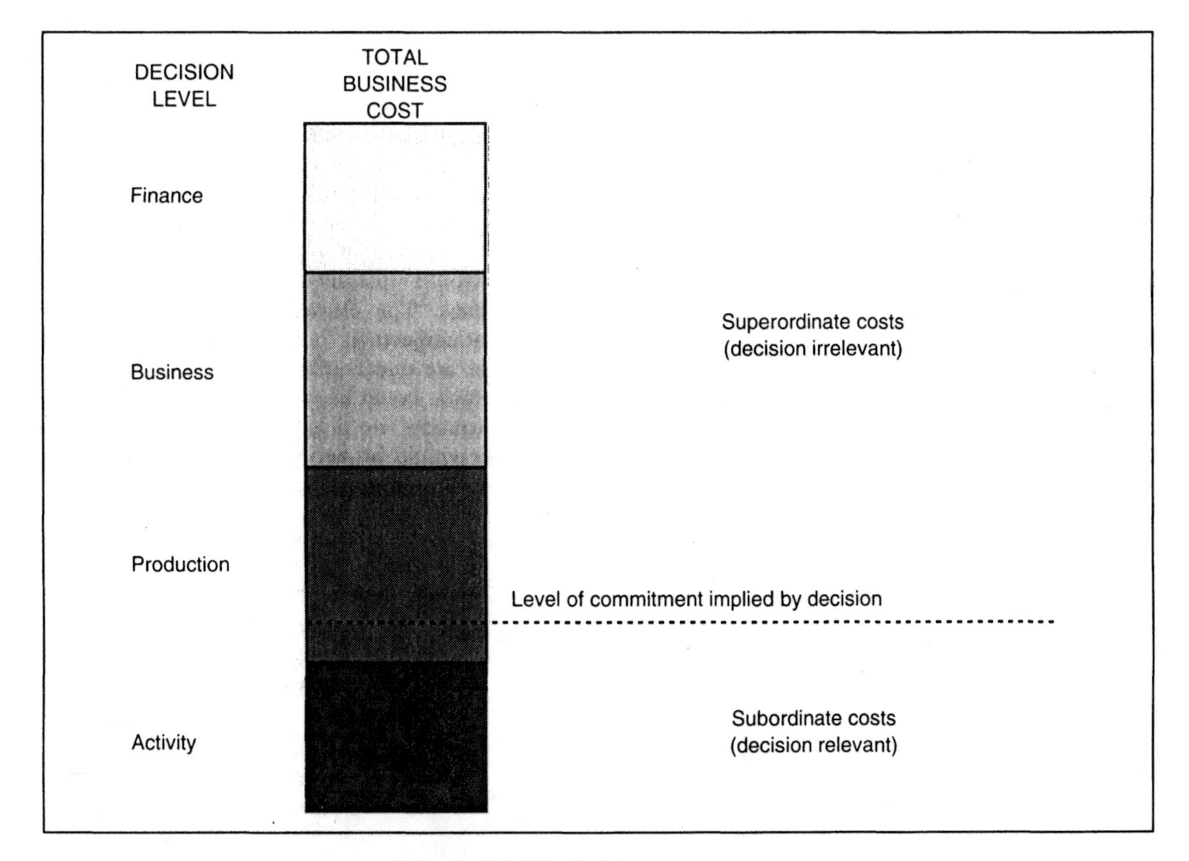

Figure 7.1 The decision–cost spectrum.

additional general business facilities compared with 5000 units, then the cost of those additional facilities would form part of the opportunity cost of 6000 units compared with 5000 units.

Another type of cost often appears in business which we would regard as irrelevant in evaluating the net cash contribution of a decision. When a business purchases a fixed asset, it is normal to provide for depreciation in the financial accounts. The purpose of depreciation is to charge fairly to a given period the cost of using the fixed asset concerned in production. So, for example, a machine costing £50 000 which has a five-year life might produce an annual charge to the production account of £10 000. As we saw in Chapter 6, such charges are purely paper transactions within the business's books of account reflecting the operation of the accruals principle. Depreciation is not a cash cost to a business (the cash was spent when the asset was purchased) so depreciation falls outside our definition of opportunity cost as articulated above.

EXAMPLE OF THE OPPORTUNITY COST CONCEPT

Alpha, an electronics company, has been asked to quote for the delivery of 100 control units to a Government agency. The units are currently in stock as 70% work in progress. The purchase price of the components within each unit were estimated at £300 each although their stock valuation (bearing their share of fixed overheads to date) is at £780 in the books. Each unit has absorbed 10 hours of labour time to date.

The units are complete with respect to materials but approximately five labour hours are required to complete each unit at a standard labour rate of £48 per hour. The company absorbs fixed overheads at the current direct hourly charge rate at 300% per labour hour. There is currently under capacity in the works although no redundancies are planned in the near future.

Direct packaging and delivery costs would be £45 per unit inclusive of the operating manual. The company has incurred contracting costs of £5000. It normally bids at a price equal to cost plus 20%.

Taking the figures at face value the cost of fulfilling this contract could be specified as in Table 7.1.

On the assumption that no other costs are involved, this contract should generate a profit of £22 300. However, supposing that Alpha is informed, in the process of its negotiations with the government agency that even though they appreciate it will not cover Alpha's costs all they are prepared to offer is £90 000 for the whole contract. Should Alpha accept what might appear to be loss-making business? In order to answer this question we need to examine exactly how much cash would flow out of the business if the contract were to be accepted. If this value should turn out to be less than the £90 000 then this contract, even at that price, would be a net cash generator for the business.

Let us take each cost element in turn. The materials consist of the part complete units. The buying-in price of the materials is £300, and this would form at least part of the opportunity cost on the assumption that the sale of these units would lead to their replacement in due course. Replacement of the stock would mean that new materials would have to be purchased at the current buying price, and this would represent the negative cash change to the business. The element of labour in stock is somewhat conjectural, however, as we are told that the works are under-utilised at the moment. Given that idle time could be spent on replacing the units for this contract, no negative cash change in respect of labour would be necessary. The labour element of the units in progress should be disregarded.

Table 7.1

Materials costs (control units in stock at valuation)	£78 000
Labour costs (using standard rate)	£24 000
Packing and delivery	£4 500
Precontract costs	£5 000
Cost of control units	£111 500
Mark-up at 20%	£22 300
Price to be charged	£133 800

Materials cost = £300 × 100 = £30 000

Following a similar line of argument, the labour required to complete the units also has a zero opportunity cost for the company. Again, the fact that the labour has idle time, and given that the company will pay its labour costs irrespective of the jobs on which they are employed in the short term, leads us to the conclusion that there will be no loss of cash to the business as a result of the decision to proceed with the contract.

Note that in this example we also come across a very common practice in many businesses where general overheads are being absorbed into labour cost at a standard rate. In this company, whenever an hour is worked, £36 (£48 less the direct wage rate which must be £12 per hour as 36/12 = 300%) is charged as a central cost to that product. We will explore this issue in more detail in a later chapter, but note for now that even if the labour was fully utilised and the direct labour charge became the opportunity cost, the overhead element would still be ignored. Why? Because that element of cost, no matter how it is absorbed into production would have been paid by the company whether the product is sold on this contract or not.

Labour cost = £0

Packaging and delivery is all opportunity cost on the presumption that the £45 per unit is a direct charge which would represent a cash expenditure by the business in order to fulfil this contract and for no other reason.

Packaging and delivery = £4500

The pre-contract costs of £5000 are sunk costs, in that they have already been incurred and remain spent no matter what course of action the company takes.

At this stage, in order to be in a position to satisfy this contract,

Company expenditure = £34 500

This is the opportunity cost of production, and on this basis, at a price of £90 000, the contract will win a positive cash contribution of £55 500 to the business and the contract should be accepted. At this stage we can hear the objections being raised!

OBJECTIONS TO THE OPPORTUNITY COST APPROACH

(i) *Opportunity costs ignore fixed costs and depreciation, but if prices are set which do not 'cover' these costs, then the business will not survive.*

There are two elements to dealing with this objection. First, prices are not determined by the producer's costs but by what the purchaser is prepared to pay in the market context in which the transaction takes place. The decision for the producer is whether the opportunity to earn revenue will generate more cash inflow than cash outflow caused necessarily by that decision. The astute business person will presumably seek to maximise the cash contributed to the business as a result of the decision he or she makes. In this way the business will maximise the contribution of cash towards the payment of its fixed costs. The second point is that the opportunity cost of a product will not always be less than the full accounting cost including absorbed fixed overheads. Indeed, in situations of resource scarcity it may be many orders higher than full accounting cost. We will explain the reason for this in the next chapter.

(ii) *Opportunity costs are subjective, whereas accounting costs are measurable facts.*

It is true that in the estimation of opportunity cost, the decision maker must assess the market value of outcomes in the future. For example, in the case of the materials above, the opportunity cost of using the units on this contract is the replacement cost of their materials. However, the business will not know the actual replacement cost until it actually makes the purchase. However, the use of the opportunity cost concept forces the decision maker to evaluate the financial consequences of the most likely outcome and also assess the possible range of errors in the costing process. If you have followed the discussion so far, you may well be convinced of the logic and the simplicity of the opportunity cost concept. The fact that the uncertainty of the evaluation process is brought forward and made explicit by the opportunity cost concept should be regarded as a strength. To repeat the old saw: it is better to be subjectively right than objectively wrong.

However, you may be surprised to learn in Chapter 22 just how much subjectivity is built into the conventional accounting approach and, in particular, in the allocation of fixed overheads to production.

(iii) The use of opportunity cost if applied to all decision making would make the decision processes intrinsically unstructured. Simple accounting costing procedures allow decisions to be delegated.

There is a real problem here in that current management wisdom argues for subsidiarity or 'enablement' in decision making. The opportunity cost concept may be simple to understand in principle but it does require quite punishing and rigorous logical analysis in many situations. This may be beyond many in management. Contrary to this argument we can make two points: first, as we shall see in Chapter 22, conventional accounting practice does bias decision making, and senior management, through its accounting policies, can favour one class of decisions over another and, indeed, one division or department over another. In many situations, therefore, the decision making is never properly delegated in a conventional accounting framework for the benefit of the organisation as a whole; rather it is manipulated in the interests of senior management. Second, there is good evidence to suggest that when management is not exposed to conventional accounting procedures, the natural process which they use is akin to the opportunity cost approach. In my experience, managers who are naively unaware of conventional accounting methods, when asked to define cost, often come up with definitions very similar to those given for opportunity cost above.

(iv) Opportunity costing is irrelevant for long-term decision making – it can only be used in the very short term.

This argument reveals a misunderstanding of the nature of long-term decisions. As we shall show in Chapter 14, effective long-term decision making presumes a sequence of consequential and feasible short-term decisions.

EXAMPLE

A More Extensive Example of the Opportunity Cost Approach

Diego plc is considering the terms of a small construction project. The building could be completed in four weeks and the client is prepared to pay a cash price, upon completion, of £30 000.

The project will involve the use of the following.

Labour

1500 unskilled labour hours will be required. Men and women capable of doing this work can be hired on subcontract at a rate of £8 per labour hour. In addition, three supervisors will be required: one supervisor is due to be served with an immediate redundancy notice which could be delayed until the end of the project; a second supervisor could be redeployed from other supervision duties which would have to be subcontracted at a cost of £450. The third supervisor would have been on 'standby' duties for the month, on full pay, as no other work is available. Each supervisor is paid £12 000 per annum (gross) inclusive of employer's pension contribution and National Insurance (NI).

Materials

The following materials will be required.

- *200 tons of concrete mix which Diego currently holds in stock. The mix was purchased two months ago at a cost of £18 per ton, but the contract on which it was to be used has fallen through. Due to the short shelf life of the mix, Diego had planned to sell it to another company at £9 per ton net.*
- *100 cubic yards of timber had been ordered, on contract, at a purchase price of £6 per cubic yard, although it is only now due for delivery. This type of timber is used on a number of different jobs within the firm. Since ordering, the purchase price has risen to £7.50 per cubic yard.*
- *Other materials will have to be purchased at a net cost of £3700.*

Stock is valued by the firm's accountants at the lower of its cost or net realisable value.

Plant and equipment

One excavator, which was due to be sold for £18 000 can be held for the life of the project. However, the renegotiated price for delivery one month late will be £17 000. The original purchase price of the excavator was £30 000. The other necessary equipment can be hired at a cost of £5500 for the duration of the project. Diego normally charges 10% of original cost of equipment as a depreciation charge in its accounts.

Other information

To date, design costs of £4800 have been spent in preparing for the new project. Diego normally allocates part of its fixed overheads to projects. In this case, Diego's accountants have decided to allocate

£6000 to this project. The managing director has estimated that he will incur an extra £800 of entertainment expenses if the project proceeds.

If we assume that the facts as given above fully reflect the problem facing Diego's management, we can proceed to identify the consequential change in cash which will occur if they decide to go ahead.

Cash outflows (cost items)

Unskilled labour will cost the firm £12 000 (1500 hours at £8 per hour). During the course of the project (or very shortly afterwards) Diego's bank account should show a payment of £12 000. This figure represents the direct cash change attributable to the use of unskilled labour following acceptance of the project.

Unskilled labour (cash outflow)	£12 000

The first supervisor was due to be made redundant. Because his redundancy payments will be made at the end of the project rather than at the beginning, no additional cash change on that account will be incurred. This supervisor will simply cost Diego £1000, being one month's salary (£12 000/12) which would not be paid if the project does not proceed. The second supervisor will be paid his salary irrespective of whether the project goes ahead or not. The only cash change which will result if this supervisor is employed upon the project is the subcontract charge of £450. The third supervisor would have been idle for the month in any event, so no cash change follows his use on the project.

First supervisor (cash outflow)	£1000
Second supervisor (cash outflow on redeployment)	£450
Third supervisor	nil

The materials costs raise slightly more complicated issues: in the case of the concrete mix, the decision to proceed with the project entails the loss of the opportunity to sell. In other words, proceeding means that £1800 (9 per ton × 200) will be forgone. The purchase price of £18 per ton is irrelevant as the company will not be replacing the concrete mix once it is used.

With the timber, the decision to proceed with the project implies that it will have to be replaced as we are told that it has a variety of other uses within the firm. As a result of its use, the replacement will cost £750, i.e. there will be a cash flow out of the firm of £750 which will have arisen as a direct result of accepting the project.

Note, however, that the original contract price of £6 per cubic yard is irrelevant as the contract has already been entered into and the commitment to pay the £6 per cubic yard already made. The figure of £6 per cubic yard will be paid irrespective of whether or not the contract proceeds. The remaining materials must be purchased at their full cost (which will represent an actual cash outflow) of £3700.

Cement mix (sale proceeds forgone)	£1800
Timber (replacement cost)	£750
Other materials (cash outflow)	£3700

The use of the excavator means that its sale must be delayed by one month, as a result of which the immediate sale price of £18 000 will be forgone and £17 000 received instead. The cash change resulting from the decision is, therefore, £1000. The remaining plant represents an actual cash flow of £5500.

Note, however, that the depreciation charge (which is shown in Diego's accounts as a deduction from the original cost of the asset and as a charge against income in the profit and loss account) does not represent a cash flow during the period. Indeed, the amount which is written off each period may bear little relationship to either the physical deterioration or economic value of the asset. Depreciation charges are usually set using the accounting conventions adopted by the firm. In this case the monthly depreciation charge of:

$$10\% \times 30\,000/12 = £250$$

is relevant for this decision.

Excavator (cash forgone through delay of sale)	£1000
Hire charges for other equipment	£5500

The design costs have already been incurred prior to the time at which the decision is being made. The design costs are, therefore, a 'sunk cost'. The sum of £4800 has already been paid out and is irrecoverable. Similarly, the allocation of £6000 for fixed overheads is an arbitrary allocation of expenses which will be incurred irrespective of whether or not the project proceeds. On the other hand, the sum of £800 for additional entertainment will only be incurred if the decision to proceed is made.

Entertainment expenses (cash outflow)	£800

We can now summarise the effect on Diego's cash flows if the option to proceed is adopted (Table 7.2).

In an overall sense we can say that accepting the project leaves Diego £3000 better off. Turning the

Table 7.2

Statement of cash changes
(cash revenues less opportunity costs)

Cash inflow from revenues		£30 000
Cash outflows:		
Unskilled labour	£12 000	
First supervisor	1 000	
Second supervisor	450	
Third supervisor		
Materials:		
Cement mix	1 800	
Timber	750	
Other materials	3 700	
Plant and equipment:		
Excavator	1 000	
Other	5 500	
Entertainment expenses	800	
		27 000
Net cash receipts to Diego		£3 000

argument around the other way, failing to accept the project would have meant that the firm's cash balances would have been £3000 lower than they would have been if the project were accepted. Thus, the figure of £3000 is the opportunity cost of not accepting the project.

We have assumed in our analysis that proceeding with the project does not entail forgoing any other productive opportunity. In only one instance, in the case we have examined, is a redeployment cost incurred. With the second supervisor a redeployment cost is incurred (the cost of subcontracting his supervision duties). Although redeployment charges such as this are cash costs incurred as a direct result of the decision to proceed with the project, they arise indirectly through the redeployment of resources internally. In the next chapter we consider in more detail the problems associated with these internal transfers of resources.

On the basis of our analysis a 'rational' manager would undertake the project concerned. By accepting the project, Diego is £3000 better off than it would have been, i.e. £3000 has been earned as a contribution to the general running costs of the business.

OPPORTUNITY COSTS AND OVERHEADS

We have argued that the most important decision-making criteria for evaluating business opportunities is whether or not that opportunity leads to a net cash contribution for the business. Further, in a situation where a business has mutually exclusive choices it should choose that option which maximises the cash contribution to the business. This idea presents a problem for many business people in that decisions may be taken which lead to a cash contribution to the business but which do not cover any allocation of overheads which may be charged to that product or project.

If business is always accepted on this basis, or prices are agreed which do not cover full cost, then overheads will not be covered, and the business will make a loss overall. However, there is a failure in logic with this argument. Note again that we suggest that the sensible business decision maker should always accept business which generates a net cash contribution, even though some of that business may not cover overheads in conventional terms. Why?

- If a business in the long run does not cover overheads, then the business will fail. However, the problem lies not with making decisions on the basis of cash contribution, but with the long run decisions which set up that capability in the first place.
- If a business opportunity fails to cover full accounting cost but makes a cash contribution, what are the alternatives to accepting that opportunity? The business could forgo the opportunity

and give up the chance of at least some contribution to fixed overheads. It could try to increase the price charged, but then what would happen if it could not sell at those higher prices? Again, it would lose the possibility of earning at least some contribution towards its fixed costs. In both cases the alternative to not accepting the net cash generating opportunity is that the chance of at least mitigating some fixed overhead is lost. In the long run, if the cash contribution which can be earned from exploiting all opportunities in the most effective way possible is greater than the pre-committed costs then the business will survive, otherwise it will fail. This is a consequence of my first law (see Chapter 5) and is shown diagramatically in Figure 7.2.

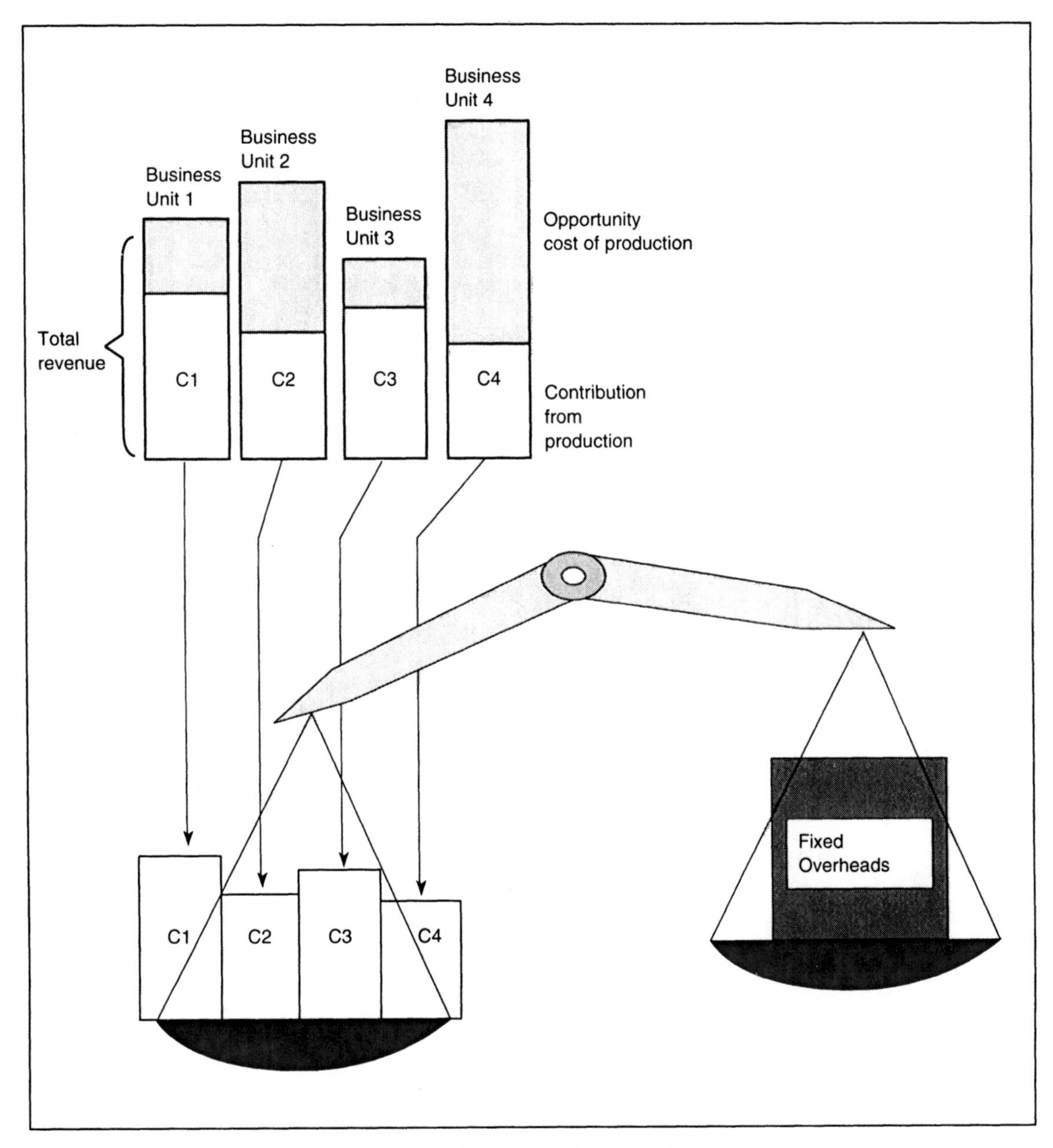

Figure 7.2 The scales of financial viability.

Because this approach departs so radically from conventional accounting wisdom, we will devote considerable space in this book to explaining conventional approaches but then pointing out how and why they can lead to defective decisions. In the next chapter, we will pursue this idea through to its conclusion and create, as we do so, a new framework for cost in the changing business environment.

CONCLUSION

In this chapter we have seen how the 'four-C' approach of opportunity accounting leads to the definition of cost. The concept of cost lies at the heart of all managerial activity, and our definition, if rigorously applied, will always lead to a clear understanding of the financial implications of any decisions an individual or business may make. There is a silly saying which you may have heard: 'accountants know the cost of everything and the value of nothing'. The sensible retort is: 'managers who think they know the value of everything and the cost of nothing go broke!'

In the next chapter we take our discussion of opportunity cost further by considering the problems of costing resources when external markets for those resources do not exist.

Chapter 8

Opportunity Costs under Scarcity

Level M

Contents

Summary

In this chapter we will extend the opportunity cost concept to deal with the situation in which one or more resources in production are in short supply. When resources are in short supply, the market price (if it exists) would understate the cash lost to the business in redeploying those resources from one area of production to another. These cash losses represent the hidden or 'shadow costs' of resourcing new business opportunities when a firm is at capacity. In the last sections of this chapter we preview an issue which re-emerges later in Chapter 22, namely that conventional costing tends to ignore these shadow prices with all the consequent problems in determining appropriate product prices.

INTRODUCTION

The opportunity cost method is often criticised because it ignores fixed overheads as irrelevant to the business decision process. However, as we have pointed out in Chapter 3, fixed overheads are predominantly the transaction costs of production through the medium of a firm rather than through markets. The current attention in management to the definition of 'core business' and the subcontracting of non-core activities to associated producers is an attempt to minimise the overhead burden to production. The opportunity cost approach, if properly developed within an organisation, can give a clearer understanding of the true cost of production and provide a benchmark against which other costing systems can be judged. In judging the usefulness of the opportunity costing approach we need to consider the following questions.

- How does opportunity cost allow us to choose between competing elements of business?
- How does opportunity cost help in measuring the benefits of policy changes, especially in terms of identify and focusing on core business?
- Is true production cost stable over long periods of time, or will such costs vary with utilisation of capacity, for example?
- Can opportunity cost be used as a substitute for fully absorbed product costs?

OPPORTUNITY COST AND COMPETING BUSINESS

Business managers are often faced with the problem that certain necessary inputs into a particular process are unavailable on the open market. This may be due to simple economic scarcity where, for example, the input in question is unavailable within the firm's planning period. However, in some situations, a resource may be unavailable because of some technological constraint. For instance, an employee who has special experience or skills can be difficult to replace except after a lengthy period of training. Limited storage facilities may also produce problems because, in the short term, the cost of expansion may be prohibitive.

In the long run, all scarcity problems can be overcome. New labour can be recruited and trained, physical plant or equipment can be extended, raw materials can be found from new sources. But in the short run, these possibilities may be unavailable to the firm.

As we have shown in Chapter 7, resources which are used as the consequence of a particular decision entail an opportunity cost. In the situation where a resource is unavailable externally, that is from the open market, the decision to use that resource can only be made if it can be diverted from an existing use within the firm.

The transfer of a resource from one use to another within the firm will not result in the actual expenditure of cash, as is the case with resources which can be readily obtained on the open market. Rather, the existing activity on which the resource is currently employed will suffer a loss of net cash contribution. It is this loss of cash contribution which gives rise to the opportunity cost of employing a scarce resource.

EXAMPLE

Taranto plc is considering bidding for a new contract to produce PXs. However, the production of PXs entails the deployment of specially trained labour which is already employed on another process, 'alpha'. Process alpha currently produces a net cash contribution to the firm of:

Sales revenue		*£180 000*
Labour costs	*£80 000*	
Materials	*24 000*	
Energy costs	*20 000*	
Variable overheads	*32 000*	
		156 000
Net cash contribution		*24 000*

We will assume for the sake of simplicity that labour, materials and overhead costs are linearly related to output. This means that there is a direct, proportionate relationship between these costs and output.

Ignoring, for the moment, any sales revenues or other costs on eventual PX production, withdrawing labour from alpha production will cause a fall in Taranto's net cash contribution. PX production will require the withdrawal of one-eighth of the labour force involved in alpha production.

The loss in net cash contribution to Taranto as a whole because of the redeployment to PX production is:

	Change
Sales revenue	£(22 500)
Labour	–
Materials	3 000
Energy costs	2 500
Variable overheads	4 000
	£(13 000)

The assumption of linearity means that sales revenue will fall by one-eighth (a cash loss) and that all of the other costs (except the labour which is still employed) will also fall by one-eighth (a cash saving). Therefore, as a direct consequence of withdrawing labour from alpha production, we see that there is a cash loss on sales revenue, although cash savings are made on materials, energy and overheads. Labour costs remain unchanged as the cash cost to Taranto of employing labour must still be incurred.

Therefore, in a situation of scarcity where a particular resource must be switched from one productive use to another, the full opportunity cost is given by the loss in cash suffered as a direct result of that decision.

In practice, the analysis of cash flows would lead to lengthy and impractical calculations. Indeed, the firm's information system may not be geared up to produce data in the form required. Using the linearity assumption, the problem can be simplified. The full cash loss (£13 000) in the above example, can be identified as the sum of two components.

(i) The market cost of the resource redeployed (or 'external opportunity cost'). In the example above the external opportunity cost of labour (EOC) is

$$EOC = 1/8 \times 80\,000 = £10\,000$$

(ii) The loss in contribution on the process forgone (or 'internal opportunity cost'). In the example above the internal opportunity cost (IOC) of redeploying labour is

$$IOC = 1/8 \times 24\,000 = £3000$$

Thus the total opportunity cost (TOC) of using a scarce resource is equal to the sum of the external and internal opportunity cost (EOC + IOC), i.e.

$$TOC = EOC + IOC$$

For Taranto, the total opportunity cost of the labour redeployed from alpha production is:

$$TOC = £10\,000 + £3000$$
$$= £13\,000$$

Given, therefore, that the current use of resources generates a cash contribution, a resource which is in short supply will have a total opportunity cost in excess of its market price. The total opportunity cost can be summarised as the sum of:

(i) the opportunity cost, *given* that the resource is freely available;
(ii) the cash contribution lost from the alternative use, *given* that the resource is not freely available and has been redeployed.

PRODUCTION PLANNING WITH A SINGLE RESOURCE IN SHORT SUPPLY

In order to develop the opportunity cost concept in more detail, we will consider the problems of production planning in a situation where a single resource is in short supply.

The production decision is concerned with allocating the firm's available resources among the various processes which the firm could, potentially, undertake. For a start, we will consider a multi-product firm where the following conditions hold.

- The firm wishes to maximise its cash contribution (the optimisation assumption).
- Costs are directly related to output (the linearity assumption).
- There are no joint products. That is, the firm's products are independent of one another – they are neither complementary nor substitute goods (the independence assumption).
- All processes are perfectly divisible, i.e. small fractions of products can be produced, or small fractions of inputs such as labour hours or materials can be utilised (the divisibility assumption).
- There are no hidden costs associated with non-production such as loss of goodwill or market coverage (the completeness assumption).
- All the inputs into the problem are known with certainty (the certainty assumption).

At this stage we will also assume that only a single resource is in short supply. All of the other inputs into the production process can be obtained in any desired amount at their stated market prices. We will also assume that there is a limit to the amount of each product that can be sold, given the current level of demand in the market. We will demonstrate, in due course, the ways in which the various assumptions outlined above can be relaxed. However, the greater the degree of realism we introduce into the methods of solution – or 'algorithms' – the more complex they become.

EXAMPLE

Taranto plc has six production processes within its plant which (to add a certain classical sophistication) are called alpha, beta, gamma, delta, epsilon and zeta. The production requirements, sales revenue and demand for each product are as specified in Table 8.1.

The materials cost is £5 per kilogram and the labour cost is £10 per labour hour. Each process uses the same materials and the same grade of labour. However, due to the special skills required by the labour force, Taranto is limited to a maximum of 1300 labour hours on these particular processes.

Table 8.1

	Alpha	Beta	Gamma	Delta	Epsilon	Zeta
Sales price (£/unit)	22.5	20	60	30	100	42
Materials (kg/unit)	1	2	4	1	6	5
Labour (labour hours/unit)	0.5	0.25	3	1	5	1
Maximum demand	200	300	200	200	200	100

The contribution per unit for each of these processes is shown in Table 8.2.

At first sight it might appear that the best way to solve this problem is to rank the products according to the contribution per unit which they generate (Table 8.3).

The labour hours used up on each product are calculated by multiplying the number of units produced by the labour requirement per unit. The total contribution for each product is calculated as:

Total contribution =
number of units produced × contribution per unit

In this production plan, a total contribution of £9500 is earned by producing all the epsilon, delta and alpha which can be sold. The remaining products are not produced.

The weakness of the technique used is that it does not focus on the efficiency of each product in converting the scarce resource into contribution. Because Taranto faces a shortage of labour, its primary concern will be to ensure that labour is used to its maximum efficiency. This line of argument suggests that instead of ranking each product in terms of contribution per unit produced we should rank according to a ratio which reflects the

Table 8.2

	Alpha £	Beta £	Gamma £	Delta £	Epsilon £	Zeta £
Sales revenue	22.50	20.00	60.00	30.00	100.00	42.00
Materials	(5.00)	(10.00)	(20.00)	(5.00)	(30.00)	(25.00)
Labour	(5.00)	(2.50)	(30.00)	(10.00)	(50.00)	(10.00)
Contribution	12.50	7.50	10.00	15.00	20.00	7.00

Table 8.3

Ranking	Product	Contribution per unit £	Labour hours employed	Total contribution £
1st	Epsilon	20	1000	4000
2nd	Delta	15	200	3000
3rd	Alpha	12.5	100	2500
			1300	9500

Table 8.4

Ranking	Product	Ranking Ratio	Labour hours employed	Total contribution £
1st	Beta	30	75	2 250
2nd	Alpha	25	100	2 500
3rd	Delta	15	200	3 000
4th	Zeta	7	100	700
5th	Epsilon	4	825	3 300
			1300	11 750
6th	Gamma	3.5	Not produced	

efficiency with which labour is converted into contribution, i.e. our ranking ratio should be:

$$\text{Contribution per unit of scarce resource} = \frac{\text{contribution per unit}}{\text{units of scarce resource per unit output}}$$

In the case of product 'alpha', half a labour hour is required to produce one unit of output. Therefore, the contribution per unit scarce resource for alpha is:

Ranking ratio (alpha) =
£12.5/0.5 = £25.0 per labour hour

Ranking all six products by their ranking ratio we obtain the result shown in Table 8.4.

The total contribution for epsilon production is found by dividing the remaining labour hours after completing zeta production by the number of labour hours required to produce each unit. This gives the total units which can be produced (825/5 = 165) which, when multiplied by the contribution per unit, gives the total contribution generated (165 × 20 = £3300).

THE SHADOW PRICE OF A SCARCE RESOURCE

The revised production programme reveals that the use of the same resources can produce an outcome which better satisfies management's objective of maximising contribution. Given that management finds this programme acceptable, we can then proceed to calculate the value to Taranto of its scarce resource. In the sequence of production priorities, the last (or 'marginal') product is epsilon. Some, but not all, of the demand for epsilon has been met. Consequently, if another labour hour could be found, it would increase Taranto's overall contribution by £4, i.e. one-fifth of an extra unit of epsilon could be produced (invoking the 'divisibility' assumption).

The figure of £4 per labour hour represents the marginal benefit which would accrue to Taranto if an extra labour hour could be found, or the contribution loss which would be suffered if, for some reason, Taranto was deprived of a labour hour. This figure of £4 is termed the 'shadow' price of labour. The 'shadow price' suggests to Taranto that it would be worth paying up to £4 above the current labour rate of £10 per hour (perhaps as an overtime rate) in order to gain extra labour. In terms of net contribution, an overtime rate of £4 per labour hour, for example, would increase the unit cost of epsilon production by £20 per unit which would give a net contribution of exactly zero on the additional units produced.

In our earlier discussion of the cost of redeploying resources from one use to another, we demonstrated that an 'internal opportunity cost' will arise when a given resource is in short supply. In this case we can see that the figure of £4 represents the contribution which would be forgone if one labour hour was diverted away from the production programme. Withdrawing one hour of labour from epsilon production gives a revised table of total contribution (Table 8.5).

The change in contribution following withdrawal of one labour hour is

£11 746 − £11 750 = (£4)

Given that total opportunity cost equals external plus internal opportunity cost, the full opportunity cost of labour is given by the market price of labour

Table 8.5

Ranking	Product	Ranking Ratio	Labour hours employed	Total contribution £
1st	Beta	30	75	2 250
2nd	Alpha	25	100	2 500
3rd	Delta	15	200	3 000
4th	Zeta	7	100	700
5th	Epsilon	4	824	3 296
			1299	11 746
6th	Gamma	3.5	Not produced	

(£10 per labour hour) plus the figure of £4 calculated above.

This concept of the contribution per unit on the marginal product is of central importance in production planning. Not only does it indicate the premium which attaches to a given resource – which may be of use in negotiating extra supplies of that resource – it also provides a means of rapidly appraising any new project that may arise after the basic plan has been formulated and accepted.

For example, after deciding to implement its production plan as discussed above, Taranto plc was asked to consider producing 50 units of pi on a special contract. No extra labour is available. The production requirements and sales revenue per unit for pi are as follows:

Sales revenue per unit	£40.0
Materials usage per unit	1.0 kg
Labour usage (hours per unit)	2.0 hours

These production requirements generate a net contribution of £15 per unit produced and sold. Given the shortage of labour, Taranto could introduce pi into its original production plan and rework the solution. As 100 labour hours will be required for pi, Taranto must forgo part of its epsilon production. The original and revised production schedules are as shown in Table 8.6. The increase in net contribution of £350 indicates that the pi contract should be accepted, even given the depletion in epsilon production.

A more direct route to this answer can be found through the use of the dual price of labour. The figure of £15 per unit net contribution for pi is calculated on the basis of a £10 per hour labour charge. However, if, in assessing the contribution for pi, we include the shadow price of labour as part of the overall labour charge we obtain:

Sales revenue per unit		£40.0
Materials cost per unit	5.00	
Labour cost per unit, $(10+4)\times 2$	28.00	
		33.0
Increase in contribution per unit		£7.0

Therefore, each unit of pi produced gives a net benefit of £7 over and above that provided by the original marginal product – epsilon. The increase in overall contribution for pi production is

$$£7.0 \times 50 = £350$$

which is exactly the result we had before.

One problem with this approach is that it only applies to small changes in the original plan. For example, in Taranto's case, any new opportunity which requires more than 825 labour hours would involve forgoing some zeta production, with a consequent change in the shadow price of labour on the marginal product. Unfortunately, what is a 'small change' is solely dependent upon the circumstances of the case and so no definite rule can be applied.

We can summarise the above as follows.

- An internal opportunity cost will only arise if a particular resource is in short supply.
- If the assumptions of linearity and divisibility apply, the internal opportunity cost is equal to the net cash contribution forgone on the marginal product.
- Marginal alterations to a production plan can be assessed by including the internal opportunity cost

Table 8.6

	Production schedule original		Production schedule including Pi	
	Labour hours	Contribution (£)	Labour hours	Contribution (£)
Beta	75	2 250	75	2 250
Alpha	100	2 500	100	2 500
Delta	200	3 000	200	3 000
Zeta	100	700	100	700
Pi	–	–	100	750
Epsilon	825	3 300	725	2 900
	1300	11 750	1300	12 100

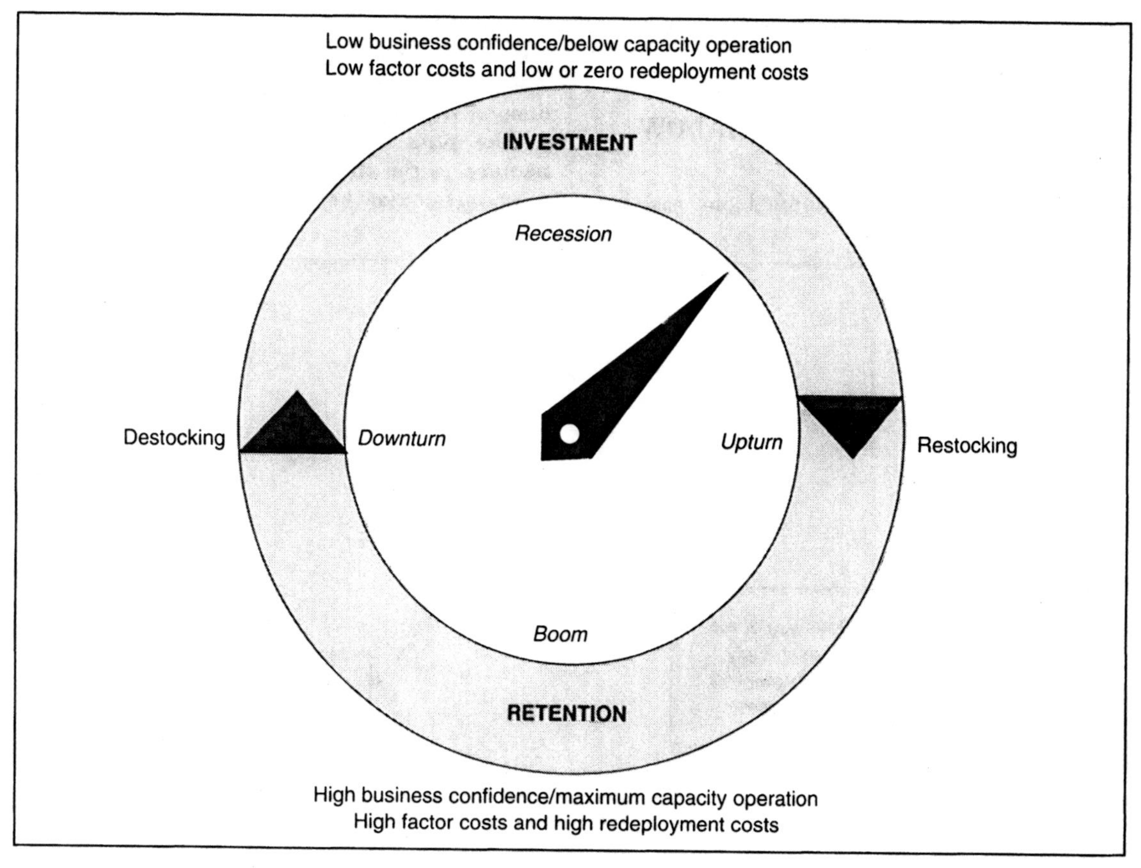

Figure 8.1 The economic cycle.

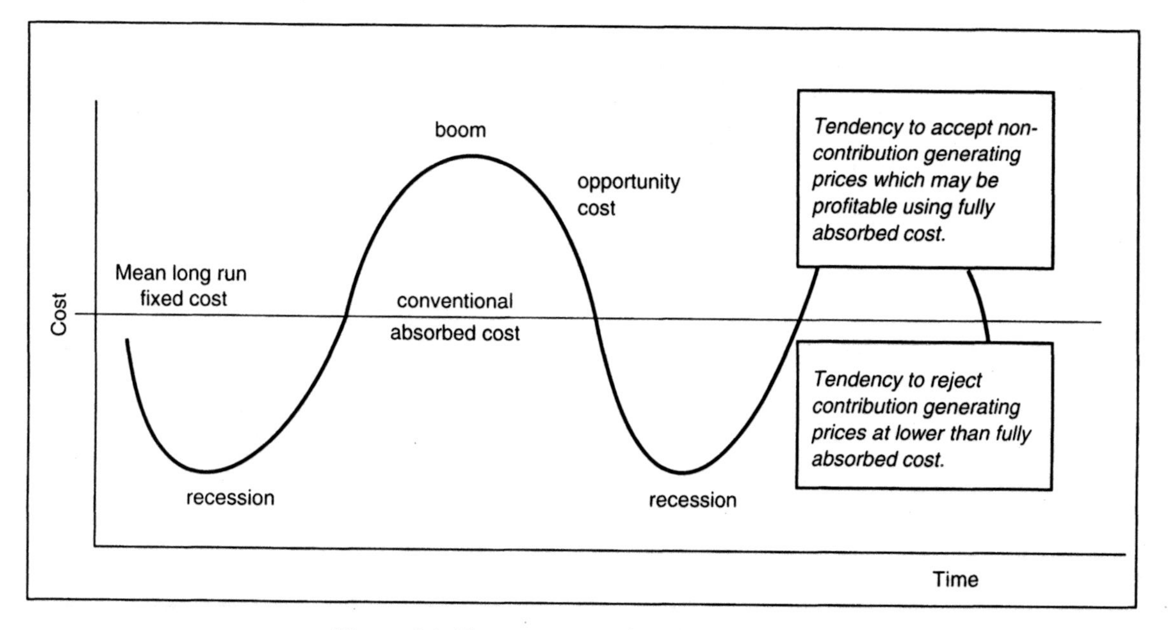

Figure 8.2 The economic cycle and cost absorbtion.

(shadow price) in the cost of the resource in short supply.

THE IMPLICATIONS OF THE SHADOW PRICE

In the example above we identified one resource (labour) which was in short supply. However, in a real business many resources will be in short supply: senior management time may be restricted and limiting their capability to search for new opportunities; plant space and machine time are a finite resource in the short run and internally produced components may be of limited availability. Such

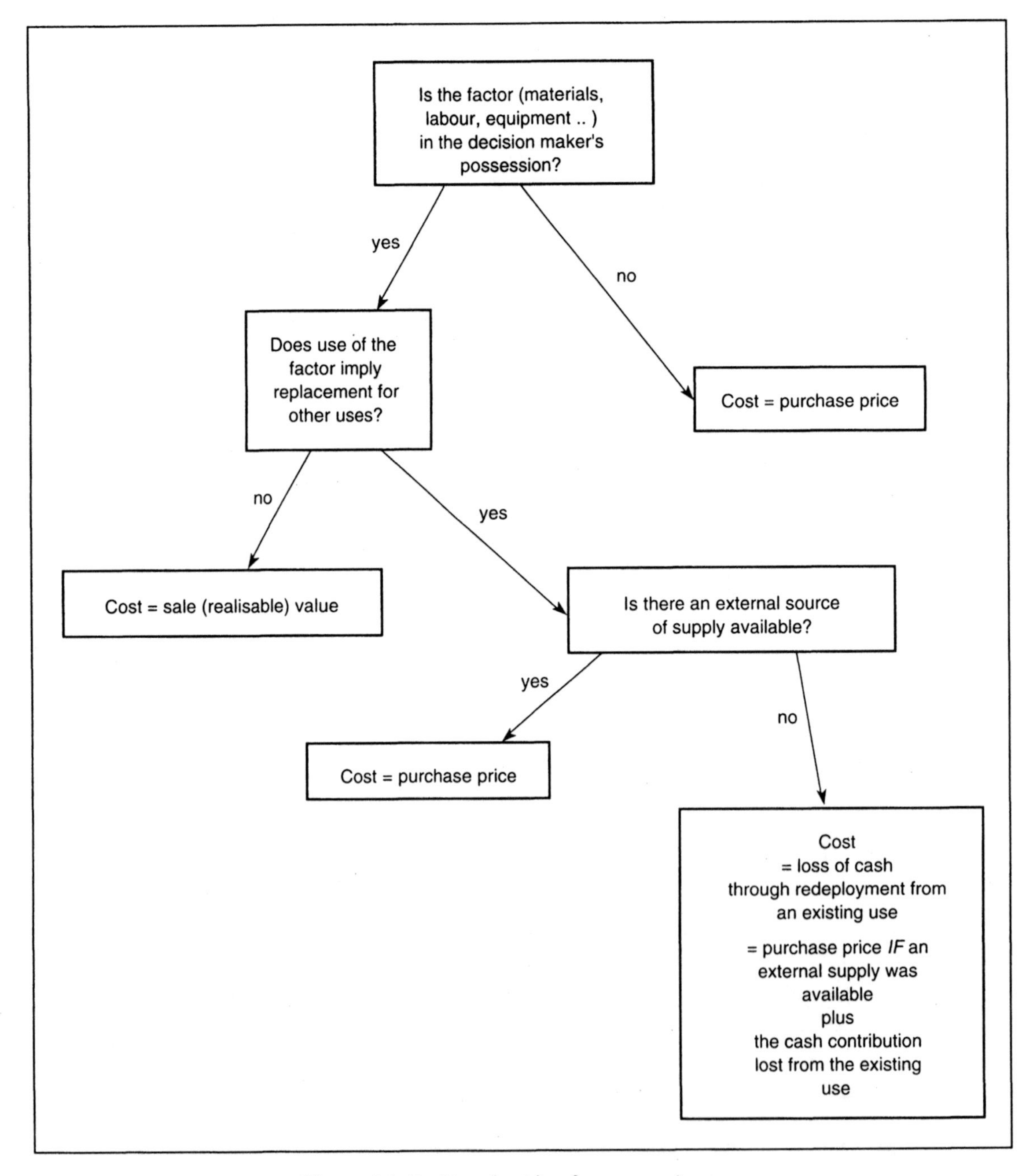

Figure 8.3 Decision algorithm for opportunity cost.

resources will have a redeployment cost or shadow price in terms of the contribution they could earn on their next best use in production. In accurately assessing the opportunity cost of a product, the shadow prices of all scarce resources should be brought into account.

At certain stages in the economic cycle, when a business is operating at maximum capacity, the shadow prices of scarce resources may be many times the external opportunity costs into production and, indeed, many times any imputed overhead loads which the conventional accounting approach might indicate. Conversely, at the other end of the economic cycle, during a recession, a business may have idle capacity and labour time in the short run (see Figure 8.1). In this situation the full opportunity cost of production will be very close to the external opportunity cost as the shadow prices of resources drop towards zero. We come, therefore, to the startling and profound conclusion that the true opportunity cost of a product is not stable but will change as a business approaches and then retreats from capacity as the economic cycle turns.

The problem with conventional allocation matching methods of establishing product costs is that they assign the external cost of maintaining a firm's capabilities to products as overhead charges without recognising that those capabilities may not be expandable or reducible in the market. They represent an average absorption of fixed costs to products, assuming full utilisation of capacity – no more and no less. However, in times when resources are under pressure and a business's capability is fully extended, these absorbed costs may significantly *understate* the true cost to the firm of redeploying that capability to a new use (see Figure 8.2).

Likewise, when capacity is under-utilised, the cost of using it on new opportunities is likely to be very low indeed. In Figure 8.2 we point out the implications of the economic cycle for the relationship between opportunity (decision-matched) cost and conventional (allocation-matched) cost for the 'average firm' in the market.

CONCLUSION

In this chapter we have completed our investigation of the principles of opportunity costs by considering the costs incurred when an external market for a scarce resource does not exist. In this situation, the cash lost by the organisation in its transactions with the external market will be the contribution lost by redeployment.

In Figure 8.3 we show the evaluation sequence for identifying the opportunity cost of any resource. This figure summarises the main conclusions of this and the previous chapter, and gives a simple procedure for deciding which cost possibility is the opportunity cost in any given circumstances.

Part II

Developing Business Capability

Chapter 9

Creating a Business Plan

Level M

Contents

Summary

In this chapter we examine the problems of developing a coherent business plan. We recommend good practice in terms of the layout of such planning documents and emphasise the need for careful market research which should be encapsulated in the marketing plan. The financial plan follows as a consequence of the preceding planning exercise, and is dependent on the specification of strategy, markets, technology and the team putting the project or business together. Finally, we explore some of the issues in valuing and appraising business plans, laying particular emphasis on the rigorous testing of assumptions.

INTRODUCTION

In this chapter we will describe the most effective ways of creating a business plan. A business plan is an integrated document relating to any new business initiative: a new product, project or whole business, and covers all the principal planning elements within business. These planning elements are: strategic, market, technological, team and financial. It is important to construct a business plan whenever:

- a new business is to be formed and capital is required;
- a new investment project is being proposed and a maximum capital need must be specified;
- new product line or project is being proposed.

In this book we concentrate upon the financial aspects of business planning. We outline the procedures for evaluating the financial merits of a business plan in the latter part of this chapter although we will defer a formal discussion of project investment appraisal until Chapter 14. The financial aspects of business planning present few serious problems compared with the marketing plan for example. However, it is difficult to stress the importance of good business planning and, in particular the ruthless testing of assumptions.

EXAMPLE

Devotees of the British TV series: 'Howard's Way' will remember the problems experienced with the Barracuda Yacht within the story line. In fact, that story line was taken from real life, and the company concerned was Sadler Yachts, a reasonably successful boat builder based in Poole, Dorset, England. The Barracuda was a 45 ft light displacement yacht, and the TV series, which was very popular, provided the company with enormous publicity. The estimated development cost of the Barracuda was planned at £200 000 in 1985. However, by 1987, the total book cost of the Barracuda moulds stood at £430 000 which, with the managerial and other resources devoted to the development of that yacht, represented a substantial development cost overrun. In addition, only 17 Barracudas were sold compared with expectations of over 100 units. The company had not researched its market nor the development costs thoroughly enough, but had been carried away on a wave of media interest which failed, as it often does, to translate into sales. Sadler failed in 1988.

Business planning forms one part of the innovation sequence where the potential of new opportunities are identified, measured and evaluated (Figure 9.1). The key output of the business planning process is the business plan itself which will be the main presentational document required to support a case for funding, either from the financial markets or from senior management within a firm.

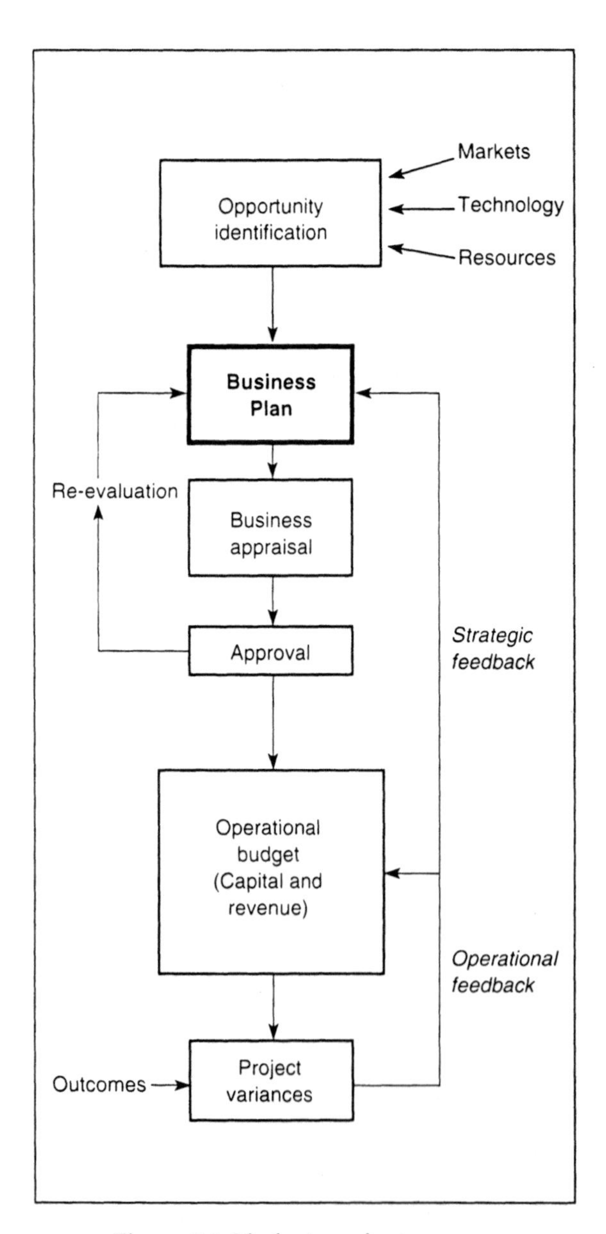

Figure 9.1 The business plan in context.

THE STRUCTURE OF THE BUSINESS PLAN

The formal business plan is a set of linked documents which follow the conventional business planning process of:

Mission → objectives → strategy → plan

In Figure 9.2 we show the layout of a business plan showing its principal elements and how they are structured.

For any given business opportunity, variations may well suggest themselves and certain layout modifications may be appropriate. However, the structure outlined here is most likely to generate the information necessary for a thorough evaluation and form a sound basis as possible for avoiding eventual failure.

The executive summary

This document should be brief. For most business propositions it will cover no more than one side of paper and should be a masterpiece of persuasive English. It is an important fact that most business proposals are not read fully by the decision makers concerned. In this area of decision making, as in most others, impression and intuition are often relied upon and any formal analysis of the proposal concerned is used as an ex-post rationalisation of the judgement made. In this context, the executive summary becomes a very important rhetorical device in the hands of the advocate of a new business proposal. Good executive summaries should contain three key elements:

- the facts of the proposal, outlining the nature of the product or service and indicating the scale and timing of the financial investment entailed;
- the benefits which will accrue to the organisation making the investment decision and, in some cases, to the individual making the decision;
- the success factors by which the investment can be judged.

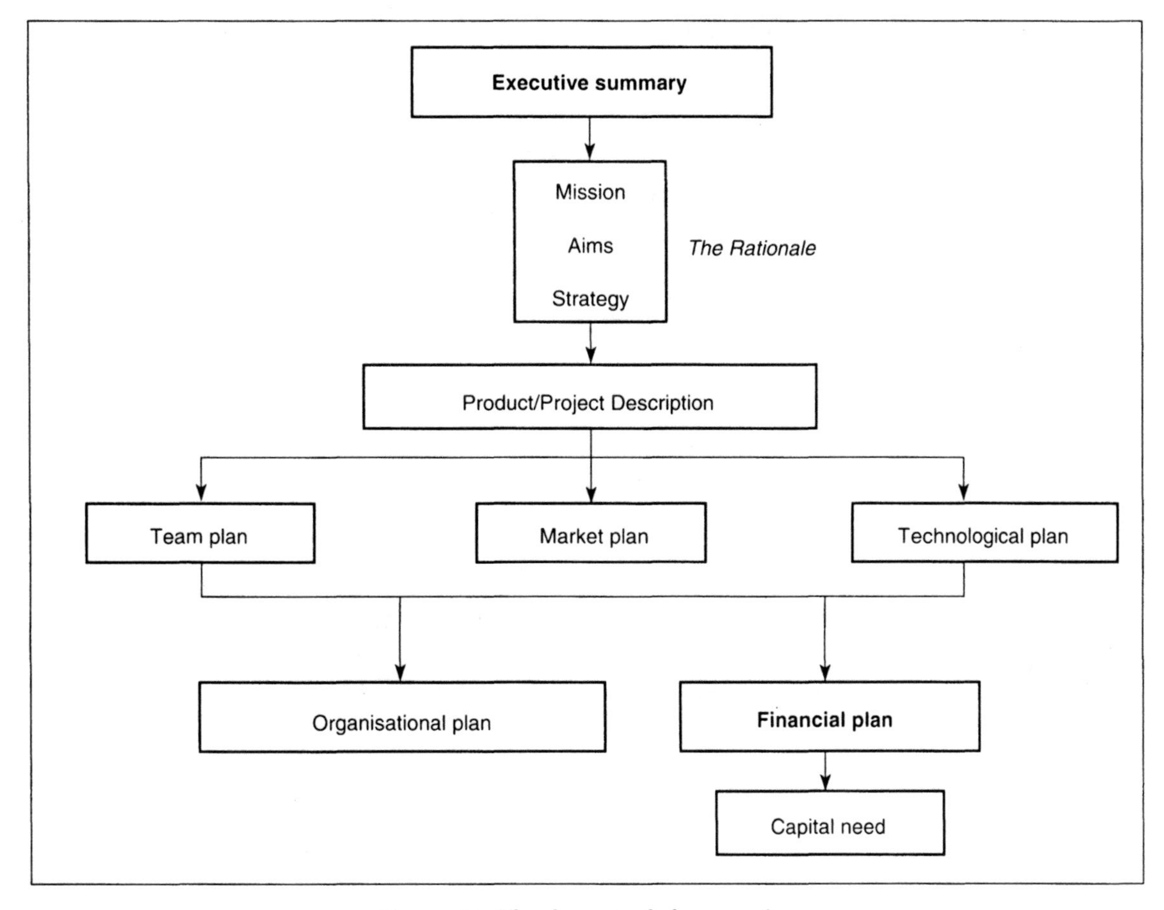

Figure 9.2 The elements of a business plan.

The rationale

The rationale for a business plan should consist of three elements: a statement of overall purpose or intention (the mission), the *objectives* which the project or business is attempting to realise and the method which will be employed to realise those objectives (the strategy). Strategic statements can be decomposed into: product and technological strategy, market strategy, human resource strategy and financial strategy. The principal attributes for judging a set of strategic proposals can be summarised as follows.

- Are the components of the strategy internally consistent and based upon reasonable assumptions of the likely future state of the world?
- Is the strategy clearly focused upon the attainment of the objectives as specified, or is some purpose lying beneath the surface of the analysis which has not been made explicit?
- Where the business plan is being prepared within the context of an existing business, does the mission, objectives and strategy fit with the overall intentions of the organisation?

In assessing a strategy, lending institutions will pose a series of questions.

(i) Is the strategic intention behind the business proposal ethical and legal?
(ii) Is the strategy logically consistent? A minimum cost strategy will be difficult to achieve alongside aspirations to become a high quality producer.
(iii) Is the strategy likely to yield competitive success given the known state of the market and the regulatory environment?
(iv) How much risk will the lender face – is there some form of downside protection in the event of failure (e.g. significant real assets which may be realised in the event of problems)?

(v) Is the strategy simple and direct in its purpose of achieving the business mission?

The product description

This element of the plan should describe to an appropriate level of detail (given the audience) the product or service being offered to the market. Sufficient detail should be presented to be convincing and to substantiate any financial implications which may be developed later in the plan. Clearly, if a non-technical audience is being addressed a technical exposition could invite non-comprehension or referral to a technical specialist for advice.

The plans

The plans can be separated into two categories:

- the development plans covering technical, market and team issues;
- the implication plans which cover the appropriate organisational and financial implications of the development plans.

Generally, non-specialist decision makers place emphasis as follows:

Team → market → financial →
organisational → technical

In other words, once they understand what is being proposed (in outline) from the executive brief, attention usually focuses on the credibility of the team presenting the case, the strength of the potential market and, then, their financial obligations. There has been little systematic research into the reaction of the financial institutions to business plans, but the level of finance is rarely seen as a critical issue and in a recent study of the venture capital market it became clear that venture investors were more concerned with ensuring an adequate level of funding for the needs of the project, rather than in being parsimonious about the level of funding which can be made available. Unplanned second wave financing is regarded as a serious problem for any business or project using the venture capital market.

In terms of practical importance the crucial plan in the above set is the market plan, and this is undoubtedly the most difficult to get right. With some products or services, thorough market research may be necessary. With other, perhaps more innovative products, consumer choice may be so uninformed that market research may reveal little that is useful. In this situation, careful analysis of complementary or substitute product markets would be necessary, supplemented by an appraisal of the potential competitive advantage offered by the new product or service.

Once the development plans have been defined as well as is practical, the financial implications can be identified, and the financial planning exercise commenced.

The financial plan

Normally, a financial plan consists of the following elements:

(i) a short-term forecast of cash flow for the next twelve months showing cash income less expenditure including financing charges using the most reasonable assumptions about demand;
(ii) a medium-term forecast over a minimum of three years, but preferably five; with
(iii) annual profit and loss and balance sheets using conventional accounting procedures for five years;
(iv) a statement of maximum financial need for the project (taken from (i));
(v) a proposal of how the project will be financed giving, if appropriate, the amount of equity which the proposer is willing to invest.

A BUSINESS CASE IN FINANCIAL PLANNING

Johnson is examining the financing requirements for the production of a master switching unit developed from novel technology flowing from his research into high capacity cable optics.

The capital cost for the project would be minimal, but production would rely upon Johnson's own technological skill. He would employ a packer assistant and his wife would run the office. During the first year he is confident that he could build monthly sales from a base contract with TCS Ltd (a large manufacturer of cable systems). This contract would be worth £40 000 per month. Their terms of trade are good but they do take up to three months to pay. Johnson hopes to build business at an average rate of 5% per month in the first year. This is an exceptional rate of growth and would be dependent upon the technology gaining early acceptance in the market place.

On average the material costs are 70% of the

selling price of each unit and Johnson tries not to produce except to order. His suppliers look for payment one month after the date of supply.

Johnson estimates his expenditures as follows:

Capital equipment (payable 1 January)	*£30 000*
Annual rent on 1000 square feet (inc. service charge payable quarterly in advance)	*£6 800*
Salary costs	*£14 400*
Rates (per annum) payable quarterly in arrears	*£6 000*
Personal living expenses (April and quarterly thereafter)	*£2 000*
Marketing costs (initial)	*£10 000*
Advertising costs (per annum)	*£18 000*
Initial stock float (to be maintained)	*£8 000*

Johnson can put £20 000 of his own cash into the business and the bank has agreed, subject to a detailed financial plan for his first year of business to finance the remainder of his financial need on an overdraft basis bearing interest at a monthly rate (calculated on the month end balance) of 0.8%. The capital equipment will depreciate over five years.

Johnson wishes to consider two situations: (i) where his business restricts itself to the core contract with TCS and (ii) where he expands sales at 5% per month.

The first stage in this exercise is to create, in columnar form, a statement of the cash flows, which will arise for the business during the year. In doing this we need to make the following assumptions.

- Sales will remain constant at £40 000 per month.
- Revenues and expenditures occur on the last day of the month in question. This will allow us to create a monthly projection of cash flow, rather than a daily projection which would be impractical and unnecessary (we assume that the capital expenditure, for example, will occur on the final day of January).

In Table 9.1 values are calculated as follows.

- *Sales*: these are projected at £40 000 per annum, but note that the first cash is received in April, three months after the first sales are made.
- *Purchases*: these more closely match production. In January, Johnson will sell £40 000 (for which he received the cash in April) but he will have to pay for the materials in February (one month after purchase). The initial stock float of £8000 must, similarly, be paid for in February.

All of the other expenses (except interest) are laid down on the spreadsheet in their respective months of payment. Note that it would be rather tempting to assume that the rates can be paid a few days late, and hence in the following month. It is not good practice, however, to engage in window dressing at this level of analysis, but rather to adhere to the assumptions made as closely as possible.

The monthly cash flow line shows cash receipts less cash payments in that month, and it is not difficult to see that quite heavy cash expenditures will be entailed in the first three months by:

- cash expenditure on initial set up;
- funding 'working capital', i.e. financing opening stocks and three months of unrecovered sales.

The interest payments are straightforward:

At 31 January –
outstanding borrowing = 24 650
monthly interest = 24 650 × 0.008 = £197

This value is then added to the month end outstanding to give a month end cumulative total.

At the end of February –
outstanding = 24 847 (Jan.) + 38 950 (Feb.)
and interest = 63 797 × 0.008 = £510

The cumulative total with interest gives the maximum financial need of the business which can be shown graphically as in Figure 9.3. In addition, the maximum financial need assuming different rates of growth per month is also included although you may wish to recalculate the spreadsheet in Table 9.1 to confirm the results.

As you can see from Figure 9.3, the financial needs of the business reach a maximum in March and then only gradually recover during the rest of the year. The depth of the 'cash trough' is heavily influenced in Johnson's case by the lengthy credit period taken by its principal customer, TCS Ltd, and much of the £100 000 of borrowing in March is taken up with financing two months sales (relative to the point at which cash is paid in settlement of purchases made).

Figure 9.3 shows one of the most paradoxical financial phenomena in business which has been the cause of more bankruptcies in the small business sector than any other financial cause – namely that in a situation where the terms of trade are in balance or positive, i.e.

$$\text{Debtor age} - \text{creditor age} \geq 0$$

Table 9.1 Cash flow statement.

Johnson's financial plan
Budgeted cash flow statement

	Jan.	Feb.	Mar.	Apr.	May	Jun.	Jul.	Aug.	Sep.	Oct.	Nov.	Dec.
Sales				40 000	40 000	40 000	40 000	40 000	40 000	40 000	40 000	40 000
Purchases		(28 000)	(28 000)	(28 000)	(28 000)	(28 000)	(28 000)	(28 000)	(28 000)	(28 000)	(28 000)	(28 000)
Purchases		(8 000)										
Wages	(1 200)	(1 200)	(1 200)	(1 200)	(1 200)	(1 200)	(1 200)	(1 200)	(1 200)	(1 200)	(1 200)	(1 200)
Office costs	(250)	(250)	(250)	(250)	(250)	(250)	(250)	(250)	(250)	(250)	(250)	(250)
Rent	(1 700)			(1 700)			(1 700)			(1 700)		
Rates			(1 500)			(1 500)			(1 500)			(1 500)
Initial marketing	(10 000)											
Advertising	(1 500)	(1 500)	(1 500)	(1 500)	(1 500)	(1 500)	(1 500)	(1 500)	(1 500)	(1 500)	(1 500)	(1 500)
Capital	20 000											
Equipment	(30 000)											
Drawings				(2 000)			(2 000)			(2 000)		
Monthly cash flow	(24 650)	(38 950)	(32 450)	5 350	9 050	7 550	5 350	9 050	7 550	5 350	9 050	755
Interest	(197)	(510)	(774)	(737)	(671)	(616)	(578)	(510)	(454)	(415)	(346)	(288)
Cum. Balance	(24 847)	(64 308)	(97 532)	(92 919)	(84 540)	(77 606)	(72 834)	(64 294)	(57 198)	(52 263)	(43 559)	(36 297)

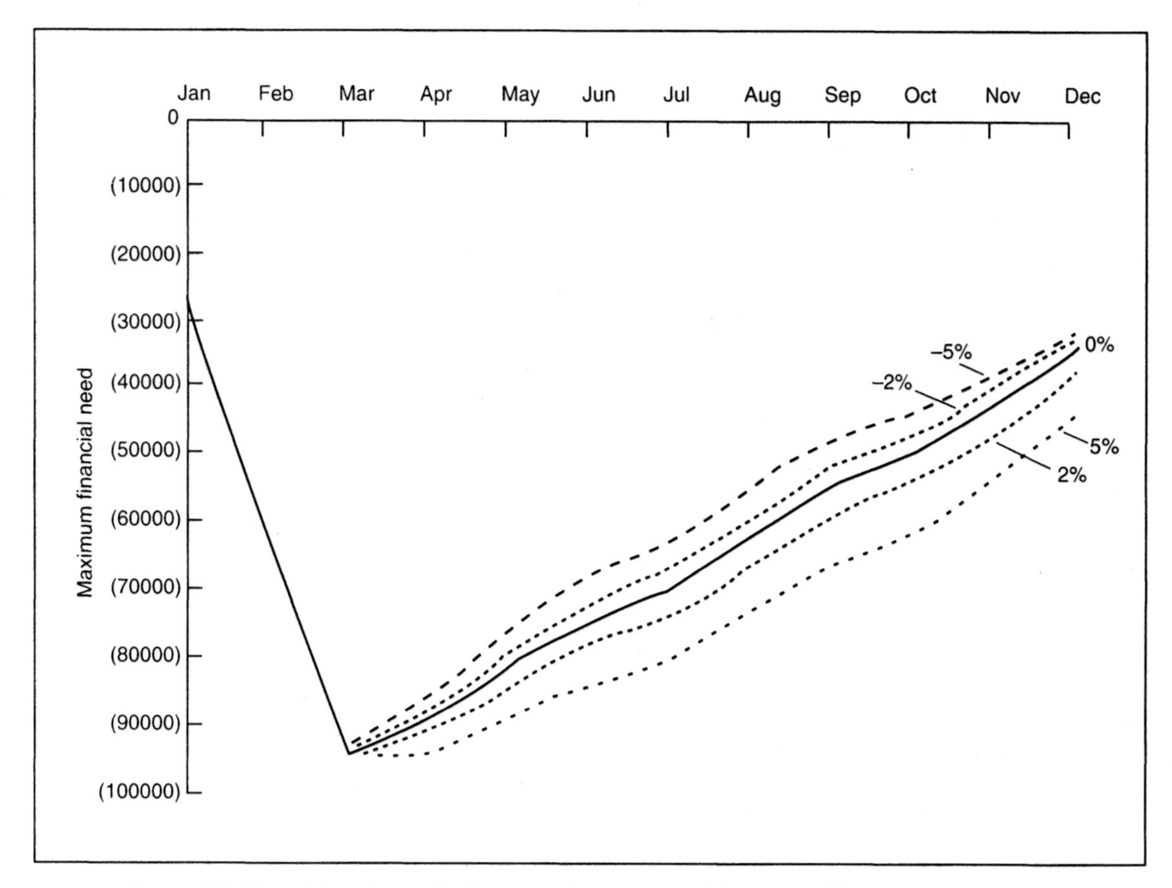

Figure 9.3 Financial need over the first year of operation at different monthly growth rates on sales.

then *expanding* sales will lead to a short-run deterioration in liquidity, but an improvement in profitability, and *contracting* sales will lead to short-run improvements in liquidity but a deterioration in profitability. However, if

$$\text{Debtor age} - \text{creditor age} < 0$$

then *contracting* sales will lead to a short-run deterioration in liquidity, and deterioration in profitability, and *expanding* sales will lead to short-run improvements in liquidity, and an improvement in profitability.

> **RYAN'S THIRD LAW**
>
> *Short-term changes in corporate liquidity are positively associated with changes in contribution-generating sales under neutral or positive terms of trade. Short-term changes in corporate liquidity are negatively associated with changes in contribution-generating sales under negative terms of trade.*

The next stage in the financial planning exercise is to consolidate the statement of cash flows above into a summary form taking into account both undischarged commitments (debtors and creditors) and temporal accruals (depreciation). In Table 9.2 we summarise the monthly cash statement into the following.

(i) An annual cash flow column which is simply the sum of all the cash flows in each month across each row.

(ii) A column of revenue less expenses for the period concerned. Notice that the total income is £480 000 of which £360 000 was discharged by customers and the remainder (£120 000) is undischarged debtor balances. With purchases £336 000 of stock was purchased to match to production (of which

£28 000 was undischarged at the end of the year) and £8000 was purchased as contingency stock and which was in hand at the end of the year. This £8000 is unmatched to the year's revenue and is therefore carried forward to the next year as a stock balance. The remainder of the expenses which can be matched to the year's revenue is then listed as given, except for depreciation which is calculated as one-sixth of the asset value which can be charged to the year concerned. All of the matched expenses when deducted from total revenue give a net profit of £74 703.

(iii) A list of outstanding assets can now be constructed. First, the net book value of the fixed asset stands at £30 000 less accumulated depreciation of £5000, i.e. £25 000. The stock of materials is £8000 and the outstanding debtors stand at £120 000.

(iv) A list of outstanding claims completes the picture with: £28 000 of creditors, capital of £20 000 (put in by Johnson) less £6000 of drawings against his capital account plus the profit accumulated by the business on his behalf which is £74 703. We have assumed that Johnson is withdrawing against his capital rather than taking a salary, which does change the apparent performance of this project (see the section on valuing a business plan below).

The revenue and expenses column can now be rearranged to form a standard profit and loss account for the business for the year (Table 9.3). Similarly, the assets and claims can be rearranged into balance sheet format. The methods of creating a balance sheet and profit and loss account are explained in much more detail in Chapter 30, although you should be able to reconstruct these two accounts for different levels of sales growth during the first year.

The projected cash flow forecast is the primary planning document as it enables management to estimate its financial needs to fund the start-up phase. It also allows management to understand the impact of the credit policies it has been able to win in the market place, and by varying some critical assumptions concerning growth, credit policy and timing of cash flows it can also provide useful information on the liquidity of the business.

In Johnson's case the profit and loss account reveals a very satisfactory return on equity capital employed (ROE):

$$\text{ROE} = \frac{\text{profit for shareholders}}{\text{average equity capital invested during the year}}$$

$$= \frac{74\,703}{(20\,000 + 88\,703)/2} \times 100 = 137\%$$

and, by the end of the year, the liquidity of the business as measured by its acid test ratio is:

$$\text{Acid test} = (\text{current assets} - \text{stocks})/\text{current liabilities}$$
$$= 120\,000/64\,297 = 1.87$$

What neither of these ratios indicates is the extent of the cash deficit which the business still faces at the end of the year and a clear question that would arise is how quickly the company can clear its overdraft. With a full financial plan, up to five years figures should be forecast using consistent assumptions about costs and revenues, and a time estimate generated for full financial recovery under those assumptions.

Graphically, Johnson's exercise reveals that full cash recovery in all but the most pessimistic sales projections will lead to full cash recovery within 15 months (Figure 9.4). Notice also that the favourable short-term benefit of the reducing sales level at −5% or −2% is lost by the end of the first year. You may wish to consider in your own mind the dynamics of what is happening here and how the picture would change if different assumptions about non-direct costs were to be made.

In summary, therefore a full financial plan for a start up business would include the following:

(i) a detailed cash forecast over the start-up phase on at least a month-by-month basis;
(ii) an estimate of maximum financial need;
(iii) summary cash flow, profit and loss and balance sheet for the first full year of activity;
(iv) annual cash flow estimates with corresponding profit and loss account and balance sheet for a minimum of three years;
(v) an estimate of the sensitivity of the projections to changes in crucial variables projecting a best and worst case scenario;
(vi) on the basis of this an estimate of the annual ROE in the business, other performance measures and the time required to obtain full cash recovery;
(vii) and finally, we come to the all important stage of valuing the financial plan.

VALUING A FINANCIAL PLAN

The approach to valuing any project or business

Table 9.2 Summary of Table 9.1.

	Annual cash flow	Revenue (expenses)	Outstanding assets	Outstanding claims
Sales	360 000	480 000	120 000	
Purchases	(308 000)	(336 000)		28 000
Purchases	(8 000)		8 000	
Wages	(14 400)	(14 400)		
Office costs	(3 000)	(3 000)		
Rent	(6 800)	(6 800)		
Rates	(6 000)	(6 000)		
Initial marketing	(10 000)	(10 000)		
Advertising	(18 000)	(18 000)		
Capital	20 000			20 000
Equipment	(30 000)	(5 000)	25 000	
Drawings				(6 000)
Annual net cash flow	(30 200)			
Accrued interest	(6 097)	(6 097)		
Overdraft account	(36 297)			36 297
	Profit =	74 703		74 703
			153 000	153 000

Table 9.3 Johnson's projected accounts for the first year of operation.

Johnson's profit and loss account

Sales		480 000
less: cost of goods sold		(336 000)
Gross profit		144 000
less: wages	(14 400)	
Office costs	(3 000)	
Rent	(6 800)	
Rates	(6 000)	
Marketing	(10 000)	
Advertising	(18 000)	
Depreciation	(5 000)	
Interest	(6 097)	
		(69 297)
Net profit		74 703

Johnson's balance sheet

Fixed assets		30 000
less: accum. depreciation		(5 000)
		25 000
Current assets		
debtors	120 000	
stock	8 000	
	128 000	
Current liabilities		
creditors	28 000	
overdraft	36 297	
	64 297	
Net current assets		63 703
		88 703
Capital employed		
Owner's equity		20 000
less: drawings		(6 000)
		14 000
Accum. profit		74 703
		88 703

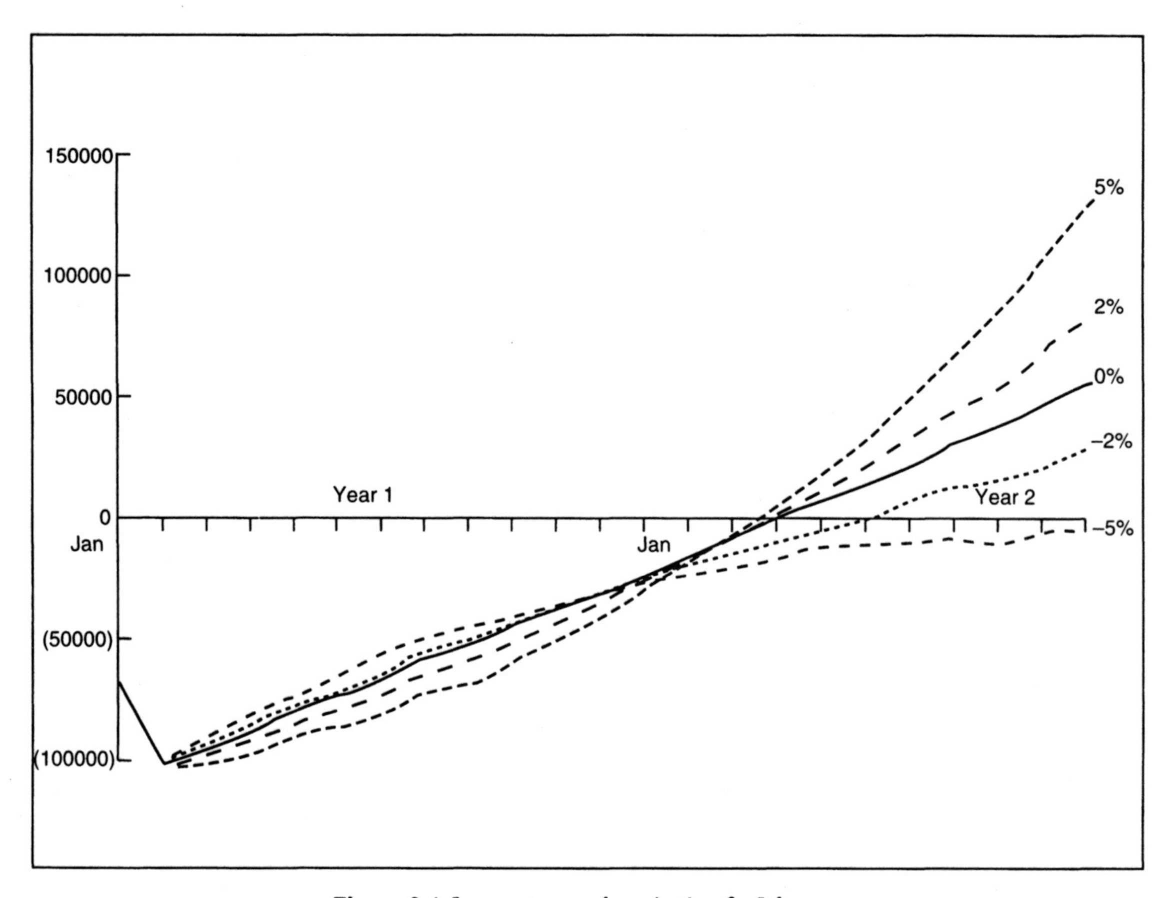

Figure 9.4 Longer-term cash projection for Johnson.

opportunity is developed and discussed in Chapter 14 where we examine in some detail the methods of investment appraisal. We will defer a more detailed discussion of the valuation of Johnson's plan until then, and just present the results here.

Our preferred technique for valuing business investments is to discount the future net cash flows (negatives and positives) of the project at the appropriate rate of discount. For this business plan we do not know Johnson's personal rate of discount, i.e. the minimum rate of return which he would look for in any business investment. However, we can take the bank rate as a proxy figure and look to see whether the business has a positive value at this rate of discount.

As we will see in Chapter 14, the net present value of this project, at a monthly rate of 0.8%, approximates to £848 400 assuming consistent sales into the future of £40 000 per annum. In Chapter 14 we explain why this figure does not include Johnson's capital input of £20 000 nor his withdrawals. Intuitively, in appraising a project we would wish to evaluate whether the project generates an adequate return on Johnson's investment. The net present value method includes all of the initial investments on equipment and working capital and tells us that the business will generate a positive benefit of £848 400 over and above the cash required to fund that investment including the minimum rate of return of 0.8% per month.

The issue of Johnson's withdrawals are more tricky to deal with. If they are assumed to be a salary payment then they would be a genuine cost and would reduce the value of the investment. In this example we have taken the view that they are withdrawals from capital and do not form a cost upon the business.

APPRAISING A BUSINESS PLAN

By now you have probably realised the importance of preparing a good business plan in defining funding requirements, the priorities of the business and in establishing a blueprint for the future. The appraisal of a business plan consists of the following stages:

(i) ensuring that all the necessary components, as described above are in place;
(ii) ensuring that the plans are internally consistent, i.e. conclusions from one plan are translated into others;
(iii) testing the assumptions within each plan and providing revised plans under different assumptions;
(iv) evaluating the conclusions of the plan, i.e. does the plan fit within the total portfolio of other activities or lending, and does it promise performance at a level which justifies investment within it?

In appraisal, a critical stage is in the testing of assumptions. Assumptions fall into a hierarchy which can be classified as follows.

- Assumptions of capability – these specify the opportunities which the business would be capable of following given the range of skills and technologies which it has at its disposal.
- Assumptions of state – these are assumptions about future values, the type of market, the market share which can be gathered at a particular price, yields on new processes, labour productivity in the future and so on.
- Assumptions of fact – these are assumptions about current conditions: market prices, demand, competitor products, current process yields, tax regimes and rates etc. In this context, what may appear to be hard data from sample surveys still generate assumptions of fact concerning the population from which those data are drawn.

A business plan which is shown to have deficiencies at any of the above levels will lose credibility in the eyes of whoever is appraising its viability. Clearly, assumptions of fact should be replaced by actual evidence if it can be found, although data rarely come free of some implicit assumptions in their measurement or in their classification. Even judgements of competitor prices rely upon assumptions about the comparability of their products with the one(s) specified in the business plan and the other customer support which might be provided. State assumptions can be backed by evidence from properly conducted trials, pilot plant experiments or market research, as the case may be. In studies on corporate failure, the absence of market research, for example, has been shown as a prime mistake by management, and one which sows the seeds of weakness within any business. Assumptions of capability are generated to a certain extent by the plan itself and will be critical in the funding decision. But, the assumption of capability in delivering the business as planned may still be insufficient to gain a lender's support if the project does not promise high enough returns or does not fit within the lender's perception of what is appropriate business to be engaged in.

CONCLUSION

In this chapter we have summarised the main issues and methods in generating business plans. We suggest a standard plan layout which has been shown to be serviceable in many contexts. As part of our analysis of the details of financial planning, we identified both the static and dynamic cash flow problems which need to be worked through for a new business or project. In particular, we urged attention on assumptions about the timing of cash flows and how variations in the assumed terms of trade for a business produced significant impacts upon the financial needs of a growing business.

Chapter 10

The Nature of Business Risk

Level G

Contents

Summary

In this chapter we will take an in-depth look at the concept of risk. The theory of risk took a major step forward in 1953 when Harry H. Markowitz produced his great work 'Portfolio Selection' in the Journal of Finance. *Until that time, risk had been viewed as an intrinsic property of a security or other claim on an asset. Markowitz produced a revolution in finance when he demonstrated that risk is also a relative property and relates to the way in which securities and claims are brought together into combinations called portfolios. This chapter is somewhat theoretical, but the insights offered by the theory of portfolio risk are of relevance for real investment decision making, whether that investment is in the form of securities, assets or in the production of different product ranges. In fact this theory also offers insights into problems of product and firm diversification, and can also throw light upon the performance of teams. In this chapter we commence our discussion with an introduction to the statistical nature of risk and uncertainty before moving on to a discussion of the assumptions, mechanics and implications of the portfolio theory of risk.*

INTRODUCTION

The notion of rational decision making presupposes the idea that future outcomes, measured in terms of their cash effects upon the firm, can be identified and measured. If we could be in the happy but unlikely position of possessing complete information on all the economic processes surrounding a particular decision, then we should be able to predict the future with complete certainty, providing, of course, that we accept the assumption that all social and economic events are causally linked to one another. However, we rarely possess complete information in this sense, and so we are forced to consider the uncertainty attached to the outcomes of our actions.

With outcomes which are very close in time to a particular decision, the link between cause and effect can be quite clear. However, the more remote the outcome, the less clear the linkages between action and consequence become, and the greater the degree of uncertainty with which the decision maker must contend. In addition, outcomes over which there is some control and/or some prior experience will be less uncertain than when the opposite is the case.

The uncertainty of an outcome can be attributed to four sources:

- the time lag between decision and outcome;
- the degree of control we have over the outcomes in question;
- the complexity of the relationship between the variables which impinge upon the decision;
- our experience of similar decision situations.

In some situations, sufficient past experience of a particular type of decision may be available to enable the decision maker to predict, with a considerable degree of certainty, the likelihood of certain events occurring. Life-insurance companies regularly predict the life expectancy of particular individuals when assessing premiums for life-insurance policies. They can do this by virtue of the large amounts of data which they have collected over the years and compiled into their actuarial tables of life expectancy. In other situations, little or no past experience of a particular type of decision is available, and subjective judgement is all that we have to make decisions. For example, an entrepreneur setting up a new business, or an existing company entering into a new market, may have very little experience upon which to base their decisions.

An insurance company, which uses the results of a large number of similar events as a basis for estimating the probabilities of particular events occurring, is in what we call a 'risk' situation. At the other extreme, a company trying to take decisions without any prior knowledge, and purely on the basis of subjective estimates, is in an 'uncertainty' situation.

The words 'risk' and 'uncertainty' denote opposite ends of the objectivity–subjectivity spectrum. In Figure 10.1 we show this risk–uncertainty spectrum with examples of decision-making situations which lie within it.

We can use the statistical concept of probability to assess the likelihood of an event occurring in both risk and uncertainty situations. In risk situations we can use objective probabilities to make statistical predictions, while in uncertainty situations we use probabilities as subjective measures of likelihood.

Probabilities are represented on a scale from 0 to 1 (or sometimes on the equivalent percentage scale of 0 to 100%). Completely certain outcomes have a probability of 1 of occurring. Absolutely impossible situations have a probability of 0 of occurring. In Figure 10.2 we show the scale of prob-abilities from 0 to 1 with some suggestions of appropriate situations and their probability of occurring.

In all decision situations a range or 'set' of possible outcomes exists and each outcome has its own probability of occurring.

EXAMPLE

To give an example from the short-term decision-making area, consider Marchena plc, which uses a raw material, olic acid, in its production processes. The material is bought from a supplier who produces olic acid as a by-product from another process. Because the production runs which produce olic acid follow a monthly cycle the supplier cannot guarantee delivery on any particular day but only within 28 days of order. Marchena's purchasing

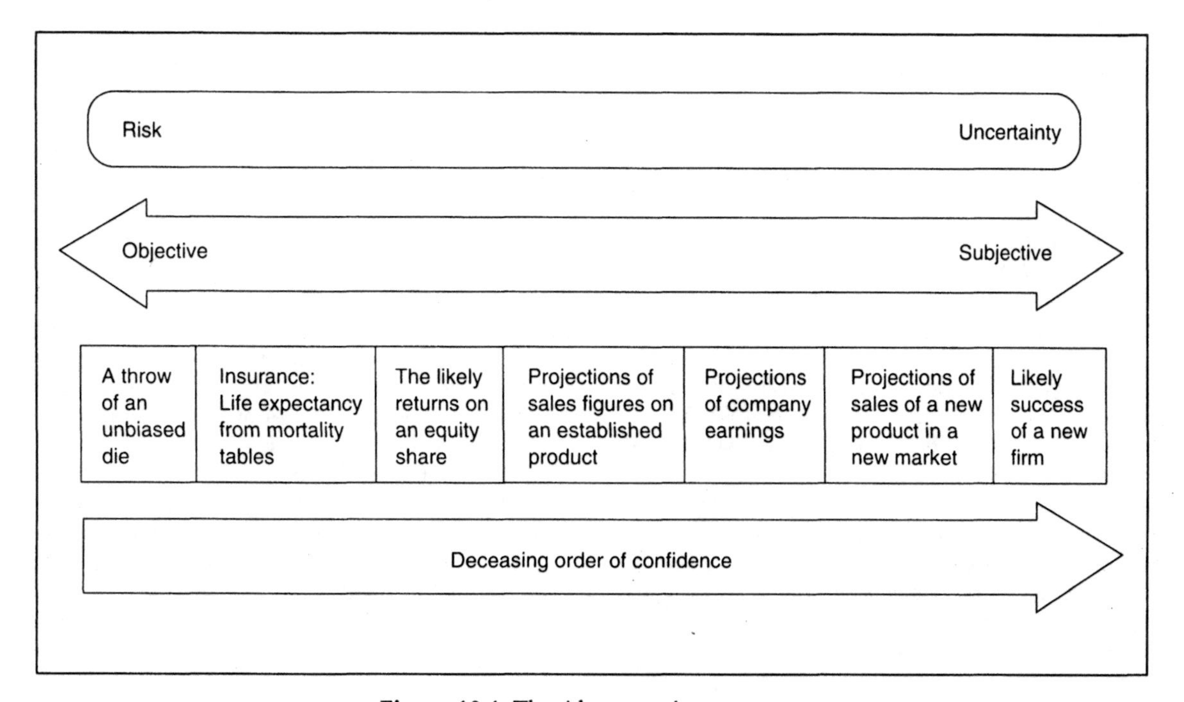

Figure 10.1 The risk–uncertainty spectrum.

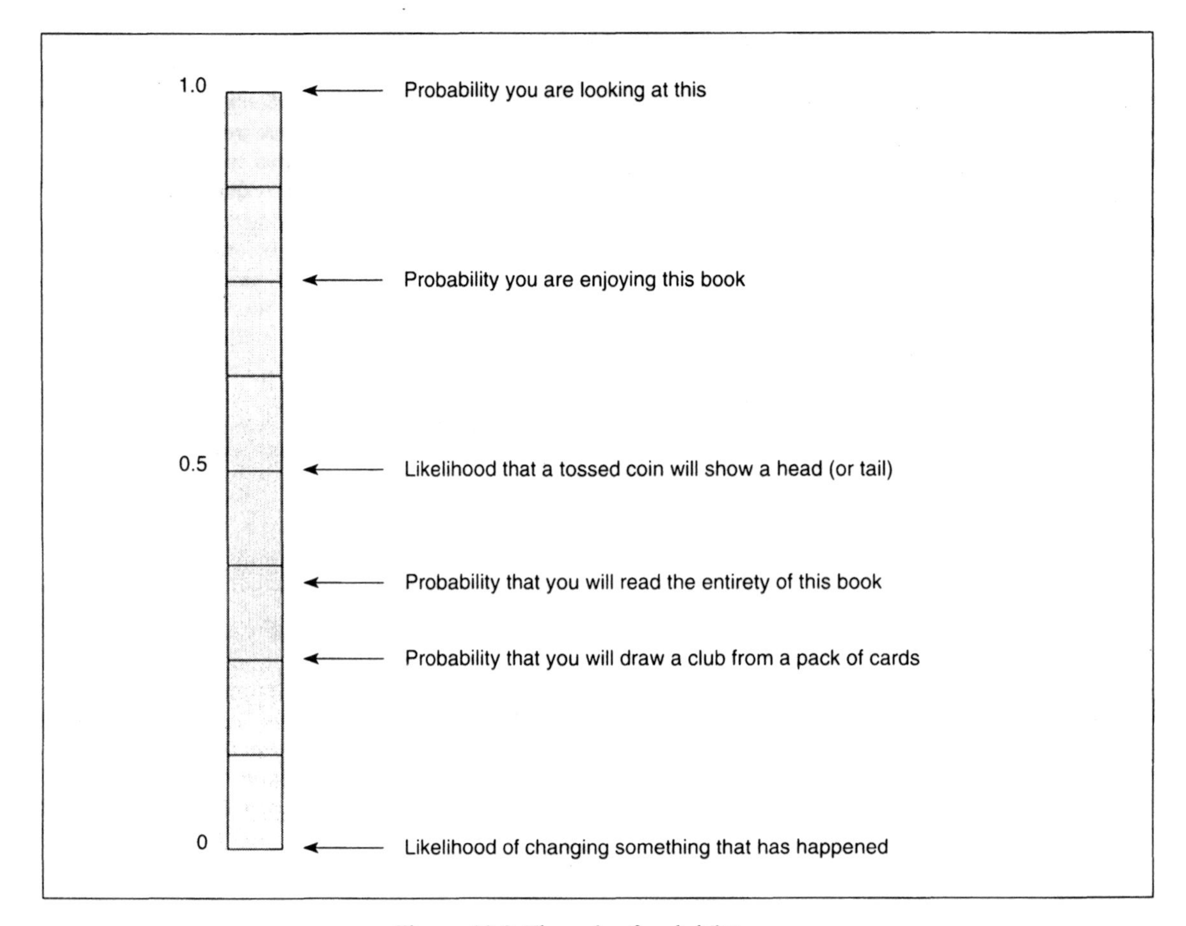

Figure 10.2 The scale of probabilities.

department has kept a note of the order to delivery time (the 'lead time') for the last 400 orders (more than one order may be placed within a particular calendar month).

They have noted that no delivery has ever been made within 10 days of order. The purchasing department's figures are summarised in Table 10.1.

By dividing the number of deliveries on a given day by the total number of orders (400) we can estimate the probability of a delivery being made on a particular day (Table 10.2).

In Figure 10.3 we show the probabilities calculated above in the form of a histogram. The y-axis carries the measure of probability and the horizontal x-axis represents the variable of interest to us which is, in this case, the number of days to delivery. If we were to connect the top of each line (whose heights represent the probability of deliveries being made on that number of days after the order) we would form an approximation of a bell-shaped curve which we call a 'continuous probability distribution'.

The shape we have drawn in Figure 10.3 closely approximates an ideal type of curve known to statisticians as a 'normal probability distribution'. The height of the curve above the x-axis at any point gives the probability of that x-value occurring. Many social, economic and physical systems generate variables which appear to be close approximations of the normal distribution. For example, the height of males (and the height of females as a separate group) in the population are distributed normally, so are the returns generated by ordinary shares. Many more examples can be found.

Only two values need to be known in order to draw a normal distribution and they are its mean value and its standard deviation. Once these two values are known the value of p can be obtained by taking any value of x and substituting it into the equation below. If this is done a sufficient number

Table 10.1

Number of days from order	Number of deliveries	Numbers of days from order	Number of deliveries
10	0	19	59
11	1	20	46
12	4	21	31
13	9	22	18
14	18	23	9
15	31	24	4
16	46	25	1
17	59	26	0
18	64	27	0

Total number of deliveries = 400

Table 10.2

Number of days from order	Probability of delivery	Number of days from order	Probability of delivery
10	0	19	0.1475
11	0.0025	20	0.1150
12	0.0100	21	0.0775
13	0.0225	22	0.0450
14	0.0450	23	0.0225
15	0.0775	24	0.0100
16	0.1150	25	0.0025
17	0.1475	26	0
18	0.1600	27	0

Note that the total probability of delivery within 28 days is exactly 1.00

of times, and the results drawn on a graph, the normal curve will emerge.

The general formula for a normal distribution is:

$$p_i = \frac{1}{\sqrt{2\pi\sigma^2}} e^{-1/2(x_i-\mu)^2/\sigma^2}$$

As we have noted above, only two items of information are needed to describe a normal distribution: its mean (μ) and standard deviation (σ).

For Marchena's problem the mean is given by:

mean (number of days from delivery to order)
= sum of: each value of x multiplied by its respective probability

In mathematical notation this becomes:

$$\mu = \sum_{1}^{n} (p_i x_i)$$

where:

μ is the mean value. This is often called the 'expected value' of the variable x and is sometimes symbolised as $E(x_i)$.

p_i is the probability of 'observing' any one of the n possible values of x_i. In this case $n = 16$.

x_i is the probabilistic variable under consideration. In this example it is the number of days from order to delivery.

Σ is a mathematical symbol which means 'the sum of' the range of values which immediately follow it. The range of values to be summed is given by the values above and below the Greek letter sigma. Therefore, in Marchena's example the summation sign indicates that we have to add n (=16) values together to get the mean value. Symbols such as the summation sign which denote a particular arithmetic or mathematical

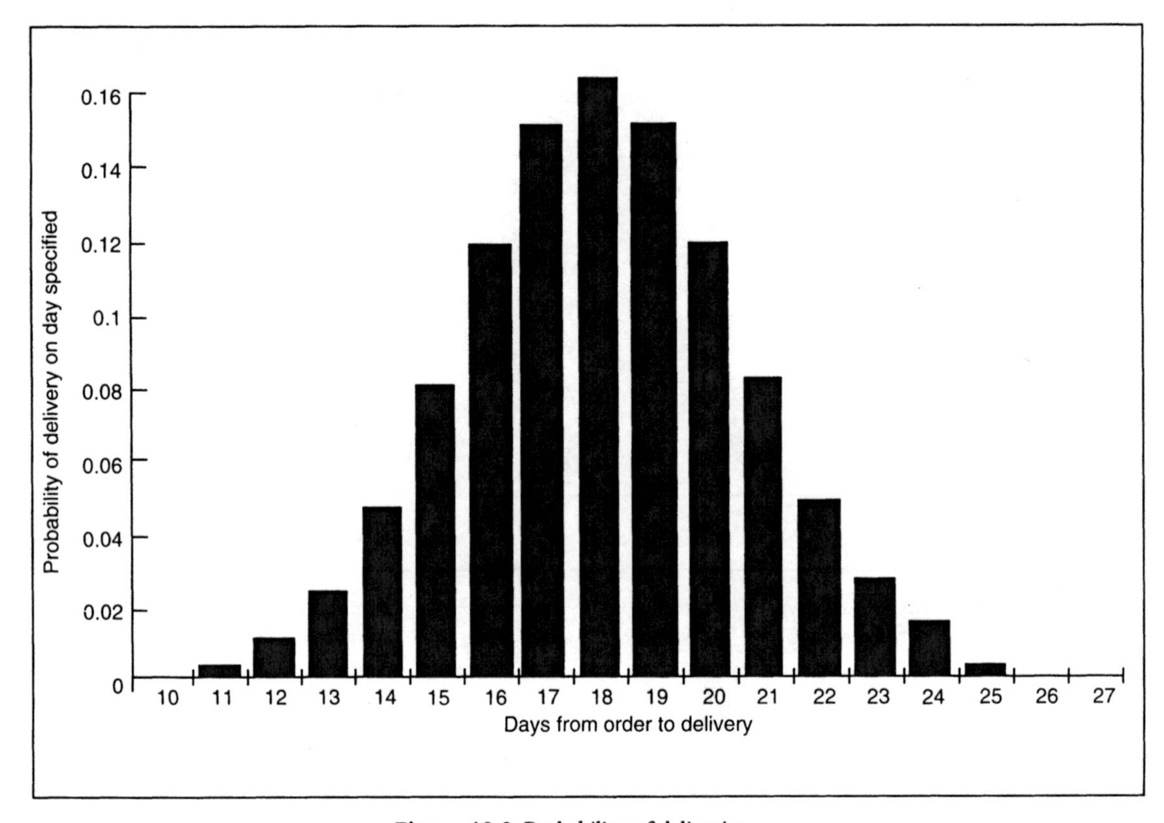

Figure 10.3 Probability of deliveries.

operation are called 'operators'. This sign is, therefore, the 'summation operator'.

Therefore, the mean number of days to delivery is given by:

$$\mu_t = 0 \times 10 + 0.0025 \times 11 + 0.01 \times 12 + 0.0225 \times 13 + 0.045 \times 14 + \ldots + 0.0250 \times 25 + 0 \times 26 + 0 \times 27$$
$$= 18 \text{ days}$$

The standard deviation gives a measure of the average deviation of the normal distribution. Because deviation is measured above and below the mean value, deviations would cancel themselves out on simple averaging as every positive would be matched by an equivalent negative. To get round this we square the values of all of the deviations (negative deviations then become positive on squaring) and then take the average of the squared deviations, before taking the square root to convert back to our 'unsquared' units of measurement.

In practice, the standard deviation measures the width of the distribution which encloses approximately 68% of the total area under the curve. The standard deviation of a normal distribution is given by:

$$\sigma = \sqrt{\sum_{1}^{n} p_i (x_i - \mu)^2}$$

where the notation is the same as that specified for the mean.

To calculate the standard deviation we deduct the mean number of days (μ_t) from each possible day. This gives the deviation of each day from the mean. Each deviation is then squared and multiplied by its respective probability. The square root of the sum of the resultant values gives the standard deviation. Normally, if we take the square root of any number we get two answers or 'roots', one plus and the other minus. However, the standard deviation is defined in terms of the absolute value of the deviation from the mean, i.e. for Marchena:

$$\sigma = \{0 \times (10-18)^2 + 0.0025 \times (11-18)^2 + 0.01 \times (12-18)^2 + \ldots + 0.0025 \times (25-18)^2 + 0 \times (26-18)^2 + 0 \times (27-18)^2\}^{1/2}$$

The power 1/2 indicates the square root of the expression within {}.

The probability with which an outcome occurs measures the risk or uncertainty attached to that outcome. Given a range of possible outcomes which approximate to the normal distribution (as in Marchena's example) the mean or expected value of the distribution gives the most likely outcome (i.e the outcome with the highest probability). The standard deviation measures the variability of possible outcomes around the mean value and is a measure of the risk attached to the distribution as a whole.

We can summarise these points on risk and uncertainty as follows.

- Risk and uncertainty arise through our imperfect attempts to predict the future.
- We use probabilities to measure the risk or uncertainty attaching to a particular outcome.
- If a range of alternative outcomes is possible, then the mean or expected value will give the most likely outcome.

If a range of alternative outcomes is normally distributed, then the standard deviation gives a measure of the risk or uncertainty attaching to that outcome.

When managers perceive that following a particular course of action entails accepting risky outcomes, they will attempt to quantify and minimise that risk as far as possible. In the last section we saw how the risk attaching to a particular outcome can be measured, making the implicit assumption that the variability of a distribution is a reliable indicator of future risk. There are, however, a number of strategies management can follow in order to minimise the level of risk.

- They can seek further information about the relationship between particular decisions and their consequences. For example, if a company decides to alter the price of its product, it may believe that there is a level of uncertainty concerning the amount it will sell. To an extent, market research can reduce that uncertainty and, indeed, may be able to quantify the situation in terms of a range of possible sales levels with probabilities attached to them.
- Management may attempt to insure against the possibility of undesirable outcomes (i.e. outcomes lower than the mean or expected value). For example, if a company perceives that a new production facility increases the risk of fire at a particular plant, it may decide to cover that increased risk by taking out extra fire-insurance cover. Similarly, if an investor sells shares he or she does not possess (a 'short sale') in the hope of earning a profit on an immediate fall in share price, that investor can insure against the possibility of an increase in share price by buying a call option'. A 'call option' represents a right to purchase the shares at a stated price at a specified future date. The risk of an increase in share price, which would entail buying back the shares at a loss, is covered by the option. Reducing risk in this way is often called 'hedging', hence the term 'hedging one's bets'.
- Finally, management can reduce risk by 'diversification'. When several outcomes are put together, their combined risk is not always a linear addition of their individual risks. The combined risk may be greater or less than a simple combination of their risks depending on the circumstances. When management takes combinations of decisions in order to obtain outcomes which reduce risk overall it is said to be following a 'diversification strategy'. We will examine this important method of risk management in the next section of this chapter.

RISK WITH MORE THAN ONE ASSET OR SECURITY

Any of the items shown in Table 10.3 can be described as an 'asset' to a business organisation with particular payoffs (return) and particular risks.

In order to explain the concepts involved in risk management we will consider the simplest case of a risky investment. It was with just such a setting that much of the theory of portfolio risk was originally developed, and the results are easy to extend to other assets. We will consider just two investments in company shares: share A and share B. We will assume that the historical annual returns for these two shares have been recorded along with the standard deviation of those returns.

The risk 'intrinsic' to each security is measured by its standard deviation. However, the risk of the combination can only be known when the standard deviation of the combined distribution of returns is known. This requires a specification of the degree of correlation between the two securities. Correlation is a measure of the degree of relationship which

Table 10.3

Asset	Return	Risk
Fixed assets	Operational performance	Substandard performance, breakdown
Product line	Optimal sales at set price	Suboptimal sales at set price
Personnel	Job performance	Substandard work, opportunism, moral hazard, adverse selection
Investments	Return – yield on dividends and capital gains	Below average returns

exists between two variables. If the returns of two securities are perfectly co-related, i.e. if the returns of each security are perfectly matched with one another (positive returns in one are associated with positive returns in the other and negative returns in one are associated with negative returns in the other) then they are perfectly correlated with a correlation coefficient of +1. Similarly, an exactly opposite extreme can be proposed where positive returns in one security are always matched by negative ones in the other. In that case the two securities will have a correlation coefficient of −1. The appendix to this chapter contains details of how the correlation coefficient is calculated.

In Figure 10.4 below the two extreme possibilities are shown. A simple way to understand the issue is to compare two shares: one company specialising in 'winter sun' holidays and the other in summer holidays only. Assume that the share market is sensitive to the seasonal performance of each business in selling holidays; then, even though there is considerable variation in the performance of each business, their combination into a single business would result in a situation where the performance is stabilised throughout the year. In this situation, we would expect sales performance and hence market performance to be highly *negatively* correlated and their combined performance to be much smoother than the performance of each business on its own.

Consider now some numerical data on our two securities A and B. The two securities have a high negative correlation of −0.8 (remember −1.0 is the theoretical limit to negative correlation). The returns and risks for each security are shown in Table 10.4.

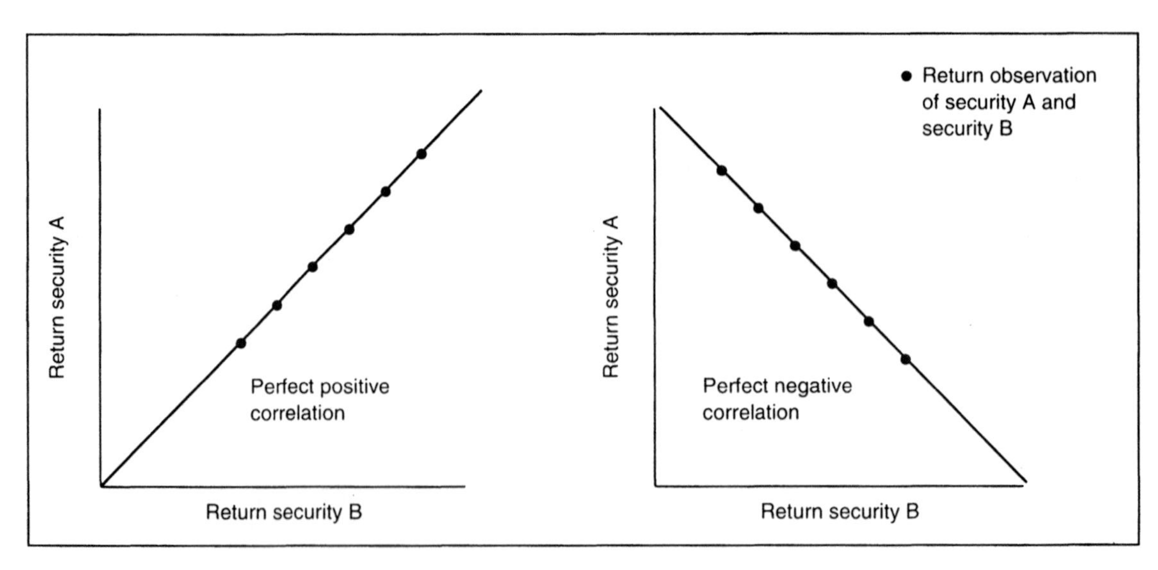

Figure 10.4 Positive and negative correlations of returns for two securities.

Table 10.4

	Return (%)	Risk (%)	Correlation
Security A	8	10	−0.8
Security B	5	4	−0.8

The return of the portfolio (r_p) is given by the formula:

$$r_p = w_A r_A + w_B r_B$$

Where w_A is the proportion *by value* of security A in the portfolio and w_A is the proportion of security B. For example, for an equally weighted portfolio w_A and $w_B = 0.5$, i.e.

$$w_A + w_A = 1$$

Therefore:

$$r_p = 0.5 \times 0.08 + 0.5 \times 0.05 = 0.065 \ (6.5\%)$$

(note that 8% and 5% shown as a decimal fraction are 0.08 and 0.05 respectively.)

The standard deviation is somewhat more cumbersome because it brings into account the degree of correlation between the two securities. The equation for the standard deviation of a two security portfolio is derived from a two-by-two variance – covariance matrix where each row and column element is added together to give the final value for the variance of returns for the portfolio:

$$\sigma_{pp} = \begin{Bmatrix} w_A w_A \sigma_{AA} + w_B w_A \sigma_{BA} \\ w_A w_B \sigma_{AB} + w_B w_B \sigma_{BB} \end{Bmatrix}$$

where σ_{AA} is the square of the standard deviation of returns (the variance) of security A (or B), and $\sigma_{AB} = \sigma_{BA} = r_{AB}\sigma_A\sigma_B$, where r_{AB} is the correlation coefficient.

Therefore for an equally weighted portfolio the variance is given by

$$\sigma_p = \begin{cases} 0.5 \times 0.5 \times 0.1 \times 0.1 & +0.5 \times 0.5 \times -0.8 \times 0.04 \times 0.1 \\ 0.5 \times 0.5 \times -0.8 \times 0.1 \times 0.04 & +0.5 \times 0.5 \times 0.04 \times 0.04 \end{cases}$$

which gives a solution matrix where the value of each component of the formula above are placed in their respective position in Table 10.5.

The risk matrix shows a portfolio risk of 3.6%

Table 10.5

Risk matrix			
	Weights	Security A	Security B
Weights	1	0.5	0.5
Security A	0.5	0.0025	−0.0008
Security B	0.5	−0.0008	0.0004
Portfolio risk		3.6055513	

which is lower than the risk of either of the two securities on their own. This is a common result when we diversify with negatively correlated securities. It is possible to repeat the above calculations for all possible combinations of A and B in the portfolio (where $w_A = 1$, $w_B = 0$ to $w_A = 0$, $w_B = 1$) and draw up a table of return and risk for any conceivable portfolio of the two securities. Graphically, a graph of these data can then be plotted and Figure 10.5 produced. This figure shows the 'possibility set' of all portfolios which can be constructed with the two securities A and B. Figure 10.5 reveals that a minimum risk portfolio of 5.7% return with a standard deviation of 1.8% above or below this figure is the best that can be achieved (in fact, a table would show this minimum risk portfolio as consisting of 25% security A and 75% security B. In practice, however, the minimum risk portfolio may not be of interest to the investor because he or she is prepared to accept some risk providing that a commensurate level of return can be earned.

THE CONCEPT OF THE EFFICIENT PORTFOLIO SET

We will assume that our investor is risk averse, that is:

(i) if two portfolios offer identical return then the portfolio offering the lowest risk will be chosen;
(ii) if two portfolios offer identical risk then the portfolio offering the highest return will be chosen.

In this situation, taking the two-security case discussed above only portfolios lying along the right of the possibility set will be chosen. For example, in Figure 10.6, portfolios M and M' are of identical risk but portfolio M' will be chosen because of principle (ii) above. The emboldened portion of the possibility set represents the most return-efficient portfolios available to the decision maker for any

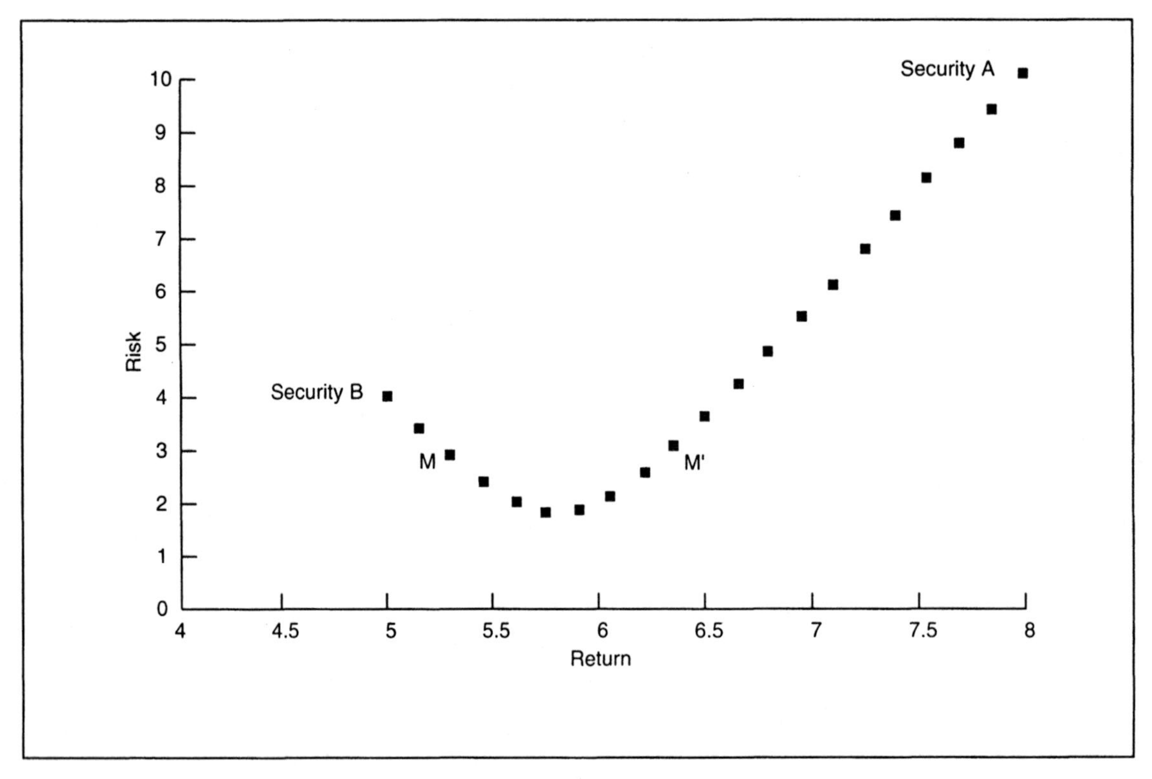

Figure 10.5 The set of possible portfolios from two securities.

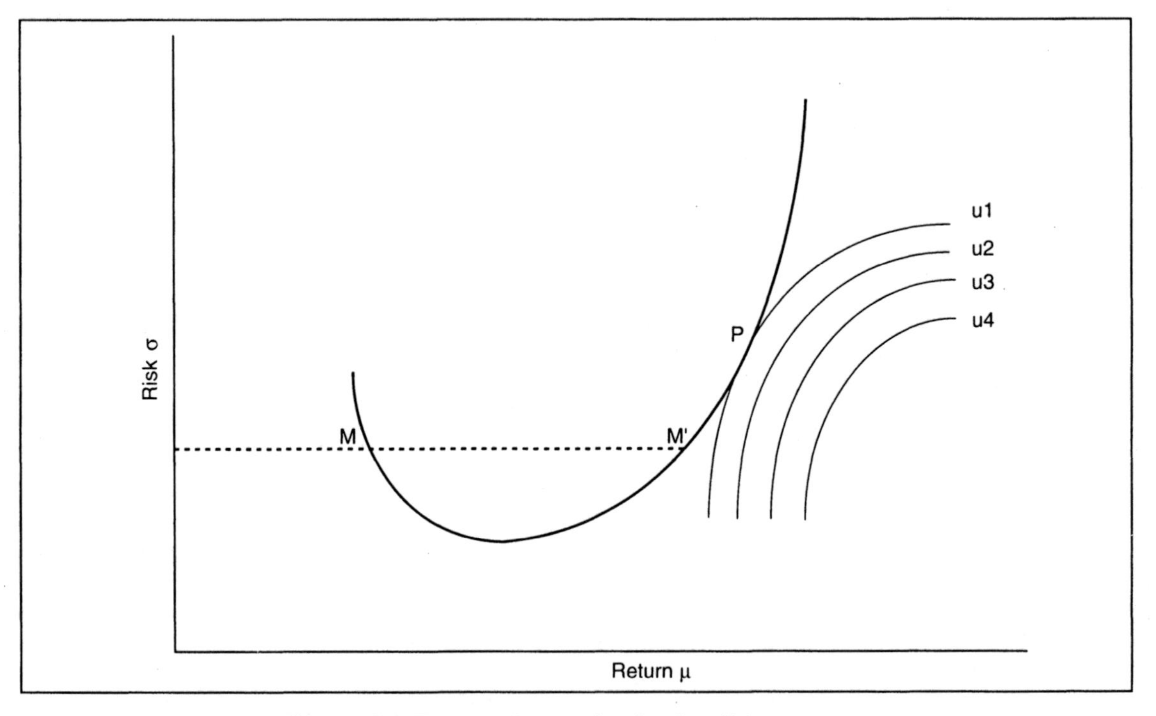

Figure 10.6 Two-security case showing the efficient set.

possible level of risk. The emboldened portion is what is termed the 'efficient portfolio set'. Portfolio P will be chosen by a decision maker with the preference function set:

$$U = \{u \mid u1, u2, u3 \ldots\}$$

You may like to check for yourself that the set of indifference curves *u*1, *u*2, *u*3 are consistent with an individual who is risk averse and that *u3* > *u2* > *u1* (where > means 'is preferred to').

THE EFFICIENT SET FOR MORE THAN TWO ASSETS

In a situation where more than two assets or securities are available to the decision maker then the return for the portfolio can be generalised as follows:

$$r_p = w_1 r_1 + w_2 r_2 + w_3 r_3 + w_4 r_4$$

(for a four-security portfolio for example), where:

r_p is the return on the portfolio;
w_n is the weight of the *n*th security or asset by value proportion in the portfolio;
r_n is the return of the *n*th security or asset.

The risk of a four-security portfolio is measured by the standard deviation of returns of the portfolio. In order to obtain the standard deviation of portfolio returns we must, first, establish the variance–covariance matrix. The variance (or square of the standard deviation) of the portfolio returns is given by:

(i) the weighted sum of the variances of each constituent security, plus
(ii) the weighted sum of each pairwise covariance for each security against one other.

The variance–covariance matrix for a four-security portfolio is given as follows:

$$\sigma = \begin{Bmatrix} w_1 w_1 \sigma_{11} + w_1 w_2 \sigma_{12} + w_1 w_3 \sigma_{13} + w_1 w_4 \sigma_{14} \\ w_2 w_1 \sigma_{21} + w_2 w_2 \sigma_{22} + w_2 w_3 \sigma_{23} + w_2 w_4 \sigma_{24} \\ w_3 w_1 \sigma_{31} + w_3 w_2 \sigma_{32} + w_3 w_3 \sigma_{33} + w_3 w_4 \sigma_{34} \\ w_4 w_1 \sigma_{41} + w_4 w_2 \sigma_{42} + w_4 w_3 \sigma_{43} + w_4 w_4 \sigma_{44} \end{Bmatrix}$$

where:

σ_{11} is the variance of returns for the first security;
σ_{12} is the covariance of returns of the first security with the second and so on;
w_n is the weight of the *n*th security in the portfolio.

The variance of returns for the four-security portfolio is given as the sum of all the terms in the above matrix. As before, the risk is given as the standard deviation which is the square root of the variance.

For a four-security portfolio we can determine the minimum risk portfolio which can be obtained for every different risk level and an efficient set can be derived. The efficient set in this case will lie on the south-east perimeter (hence the term 'efficient frontier') of the feasible set of portfolios which can be constructed from those four securities, and it is one of these portfolios which an economically rational individual would seek out, given that he or she was searching for the best available return for any given level of risk or the minimum risk for any given level of return.

In practice, the data requirements for a portfolio analysis of any more than a handful of securities led researchers to develop more efficient means of identifying risk–return optimising portfolios. We will return to these methods in the next chapter. However, staying at the general level and ignoring the problems of measurement, portfolio analysis provides some extremely useful theoretical insights which can guide investment practice.

THE ASSUMPTIONS OF PORTFOLIO ANALYSIS

It would be easy to dismiss portfolio analysis as impracticable if it were not for the wealth of theoretical insight which it offers about investment behaviour under risk. The theory of portfolio risk (portfolio theory) developed by Markowitz and others makes a number of assumptions as follows. First, it is necessary to conceive of an efficient set diagram which consists of the risk–return points for all securities in the capital market and all conceivable portfolios derived from those securities. Such a diagram for an individual would be as shown in Figure 10.7. The efficient set in this case is a theoretical construction of the most return-efficient portfolios which can be constructed for any given risk level, and it will lie on the extreme edge of the lower right quadrant of the total set of all securities and portfolios.

The next stage in the theoretical analysis assumes that all investors:

(i) have identical beliefs about the risk and return of all securities;

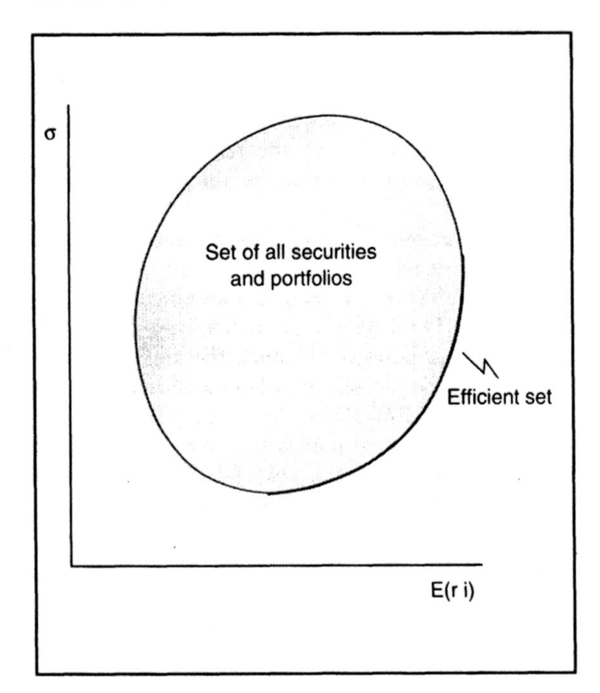

Figure 10.7 The set of all risky assets in the market place.

(ii) have equal access to costless information about all securities in the market place;
(iii) can trade free of transactions costs, taxes and other burdens.

These are the normal perfect competition assumptions applied to the capital markets. In practice, they represent an ideal to which any capitalist economy should aspire, as it is a principal consideration of such an economy that the allocation of capital funds via the pricing mechanism should be as perfect as possible. In practice, of course transactions costs do occur, although these are not particularly difficult to handle analytically.

However, the assumption of free access to information on the part of investors is somewhat difficult to justify in practice, and this may lead to discrepancies between investors about what they believe is the appropriate risk and return for each and every security. Indeed, on first sight it might appear to be a somewhat restrictive assumption that all investors hold identical beliefs about the risk and return for each security in the capital market. On reflection, however, some commonality of belief must exist for trading to occur, and this degree of practical agreement is probably all that is needed for the theory to become a reasonable approximation to reality.

Finally, it is assumed that investors have the ability to deposit cash or borrow at a common risk-free rate of interest.

THE PORTFOLIO THEORY MODEL

Given all of the above assumptions, all investors will perceive a common efficient set of portfolios in the market place, and in the absence of a risk-free borrowing or lending rate will choose a single portfolio somewhere along the efficient frontier.

Once the possibility of borrowing or lending at a risk-free rate is invoked, some rather startling conclusions arise.

(i) All investors will choose portfolio 'M' – the so-called 'efficient market portfolio' – which lies at the point of tangency with a straight line representing the 'geared portfolios' of M and R (see Figure 10.8).
(ii) All investors will construct an overall holding (a 'geared portfolio') consisting exclusively of M and R in proportions dictated by their personal risk preferences. We can calculate the risk and returns of different proportions of M and R as follows:

The returns of any combination (r_c) of M and R will be given by:

$$r_c = w_M r_M + w_R r_R$$

and the variance of the combination will be given as:

$$\sigma_{cc} = \begin{cases} w_R w_R \sigma_{RR} + w_R w_M \sigma_{RM} \\ w_M w_R \sigma_{MR} + w_M w_M \sigma_{MM} \end{cases}$$

but as the variance of a risk-free security must be zero by definition then its covariance with any other security must be zero also. Given this the expression above becomes:

$$\sigma_{cc} = \begin{cases} 0 + 0 \\ 0 + w_M w_M \sigma_{MM} \end{cases}$$

or, the standard deviation (which is, remember, the square root of the variance σ_{cc}) becomes

$$\sigma_c = w_M \sigma_M$$

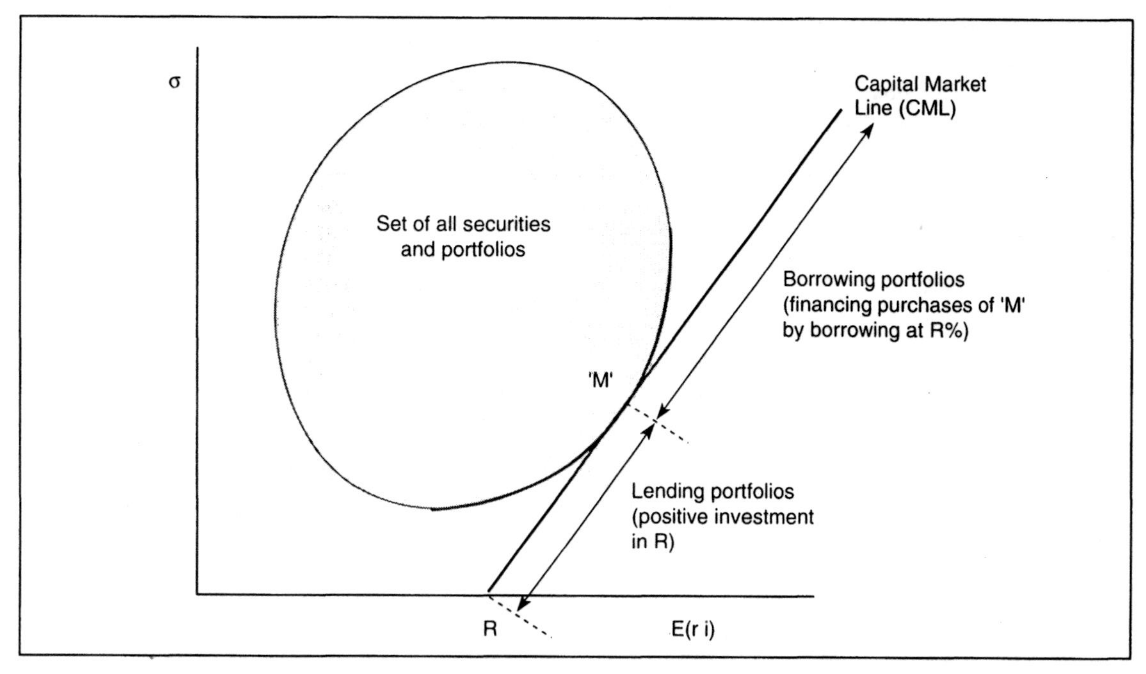

Figure 10.8 The efficient market portfolio with risk-free borrowing and lending.

So, for example, if:

(i) the estimated return of the efficient market portfolio was 12% per annum with a risk of standard deviation of 5% of that figure;
(ii) the risk-free rate of return was 6% per annum;

then the returns and risk for portfolios of different gearing would be as shown in Table 10.6.

As the level of adoption of the risky market portfolio (M) increases the return on the holding increases and so does the risk.

Indeed, the rate of substitution of risk for return is the slope of the capital market line in Figure 10.8. Beyond a 100% holding in M, the investor has the possibility of borrowing to finance additional holding of M indefinitely. The limit of Table 10.6 shows a 300% holding in M with an expected rate of return of 24% and an expected standard deviation of returns of 15%.

The actual combination of risk-free borrowing or lending (deposits) which the individual investor will choose depends upon the preferences of risk or return possessed by that individual. Highly risk-aggressive investors (but who are still risk averse in the sense that they will not take on risk without some positive reward) would choose a holding with some level of borrowing at the risk-free rate of interest. More cautious investors may well choose to deposit some of their wealth at the risk-free rate with the balance in the risky portfolio M.

THE MARKOWITZ SEPARATION THEOREM

This theorem states that, given the perfect capital market assumptions outlined on pages 97 and 98, an investor's decision concerning the optimal portfolio is separated from the decision about how he or she attains an ideal holding in terms of risk and return. In other words, all investors should choose the efficient market portfolio (M) as their preferred vehicle for risky investment and then gear themselves by borrowing or depositing at the risk-free rate in order to achieve their ideal trade off between risk and return. This strategy will achieve a superior outcome than investing in a risky portfolio on the efficient frontier of greater or lesser risk than the efficient market portfolio M.

In practice, all of the assumptions above are likely to be violated to a greater or lesser extent. There is also the practical problem of interpreting in practice what the efficient market portfolio M might be. If, however, we assume that all investors consistently translate their beliefs and expectations into real buy or sell decisions then the prices in the market should reflect consensus expectations in the market.

Table 10.6

Proportion of risk-free lending w_R	Proportion of risk-free borrowing w_R	Proportion of risky portfolio w_M	Expected return	Expected risk
1		0	0.06	0
0.8		0.2	0.072	0.01
0.6		0.4	0.084	0.02
0.4		0.6	0.096	0.03
0.2		0.8	0.108	0.04
0		1	0.12	0.05
	0.2	1.2	0.132	0.06
	0.4	1.4	0.144	0.07
	0.6	1.6	0.156	0.08
	0.8	1.8	0.168	0.09
	1	2	0.18	0.1
	1.2	2.2	0.192	0.11
	1.4	2.4	0.204	0.12
	1.6	2.6	0.216	0.13
	1.8	2.8	0.228	0.14
	2	3	0.24	0.15

Consequently, the level of an all-share index such as the FT All-Share Index in the UK or the Dow-Jones Index in the United States should represent the performance of a broadly based market portfolio. Further, if we assume all investors are rational and that they know all there is to know about the securities in which they deal, then it is not hard to accept the idea that the performance of the all-share index is a good proxy for the theoretically efficient market portfolio M.

Although the theoretical abstractions implicit in this analysis do appear far fetched we will discuss the development of a risk–return model in the next chapter which is derivable from Markowitz Portfolio Theory on the assumption that all investors hold identical expectations. That capital asset, risk-pricing model does make quite robust predictions about the operation of the capital market which give us some comfort that the assumptions made in deriving the Markowitz model and the separation theorem are not gross violations of reality.

THE RELEVANCE OF PORTFOLIO THEORY FOR REAL INVESTMENT DECISIONS

If an investor were able to estimate the average returns and construct a variance–covariance matrix for those returns for all securities in the market place then he or she would be able to construct an efficient set for those securities. Assuming that there is also a risk-free borrowing or lending opportunity in the market then the investor should be able to identify a single portfolio along the efficient set which has the same risk–return characteristics as the capital market line (it will be that portfolio which is at the point of tangency of the capital market line and the efficient set).

This tangency portfolio is the portfolio which the risk averse investor should choose in some combination or other with the risk-free security.

Now, if all investors analyse past security returns in the same way then a single unique tangency portfolio consisting of all securities in the market place in some proportion or other will be the only risky investment which they will choose, and that portfolio will be representative of the whole market. It is a large assumption to accept that all investors behave in this way, but we only have to believe that this assumption lies at the core of rational behaviour in the market for the separation theorem to hold and for the efficient market portfolio to dominate all others. Why? Because presumably irrational behaviour will be idiosyncratic and tend to cancel itself out in the real market, leaving rational behaviour as the behaviour which dominates the market and pricing within that market.

If Markowitz portfolio theory holds in explaining individual investor behaviour (or at least in

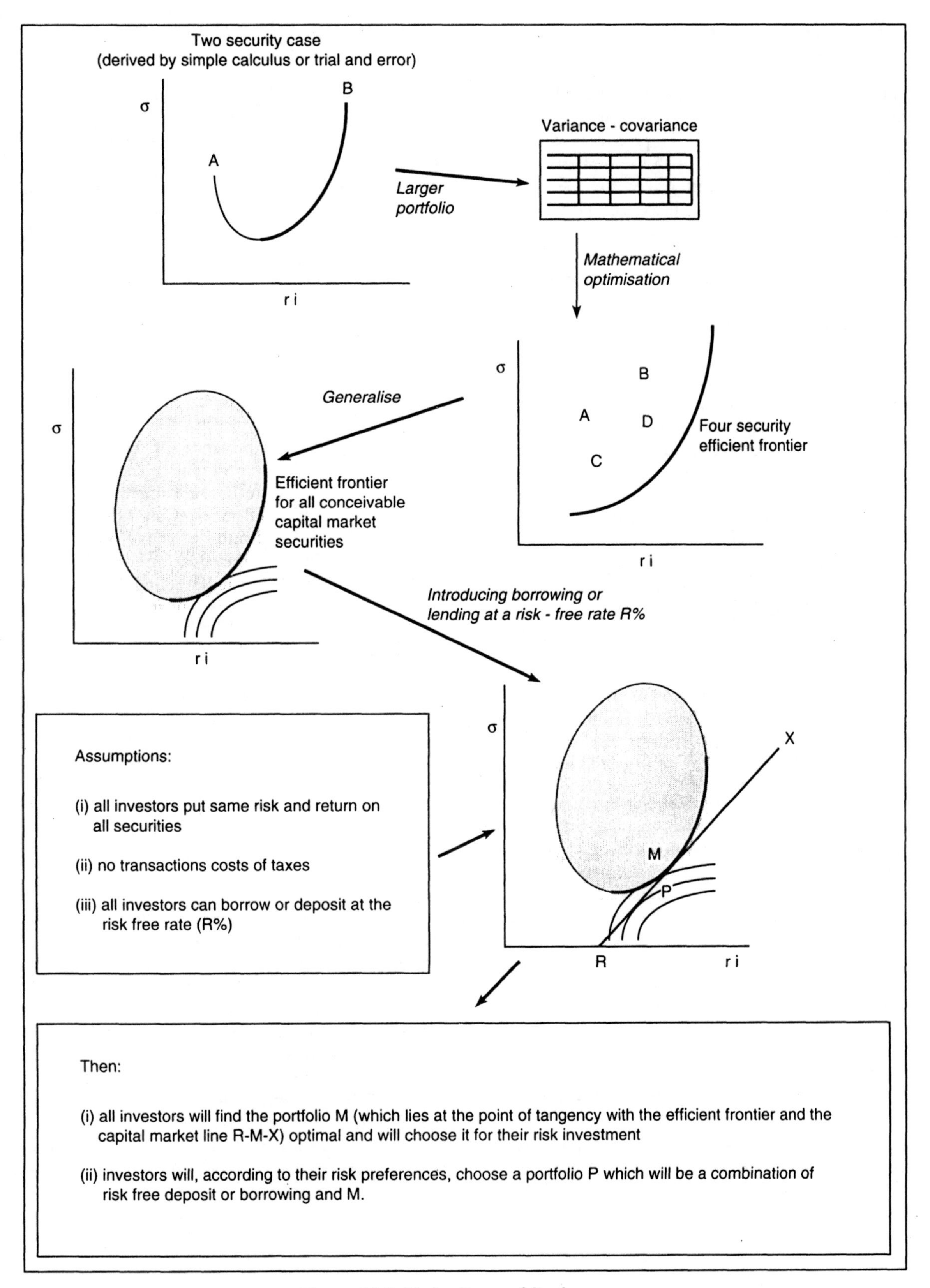

Figure 10.9 Markowitz portfolio theory.

explaining core rationality within the market) then the question arises as to how we identify the efficient market portfolio. In practice, we would argue that an all-share index in the domestic capital market would be the best proxy for the efficient market portfolio given that prices should be rationally set and the weightings of each share by its capitalisation is likely to be as optimal a weighting for an efficient portfolio as one can obtain. The natural theoretical deduction is that the most efficient long-run investment behaviour can be summarised as follows.

- The investor should choose a widely diversified proxy for total market behaviour as his or her medium for risky investment. An all-share index fund or indexed unit trust is probably the best choice although, as we show in the next chapter, it is possible to construct a reasonable market fund to map the index by direct investment in equities.
- The investor should optimise to his or her ideal risk–return position by depositing some investment funds in as risk-free form of saving as he or she can find or, by borrowing at as close to the risk-free rate of interest as can be achieved in the market place.

This strategy of investing solely in an index fund and adjusting risk or return by borrowing or lending at as close to the risk-free rate as can be obtained is not the most exciting strategy for investment. However, research indicates that it is likely to yield higher long-run average performance for any chosen level of risk than active portfolio management where securities are traded in and out of the portfolio according to whether they are perceived to be under- or overvalued in the market. As we will see later, there is strong evidence to support the belief that searching for under- or overvalued securities is a fruitless task in that the market pricing mechanisms are simply too efficient for the normal investor to be able to 'outguess' or 'outperform' the market.

THE EXTENSION OF PORTFOLIO THEORY TO OTHER ASSETS HOLDINGS

As we outlined in the first part of this chapter, a business may hold investment assets in many forms. They may hold shares in other companies although more likely they will hold portfolios of products, people and plant. All of these asset types can be represented on a two-dimensional diagram of risk and return, and Markowitz points out that risk can be minimised by choosing combinations of products, people or plant, as the case may be, in combinations which work to cancel out risk. British Gas, for example, came up with the idea that the market for gas could best be developed by expanding the market for air conditioning, barbecues and outdoor lighting. They expected these market areas to counter-vary with performance in their primary heating and energy markets.

At the other extreme, researchers in the areas of team work, such as Meredith Belbin, have discovered that the performance of teams can be enhanced when counter-varying characteristics in peoples' personalities are brought together. Belbin's work developed the ideas of Carl Gustav Jung, namely that people fall into distinctive types which can be combined together to form much more productive teams than can be found by choosing people at random or because they are all particularly good at some particular job.

Both of these examples can be understood in terms of portfolio theory which gives some insight into how performance risk can be mitigated by judicious combinations. In Figure 10.9 we show a theory diagram showing how Markowitz portfolio theory is put together and which summarises the flow of ideas in the core of this chapter.

CONCLUSION

In this chapter we have examined the problem of risk, and especially how risk is relative to the combinations in which assets are brought together. Formally, we have shown that portfolios of assets will have lower risk on their own if the benefits derived from those assets negatively covary with one another. This concept is particularly relevant when any diversification strategy is being formulated, whether it be for investments in financial securities, products or, indeed, people. In the next chapter of this book we extend the notion of risk and its management through hedging with option contracts.

Chapter 11

Options and Risk

Level D

Contents

Summary

In the previous chapter we examined the notion of risk at some length. We presented the idea that portfolio diversification is one way in which the risk to which an individual or business is exposed can be managed. In this chapter we will examine another method for handling risk through options. The theory of options has now been well developed in finance, and what is of interest to us is just how business opportunities can be exploited, managing the risk through an option contract of some form or another. We will commence our discussion in the context of options on ordinary shares and then extend the ideas to other assets.

CALL AND PUT OPTIONS

An option is a 'contingent contract' where the holder (who has purchased the option) has either the right to buy or to sell (depending on the contract) the asset at a particular price at a particular date. The advantage of such contracts is that they allow the holder to insure themselves against the risk of adverse price movements in the underlying asset.

An option is a legally enforceable contract between an 'option writer' and a purchaser (who becomes the 'holder') giving the holder the right to transact in an asset at a given time for a given price. In order for any contract to be enforceable some consideration must be exchanged for the right to the option. This is termed the 'option premium'.

A *call* option gives the right to the holder to buy the asset concerned and a *put* option gives the right to sell. The holder is not required to exercise the option if it would be disadvantageous to do so. The price at which the holder can buy or sell is termed the 'exercise price' (sometimes the 'striking' price) and the date upon which the option must be exercised is the 'exercise date'. A European option must be exercised on the exercise date. An 'American' option may be exercised at any time up to and including the exercise date. A European option is easier to handle conceptually than an American and our discussion of options will concentrate on the former.

For example: a portfolio manager decides to buy a 30-day call option in XYZ Ltd ordinary shares with an exercise price of 100p for a premium of 5p each. The following conditions can occur.

(i) The actual price of XYZ is less than 100p in 30 days time – do not exercise.
(ii) The actual price of XYZ is greater than 100p in 30 days time – exercise.

In the first case all she will have lost is the value of the premium. In the second case she can buy back the shares under the option if their actual price exceeds 100p.

In Table 11.1 the first row shows a range of prices (in 5p increments, although any value is possible) which might hold at the exercise date. The second row gives the exercise price of 100p established in the option contract. As a result, at exercise date, the value of the option will either be zero for actual prices up to 100p (as the holder would not exercise) or positive for prices in excess of 100p. The premium is a sunk cost at the exercise date and therefore is not a factor in the decision whether or not to exercise. The profit or loss on the contract overall shows the potential benefit to the fund manager as she considers whether to engage in the contract.

Notice also the very high percentage return which the option offers to the potential holder – a 10% increase in the value of the underlying share generates a 100% return over the premium invested. Similarly, a 30% increase offers a 500% return over the premium invested. In Figure 11.1 we translate these profits or losses into graphical form to give the characteristic profit chart for a call option.

Clearly, as a speculative investment, options can offer enormous returns with a fixed, downside risk of losing the whole of the premium to be invested. But what is the benefit for the option writer? Simply the inverse of the profit or loss to the holder. If the price of the asset is below the exercise price at the exercise date the option holder will not exercise and the writer gains the premium. If the actual price is in excess of the exercise price, the writer is forced to transfer the share to the holder at the exercise price which is lower than that which could be obtained on open sale.

Table 11.1 Profit or loss on an option contract.

Actual price at exercise date	80	85	90	85	100	105	110	115	120	125	130	135
Exercise price	100	100	100	100	100	100	100	100	100	100	100	100
Value of option on exercise	0	0	0	0	0	5	10	15	20	25	30	35
Premium	5	5	5	5	5	5	5	5	5	5	5	5
Profit or loss on option contract	(5)	(5)	(5)	(5)	(5)	0	5	10	15	20	25	30
Percentage profit or loss/premium	(100)	(100)	(100)	(100)	(100)	0	100	200	300	400	500	600

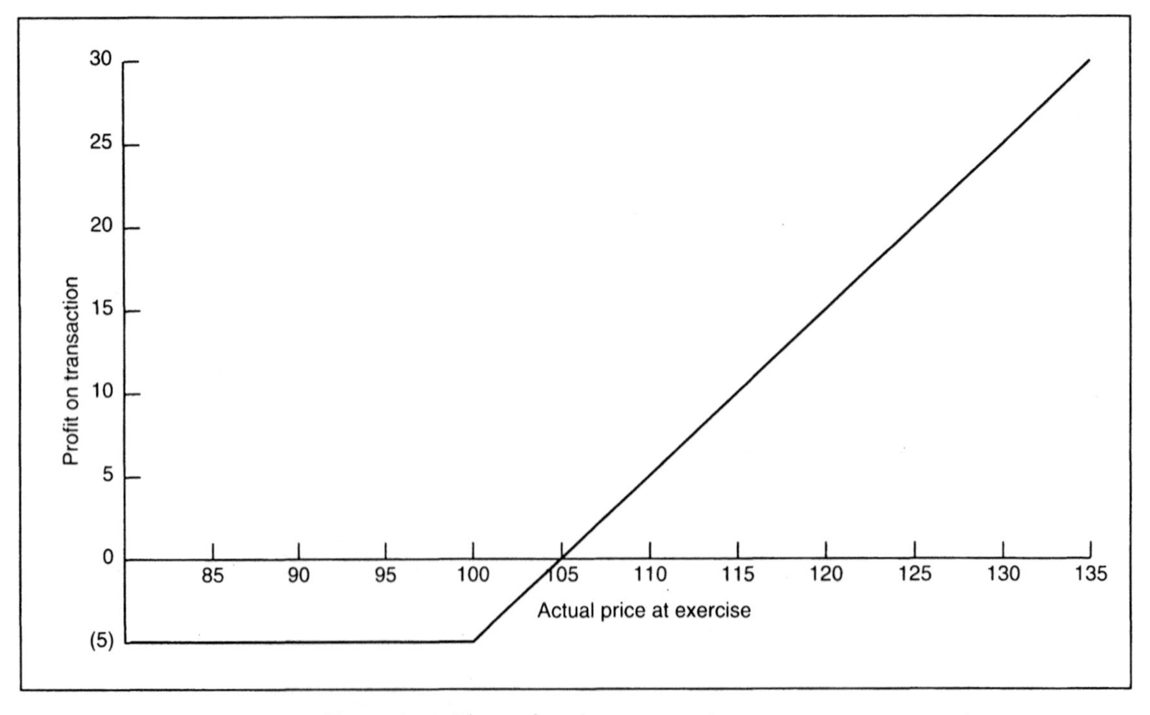

Figure 11.1 The profit or loss on an option contract.

Consider now the case where, instead of purchasing a call option contract as a speculative investment in its own right, the portfolio fund manager purchases the option to insure against a loss in a 'short sale' of the underlying security. A 'short sale' is one where an investor sells a share with the intention of purchasing that share at a later date at a lower price. Because Stock Exchanges permit any trades to be conducted within a period of account (usually two weeks) it is possible to sell shares at a high price and buy them back later at a lower price to cover the original sale contract and make a profit (or make a loss if the price goes the wrong way!). With short sales, the potential loss to an investor is unlimited as are the gains. The point about a short sale is that the investor only gains if the price falls. If the price rises the investor must purchase the stock back at a higher price to clear the transaction and hence a loss is made.

In Figure 11.3, we show the profit graph for a short sale and the profit graph for a call option where the exercise price set is equal to the current price. Putting both together we obtain a composite function ABC which shows that the unlimited loss is eliminated by the ability under the option to buy back the shares at the exercise price. The penalty is that the net loss (if the share price should rise) is the value of the premium and the profit (if the share price should fall) is reduced by the premium.

THE VALUATION OF OPTIONS

There are a number of ways in which options can be valued. One of the most popular methods was developed by two American academics, Fisher Black and Myron Scholes, and relies upon continuous time mathematics for its derivation. This model, although a gross simplification of reality, is widely accepted in professional circles.

The first and most simple assumption we can make is that the world is perfectly certain, that there

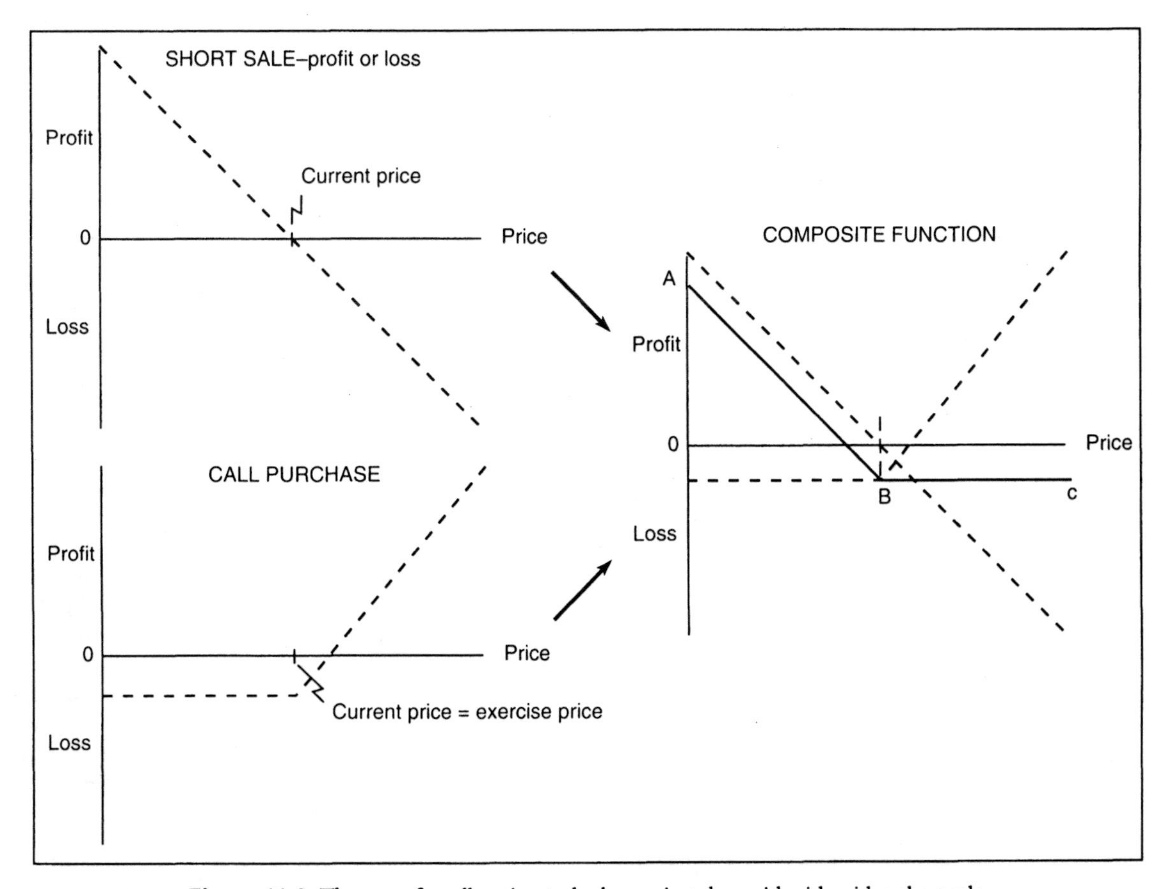

Figure 11.2 The use of a call option to hedge against downside risk with a short sale.

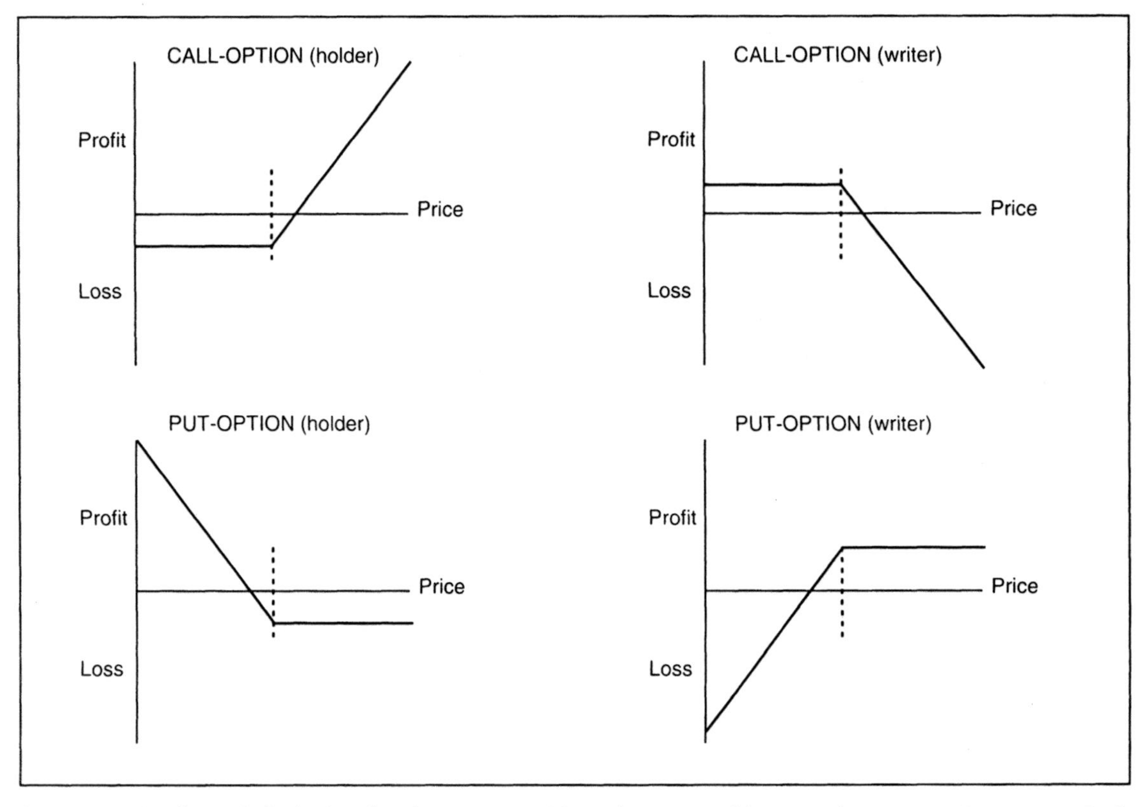

Figure 11.3 Profit graph for both call and put options. Note: the gains and losses to the option writer are exactly the opposite to those of the holder. If there are no transactions costs then an option is a *zero sum* game between the holder and the writer. What the one loses, the other gains and so on.

are no transactions costs and the company will not pay a dividend. This gives us the 'certainty equivalent' of the Black and Scholes option pricing formula:

$$p_o = p_a - p_e e^{-rt}$$

where:

p_o is the option premium;
p_a is the actual price of the share;
p_e is the exercise price;
r is the risk-free rate of interest (annual);
t is the time to exercise as a fraction of a year.

EXAMPLE

A share has a current price of 60p and a 90-day call option on that share is offered at an exercise price of 55p. The annual risk-free rate of interest is estimated at 4% per annum.

The value of the option in a risk-free environment is:

$$\begin{aligned} p_o &= 60 - 55 \times e^{-(0.04 \times 90/365)} \\ &= 60 - 55 \times 0.9902 \\ &= 5.54\text{p} \end{aligned}$$

This approach to valuing the option equates the value or option premium to the present value of the certain payoff to the investor. However, this formula excludes the one real-world factor which makes options interesting, namely their ability to absorb risk in the underlying share. The breakthrough which Black and Scholes achieved in pricing options was in realising that a call option is equivalent to the purchase of equity shares combined with borrowing in such a way as to give an identical payoff (a duplicating transaction). To avoid the possibility of an arbitrage opportunity:

Value of the call option =
cost of acquiring the shares less cost of borrowing on the duplicating transaction

In order to explain the intuition behind their model we will take a very simple example where only two future states of the world are possible for the share price.

EXAMPLE

A share has a current price of 100p and a 90-day call option is available with an exercise price of 100p. The current rate of interest on borrowing is 10% per annum. To simplify matters we will assume that risk impacts upon the share in the following way: at 90 days the share will either be valued at 80p or 120p.

We will now attempt to establish the value of a call 'contract' upon 1000 shares.

Share price	*80p*	*120p*
The payoffs on a call option in 90 days	*0*	*£200*

If the price were to fall to 80p the option would be worthless; if the price rises to 120p, the holder of the call would be able to exercise at 100p and sell at 120p which, on 1000 shares, would give a payoff of £200.

Now consider what combination of share purchase now and sale in 90 days financed by borrowing could give an identical payoff to the call. This is quite a brain teaser, but we are looking for a number of shares (N) which, if sold for £0.80, would permit repayment of an identical value loan with zero payoff:

$0.80N$ − loan = 0 (zero payoff if price falls to 80p) (i)

and the same number of shares which, if sold for £1.20 would give a payoff of £200 after repayment of the loan:

$1.20N$ − loan = 200 (£200 payoff if price rises to 120p) (ii)

Therefore:

Loan = $0.80N$ (from equation (i))

Therefore substituting into (ii):

$$1.20N - 0.80N = 200$$
$$N = 200/0.4$$
$$N = 500 \text{ shares}$$

and by substitution, Loan = £400

We can now construct a payoff table for our duplicating strategy:

Share price	80p	120p
Sell 500 shares	£400	£600
Repay loan	£400	£400
Payoff	0	£200

So purchasing 500 shares and taking a loan with a repayment value including interest of £400 gives an identical payoff in 90 days to a 1000 share call contract. The cost to the investor of the duplicating transaction is the cost of the shares purchased less the amount of present borrowing, which would entail a repayment in 90 days of £400, assuming a 10% annual rate of interest:

Share purchase 500 × £1.00	= £500.00
Less present value of loan $400 \times e^{-0.1 \times 90/365}$	= £390.26
Cost of the duplicating transaction	= £109.74

There are three learning points to note from this example.

(i) The value of an option is governed by the rate of interest and the length of time until exercise. A higher rate of interest or a longer time to exercise would have the effect of decreasing the present value of the loan, hence increasing the cost of the duplicating transaction.

(ii) The value of the option is taken as the cost of a duplicating transaction in the underlying share, where the risk of the duplicating transaction is matched to that in the option by borrowing (i.e. identical payoffs under all states of the world are achieved). We know from the arbitrage law that two securities offering identical returns and risk must trade at the same price or a 'money machine' will be created. Here we have in effect two securities, (a) an option contract and (b) a matched transaction of identical payoff and risk.

(iii) The duplicating transaction requires 500 shares, whilst the option contract is for 1000. Taking the converse of our arbitrage argument, a 2 : 1 ratio of options to shares will nullify the risk inherent in purchasing those shares for 100p with possible future prices of 80p and 120p. The value of 2 : 1 is the *hedge ratio*, and it represents the number of options to underlying shares required to eliminate the risk in the underlying transaction. The value of this perfect hedge, which is the value of the option contract, will be governed by the risk in the underlying transaction.

In practice, of course, a share will have a whole distribution of possible future prices rather than just two. The option pricing model developed by Black and Scholes develops the above idea, but assumes that:

(i) share prices follow a random pattern called a 'random walk';
(ii) prices change continuously without instantaneous jumps;
(iii) distribution of prices is log-normal.

If these conditions hold and there are no transaction costs or penalties for short selling in the underlying security, nor any dividends paid, then the following formula specifies the price of a European call option, which will be the value of shares purchased in the duplicating transaction, less the loan value taken in the duplicating transaction:

$$p_o = N(d_1)p_a - N(d_2)p_e e^{-rt}$$

where

$$d_1 = [\ln(p_a/p_e) + (r + 0.5\sigma^2)t]/\sqrt{(\sigma^2 t)}$$
$$d_2 = d_1 - \sqrt{(\sigma^2 t)}$$

The variables in the two risk factors are as in the certainty formula above, except for σ^2 which is the variance of the continuous return (annualised) on the share. Note that 'ln' is the natural logarithm.

N indicates that the values d_1 and d_2 should be converted to a probability value representing the probability that a standardised normally distributed random variable is less than or equal to d_1 and d_2 respectively. $N(d_1)$ is the hedge ratio and $N(d_2)$ is the proportion of the present value of the exercise price which should be borrowed.

This formula is somewhat cumbersome, although it is now part of the standard repertoire of finance professionals and is built into basic finance calculators. In addition, even given the assumptions upon which it is based, it does appear to be a good predictor of actual option prices in the organised secondary markets for shares options which have developed in the United Kingdom and the United States. The only problematic element within the formula is that one variable – the continuous variance of returns – must be estimated.

EXAMPLE

The current share price for TEC Ltd 25p ordinary shares is 155p per share. A 90-day option is available with an exercise price of 150p. The variance of its continuously distributed returns is 14% and the risk-free rate of interest is estimated to be 5%.

$$d_1 = \frac{[\ln(155/150) + (0.05 + 0.5 \times 0.14) \times (90/365)]}{\sqrt{0.14 \times (90/365)}}$$
$$= [0.03279 + 0.02959]/0.18580$$
$$= 0.33574 \text{ and } N(d_1) = 0.63147$$

$$d_2 = 0.33574 - 0.18580$$
$$= 0.14994 \text{ and } N(d_2) = 0.55968$$

Substituting into the main formula:

$$p_o = 155 \times 0.63147 - 0.55968 \times 150 \times e^{-0.05 \times 90/365}$$
$$= 14.95\text{p}$$

Now that we have a model for valuing an option, we can make some final comments about the boundaries on the value of a call option to an investor. First, the option's value will never exceed the current price of the underlying share (at this point the exercise price component of the valuation formula above would have to be zero). Second, the value of the option must be bounded at the lower end by zero (if the exercise price equals or is less than the current price) or by the difference between the exercise price and the current price on immediate exercise.

Graphically we can represent the zone of possible option values as the shaded region in Figure 11.4 below. The actual value of the option within that range will be determined by the factors outlined above. At the point of a zero share price the value of any option against that share will also be zero. At the other extreme, as the share price rises so far above the exercise price that the risk of not exercising the option approaches zero, then the value of the option will approach the payoff on exercise alone. However, in intermediate regions where the volatility of the share is such that likelihood of non-exercise is significant, the value of the option will be at its greatest.

Note: the value of a *PUT* option is the converse of the value of a call. From Figure 11.3 you should be able to see that a put option only has value if the price of the underlying share falls below the exercise price.

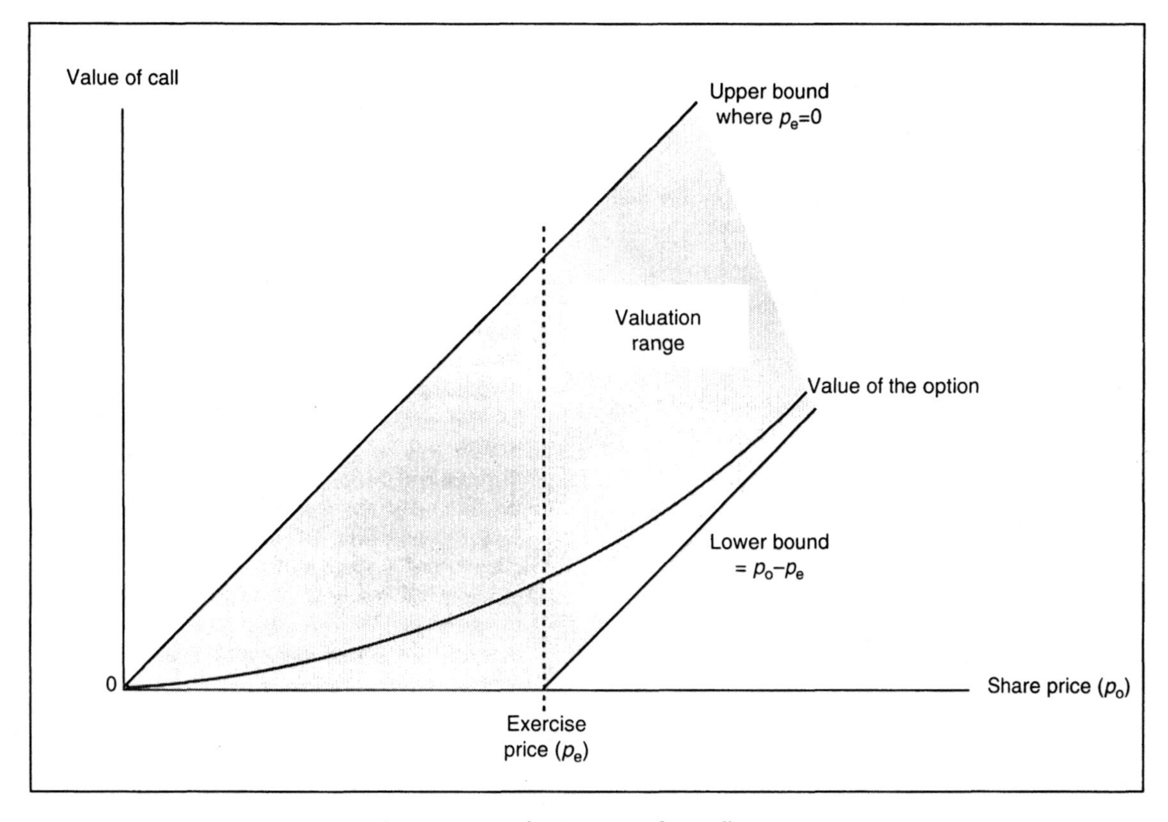

Figure 11.4 Valuation range for a call option.

THE ROLE OF OPTION PRICING THEORY IN PRICING OTHER SECURITIES

We now have a powerful model for valuing options. If that was all there was to it, the only point to our work would be in presenting you with a method of pricing a particular type of security which you may never come across in your professional life and would probably be wise not to speculate with in your private life. However, Black and Scholes, when developing their model, realised that the option pricing approach could also be used to value the equity shares in a company which also has debt. This approach to equity valuation rests on the following insight.

(i) When equity shareholders accept debt finance they are, in effect, transferring the rights in the firms assets to the debt holders until the debt is redeemed.
(ii) At the redemption date the shareholders can choose between two courses of action. They can either:

- redeem the debt and keep the assets if the asset value is in excess of the debt, or
- default on redemption and allow the debt holders to liquidate the assets to their own advantage.

Does this sound familiar? What appears to be the case is that the shareholders have a call option on the assets of the company, and the exercise price is the value of the outstanding debt at redemption. The only condition is that the equity shareholders must have limited liability or they face the downside risk on default.

EXAMPLE

A firm has £40 000 of debt which is redeemable in one year. The net assets of the firm are currently valued at £50 000. The volatility of net assets with the market conditions over the next year is 40% (measured as the variance of returns) and the risk free return is estimated at 5%.

Using the risk-free model, the value of the call option on the underlying assets is as follows:

$$p_o = p_a - p_e e^{-rt}$$
$$= 50\,000 - 40\,000 \times e^{-(0.05 \times 1)}$$
$$= 11\,951$$

Now taking into account the effect of risk we can compute the risk weights:

$$d_1 = [\ln(p_a/p_e) + (r + 0.5\sigma^2)t]/\sqrt{(\sigma^2 t)}$$
$$= [\ln(50\,000/40\,000) + (0.05 + 0.5 \times 0.4) \times 1]/\sqrt{(0.4 \times 1)}$$
$$= [0.2231 + 0.25]/0.6325$$
$$= 0.7480$$

$$d_2 = d_1 - \sqrt{(\sigma^2 t)}$$
$$= 0.7480 - 0.6325$$
$$= 0.1155$$

Calculating the normal distribution values as we did previously:

$$N(d_1) = 0.772768$$
$$N(d_2) = 0.545975$$

and substituting into the Black–Scholes model we can obtain the value of the equity claim on the assets as a call option:

$$p_o = 0.772768 \times 50\,000 - 0.545975 \times 40\,000 \times e^{-0.05 \times 1}$$
$$= 17\,865$$

The difference between this value and that in the certainty case above is due to the risk element in the equity contract, i.e.

$$\text{Risk premium} = 17\,865 - 11\,951 = £5914$$

There are a number of practical problems with the use of this model for valuing an equity claim in a limited company which detract from its usefulness, although theoretically the approach embodied within the Black–Scholes formula make minimal assumptions about the way the world works.

(i) The model assumes an unambiguous current valuation of the assets of the business. However, as we shall see in the final chapters of this book, many possible asset valuations can arise. The most conservative estimate would rely upon the realisable value of the assets under a forced sale. However, such a value would not incorporate intangible assets unless 'forced sale' is deemed to be as a going concern rather than break-up value. The only valuation which would fully incorporate the wealth-generating potential of all assets is the net present value of all net cash flows to the business over its expected life. However, this valuation should equal the value of the equity (assuming away any imperfections) less the value of the outstanding debt claim on the business which will be equal to the value generated by the Black–Scholes model.
(ii) It relies upon the firm being able to estimate the future variability of its asset values. In the absence of a clear understanding of the determinants of value it is even more difficult to progress to the secondary problem of how to evaluate the risk of those asset values.

Given these problems you might ask what the value of this approach is in practice. For small firms without organised markets for their equity then the procedure can apply very well. Similarly, when a firm has a large proportion of debt to total asset value, the call element in the firm's equity will become very important. The more important aspect of this approach to valuation is it forces you to think of equity (which is a claim against the future value of the business) as an option against that claim. Where the liability of the investor is unlimited (as in, say, a private business or partnership) then there is no call element in the equity of the firm. Once limited liability is introduced, then a call element begins to emerge because the shareholder is always able to avoid loss in excess of his or her investment (the premium) by a member's voluntary liquidation. This type of option on the future value of the business is always there. When a debt element is introduced, this has the effect of creating a definitive exercise date, namely when the debt must be redeemed.

VALUING OTHER SECURITIES

Although a detailed discussion of the valuation details is beyond the scope of this book, it is important to be aware of the implicit options which lie within many other business securities.

(i) Rights issues – the allotment letter sent to existing shareholders to subscribe to new equity shares at a stated price is an American call option on those shares. If the actual share price is less than the offer price, the holder of the letter will simply not subscribe. Presumably, if the share price is in excess of the offer price then the rights can be exercised for a potential profit. Even if the shareholder does not wish to exercise the rights under those conditions, the allotment letter has value in its own right and can be disposed of to a broker.
(ii) Convertible debt – this type of debt is issued by a company who offers the holder the right to convert that debt to equity at some future date. The convertible will specify the number of equity shares which can be taken in exchange for the bond value.

EXAMPLE

ABD plc issued a convertible bond of £100 nominal value, convertible in three years' time into twenty 25p ordinary shares. Non-conversion would entitle the bond holder to the immediate repayment of the debt at its par or nominal value.

Conversation ratio = 20
Conversion price = 100/20 = £5.00

The conversion price is, in effect the exercise price, and if the actual share price at conversion date was in excess of £5.00, conversion would be sensible, otherwise redemption would be the best course to take. The value of the convertible can be expressed as follows:

Value = present value (interest received to maturity
+ redemption value of bond)
+ call value of option on the equity
received on exercise of conversion

THE ROLE OF OPTION PRICING IN VALUING STRATEGIC OPTIONS

As we have now discovered, an option element lies at the heart of the equity claim on a business and begins to dominate its value when a company's gearing ratio is high. Option theory also has significance when we are valuing the benefits of strategies which offer the possibility of future choice to management.

- Case 1: a large engineering company had developed a capability within a specialist division for the manufacture of valves for the chemical industry. The market had been stagnant for a number of years, but future and sudden growth in the application of that technology could not be ruled out by management. The business is considering abandoning this aspect of manufacturing, perhaps selling its know-how and capability to another company. What options are available here and what factors would be involved in valuing them?
- Case 2: a company is considering a new high risk investment project which currently has a very small net present value. It could delay investment for one year, by which time the eventual payoff in the market would be much clearer. What type of option is available here and how would management value the option of delaying its investment decision for one year?

In each of these cases, option pricing theory gives us a method of valuing the contingent element within each project. However, even if management should choose not to attempt a valuation as such, the theory does allow them to identify the variables such as risk, time, financial cost and payoffs which such options offer.

CONCLUSION

In this chapter we have dealt with the second of the two most important ways of dealing with risk. Option pricing methods, developed in the theory of finance have a surprisingly wide variety of applications some of which are only now being recognised and developed within the management literature. We have demonstrated how option contracts can be valued, and how such valuation methods can be extended to equity shares and strategic options.

Chapter 12

The Financial Markets and the Financing Decision

Level M

Contents

Summary

Within the Western economies, firms operate in what have become global capital markets, where the shares and other corporate stock of large companies are traded throughout the world. For smaller companies a wide variety of sources of finance exist, from purely private sources through to listing on the Stock Exchange as a public limited company.

In this chapter we examine the characteristic features of the market for capital funds and discuss the relative merits of different types of finance. In the first section we show how the financial markets operate and then discuss some of the evidence supporting the idea that those markets are efficient in helping firms to find finance at the most competitive price. We then proceed to a discussion of the distinction between equity and debt and how capital gearing is measured.

SUPPLY OF CAPITAL AND THE ROLE OF THE CAPITAL MARKET

Capital is traded in the capital market in the form of financial securities. A financial security is any item which is a transferable store of wealth. A share certificate is a capital market security, as it can be sold by its holder to anyone who wishes to purchase it. Indeed, any item can act as a capital-market security provided it can be used as a store of wealth. For example, fine wines, held with a view to future sale rather than for consumption, can be regarded as a capital-market security. The trading in capital-market securities makes up the capital market, and it is to this market that firms have to go in order to raise new finance.

Any firm requiring capital for investment can obtain that capital in one of two ways.

- It can sell an ownership stake in the business for cash. Ownership of a part of a business is termed a 'share'. Firms are under no obligation to return the funds which they realise through the sale of their shares and are not under any compulsion to pay a dividend. The point to note here is that the shareholder investor is not 'lending' money to the firm. The shareholder is purchasing a legal claim to part of the business and, therefore, to part of the surplus which the firm may generate.
- It can borrow money, either indefinitely, or for a fixed term. In the case of fixed-term loans, the borrowing must be repaid at the due date of redemption and the agreed rate of interest must be paid when it falls due. In essence, borrowing money is like a hire agreement where the article hired is a capital sum and the rental is the interest paid.

Later in this chapter we will consider these two sources of finance in more detail.

A capital market exists to bring together savers, who may not have any direct productive investment opportunities open to them, and firms who have the investment opportunities but lack the necessary funds to undertake them. A firm seeking funds for investment raises new money through what is often termed the 'primary capital market'. However, investing firms typically require funds for the long term, while individual savers generally require a degree of liquidity to finance their changing patterns of consumption. This conflict between the long-term needs of firms and the short-term requirements of their investors has given rise to a 'secondary capital market' where share and loan certificates are traded independently of the companies in which they are held.

In Figure 12.1 we show, as a circular flow, the movement of cash between firms and individual investors. Firms use their cash resources in productive investment opportunities, in investment in working capital (stocks, debtors and short-term cash balances) and in interest and dividend payments (which we call capital charges). These capital charges represent the reward to the individual investors for their investment in the firm concerned. Also note in Figure 12.1 that in the link between investors and firms, intermediaries called 'underwriters' may intervene. These underwriters, who are usually financial institutions, assist in the acquisition of new funds by guaranteeing the uptake of a new share issue by investors.

As far as companies are concerned, the capital market is represented by all possible sources of funds which are available to them.

For large public limited companies the range of sources of new funds is very wide indeed. The banks and other financial institutions as well as private and institutional investors all provide finance for such companies. For small, private limited companies and other small firms the range of possible

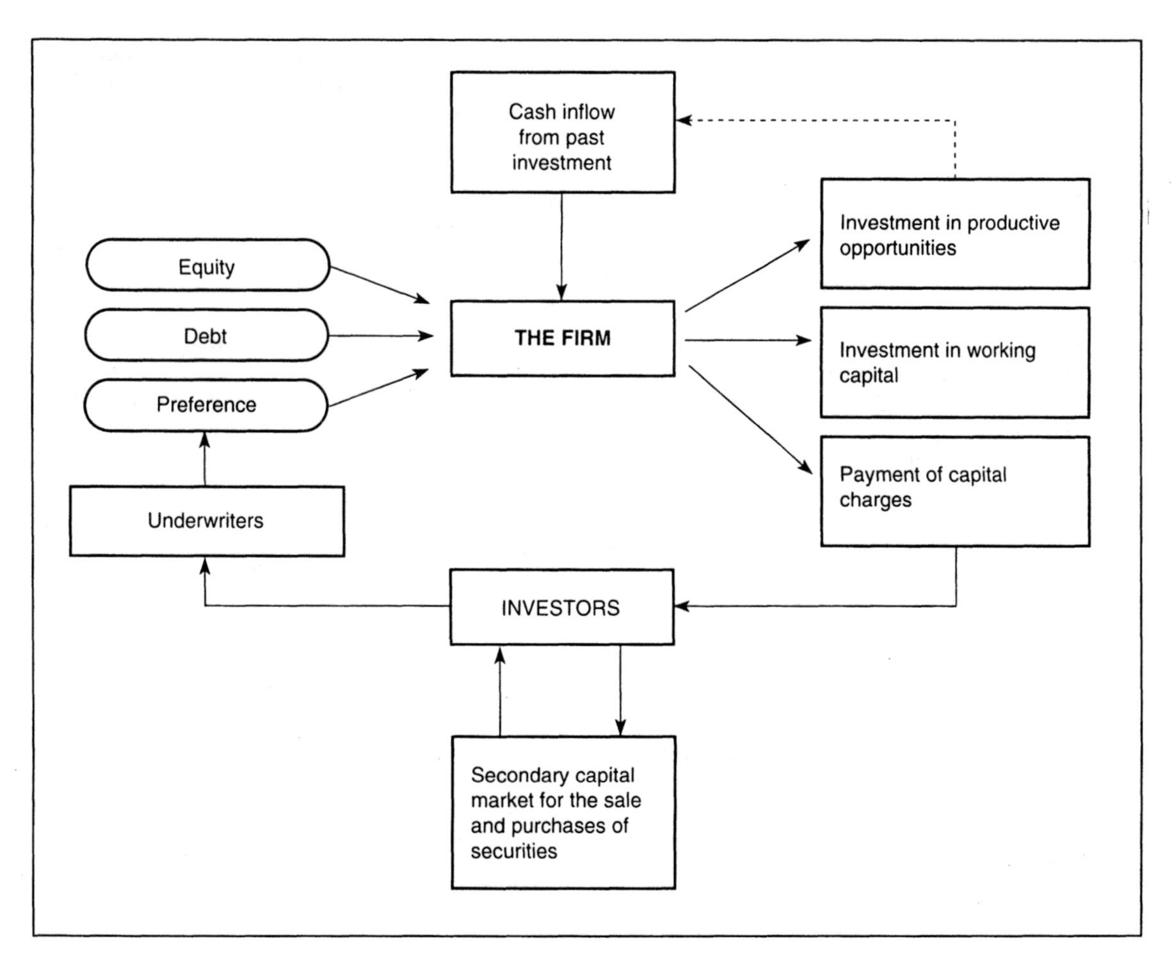

Figure 12.1 The capital-market cycle.

of finance is much smaller. Private limited companies, for instance, do not have access to finance through the stock market and would also find it very difficult to raise long-term loans from the major financial institutions. Such companies normally have to rely on the personal resources of their owners, managers and bank finance. However, no matter how large or small the firm concerned, the rate of return (in the form of interest or dividends), which will be required by the suppliers of the finance, is governed by the following factors:

- the degree of risk which the supplier perceives is attached to either the payment of interest or dividends or to the repayment of the original;
- the rate of change in the supplier's purchasing power (which in general terms is called 'inflation') and the degree of uncertainty which attaches to that rate of change;
- the rate of return which the supplier of finance can earn on equivalent investments elsewhere. As we shall see later, equivalence in this context can be taken to mean 'investments of equivalent risk'.

FUNCTION AND OPERATION OF THE STOCK MARKET

The focus of the secondary capital market in the UK is the London Stock Exchange where share and debt stock are traded. Similar institutions exist in all of the major financial centres in the world. The London Stock Exchange is not only an important secondary market, but it also serves as an important primary market where public limited companies can raise new finance.

In order to be effective as a capital market, those investors who can make the highest return from the capital available to them should be able to acquire the finance they need at the cheapest rate. It is also important that the price of a company's shares in the market represent a fair valuation of the business concerned. This will mean that the company's managers will be able to make capital resourcing and allocation decisions confident that the price they are paying, in the capital market, for the firm's financial resources is a fair price given the business prospects and risk which it faces. In order to ensure this, the capital market must be competitively perfect in that no market trader has any monopoly power over the shares of the business. A perfect capital market is one where the following occur.

- Individual traders in the market are unable to influence the price of a particular share through their own transactions. This will only occur if there are a large number of shares spread amongst a large number of investors.
- There are no transaction costs or capital taxes which would make small transactions unprofitable and eliminate the possibility of investors taking small profit-making opportunities.
- There are no 'barriers to entry' to the market either in the form of transaction costs, as mentioned above, or in the form of institutional constraints on those who wish to trade.
- There is costless access to information about the market and about individual securities for both actual and potential investors.

In fact, all of these conditions are violated to a greater or lesser degree in the real capital market, although it is an open question whether the imperfections which do exist substantially affect the efficiency with which capital funds are allocated by the market. Certainly, on the London Stock Exchange, small investors can face severe transactions costs. Indeed, the levels of transactions costs which are imposed by market dealers are often sufficient to nullify the gains which can be made on small portfolios. In addition, the existence of capital transfer taxes also creates a substantial imperfection in the market.

However, the more important problem with which we have to deal is the efficiency with which the stock market translates new information about particular companies into changes in security prices. The efficiency of the capital market, and more specifically the stock market, is a core issue in finance because, as we have suggested above, it is important that shares are not mispriced with respect to what is known about the affairs of the company concerned. There are two ways of understanding efficiency.

(i) In an efficient market, prices of all securities traded in that market respond instantly and without bias to any new items of information. In the absence of new information, share price movement will be purely random.
(ii) In a perfectly efficient market it would be impossible for any investor to use information consistently to 'beat' the level of return on investment which the market sets for a security of that level of risk.

More precisely, a perfectly efficient market with respect to a single item of information (an information signal) about a security, would be one where the price of that security jumped instantaneously from the already existing price to the price which would have existed, had the market known about the information signal all along. In Figure 12.2 we show this diagrammatically. If the price of a security does not respond to new, economically significant information about the company concerned, then the market in that security is completely inefficient. However, in practice, the efficiency of the market for individual securities will lie somewhere between these two extremes, as shown in Figure 12.2.

A considerable amount of research, much of which is highly technical, has been done into the efficiency of the stock markets in both the USA and the UK. Most of this work has been done on the efficiency of the market with respect to the pricing of equity shares, which are usually more actively traded than loan stocks. In general, the following conclusions can be drawn from this voluminous research literature.

(i) Prices of shares in these markets fully reflect all past information. In other words, the current price of a given share faithfully represents the value which market traders have placed upon that share, given the information which has already been disclosed about the company concerned. A moment's thought will show that the corollary of this is that past price information concerning a share cannot be used to predict its future price movements as the current price is a fair valuation based upon all that is known concerning that share.

Given the absence of any new information concerning a share, the only movements which will occur in its price will be random effects caused by traders buying and selling for other reasons than the arrival of new information. Many statistical studies have been done on the behaviour of share prices over time and the general conclusion is that share prices do appear to move randomly. When the market is efficient with respect to past information it is said to be 'weak-form' efficient.

(ii) The prices of shares in the UK and USA stock markets do appear to adjust extremely rapidly to the economic content of information which is made publicly available. Indeed, evidence would suggest that it is very difficult to make excess gains from investment in shares by combing the press for tips, reading company accounts and other handouts or, indeed, taking the advice of a stockbroker! In fact there is evidence to suggest the market appears to predict future information signals and 'discount' the economic content of certain types of information many months before it is actually released. A market which is perfectly efficient with respect to publicly available information is said to be 'semi-strong form' efficient.

(iii) Finally, it may well be possible to use privately available or 'insider' information to make excess gains through share dealing on the UK or USA stock exchanges. However, few investors are likely to confess to such sources of information, and hence the proposition that the market is efficient in this 'strong form' is extremely difficult to prove. It does appear, however, that investors who are most likely to have access to

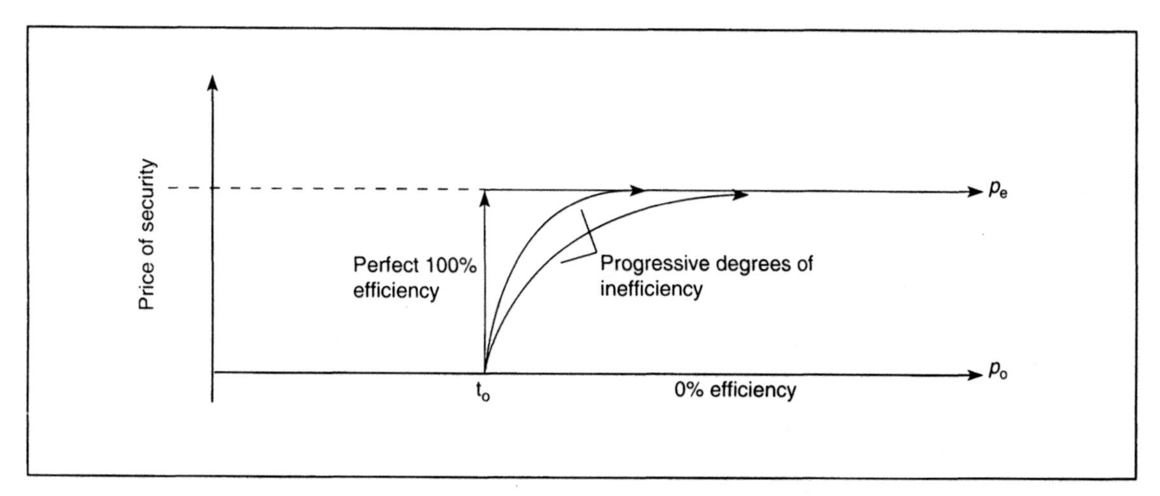

Figure 12.2 Degrees of market efficiency (p_o = equilibrium price in the absence of information, p_e = price which would have ruled if the entire market new of the information; t_o = time of arrival of information to the market).

such private information (if it could be obtained) do not systematically produce better than average returns for the funds on whose behalf they deal. Such investors are the highly professional dealers who specialise in particular investments on behalf of institutions such as pension funds, unit-trust companies, insurance companies and so on. Studies show that no UK unit-trust or pension fund managers rarely outperform, over the long term, what one would expect from a randomly drawn portfolio of equivalent risk. This leads us to the rather weak conclusion that even those investors who we would expect, through their expertise, could gain access to generally unavailable information, cannot convert that expertise into consistently better results than can be obtained from a random selection of shares.

ARE THE CAPITAL MARKETS REALLY RANDOM?

However, compelling as it may seem, there have been a number of studies which contradict the view that the capital market is a perfect exchange for information and that significant imperfections may exist. For example:

- small firms tend to generate abnormally high returns given their risk;
- market returns tend to be higher in January than in any other month of the year, and this is especially true for the small-firm sector;
- there appears to be a day-of-the-week effect, with both Mondays and Fridays showing abnormal returns.

Surprisingly, these abnormalities appear to persist, even though the market is well aware of their existence and presumably should be active in trading the benefit of their existence away. This would seem to indicate that these irregularities are structural and represent some underlying attribute in the pricing process itself. In order to understand this, market theorists are attempting to model the way the market works by a new branch of mathematics called dynamical systems theory or, as it is popularly known, chaos theory. Comparison of chaotic models rather than statistical models of price behaviour with real-world prices shows some startling similarities.

Chaotic processes follow basic structural laws of feedback which can appear random when viewed simply as a time series. For example, one structural law would be that if the price of a share were to rise too high, then demand for that share will fall and there would be corresponding negative pressure on the price. Similarly, if its price were to fall too low, demand would rise, the fall would stop and the share would 'bounce back'. Let us assume that the price of a share on a given day is p_t and that market makers attempt to push the share price up on day $t+1$ to p_{t+1}. The price relationship between the consecutive days would then be given by:

$$p_{t+1} = Xp_t$$

where X is the factor by which the share price is increased.

However, the effect of buyer resistance to this forced price increase can be represented by a 'price deceleration' term which we describe as Yp_t such that:

$$p_{t+1} = Xp_t - Yp_t = (X - Y)p_t$$

If $(X - Y) > 1$ then this equation leads to the conclusion that share prices will continue to rise, whereas if $(X - Y) < 1$ then the price will fall. As it stands, therefore this equation clearly does not explain the complexities of real share price behaviour. However, if we replace the deceleration term Yp_t by a power term in X then the model begins to produce some startling results. Let $Yp_t = Xp_t^2$ then:

$$p_{t+1} = Xp_t - Xp_t^2$$

Now this is a simple quadratic equation which is a negative inverted parabola of height dependent upon the value of X chosen. However, assuming different values of X we can see what happens to subsequent day share prices. In Figure 12.3(a), the deceleration term is as shown above (to the squared power) and in Figure 12.3(b) we have modified the power term shown to cubed power Xp_t^3.

In reality we do not know exactly what mathematical form the deceleration or feedback term will take, although even in the very simple mathematical cases shown above, what looks to be a random process arises, and indeed, simple serial correlation would appear to show that there is a low or zero correlation between one day's price and the next. It is fun to play with simple price adjustment formulae on a spreadsheet and demonstrate how even tiny variations in the deceleration term or the starting value for the series can produce quite startlingly different patterns.

The results of chaos theory indicate that although the market appears to be random, there may be an

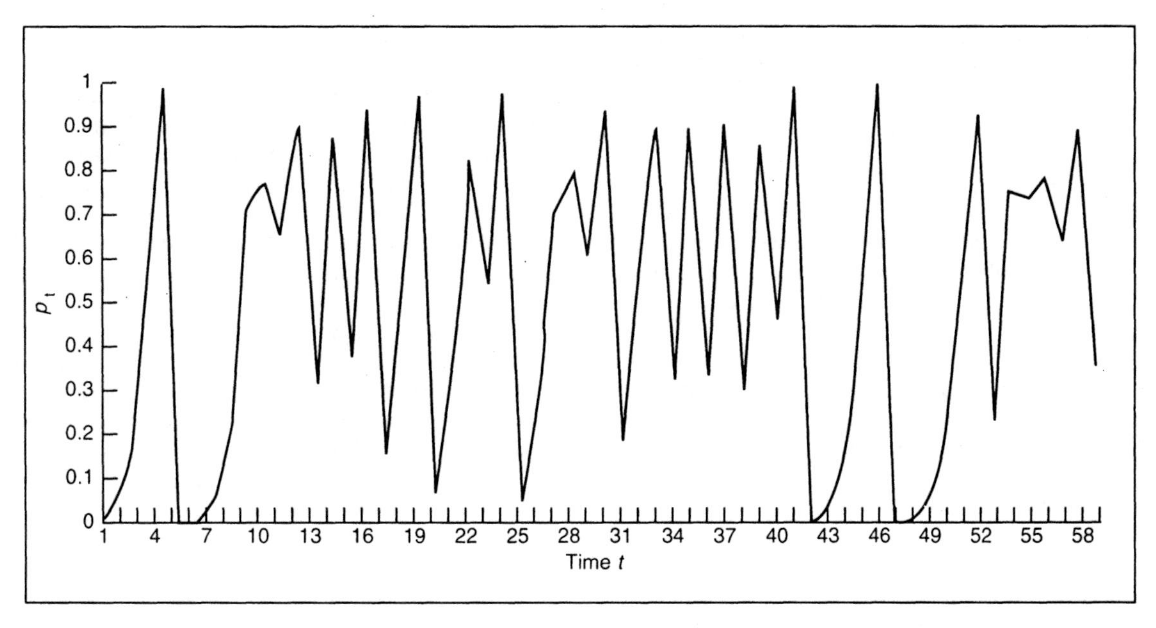

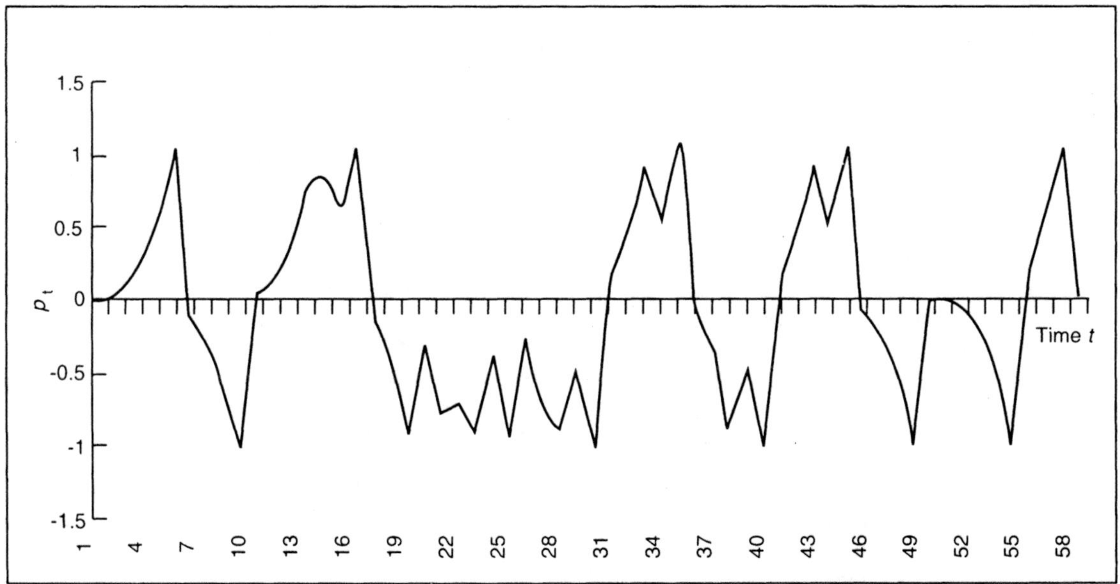

Figure 12.3 Time series of price data using (a) $X = 4$ and function $p_{t+1} = Xp_t - Xp_t^2$; (b) $X = 2.7$ and function $p_{t+1} = Xp_t - Xp_t^3$.

underlying structure within the price-setting process which gives the recurrent behaviour exhibited by the January effect and other non-random behaviour mentioned in the previous section. At this stage we do not fully understand the dynamics of share price movements, although the earlier assumptions that share markets are perfectly efficient and represent purely random processes in the absence of new information may be only an approximation at best.

ADVANTAGES AND DISADVANTAGES OF DIFFERENT TYPES OF FINANCE

In this section we will consider the various types of finance which are available within the two subdivisions of equity and debt, and the relative merits of each type will be discussed. Certain types of finance, such as preference shares and convertible loans, have some of the properties of equity capital and some of the properties of debt capital. A detailed consideration of these hybrid securities is beyond the scope of this book.

Equity finance

Both public and private companies raise equity finance by issuing 'ordinary shares' (called 'common stock' in the USA). It is normal in the UK to attach a nominal value to each ordinary share (usually 25p, 50p or £1). This figure has no real significance, as ordinary shares are invariably issued to the market at much higher figures per share than the nominal value. The excess is termed the 'share premium'. Furthermore, the nominal value has no significance for the price at which any given share is traded. The only time the nominal value of a share matters is if the market value falls below the nominal value. In this case the company would not be able to raise new equity finance of the same type, as it would entail issuing shares at a discount, which is illegal under UK company law.

Raising equity by an issue of ordinary shares can be accomplished in a number of ways.

By a prospectus issue

With a prospectus issue the company concerned (which must be a public limited company) invites applications for its shares from the general public. The invitation to subscribe for shares must be accompanied by a prospectus, which is a document designed to advertise the affairs of the company in a prescribed fashion to prospective investors. The contents of the prospectus are prescribed by the Companies Acts and, for those companies issuing shares through the London Stock Exchange, by the Stock Exchange 'Yellow Book' *Admission of Securities to Listing*. The principal legal requirements are that the prospectus should contain a five-year financial history, a statement of the directors' financial interests in the company and certain other information concerning the issuing company's financial affairs.

By an offer for sale

With an offer for sale an independent institution takes up the shares to be issued and then administers the sale of those shares on behalf of the public limited company concerned. In 1983 the British Government privatised British Aerospace (which had been a nationalised concern) as a part of its programme of selling off the profitable parts of British industry in public ownership. The offer was made as an 'offer for sale' of 100 million ordinary shares of nominal value 50p at a price of 150p per share. The administrating agent who made the 'offer for sale' itself was the merchant bank Kleinwort Benson Ltd. The 'offer for sale' document, in such a situation, is deemed to be the prospectus, and it must present the same information as that required for a prospectus under the Companies Acts and the Stock Exchange regulations.

In addition, several companies (including Kleinwort Benson) underwrote the issue of the British Aerospace shares. That is, they agreed (for a commission) to take up any shares not taken up by the public. Such an 'underwriting agreement' is an important guarantee to a company (or to the government in the particular circumstances of the British Aerospace flotation) that it will be able to obtain its full financial requirements from the issue. However, the costs of underwriting commission can be very high, thus substantially raising the costs of obtaining this type of finance.

By a rights issue

With a rights issue, a company's existing shareholders are offered new shares in proportion to their current holdings. The offer can often be very attractive to shareholders, as the new shares are usually offered at a considerable discount on the existing share's current market price. With a rights issue, the company will send to its shareholders a 'revocable letter of allotment' for the shares being offered which the individual concerned (or any individual to whom the shareholder sells the letter of allotment) must accept within a specified period of time. These letters of allotment have value in their own right if the shares are being issued at a discount on the current market price. The holder of the letter can sell it on the market.

By an open offer

This is similar to a rights issue except that existing shareholders may apply for any number of shares irrespective of their current holding. This method is not particularly popular, apart from very small privately owned companies where the offer is put out to family members and close friends who are shareholders already.

All of these methods of raising finance can be very costly to the company, especially when the amounts of finance being sought are relatively small. The costs of administering a share issue can be high, especially for an offer to the general public where a large number of individual investors may be involved. On top of this, the yield of cash from a share issue can be significantly reduced if underwriting commission must be deducted. For this reason, of all the possible ways for raising equity finance which exist, rights issues have been the most popular with companies in the UK.

However, the full cost of equity capital to a firm will depend upon other factors apart from the cost of actually raising funds. Most importantly, the company must consider the 'opportunity cost' of equity finance – a concept we will consider in Chapter 13.

Debt finance

The other main form of finance is debt or loan finance. Debt finance can be broadly categorised into either redeemable (where the company promises to repay the capital sum to its debt holders at a given future date) or irredeemable (where no such promise is made). In addition, debt can be either secured or unsecured. A debt is secured where the firm 'pledges' or 'mortgages' part of its real assets (usually land or buildings but stocks are sometimes used with short-term debt) to the lender. If the company fails to honour the conditions of its debt contract, perhaps by not paying interest or not repaying capital on the due date, then the lenders of secured debt have the right to foreclose and sell the pledged or mortgaged assets forming their security to settle their claim.

Public limited companies can issue loan stock in just the same way as they issue shares, i.e. through a stock exchange. In such cases, the formal procedure for the issue of debt is very similar to that for equity. A prospectus must be published and the issue can be underwritten. It is normal for such publicly subscribed debt to be issued in nominal £100 units. In the case of debt, the nominal value is usually the issue value and will be the amount repaid to the debt holder on redemption. The nominal value of a stock is usually referred to as its 'par' value and this is the amount upon which interest payments are calculated.

For smaller companies, the more usual sources of debt finance are the clearing banks, merchant banks, company directors (and their relatives) and government-financed loan schemes for small businesses. Unfortunately, the latter tend to change with the Chancellor of the Exchequer, if not more frequently! Various 'Government Loan Guarantee Schemes' have existed in the past where certain financial institutions, including the clearing banks, offer loans to existing and new businesses which are guaranteed by the government. Because the loan is guaranteed, the financial institutions offering the loans can offer them at a lower rate than would otherwise be the case.

The great advantage of these sources of finance for small businesses is that they do not require the degree of disclosure required for debt issued to the public, although banks do require a very full statement of a client company's affairs and prospects.

Bank lending has, historically, been for medium or short-term finance rather than for the longer term. This is now changing, however, as the banking sector has responded to criticism of its somewhat conservative lending policies levied against it by, among others, the Wilson Committee Report on City Institutions.

Bank lending comes in one of two forms.

(i) A loan: this is usually for a fixed term, bearing interest at some agreed rate above the Inter-Bank Base Rate. For a very low-risk company, the premium above base rate may be as low as 1% to 1.5%. Unlike a redeemable debenture raised through the market, bank borrowing is normally repaid on a schedule of instalments rather than in a final lump sum.

(ii) Through an overdraft: this may be for an agreed or for an indefinite term. An overdraft simply allows a business to spend over the balance on its bank current account. The rate of interest on overdraft account is much higher than for equivalent sums borrowed on fixed loan. In addition, the banks have the right to call in an overdraft at any point in time, that is to ask for the overdrawn customer to bring the account into immediate credit.

THE CONCEPT OF 'GEARING' AND FINANCIAL RISK

The introduction of debt into a firm's capital is called 'gearing' in the UK and 'leverage' in the USA. The gearing ratio measures the proportion of debt in a firm's capital structure and is given by the formula:

Book value gearing =
[(book value of all debt plus overdrafts not covered by cash balances in hand)/
(book value of all equity including retained earnings and provision for deferred taxation)] × 100

Market gearing =
[(market value of all outstanding debt plus
overdrafts not covered by cash in hand)/
(market value of all equity shares)] × 100

Sometimes the denominator of each of the above ratios is taken as the sum of the debt (as given by the numerator) plus the equity (as given by the denominator). This gives a gearing range from 0% to 100% which many people find easier to understand.

Although debt is often cheaper to raise than equity (and, some would argue, it has a cheaper long-run cost as well) it does have one significant disadvantage. Because debt involves a contractual commitment on the part of the lender to pay interest and repay capital on the due date, the penalties for default are high.

If a company fails to pay a dividend on equity, all that is likely to happen is that its share price will decline as disgruntled investors sell their shares. However, non-payment of debt interest is a serious matter, in that the majority of industrial and commercial loan agreements give the lenders the right to appoint a receiver in such circumstances to manage the affairs of the company on their behalf. The appointment of a receiver is usually the precursor of either corporate bankruptcy (where the company is forced into 'liquidation') or the sale of a substantial part (or even the whole) of the company in order to redeem its debts.

The additional risk brought about by gearing arises by virtue of the power of foreclosure on the part of lenders. We call the risk 'financial risk' as opposed to the normal 'business risk' which the company faces through its operations.

EXAMPLE

In order to quantify and understand the concept of financial risk consider two companies, A and B, the first of which is financed entirely by equity and the second which has a geared capital structure. Both companies earn an average of £100 000 per annum and both have a standard deviation on their earnings of plus or minus £40 000. Both companies distribute their earnings in full, A to its equity shareholders and B to both its debt and equity investors. Company B pays interest of £30 000 per annum to service its debt capital.

In order to get a relative measure of the risk to the equity investors (as both companies have different average after-interest returns) we will use a standardised measure of risk. As we outlined in Chapter 10, risk can be measured by the standard deviation of the relevant variable. However, a problem arises when we try to compare two or more distributions with widely different mean values. To avoid this difficulty, standardised risk measures the amount of risk (measured in pounds sterling of standard deviation) per pound sterling of average value.

Standardised risk (Z) =
standard deviation per unit of mean

For company A,

$$Z = 40\,000/100\,000 = 0.4$$

For company B,

$$Z = 40\,000/70\,000 = 0.57$$

Therefore, company B has relatively more risk (measured in standardised units of risk) than company A. This extra risk has been brought about by the higher level of gearing in company B as compared with company A. We can see the result diagrammatically in Figure 12.4.

Intuitively, this means that the more highly geared a company becomes, the greater the chance that a poor year's trading performance will leave it in a situation where its debt interest cannot be paid and the consequent possibility that a receiver will be appointed. Although gearing can be a source of trouble in poor trading situations, in good times the equity shareholders, in a geared firm, will earn higher equity returns as the full benefit of the increased earnings will accrue to their smaller equity base compared with the ungeared firm.

High levels of gearing can be especially dangerous where the rate of interest is not fixed, but can vary with changing economic circumstances, as is usually the case with bank loans. Nationally, a dramatic example of this danger materialised when the British Government attempted to reduce the money supply by pushing up interest rates in 1981. As a result debt became very expensive and many small companies (as well as some larger ones), who were competitive in every other way, were forced out of business. Furthermore, because the increased interest payments consumed a greater proportion of company value added less resources were available for labour and thus companies were forced to lay off employees in order to survive. The British Government was constrained to follow the same policy in 1989 to 1992 due to its high exchange rate commitment

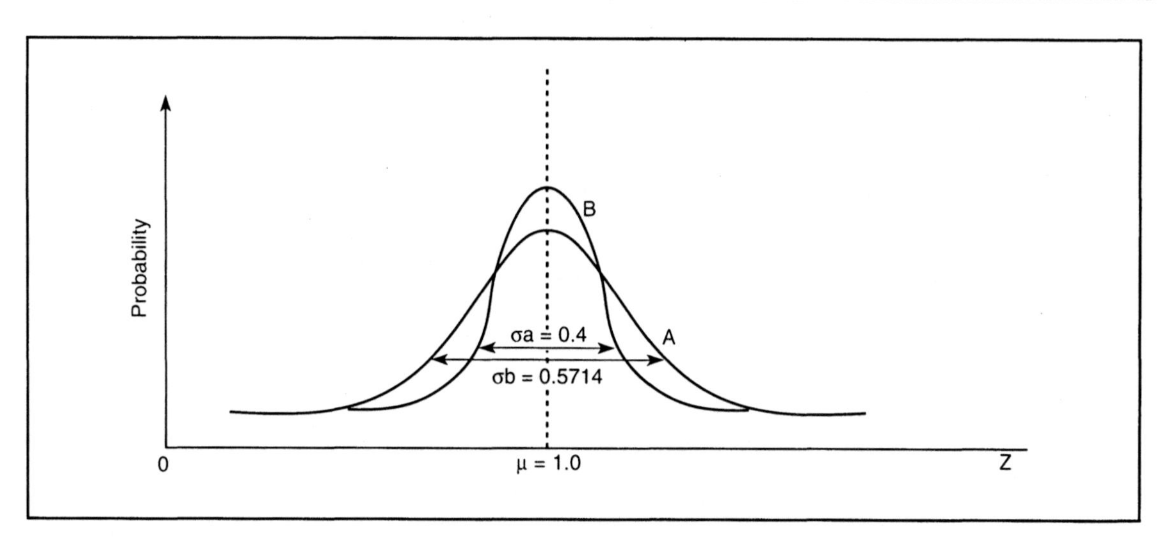

Figure 12.4 Standardised earnings risk as a result of increased gearing.

to the European Monetary System within the Exchange Rate Mechanism (ERM). The result was the longest corporate recession since the 1930s.

We will defer a discussion of the balance between equity and debt which a company should choose until the next chapter.

CONCLUSION

In this chapter we have reviewed the nature of the financial markets which a business faces and the sorts of opportunities which those markets offer to managers. In particular we have considered the most important ways in which businesses can raise finance for long-term investment and the factors management would have to bear in mind when entering the financial markets. Finally, we have examined the problem of financial risk and raised an issue which we will deal with in detail in the next chapter, namely the optimal level of gearing which a company should choose.

Chapter 13

Costing the Firm's Capital Resources

Level M

Contents

Summary

Different types of finance have different costs depending upon the risk associated with them. In this chapter we define the opportunity cost of capital as the minimum rate of return which a firm must offer to the market in order to raise new capital to replace that used in investment. Only in exceptional circumstances will this 'replacement cost' of capital not be its opportunity cost. We then develop these ideas to consider the opportunity cost of capital for a geared firm, i.e. a firm financed by a mixture of equity and debt capital. Finally, we consider whether an optimal level of gearing exists at which a firm's opportunity cost of capital can be minimised.

INTRODUCTION

In Chapter 7 the concept of 'opportunity cost' was introduced to describe the impact on current and future cash balances of the decision to use scarce resources such as labour and materials. Capital is also a productive resource, and in most respects its treatment is just like any other resource the firm may use.

To assess the opportunity cost of capital we must establish the net cash loss to a firm when it decides to use up capital on a particular investment (a project). This cash loss is not measured in absolute terms when applied to capital, as was the case with other resources, but rather in terms of a percentage rate on the capital used up. However, as with other resources, the opportunity cost of capital is dependent upon its nearest available alternative use.

If a firm has capital which is surplus to its requirements, its opportunity cost of capital will be the higher of:

(i) the best available rate of interest on external investment (say, on a short-term deposit);

(ii) the rate which its equity investors can earn on their best alternative investment (of equivalent risk).

We assume that, if the managers of a firm have no further use for the capital funds at their disposal and cannot earn a rate of return on external investment in excess of the return their investors can earn elsewhere, they will distribute those surplus funds to the shareholders. The rate of return which a firm's investors can obtain on be their best alternative investment opportunity (of equivalent risk) is deemed to be the minimum required rate of return on their investment in the firm (we will clarify this notion a little later in this chapter).

If, however, a firm is currently fully utilising the capital within its business then the decision to use up more capital on further projects will mean that new capital funds will have to be raised from the market. This follows from the idea in Chapter 8 that when a decision is made to consume a useful resource, the cash loss to the firm is the replacement cost of that resource. With capital its 'replacement cost' will be the minimum rate of return (in the form of dividends and interest) the firm will have to pay in order to attract new capital funds in its current gearing ratio.

On occasions a firm may find itself in need of capital which cannot be obtained on the open market. In such a situation of 'capital rationing', as it is usually called, the firm will have to redeploy its existing capital internally. We will discuss the concept of the internal opportunity cost or 'dual price' of capital in the next chapter.

Note: We always assume that a firm will keep its financing decision separate from its project selection (investment) decision. In this way the company can avoid the situation of accepting relatively poor investment opportunities at one point in time because finance is cheap, while rejecting much better opportunities later because finance has become expensive. When costing the capital required for a particular investment we assume that the firm will finance the project in the current gearing ratio. By doing this the firm is able to assess the merits of the investment project independently of its capital structure. Consequently, we take the average cost of capital for the firm rather than the marginal cost which could be the rate of interest on the cheapest source of available funds.

In order to decide between the alternative bases for determining the opportunity cost of capital we have constructed a diagram (Figure 13.1) which is very similar to that shown in Chapter 8.

We will now consider how the external opportunity cost of capital can be determined when:

- the firm is financed solely through equity;
- the firm is financed solely by debt;
- the firm has a geared capital structure.

In this book we will consider the most usual circumstances where the investor's minimum rate of return determines the opportunity cost of capital.

THE COST OF CAPITAL IN THE PURE EQUITY FIRM

If a pure equity firm wishes to replenish the capital used up in investment, it must offer to potential new investors a rate of return equal to, or in excess of, the minimum acceptable rate, in the market, for equity shares of the same risk class.

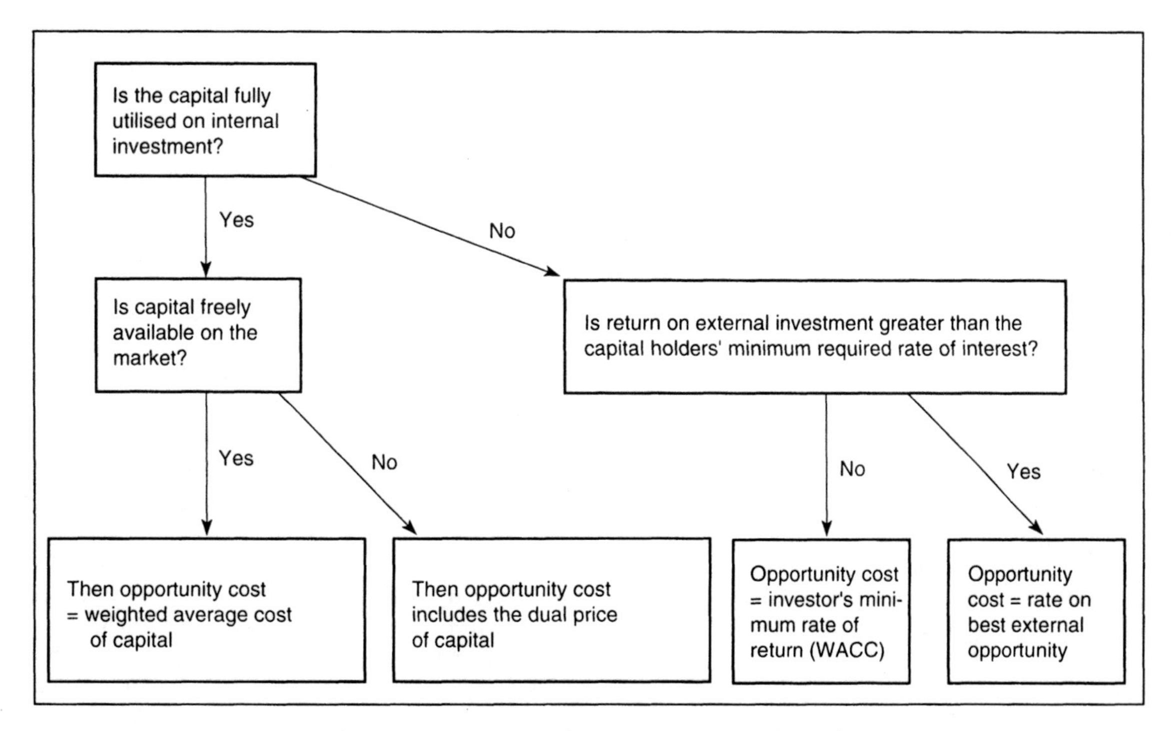

Figure 13.1 Evaluating the opportunity cost of capital.

For this purpose, 'return' is defined as the capital gain on a share plus its dividend yield, i.e.

$$\text{Return} = \frac{p_1 - p_0}{p_0} + \frac{d_0}{p_0}$$

$$= \frac{p_1 - p_0 + d_0}{p_0}$$

where p_1 is the price at the end of a given period of time, p_0 is the price at the beginning of the period and d_0 is any dividend declared in the period.

The period chosen for calculating the return on an equity share can be any length of time we wish. For example daily, weekly, monthly or annual returns can be calculated. If sufficient (say weekly) return measures are available then an average (weekly) return can be calculated also. Note also that return is inversely related to opening price p_0, i.e. the higher the price the lower the return and vice versa.

EXAMPLE

The shares of Montoya plc were quoted at the following prices (per share):

1 January 19x3	*160p*
31 January 19x3	*166p*

A dividend of 10p per share was paid in the month of January.

The return on Montoya's shares in January were as follows:

$$\text{Return} = \frac{166 - 160 + 10}{160}$$

$$= 16/160$$

$$= 0.1 \text{ (or } 10\%)$$

This figure is the return over one month. However, we often prefer to show returns annualised, that is, how they would be if the same monthly return was achieved over each month during the year and the equivalent annual return produced. Because the returns are compounded, the equivalent annual return, given a monthly return figure (r) expressed as a decimal, is:

$$\text{Annual return} = (1 + r)^{12} - 1$$

Therefore:

$$\text{Annual return} = (1 + 0.1)^{12} - 1$$

$$= 3.1384 - 1$$

$$= 2.1384 (213.84\%)$$

In this case a relatively small increase in price, combined with a dividend payment, appears to give a very large annual return. However, in practice, the share's performance in other months is unlikely to be so good, and the net effect, over the year, will be a much lower annual return.

On the basis of a series of (say) monthly return figures the investor will form an 'expectation' of what the average rate of monthly return should be on those shares in the future. If that expected return is high enough, the investor will consider buying. Conversely, if the expected rate is lower than the investor's minimum required rate of return, the investor will not buy the shares concerned and, indeed, should sell those shares which he or she possesses at that point in time. It would be very difficult for a firm to determine the minimum rate of return which investors, within the market place, require for its shares by going and asking them. The only realistic way to find the appropriate rate is to infer it from their buying and selling behaviour on the basis of some simple assumptions about the way they make decisions.

The model we present below, for estimating the minimum rate of return required by investors, is based upon the axioms of 'rational economic man' plus the following assumptions:

- Investors hold individual shares in well-diversified portfolios.
- Investors are only concerned about the average rate of return that they can earn on their investments and the riskiness of that return (as measured by the standard deviation of returns).
- There are no transaction costs or taxes which will prevent the prices of individual shares reaching equilibrium.
- Investors have free access to all information concerning the shares in question.

The theory of investor behaviour, at the heart of the model described below, suggests that investors can best evaluate the performance of their share holdings by comparing them with some 'yardstick' of performance. In theory this yardstick is the average return and risk of all possible securities in the capital market combined together into a giant, representative portfolio. In practice the performance of this market portfolio is approximated by the performance of a broadly based stock market index (the level of which can be taken to be the price of a portfolio of the shares contained in the index). Such an index could be the Financial Times' Actuaries All Share Index.

The model we will use relates the expected return on an individual share to:

- the return an investor would expect from an investment in a completely risk-free security – the 'risk-free rate of return';
- the extra element of return needed to induce an investor to bear the risk entailed in holding the share concerned – the risk premium.

The risk premium is measured by comparison with the index of market performance. If movements in the periodic returns of the individual share are a perfect reflection of movements in the returns of the market portfolio (as shown by changes in the market index) then that share has the same risk as the market. As a result, investors will expect the same average return from that share as from the market portfolio.

More precisely, these two components (the risk-free rate and the risk premium) can be expressed by a simple formula which explains the expected rate of return on a security when the supply and demand for that security are in equilibrium.

Expected return on security '*i*' =
risk-free rate of interest
+ $\beta \times$ [(expected return on the market portfolio) – (risk-free rate of interest)]

where β is the market risk loading factor for security *i* which we will explain in detail below.

The formula above, when put into mathematical form is:

$$E(r_i) = R + \beta i\,[E(r_m) - R]$$

This model is known in the theory of finance as the Capital Asset Pricing Model (CAPM). This is one of the most important models in the theory of finance, and has been shown to be remarkably robust at explaining the average return earned on shares and other securities.

If a share has a return which is exactly as risky as the market (i.e. where the share returns move up and down exactly in line with movements in the index), then that share's β value will be exactly 1. In this case, investors will expect to earn exactly the same level of return on the share as they could earn by holding a portfolio containing all the shares in the market.

The value of β for a given share tells us how volatile the returns on that share are in comparison with the returns on the market portfolio. Once we know the value of β for a firm's shares we can then predict the expected return that share should earn given a value for the expected return on the market portfolio and the risk-free rate of interest.

Therefore:

- if $\beta = 1$ then the security is exactly as risky as the market;
- if $\beta > 1$ then the security is more risky than the market;
- if $\beta < 1$ then the security is less risky than the market.

In Figure 13.2 we show this relationship between the return which can be expected on a share and the market risk loading factor, β. In practice β values for individual shares are calculated using linear regression techniques on the shares' past returns against the returns of the market index. In the UK, values of β for British shares can be obtained from the London Business School's Risk Measurement Service which is revised and published quarterly.

In order to see how the CAPM can be used to estimate the minimum required rate of return on an equity share consider the following example.

EXAMPLE

On average the return on a broadly based market index is 14% per annum and the return on 90-day government 'tap' stock (the nearest thing to a risk-free rate of interest) is 8% per annum. Determine the minimum rate of return on a share which has (i) 20% more risk, (ii) 20% less risk and (iii) the same risk as the market.

(i) 20% more risk means that $\beta = 1.2$:

Expected return = 0.08 + 1.2 × (0.14 – 0.08)
= 0.152 (=15.2% per annum)

(ii) 20% less risk means that $\beta = 0.8$:

Expected return = 0.08 + 0.8 × (0.14 – 0.08)
= 0.128 (12.8% per annum)

(iii) the same risk means that $\beta = 1.0$:

Expected return = 0.08 + 1.0 × (0.14 – 0.08)
= 0.14 (=14.0% per annum)

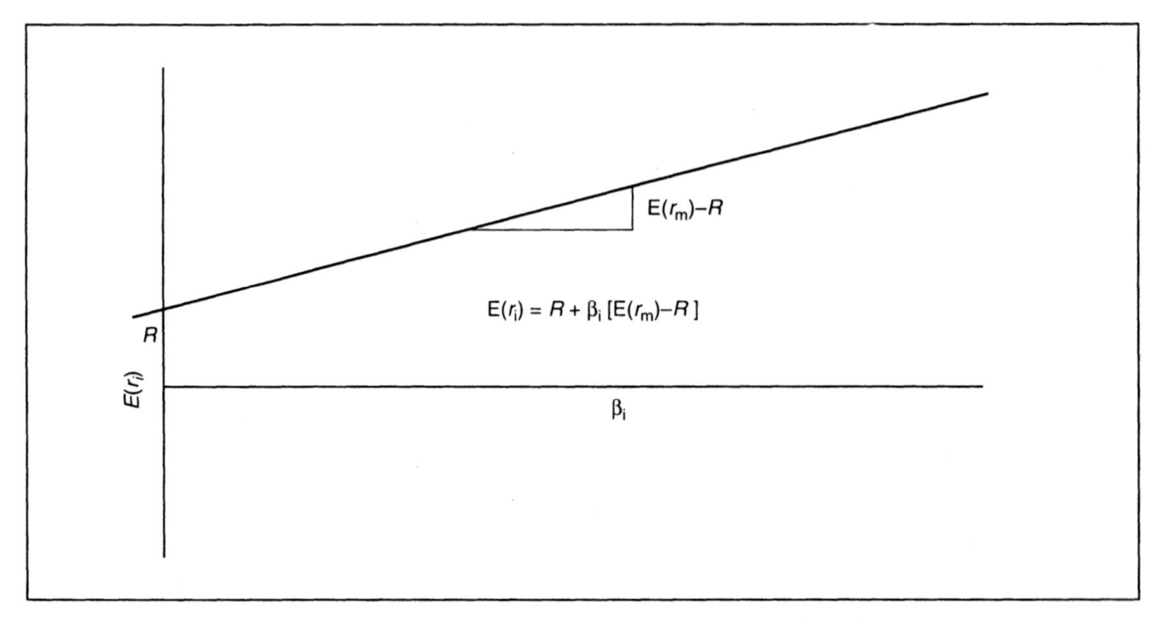

Figure 13.2 Expected return on a security against market risk.

Mapping these figures onto a graph of return and market risk we obtain Figure 13.3.

There are three points to note about this discussion of the equity rate of return and the nature of risk.

- The only variable which relates to the individual firm is the β factor. The value for an individual share measures the response of that security to change in market-wide conditions. It is, therefore, an indication of the part of the security's

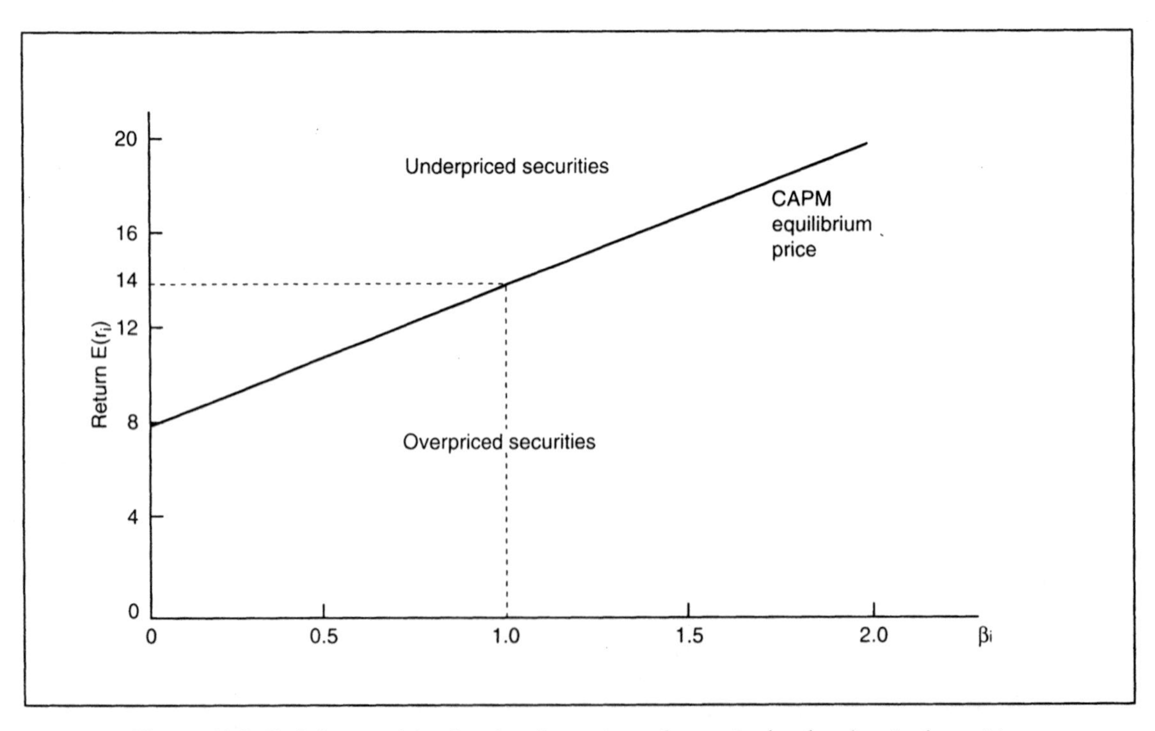

Figure 13.3 Capital asset pricing line showing regions of overpriced and underpriced securities.

overall variability of returns which is caused by market-wide influences such as changes in interest rates, exchange rates, government fiscal and monetary policies, etc. All of these factors will affect the security's price and hence its return.

- Because expected return is inversely related to price, we can say that any security which has a return above the line in Figure 13.3 is underpriced and any security which has a return below the line is overpriced. The theory of the CAPM suggests that, at equilibrium, all securities have returns which lie somewhere along the line.
- If an investor holds a widely diversified portfolio, the most crucial consideration concerning an ordinary share is how that security performs in relation to the total market. In fact, the 'averaging' process which occurs when shares are combined into portfolios tends to eliminate the effect of the risk which is caused by factors peculiar to the individual firms rather than to the market as a whole. The only component of a security's risk which appears in the risk of a well-diversified portfolio is its market risk, i.e. the risk caused by market-wide rather than firm-specific factors.

That part of a security's overall risk which is caused by general market influences is often referred to as 'systematic risk'. Firm-specific risk, on the other hand, is referred to as 'unsystematic risk'. In Figure 13.4 we show how diversification reduces the risk of a portfolio. The graph in Figure 13.4 is based upon empirical studies which show that as the size of a portfolio is increased (in terms of the number of securities contained within it) its risk decreases.

Notice that the total risk does not fall to zero but diminishes to a constant value. This constant value is the level of market or systematic risk. Obviously, if a portfolio were to be diversified continuously, it would eventually come to resemble the market portfolio and would then possess a level of risk very close to that of the market portfolio itself.

Surprisingly, the empirical evidence indicates that the benefits of risk reduction through increased diversification are mostly gained by the time 15 or so securities equally weighted by value have been added into the portfolio. Building portfolios of larger size just wastes transaction costs such as management costs, brokerage fees and so forth. This is true no matter how much is invested, in value terms, in the portfolio.

THE COST OF CAPITAL IN THE PURE DEBT FIRM

In principle, every company must have an ownership interest. However, it is possible that a firm could acquire so much debt that it becomes

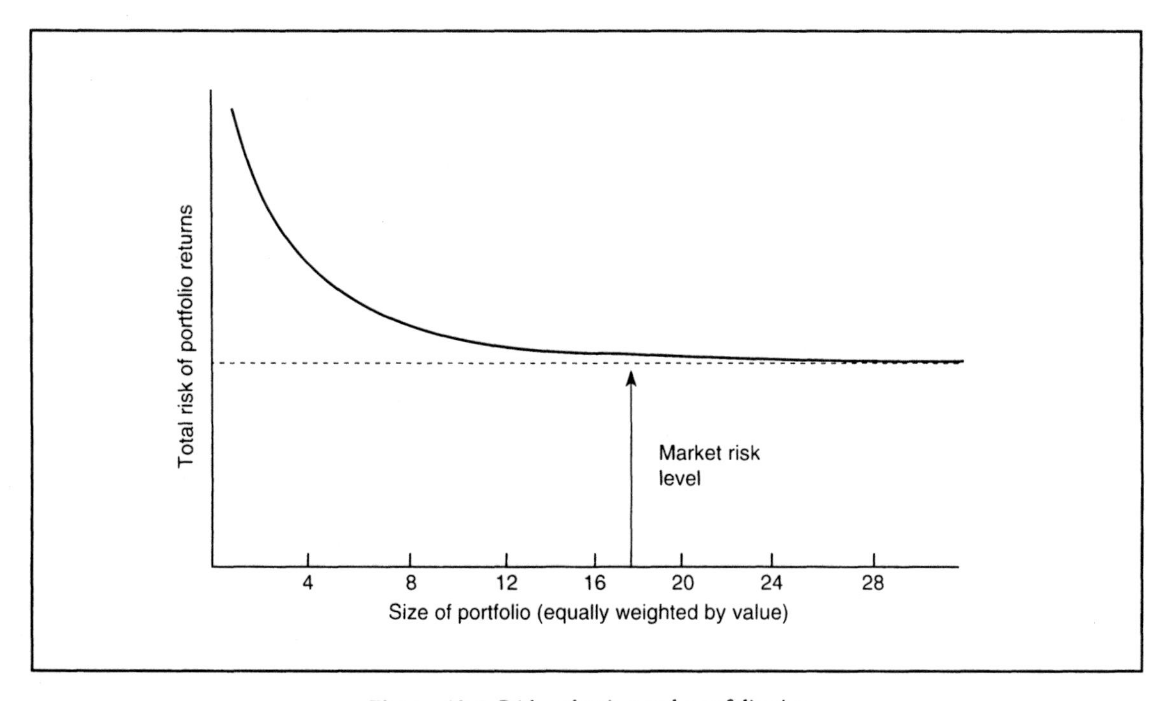

Figure 13.4 Risk reduction and portfolio size.

effectively fully geared. Also, with many small, private companies the shareholding is restricted to a few controlling individuals who would not consider expansion of the firm's equity capital in any event.

If a firm's debt finance comes solely from bank lending the opportunity cost of its capital is the current rate of interest required to obtain new funds. In this case the rate is likely to be that which a bank would charge upon a new loan.

If, on the other hand, the debt had been raised on the market through the issue of loan stock then the opportunity cost of capital would be the rate of interest which the company would have to offer to the market on a new issue in order for it to be fully taken up. Where a loan stock is freely traded in the capital market it is reasonably easy to establish this rate. This is the situation which we will consider first.

Let us examine two cases: (i) where the loan stock is irredeemable and (ii) where it is redeemable.

The cost of irredeemable loan stock

We will assume that when investors value loan stock they discount cash receipts they expect from that loan at their required rate of return for stock of that type.
On average, therefore,

Market value (ex-div) =

$$\frac{I}{(1+r)^1} + \frac{I}{(1+r)^2} + \frac{I}{(1+r)^3} + \frac{I}{(1+r)^4} + \cdots$$

where r is the minimum required rate of return for this type of loan stock and I is the interest paid per unit of stock (i.e. the 'coupon' or 'nominal' rate). This type of formula is a perpetual geometric progression which simplifies to:

$$\text{Market value} = I/r$$

EXAMPLE

A firm's quoted loan stock has a coupon rate of interest of 10% per annum and a market value of £86.00% (which is a way of saying '£86 per £100 nominal stock unit').

Therefore:

$$\text{Market value} = £86.00 = 10/r$$

Rearranging, the implied value of r, the minimum required rate of return, is given by

$$\begin{aligned} r &= 10/86 \\ &= 0.1163 \ (=11.63\%) \end{aligned}$$

This means that if the firm wished to issue new loan capital it would have to offer a coupon rate of at least 11.63% per annum in order to induce investors to take up the new stock at its par value of £100 per unit.

The cost of redeemable loan stock

In this case interest payments will be received up to the date of redemption whereupon repayment of the original amount will be made. Therefore, the market value of this type of stock is given by:

Market value (ex-div) =

$$\frac{I}{(1+r)^1} + \frac{I}{(1+r)^2} + \cdots + \frac{100+I}{(1+r)^n}$$

where n is the number of years which must elapse until redemption.

EXAMPLE

Consider a firm with 10% redeemable loan stock which has a market value of £86.00%. The firm has agreed in the loan deed to redeem the loan in four years' time at par.

Therefore:

$$86.00 = \frac{10}{(1+r)^1} + \frac{10}{(1+r)^2} + \frac{10}{(1+r)^3} + \frac{110}{(1+r)^4}$$

We now have to find the value of r which satisfies the above equation. The easiest way of doing this is by substituting increasing values of r into the equation and plotting these values of r against the resultant market value. Where the graph cuts through the value of £86 we have, at the crossover point, the minimum required rate of return for this type of loan stock.

In Figure 13.5 we have drawn the graph of the above equation. The value of r is 15% at the market value of £86.

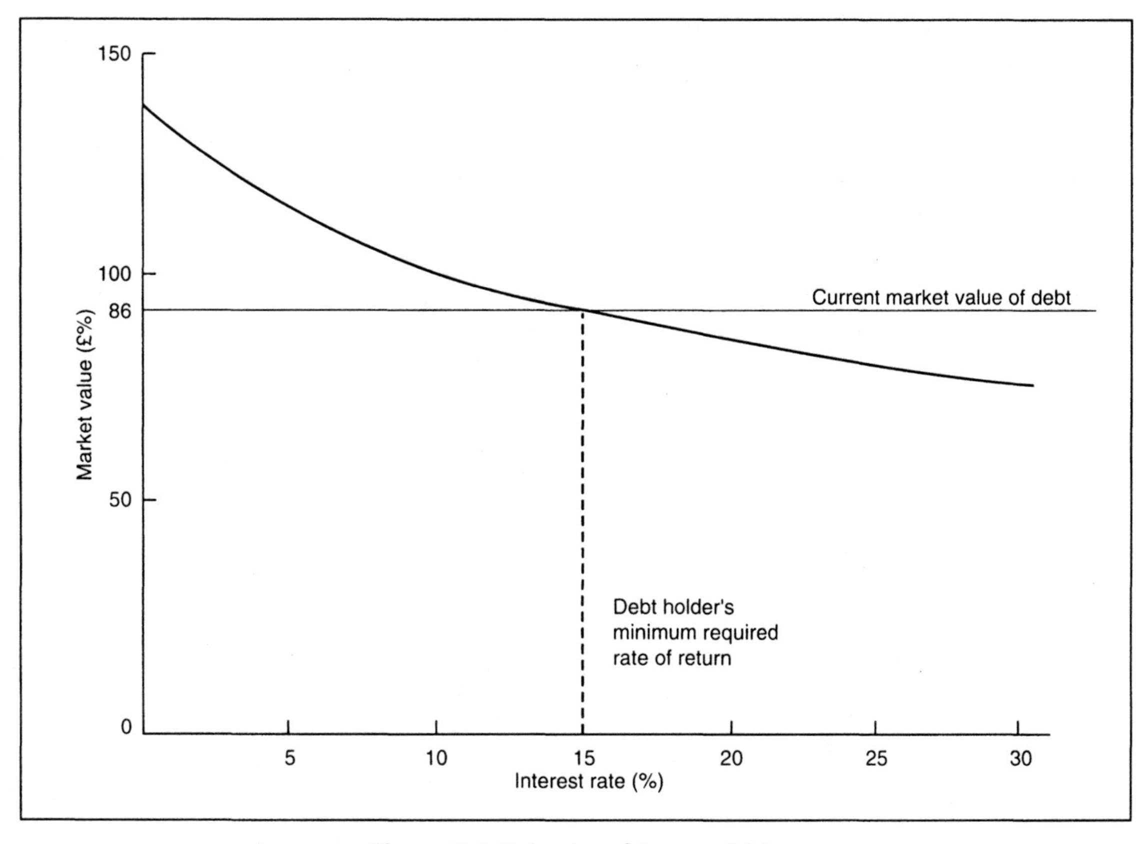

Figure 13.5 Estimation of the cost of debt.

In some situations a firm's loan stock may not have a recognised market value because it is not traded on the open market. There are two ways in which an approximation to the opportunity cost of debt capital can be derived:

- by obtaining estimates from merchant banks and other long-term lenders of the appropriate rate for new borrowing given the firm's size and current level of gearing;
- by using the market value of an equivalent government gilt-edged security. The gilt-edged security used for comparison purposes should have the same nominal rate of interest and redemption date as the loan stock concerned. The prices of government gilt-edged securities can be obtained from the daily publication of security prices in the *Financial Times* or other quality newspapers in the UK.

The cost of capital in a geared firm

We are now in a position to calculate the average return which must be offered to a firm's investors where it has both equity and debt in its capital structure. The opportunity cost of each type of capital is calculated as described above. The average rate is then calculated by weighting each type of capital according to the relative proportions of each type in the firm's capital structure. The proportion (w) of each capital type is calculated as the ratio of the market value of that capital type to the total market value of all the firm's capital.

EXAMPLE

Consider a firm which has three components of capital in its capital structure:

- *Equity shares: 1 000 000 ordinary shares, market value 270p each, opportunity cost 18% per annum.*
- *Redeemable loan stock: 12 000 £100 units, market value £86%, opportunity cost 15% per annum.*

- *Irredeemable loan stock: 50 000 £100 units, market value 90%, opportunity cost 16% per annum.*

The total market value and the proportion of each type of capital in the firm's capital structure is given in Table 13.1.

The weighting (w) of each component is, therefore:

- equity shares,

$$w_e = \frac{2\,700\,000}{8\,232\,000} = 0.328$$

- redeemable debt,

$$w_d = \frac{1\,032\,000}{8\,232\,000} = 0.125$$

- irredeemable debt,

$$w_{irr} = \frac{4\,500\,000}{8\,232\,000} = 0.547$$

Note that the sum of the weights is 1.

The weighted average cost of capital (WACC) for this firm is given by:

$$\begin{aligned} \text{WACC} &= w_e \times r_e + w_d \times r_d + w_{irr} \times r_{irr} \\ &= 0.328 \times 0.18 + 0.125 \times 0.15 + 0.547 \times 0.16 \\ &= 0.1653 \; (=16.53\%) \end{aligned}$$

We conclude that this firm would need to pay its investors and lenders an average rate of 16.53%. To its equity investors (who account for 32.8% of the total) it will pay 18%, similarly it will pay the appropriate rate to the other two classes of capital subscriber in their respective proportions. On average, the rate of 16.53% is the minimum rate which investors and lenders would require to provide further finance for the company. In the next chapter we will consider in some detail how a company should use the weighted average cost of capital in its investment decision making.

Table 13.1

Security	Total market value £
Equity	1 000 000 × 270p = 2 700 000
Redeemable debt	12 000 × £86 = 1 032 000
Irredeemable debt	50 000 × £90 = 4 500 000
Total capital value	8 232 000

THE PROBLEM OF OPTIMAL GEARING

The fact that debt finance usually has a lower opportunity cost of capital than equity finance may seem to suggest that a firm should gear itself up as quickly as possible thus reducing its overall cost of capital. However, very high gearing can bring about high levels of financial risk and this would mean that equity investors would require a higher return as compensation for the extra risk they have to bear.

When a company increases its gearing there is a

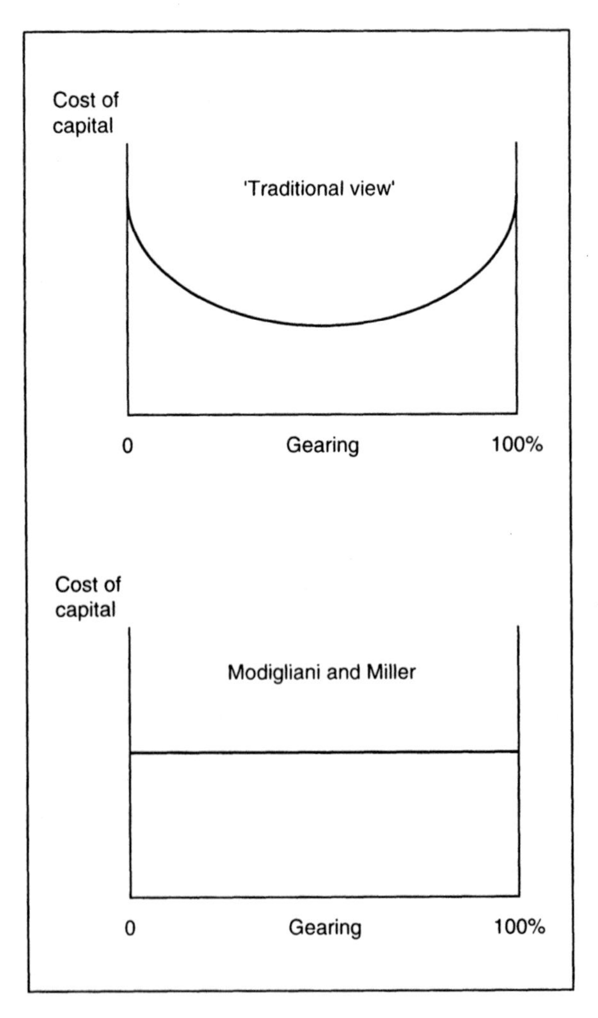

Figure 13.6 The relationship of cost of capital to gearing.

shift in risk from one class of capital investor (the debtholders) to another (the shareholders).

One view, put forward by two theorists in this field, Modigliani and Miller, is that the capital market is perfectly efficient in the way it allocates the appropriate level of return to a given level of risk. In other words the lower return required by debt holders for the lower risk of holding debt is exactly counterbalanced by the extra return required by the equity investors for holding the increased financial risk. In Modigliani and Miller's view, if there are no taxation benefits in holding debt, then a firm's weighted average cost of capital will remain constant as the firm increases its level of gearing. Therefore, there is no optimal level of gearing.

Another view is that the capital market is not perfectly efficient in the way it allocates return to holders of different levels of risk. Up to a certain point increased levels of gearing bring about a reduction in a firm's weighted average cost of capital. However, beyond a certain point, the increased return required by equity investors as compensation for the higher levels of financial risk which accrue with very high gearing, exceed the cost savings associated with holding debt. As a result the net effect is that the weighted average cost of capital will rise again. In Figure 13.6 we show these two views in graphical form.

Because the weighted average cost of capital is inversely related to the market value of a firm it follows, if the traditional view is correct, that alterations in gearing will cause alterations in the value of the firm. In other words, if a level of gearing can be found which minimises a firm's cost of capital then that level of gearing must also be the position at which the firm's total capital) value is maximised. Modigliani and Miller's view, on the other hand, is that the value of a firm is solely dependent upon its business performance and the level of business risk which it faces. Altering the financing of a firm will have no effect upon its valuation.

There has been considerable debate concerning these two views. However, the theoretical argument is still not reconciled one way or the other, although some useful insights into the capital gearing problem have been put forward by proponents of Transactions Cost Economics. In Chapter 3 we pointed out that the structure that firms take on is largely dependent upon the ability of a firm to redeploy its assets from one use to another. Highly specific assets favour unitary structures and less-specialised assets favour market type solutions. We can extend this line of reasoning to consider the type of capital which a firm will find most favourable in any particular circumstances. First, we know that loan capital is most easy to secure upon real physical assets which have a high degree of mobility in use.

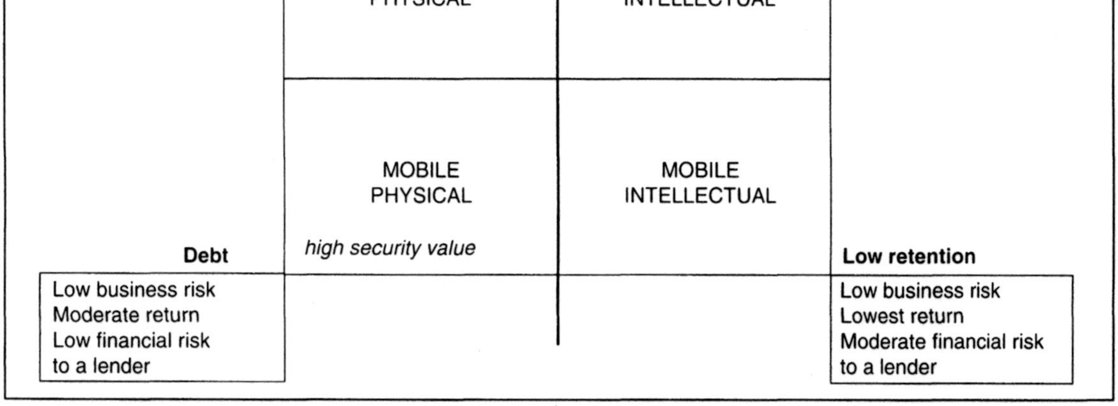

High business risk
High return
High financial risk to a lender

CAPITAL SIDE

REVENUE SIDE

High business risk
Highest return
Highest financial risk to a lender

Equity

low security value

High retention

SPECIFIC PHYSICAL

SPECIFIC INTELLECTUAL

MOBILE PHYSICAL

MOBILE INTELLECTUAL

high security value

Debt

Low retention

Low business risk
Moderate return
Low financial risk to a lender

Low business risk
Lowest return
Moderate financial risk to a lender

Figure 13.7 The corporate funding policy matrix.

Normally, such assets find a ready market in the event of a forced sale. Second, intangible or 'intellectual' assets of a highly specific nature are unlikely to attract cheap debt finance and may not be attractive to equity investment.

In Figure 13.7 we show the typical ways in which business will be able to fund assets of different types. The highly specific physical assets whose use is constrained will need to be funded by ownership capital and will, incidentally, be managed within the context of a unitary, highly controlled organisation. Such assets offer poor security to a lender and would increase their perception of the risks involved. With highly mobile physical assets which can be substituted from one use to another (such as general purpose land and buildings) debt finance is likely to be readily available at relatively cheap cost as such assets tend to have high value as security.

On the other side of the matrix, highly specific intellectual assets tend to take time to create and are normally funded by revenue retention. Where such assets (such as brands and patents) are acquired by a company via takeover then equity financing is likely to be preferred. Mobile intellectual assets have the lowest value in the market place and can normally be expanded or contracted through normal market mechanisms. For most businesses, such assets can also be funded through current rather than capital expenditure.

From a TCE perspective, therefore, the issue of the type of finance which a company should adopt (or indeed will be able to obtain) is largely governed by the type of assets which that company uses in production. The optimal mix of funding will be dependent upon the mix of assets and misfunding can be a significant source of misalignment cost (see Chapter 3) for a business.

CONCLUSION

In this chapter we have examined the different sources of finance which are available to a firm and their relative advantages and disadvantages. In addition, we have demonstrated ways in which a firm can estimate the opportunity cost of the various types of capital it chooses to use in its investment programmes.

This material forms an important background to the financing decisions made by firms and a necessary precursor to our study of investment decision making in the next chapter.

Chapter 14

The Investment Decision

Level M

Contents

*The Nature of Investment Decisions * The Net Present Value (NPV) Rule * Other Methods of Investment Appraisal * Choosing Between Projects when Capital Funds are Scarce * General Problems of Capital Investment*

Summary

In this chapter we consider a number of techniques for analysing the value of new investment projects to a firm. The validity of individual techniques relies upon the rigour and consistency with which they treat the available information and the limitations of the assumptions upon which they are based. We argue that the net present value method, of all the techniques considered in this chapter, is the one which most clearly measures the increment in wealth which will accrue to an individual or firm as a result of the decision to adopt a particular project. However, the net present value method does rest upon a number of assumptions which are unlikely to fully hold in practice. In particular, the NPV method cannot be used to rank projects in a capital rationing situation but must be modified to account for the relative efficiency with which a given project converts capital expenditure into increased wealth. Finally, we make some observations on the general problems which face managers in investment decision making and, especially, to throw some light on the reasons why managers prefer projects which recoup their capital outlay quickly rather than others which do not.

THE NATURE OF INVESTMENT DECISIONS

By now you should be familiar with the idea that investment entails giving up current cash balances in the hope of earning future cash flows. In Chapter 5 we outlined how an individual can convert expected future cash flows into an estimate of current wealth by discounting the future cash flows using his or her 'time value' for cash.

In practice, we can characterise the typical investment decision as a five-stage process:

- an opportunity identification stage, where new production projects are identified following an analysis of some commercial opportunities or the recognition of some production problem;
- a development stage, where the anticipated outcomes from the project are evaluated and cash-flow projections made;
- a selection stage, where a choice is made between those opportunities which are available to the firm;
- an implementation stage, where the capital expenditure is made, any appropriate construction work undertaken and the process commenced;
- a post-project audit stage, where the project's actual performance is monitored and compared with the projected cash flows.

These five stages can be superimposed upon the stages of the investment's overall life which we depict in Figure 14.1.

The process from project evaluation to project wind-down is referred to as the project 'life cycle'. The actual decision concerning the investment of

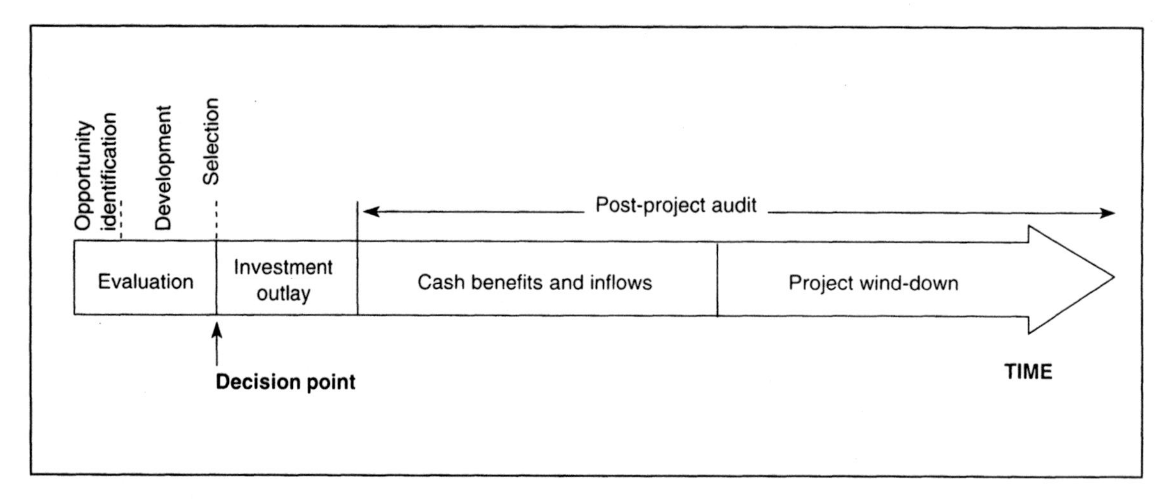

Figure 14.1 Life cycle of an investment project.

capital may well occur quite a way through the evaluation phase of the project and, by this time, a considerable part of the evaluation expenditure may well have been made. This evaluation expenditure will then be a sunk cost with respect to the decision.

In principle, all capital investment projects can be evaluated by deducting the necessary investment outlay from the present value of the future cash flows generated by the project. In Figure 14.2 we show a graph which typifies the types of cash flow profile we can expect from investment.

Investment A is a project of very short-term duration with an immediate return on the capital invested. An example of this type of project would be a short-term construction project where funds are invested in development, design and the purchase of capital equipment which is followed by cash inflows over a relatively short time period (say one to four years). Projects like this are regarded as investment decisions only when the timing effects upon future cash flows are likely to be significant. At the other extreme we have projects such as B in Figure 14.2 where there is a considerable time lag between investment and the return of cash surpluses. Examples of this type of project can be found in the aerospace and energy-supply industries.

However, the majority of investment projects fall between these two extremes. For example, a firm setting up a new plant to produce a widely used chemical compound would expect to earn cash surpluses within a reasonable time of the commissioning of the plant and would hope that those surpluses could be sustained for a substantial period of time before the plant had to be taken out of service.

Generally speaking, the capital investment and operating costs entailed in the production of completely new market products are larger than that required for the production of more mature products. The reasons for this are as follows.

- New products often entail new production technologies which are themselves expensive. However, as competing manufacturers enter the market, the increased demand for the necessary production equipment will bring down its price.
- With completely new products, the technology of production may not be optimised and this means that the new producers have to hear the costs associated with this sub-optimality – costs which will not have to be borne by later entrants to the market.
- Quality control and performance measures may well be difficult to establish with new products where their technology of production is still in its infancy. As a result the new producer will have to bear the additional costs of production which will be incurred.

Considerations such as these have led to a view which is very common among managers in manufacturing industry, that it is often best to be second into a new market. We will examine the validity of this approach in the next chapter.

Below we give some examples of common long-term investment decisions within industry:

- investment in the expansion of current production facilities;
- investment for entrance into new product markets;

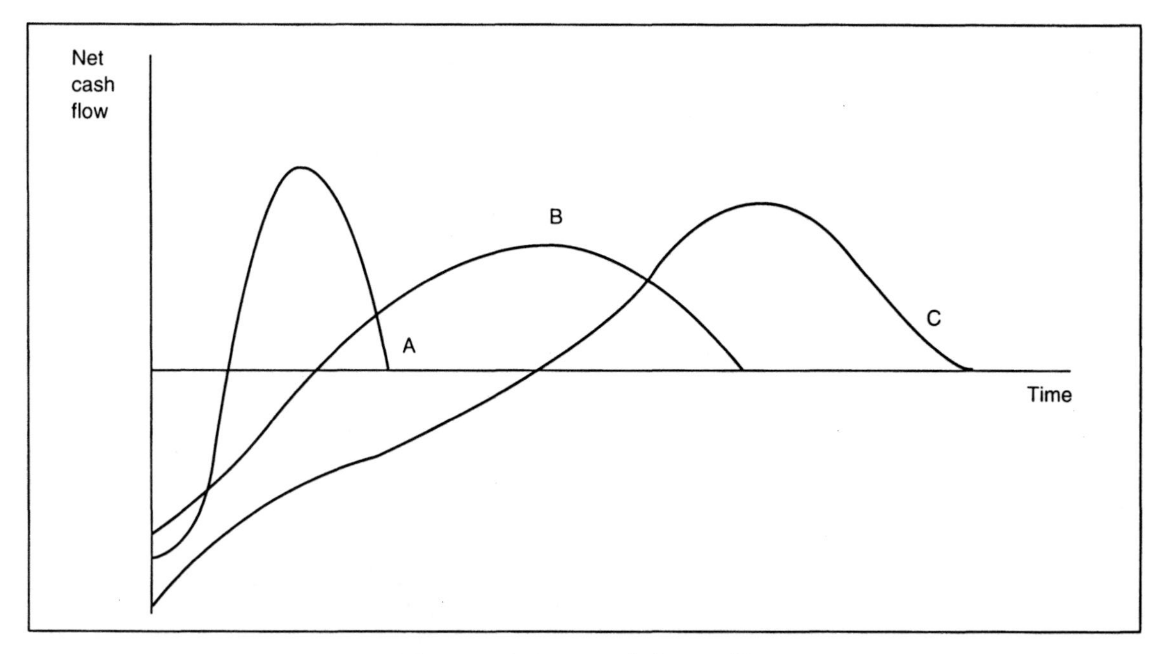

Figure 14.2 Project cash flow profiles.

- investment in the maintenance and replacement of existing plant and machinery;
- investment in long-term advertising campaigns and in research and development;
- investment in administrative facilities;
- investment in 'human capital' through training, education, etc.

The area of investment decision-making is particularly complex in that choices have to be made on the basis of projected outcomes which may be very uncertain. It is also true that in highly competitive (technologically and economically) industrial environments worthwhile investment projects are very hard to find. Naturally, if such projects were easy to find there would be far fewer company failures than there are! In such highly competitive environments most projects will have net present values of approximately zero as firms compete away their technological and economic advantages and hence their potential for earning excess profits.

THE NET PRESENT VALUE (NPV) RULE

In Chapter 5 we introduced the concept of present value when examining cash dynamics over time. In ideal market conditions, the net present value (NPV) for a project gives us important information about the benefit of that project to the decision maker. These ideal conditions are:

- A single market rate of interest exists for both borrowing and lending.
- An individual can borrow or lend any amount of money at the market rate of interest.
- There are no transaction costs or taxes, i.e. the market is 'frictionless'.
- There is perfect certainty concerning future cash flows.

If these conditions hold, the NPV of the future cash flows which accrue to an individual represent an absolute increase in wealth for immediate consumption. Consider a simple project spanning three year which entails an investment of £10 000 followed by net cash inflows of £5000, £4000 and £3000 in each of the subsequent three years. In Table 14.1 we show the NPV of this project which is positive.

The value of £440 represents the actual increase in disposable cash to the investor which is realisable immediately by borrowing, *providing* the capital market conditions outlined above exist. It would be possible for the investor to borrow the investment of £10 000 plus the NPV of the project and allow the subsequent project cash flows to repay his or her borrowing.

As the account schedule in Table 14.2 shows, the investor can borrow £10 440 for the purpose of the

Table 14.1

Rate of Interest	0.08			
Period	0	1	2	3
Project cash flow	(10 000)	5000	4000	3000
Year 1 DCF	4 630 ←			
Year 2 DCF	3 429 ←			
Year 3 DCF	2 381 ←			
Net present value	440			

Table 14.2

	Cash flows
Original investment plus NPV	(10 440)
First year interest	(835)
Outstanding at the end of year 1	(11 276)
Repayment from project	5 000
Balance to year 2	(6 276)
Second year interest	(502)
Outstanding at the end of year	(6 778)
Repayment from project	4 000
Balance to year 3	(2 778)
Third year interest	(222)
Outstanding at the end of year 3	(3 000)
Repayment from project	3 000
Balance at project end	0

investment (£10 000) and immediate consumption (£440) even before the project commences earning cash flows. This gives rise to two important principles.

(i) In a perfect world the issue of the valuation of a project and the consequential decision to invest is separated from the decision about how to finance the project. In this case the decision maker could have financed the project from his or her own resources, retained earnings or borrowing.
(ii) The wealth of the investor rises as soon as a positive NPV project is identified and the decision to proceed is made.

In the real world, the first principle is unlikely to hold, although it does give us limiting case behaviour. The second principle will hold, although there may be considerable uncertainty about the actual magnitude of the NPV.

With corporate investment decision making, additional issues arise. As firms are made up of a diverse set of interest groups, it may well not be appropriate to extend the model for individual decision making directly into the corporate environment. However, even assuming a situation where the sole objective of a firm is to maximise the wealth of its investors, there are a number of difficulties involved in using simple present value techniques.

Initially, we will examine the usefulness and difficulties of NPV techniques, assuming the objective of shareholder supremacy. Later, we will discuss the wider problems associated with the NPV model when we make more realistic assumptions about the firm.

The NPV model states that for an individual investor a project will only be acceptable if it increases his or her current wealth, i.e.

$$W_f - W_o \geq 0$$

- W_f is the present value of the future receivable net cash flows generated by the investment. As we have stated above, the present value of these future cash flows represents the increment of current wealth which accrues to the investor once the investment's potential is recognised.
- W_o is the current wealth given up to undertake the investment. We sometimes talk about this amount as the investment 'outlay'.

For example, an investment entailing an outlay of £25 000 followed by net cash returns of £12 500 over three years could be evaluated as shown in

Table 14.3. We will assume a minimum rate of return required by the investor of 10% per annum.

This project increases the investor's wealth by the NPV of £6086. Any project such as this with a positive NPV would be worthwhile to the investor.

The main technical problem to be resolved, before we can apply this technique directly to a firm's investment decisions, concerns the nature of the discount rate. Because a firm may have a large number of shareholders, the discount rate of interest must offer a rate of return which will satisfy the minimum return requirements of all those individuals. The discount rate, therefore, should be equivalent to the average minimum rate for the firm's investors. In the light of our discussion in the last chapter, this average rate is the same as the opportunity cost of equity capital.

Accordingly, the opportunity cost of equity capital will be the appropriate discount rate for a pure equity firm. In a geared firm, however, the discount rate should offer a return which will satisfy all types of investor (equity and debt) within the firm. Therefore, the weighted average cost of capital will be the appropriate discount rate for such a firm.

If the market value of a firm is a perfect reflection of the total wealth invested within the firm then, given perfect access to information on the part of investors, the acceptance of a new project by the firm's management should bring about an increase in the market value of the firm equal to the project's NPV. In this situation the secondary capital market will fulfil the role of a perfect money market bank as the investor can realise the increase in wealth following the project's acceptance by judicious selling of his or her investment for cash. This assumes, of course, that the stock market is, itself, competitively efficient.

As you can see, the validity of the NPV model as a measure of project worth is hedged around by a number of assumptions which we would not expect to be realised in reality. Over the last 30 years, considerable theoretical developments have been made in the area of investment appraisal although the practical application of these developments has been very difficult. However, discounting methods based upon the simple NPV model described above are widely used in industry. But the limitations of these methods and the restrictiveness of the underlying assumptions do not seem to be widely recognised.

In order to discuss the problems of investment appraisal we will set up an example which we will use as the basis of our discussion throughout the remainder of this chapter. This is an extensive problem employing a number of data manipulation techniques.

EXAMPLE

Martinez plc is considering the construction of a chemical plant to produce a staple product used widely in the chemical industry, called alpha-nievene. The production process is continuous and the expected life of the plant is five years. The plant capacity will be 65 000 tons in the first year, but this will rise by 10% per annum over the following two years before levelling off at a constant capacity for the remainder of the plant's life.

The selling price of alpha-nievene is currently £100 per ton, and this is expected to rise by 8% per

Table 14.3

	t_0	t_1	t_2	t_3
Cash inflows		12 500	12 500	12 500
Discount factors		1/1.1	$1/(1.1)^2$	$1/(1.1)^3$
Present value				
t_1	11 364 ←			
t_2	10 331 ←			
t_3	9 391 ←			
Present value of cash inflows, W_f =	31 086			
Cash outlay, W_o =	25000			
Net present value =	6 086			

annum over the plant's life. The total market for the product currently stands at 550 000 tons per annum, which is rising by 5% per annum. Martinez expects to hold its market share of 10% into the indefinite future. The raw material cost is £30 per ton bought in, and the expected conversion ratio is 0.7 tons of finished chemical for every ton of raw material input. Raw-material costs are expected to rise at a rate of 12% per annum over the life of the project.

While output is rising, labour costs are expected to be directly related to output. The wage rate is currently £25 per ton of finished product and this rate is expected to increase by 6% per annum. Half of the labour force committed to this project are on the permanent establishment and will have to be replaced by direct recruitment. Half of these permanent staff have special skills and their redeployment from other activities within the firm will bring about a loss of £75 000 contribution in the first year. The newly recruited staff should have acquired the necessary skills after their first year of employment. The remainder of the staff necessary for this project will be recruited on short-term contracts.

Current energy costs for the chemical process are £6 per ton produced and are expected to rise by 5% per annum.

The firm depreciates its plant and equipment on a straightline basis over its expected life. Development and pilot plant experimentation have already incurred costs of £80 000. The capital cost of the plant is £6 250 000 which will be spent immediately and the plant will be commissioned and fully operational for the current production year. The plant will be scrapped and dismantled at the end of its life at a net cost of £30 000. All cash flows, except the immediate capital outlay, can be assumed to be incurred at the end of the year in question.

Martinez would like to plan on the basis of full capacity operation each year with any final stock balances being sold in the sixth year. Martinez has an opportunity cost of capital of 10% per annum. The Retail Price Index is expected to continue growing at 4% per annum over the indefinite future.

This example is primarily concerned with the problem of projecting cash flows and the correct application of the various investment appraisal methods. Our first task is to project the cash flows which occur beyond the decision point ignoring any costs and revenues which do not alter with the decision.

Each item of information given above was expressed in terms of current quantities or prices.

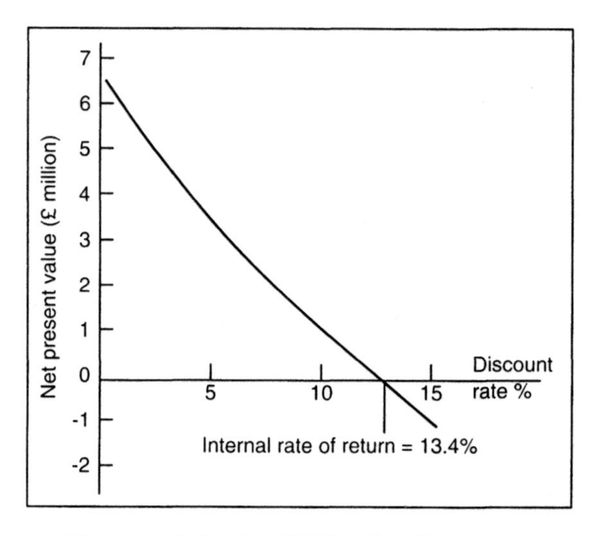

Figure 14.3 Graph of NPV against discount rate.

Using the expected rates of change for each item the future cash flows can be estimated as shown in Figure 14.3.

Plant capacity has been set at 65 000 tons for the first year of operation and then expanded by 10% in each of the following two years:

Year t_1: = 65 000 tons
Year t_2: $65\ 000 \times 1.1$ = 71 500 tons
Year t_3: $65\ 000 \times (1.1^2)$ = 78 650 tons

In years t_4 and t_5 the capacity will remain constant at 78 650 tons. Martinez's share of the annual demand for alpha-nievene is expected to be 10% of a total market which is rising by 5% per annum. The demand in the first three years of the project can be estimated as follows:

Year t_1: $550\ 000 \times 0.1$ = 55 000 tons
Year t_2: $550\ 000 \times 0.1 \times 1.05$ = 57 750 tons
Year t_3: $550\ 000 \times 0.1 \times (1.05^2)$ = 60 638 tons

Demand for each of the remaining years of the project is calculated in a similar fashion.

The firm's actual sales of alpha-nievene in each of the five years of the project will be the lower of demand and plant capacity. The total production throughout the life of the project is expected to be 372 450 tons, while the actual sales will be 303 910 (see Table 14.4). Given that management operate at full capacity throughout the life of the project and clear the remaining stocks of chemical in the sixth year, we can project a figure for sales of 68 540 tons for that year.

The sale price per ton has been compounded from its current price of £100 per ton at the rate of

8% per annum. This figure is then multiplied by the projected sales figure to obtain an estimate of total revenue. The same procedure has been applied to the materials cost per ton, except that with materials a yield ratio of 0.7 must be applied to the material price and the resultant figure multiplied by the estimated production rather than sales. Therefore, in the first year material costs are given by:

$$\text{Materials } t_1 = £30/0.7 \times 1.12 \times 65\ 000$$
$$= £3\ 120\ 000$$

A yield ratio of 0.7 means that 0.7 tons of alpha-nievene are produced from one ton of raw material input. Therefore, we divide the material cost per ton by 0.7 in order to determine the cost of the materials required to produce one ton of final product.

Labour costs are calculated on the basis of expected production although in the first year we also include the internal opportunity cost incurred through redeployment of labour with special skills. Because the labour force on the permanent establishment must be replaced the cost of their replacement is an opportunity cost of production. We assume that the rate of £25 per ton of finished product is also appropriate for the replacement labour.

Current energy costs are increased by the specified rate of 5% per annum.

As we noted in Chapter 6, depreciation is not a true economic cost because it is independent of any decision concerning the machinery to which it relates. However, the cost of scrapping the plant at the end of its life is a true cash change to the firm brought about by the investment decision. Therefore, the cost of scrapping the plant has been applied as a cost in year t_6 of the project. The costs incurred for project development are sunk costs at the point at which the decision is made. No matter what choice is made, the development costs and pilot plant expenses have already been incurred and cannot be recovered.

In Table 14.4 we deduct the total opportunity costs of production from total revenues in each year, to give a projected estimate of the annual net cash contribution generated by the project. Because the net cash contribution earned each year represents the cash change brought about as a direct consequence of the decision to invest, it represents a direct change in the investors' future anticipated cash stream. Further, all of these cash changes are expressed in the actual money value appropriate for the years in which they arise.

Table 14.4

	0	1	2	3	4	5	6	Total
Plant capacity (tons)		65 000	71 500	78 650	78 650	78 650		372 450
Demand (tons)		55 000	57 750	60 638	63 669	66 853		303 910
Actual sales (tons)		55 000	57 750	60 638	63 669	66 853	68 540	68 540
Price per unit	100	108	117	126	136	147	159	
Total revenue		**5 940 000**	**6 735 960**	**7 638 579**	**8 662 148**	**9 822 876**	**10 876 481**	
Materials cost		3 120 000	3 843 840	4 735 611	5 303 884	5 940 350		
Labour cost								
Internal opportunity cost		75 000						
Wages		1 722 500	2 008 435	2 341 835	2 482 345	2 631 286		
Energy costs		409 500	472 973	546 283	573 597	602 277		
Scrap cost							30 000	
Total cost		**5 327 000**	**6 325 248**	**7 623 729**	**8 359 827**	**9 173 914**	**30 000**	
Net contribution		613 000	410 713	14 849	302 321	648 962	10 846 481	
Discount factor		.9091	.8264	.7513	.6830	.6209	.5645	
Discounted cash flow		557 273	339 432	11 157	206 489	402 955	6 122 556	7 639 861
Capital cost	(6 250 000)							(6 250 000)
Net present value								**1 389 861**
Real cash flows	(6 250 000)	589 423	379 727	13 201	258 425	533 400	8 572 132	
Discounted real cash Flow (at 5.77%)	−6 250 000	557 273	339 432	11 157	206 489	402 955	6 122 556	1 389 861

Table 14.5 Money to real cash flow conversion

Year	Future money cash flow £	Discount at inflation rate	Future money flow expressed in real terms £
1	613 000	$1/(1.04)^1$	589 423
2	410 713	$1/(1.04)^2$	379 727
3	14 849	$1/(1.04)^3$	13 201
4	302 321	$1/(1.04)^4$	258 425
5	648 962	$1/(1.04)^5$	533 400
6	10 846 481	$1/(1.04)^6$	8 572 132

As the project has a positive NPV it is acceptable to the firm.

A second way of handling a series of future net cash flows when prices are rising is to restate them in current prices. In the Martinez example the first cash flow of £613 000 represents money receivable in one year's time. It is possible to calculate the sum of money which, at the purchasing power of time t_0, will buy the same basket of goods as that future cash flow. We can calculate the current purchasing power equivalent or 'real' value of a future cash flow by discounting the future cash sum over the number of years concerned at the rate of inflation.

In Table 14.5 we show the series of real cash flows for all of the years of the project. It should be reasonably easy to see that if we have converted the money cash flows to their equivalent value expressed in current prices, the rate of discount required to calculate the NPV should not be the same as that used to discount the money cash flows. The rate of 10% used previously represents the rate of return required by investors in an inflationary environment. However, if the effect of that inflation has been eliminated from the net cash flows which those investors will receive then the appropriate rate of discount should also have the inflationary element removed.

You should now know that a discount rate of 10% implies that £1 is the present value of £1.10 receivable in one year. However, the real value of £1.10 receivable in one year (i.e. the sum of money which will buy the same basket of goods in current prices as £1.10 will buy in one year's time) is obtained by discounting the £1.10 at the rare of inflation: i.e.

Real equivalent to a money discount rate of 10%

$$= 1.10/1.04$$
$$= 1.0577$$

which is equivalent to 5.77%. Note, the rate is not simply the difference between 10% and 4%!

If we use this real rate of discount to discount the real cash flows, we arrive at exactly the same answer as we had with the money analysis, namely a project NPV of £1 389 861.

We have shown this second method of analysis because many industrial managers do prefer to think, and make projections, in terms of current prices. A study, conducted in the UK in the mid-1970s, suggested that managers in industry attempt to discount real cash flows using discount rates incorporating a return for the inflationary expectations of investors (the money rate). This is wrong, and if discounting procedures are an important component of senior management's decision making, then this mistake will lead to systematic underinvestment in the firms concerned.

At the end of this book we provide a reference to the study cited above (Carsberg and Hope, 1976).

To summarise, we can make the following assertions concerning the benefits of the NPV technique for investment appraisal.

- In a world of perfect money markets the NPV of a project represents the absolute increase in the wealth of the firm's investors.
- On the assumption that a firm's investment capital is not in short supply (which is implicit in the perfection assumptions), the net-present-value rule is extremely easy to apply. All the decision maker need do is determine whether a single number (the project's NPV) is positive or negative.

The NPV rule has given us a simple means of structuring a complex and what appeared to be a very unstructured decision situation. It is for this reason that managers are often prepared to follow this rule, and decision rules like it, even when the assumptions supporting them are not satisfied in practice. However, the reliability of decision-making techniques such as the NPV rule are largely dependent upon the quality of the forecasting procedures employed to estimate the future cash flows. A decision rule can only ever be as good as the forecasted information on which it is used.

OTHER METHODS OF INVESTMENT APPRAISAL

In one respect or other, all of the techniques which we will outline in the following section are deficient when compared with the NPV rule. However, all of the techniques outlined below are popular in practice and we will suggest some reasons why this may be so.

The internal rate-of-return criterion

The internal rate of return of an investment project is that rate of discount which sets the project's NPV to zero. If a project has an outlay A_0 and net cash inflows of A_1, A_2, to A_n, where n is the number of years the project is expected to run, then the internal rate of return is the value of i which satisfies the following equation:

$$-A_0 + \frac{A_1}{(1+i)^1} + \frac{A_2}{(1+i)^2} + \cdots + \frac{A_n}{(1+i)^n} = 0$$

If the value of i which solves this equation is greater than the firm's opportunity cost of capital the project is acceptable.

Given Martinez's problem, the internal rate of return of the project is given by the solution of the following equation:

$$-6\,250\,000 + \frac{613\,000}{(1+i)^1} + \frac{410\,713}{(1+i)^2} + \frac{14\,849}{(1+i)^3} + \frac{302\,321}{(1+i)^4} + \frac{648\,962}{(1+i)^5} + \frac{10\,846\,481}{(1+i)^6} = 0$$

It is difficult to solve such polynomial equations directly, indeed, it is difficult enough even when the length of the project is only two years and a quadratic equation is involved. The easiest way of arriving at a solution to the above equation is to graph the NPVs obtained using a range of discount rates. In Table 14.6 we show the NPVs obtained using a range of discount rates.

Table 14.6

Rate of discount (%)	Net present value £
0	6 586 326
4	4 096 307
8	2 180 511
10	1 389 860
12	690 842
16	(479 009)

Clearly, a zero NPV will be obtained for this project if a discount rate of between 12% and 16% is used. In fact, as Figure 14.3 shows, the internal rate of return is approximately 13.4%. As the internal rate of return for the project is in excess of 10% (the firm's opportunity cost of capital), the project is acceptable.

There are a number of reasons why the internal rate-of-return criterion can give misleading results compared with those obtained using the NPV rule.

First, for a project with an unusual pattern of cash flows (i.e. ones where some of the future cash flows are negative) the internal rate of return may have more than one value. This is because equations such as the six-term discounting formula given above can have a number of solutions. Even an equation for a two-year project which will, therefore, contain a squared term (to give a quadratic equation) can have two answers or 'roots'.

Second, because the internal rate of return measure is a percentage it does not give an absolute measure of a project's worth as does NPV, but rather gives a relative measure of return against outlay. Other things being equal, therefore, internal rate of return will favour projects with small rather than large outlays.

For example, consider the two, mutually exclusive, projects shown in Table 14.7.

Table 14.7

	t_0	t_1	t_2
Project (i) net cash flow	−100 000	70 000	80 000
Project (ii) net cash flow	−20 000	19 000	18 000

The NPV of the two projects (assuming the investor has an opportunity cost of capital of 10% per annum) are as follows:

$$\text{NPV(i)} = -100\,000 + \frac{70\,000}{(1+i)} + \frac{80\,000}{(1+i)^2} = +29\,752$$

and

$$\text{NPV(ii)} = -20\,000 + \frac{19\,000}{(1+i)} + \frac{18\,000}{(1+i)^2} = +12\,148$$

Project (i) has the greater present value and, under the assumptions required for the NPV to be valid, will bring about the greater increase in the investor's wealth. However, the internal rate-of-return criterion ranks project (ii) over project (i):

Project (i) internal rate of return = 31.05%
Project (ii) internal rate of return = 53.60%

Two graphs of NPV against discount rate are shown in Figure 14.4. As we can see, because the investor's cost of capital is less than the interest rate at the crossover point, the internal rate of return and the NPV criteria disagree on the relative ranking of the two projects although both projects are acceptable in themselves.

The NPV rule is regarded as the safest guide in the situation where a choice has to be made between two or more mutually exclusive investment projects.

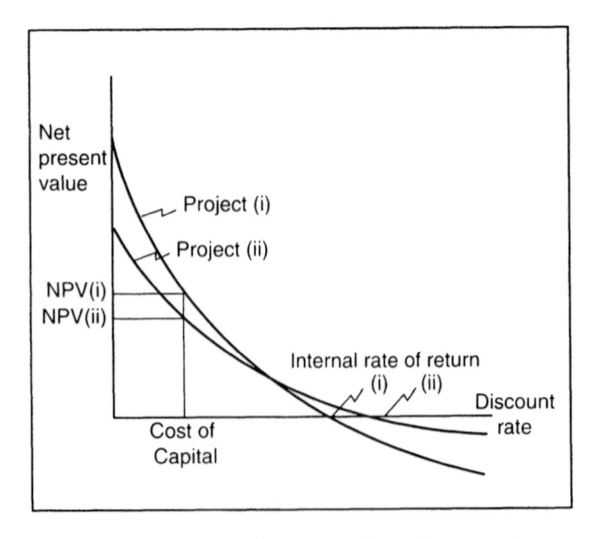

Figure 14.4 NPVs of two mutually exclusive projects.

The payback criterion

With new projects, managers often wish to know how quickly the original cash investment will be repaid by the anticipated future cash flows. In a situation of perfect money markets this question is irrelevant, because in such markets it is assumed that the investing firm has access to an unlimited supply of funds which it can use to fund any project which has a positive NPV. Sadly, the real world is not perfect, and lending institutions often question how quickly an investment can be repaid. Lenders normally attribute a higher degree of risk to long-term projects than they do to short-term projects and will assess the appropriate rate of interest to charge on the loan accordingly. The payback period on any project is, therefore, an important piece of negotiating information.

In Martinez's case we can calculate the payback period on both the money and the discounted cash flows, as shown in Table 14.8.

The above analysis shows that this project will only finish repaying its initial investment in the sixth year when the accumulated stocks are finally sold off. The payback period (for both money and discounted cash) can be calculated exactly as follows. The payback period lies somewhere in the sixth year on both the money and discounted cash-flow basis. Taking the money cash flows first, the proportion of the cash balance outstanding at the end of the fifth year (£4 270 155) to the amount paid back in the sixth year (£10 846 481) gives the payback time in the sixth year:

$$\text{Payback in money cash flows} = 5 + \frac{4\,260\,154}{10\,846\,481}$$

$$= 5.394 \text{ years (5 years 4.71 months)}$$

Similarly

$$\text{Payback in discounted cash flows} = 5 + \frac{4\,732\,695}{6\,122\,556}$$

$$= 5.773 \text{ years (5 years 9.28 months)}$$

The problem with payback based upon the money cash flows is that it ignores the opportunity cost of the capital used to fund the investment and emphasises the benefits of short-term projects with immediate positive initial cash flows. Payback can also be misleading in that it ignores any cash flows (positive or negative) which occur after the payback period irrespective of the magnitude of those later flows.

Table 14.8

Year	Cash flow £	Cumulative cash flow £	Discounted cash flow £	Cumulative discounted cash flow £
0	(6 250 000)	(6 250 000)	(6 250 000)	(6 250 000)
1	613 000	(5 637 000)	557 273	(5 692 727)
2	410 713	(5 226 288)	339 432	(5 353 295)
3	14 849	(5 211 438)	11 157	(5 342 139)
4	302 321	(4 909 117)	206 489	(5 135 649)
5	648 962	(4 260 154)	402 955	(4 732 695)
6	10 846 481	6 586 327	6 122 556	1 389 861

Discounted payback surmounts the principal deficiency of simple money payback in that it does incorporate the opportunity cost capital. However, like the internal rate of return criterion discounted payback may not give the same advice as the NPV rule when a choice has to be made between mutually exclusive projects. This is because the payback criterion ignores the magnitude of any cash flows which arise subsequent to the payback period. For example, consider the projects (i) and (ii) discussed above. Their discounted payback, given a discount rate of 10%, is shown in Table 14.9.

Discounted payback for project (i) =

$$1 + \frac{36\,364}{66\,116} = 1.55 \text{ years}$$

Discounted payback for project (ii) =

$$1 + \frac{2727}{14\,876} = 1.18 \text{ years}$$

As with the internal rate-of-return criterion, discounted payback has favoured the project with the lower NPV. However, with the payback criterion it is not the magnitude of the outlays which is important, but the speed with which they are paid back.

Given the unreliability of the payback criterion, even in its discounted form, one may wonder why it is as widely used as it is. We conclude our discussion of payback by advancing the following reasons for its popularity.

- Lending institutions often place a premium on projects which can be repaid quickly. Indeed, the main clearing banks lend primarily to short- or medium-term borrowers. For this reason, any investing firm which seeks funds from institutions like the banks must be aware of the payback period on its proposed projects.
- Where capital funds are in short supply and the future is highly uncertain, projects promising quick cash returns will be highly favoured by firms.

Table 14.9

	Project (i)			Project (ii)		
Year	Cash flow £	Discounted cash flow £	Cumulative cash flow £	Cash flow £	Discounted cash flow £	Cumulative cash flow £
0	(100 000)	(100 000)	(100 000)	(20 000)	(20 000)	(20 000)
1	70 000	63 636	(36 364)	19 000	17 273	(2 727)
2	80 000	66 116	29 752	18 000	14 876	12 149

- Managers are often judged according to the returns which are generated by the projects they have initiated. This, coupled with the fact that many managers perceive that they may never see the full fruits of their company's long-term investments, means that there will be a bias in managerial choice toward short-payback projects.

The accounting rate of return

It is quite a common practice in investment appraisal to determine the effect a project will have on the company's accounts. Such effects are generally measured by a project's accounting rate of return (ARR). Naturally, because senior managers are judged in terms of their performance, as revealed by their firm's financial accounts, they will pay particular attention to this measure of project viability, even though other criteria may lead to better decision-making overall. We define the accounting rate of return as:

$$\text{ARR} = \frac{\text{average annual profits generated by the project}}{\text{average investment over project life}}$$

Unlike the appraisal methods discussed up until now, the accounting rate of return is based upon measures of profit rather than cash flow. This has the effect of introducing non-cash costs such as depreciation into the calculation. For projects (i) and (ii) above, assuming straight-line depreciation over the investment life, we can calculate the accounting rate of return as follows:

$$\text{ARR} = \frac{\text{average annual cash flows less depreciation}}{\text{average investment in project}}$$

The annual depreciation charge for each project is as follows:

$$\text{Project (i) depreciation} = \frac{100\,000}{2} = £50\,000$$

$$\text{Project (ii) depreciation} = \frac{20\,000}{2} = £10\,000$$

Therefore,

$$\text{ARR(i)} = \frac{((70\,000 - 50\,000) + (80\,000 - 50\,000))/2}{(100\,000 + 0)/2}$$

$$= 0.5 \text{ (50\%) for project (i)}$$

$$\text{ARR(ii)} = \frac{((19\,000 - 10\,000) + (18\,000 - 10\,000))/2}{(20\,000 + 0)/2}$$

$$= 0.85 \text{ (85\%) for project (ii)}$$

Note that the average capital investment is taken by averaging the value of the asset at the beginning and at the end of its life.

Again, we can note the same problem with accounting rate of return as was found by the internal rate-of-return measure discussed earlier. Both methods are measured relative to the investment outlay and this has the effect of favouring the smaller of the two projects. In addition, accounting rate of return suffers from the fact that it ignores the cost of financing the capital investment and includes non-cash costs such as depreciation which are arbitrarily defined.

CHOOSING BETWEEN PROJECTS WHEN CAPITAL FUNDS ARE SCARCE

It may well be that, in any particular period, a firm may experience a short-term shortage of investment funds which restricts the range of investment projects which it can adopt. There may be a number of reasons why such a 'capital rationing' problem may arise. However, such rationing problems can usually be overcome if worthwhile investments are available.

Of course, the problem can be more pronounced for smaller companies, which generally do not have the wide range of financial sources open to larger companies. In this book we will only consider the case where capital is rationed for one period only.

Consider a firm that has a range of projects with the following cash flows and NPVs when discounted at the firm's opportunity cost of capital of 10%.

We will assume that the company can scale down each project by any factor it wishes, although the magnitudes of the cash flows shown are the maximum size of project permissible. We also know that

Table 14.10

Project	Cash flows (£)					Net present value (£)
	t_0	t_1	t_2	t_3	t_4	
A	(46 000)	5000	21 780	26 620	17 855	8741
B	(24 000)	4100	14 250	10 648	7 987	4959
C	(10 500)	5100	4 599	3 250	2 854	2328
D	(13 000)	650	3 980	8 225	6 280	1349

the company is limited to £50 000 of investable funds. Our first reaction may be to accept the project which gives the largest positive NPV – project A in this case – and to invest the remaining £4000 in project B. However, you may remember that in Chapter 8 we considered an analogous problem where a company had a single limiting scarce resource. In Chapter 8 we discovered that contribution could be maximised by choosing products which were most efficient at converting scarce resources into contribution. In this case we are not seeking to maximise contribution *per se*, but rather to maximise NPV. We can achieve this objective by ranking the projects according to the ratio of NPV to unit of capital outlay (Table 14.11). Projects not included in the investment plan are shown in Table 14.12.

Note that only part of project A has been accepted. We calculated the appropriate proportion as follows:

$$\text{Proportion of A accepted} = \frac{\text{cash remaining for the marginal project}}{\text{outlay required for the marginal project}}$$

Table 14.11

Project	NPV Outlay	Outlay £	NPV £
C	2328/10 500 = 0.2217	10 500	2 328
B	3959/24 000 = 0.2066	24 000	4 959
A	8740/46 000 = 0.1900	15 500	2 945
	Outlay =	50 000	
	NPV =		10 232

Table 14.12

Project	NPV/Outlay	Outlay £	NPV £
A	8740/46 000 = 0.1900	30 500	5795
D	1349/13 000 = 0.1037	13 000	1349

The NPV of this proportion of project A is:

Proportion of A's NPV = 0.337 × 8740 = £2945

If an extra £1 of capital is obtained in t_0, the NPV of the firm would rise by £0.19, as this extra £1 would be invested in the marginal project, namely project A. Similarly, if £1 had to be diverted from this set of projects to some other use, then the total NPV would fall by £0.19 per £1 or 19%. The total opportunity cost of the firm's capital is:

Total opportunity cost
= external opportunity cost
+ internal opportunity cost
= 0.10 + 0.19
= 0.29 (29%)

This firm should be prepared to pay up to 29% per annum for the remaining £30 500 required to exhaust project A and then 20.37% (0.10 + 0.1037) for the additional funds required for project D.

GENERAL PROBLEMS OF CAPITAL INVESTMENT

We conclude this chapter with some general remarks about the problems of investment faced by management.

(i) The effectiveness of the methods outlined above depend upon a number of assumptions about how the capital market operates and about the efficiency with which information concerning new projects is transmitted to the market. We have already pointed out that discounting procedures depend upon a number of highly restrictive assumptions about the market. We should also note that the method depends upon a specific notion of the value of the firm; namely the capital-market valuation. This valuation relies upon the market appreciating that a new investment project is being undertaken and agrees with management's projections of the future cash flows.

The difficulty is that management is unlikely to disclose publicly its projections of cash flows for a new project. Further, the company's published accounts provide a picture of what has passed rather than of what is to come. As a result of this, even if the firm's investors appreciated that a new investment was under way, they would not have access to the necessary information to revalue the firm and might, indeed, react adversely if they observed inexplicably negative cash flows in the early years of a project.

These rather pessimistic comments lead us to the conclusion that management will be biased against any investment project which, even for a period, happens to be a drain on a firm's cash flow and reported earnings.

(ii) The general level of uncertainty which managers feel will undoubtedly affect their investment decision-making attitudes. Changes in government macroeconomic policy, for example, can radically influence the environment in which investment decisions are made. Money-market interest rates, as we have observed before, feed through into a company's opportunity cost of capital, and sudden changes in interest rates can turn otherwise viable investments into liabilities. Changes in taxation policy can also have a profound effect on the viability of projects. We have not discussed the impact of taxation on investment appraisal in this book, but it is not hard to see that if government changes the basis upon which tax reliefs and Corporation Tax are calculated, this will disturb even the most carefully laid investment plans.

(iii) Finally, new investment often brings problems with employees, especially if the investment is not designed to increase the firm's productivity as a whole, but rather to get the same level of production with less labour. Union negotiators may well put the point that this is really just an attempt by the owners of capital to appropriate more of the surplus value from labour. In other words, if management views labour just as a cost to the minimised by whatever means available, it is unlikely to meet a favourable response from its employees' representatives. If, on the other hand, the new investment is designed to increase the productivity of the firm overall, the labour negotiators will want to see a fair proportion of the resultant value added being passed on to the labour force in the form of higher wage benefits.

CONCLUSION

In this chapter we have reviewed the methods of investment appraisal available to managers and discussed the advantages and disadvantages attached to each. The net present value rule, for a number of reasons explored in this chapter, has fewer problems associated with it than any of the other methods considered. It is, however, only a tool of decision making in that it allows managers to collect a number of different variables within a single criterion. It does not dispense with the manager's need to be critical and to make wise decisions about the deployment of long-term resources which can commit the firm for a considerable time in the future.

Chapter 15

Product Portfolios and Product Life Cycles

Level E

Contents

Summary

In this chapter we examine the life cycle of products, both in their market and in terms of the positioning of an individual producer. The product life cycle is developed as a four-stage representation of the genesis of a product, its movement through the stages of growth and market maturity terminating in the fourth stage of product decline. We develop the conventional product portfolio approach by reinterpreting product strategy in terms of the Markowitz Portfolio Model explored in Chapter 10 and in terms of an extended product portfolio matrix which includes not only the position of the product in the market place but also the firm's position with respect to that product. Finally, we outline the method of life cycle costing.

THE PRODUCT LIFE CYCLE

A key element in developing business opportunities is understanding the nature of the business product to be sold and the peculiarities of its market place. There is a perception in many popular strategic planning books that strategy should drive products and, indeed, as we have discussed in Chapter 4, so it should. However, as we argued in that chapter, the definition of a business's core capability in terms of those products and services in which it has a true comparative advantage in producing and selling, is the most important step in forming a strategy. To an extent, strategy is inevitably driven by what the business is good at and this encompasses the range of products which it has in its current catalogue as well as those it can create in the future.

The product of a business is its output, and it is important for any business to understand what that output is and how it fits into the market place. We can define products in different ways.

(i) *Technological characteristics.* This would include a full specification of a product's physical and operational characteristics. For an industrial chemical such as benzene, for example, its chemical nature is well known and its specification would be described in terms of its percentage of impurity and the principal components of that impurity on assay. For a piece of consumer electronics, such as a portable CD player, the specification would be much more detailed and subject to numerous patents.

(ii) *Functional capability.* This would define the product in terms of those functions it can perform. Quite physically dissimilar products, such as a book and a CD ROM system, can perform very similar functions. Defining a product this way does not pre-empt the use to which a product will actually be put by consumers – indeed, consumers are very adept at finding new uses for old products.

(iii) *Benefit in use to the consumer.* This is a definition of a product in terms of the use to which a product can be put in the market place. It requires a specification of the benefit which different classes of consumer can derive from a particular product.

When engineers and management accountants talk about products they tend to talk in terms of (i) above. How is the product made, how can its physical characteristics be improved and how much does it cost? Marketing specialists tend to describe products in terms of (iii) above. Neither approach is right, and neither is wrong; they are simply different ways of describing the same thing.

Products usually follow a well-defined life cycle, and this is certainly the case at the consumer end of the production chain. There is some doubt whether primary products and necessary goods will ever complete a life cycle as such. For example the long-playing record has clearly passed into the terminal stage of its life cycle, whereas Marmite will continue to exist and will find a reasonable market for as long as the Marmite Corporation is prepared to produce it.

A product life cycle can be divided into four distinct phases (Figure 15.1).

(i) The product invention and innovation phase can take an extensive period of time if the product is being developed from novel science or technology. It is usually regarded as being complete when a product has survived market and pilot production trials and is in a fit state to enter full production.

(ii) The market acceptance or market development phase is where consumers become aware of the existence of the new product and make their first purchase decisions. Sales will grow on a period-by-period basis following the familiar 'S'-shaped growth curve. The steepness of the curve indicates the priority which consumers place on the acquisition of the product and the rate at which awareness can be stimulated by marketing activity.

(iii) The product maturity phase is where sales reach a constant level on a period-by-period basis. Market awareness of the product is high and is not the overriding issue in marketing terms. There may be a high degree of replacement purchasing being undertaken in this phase, especially where consumer durables are concerned.

(iv) The product decline phase occurs when a new and more efficient means of satisfying the need concerned arises in the market, and the product becomes superseded. As we have suggested above, this stage may never be reached by certain products.

THE LIFE CYCLE PRODUCT MATRIX

It is possible to reconstruct the life cycle as a two-by-two matrix with two cells concerned with the 'flat' phases of the cycle (the innovation and maturity phases) and the other two with the 'change' phases (the market acceptance and decline phases).

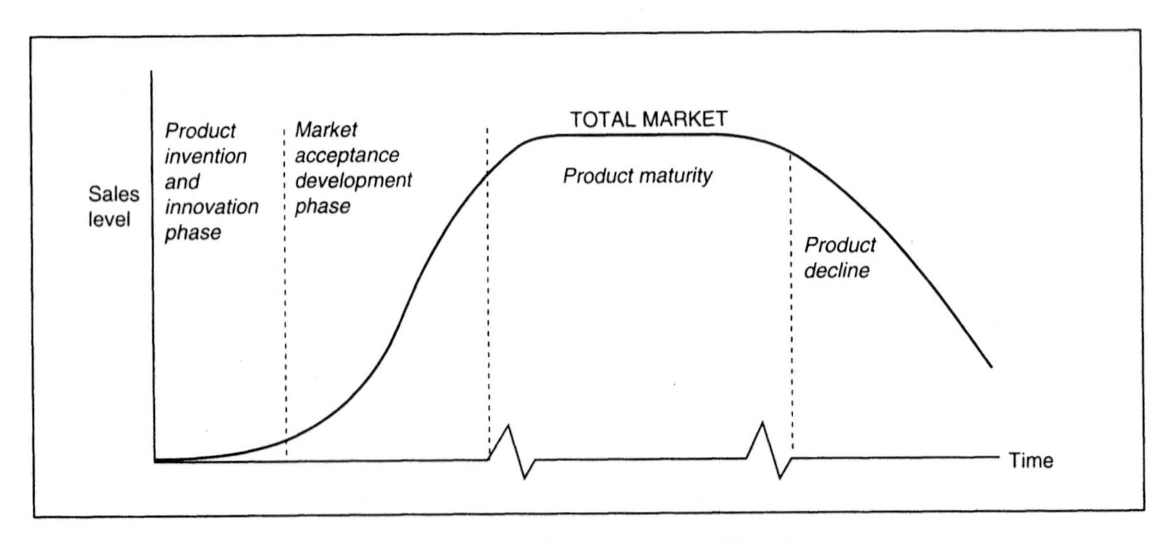

Figure 15.1 The four-phase product life cycle.

This matrix was originally devised by the Boston Consulting Group and has as its two vectors:

- the market share held by a particular firm (usually expressed as a relative value);
- the market growth rate.

In our analysis we choose product contribution as a more meaningful measure of a product's financial performance. In Figure 15.2 we also show contribution per unit as an important measure of the stage a product has reached in its life cycle. Figure 15.2 shows a product matrix. The 'wild-card' product is the new untested idea which a firm is bringing to the market for the first time. As the market innova-

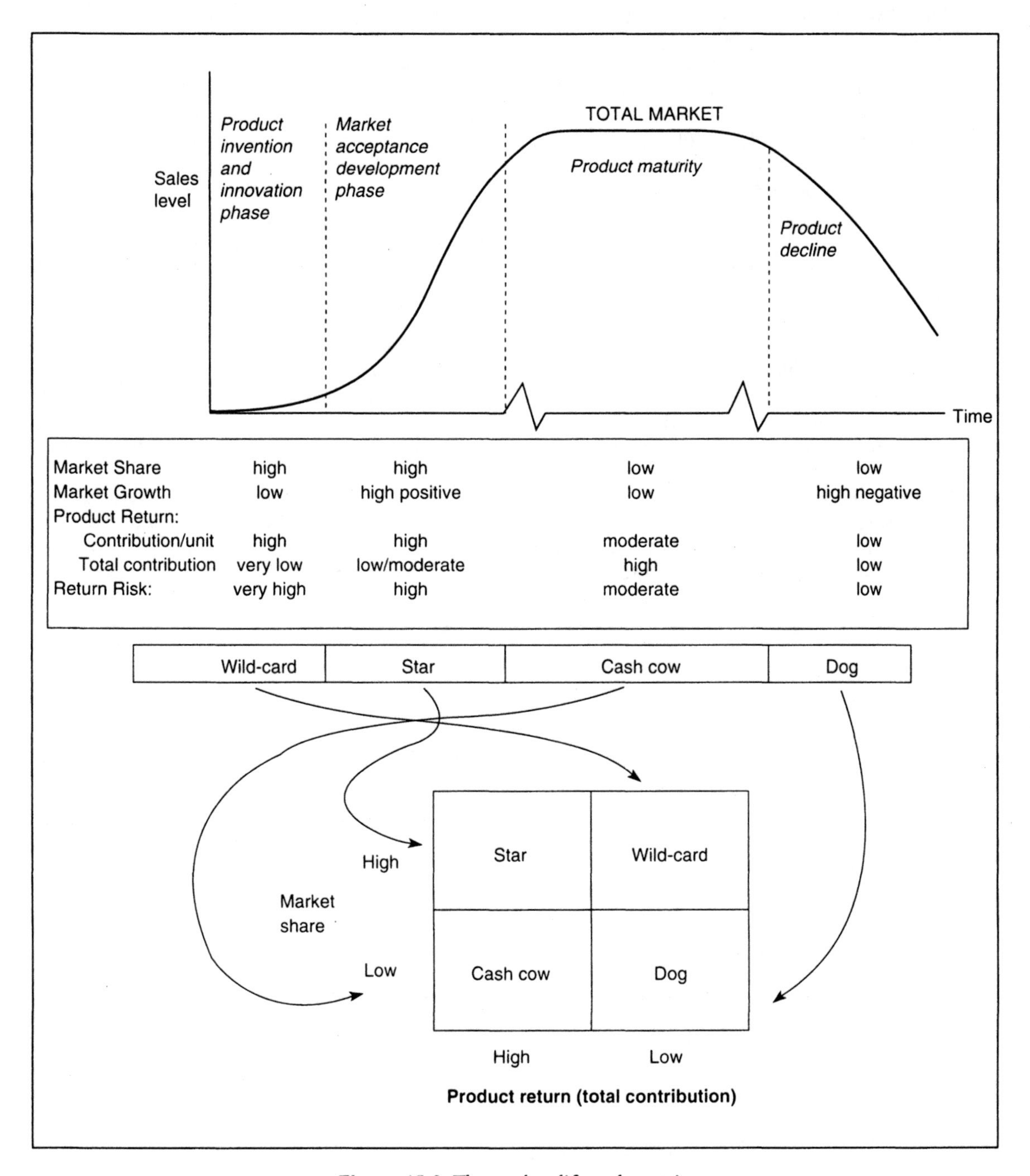

Figure 15.2 The product life cycle matrix.

tor it will hold a 100% market share for that product by definition. During this stage the product should offer a very high contribution per unit sold, but because sales are likely to be close to zero the total contribution to the firm will be very low.

A product in the high positive growth phase of the cycle is referred to as a 'star' and should enjoy very high rates of product return (measured as contribution per unit), although in the early stages the relatively low volume of sales will entail low total contribution. The market maturity phase is that of the 'cash cow' – the product which enjoys stable and perhaps long-running levels of return with a relatively constant market share. If the company has been successful this should be the stage where it generates the bulk of its cash contribution from the product because even though the maturing market demand curve may bring downward price pressure, sales volume will be at its peak.

Finally, the product will enter its terminal stage and enjoys the title of a 'dog'. A dog in the product sense is one which appears to have exhausted its potential to generate return and which can only be further justified through some technological innovation. In Figure 15.3 we show the typical pattern of contribution per unit that we would expect to see over the life cycle of a product.

The conventional office typewriter has turned into a dog product for many office equipment manufacturers, some of whom have attempted to sustain the products life by introducing word-processing characteristics into the basic machine. Similarly, the computer mainframe market appears to be slipping towards the dog status, with many computer hardware manufacturers finding their business under severe pressure. IBM, for example, seriously misread the market in the early 1980s and failed to realise that the mainframe computer, which was the mainstay of their business, would collapse by the end of that decade.

This approach to the analysis of products in markets is often referred to as 'portfolio analysis', although, on first inspection it appears to bear little relationship to the portfolio analysis developed in Chapter 10. The Markowitz approach would interpret product performance in terms of product return and risk of return. The combination of products within a product portfolio will produce the following possibilities.

- Complementary products: those whose sales performances are expected to be closely associated with one another – cameras and photographic film are an obvious example. The returns from such products are likely to be highly positively correlated.
- Counter-cyclical products: those where common systematic factors effect the sales and hence the total return from the two products in contrary ways. We have already mentioned the example of

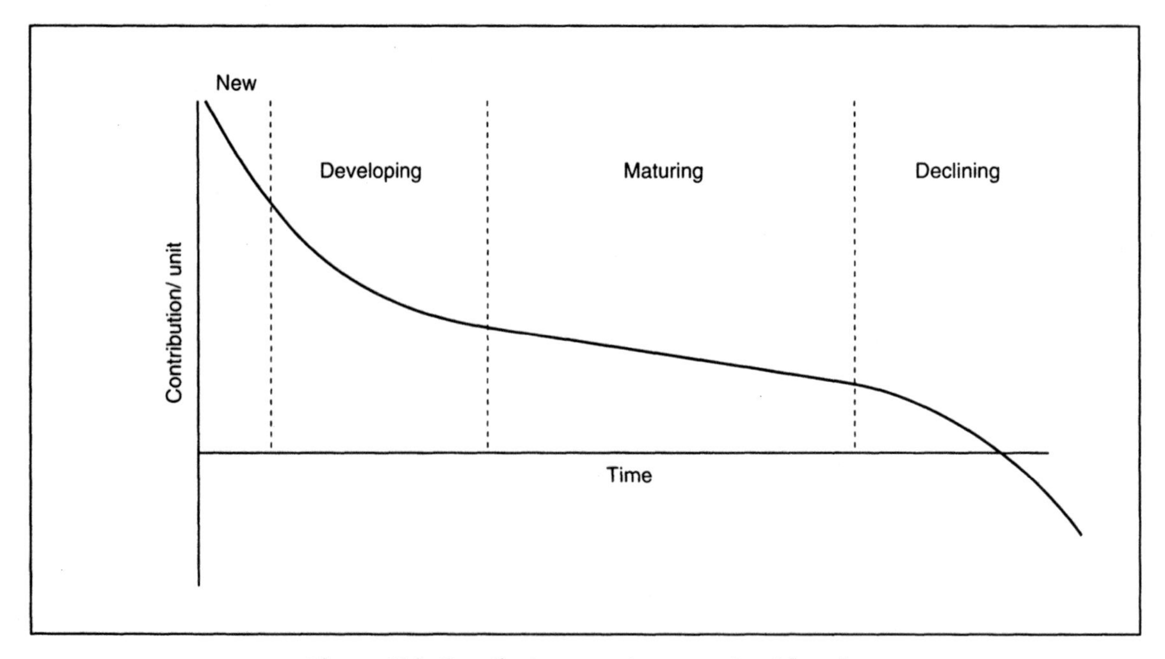

Figure 15.3 Contribution per unit over product life cycle.

British Gas which is exploiting its product in counter-cyclical markets, but essentially any two products which can support one another as one fails the other succeeds, and vice-versa, will qualify.

A business's product range can be described as a portfolio of assets, with each product offering a particular return over a period with a degree of risk associated with that return. The combination will produce an efficient set of products which is that combination of sales during a period which will generate the highest level of return commensurate with a given level of revenue risk.

In Figure 15.4 we identify wild-cards as presenting the highest level of product failure risk and with very low current returns (measured as total contribution from sales). Cash cows are those products which offer high consistent levels of return at relatively low risk and as such will occupy a central position in the product set. Stars lie in between, whilst dogs lie at the opposite extreme as low-return, perhaps risky, products which can, if not dealt with, lead to substantial depletion in business resources.

We know from Markowitz portfolio theory that a firm will attempt to create an actual product portfolio which lies on the extreme of the efficient set. It can achieve this through the following strategy:

- by focusing energy into the development of cash cows and their rigorous maintenance through quality enhancement programmes, cost economy where possible and the exploitation of new markets;
- by seeking counter-cyclical products and counter-cyclical product use markets to exploit the risk reduction effect.

In Figure 15.4 we show the vectors along which particular product combinations will take the firm: complementary products towards the high risk area of the set, counter-cyclical products towards the low risk area.

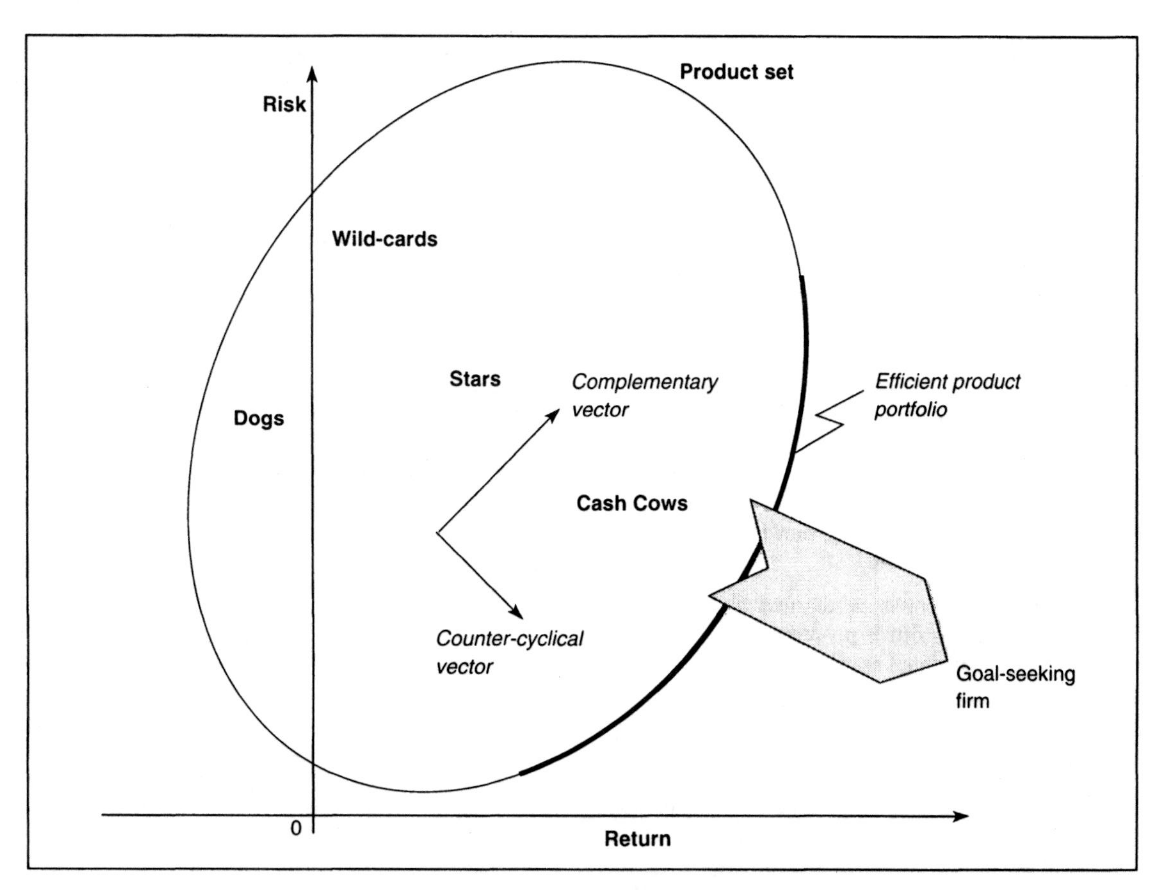

Figure 15.4 The product portfolio as a Markowitz set.

THE EXTENDED PRODUCT PORTFOLIO MATRIX

In the last section we developed the portfolio model to consider the two by two product matrix in the market. The problem with this analysis is that ignores some important issues.

(i) The product cycle faced by a firm is different from the market cycle in normal situations, and product strategy must be formed in recognition of a firm's point of entry into a market.
(ii) There are real problems in defining the concept of the market for a product and hence the notion of market share. By being highly restrictive in defining a market's need, it is possible for a firm to argue that its product is unique in satisfying that need, and hence it holds a 100% market share.

The approach which we will now develop deals with the first problem but leaves the second unresolved. Most approaches to product strategy define market in terms of a particular cluster of needs or problems which a range of products may be able to solve. It is difficult to define market boundaries, but the following pointers may be helpful.

- Is the need differentiable from other needs which consumers may have? Problems of eyesight failure are often associated with ageing, which has a large cluster of associated needs, but which can be separated from those needs and treated by eyeglasses, contact lenses and, in some cases, surgery.
- Is the need one which a substantial number of potential product consumers are prepared to convert into wants (which ultimately drive the purchase decision)? For example, it may be argued that a substantial section of the adult population needs continuing education although a much smaller proportion is prepared to convert that need into a want.
- Is the need capable of being met by a product or combination of products?

The product life cycle as defined above can be complemented by a firm's product cycle signifying its entry into a product market, its phase of sales growth within the market, the establishment of a stable market position and, ultimately, its withdrawal from that market place.

The combination of the market product life cycle and the firm's product cycle creates an enlarged matrix of possibilities, as shown in Figure 15.5.

Each element of the matrix represents position possibilities for a firm with its product in the market place. A sequence of moves from one cell of the matrix to another represents a product strategy. An EN product, for example, is where the firm concerned is leading the product innovation and development and is creating a new market. Sony were in this position when they developed the first Walkman. This is the highest product risk posture for a company to take: the market is new and the product is new, as may be the technology for its fabrication. Of the 16 possible positions, four are what we refer to as the 'main-line' product sequence and they form the diagonal: EN–GD–CM–WX. The main-line sequence can be characterised as follows.

- The firm is leading the development of the market and is in the best position to become the market leader for that product. At the EN stage it would be an early entrant to the market, and may be responsible for the creation of the product and the definition of a unique market. It should be in a position to dominate the market development phase by growing its own productive capacity to match (the GD stage). If all is well, the company should find itself in the position of dominating and continuing to define the market during the maturity (CM) phase; finally, if it reads the market correctly it should be able to make the most efficient withdrawal from that market. Sony, with its Walkman range, has followed the main-line.
- As the first entrant, the firm may be able to create a brand image which defines the market. Indeed, names such as 'Biro' and 'Hoover' have entered the language as product descriptions rather than brand names and in the former case the market has been taken over by Parker, Schaeffer and BIC.
- As the first entrant, the firm may be the first to commit itself to novel technology which may be rapidly superseded. If this happens, the company may face severe cost competition in the latter part of the GD and in the CM and WX phases of the main-line.
- Its posture will tend to be defensive in the latter stages of the main-line as predatorial competitors seek to take market share.

The lower left-hand portion of the matrix represents a set of 'forbidden' possibilities, i.e. possibilities which are logically impossible such as a firm growing, establishing or withdrawing from a market where the product is passing through the market invention and innovation phase. Others of these forbidden possibilities represent the rectification of previous 'mistakes', e.g. withdrawing from a developing or a mature market.

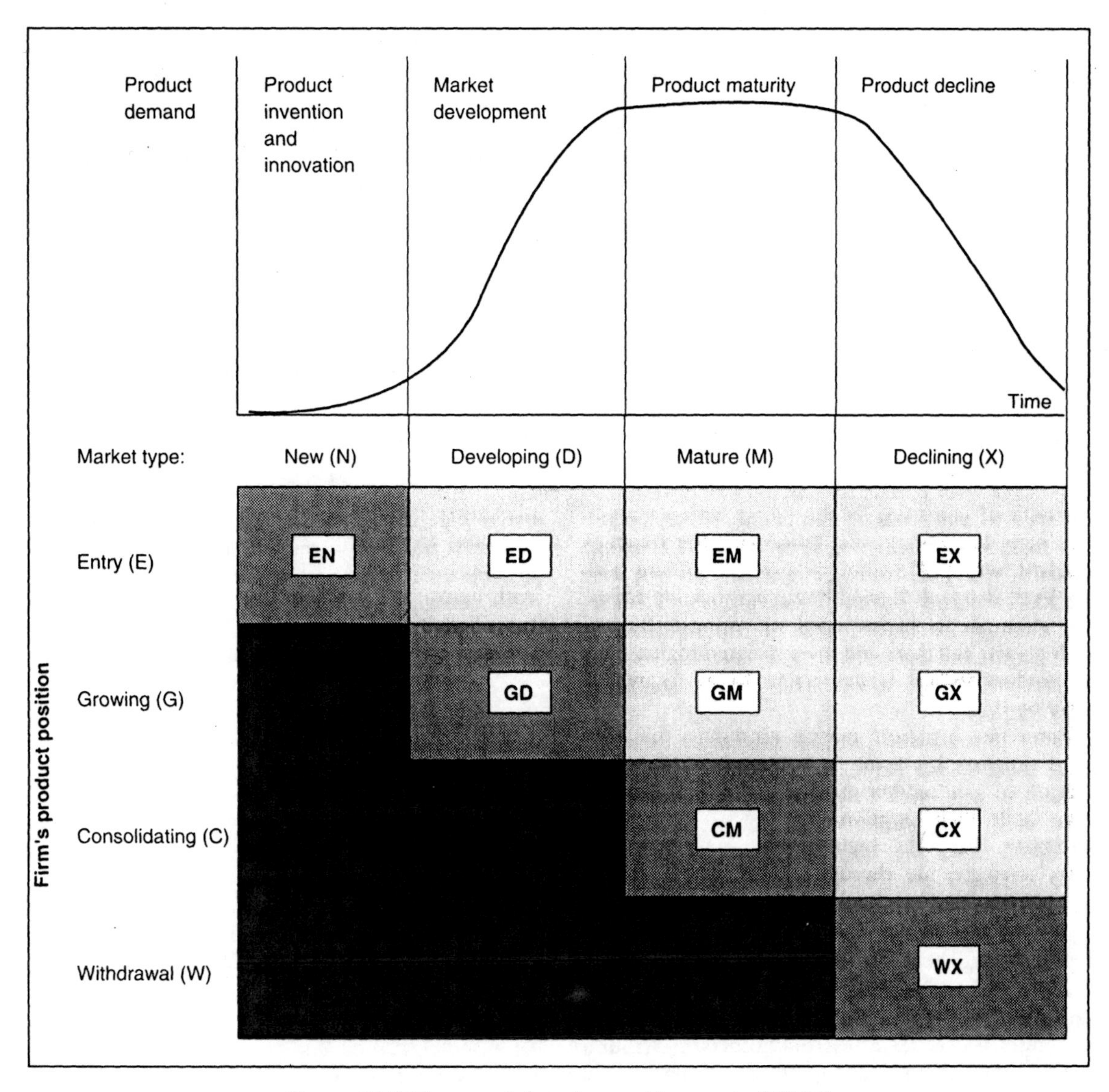

Figure 15.5 The extended product position matrix (EPPM).

The upper right-hand portion of the matrix represents the range of 'second-line' product positions and strategies for a firm, some of which govern entry, others product development and consolidation and others withdrawal.

We have already discussed main-line entry above. Three other entry possibilities are also available to the firm with associated possibilities for growing the product market, as shown in Figure 15.6.

Entry into a developing market represents the classical second entry position. By this stage, the nature of the product and its technological possibilities and characteristics should be established although the main-line entrant may well have secure patents and copyright. In this case the creation of a competing product may well involve the second entrant firm in the creation of a new alternative technology of production with all the risks associated with that approach. The opportunity is also available for the second entrant to devise significant improvements to the product and to use that edge to gain market share from the main-line competitor. However, second entrants at any stage must take an aggressive approach to gaining market share because at that stage of the game the market is 'held' by the main-line entrant. A clear example of

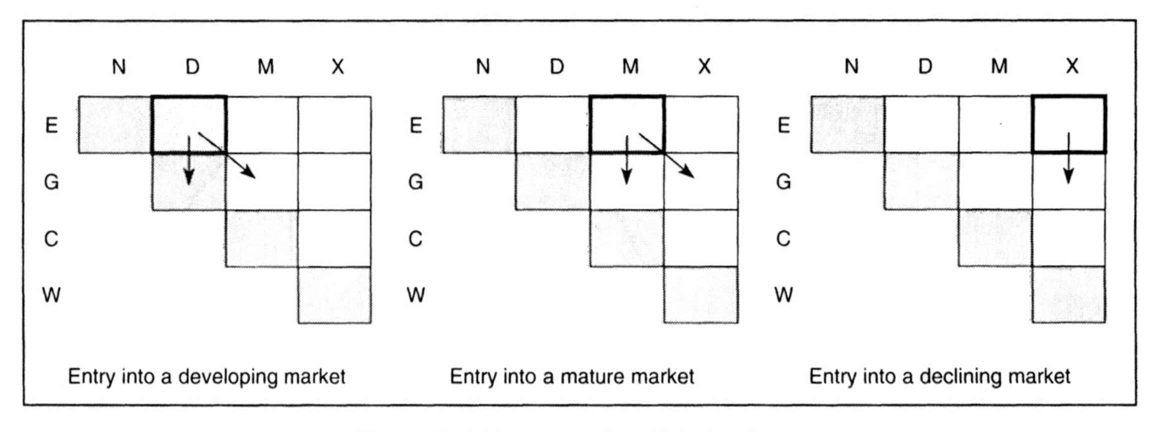

Figure 15.6 Entry strategies within the EPPM.

this type of entry was in the young video market. The main-line entrant was Sony with the Betamax standard, with JVC coming as a second entrant with the VHS standard. Betamax was significantly superior, although its higher level of sophistication in both players and tapes and the associated higher costs of production left it vulnerable to an aggressive entry by JVC.

Entry into a mature market represents the most usual situation for firms. It is, however, the most difficult to gain market share as earlier entrants will have built their position and, to use a military metaphor, hold the high ground. The favourite entry strategies are through either cost leadership through refined technology, or through some significant improvement in quality or performance which the market is able to recognise and accept.

Entry into a declining market is a sophisticated 'end game' strategy for the opportunistic firm which recognises that larger firms are withdrawing from a market and that short-run profit opportunities are available using, perhaps, more mobile assets. It is not a strategy to undertake by mistake, although it is surprising how many businesses do attempt to enter markets when the 'fashion' for a particular product has passed through, and wiser firms have seen the trend and are withdrawing.

For each of these entry positions the firm may choose to seek to enter the main-line by a rapid market assault, and certainly in the early stages of the market life cycle it is easier for a second entrant firm to 'catch up' than in the latter stages of the cycle. However, when entry lead times are of lengthy duration and products can be successfully protected by patents, second entry strategies may have to be much more cautious. Glaxo's development of the ulcer drug 'Zantac' and its successful marketing has led to the company cornering this particular and highly lucrative market. Only now are generic manufacturers beginning to make an entry with derivatives although the market must wait for the Glaxo's patents to expire before there is any prospect of direct competitor entry.

LIFE CYCLE COSTING

Over the life cycle of a product we can predict certain typical patterns of cost as a firm moves from entry to eventual withdrawal. Life cycle costing considers costs not on a period-by-period basis, but over the whole product life, however long that may be. It is the direct corollary of life cycle budgeting which we consider in Chapter 25.

Life cycle costing has the following characteristics.

- It takes into account all costs committed to a given product over its whole life. It does not include business committed costs which are not directly related to the product manufacturing decision. However, a life cycle costing would include R&D expenditure, capital investment and maintenance, quality costs, product marketing costs and all the activity associated costs such as direct labour, materials and energy costs.
- Final product profitability or the contribution the product has made to a firm's committed business costs cannot be determined until the product completes its full life cycle. During the progress of the life cycle all that can be measured is variation from the predetermined life cycle budget.
- The life cycle budget will be dependent upon the product position and strategy adopted through the

EPPM. A first entrant to a market following the main-line product sequence is likely to show a different pattern of life cycle cost to a later entrant. Similarly, the technology chosen will have a profound affect on life cycle costs.

- Life cycle costs will include the benefits of 'learning' in production. Learning effects can be summarised by a typical 'experience' curve (Figure 15.7).

During the four stages of the life cycle we can expect the following costs to be dominant.

(i) Invention and innovation:
    research and development;
    design;
    market research and testing;
    pilot plant costs or prototype fabrication costs;
    capital expenditure costs on production facility.

(ii) Market development:
    marketing costs – awareness development;
    continuing product development;
    quality checking;
    production materials and components;
    production labour;
    downtime costs (plant maintenance, work-in-progress holding costs etc.).

(iii) Product maturity:
    production materials and components;
    production labour;
    quality control;
    product improvement;
    downtime costs (plant maintenance, work-in-progress holding costs etc.).

(iv) Product decline:
    production materials and components;
    production labour;
    quality control;
    product improvement;
    downtime costs (plant maintenance, work-in- progress holding costs etc.);
    decommissioning costs.

The exact life cycle profile of cost is dependent upon the point at which the company enters into the market and its strategy for building and holding market position. As we indicated in the previous section, first entrants tend to suffer relatively high capital costs compared to later entrants if new emergent technology is required to fabricate the product. In addition, marketing costs will tend to be higher for the first entrant compared with followers, given that the problem of building product awareness will principally fall to that supplier.

Unlike conventional period accrued costs, life cycle costs fully reveal the production costs actually incurred by a product over its life time. Comparing product by product, it is easy to see the effect of choosing different technology, various quality costs and other costs which tend to be hidden or distorted by the conventional approach.

CONCLUSION

In this chapter we have explored the problems of formulating product strategies. In our view, products should be analysed in a portfolio context where a number of interrelated issues can be considered. We have extended the portfolio model in

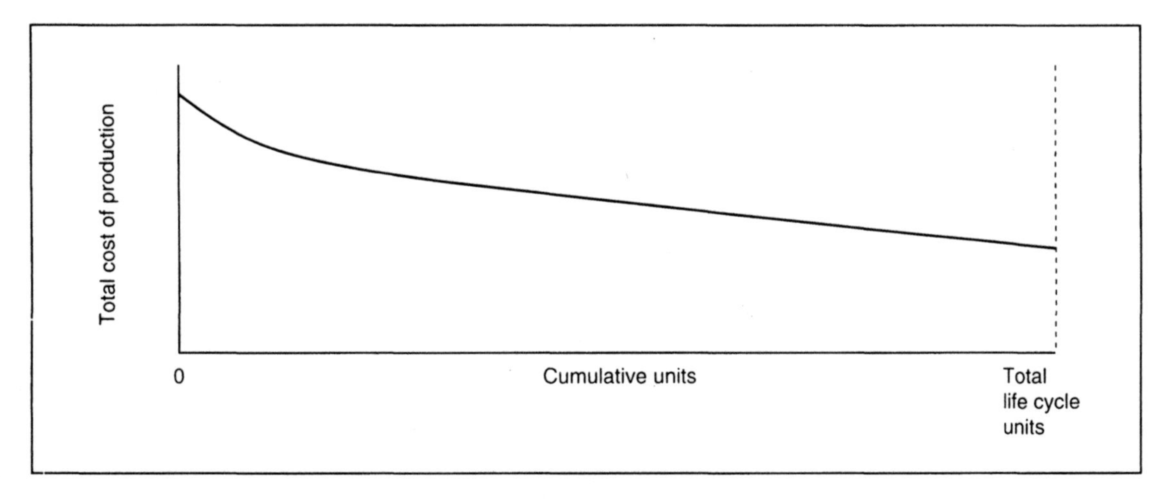

Figure 15.7 The experience cost curve.

Chapter 10 to the firm's product range and suggested that the risk of a product can have a covariance property which can be exploited. We then developed an extended product portfolio model using our 'extended product position matrix' and proposed a number of contingent product development strategies which can be followed, depending upon the stage at which a firm enters a given market. Finally we have reviewed some of the basic ideas in life cycle costing.

Chapter 16

Valuing the Firm and Building Value

Level M

Contents

Summary

In this chapter we discuss the concept of firm value and how, in principle a value can be derived for a company as a whole and for an individual share. We look at value in two ways: (i) the value of a company in terms of the economic benefits which it can generate (which is measured in terms of the net cash flows it can produce over its lifetime) and (ii) the market value of its assets. Our approach to valuation stresses what needs to be done to raise the value of the business and, in particular, that value increases will only be realised if projects (whether in terms of capital investment or in the exploitation of markets) generate positive net present values at the company's cost of capital. We use the approach to valuation in this chapter to develop a simple share valuation model which can be used to translate the important characteristics of a company's performance into a share price.

INTRODUCTION

When valuing a business, certain questions arise.

(i) What do we mean by 'value'?
(ii) Which implies value to who?
(iii) Even if we agree on what 'value' means, how do we measure it?

In this chapter we will discuss value in terms of value to the owner group, i.e. the value of the business, assuming that all prior claims on the business have been discharged. In many respects, valuing a business for the owner group is the simplest and least conjectural way of doing it, as the owners' claim is a 'residual claim', i.e. a claim after all other claims have been recovered. We will also only consider the financial aspects of valuation in this chapter. The social value of a business can be very important, but such valuation takes us out of the realms of finance and into political and social judgement, which is a much more skilled business than this book presumes to teach.

THE CONCEPT OF VALUE

There is no agreement as to what constitutes 'the value' of a business – even to its shareholders. Ultimately, the only true value of a business, in the financial sense is how much it would realise if sold at the best price in the market place. Note, however, that this is not just the product of the share price and the number of shares in issue. The current share price is determined by the transaction between a buyer and seller in the market place who are dealing in marginal quantities of the shares concerned. In the context of a publicly quoted company subject to a takeover bid, the predator would have to offer existing shareholders a price in excess of their current share price to induce them to sell and thus, at any point in time, it is likely that the current share price would be less than the bid price. Conversely, if an investor wished to sell a large number of shares in the market it is unlikely that he or she would be able to realise the published share price as unloading a non-marginal quantity would significantly increase the supply and hence reduce the market price.

We should think about the value of a business in three ways:

(i) the market value of the business if it was sold as a whole and as a going concern (V_g);
(ii) the market value of the business if the assets were broken up and sold (V_r);
(iii) the market value of the business's share capital (V_m).

These three values are unlikely to be the same. However, we can make some observations about the relationship between these values. For convenience we will regard each as a total market value, which in the case of (iii) means that:

$$V_m = \text{price per share} \times \text{number of shares issued}$$

The normal case for a business is that:

$V_g > V_m > V_r$ (where > mean 'greater than')

Clearly, if $V_r > V_g$ then there would be no point in operating the business as a going concern. It would make sense for the owners to close down the business and sell their assets. The premium of the going concern value over the value of the assets if broken up and sold we call the business 'value added'. In other words, it is the value added to the business by maintaining and valuing the assets of the business in combination and as a going, concern rather than doing the next best alternative which is to sell them off on the open market, i.e.

$$\text{Business value added } (\Delta V_g) = V_g - V_r$$

Similarly, if $V_r > V_m$ it would be to the benefit of the shareholders for the company's assets to be sold individually, and hence they would realise an immediate profit.

In order to understand how to build value we need to understand the determinants of value.

GOING CONCERN VALUATION

In financial terms, the value of a business is equal to the present value of the net cash generated for the benefit of shareholders by that business over its lifetime. So,

$$V_g = \frac{C_1}{(1+r)^1} + \frac{C_2}{(1+r)^2} + \frac{C_3}{(1+r)^3} \cdots \infty \qquad \text{(i)}$$

where:

C_1, C_2, C_3, etc. are the annual net cash flows generated for and in principle available for distribution to the shareholders by the business operating as a going concern;
r is the cost of equity capital adjusted for the perceived risk attaching to the cash flows;
∞ is the sign indicating that a perpetual series of cash flows is anticipated (otherwise we would not be assuming a going concern).

This model is an 'ex-div' valuation model in that it assumes that a cash distribution to investors has just been made. A 'cum div' valuation model would be as follows:

$$V_{g(c)} = C_0 + \frac{C_1}{(1+r)^1} + \frac{C_2}{(1+r)^2} + \frac{C_3}{(1+r)^3} \cdots \infty$$

which implies that the immediate cash flow C_0 is just about to be received compared with the 'ex-div' model which would assume that the cash flow has just *been* received.

We can easily see the conditions under which an increase in the going concern value of a business will occur. Consider an investment project to be funded by the issue of new shares to the value A_0 which will generate additional *incremental* cash flows to the owners over three years of A_1, A_2, and A_3 respectively. The going concern value of the firm after acceptance of the project would be V'_g:

$$V'_g =$$

$$-A_0 + \frac{C_1 + A_1}{(1+r)^1} + \frac{C_2 + A_2}{(1+r)^2} + \frac{C_3 + A_3}{(1+r)^3} + \frac{C_4}{(1+r)^4} \cdots \infty$$

Separating out like terms:

$$V'_g = -A_0 + \frac{A_1}{(1+r)^1} + \frac{A_2}{(1+r)^2} + \frac{A_3}{(1+r)^3}$$

$$+ \frac{C_1}{(1+r)^1} + \frac{C_2}{(1+r)^2} + \frac{C_3}{(1+r)^3} + \frac{C_4}{(1+r)^4} \cdots \infty$$

Substituting the original ex-div value of the firm V_g

$$V_g' = -A_0 + \frac{A_1}{(1+r)^1} + \frac{A_2}{(1+r)^2} + \frac{A_3}{(1+r)^3} + V_g$$

and rearranging:

$$V_g' - V_g = -A_0 + \frac{A_1}{(1+r)^1} + \frac{A_2}{(1+r)^2} + \frac{A_3}{(1+r)^3}$$

You may recognise this formula as the net present value formula developed in Chapter 14 expressed in a slightly different way. What this result shows is that the going concern value of a firm will only increase if a project is accepted whose incremental cash flows, to the owners, have a net present value greater than zero when discounted as the equity cost of capital given their risk. So, in order to build value, a firm's management must seek out projects which offer a positive net present value.

Valuing a firm using the basic valuation model (i) presents a number of problems:

(i) the difficulty of valuing what would amount to an infinite series of future cash flows;
(ii) identifying an appropriate discount rate which reflects the owner's preferences for current as opposed to future cash and the riskiness of the future cash flows.

However, in theory at least, the basic valuation model tells us the true 'economic value' of the business, even though that economic value may be unmeasurable in practice. In practice, the valuation of a whole business is approximated in one or more of the following ways.

Valuing all of the assets at their opportunity cost

This would be a replacement cost value on the open market for a business operating as a going concern. However, there are three profound problems with this approach.

- It may be very difficult to replace certain assets on the open market. Brands, patents, highly specialised staff, the exact location for production etc. may not be reproducible in the market.
- It may be difficult to replace even fixed assets in exactly the same form – a decision would have to be made between valuing at the cost of a new or second-hand asset of exactly the same life expectancy or valuing by replacement with a technologically equivalent asset.
- Assets gain their economic value to a firm in combination, and the sum of a firm's assets will not equal the value of the whole.

Valuing at sale (realisable) value

This will only represent a going concern valuation if the business is being sold as a whole rather than broken up into constituent parts. Realisable value (after taking into account transaction costs) should give the cash value of the business in liquidation which may be an important component of the owner's valuation process, especially if he or she is determining what the minimum value for the business should be at any point in time. However, estimates of realisable value have their problems in the absence of an actual market sale:

- Is the realisable value being estimated for the sale of the whole business or broken up into its constituent assets?
- Is the business being valued on the basis of a 'forced sale' or one conducted under the most favourable selling conditions?
- Are all of the transactions costs (which can count up to 15% of total value) recognised within the valuation process?

Valuing on the basis of historical cost

This is the basis of a conventional balance sheet valuation. We discuss the construction of the balance sheet in the final section of this book. At this point you should simply note the following.

- Historical cost represents the original purchase price of the asset concerned which may be significantly different from their current value, whether estimated on a replacement cost or a realisable value basis.
- Historical cost values consider assets as individual entities rather than as a portfolio of assets in use.
- The conventional balance sheet values do not incorporate a wide range of intangible assets which may be the most substantial assets the company possesses. Such assets are: the brands held by the business, the company's name, the skilled people the company employs, the range of customers the business attracts and the intellectual copyright the company holds on processes and through patents.

Although the historical cost accounts may be of little use in valuing a business, they do have a reasonable role in the practical assessment of value changes. We will consider this issue in the final part of this book.

A SHAREHOLDER VALUATION MODEL

We will assume that we are dealing with shareholders who have no other pecuniary interest in the firm other than their shareholding. In that case, the value of their shareholding will be dependent upon the cash 'stream' which the investors expect to receive from the business over its lifetime. This cash stream will be realised in the form of a series of cash dividends. In valuing those dividends, the firm's investors will need to make a judgement about their future value and rate of growth.

Using the valuation model described before:

$$V_m = \frac{D_1}{(1+r)^1} + \frac{D_2}{(1+r)^2} + \frac{D_3}{(1+r)^3} + \cdots \infty \qquad \text{(ii)}$$

where D_n are the dividends receivable on a share in year n.

Let us assume no growth in dividends over what has just been issued, i.e. $D_1 = D_0$, $D_2 = D_0$ etc., then:

$$V_m = \frac{D_0}{(1+r)^1} + \frac{D_0}{(1+r)^2} + \frac{D_0}{(1+r)^3} + \cdots \infty \qquad \text{(iii)}$$

This formula can be simplified by first multiplying both the left hand and the right hand sides of the equation by $(1+r)$:

$$V_m(1+r) = \frac{D_0(1+r)}{(1+r)^1} + \frac{D_0(1+r)}{(1+r)^2} + \frac{D_0(1+r)}{(1+r)^3} + \cdots \infty$$

Cancelling down terms on the right hand side:

$$V_m(1+r) = D_0 + \frac{D_0}{(1+r)^1} + \frac{D_0}{(1+r)^2} + \frac{D_0}{(1+r)^3} + \cdots \infty$$

and substituting V_m from equation (iii)

$$V_m(1+r) = D_0 + V_m$$

which on rearrangement gives:

$$V_m = \frac{D_0}{r}$$

EXAMPLE

Peelet plc is only expected to maintain its dividend at its current value into the foreseeable future. The last dividend paid net of tax was 8p per share. The estimated rate of return required by Peelet's equity investors is 10% per annum.

Using the no-growth valuation formula we have:

$$V_m = \frac{D_0}{r}$$
$$= 8/0.1$$
$$= 80\text{p}$$

The more realistic situation is where some growth in dividends (g% per annum) is anticipated:

$$D_1 = D_0(1+g),\ D_2 = D_0(1+g)^2 \text{ etc.}$$

then substituting into equation (ii):

$$V_m = \frac{D_0(1+g)^1}{(1+r)^1} + \frac{D_0(1+g)^2}{(1+r)^2} + \frac{D_0(1+g)^3}{(1+r)^3} + \cdots \infty \qquad \text{(iv)}$$

Multiplying both sides of the equation throughout by $(1+r)$ and dividing by $(1+g)$ we have:

$$V_m \frac{(1+r)}{(1+g)} = \frac{D_0(1+g)^1(1+r)}{(1+r)^1(1+g)} + \frac{D_0(1+g)^2(1+r)}{(1+r)^2(1+g)} + \frac{D_0(1+g)^3(1+r)}{(1+r)^3(1+g)} + \cdots \infty$$

Cancelling terms on the right-hand side:

$$V_m \frac{(1+r)}{(1+g)} = D_0 + \frac{D_0(1+g)^1}{(1+r)^1} + \frac{D_0(1+g)^2}{(1+r)^2} + \frac{D_0(1+g)^3}{(1+r)^3} + \cdots \infty$$

and substituting V_m from equation (iv) into the right-hand side:

$$V_m \frac{(1+r)}{(1+g)} = D_0 + V_m$$

Rearranging:

$$V_m = \frac{D_0(1+g)}{(r-g)}$$

This is an important model first developed by the financial economist Myron Gordon and it expresses the value of a firm's share as a function of its dividend, the anticipated growth in those dividends and the rate of return (r) required by the firm's equity investors.

EXAMPLE

The Greenall Group Ltd paid a dividend of 11.8p per share in 1992. Dividend growth was expected at 4.7% in the subsequent year and the risk adjusted interest rate, appropriate for Greenalls was estimated at 8% per annum.

$$V_m = \frac{11.8(1.047)}{(0.08-0.047)}$$

$$= 374\text{p per share}$$

In fact, the Greenall share price ranged between 400p and 360p during the first three quarters of 1993.

The valuation model makes a number of assumptions.

- The principal determinant of share price is the cash dividends receivable by investors over the lifetime of the business. This is not a fanciful assumption if we (i) accept that the business is operating as a going concern and (ii) recognise that no other benefit accrues to an investor apart from the cash dividends he or she can expect to receive. It is sometimes suggested that the investor also receives the possibility of a capital gain on eventual sale of the shares. However, a future share price on sale simply reflects the market's estimate at that time of the discounted value of future dividends which is implicit in the model in any event.
- The discount rate is the required rate of return by equity shareholders in the market and is expected to be stable over time. This is a reasonable assumption in that much of the evidence we have about market processes indicates that a current

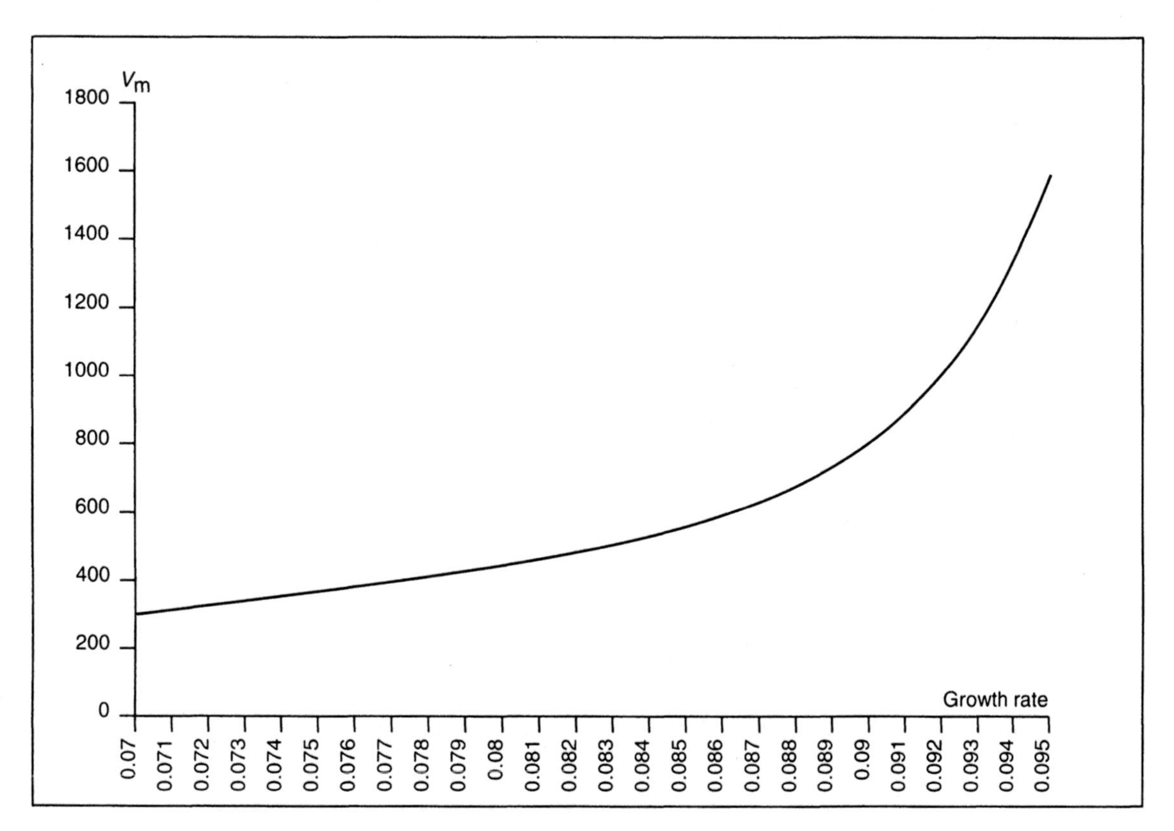

Figure 16.1 The value of a share with different assumed growth rates.

estimate of the value concerned is the best estimate of future values.

- The growth rate in dividends is constant into the future and will not vary over time. Clearly this will be an unreasonable assumption in practice, although at the point a valuation is undertaken it may be the best that can be achieved.

In Figure 16.1 we examine the sensitivity of market valuation to estimates of the growth rate in dividends. In that example we show the market value of a share offering a dividend of 8p per share, a required rate of return of 10% per annum and variable growth rates.

At relatively low rates of growth, the sensitivity of market value to changes in growth (as given by the slope of the curve in Figure 16.1) will be low. However, as the rate of assumed growth approaches the rate of return, the value of the share will rise asymptotically towards an infinite value as the rate of return is approached.

This valuation model has a mathematical form, as shown in Figure 16.2 which generalises the graphical result from the example in Figure 16.1.

From this model we can make some simple deductions about how share prices are likely to behave under different conditions.

- Relatively low growth firms are likely to exhibit low share price volatility than high growth firms where growth is measured relative to the minimum required rate of return (*r*). With high growth firms, tiny changes in growth can produce disproportionate changes in share price.
- As minimum required rates of return fall towards the norm of corporate growth rates, we would anticipate that share prices would begin to rise at an increasing rate.

In Figure 16.3 we lay down the sequence of activities required to estimate the market value of a share using the growth model.

Of all the values in the growth model, the anticipated rate of dividend growth is the most important value to get right. It encapsulates the investor's estimate of the future growth potential of the business and is the parameter within the model which is most dependent upon the subjective evaluation skills of the valuer. The following factors are likely to influence the value of dividend growth:

- the strength of the business's product range and customer base;
- the skill of management in identifying new opportunities which will enhance the core capability of the business;
- the economic and political climate for the business;
- the strength of the competition for the business in its market place.

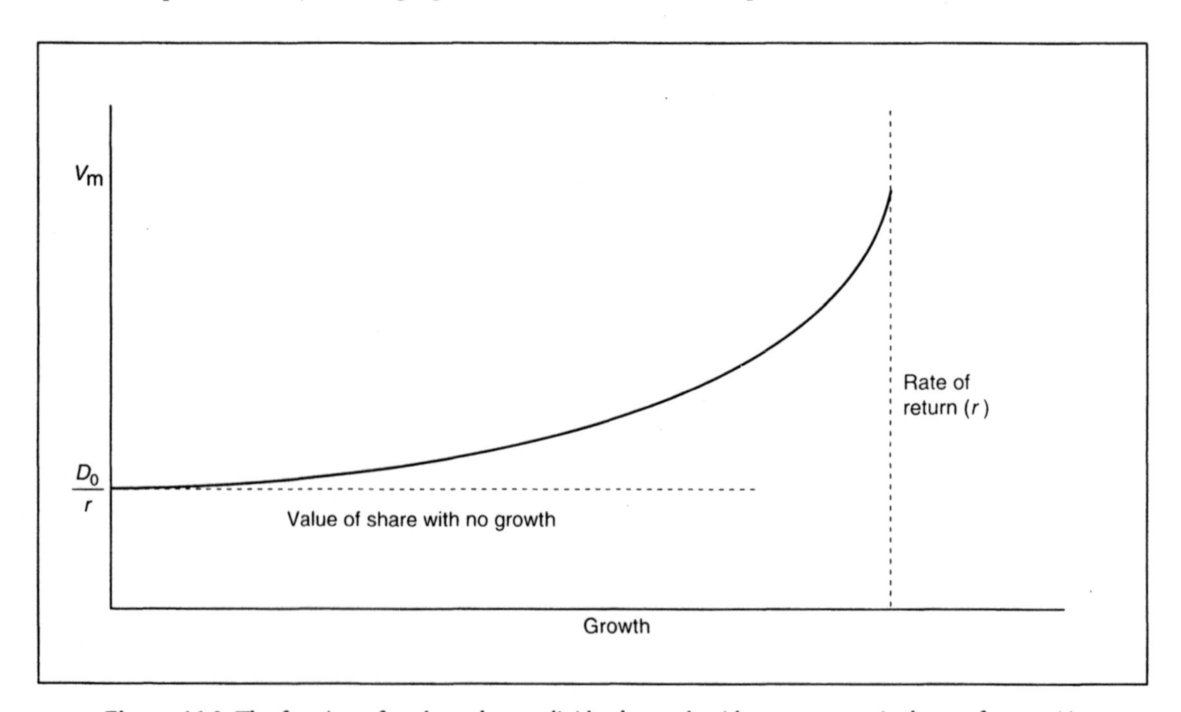

Figure 16.2 The function of market value vs. dividend growth with constant required rate of return (*r*).

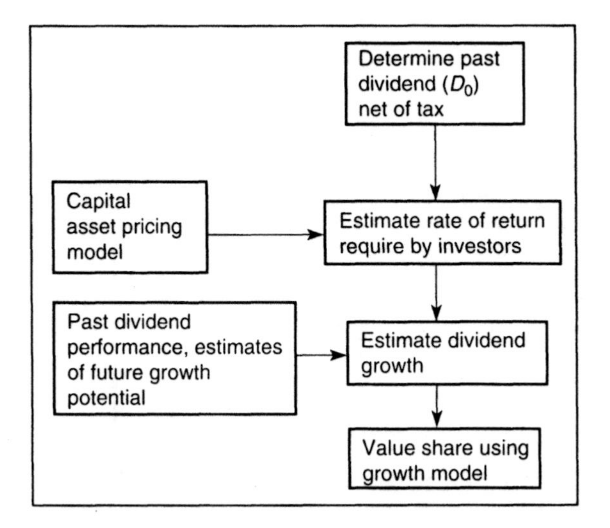

Figure 16.3 Estimating the dividend growth rate.

It is possible to estimate past dividend growth from the published accounting data for a company.

EXAMPLE

Deltcorn plc reported the dividends shown in Table 16.1 on its 25p ordinary shares over a five-year period.

Using the five annual dividend figures we have calculated:

(i) the annual growth using the formula:

$$D_{1991}(1+g) = D_{1992}$$

and thus

$$\begin{aligned} g &= D_{1992}/D_{1991} - 1 \\ &= 16.4/15.1 - 1 \\ &= 0.0861\ (8.61\%) \end{aligned}$$

which is then repeated down through the subsequent years.

(ii) the biannual growth using the formula

$$D_{1990}(1+g)^2 = D_{1992}$$

and thus

$$g = \sqrt{(D_{1992}/D_{1991})} - 1$$

and similarly for the three-year and four-year growths;

(iii) the average of each of the ten annualised growth values to give an annual percentage growth of 5.3% per annum.

HOW THE MODEL WORKS IN PRACTICE

The simple dividend valuation model can be applied to any company's shares. In the analysis below we consider a small sample of electricity companies in the UK and assume that expected growth and the risk adjusted discount rate is the same for all of them (Table 16.2). The declared dividends for each company were calculated net of standard rate of tax, and the expected growth in dividends for the sector was conditioned by a number of factors, of which the following were regarded as very important:

(i) the actual growth in dividends since nationalisation within the industry;

Table 16.1

	1988 £ million	1989 £ million	1990 £ million	1991 £ million	1992 £ million
Dividend/share	13.2	14.0	14.5	15.1	16.4
Annual growth		0.0606	0.0357	0.0414	0.0861
Biannual growth annualised			0.0481	0.0385	0.0635
Three-year growth annualised				0.0458	0.0542
Four-year growth annualised					0.0558
Average growth	0.0530				

Table 16.2

	Real growth	Growth	*r*	Div.	Estimated value/share	Actual value/share
National Power	0.0225	0.0634	0.095	18.58	625	652
SeeBoard	0.0225	0.0634	0.095	18.84	634	644
Manweb	0.0225	0.0634	0.095	19.50	656	650
Midlands	0.0225	0.0634	0.095	18.82	633	612
Scottish Power	0.0225	0.0634	0.095	10.99	370	407
Yorkshire	0.0225	0.0634	0.095	19.28	649	627
Norweb	0.0225	0.0634	0.095	18.58	625	652

(ii) expectations of economic growth within the industry to which energy consumption is highly correlated;
(iii) expectations of the comparative performance of the electricity industry as a supplier of energy within the economy.

Both energy producers and regional energy distributors were included in the sample studied and values were taken from the *Financial Times* (26 November 1993). The following parameters were incorporated:

- inflation at 4%;
- interest rate at 5.5%.

For the purposes of a first estimation of share value in each case, real growth in dividends was projected at 2.25% above the RPI over the foreseeable future. This accommodated Treasury expectation of economic growth in the British economy and was taken as a reasonable proxy for the expected growth in activity and hence energy consumption. The cost of money in the economy at the date of the study was, as given by the inter-bank rate, 5.5%. A 4% risk premium was then added to reflect the average cost of finance for this industry. The estimated value per share was then calculated as follows for National Power.

Nominal growth =

$$(1.0225 \times 1.04) - 1 = 0.0634 \ (6.34\%)$$

(i.e. the real rate of growth compounded by the inflation rate.)

$$V_m = \frac{D_0(1+g)}{(r-g)}$$

$$= \frac{18.58 \times (1.0634)}{(0.095 - 0.0634)}$$

$$= 625\text{p per share}$$

Taking the range of stocks chosen and the parameters as specified, the model sets a share price close to the market price and, indeed, the average error is only slightly in excess of 3.5% of the market value.

Repeated studies with this model show that it provides a reasonable basis for estimating the value of a share for a wide range of stocks. However, some caveats are in order.

- The assumptions upon which the model is based are restrictive because, although we are fairly confident that it traps the important variables in the actual pricing process, it does assume that constant values are expected in the future. The estimated price can be highly sensitive to these variables, and growth estimation from past dividend predictions has a high degree of uncertainty attached to it.
- The parameters are quite difficult to estimate in practice, and will always incorporate some soft judgements about a firm's expected growth and its relative risk. We have discussed in Chapter 13 how such risk estimation may be conducted in practice, although for small companies this estimation process can be difficult in the extreme.

The model is, however, particularly useful in valuing small businesses where industry norms can be established for the sector and the risk-adjusted discount rate inferred from similar companies of similar gearing and risk. In building an estimate of share value, any model relies upon the quality of the judgements required to estimate its parameters. If an investor is confident that his or her estimates are reasonable, given what is known about the business in its markets and economic environment, and the actual share price is markedly different from what the model predicts, then that would throw doubt upon the reasonableness of the market pricing process itself.

BUILDING THE VALUE OF A BUSINESS

Our discussion above has centred on the importance of the economic valuation model and how it can be applied to examine the value of the business as a whole or as individual marketable shares. We have also concluded that the way that a company can add to its business value is by seeking out and accepting projects which have a positive net present value. In other words, any investment opportunity which has not been anticipated by the market will lead to an upwards revision of the market value of the business:

- providing the market becomes aware that such an investment opportunity has been identified and accepted by the company;
- the market has the same beliefs as management about the merit of the opportunity concerned;
- the market believes that the company and management are capable of realising the value of the opportunity;
- the opportunity has a positive net present value when discounted at the company's ruling cost of capital.

There are a wide range of strategies for improving the value of a business, as we outline on a mapping of NPV/outlay to risk in Figure 16.4.

Invariably, the elimination of wasteful expenditure and mismanagement costs have the most profound effect on any business. Cost cutting is only risk free if management understand what they are doing, and only and always seek the minimum cost solution to the production of the intended product at the quality required. Inappropriate management and governance structures impose a severe cost overhead on any firm, and in themselves can be sufficient to obliterate any competitive advantage the firm may have by virtue of its products or superior market strategy. For this reason, we place great emphasis on cost management and economising strategies as means of sustaining the power of a business in its markets.

There are many and varying strategies which a company can pursue to build value. You may like to consider their likely positioning in Figure 16.4.

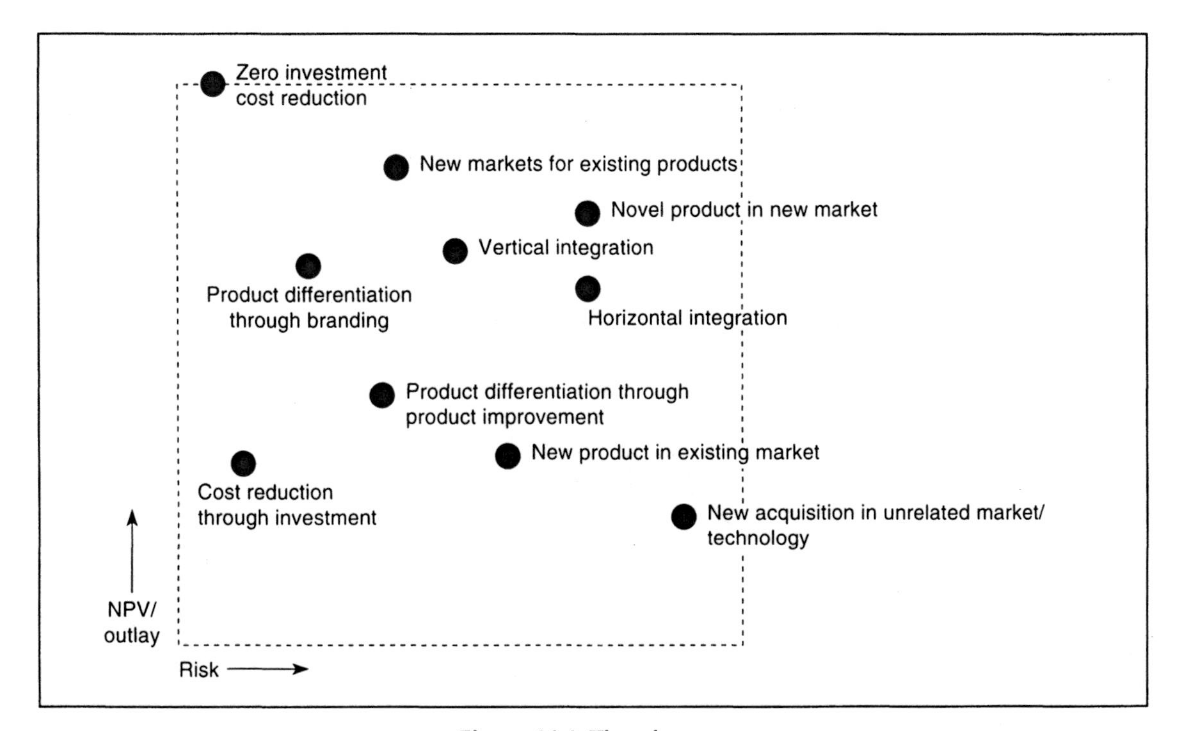

Figure 16.4 The value map.

CONCLUSION

In this chapter we have drawn together a number of threads from earlier chapters in demonstrating the basis upon which shareholders value firms. Using some simple assumptions about the components of a shareholder's valuation model based upon dividends and growth, we have been able to make reasonable estimates about actual price levels in the market. From these, we have then been able to draw some conclusions about how firms can build their value, which neatly reinforces our analysis of the cash mechanics of a business in Chapter 5.

Part III

Exploiting Business Capability

Chapter 17

The Output Decision

Level G

Contents

Summary

In this chapter we examine the output decision. This is the choice which management must make between the various levels of output which are available to it. We commence our discussion by examining how costs and revenues vary with output level, point out that both are unlikely to exhibit neat linear relationships with output. We then develop a simple technique called break-even analysis which exploits graphical techniques to help the manager make sensible output decisions. We then proceed to a discussion of the methods of marginal analysis and flexible budgeting.

THE BASICS OF THE OUTPUT DECISION

The output decision is a short-run decision because, first, it presumes that some prior long-run decision (in this case the decision to produce) has already been made and, second, we can normally disregard the timing problem when measuring the impact of output changes upon their value.

In order to make output decisions we need to understand two things:

- the way in which revenues vary with output (which is linked to the pricing decision).
- the way in which costs vary with output.

The aims and objectives of the output decision

As we noted in Chapter 3, the single-minded pursuit of optimising goals may not be really representative of typical decision-making behaviour. It may well be that under stress, or, indeed, in situations of imperfect knowledge, decision makers will opt for satisfactory rather than optimal solutions. In this chapter we will examine an important technique in output decision making called 'break-even' analysis. This technique can be regarded, for reasons we will discuss later, as a 'satisficing' procedure.

Following our discussion of break-even analysis we will consider how output decisions can be made in an optimising framework using a very simple form of mathematical analysis. The optimising model we use assumes that management wishes to maximise its firm's economic profit, given that output can be set at any level within the capacity of the production system.

The time period of the output decision

In continuous-production systems such as an oil refinery, a chemical plant or a continuous car-production line, the output decision must be made over an arbitrary time period. In batch processes, however, the period defined by the beginning and the end of the batch may form a more natural decision-making period. The time period chosen is important on two counts: first, the length of time determines the maximum physical output possible on a particular production process and, therefore, the basis upon which output is measured; second, the function of stocks as an intermediary between production and the firm's product market becomes more important as we move from continuous-time to discrete-time (batch) processes.

VARIATION OF REVENUES WITH OUTPUT LEVEL

The revenue gained from selling a particular quantity of product is directly related to the number of units sold:

Total revenue =
price per unit sold × total number of units sold

Consider a demand curve for video recorders facing an electronics company (Figure 17.1). The straight line relating price per unit (p) to the quantity sold (Q) can be defined by the formula

$$p = a - bQ$$

where a is the point where the line relating price to quantity cuts the price axis of the graph and b is the slope of the line and the negative sign indicates that there is a negative relationship between price and quantity, i.e. as the price of the product rises the quantity demanded in the market, and therefore sold, falls. Similarly, as the price falls so the quantity sold will rise.

You will note that the formula above is similar to the general formula for any straight line,

$$y = a + bx$$

where y and x are the two variables which are linearly related to one another and a and b are the point of intercept with the y-axis and the slope of the line, respectively. The sign (plus or minus) which attaches to the slope coefficient b tells us whether the line expresses an upward-sloping (positive) or a downward-sloping (negative) relationship between the two variables.

Given the definition of total revenue as price per unit times the quantity sold we can restate total revenue using the demand relationship above:

$$\text{Total revenue} = \text{price} \times \text{quantity}$$
$$= p \times Q$$

but, using the demand relationship, $p = a - bQ$, it follows that

$$\text{Total revenue} = (a - bQ)\,Q$$
$$= aQ - bQ^2$$

This formula represents an inverted quadratic relationship between total revenue and quantity as shown in Figure 17.2. The conclusion to be drawn

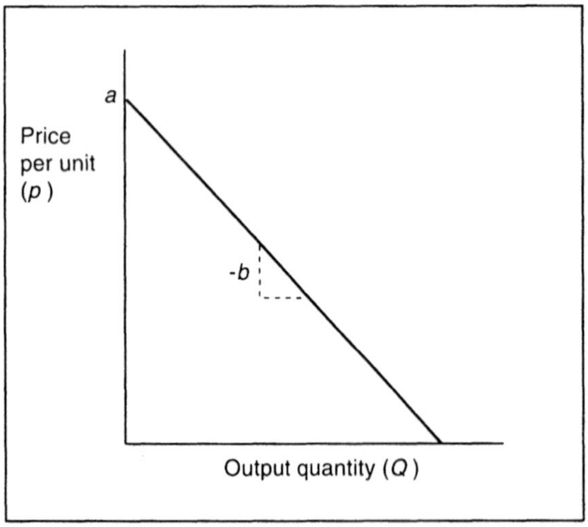

Figure 17.1 A linear demand curve.

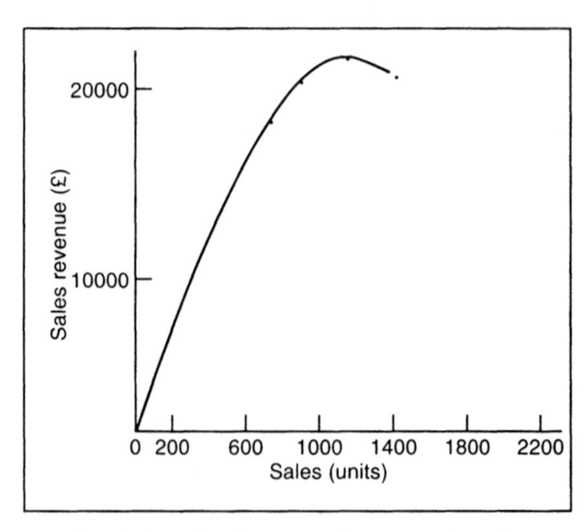

Figure 17.2 Total revenue from typewriter sales.

from this curve is that the curve will produce a total revenue function which is upward sloping over the first part of its range and then, after reaching a point of maximum total revenue, turns down giving decreasing total revenue with increasing output.

EXAMPLE

Almeria plc produces typewriters. Almeria's market research department believes that the price quantity relationship for its typewriters is as follows:

$$p = 290 - 0.1Q$$

where p is the price of each typewriter sold at the output quantity Q. Therefore, if 500 units are placed on the market, the price at which they can be sold is given by:

$$\begin{aligned} p(500) &= 290 - 0.1 \times 500 \\ &= £240 \text{ per unit} \end{aligned}$$

Given the price–quantity relationship expressed by this demand curve, we can draw up a table of prices and total revenues which will result from different levels of sales (Table 17.1).

Almeria's total revenue function is given by

$$\begin{aligned} \text{Total revenue} &= pQ \\ &= (290 - 0.1\,Q)\,Q \\ &= 290\,Q - 0.1\,Q^2 \end{aligned}$$

The graph of total revenue from sales is shown in Figure 17.2. The shape of any total revenue function is determined by the shape of the underlying relationship between price and output which a firm faces in the relevant product market. The quadratic function shown in Figure 17.2 is derived from the simplest type of demand curve. More complicated functions generate more complex relationships between total revenue and output.

Table 17.1

Sales of typewriters	Price at specified level of sales (£)	Total revenue from sales
0	290	0
250	265	66 250
500	240	120 000
750	215	161 250
1000	190	190 000
1250	165	206 250
1500	140	210 000
1750	115	201 250

THE CONCEPT OF ELASTICITY

The sensitivity of the amount demanded of a particular product to changes in its price is measured by its price elasticity of demand. The price elasticity of demand measures the proportionate change in the quantity of a product demanded by the market following a small change in the product's price.

It is also possible to measure the elasticity of demand with respect to other variables: advertising expenditure is one example, changes in the levels of consumer income is another.

If Almeria's typewriters currently retail at £240 and their price is reduced to £215 then the proportionate change in price is given by

$$\frac{\text{New price} - \text{current price}}{\text{current price}} = \frac{\Delta p}{p} = \frac{215 - 240}{240} = -0.10417$$

As a consequence of this fall in price the demand for Almeria's typewriters will rise. The corresponding proportionate change in demand is, therefore

$$\frac{\text{Demand at new price} - \text{demand at current price}}{\text{demand at current price}} = \frac{\Delta Q}{Q} = \frac{750 - 500}{500} = 0.5$$

The demand levels at a price of £215 and £240 can be read from Table 17.1.

The price elasticity of demand at the point on Almeria's demand curve where price = £240 and quantity = 500 units is given by the ratio of the two proportionate changes:

$$\text{Elasticity at point } (p, Q) = \frac{\Delta Q/Q}{\Delta p/p} = \frac{\Delta Q}{\Delta p} \times \frac{p}{Q}$$

therefore

$$e(240{,}500) = 0.5/0.10417 = 4.80$$

where $e(240{,}500)$ is the point price elasticity of demand at a price of £240 and an output quantity of 500 units. Note that, by convention, price elasticity of demand is usually expressed as a positive value, irrespective of the sign of its component ratios.

An elasticity of 4.80 indicates that, for small price changes only, every percentage change from the price of £240 will bring about a 4.80% change in the quantity demanded.

When a product has 'price-inelastic' demand any fall in its price will bring about a fall in total revenue. Inelasticity is defined by the range of values from unity to zero, i.e.

$$0 < e(p, Q) < 1 \text{ (inelastic demand condition)}$$

while 'price-elastic' demand is where price increases bring about increases in total revenue, i.e.

$$1 < e(p, Q) < \infty \text{ (elastic demand condition)}$$

'Perfect elasticity' means that a demand curve is infinitely inelastic along its entire length. 'Perfectly inelastic' demand curves are of zero elasticity along their entire length.

When the point elasticity of a demand curve is unity ($e(p, Q) = 1$) a small change in price will bring about an equivalent proportionate change in demand. At this point, therefore, tiny increases or decreases in price will be matched by corresponding decreases or increases in quantity. Because the increase (or decrease) in revenue, caused by the price change, is exactly netted off by the decrease (or increase) in revenue, caused by the quantity change, there will be no alteration in total revenue and this (referring back to Figure 17.2) can only occur when total revenue is at a maximum.

We can determine the maximum total revenue for a linear demand curve as follows:

$$e(p, Q) = 1 \quad \text{(at maximum total revenue)}$$

then

$$\frac{\Delta Q}{\Delta p} \times \frac{p}{Q} = 1 \tag{i}$$

For Almeria, the slope of the demand curve is 0.1, i.e.

$$\frac{\Delta p}{\Delta Q} = 0.1$$

therefore

$$\frac{\Delta Q}{\Delta p} = 1/0.1 = 10$$

Substituting in (i) above:

$$10 \times p/Q = 1$$

therefore

$$p/Q = 0.1 \quad \text{(at maximum revenue)}$$

or

$$Q = p/0.1 \tag{ii}$$

Almeria's demand curve is

$$p = 290 - 0.1 \times Q$$

Substituting for Q using equation (ii):

$$p = 290 - 0.1 \times p/0.1$$
$$p = 290 - p$$

therefore

$$2p = 290$$
$$p = £145$$

At a price of £145, the demand (Q) is given by rearranging the demand curve equation:

$$p = 290 - 0.1 \times Q$$

therefore

$$Q = \frac{290 - p}{0.1}$$

Substituting for p

$$Q = (290 - 145)/0.1 = 1450 \text{ units}$$

Therefore, at maximum revenue, price is £145 and demand 1450 units.

In a situation where a company faces a perfectly elastic demand curve, the price which the company can obtain for its product is completely independent of the quantity it produces and sells to the market. This state of affairs exists only in perfectly competitive product markets.

VARIATION OF COSTS WITH OUTPUT LEVEL

We have noted before that the long-run decision to produce a particular product will commit the firm to a certain level of fixed costs. Because these costs are invariate with the output level chosen they cannot influence the output decision. Such costs are: rent,

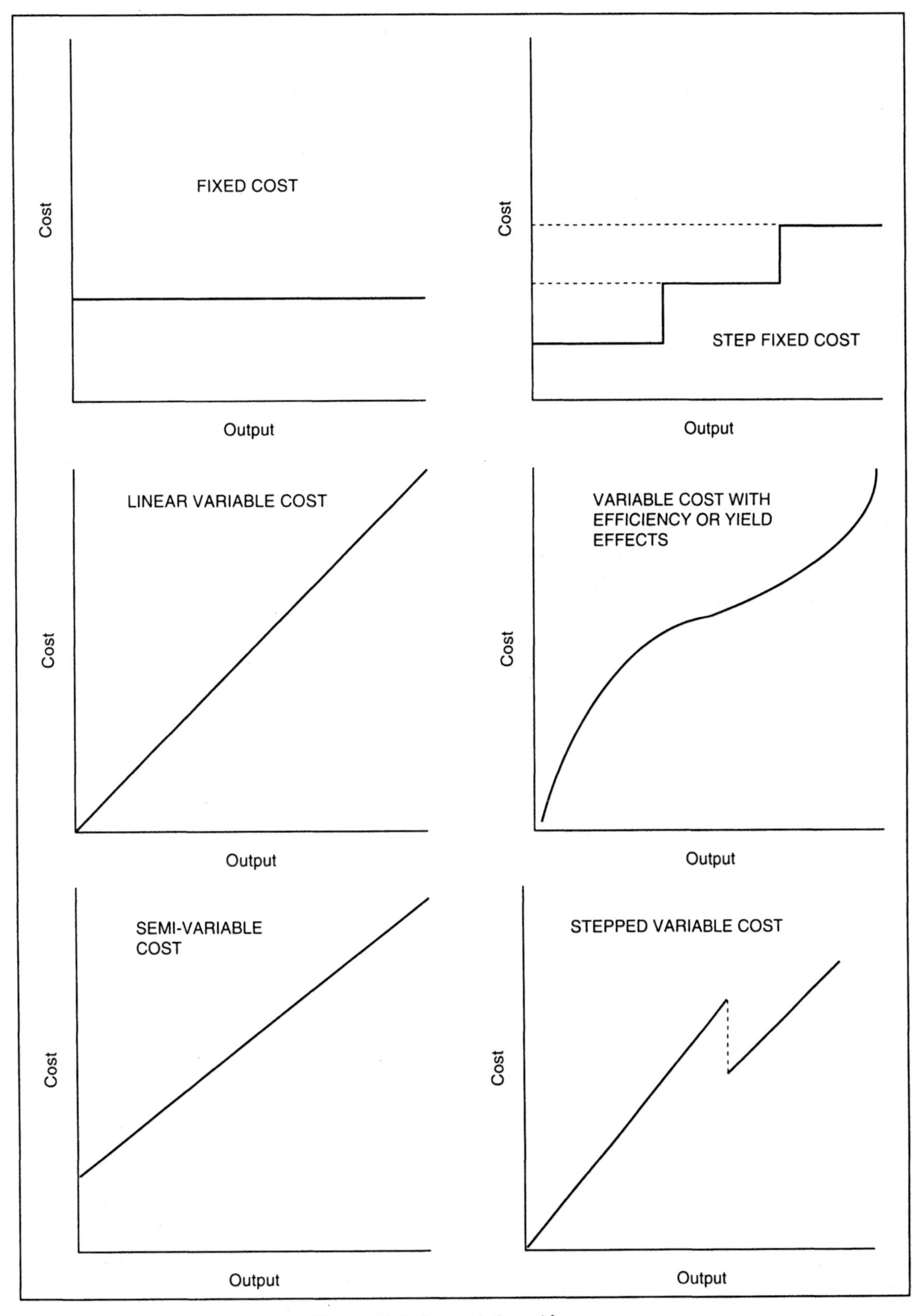

Figure 17.3 Cost variation with output.

rates, heating (in so far as it relates to the premises rather than the production process itself), lighting and the salaries of all of those who are not involved directly in production. A graphical representation of this type of cost is shown in Figure 17.3.

However, certain costs may appear fixed over certain specified ranges of output, although these ranges are separated by 'steps' or discontinuities. An example of such a cost is labour charges, where an additional plant or process operator is hired as production passes through fixed points on the increasing range of output. In fact, labour costs exhibit a 'ratchet' effect, in that they are stepped going up, but appear fixed coming down through the range of output. In other words, hiring labour is often treated and appears as a short-term decision, but firing labour is invariably a long-run decision, given the employment protection for employees in UK law.

Certain costs vary directly with output level, in that zero cost is incurred at zero output and there is a constant rise in the cost of the resource concerned through the entire range of output. In practice, few costs behave in quite such a tidy way. Material costs (ignoring changes in stock levels) are one example, packaging costs are another. In some production systems, especially those based upon continuous processes, material costs can vary in quite peculiar ways with output. Over initial ranges of output, material costs may well be directly variable. However, as the plant comes up to its most efficient operating conditions, yields may well improve and the rate of material usage fall off. At extremely high operating conditions, however, the efficiency of the conversion of materials into finished products usually falls off and material costs rise rapidly. In Figure 17.3 we show a 'well-behaved' variable cost curve, that is one which is linear throughout its entire range of output and we also show the less well-behaved pattern of variation described above.

Certain variable costs have an initial fixed cost which is incurred irrespective of the output level. Sometimes material costs are of this type where a certain quantity of material is required to prime the production process. Many chemical plants have to be primed in this way. Just as a motor-car requires a certain amount of petrol to fill the carburettor before its engine will fire, some chemical plants require a certain level of raw materials in their input system before the reactions can proceed. In Figure 17.3 we show the typical pattern of behaviour associated with such 'semi-variable' costs. As with fixed costs it is possible to get steps in variable-cost patterns. For example, if a supplier offers a discount on raw materials for deliveries in excess of a certain agreed figure in a given period, then a downward step will occur at that level. In Figure 17.3 we show an example of a stepped variable cost.

THE ROLE OF STOCKS IN PRODUCTION PLANNING

Managers often feel uncomfortable with the idea that their output decisions are completely at the mercy of the demand curve for the products they are attempting to sell. In fact, we have oversimplified our discussion to a certain extent. Managers can, in the short term, escape from the constraints of the market demand for their product by creating or reducing stocks. Such stock management is of importance in two situations.

- Where the product concerned is produced by a batch process: stocks of the finished good can be made at the most efficient level of production for the particular plant involved and then stored until it can be sold at the best price.
- Where there is a significant degree of seasonality in the demand for the particular product: the output from the production process can be stored (whether it is produced on a batch or continuous process) until the best price can be obtained.

With many products their demand curves change seasonally (see Chapter 19). For example, in the two months prior to Christmas we would expect an increase in consumer preferences for toys and games relative to other goods. Consequently, we would expect a seasonal shift in the demand curve for these products. A toy manufacturer will, therefore, be concerned with creating sufficient stocks during the production year to satisfy both the normal and the exceptional demand prior to Christmas.

There are costs associated with stock holding, however. Investing resources in stocks means that those resources cannot be used elsewhere. The frequency and size of the production runs will have a significant effect upon the costs of holding stocks.

BREAK-EVEN ANALYSIS AND ITS APPLICATION

Break-even analysis is a long-established technique for analysing the output problem. The traditional accounting approach is to assume that price is invariate with output and that costs can be represented as linear relationships with output. A simple

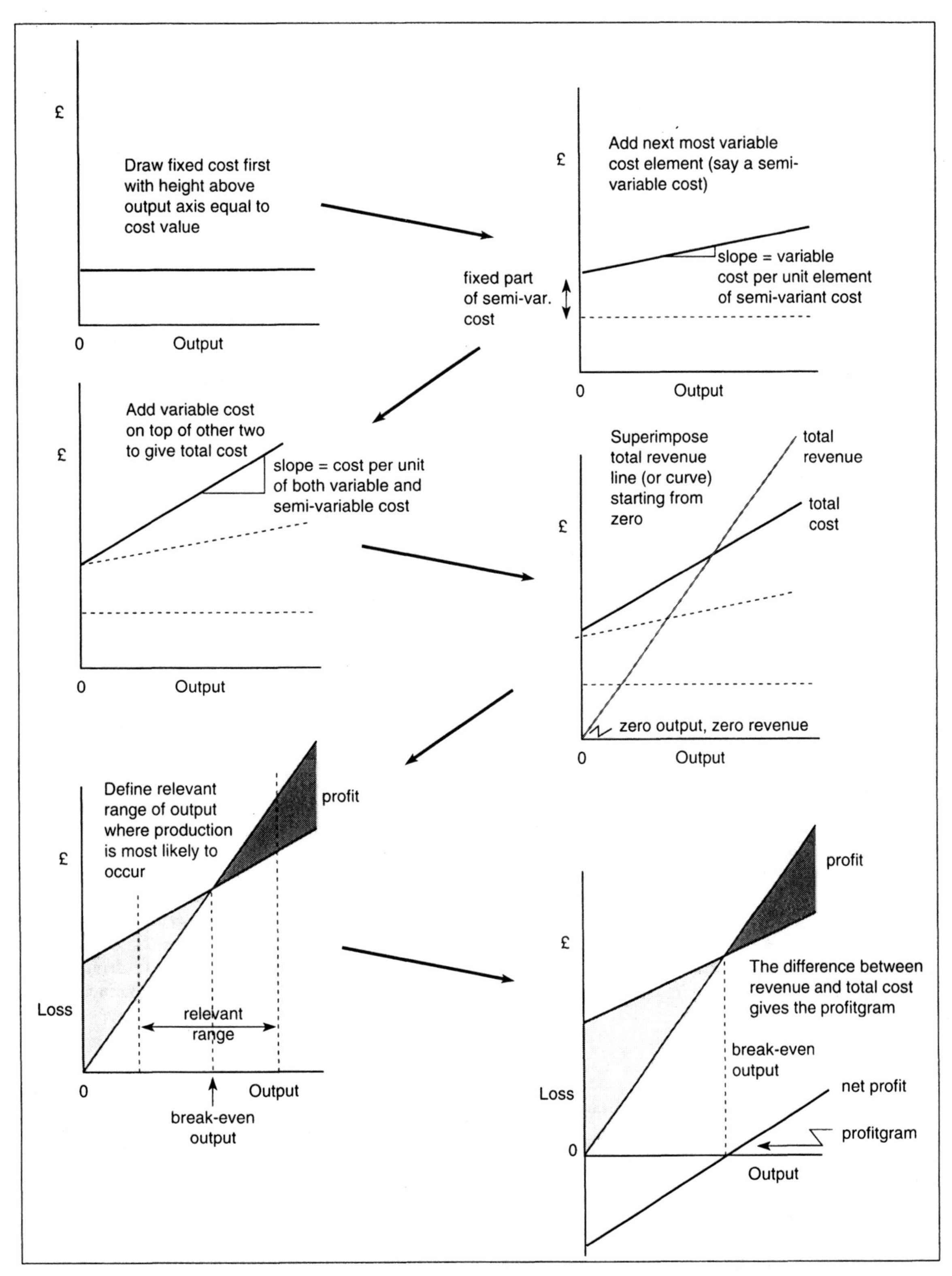

Figure 17.4 Stages in the development of a break-even chart and profitgram.

example of a break-even curve for a particular process is given in Figure 17.4. The difference between total cost and revenue at any particular output level can be mapped as a 'profitgram'. This is a simple graphical analysis superimposing a total revenue line or curve onto a graph of total cost. The assumptions of this type of analysis are:

- increasing profits will be made the greater the output;
- any production level in excess of that required to break-even is a 'satisfactory' level of output.

An unquestioning approach to the assumption of linearity in cost or revenue behaviour can lead to suboptimal decisions, with an overemphasis on a range of acceptable outputs, and little attention given to the search for an optimal solution. However, it may well be that management is quite prepared to accept the degree of approximation inherent in such a linear analysis because any refinement of the analysis would entail high and unacceptable search and information processing costs to the firm. Also, it may be that management is of the opinion that, over the likely output range (the relevant range), linearity is a reasonable assumption to make.

But, as we shall now show, the assumption of linearity can lead to significant distortions in the decision-making process. Whether the losses which arise from such distortions are offset by the higher information collection and processing costs implied by the type of analysis we are about to describe, is very difficult to say. Some firms with well-developed management information systems may be able to collect the additional information at little extra cost. Others may find the cost of obtaining and processing the additional information prohibitively expensive.

The first area of sophistication which can be brought to break-even analysis involves dropping the assumption of linearity in the total revenue function.

EXAMPLE

The total production cost for Almeria plc can be represented by the relationship

$$\textit{Production cost} = 69\ 780 + 66.90 \times Q$$

(Note: we show how such a cost relationship can be estimated in Chapter 18.)

The total revenue function is of the form

$$\textit{Total revenue} = 290Q - 0.1Q^2$$

where Q is the output quantity demanded and sold.

We can plot these two functions and their associated profitgram as shown in Figure 17.5. Unlike the simple break-even analysis illustrated in Figure 17.4 where a single break-even point was revealed, Figure 17.5 has two such points: a lower break-even point where, for the first time, total revenue exceeds total cost; and an upper break-even point where the effect of the declining demand curve has taken total revenue below total cost again.

The profitgram now has a clear maximum, i.e. that point at the top of the profit curve where its slope is zero. At this 'turning point' on the profitgram, the rate of increase in profit following marginal changes in output is zero (that is, marginal profit is zero). This is implied by the statement that the slope of the profitgram is zero at maximum profit. Mathematically, this point of maximum profit is reached when the marginal change in total cost with respect to a marginal change in output (the slope of the cost function at a particular output) is equal to the marginal change of total revenue with respect to a marginal change in output.

To summarise this analysis, we can say that a profit-maximising producer should set an output level where marginal cost and marginal revenue are equated. In Almeria's example we can easily determine the value of the marginal cost of production. In the case of a linear cost function, marginal cost will be the same as the variable cost per unit:

$$\text{Marginal cost} = £66.90$$

Any additional unit of output incurs an incremental cost of £66.90 for the firm. Marginal revenue is slightly more complex as it changes with increasing output level. The slope (mathematically the first differential) of Almeria's total revenue function is given by

$$\text{Marginal revenue} = 290 - 0.2 \times Q$$

At the optimum output, therefore

$$\text{Marginal cost} = \text{marginal revenue}$$
$$\text{i.e.} \quad 66.90 = 290 - 0.2 \times Q$$

Therefore, by rearrangement:

$$Q = (290 - 66.90)/0.2 = 1115.5 \text{ units}$$

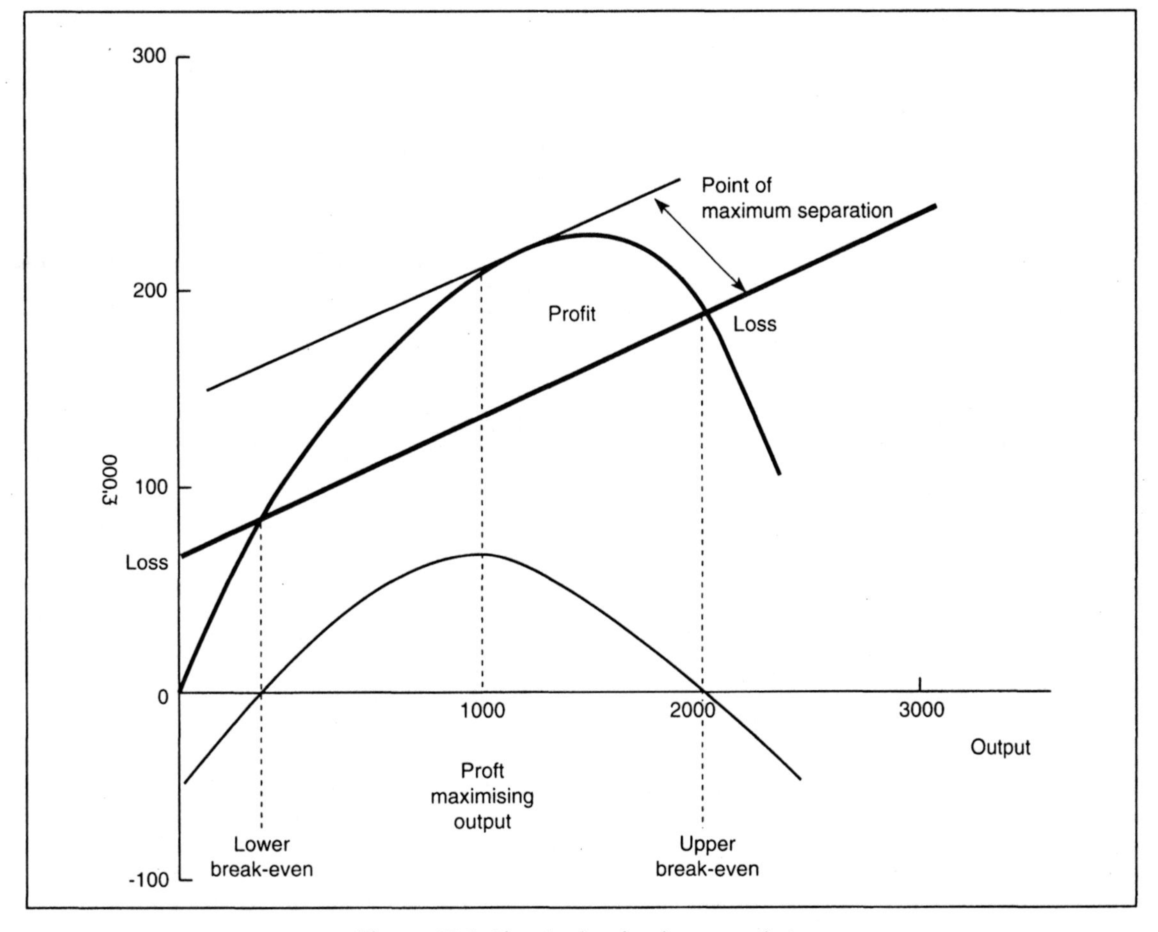

Figure 17.5 Almeria plc – break-even analysis.

At this level of output profit,

$$\begin{aligned}\text{Total profit} &= \text{total revenue} - \text{total cost}\\ &= (290 \times 1115.5 - 0.1 \times 1115.5^2)\\ &\quad - (69\,780 + 66.90 \times 1115.5)\\ &= £54\,654\end{aligned}$$

Marginal analysis of this type presents two problems for practical application.

- The objective of profit maximisation may be inappropriate for the firm.
- The technique can only work where the underlying cost and revenue functions are smooth without 'discontinuities'. But discontinuities occur if there are steps in the cost functions or 'kinks' in the revenue functions. In the presence of such discontinuities only a graphical analysis can bring out the full complexities of the problem.

For example, assume that Almeria's fixed costs consist of two elements:

Established fixed costs	£50 000
Fixed component of semi-variable cost	£19 780
Total fixed cost	£69 780

However, Almeria's management believes that, in the future, while the variable component of cost will remain the same as at present, the established fixed cost will increase at higher output levels:

Output level (units)	Fixed cost
0–499	50 000
500–999	75 000
1000–1499	100 000

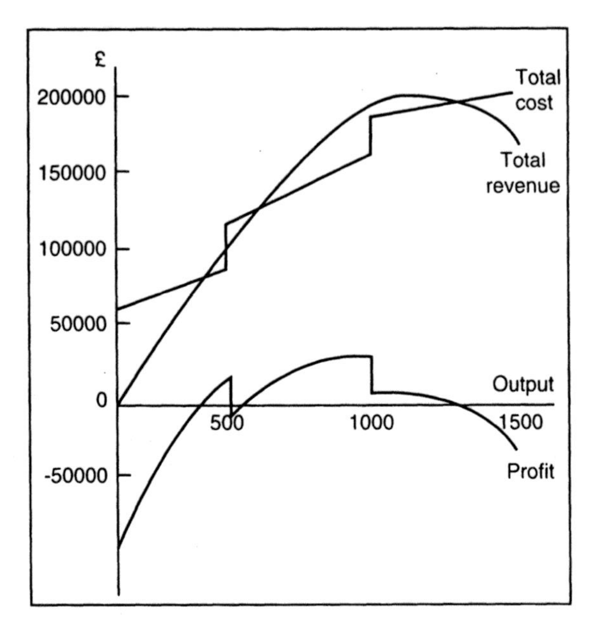

Figure 17.6 Almeria plc – break-even analysis with discontinuities.

In Figure 17.6 we introduce these steps into the total cost structure. Notice that instead of two break-even points we now have four and, most important of all, a discontinuity has appeared at a lower output level than the profit-maximising output revealed by our marginal analysis above. The new profitgram shows that profit is maximised at 1000 units. Any increase beyond this output level brings an immediate and dramatic reduction in profit. In addition, the graph reveals a new loss-making area between 500 and 580 units of output.

Our analysis now incorporates two significant improvements over the simple, linear break-even graph. First, we have dispensed with the unrealistic assumption of a linear total-revenue function. Second, we have shown how discontinuities in the basic cost functions can be incorporated into the break-even graph. The introduction of discontinuities into our analysis has highlighted the weakness of simple mathematical methods in that they assume smooth, continuous functions which are mathematically well behaved.

FLEXIBLE BUDGETING AND BREAK-EVEN ANALYSIS

A break-even graph represents, in diagrammatic form, the possibilities open to management in their output decision making. With a flexible budget the break-even graph is recast in columnar form usually on a spreadsheet. Indeed, modern computer spreadsheet packages make the process of flexible budgeting very straightforward.

A flexible budget is a translation of a break-even graph into a statement of revenue and costs at various specified output levels. These output levels will be set at discrete intervals which may or may not include either the points of break-even or the positions of maximum profit. The purpose of a flexible budget is that it permits the creation of different operational budgets based upon different output-level assumptions. These operational budgets can be consolidated later into the master budget. This procedure allows management to measure the sensitivity of the master budget to different output-level assumptions.

Table 17.2

	Output level (units)						
	200 £	400 £	600 £	800 £	1 000 £	1 200 £	1 400 £
Total revenue	54 000	100 000	138 000	168 000	190 000	204 000	210 000
Variable component cost	(5 020)	(10 040)	(15 060)	(20 080)	(25 100)	(30 120)	(35 140)
Variable labour charge	(6 680)	(13 360)	(20 040)	(26 720)	(33 400)	(40 080)	(46 760)
Variable overheads	(1 680)	(3 360)	(5 040)	(6 720)	(8 400)	(10 080)	(11 760)
Total fixed cost	(69 780)	(69 780)	(94 780)	(94 780)	(119 780)	(119 780)	(119 780)
Profit/loss	(29 160)	3 460	3 080	19 700	3 320	3 940	(3 440)

For example, Almeria plc has completed a detailed analysis of its components of total production cost. The variable and fixed costs of production are as follows:

Variable component cost	£25.10
Variable labour charge	£33.40
Variable overheads	£8.40
Total fixed cost (0–499 units)	£69 780.00
(500–999 units)	£94 780.00
(1000–11499 units)	£119 780.00

A flexible budget at incremental levels of output of 200 units would then appear as shown in Table 17.2.

Total revenues have been derived from Almeria's demand curve given the specified output levels.

Note, however, that the flexible budget has lost a lot of the information contained in the original break-even graph, although numerical analysis will give more precise results than can be read from a graph. We will discover, in Chapter 26, the usefulness of flexible budgeting as a method of restating budgets under different output assumptions, and as a method for determining whether differences between actual and budgeted figures are due to changes in overall output level, or due to changes in the efficiency with which resources are used.

CONCLUSION

In this chapter we have reviewed the problems associated with decisions about output. Output decisions are of a short-term nature and they require a careful analysis of the ways in which costs and revenues vary with activity. We have discussed simple break-even analysis and its numerical analogue, flexible budgeting, in some detail. However, these techniques of themselves do not provide guidance to management about 'optimum' levels of output; to achieve that we have discussed the methods of marginal analysis. In the next chapter we continue our discussion of this topic with a review of the practicalities of cost estimation.

Chapter 18

The Practical Estimation of Cost–Output Relationships

Level D

Contents

Summary

In this chapter we examine two methods of statistical cost estimation which can be useful, in practice, when managers wish to understand how their costs of production vary with output levels. First, we consider analytical cost analysis, which presupposes that the mechanisms by which costs are created can be understood and priced by appeal to external market prices. Second, we examine the method of statistical cost estimation using ordinary least squares linear regression, and point out the uses and limitations of that method. Finally, we look at the statistical tests of goodness of fit, which are useful in gaining confidence in the applicability of the estimation process.

INTRODUCTION

In order to make decisions concerning output levels, we need to know the current relationship which exists between cost and output for the process concerned. Unfortunately, past costs will not, necessarily, provide a good indication of either current or future cost–output relationships on that particular plant or process. As far as possible, output decisions should be made on the basis of up-to-date estimates of cost; however, in certain circumstances, reliance may have to be placed on projections based upon past figures.

In principle, two methods are available to help us estimate the relationship between cost and output:

- analytically, from the plant's or process's technological characteristics;
- statistically, from past cost–output data from the plant or process concerned.

ANALYTICAL PROCESS ANALYSIS

All physical processes require inputs of raw materials, energy and technical knowledge in order to produce outputs. In many physical systems this conversion of inputs to outputs can be understood with a high degree of accuracy. For example, an engineer in an oil refinery may well be able to predict, with considerable accuracy, the proportions of different types of petroleum spirit which can be 'cracked' from a given type of crude oil. Similarly, a whisky distiller can tell, given a fermented mash of a certain specific gravity, the number of litres of distilled spirit which can be produced. However, because all physical products are susceptible to random fluctuations in performance, the conversion of input to output can only be described in the form of a probability distribution of yields.

A firm's production engineers can usually specify the relevant conversion ratio for input to output on a particular plant or process and can provide estimates of the amount of labour required to operate and control the system. For example, a raw-materials conversion ratio for a chemical plant would be as follows:

$$\text{Conversion ratio} = \frac{\text{number of kilograms of raw material}}{\text{number of kilograms of principal output product}}$$

This conversion ratio can be altered to accommodate the situation where some raw material is recovered from the waste effluent during the product's purification stage.

An analytical approach to the problem of determining the relationship between cost and output means that the management accountant must be heavily dependent upon the technical expertise of the firm's engineering staff. However, it is important to appreciate that even the best estimates provided by the engineering staff can be subject to error because of the following.

- Differences in the quality of raw materials between one batch and another, even minor variations, can have a dramatic impact upon a production system's ability to convert that raw material into final product.
- Variations in the operating procedures of the plant or process, again, even minor variations in, for example, ambient temperatures or stirring rates in a chemical reactor, can cause major changes in process yields.
- There is inherent unpredictability in many natural processes. Often the laws which govern physical processes are probabilistic and so predictions can only be made to certain degrees of confidence.
- The inputs to a particular process and hence the input costs may be dependent upon other variables as well as plant output, such as product quality, labour input, etc.

In many cases the direct examination of a cost–output relationship may be impossible. It may simply be that the manufacturing plant records are insufficiently accurate or that the process has only been attempted at the pilot-plant level and not as yet commissioned on a full-scale plant. In the first case, the management accountant will have to attempt a statistical analysis of the firm's past production records. In the second case, the management accountant will have no alternative but to conduct a similar statistical analysis on the results of any pilot-plant experiments which have been carried out.

STATISTICAL COST ANALYSIS

Statistical cost analysis involves the following four steps.

- The collection of past input costs and output data over as long a period as possible.
- The adjustment of the past data to render them comparable in terms of current input prices.
- The statistical analysis of the collected data into fixed and variable components.
- The estimation of the degree of confidence which can be placed on the results of the analysis.

The collection of past input costs and output data

In order to ensure statistical reliability, the largest possible body of comparable data should be collected. For a particular production process a number of sources of data may be available to the management accountant:

- stock records of inputs and outputs from a particular process;
- suppliers' price lists and purchasing department records;
- process log sheets and operator work sheets;
- cost accounts of raw material or component usages and accounts of process outputs.

In any given situation the management accountant may be forced to use data which are either aggregated (and will need detailed analysis) or are incomplete. In both situations any source of supporting information which can be found will be useful for checking analyses and estimates.

The adjustment of past costs

The accountant's aim, as far as possible, is to create a picture of the current relationship between cost and output. Economists refer to the graphical representation of such a relationship as an 'analytical' cost curve. Such a relationship can be regarded as a cost 'snapshot' of a particular plant's or process's operating potential in that it gives a cost–output relationship over the operating range of output at a particular instant in time.

Three problems can arise with the use of past data:

- The plant's or process's operating procedures may have altered in some way or other which is not obvious from the past cost data. This difficulty can be surmounted by discussion with the firm's technical staff.

- There may have been a step in the input costs at some time in the past, brought about by a price rise such as an increase in labour costs following a successful wage claim.
- There may have been a continuous pattern of changing input prices. Specific price inflation affects different input costs in different ways.

EXAMPLE

Almeria plc has collected the following costs from its typewriter factory for the last six months of production. We can assume that the costs arise on the last day of the month in question (Table 18.1).

During our analysis of production costs we discover that the costs of the components have risen during the course of the previous six months at an average rate of 2% per month. In addition, we discover that a 10% wage increase was negotiated for all production staff to take effect from the beginning of September.

Given the facts, as stated above, two adjustments need to be made in order to make all six months' figures comparable. November's component cost figure is based upon purchase prices which are one month out of date. With a 2% monthly increase the November cost, restated in December prices, is

November component charge =
£34 560 × 1.02 = £35 250

October's component cost figure is two months out of date. To make the October figure comparable with November we must raise it by 2% and then by a further 2% to bring it to December prices:

October component charge = £32 440 × 1.02 × 1.02
= £32 440 × 1.02^2
= £33 750

On the same basis we can revise the remaining component charges for the six-month period as follows:

	Original	Revised
December	41 630	= 41 630
November	34 560 × 1.02^1	= 35 250
October	32 440 × 1.02^2	= 33 750
September	27 205 × 1.02^3	= 28 870
August	17 320 × 1.02^4	= 18 750
July	24 455 × 1.02^5	= 27 000

The wage-rate increase raises a slightly different problem in that the increase affected all wage levels from September onwards. Neither the August nor the July figures contained the increase of 10% in the labour rate. Therefore, to make these two months comparable with the months that follow we should increase their respective labour costs by 10%:

August labour cost = £22 730 × 1.1 = £25 000
July labour cost = £32 730 × 1.1 = £36 000

Note that with labour costs we are not concerned with a rate of increase as we were with component charges. A rate of increase implies that each month's cost figures are increased by the specified percentage rate. With labour costs we are dealing with a single step rise in the level of labour costs.

Using the corrected component and labour costs we can now create a revised schedule of production costs against output level (Table 18.2). But now the month in which the costs arose is irrelevant. We have removed all the timing effects that we know about and are left with a series of production costs (stated in current, December prices).

Table 18.1

	Jul.	Aug.	Sept.	Oct.	Nov.	Dec.
Components	24 455	17 320	27 205	32 440	34 560	41 630
Labour	32 730	22 730	38 500	45 000	47 000	55 500
Variable overheads	9 000	6 250	9 630	11 250	11 750	13 870
Fixed overheads	50 000	50 000	50 000	50 000	50 000	50 000
Total production costs	116 185	96 300	125 335	138 690	143 310	161 000
Output (units)	710	500	900	1 100	1 250	1 150

Table 18.2

Output level	710	500	900	1 100	1 250	1 150
Component cost (revised) (£)	27 000	18 750	28 870	33 750	35 250	41 630
Labour cost (revised) (£)	36 000	25 000	38 500	45 000	47 000	55 500
Variable overheads (£)	9 000	6 250	9 630	11 250	11 750	13 870
Fixed overheads (£)	50 000	50 000	50 000	50 000	50 000	50 000
Total production costs (£)	122 000	100 000	127 000	140 000	144 000	161 000

We have noted that the relationship between cost and output may not, of necessity, be exact and, indeed, if we plot the data on a graph (see Figure 18.1) we notice that the points are scattered around what appears to be an upward rising trend.

The question which now arises is: given that the cost–output data do not fall on a straight line, how do we go about judging the line which best represents the data?

The statistical analysis of past data

In practice, just six data points would not form a particularly promising basis for any form of statistical analysis, unless they all clearly fell upon a line or some other smooth function. The greater the degree of dispersion of the points, the more data will be required to gain useful results. However, given the data we do have we will now turn to a very simple statistical technique for its analysis.

We will make the simplest assumption possible concerning the relationship between production cost and output, namely that the data fall upon a straight line which can best be described by the relationship:

Production cost = fixed cost + (variable cost per unit × output quantity)

which is a relationship of the linear form:

$$y = a + bx$$

where:

a is the intercept with the vertical (y) axis (which, in this case, will be an estimate of the fixed cost);
b is the slope of the line relating production cost to quantity (which, in this case, will be an estimate of the variable cost per unit).

The technique of 'linear regression' allows us to convert raw data points on a graph into values of a and b which define the line of best fit for those data points. From a series of n data points ($n = 6$ in Almeria's example), the line of best fit can be estimated by solution of the following pair of simultaneous equations:

$$\Sigma y = na + b\Sigma x \quad \text{(i)}$$

$$\Sigma(xy) = a\Sigma x + b\Sigma x^2 \quad \text{(ii)}$$

These two equations are similar in structure to the equations of the line itself and are not too difficult to memorise. Their derivation can be found in most statistical textbooks. Remember, the operator Σ means 'sum of'.

We can convert the production cost–output data into a form suitable for inclusion in the two simultaneous equations given above by constructing Table 18.3. Substituting the totals from this table into the two simultaneous equations we have

$$794\,000 = 6a + 5610b \quad \text{(iii)}$$

$$770\,070\,000 = 5610a + 5\,659\,100b \quad \text{(iv)}$$

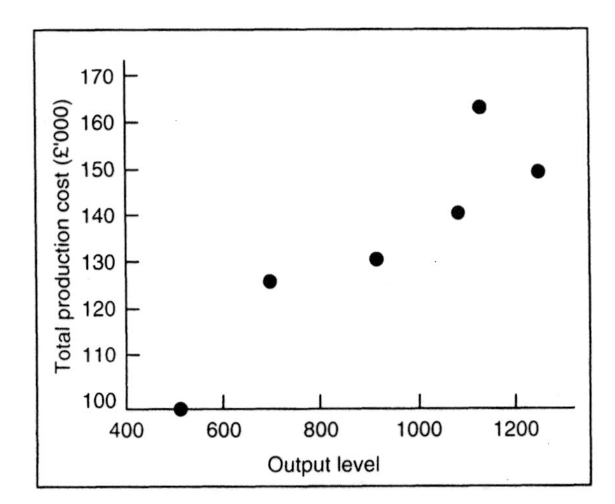

Figure 18.1 Almeria plc – scatter diagram of production cost against output level.

Table 18.3

	Production cost, output		
y(£)	x	xy	x^2
122 000	710	86 620 000	504 100
100 000	500	50 000 000	250 000
127 000	900	114 300 000	810 000
140 000	1100	154 000 000	1 210 000
144 000	1250	180 000 000	1 562 500
161 000	1150	185 150 000	1 322 500
Σ794 000	$\Sigma x = 5610$	$\Sigma(xy) = 770\,070\,000$	$\Sigma x^2 = 5\,659\,100$

In order to solve these two equations we need to bring the coefficients of one variable to a common figure so that when one equation is taken from the other one variable drops out. If we multiply equation (iii) by 935 (i.e. 5610/6) we get a revised equation (v):

$$742\,390\,000 = 5610a + 5245\,350b \qquad \text{(v)}$$

Equation (v) is a transformed version of equation (iii); it expresses the same mathematical relationship as equation (iii) except on a larger scale. If we subtract (v) from (iv) we get

$$770\,070\,000 = 5610a + 5659\,100b$$

$$742\,390\,000 = 5610a + 5245\,350b$$

$$27\,680\,000 = \quad 0 \; + \; 413\,750b \qquad \text{(vi)}$$

Equation (vi) when rearranged gives

$$b = 27\,680\,000/413\,750$$
$$= £66.90 \text{ per unit of output}$$

By substituting the value of b (the variable cost per unit) into either equation (iii), (vi) or (v), the value of the fixed costs (a) can be derived.

Using Equation (iii):

$$a = \frac{794\,000 - 5610 \times 66.90}{6}$$

$$= £69\,780$$

The result of our analysis is that the production cost–output relationship can be described by the linear relationship

Production cost = 69 780 + 66.90 × output quantity

We show this relationship between production cost and output in Figure 18.2.

Note the estimated fixed costs are greater than the fixed costs of £50 000 specified in the example. This could mean that there is a fixed element in one or more of the other cost classifications. However, with only six observations of the cost–output relationship, our estimation of the overall fixed cost will not be particularly reliable.

Linear regression is a straightforward technique for analysing the relationships which exist between pairs of variables. It is, in essence, a method for putting a ruled line through a series of data points to give the best line of fit. As we shall see in Chapter 20, linear regression has other uses for the management accountant. For this reason it is important to note some of the limitations of the technique (apart from the presumption that the underlying relationship is linear).

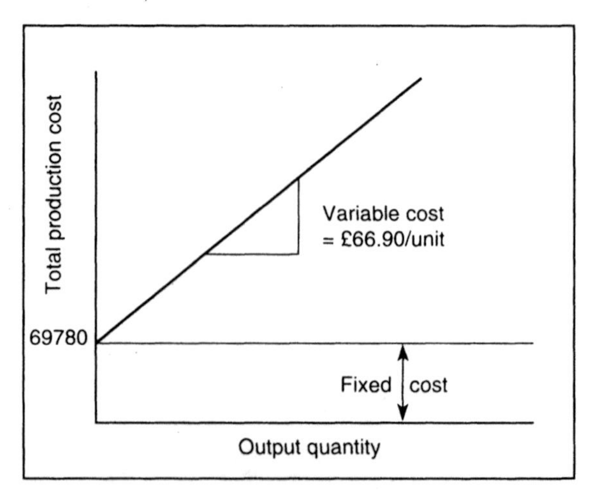

Figure 18.2 Estimated relationship between total production cost and output.

The limitations of linear regression arise from the assumptions upon which the two simultaneous equations (iii) and (vi) are based.

- The line of best fit is that one which minimises the sum of the squared values of the differences between that best fit line and the individual data points. For this reason, linear regression is often referred to as 'ordinary least squares regression'.
- The average value of the deviations of each data point from the line of best fit is zero. Obviously some data points will lie above and some lie below the line of best fit; this assumption means that the differences above and below the line should net out to zero.
- Production costs in any given period are solely dependent upon output quantity in that period; any differences between individual data points and the best fit line are caused by purely random effects and are independent of one another.
- If the production cost could be measured a large number of times at each possible output quantity (i.e. at each possible x-value) then the spread of production costs around the best fit line would be constant along its entire length.

Given all of these assumptions, one would be forgiven for dismissing the technique as too restrictive. Like all mathematical and statistical techniques, linear regression is only as good as the assumptions which support it. However, in most cost estimation problems the assumptions given above are unlikely to be too restrictive, and the technique of linear regression has the great advantage of removing an element of subjective judgement from cost estimation.

The final stage of regression analysis is that of determining the confidence which can be placed in the results obtained.

STATISTICAL MEASURES OF GOODNESS OF FIT

With any linear regression between two variables the first problem is to identify how well the line of best fit represents the data. We can do this by determining the strength of the relationship between the variables. Two variables which are perfectly correlated with one another would have all of their data points lying along the line of best fit. A statistic called the 'correlation coefficient' (which is symbolised as r) takes the value of one if such a perfect fit exists. If the two variables are positively related (i.e. the slope coefficient has a positive sign) then the correlation coefficient would be plus one given a perfect fit. If, on the other hand, the relationship is negative (as we saw in the relationship between price and demand) then the correlation coefficient for a perfect fit is minus one.

The correlation coefficient (r) can have any value between plus and minus one. Completely uncorrelated variables have a correlation coefficient of zero. The closer the correlation coefficient is to its extreme value of plus or minus one, the more confident we can be that the relationship between the two variables is dependable and that the line of best fit is a good representation of the data.

The formula for calculating the correlation coefficient is quite simple:

Correlation coefficient = the slope of the line of best fit multiplied by the ratio of the standard deviations of the x- and y-variables $= b \times \sigma(x)/\sigma(y)$

where $\sigma(x)$ is the standard deviation of the x-variable (output quantity in Almeria's example) and $\sigma(y)$ is the standard deviation of the y-variable (total production cost in Almeria's example).

The standard deviation of the x-variable is given by

$$\sigma(x) = \sqrt{\left\{\frac{(\Sigma(x - \Sigma x/n)^2}{n}\right\}}$$

$$= \sqrt{\left\{\frac{(710 - 5610/6)^2 + (500 - 5610/6)^2 + \cdots + (1150 - 5610/6)^2}{6}\right\}}$$

$$= \sqrt{\left\{\frac{50\,625 + 189\,225 + \cdots + 46\,225}{6}\right\}}$$

$$= 262.20$$

Similarly, the standard deviation of the y-variable can be calculated:

$$\sigma(y) = 19\,136.93$$

The correlation coefficient is given by

$$r = +66.90 \times 262.30/19\,136.93$$
$$= +0.917$$

A statistic closely related to the correlation coefficient is the 'coefficient of statistical determination' or r^2. This statistic is calculated as the square of the correlation coefficient and represents the proportion of variability in the independent variable (y) caused by variation in the dependent variable (x).

For Almeria:

$$r^2 = 0.917^2$$
$$= 0.841 \ (= 84.1\%)$$

The correlation coefficient of 0.917 indicates that there is a strong relationship between production cost and output quantity, and the coefficient of statistical determination tells us that 84.1% of the variability of production cost is explained by changes in output quantity. Therefore, the remaining 15.9% variation must be attributable to other factors, for example the following.

- Step costs may be present in one or more of the cost functions which underlie total production cost. Steps will produce a lowering of the correlation coefficient, although their existence may well be quite predictable.
- Random operating variables may be present, as discussed above.

Combining together simple regression analysis and statistical measures of goodness of fit, it is possible for management to gain a good understanding of how their costs have varied with output in the past and, given appropriate caution, estimate how those costs are likely to vary in the future.

CONCLUSION

In this chapter we have described a statistical method for the analysis of cost data which allows us to convert historically derived cost figures into cost relationships. We have supplemented the method with a review of the statistics of correlation and determination which allow us to place some confidence on the goodness of fit of a set of data points.

Chapter 19

The Economics of the Pricing Decision

Level M

Contents

Summary

This chapter, in conjunction with the last, demonstrates the heavy interaction between the output and pricing decision. These two classes of decision are closely related, and price is heavily influenced by the market conditions under which the firm operates. In many respects the problems outlined in these chapters bring strategic accounting into very close alignment with the microeconomic theories of consumer behaviour and the firm. In this chapter, we give a brief introduction to the economics of the pricing decision. We outline the different market types with which the firm may be faced and identify the sorts of information which will be relevant in pricing decisions. Finally, we discuss the problems of pricing in markets where market concentration distorts the pricing process.

INTRODUCTION

The pricing decision is one of the most complex problems faced by management. As we have emphasised before, in most situations, the price of a product is determined by factors outside the firm's immediate control. The principal determining factor of price is the supply and demand for the product concerned. More specifically, the following factors all have an important bearing upon the pricing decision:

- the ability of the firm to differentiate in the eyes of its customers its own products from the products of its competitors;
- the advertising and other marketing methods which the firm uses to alter the tastes of its customers;
- the credit facilities and other terms of trade (such as guarantees and after-sales service) which the firm can offer its customers;
- the ability of the firm to minimise its transaction costs in selling its products and its willingness to pass on the cost savings to its customers in the form of lower prices.

A product will only be purchased if it 'adds value' to the customer by satisfying a perceived need at a particular point in time. The added-value equation which motivates purchase is where the benefit (moderated by the benefit risk) to the consumer exceeds the unit price. As we will discuss in detail in Chapter 21, increased added value arises by creating products which offer higher product capability or greater functional simplicity in use. The greater the difference between consumer's evaluation of benefit (under constant benefit risk) and the price the greater will be the demand for the product in the market. It is the analysis of the relationship of demand to benefit and price which underlies the economic theory of demand.

In Figure 19.1 we show the principal factors affecting demand in terms of the functional benefit a product offers to the consumer. From Figure 19.1, if the benefit component of the demand relationship is held constant then it follows that demand and price should be negatively related, i.e.

$$\text{demand} = \text{constant} - f_d\ (\text{price})$$

where f_d is the functional relationship between demand and price.

Conversely, for the producer the level of supply will be governed by the unit price less the average unit production cost (moderated by cost risk) at the level of supply chosen (Figure 19.2).

Given constant unit average production cost there will be a positive relationship between the number of units supplied and the price.

$$\text{Supply} = f_s\ (\text{price}) - \text{constant}$$

Given the absence of any intermediaries between producers and consumers (in which case the price to the supplier will be different to the price paid by the consumer) market equilibrium will be achieved when the quantity supplied equals the quantity demanded.

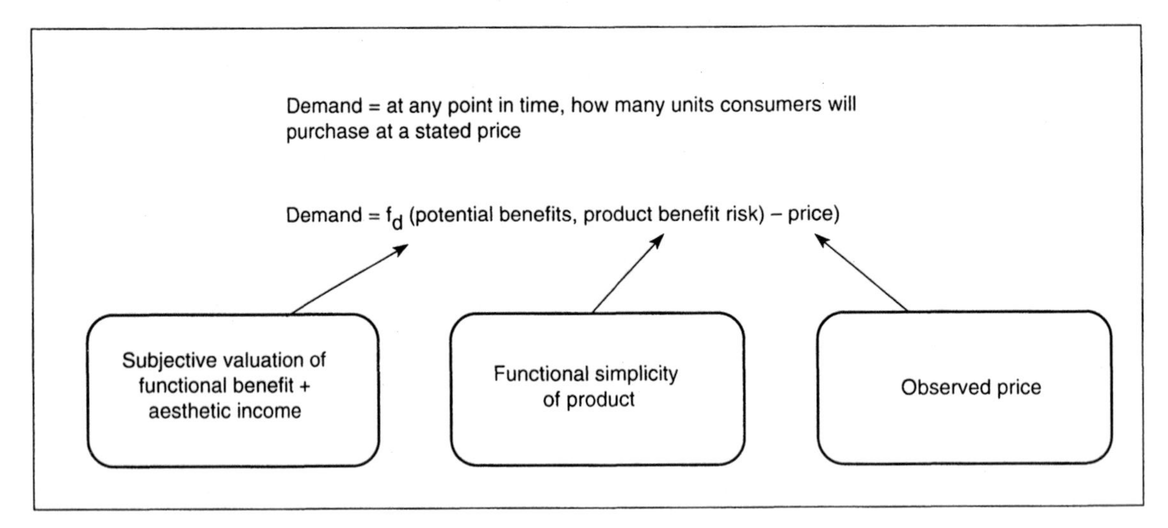

Figure 19.1 The demand function.

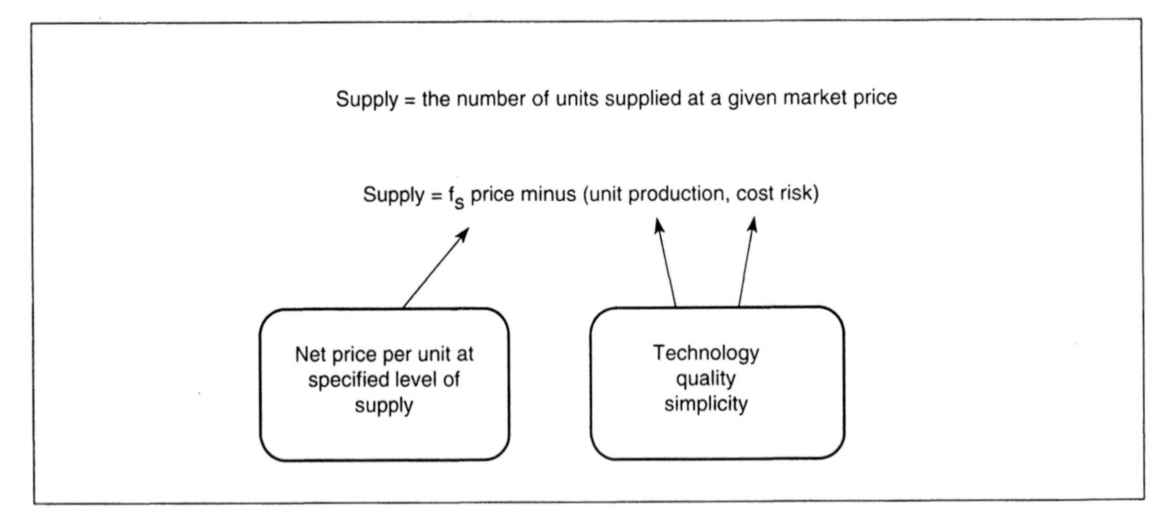

Figure 19.2 The supply function.

THE ROLE OF THE MARKET IN DETERMINING PRICE

The supply curve for a particular product should, therefore, represent an upward-sloping relationship between quantity and price. In Figure 19.3 we show these two relationships superimposed upon one another. P_e is the price and Q_e is the output level for a particular product when its demand and supply are in equilibrium.

The two curves in Figure 19.3 represent the supply and demand for a product in the context of its total market. The supply and demand relationship represents the basis of pricing analysis for managers in firms and is heavily dependent upon the identified elements in the pricing equations, which can be summarised as:

- the valuation of the product by consumers in rela-tion to their perceived needs and the alternative means of satisfying those needs (the demand function);
- the costs of production and other aspects of supply (the supply function).

THE MARKET CONTEXT FOR A PRODUCT

The economists' classification of market types is a useful starting point for understanding the problems of pricing. This classification can be characterised by the following.

- The number of suppliers in the market.
- The number of buyers or consumers in the market.
- The type of product (i.e. whether it is a uniform commodity, one unit of which cannot be distinguished from another, or whether it is a product which can be given special characteristics which will separate it from the competition).

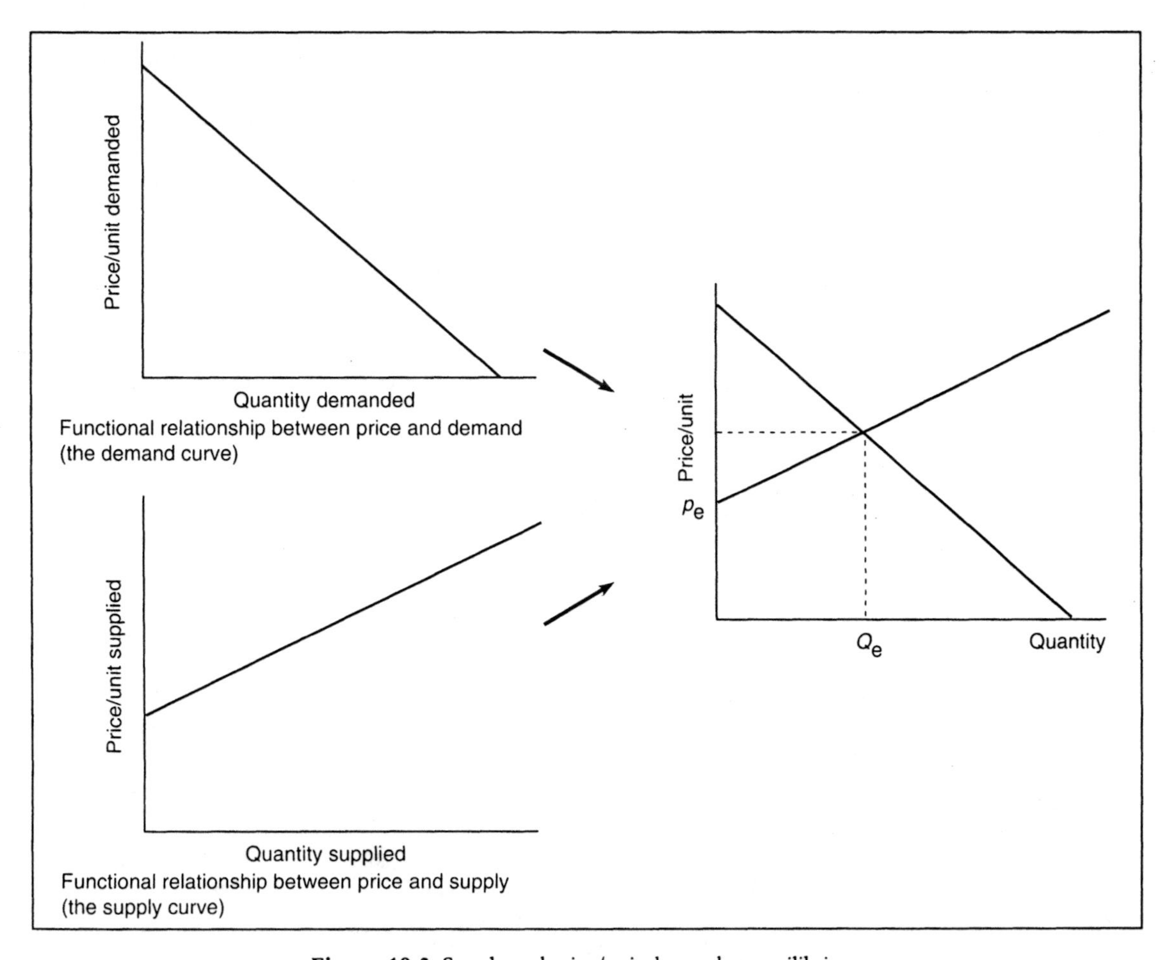

Figure 19.3 Supply and price/unit demand at equilibrium.

- The barriers to entry for potential new competitors in the market. A 'barrier to entry' is simply the levels of non-direct, investment cost required to enter and transact in the particular market. A seller of matches on a street corner faces very low costs in entering that particular business (providing he or she does it legally) whilst the seller of telecommunications services will find very high capital and regulatory costs impeding entry into those particular markets.
- The degree of discretion which the management of the supplying firm has over the product's price.

In Table 19.1 we show the six principal categories of market.

The assumptions implicit within both the agency and TCE approaches to the firm (see Chapter 3) that managers will always attempt to maximise their discretion leads to the consequence that they will seek the greatest degree of monopoly power possible within the markets in which they operate. Monopoly gives an exceptional profit reward to the supplier compared with a perfectly competitive situation (where no exceptional profit can be earned over and above the full opportunity cost of production). Creating value added for a firm is synonymous with gaining some monopoly power by one or both of the following:

- increased product differentiation (which is translated into net benefit to the consumer);
- reducing the average unit cost of production.

Monopoly and perfect competition are competitive limiting cases. In the overwhelming majority of cases, normal markets are characterised by products or services which are not exact and perfect substitutes (monopolistic competition) and where some degree of supply-side concentration exists (i.e. a limited number of competing suppliers). As we have discussed before, strategy is the game of realising sustainable competitive advantage in such market contexts.

In a situation of perfect competition the producing firm is a price taker and, even though the demand for the total supply of the product within the market will be downward sloping, the individual firm will face a flat demand curve where price is independent of output quantity. In this situation the firm can do nothing to affect the price of its product and should set its output level at the point where the increase in total cost incurred through producing one extra unit of output (the product's marginal cost) is equal to marginal revenue, which is, in this case, the market price per unit at all output levels.

This analysis of the behaviour of a producer in a perfectly competitive market assumes that producers and consumers are physically separated from their point of sale, in which case such producers will have to include their transport costs in their marginal cost of production. Similarly, if other transaction costs are incurred (perhaps through the use of wholesalers or brokers in the market) then those transaction costs must also be included as part of the cost of production. Later on in this chapter we investigate how pricing affects the decision whether to sell through intermediaries (where distribution costs are borne out of the price differential that a firm can earn compared with that paid by its ultimate

Table 19.1 Characteristics of competitive markets

	Number of suppliers	Number of consumers	Barriers to entry	Supplier's discretion over price	Product type
Perfect competition	Many	Many	None	None	Homogeneous
Monopolistic competition	Many	Many	Low	Some	Heterogeneous
Monopoly	One	Many	High	Very high	Homogeneous
Oligopolistic competition	Few	Many	Significant	Considerable	Homo/heterogeneous
Monopsony	More than one	One	High	Some	Homogeneous
Bilateral monopsony	One	One	High	Some	Homogeneous

customers) or engage in direct selling (where distribution forms part of the producer's costs).

Market monitoring in a perfect market is restricted to establishing three facts concerning the product:

- the price of the product, which will be in a state of continual change;
- the marginal cost of the product concerned;
- any transaction costs incurred in selling the product.

Management, in its search for some degree of monopoly power, will attempt, as far as possible, to differentiate its product(s) from the competition. In the retail trade, for example, producers often attempt to create a distinction between their products and those of their competitors by some minor physical modification. Such modifications might be achieved through different packaging, brand advertising or any other marketing ploys that the firm can dream up. The firm's intention is to create some sense of brand identification in the consumer's mind which will lead to a situation where higher prices can be charged than would otherwise be the case. The type of market where products are differentiated in minor ways is called 'monopolistic competition'. Naturally, if a producer manages to reap exceptional profits in the short term we would expect competitors to move into the market as the barriers to entry are typically quite low.

A monopolistically competitive firm faces a downward sloping demand curve for its product although it may be highly price elastic (remember that in a perfectly competitive market each producer faces a perfectly price elastic demand curve). Consequently, such a firm faces both a downward-sloping demand curve and a downward-sloping marginal-revenue function, and maximises its profits when marginal revenue equals marginal cost.

In the short run, a producer in a monopolistically competitive market will be able to take advantage of the benefits of product differentiation and make greater than normal profits. One strategy for doing this is to reduce output in order to gain a higher price. Indeed, simple economic analysis indicates that the optimising price–output combination for a firm with a competitive advantage will be set at a lower output than would be the case if that firm were in a perfectly competitive market.

Monopoly is that situation where barriers to entry are so high that potential competitors are dissuaded from entering a particular market. A monopolistic firm is, effectively, the 'industry' for the supply of the product concerned. Again, as with the two previous market types, the monopolist should set a price output combination which equates marginal revenue with marginal cost. The optimal position for a pure monopolist will be at a lower output level than would hold if the product was supplied through the medium of a perfectly competitive market.

Monopolies can occur for the following reasons.

- Some technical barrier exists which would impose unacceptably high set-up costs for a potential competitor. For example, since the early 1980s the US Government through NASA held a monopoly on satellite-recovery services. At the time, only the USA had the technology in the form of the Space Shuttle to track and recover damaged or off-course satellites. The costs which would be faced by any potential competitor would be prohibitively high even if a viable market for such services could be established.
- The government believes (for public policy reasons) that certain products should be supplied by the state or under state control. For example, the government in the UK and in most other countries as well, is a monopoly supplier of defence and policing (although in the latter case certain aspects of police work are available from specialist security firms).
- The grant of a patent or copyright has given a producer the legal right to monopoly selling of his or her product. Such a legal monopoly right is usually granted for a fixed number of years only.
- Certain products or services are held under monopoly control by the government. For example, in the UK the government controls (or has controlled in the past) either directly or through the medium of public corporations such services as telecommunications, the post, gas, electricity and water.

Oligopoly, along with monopolistic competition, forms by far the most usual market situation. Oligopoly exists where a few large firms (relative to the market's size) account for a large proportion of the total supply of the product concerned. There may be a large number of smaller firms in the market as well, although they will be price takers and of little significance in the context of the market as a whole. The existence of a small group of large, competing firms makes oligopoly a very interesting market type.

Oligopolies are interesting because they permit the possibility of collusion (overt and covert) between the participants and also the possibility of interdependent reactions which have more to do with psychology than economics. It is in oligopolies (and in monopolistically competitive markets to a lesser extent) that competitive action, in the colloquial sense, can be fiercest. In perfect markets, competition is automatic and almost inhuman. Indeed, the great Scottish economist, Adam Smith, referred to such market mechanisms as the 'operation of an invisible hand'. With oligopolies it is just the opposite.

Oligopolies can occur through geographical factors. For example, petrol stations within a particular vicinity can form a small oligopoly for the supply of petrol and other motor products. Many trading situations exist where such localised oligopolies can form. At the other extreme, the clearing banks and the major oil companies have arisen as national oligopolies in the UK.

Two particular phenomena associated with oligopolies, and to a lesser extent monopolistic competition, are relevant to the managerial decision maker. First, the role of advertising and its effect upon the demand curve for a product and, second, the problem of 'sticky' prices.

THE ROLE OF ADVERTISING AND OTHER METHODS OF PRODUCT PROMOTION

In perfectly competitive and monopolistic markets there is little incentive to advertise. Advertising is principally a marketing technique for the oligopolistic or monopolistically competitive firm. Advertising serves a number of functions.

- It can be used to inform potential consumers of a new product and to give details of the product's price, function and physical characteristics.
- It can be used to alter the shape of the product's demand curve. Usually, advertising will be used to push the demand curve to the right and to make the demand for the product less elastic. A steeper demand curve (i.e. a less elastic demand curve) will give a higher marginal revenue and therefore increase the maximum profit at constant marginal cost. In practice this increased profit will be partly offset by the increased advertising costs so incurred.
- It can be used to create product differentiation by stressing a product's virtues compared with the competition.
- It can be used to create a brand image and brand loyalty. Much advertising is directed at the individual who is already an established customer for the firm's products. Some advertising is also aimed at reducing the 'cognitive dissonance' (see below) of customers after sale. Many people feel uncomfortable after a major purchase and actively seek out reinforcing advertising for the product concerned.

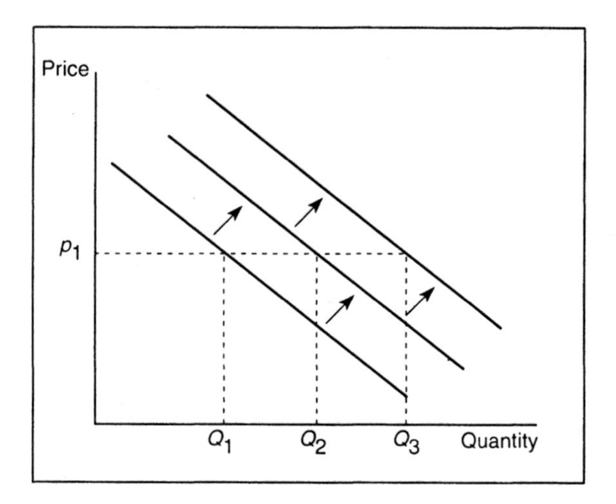

Figure 19.4 Demand shifts with advertising.

Advertising expenditure brings a further dimension to the price–demand relationship. In Figure 19.4 we show the effect of different levels of advertising expenditure upon sales and the different demand curves which follow.

THE PROBLEM OF STICKY PRICES

The phenomenon of sticky prices is found in oligopolistic markets where there is often considerable resistance to downward movement in prices.

This resistance can be apparent even in the face of changes in demand or government action, such as changes in the ease with which credit can be obtained.

To understand the problem of sticky prices, consider the situation of an oligopolistic competitor who decides, unilaterally, to cut the price of the product concerned. If none of the other competitors was to respond and follow the price decrease, the price-cutting competitor might be able to increase both market share and total revenue (although this would depend on the point elasticity of demand facing the price-cutting firm at that point in time). However, it would be unusual for competing firms not to take some form of retaliatory action in order to hold their respective market shares. It is very unlikely that a price-cutting firm would be able to gain a real volume increase from a cut in price;

therefore, downward price movements will be along a relatively price-inelastic demand curve.

On the other hand, if our single competitor were, unilaterally, to increase the price of the product concerned, especially if it was a real price increase, i.e. one over and above that justified by the rate of inflation, then the other competitors would be unlikely to follow suit. As a consequence, price increases tend to follow a relatively elastic demand curve. The oligopolistic competitor is faced by two demand curves: one, which is relatively inelastic, governs price reductions and the other, which is relatively elastic, governs price increases. In effect, therefore, the oligopolist faces a 'kinked demand curve', with the kink at the current price–output relationship (Figure 19.5).

At the producer's current price–quantity relationship downward price movements will be along the section O, B2 of demand curve B1, B2. Likewise, price increases will be along the more elastic demand curve A1, A2. These two demand curves will give rise to two different, intersecting total-revenue curves and, therefore, at the firm's current output level, to a 'mobile discontinuity'. At whatever level the firm chooses to sell its product or service it will face one demand curve for subsequent price decreases and another for subsequent price increases. In other words, the 'kink' in the demand curve will follow price changes as they are made. This discontinuity in the firm's total-revenue function adds a further level of possible sophistication to the break-even analysis developed in the last chapter.

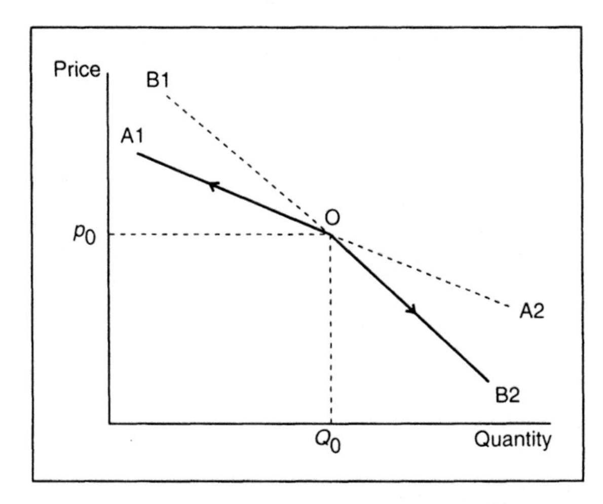

Figure 19.5 'Kinked' demand curve. P_0 = the price at which current quantity demanded (Q_0) is sold.

The kinked demand-curve model goes some way toward explaining why some products (such as motor-cars for example) change price infrequently while other products (such as commodities and ordinary shares for example) change price almost by the minute. A number of other models have been developed which attempt to explain how oligopolies behave. Some models are based upon theories of price leadership, where one firm traditionally sets the price and the other competitors follow suit. Other theories assume interdependencies in behaviour as each competitor attempts to take into account the behaviour of other firms in the market.

One of the most sophisticated attempts to deal with the problem of oligopolies uses the Theory of Games developed by the two mathematicians von Neumann and Morgenstern. This approach is based upon the idea that, in every competitive situation between two or more 'players', each will act in the most rational way. Indeed, it may well be that in certain situations the most rational action will be to deceive the other player by making an irrational choice! In an oligopolistic situation, the game played is, in the terminology of games theory, a 'zero-sum' game where the gains of one competitor will be the loss of the other (assuming, of course, a constant total market). Each competitor can build up a table of payoffs which follow from each possible action it can take given the possible retaliatory move of the opposition. Certain strategies can then be followed which dictate the action the competitor should take. The bibliography given at the end of this book will help you if you wish to pursue this topic.

We will defer discussion of monopsony and bilateral monopsony until we deal with contract pricing later in the next chapter.

CONCLUSION

In this chapter we have examined the economics of the pricing decision and the complexities caused by different market contexts. We have accepted the general economic position that markets will establish equilibrium prices which clear supply and demand. We have considered the special problems of monopolistic markets and pricing in other types of imperfect market. In the next chapter we will build upon this analysis and consider the problems of price setting in practice.

Chapter 20

The Practical Evaluation of Price

Level M

Contents

Summary

In the last chapter, we examined the microeconomics of the pricing decision. In this chapter we turn our attention to the practical evaluation of price using both cost and market research methods. In addition, we outline the problems which face a firm bidding for a contract to supply goods or services to a single buyer. Unfortunately, many of the problems of pricing are unstructured. That is, the accumulated wisdom of management (or textbooks) may be of little use when it comes down to setting the price for a product in a new market context. For this reason we stress that effective pricing must utilise a variety of different theoretical and practical skills.

PRICE EVALUATION IN PRACTICE

Most firms who survive for any length of time in a competitive market recognise the impact of their market situation upon the prices they can charge. However, many managers would appear, by their behaviour, to believe that an important component of the pricing decision is the so-called 'full cost of production'. Classical economic approaches to pricing take a rigorous market-based approach, and argue what amounts to little more than a truism that, in competitive market environments, it is the market which determines the price which can be charged for a given product at a given level of output.

However, there are two ways of attempting to evaluate the price which can be justified in terms of economics:

(i) external market analysis, where the firm attempts to determine the demand curve for its product;

(ii) internal factor and competitive position analysis, where the firm imputes a price from its factor costs and market position;

Two further approaches are also available:

(iii) accounting cost-based procedures, which are based upon some notion of cost recovery plus a fair return;

(iv) 'gut feel' pricing, which relies upon the fuzzy judgements of expert managers who may have some concept of what is a reasonable price to charge in particular circumstances.

We will now consider each of these approaches in turn.

Demand analysis

One of the crucial requirements of market research is to be able to convert its conclusions into the pricing and output decision and to indicate strategies for the maximisation of a firm's or product's competitive position in the market place. Both of these areas can be summarised into a price algorithm which relates product price to output and other product attributes which influence consumer's perceptions of the value to them of the product concerned. In this section we will look exclusively at the relationship between product price and the level of demand. In Chapter 21 we explore the pricing significance of quality variables.

Test marketing

For many commodities in the retail sector it is possible to measure the demand for a product at given locations using different prices. If the research is controlled for time (i.e. testing markets at the same point in time), social mix of the local population, product display and promotion it is possible to infer a demand curve from sales levels (normalised to a certain population size). Such an analysis would only have relevance over a limited range of demand and could only be extended outside the data range by statistical interpolation (and great care) and within markets of particular spending preferences (see Figure 20.1).

EXAMPLE

A national retailing chain was offering a new range of oriental style convenience foods. This chain's stores are located in towns with a high preponderance of A, B and C in their social groupings. The prices were set in a sample of ten stores of common size with equivalent display and in-store promotional activity. No other advertising took place for the product line. The weekly returns over a six-month trial period showed average weekly sales in each store, as shown in Table 20.1.

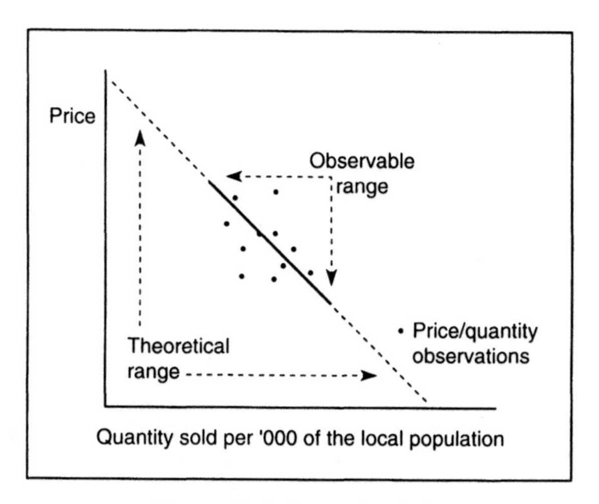

Figure 20.1 Demand analysis.

In Table 20.1, the values for the slope of the demand curve and the intercept with the price axis were calculated using OLS linear regression (see Chapter 19) to generate a price (p)/demand (Q) relationship as follows:

$$p = 6.34735 - 0.00313Q$$

The degree of goodness of fit (as measured by the correlation coefficient (r)) is -0.91033, which indicates that there is a high degree of association between the two variables.

We have drawn the scattergram of the data in Figure 20.2 and overlaid the line of best fit. This result then gives management the ability to estimate the likely weekly sales and total revenue which can be earned from any price set within the range.

The problems with test marketing is that it relies on the quality of the experimental design in controlling other determinants of demand apart from price. It also relies upon a producer being able to identify a selection of comparable test outlets which is normally only feasible with products entering the retail sector in some volume.

Where this type of experimental situation cannot be constructed it is sometimes possible for a

Table 20.1 Sales, price and statistical data for a test market survey

Store	Sales	Price
1	350	5.30
2	321	5.35
3	270	5.40
4	278	5.45
5	264	5.50
6	235	5.55
7	245	5.60
8	188	5.70
9	210	5.75
10	220	5.80

$b = -0.00313$
$a = 6.34735$
$r = -0.91033$

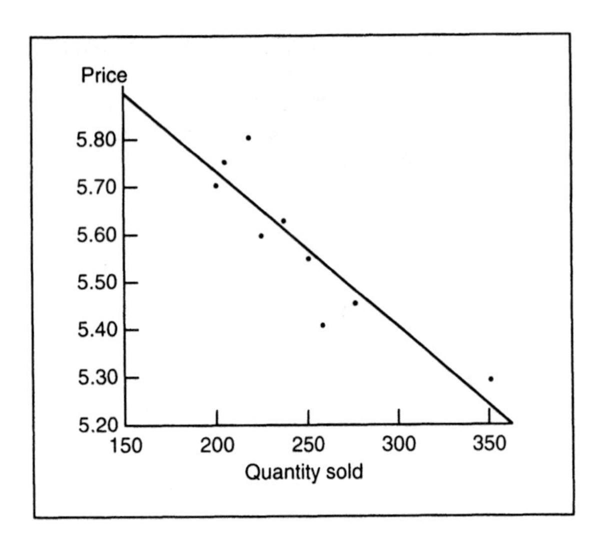

Figure 20.2 Line of best fit on demand data.

producer to look at past price (corrected to real terms) and sales volume data and to perform a regression analysis on that data to see if there is a reasonable relationship from which a current demand curve can be created.

ECONOMIC COST-BASED PRICE EVALUATION

In a perfectly competitive market, the efficient firm will be able to determine its price either by direct observation of market price levels or by the measurement of the full opportunity cost of all of its own factors of production. Because in a perfectly competitive market there are zero information, transaction and contracting costs, the consumer is purchasing all of the factors which go into a given product at their opportunity cost. A perfectly efficient firm by inspection of its opportunity costs of production will be able to observe the ruling market price.

In an imperfectly competitive market, the consumer is purchasing all of the factors which go into a given product at their opportunity cost, plus an element (which we call 'super profit') which is the market imperfection cost borne by the consumer and which the consumer is prepared to tolerate, rather than choose his or her next best alternative in finding another source of supply, or entering into the 'do it yourself' business. In order to develop this pricing procedure, the firm must evaluate the full opportunity cost to the individual consumer who chose to use direct market contracting to fabricate the product or service to an identical standard, rather than purchasing the finished product or service from the firm concerned. Such an individual we will call a 'naive consumer', in that we assume that they will have to contract for all of the factors of production, with no specialist knowledge at their disposal. In Figure 20.3 we describe an evaluation procedure for assembling the components of the maximum price which a consumer would be prepared to pay to a firm as a producer, rather than engage in production on his or her own account.

This evaluation procedure consists of two elements. First, the firm must evaluate the opportunity costs to itself of all factors which an individual would expect to bear, but excluding any marketing or final stock holding costs. These are components of a firm's cost which cannot be borne by a market. They do not arise for the single unit consumer/producer and must be offset against any relative cost advantage which a firm may have.

Second, the firm should then evaluate any additional costs and benefits which would be borne by an individual producing, by individual market contracts, over and above that which would be borne by a firm in achieving the same ends.

The combination of these two elements represent the maximum price which an individual should be prepared to pay to a producing firm rather than engage in production on their own account. Clearly, a firm will only be able to win this price if two conditions hold.

(i) There is no competing and undercutting source of supply for an identical product.
(ii) The consumer is fully informed of the costs which he or she would have to bear in production by direct market contracting.

In practice, direct contracting may not be a viable alternative for consumers, especially if there are gross imperfections in the input markets, and where information costs are very high. However, this comparative pricing procedure is an effective method (and one which many businesses employ intuitively) and is just as likely to deliver high quality pricing as demand analysis based upon market research (the cost of which cannot be passed on to consumers) or 'gut feel' pricing approaches.

The new housing market brings home the point we are making here. A house buyer in this market is faced with two choices: either purchase a new house from a house builder or build the house themselves. Consider the situation where the prospective purchaser has found a piece of land with the requisite planning consent. The purchaser could attempt to

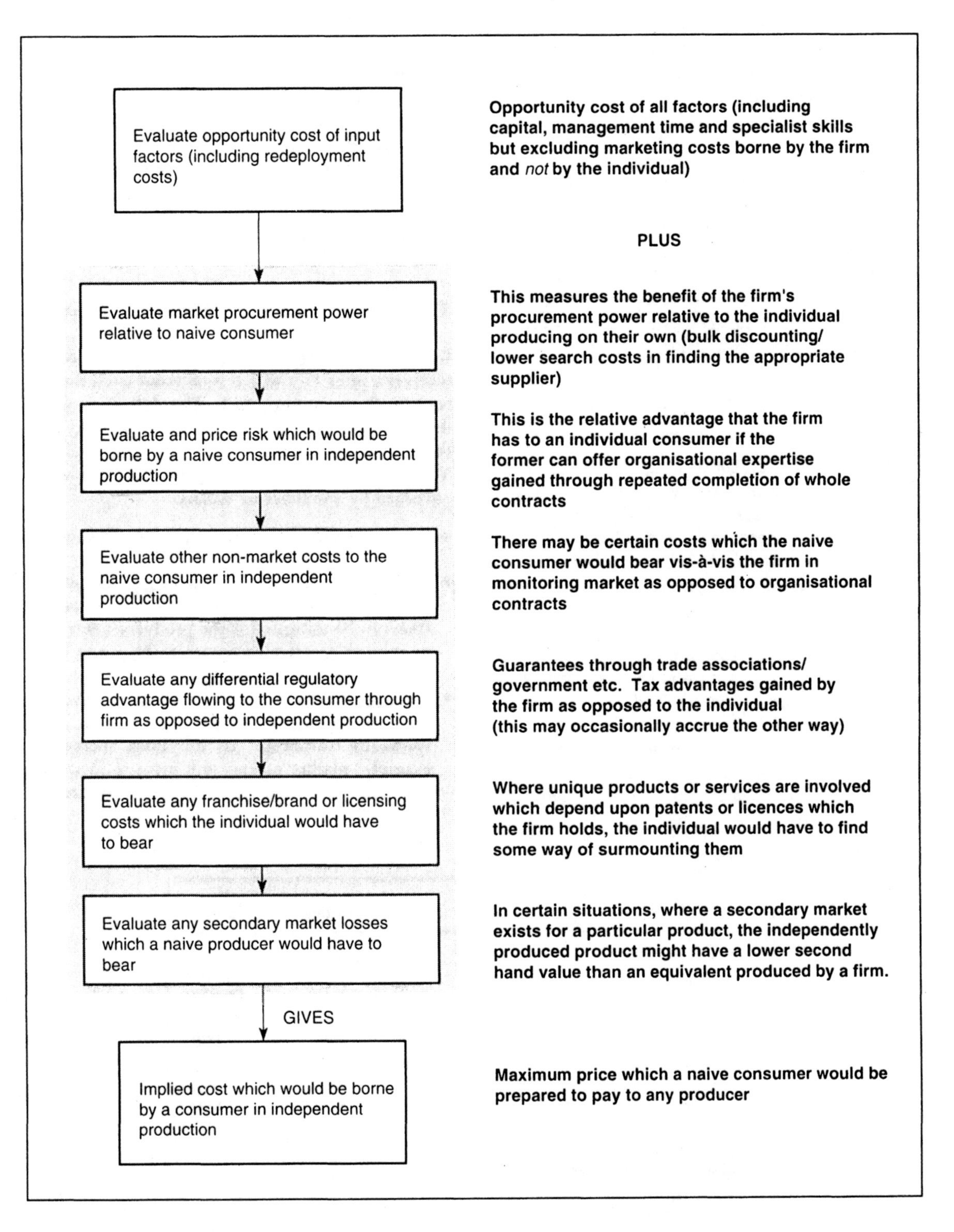

Figure 20.3 The evaluation of price.

collect all of the materials, labour and technical skills (architects and surveyors) necessary to construct the building by direct market transacting. Alternatively, he or she could contract a building firm to achieve the same end. The price such a firm would charge would be:

(i) its opportunity cost of construction (which may be less than the sum of the factor costs which the purchaser would face in a 'self build' project because of its market power in procurement);
(ii) a knowledge- and risk-sharing premium, because it is able use its superior experience to manage the resource collection and construction at a lower cost than a 'naive' purchaser.

EXAMPLE

A house builder is considering the price to be charged for a 200 m² dwelling to be constructed on a one fifth of a hectare site. In evaluating the price to be charged he takes the factors in Table 20.2 into account as the cost which would be incurred by an individual building the property on their own account.

The builder could also impute, as a cost to the individual building their own house, a realistic value of the personal time cost involved and some compensation value for the risk and effort which the individual would have to bear. This, with the £114 500, gives the maximum which a reasonable individual would be prepared to pay to avoid the task of building their own house through direct contracting. In comparison with his own opportunity cost of production, the builder enjoys, on the basis of the figures in Table 20.2, a 31.1% margin which can be exploited in pricing a house of this type. Ignoring capital costs for both parties, the value of £87 300 also represents the minimum price which the builder should charge. A lower price would be a value loss price for the firm. We will return to this issue later in this chapter.

THE PROBLEM OF INTERMEDIARIES

In the majority of market situations the producer receives a price (p_s) which is different from the price paid by the consumer (p_d). The difference will be the turn taken by a wholesaler or broker who acts as the market intermediary in the situation concerned. The magnitude of the intermediary's charge will be governed by a number of factors:

- the cost to the intermediary of performing the service;
- the risk which the intermediary perceives as inherent in the brokerage or wholesaling contract (risk can be mitigated if the producer offers a 'sale or return' contract or agrees to bear part of the intermediary's stockholding cost);
- a situation where the intermediary believes that either the producer or the customer has an information advantage. In the stock market, for example, market makers will increase their 'turn' (i.e. the price difference between buying and

Table 20.2

	Individual	Firm
Land (at auction)	£14 000	£14 000
Building materials	55 000	43 000
Direct contract labour cost	22 000	18 000
Surveyor's fee (for construction planning and management)	10 000	3 000
Architect's fee for drawings and periodic reports	4 000	–
Local Authority costs and planning fees	2 000	2 000
Plant hire and scaffolding costs	5 000	5 000
Legal fees and duties	1 500	1 500
Mortgage surveyor's fees	700	700
Building guarantee registration fee:		
non-registered builders	350	
registered builder		100
Estimated 'one-off' construction cost	£114 550	£87 300

selling) if they believe that there are market traders in the market who may possess some specialist knowledge that they do not or have access to information of which may be denied to them.

Generally, if the cost of direct selling (C_d) to a producer is less than the difference taken by the intermediary $p_d - p_s$ then direct selling will be preferred. Similarly, direct selling will not be preferred over an intermediary's services if the difference taken is likely to be less than the cost of direct selling.

ACCOUNTING-BASED PRICING METHODS

A number of full-costing techniques exist, although most are just simple variants of the two main types we will discuss here:

- cost-plus pricing;
- target rate-of-return pricing.

Cost-plus pricing

With cost-plus pricing the price of a product is built up from the sum of:

- the variable costs of production;
- a proportion of the firm's long-run costs (which will be fixed in the short term);
- a specified margin which is usually set as a proportion of the total costs derived for the product.

EXAMPLE

Almeria Ltd's monthly production figures for typewriters are as follows:

Variable components cost	*£25.10 per unit*
Variable labour cost (5 hours)	*£33.40 per unit*
Variable overheads	*£8.40 per unit*
	£66.90 per unit
Total labour hours in production	*4000 hours*
Total fixed cost at a planned output of 800 units	*£94 780.00*

Almeria's management would like to set its prices at such a level that a 20% profit is made on full cost. It is company policy to allocate fixed overheads on the basis of the labour hours employed in production.

The unit price per typewriter will be made up as follows:

Variable cost per unit produced cost
\+
fixed cost allocated to each unit produced
\+
percentage of fixed plus variation cost per unit
=
price per unit

This technique is straightforward except for the calculation of the fixed cost allocation per unit. In Almeria's case, management has decided that the appropriate allocation base is the number of labour hours in production. In practice, any base could be used for allocating the fixed overhead charge. Depending upon the circumstances and the nature of the fixed overheads, machine hours used or floor space occupied by the production facility might be more appropriate. With a labour-intensive process, for example, an overhead allocation based upon labour hours employed in production might be deemed most appropriate. On the other hand, a capital-intensive process which uses expensive equipment in production may indicate an allocation based upon machine hours employed in production.

The allocated overhead charge per unit is calculated as follows:

$$\text{fixed overhead charge per unit} = \frac{\text{total fixed overhead to be allocated}}{\text{total labour hours employed in production}} \times \text{number of labour hours required to produce each unit}$$

which for Almeria gives

$$\text{fixed overhead charge per unit} = \frac{94\,780}{4000} \times 5 = £118.48 \text{ per unit}$$

Therefore, the cost per typewriter produced is:

Variable component cost	£25.10
Variable labour cost	£33.40
Variable overhead cost	£8.40
Allocated fixed overhead charge	£118.48
Full production cost	£185.38
Plus mark-up at 20%	£37.07
Price per unit	£222.45

The use of the particular cost-plus formula laid down by Almeria's management gives a price per typewriter of £222.45. Before we consider the implications of this pricing policy, we will outline the method of pricing using target rates of return.

Target rate-of-return pricing

EXAMPLE

Upon further consideration, Almeria's management decides that the most appropriate pricing policy would be one which returns, at the targeted monthly output of 800 typewriters, a rate of return on capital employed of 10% per annum. Almeria's total capital employed in its typewriter business is £2 495 000 and the expected total cost of typewriter production for the year is expected to be £1 450 580.

This method of pricing is similar to the cost-plus method outlined above except that the mark-up applied to cost is based upon the desired rate of return on capital employed rather than upon a simple rate applied to cost.

A target rate of return 10% per annum means that on a total capital employed of £2 495 000 a profit of £249 500 must be earned as:

$$\text{rate of return on capital employed} = \frac{\text{annual net profit}}{\text{capital employed}} \times 100$$

therefore:

$$\text{annual net profit} = \frac{\text{rate of return on capital employed}}{100} \times \text{capital employed}$$

$$= 0.1 \times 2\,495\,000$$

$$= £249\,500$$

From this we can calculate that on total typewriter production a profit mark-up of 17.2% will be required as:

$$\text{Percentage mark-up} = \frac{\text{target profit}}{\text{total production cost}} \times 100$$

$$= \frac{249\,500}{1\,450\,580} \times 100$$

$$= 17.2\%$$

Using this rate of mark-up we can calculate the price per typewriter as follows:

Variable component cost	£25.10
Variable labour cost	£33.40
Variable overheads	£8.40
Allocated fixed cost	£118.48
Full cost	£185.38
Plus: mark-up to give a 10% rate of return on capital employed, £185.38 × 0.172	£31.89
Price per unit	£217.27

The question which now remains is how do these two pricing systems compare with a pricing policy based upon a knowledge of the firm's demand curve. From Chapter 18 where we first encountered Almeria's problems we know that the product demand curve is given by the formula

$$p = 290 - 0.1Q$$

where p and Q are the price per unit and the number of units output, respectively.

The demand curve indicates that a planned output of 800 units can be sold at a price of £210 per unit as

$$p = 290 - 0.1 \times 800$$
$$= £210$$

At this price, Almeria will earn a total revenue from sales of

$$\text{Total revenue} = £210 \times 800$$
$$= £168\,000$$

In Table 20.3 we compare this result with that obtained using both the cost-plus and the target rate-of-return formulae.

In each case, the total cost of production is calculated as

$$\text{Total cost} = \text{total unit cost} \times \text{quantity produced} - \text{fixed costs}$$

Using Almeria's demand curve we have calculated the level of output which will be sold at each price. Given the output level and the price, it is then a straightforward matter to calculate the total revenue.

Clearly, pricing a product without understanding the market implications of the price cannot

Table 20.3

	Market pricing	Cost-plus	Rate of return
Price per unit (£)	210.00	222.45	217.27
Number sold using the formula $p = 290 - 0.1\,Q$ (units)	800.00	675.50	727.30
Total revenue (£)	168 000.00	150 264.97	158 020.47
Total cost of production (£)	148 300.00	139 970.95	143 436.37
Net profit (£)	19 700.00	10 294.02	14 584.10

guarantee that the best price will be obtained for a given output level. However, many managers advocate cost-based pricing techniques, or variants of them, for pricing in practice. A number of reasons can be put forward for this behaviour.

- It is sometimes suggested that it is often impossible to determine the shape of a product's demand curve in the time scale in which a pricing decision must be made by management. This argument has particular force in rapidly changing markets such as the fashion industry or the computer industry. It may also be that a producer racing to get a new product onto the market before the competition may not be able to undertake the market research and draw up a demand curve for the product concerned in the time available.
- Another argument which is often put forward points out that a firm's prices, in the long run, must cover its fixed costs of production, or the business will not be viable. However, as we have seen in Almeria's example above, the company would clearly have done better, in the long run, to price the product at the price which would just clear its total production. In fact, we could argue that fixed-formula pricing will lead management to forget the linkage which always exists between pricing and output decisions in practice.
- A more sophisticated argument sometimes put forward claims that fixed-formula pricing is an imperfect attempt to reach the 'economic' price for a product in a competitive environment where zero economic profits will be earned. Full cost, in this case, will include, in a very approximate way, the opportunity cost of all the scarce resources involved in production, including those attributable to the entrepreneurial skills of senior management (the allocated fixed cost) and the cost of the capital employed in production (the profit mark-up).

This last argument has some force, in that it may give some economic justification for the fact that many firms who apparently use inferior pricing rules still manage to survive in competitive environments. However, at best, fixed-price formulae can only provide a rough and ready approximation to the price which a company should, either through market demand analysis or economic cost evaluation, charge for its products. Understanding the role of the market in the pricing decision will indicate areas in which new information can be profitably gathered for a particular product. It should focus management's attention upon the relationship between price and output within the context of the firm's product markets.

SETTING THE MINIMUM PRICE FOR A PRODUCT

Up to this point we have discussed the problem of determining the price at which a product will sell and clear the chosen level of production. The price–output combination for a producer is found where marginal revenue equals marginal cost, although this rule depends upon rather restrictive assumptions which may not always represent reality. However, the question often arises as to what is the minimum price below which production is no longer worthwhile. In perfect product markets there is little problem. The perfectly competitive firm cannot expect to make, in the long run, a return in excess of its full opportunity cost of production. An inefficient firm will be forced out of such a market because, in the long term, its opportunity cost of production will exceed its total revenue.

In reality, market perfection rarely exists and where it does it is rarely more than a transient market phenomenon. Market imperfection generally means that some opportunity exists for producers to make economic profits, i.e. some surplus over their full opportunity cost of production. In this situation, the opportunity cost of production represents the minimum threshold price below which production will not be worthwhile.

In Chapters 7 and 8 we outlined a method for determining the opportunity cost of decisions with short-term cost as the net cash change to the decision-making entity which results from choosing one particular course of action. However, this definition of the opportunity cost concept only applies to decisions which have short-term consequences. The opportunity cost of a long-term decision must also include the effect of differences in the timing of future cash flows.

No simple short-run criterion exists for establishing a minimum viable price for a product, because the question of product viability is invariably a long-run decision, while the pricing decision is governed by short-term market factors.

However, as we shall see, the same argument need not apply where a sale is made under contract. With most contract sales the production implications are often only of a short-term nature.

Gut-feel pricing

'Gut feel' pricing is used by many managers as a way of coping with the uncertainties of the market and without relying upon any more than casual market research. Few managers, in practice, would rely upon gut feel pricing for significant jobs, projects or contracts, but many do employ it in situations of continuous supply of an identical product or service. In this sense it relies upon an incremental approach, where some assumption about the changing state of the market is made and about the capacity of supply which is available and should be sold. It is usually pursued through exploration of possible prices and testing the market's response to them.

EXAMPLE

The marketing and sales manager of a 100-bed conference facility was convinced that price was a primary quality signal to the market. The conference facility had been established to a high standard and was competing with a number of other conference hotels in the locality. The conference day rate had been established when the facility opened in 1990 at £124 which was slightly under the competitive rate. The facility required an average of 65% occupancy to cover costs and finance charges. The marketing manager refused to engage in any significant price discounting during the recessionary years of 1991 and 1992 whilst other conference centres were bringing their discounted prices down to £60 per day. Occupancy during 1991 and 1992 was 24% and 35% respectively which was comparable with the competition. How can the marketing manager's pricing behaviour be justified and would another strategy have been more sensible in the conditions?

Pricing contracts

In the introduction to this chapter we introduced two types of market which involved a single buyer. In the first case, where there is more than one seller, we have a 'monopsony'; in the second case, with only one seller, we have a 'bilateral monopsony'. In the first case, selling usually proceeds through the submission of tenders which, in most situations, involves the submission of sealed bids. In the second case, negotiation proceeds through offer and counter-offer in the light of the seller's perception of the buyer's 'ability to pay' and the buyer's perception of the seller's lowest acceptable price.

Monopsony (where there is a single buyer and more than one seller) occurs in the following situations.

- In central and local government, where contracts for public services are offered for tender by potential suppliers: defence contracts are a particular example of this.
- Where a certain industry is itself under monopoly, or near monopoly control: for example, the railways, postal services and public utilities, such as electricity, gas and water, are either public sector or privatised monopolies in the UK. Organisations of this type act as monopsonist buyers of the specialised goods and services which they require.
- Where a particular individual or firm holds the patent or copyright on a particular product which can be made on its behalf by one or more suppliers.

The usual procedure for supply in a monopsony market is for the monopsonist to publish an invitation to tender. In the case of a local government contract, for example, this invitation may be published in the local and national newspapers. A private firm, on the other hand, may be more selective, and publish in a trade journal or magazine, or simply write to a number of possible suppliers giving the terms and conditions of supply.

For the specialised product, the supplier must then 'tender' to the buyer, including in the tender the following information:

- a detailed specification of the product to be supplied;
- an estimated delivery date;
  references from previous customers and/or samples of similar work performed by the supplier;
- the full price at which the product will be supplied, including any transport costs which the supplier is willing to bear;
- any credit terms which will be made available to the customer.

The tender documents, when submitted to the buyer, represent a legal offer to sell which will form the basis of the contract between the buyer and seller. The law of contract governs the rights and responsibilities of each party to the contract. The sale of certain items such as land require a written acceptance by the buyer to become legally enforceable. An offer to sell many other types of product can be accepted verbally (although this is not normal practice with commercial contracts).

The buyer will weigh up the conditions of sale before accepting a particular supplier's bid. Rarely will a buyer accept a bid purely on the grounds that it offers the lowest price. Other factors such as delivery date, the reputation of the supplier, after-sales service and so on are all important.

In a competitive bid situation the various suppliers may have a good idea who their competitors are, although there is no obligation on the part of the buyer to reveal such information. In order to set the price, each supplier will need to know the following:

- the minimum price at which the product could be sold (as we have discussed before, the opportunity cost of supply is the minimum acceptable price using purely financial criteria);
- the bid prices on similar contracts which failed including, if possible, the prices submitted on the bids placed by those competitors who succeeded;
- the likely cost structure of the other firms which are to compete for the contract taking into account any technological advantage they may possess.

THE SIZE AND TYPE OF PRODUCT MARKET

An important aspect of the output and pricing decision is the determination of the size of the product's total market which is available to the firm and the responsiveness of that market to different marketing strategies. A variety of different sources of information are available to the producing firm:

- published government statistics such as the annual abstract of statistics, the various censuses of production and distribution, the National Income and Expenditure Blue Book including the various surveys of household expenditure;
- statistics of overseas trade and the various publications of the Organisation for Economic Cooperation and Development (OECD);
- the Business Monitor series and publications from trade and professional organisations;
- publications in the fields of market research and general marketing.

The estimation of the potential market size for a given product, especially if the product has a highly specialised use, can be a lengthy and imprecise task. Below we lay out a series of steps which may be useful in those situations where relevant information can be discovered.

(i) Identify the product's classification in the light of the available statistics of market segmentation. For example, a producer of video recorders would sell into the market area defined as 'durable consumer goods' reference 63: 'television, radio and musical instruments including repairs' in the Family Expenditure Survey published by HMSO.
(ii) Estimate the total expenditure in the market segment identified in (i) above, splitting the analysis between home and export market sales. Most UK published figures give total domestic expenditure on a particular market segment as a proportion of household income. Published numbers of households within the firm's marketing area and figures of net household income will give an approximate measure of the market expenditure on the class of goods concerned.
(iii) Identify the proportion of the market segment taken by the particular type of good being produced and its close market substitutes (if any).

(iv) Analyse the pattern of supply for the product type concerned, including the identity and output of the firm's immediate competitors (taking into account the suppliers of any close market substitutes).

Up to this point we have conducted a static analysis of the current market structure for the product concerned. However, the supplier of a new product, or indeed of a product with an established market, would also have to consider ways and means of expanding the market available or creating a new market area. A variety of marketing strategies are possible, including product differentiation and advertising (both of which we have already discussed), altering the pattern of supply through middlemen, wholesalers etc., changes in credit policy and other terms of trade.

CONCLUSION

In this chapter we have considered the practical issues facing managers in choosing an appropriate price level or a product. There are in essence two approaches to the problem. The first is through a systematic analysis of the chosen market using test market data and statistical analysis of the results. The second approach is more introspective, looking at the firm and its customers, and attempting to make reasonable deductions about what the market will bear.

Chapter 21

Quality Evaluation and Costing

Level D

Contents

Summary

In this chapter we will consider the problem of evaluating the functional quality of a given product to the customer. Improvement in this level of quality creates value to the customer by increasing his or her level of certainty that the product will satisfy his or her needs. It is from this added value that the company can realise the opportunity of achieving improved competitive advantage. However, functional quality improvements can incur investment in design and manufacture and it is important to target priorities for potential quality improvement and hence to evaluate the marginal benefits to the business of those quality improvements.

INTRODUCTION

In Chapter 2 we defined the meaning of quality in terms of agreement between three states:

- formal quality, which describes the agreement of a product/service with its design specification;
- functional quality, which describes the agreement of a product/service with the functional requirements of the customer;
- ethical quality, which defines the agreement of a product/service with the total ethical parameters of the business.

In this chapter we will investigate the concept of functional quality, i.e. the quality perceived by the customer when using a product or service. To amplify the concepts involved, we will consider a camera, which is a product most people are familiar with some degree or other.

FUNCTIONAL QUALITY

Functional quality is concerned with uniting the world of product fabrication with the wants of the potential consumer. Quality at the functional level combines three concepts (Figure 21.1):

(i) capability in achieving a given purpose;
(ii) simplicity in achieving that purpose;
(iii) the non-functional aesthetic income of the product to the user.

We presume that a customer purchases a product or service in order to satisfy a perceived need by that individual. We also assume that individuals are rational in their purchasing behaviour, in that they are effort minimisers. This means:

- if two products are equally capable of achieving a desired purpose, then the product which requires the least effort in use will be chosen; or

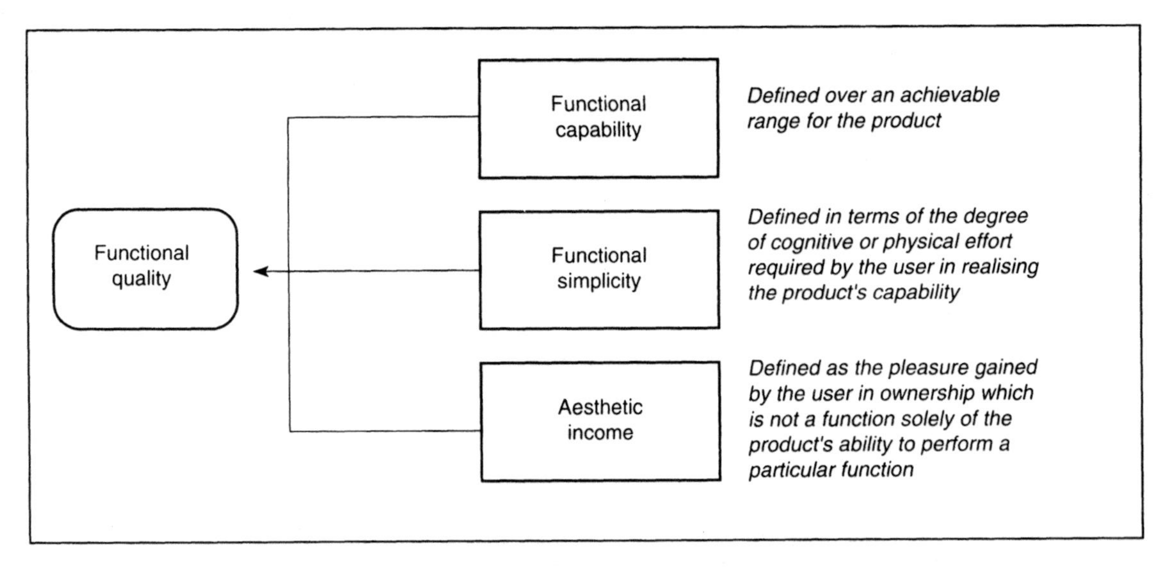

Figure 21.1 The three elements of functional quality.

- if two products entail identical effort in use, then the one that is most capable in achieving a given purpose will be chosen.

Functional range for a product or service

For a given product, the payoff, in use to the customer, is measured by the capability of that product to satisfy the customer's perceived needs. This creates positive 'value in use' to the customer and represents an economic 'good'. Increasing complexity in use is, however, an economic 'bad' for an effort minimiser, in that greater cognitive effort is required to use a complex, as opposed to a simple, product. However, the typical user of any product or service will expect to use that product over a range of conditions. This is what we term 'the functional range' of a product. This range can be defined in a number of different ways (Figure 21.2).

For any given purpose, a given product's capability will be measured in terms of what is achievable (the achievable range) against:

(i) a feasible range which represents the theoretical limits over which a function can be exercised. For example, the feasible range of lighting conditions over which a camera would be required to operate would be full sunlight to complete darkness. With some products their range of performance is theoretically unbounded although, in reality, limits exist.
(ii) a desired range which covers that part of the functional range which will satisfy the users anticipated needs perceived at the point of

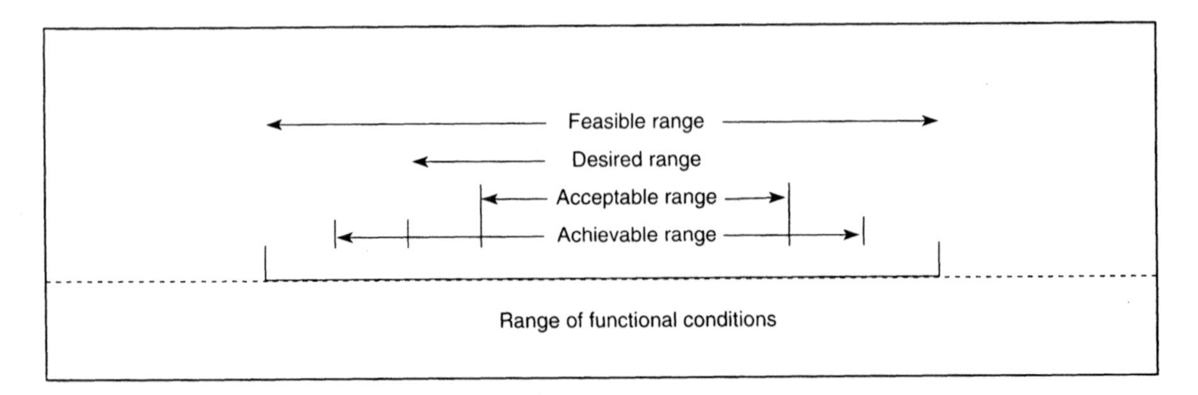

Figure 21.2 The functional range of a product.

evaluation and purchase. For most camera users the desired range will be dependent upon the type of photography which the user can visualise undertaking. If he or she is keen on interiors or portrait photography, then the desired range would be more extensive than a user purchasing a camera for holiday snapshots.

(iii) an acceptable range which is the minimum the user is prepared to accept as necessary to cover his or her most likely needs.

Clearly, we can conclude the following.

- If the acceptable range is in excess of the achievable range, then it is unlikely that a product will be purchased under any circumstances.
- If the achievable range is in excess of the acceptable range, but less than the desirable range, then purchase is possible, but inherent expectations cannot be fulfilled completely by the product, and there will be a *quality deficit* for this functional range.
- If the desirable range is exceeded by the product's achievable range then there will be a *quality surplus* in the product for the particular user over the functional range concerned.

For example, the primary function of a camera is to take photographs, and we presume that picture quality in terms of its clarity, colour and closeness to what was being photographed is the principal attribute in the mind of the user. However, the photographic purpose for the user may range over:

- lighting conditions from full sunlight to complete darkness;
- proximity of the subject(s);
- speed of the subject(s);
- resolution desired, ranging from full enlargement down to coarse-grained effects;
- a wide range of ambient conditions (from mountain top to sea bottom!).

A camera which is capable of delivering high quality photographs against any combinations of extreme purpose would have to be mechanically adaptable to a very high degree. There would be an inherently high order of complexity in such a product.

FUNCTIONAL QUALITY AND THE CAPABILITY/COMPLEXITY TRADE-OFF

Generally, the more capable a product is of fulfilling a range of needs the more complex it will be. In practice, each individual will make their consumption choices according to their tolerance for complexity as represented in Figure 21.3. The utility functions (u_1, u_2, $u_3 \ldots$) for the individual represent their indifference patterns between capability and complexity. For example, all combinations of capability and complexity along u_1 are of identical value to the individual concerned.

However, complexity can be mitigated by the 'intelligent ordering' of a product's capability. Intelligent ordering can be achieved either through simplification of a product's form (formal simplification) for a given level of capability, or through simplification of a product's operation in use (functional simplification). In the modern camera, what were once complex instruments functionally have been simplified in operation by intelligent micro-electronic control systems. With the modern camera, functional simplicity for a given capability has been won by manufacturers at the expense of increased formal complexity. Generally, formal simplification adds value to the manufacturing stage of a product, functional simplicity adds value to the customer. In many situations, as we have described for the camera, the problem comes in trading off one against the other.

Theoretically, a product (p_2) offering a combination of capability and complexity C' is preferred and, therefore, valued more highly by the user than a product (p_1) offering combination C. The only difference between p_2 and p_1 is that p_2 is functionally the simpler product along the full range of capability. Interestingly, this theory of the value of quality predicts, that functional simplification in a

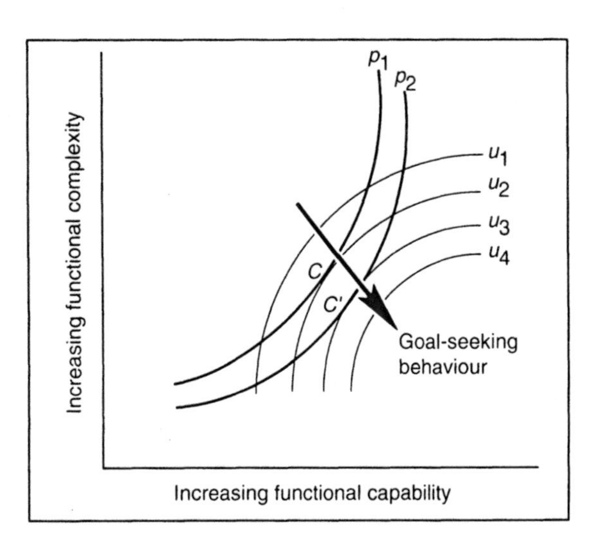

Figure 21.3 Functional complexity versus functional capability.

product will result in it being used over a higher range of capability. This makes intuitive sense. For example, as cameras have been simplified at the functional level through the introduction of intelligent micro-electronic control systems, the typical user has been able to exploit the instrument's capability to a higher level.

EXAMPLE

The spreadsheet first appeared as an application program in the late 1970s as a product called 'VisiCalc' on the Apple II microcomputer. Its value to the hard-pressed financial executive was immediately recognised, and it is said that VisiCalc alone sold many thousands of Apple II computers and helped establish the Apple company. Since that time, products such as SuperCalc, Lotus 123 and EXCEL have appeared, and VisiCalc has long since disappeared.

EXCEL has been regarded as the premier spreadsheet for the Apple Macintosh, and has also been successfully launched on the IBM and IBM compatible microcomputers, even though it has had to compete against an established product, Lotus 123, which had gained an overwhelming market share. The EXCEL program is much more sophisticated than its competitors: the code takes more memory and the program interacts with the host computer's operating systems in many subtle ways. It is, formally, an extremely complex product. However, the virtue of this formal complexity is that it delivers functional simplicity to the user with its 'point and click' user interface and a range of inbuilt functions which enable it to perform much more complicated analyses without special programming.

The competitive advantage of EXCEL was that it offered both a greater functional capability and a greater functional simplicity over its principal competitor. This product advantage was such that EXCEL has managed to topple Lotus 123 from its position and has taken over as the leading quality spreadsheet on the market. A further advantage of the higher functional simplicity is that the learning curve for new users is much more rapid, and more sophisticated users can more easily gain access to the product's special features.

AESTHETIC INCOME

Neither the capability of a particular product or service nor its simplicity completely encompasses the concept of functional quality to the user. Users often purchase particular products or services of inferior performance to others because of considerations of status, or the attractiveness of the non-functional aspects of design and so forth. Aesthetic income is the name we give to the payoff which the user receives from a product in satisfying his or her status, aesthetic or ethical needs. Indeed, consumer products are rarely purchased for their functional attributes alone, but it is difficult to predict the degree of aesthetic income which is gained from a particular product. This is very much the 'wild-card' in quality development.

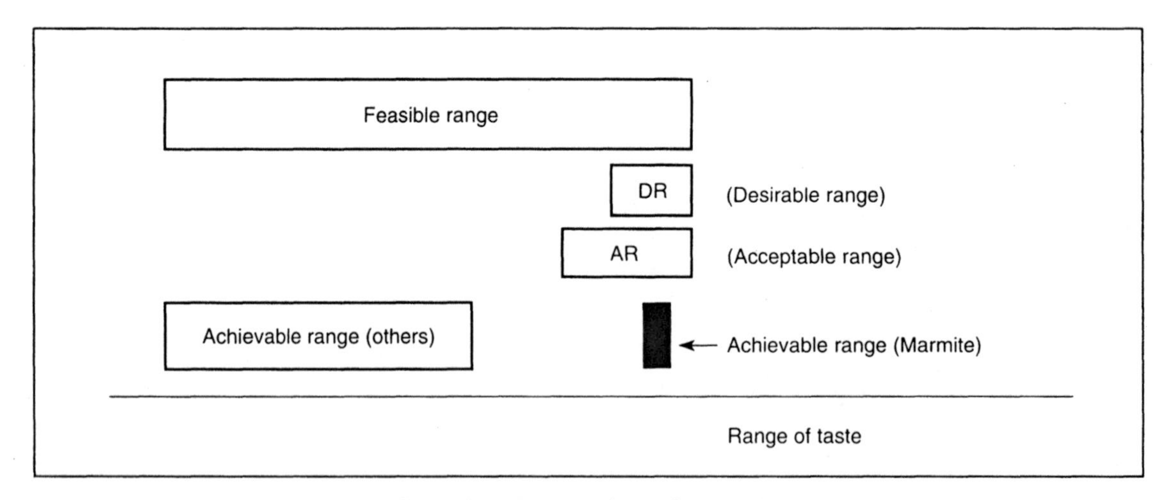

Figure 21.4 Functional map for Marmite.

QUALITY AND BRANDING

The development of a strong brand image for a product is an attempt to consolidate buyer loyalty and ensure repeat sales. Indeed, as we discuss in Chapter 19, brand loyalty, when strongly developed, can produce an almost insurmountable barrier to entry for new market entrants. For example, Marmite has established itself as the leading savoury spread in the food market, although many hydrolysed yeast spreads have been promoted by different suppliers. However, Marmite has defined what a yeast spread should taste like and has created a functional range map (Figure 21.4).

Given a feasible range of taste from hydrolysed yeast, there is a certain range of taste which is desirable. With some food and drink products, specialist tasters can clearly specify what is desirable and, slightly more broadly, what is acceptable for their product. Marmite can achieve a taste, batch after batch, year after year, which falls within what seasoned spread eaters will regard as acceptable and, indeed, what is desirable. Other manufacturers cannot achieve a product which is even acceptable, never mind desirable, as a substitute.

QUALITY AND RELIABILITY

Reliability is regarded as an important concept within quality. However, taking the idea of quality as 'negative entropy' within a product or service, reliability is simply a reduction in the probability of failure in use. Reliability is, therefore, the idea of functional simplification manifesting itself in a particular way – an unreliable product is a complex product for the consumer, in that he or she has to take insuring action, either by using the product at less than maximum levels of operation, or by employing fail-safe mechanisms or redundancy systems. The emphasis in the quality literature on the risk of failure has traditionally been focused on minimising the number of defects in a batch at various 'sigma' levels (Table 21.1).

Table 21.1

Sigma	One failure in:
3	15
4	161
5	4 292
6	294 118

These sigma levels are calculated as follows:

$$\text{Sigma failure rate} = (1 - F(z))^{-1}$$

where $z = \text{sigma} - 1.5$ and z is the number of standard deviations from which the probability of failure is to be calculated.

So, from cumulative normal probability tables, sigma 4, for example has a z-value of 2.5 and an $F(z)$ of 0.9937903. This means that the probability of a randomly drawn value occurring more than 2.5 standard deviations from the mean is given by

$$\begin{aligned} 1 - F(z) &= 1 - 0.9937903 \\ &= 0.0062097 \end{aligned}$$

Taking the reciprocal:

$$(1 - F(z))^{-1} = 161.04$$

Statistical standards of quality are usually denoted in terms of the sigma level attained, and sigma 6 is taken as zero defects for all practical purposes.

THE MEASUREMENT OF QUALITY

The problem faced by the quality manufacturer is to determine:

- how sensitive product demand is to quality as a variable;
- which attributes of a product or service to focus attention upon when deciding issues of product improvement and investment.

If the demands of the customer are the only criteria for choosing product improvement strategies and the value of investment, then the producer's choice would be simple: improve the product's functional capability and reduce its complexity. However, in the real world, manufacturers must trade off the demands of their customers against the need to justify further financial investment in any given product.

In Figure 21.5 we show the change in the quality elasticity of demand (e_Z) assuming constant price. Note that below a certain threshold level of acceptability, the quantity demanded of the product will be zero. At the other extreme, where quality as functional capability moves above that which is desirable, elasticity will again turn to zero. We can identify a range of quality which we define as the range of 'quality deficit', where the elasticity will become more elastic (i.e. demand will increase

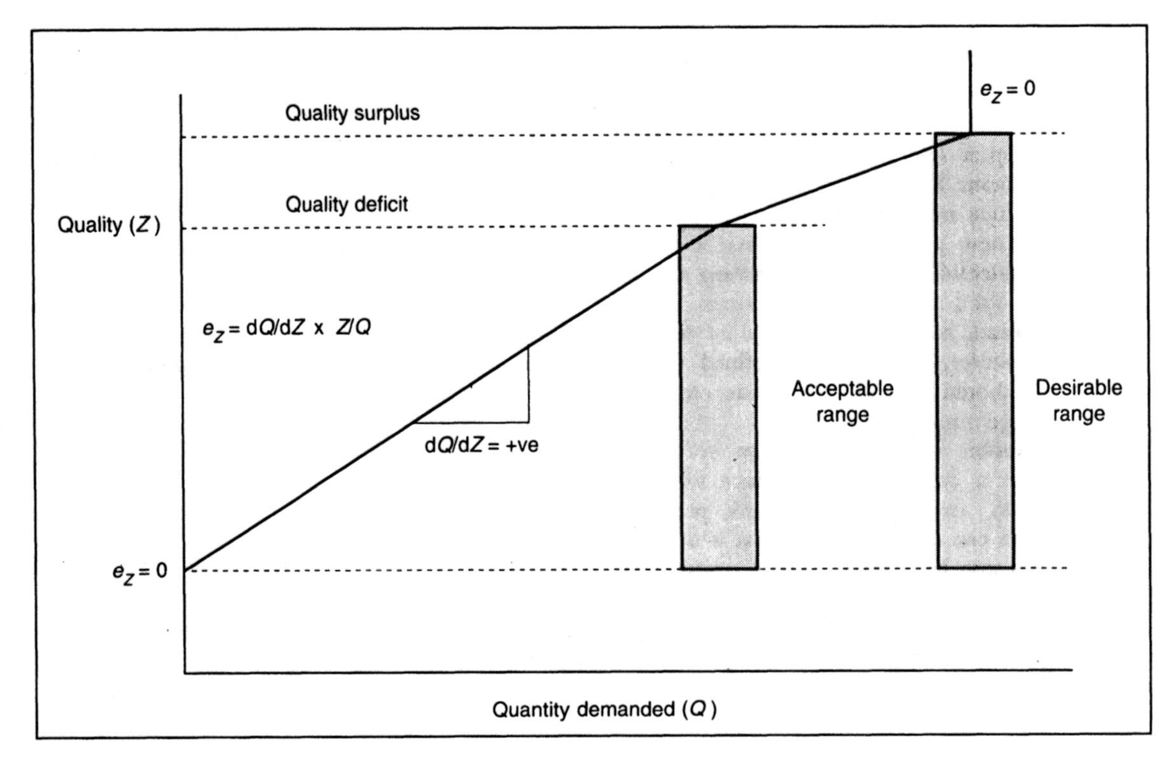

Figure 21.5 The quality elasticity of demand.

proportionately more with each quality increment than at lower levels).

The problem with demand curves is that, although they present some interesting theoretical implications, they are exceedingly difficult to define in practice. You may remember our discussion in Chapter 19 on the issue of price and demand where both variables are reasonably easily measured. Quality is an intensely subjective variable, and we must turn to more subtle methods of analysis.

Bayesian quality analysis

In measuring the functional quality of a product we need to make the following assumptions.

(i) Functional quality consists of three variables: functional capability, functional simplicity and aesthetic income.
(ii) These three variables are, to a certain degree, substitutes for one another; that is, they are 'primary quality attributes' which can be identified in any product and which in sum make up the total of what we call 'quality'.

One approach to measuring quality would be through a simple 'Bayesian approach'. This is a three-stage procedure (Figure 21.6).

- Stage 1: potential customers are requested to rank a set of key quality attributes for the product concerned. This ranking is achieved by asking each subject to distribute 100 points across the attributes concerned. The question should be asked in terms of 'given these attributes, rank them in importance when judging the quality of product X'.
- Stage 2: actual customers are asked to score out of 10 each of the quality attributes within a particular product. This places an ordinal value upon the attribute concerned. The question should be asked: 'given that you have ranked this attribute *n*th, how would you score it on a scale of 0 to 10, taking 10 as the perfect score for each attribute?'
- Stage 3: finally, a posterior distribution can be created which weights the scores from stage 2 by the prior distribution values from stage 1. These values can then be reported as percentage values which will total to the perceived quality of the product relative to its ideal.

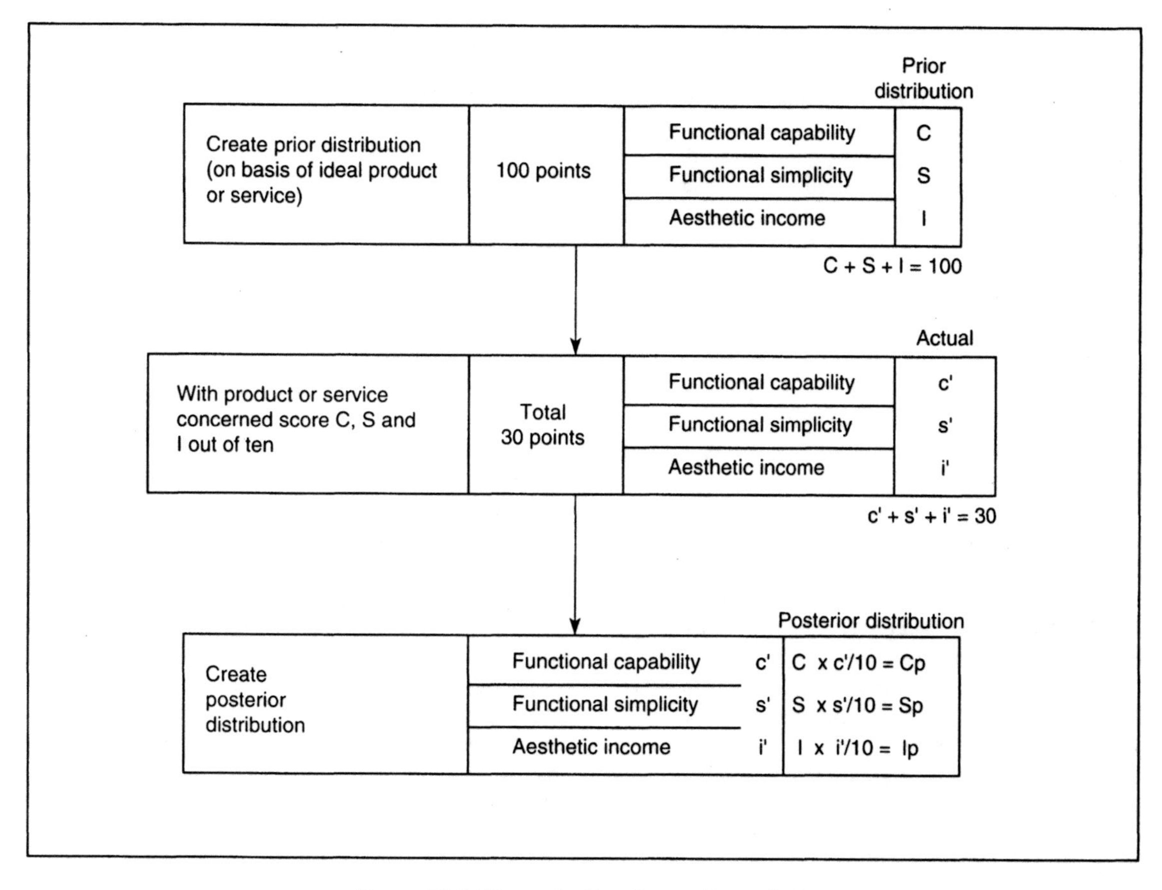

Figure 21.6 First-order Bayesian quality analysis.

It is then possible to take each one of the primary quality attributes: functional capability, simplicity and aesthetic income, and subdivide each of these into a set of secondary characteristics.

In order to understand the technique more fully, we will consider the case of a camera manufacturer faced with the problem of deciding where to focus (!) his or her product improvement. The modern camera is a striking example of the development of functional simplicity as a design attribute with enhancements in capability. This process has been improved by developments in two quite dissimilar technologies: optics and micro-electronics. The leading-edge cameras of the 1960s were largely mechanical instruments, such as the Leica M3 or the Rolliflex. The modern Pentax or Canon is largely controlled by micro-electronics, and features facilities such as automatic exposure, focusing, automatic rewind and zoom lenses.

A pool of potential camera purchasers were asked to distribute 100 points over the three primary functional attributes to create a prior distribution. That prior distribution is shown in Table 21.2.

The idea of 'picture quality' over a range of possible lighting and ambient conditions relates to the concept 'functional capability' for this particular product. 'Functional simplicity' is as we have described it above, and 'design aesthetics' relates to consumers' concerns about the 'look and feel' of the

Table 21.2

Primary quality attribute	Prior dist.	Score	Posterior dist.
Functional capability	40.00	10.00	40.00
Functional simplicity	30.00	5.00	15.00
Aesthetic income	30.00	5.00	15.00
	100.00		70.00

camera apart from its ability to take good photographs. The values for the prior distribution are taken as an average from the sample of consumers tested. In this case, given 100 points, consumers ranked the capability of taking good pictures as the most important variable in deciding between cameras, but not by much – with functional simplicity and design aesthetics ranking joint second with 30 points each.

The consumers were then faced with a given product and asked to rate its picture-taking capability on a 10-point scale, awarding 10 to a perfect score and zero to the lowest possible picture-taking performance. Each of the three quality variables was evaluated in the same way, and their average scores weighted by the prior values.

This analysis indicates that the particular camera under test was subjectively evaluated at 70% of the functional quality compared with the ideal, with picture quality being declared perfect, but with significant room for improvement on both design aesthetics and simplicity. This analysis can be repeated at intervals and a quality evaluation map drawn for each trial, where the functional capability, C, simplicity, S, and aesthetic income, A, are shown as three radial points on a set of concentric circles of increasing quality value (see Figure 21.7).

Trial 1 provides a summary of the data in Table 21.2, and we can see clearly the quality deficiencies in the product. In Trial 2, some improvements in simplicity of operation have been introduced against a stable prior distribution of quality which would represent a genuine product improvement. Interestingly, in the final trial shown, the aesthetic quality has been improved, but against some underlying shift in the prior ranking of attributes.

The analysis above focuses on the three generic attributes of functional quality identified so far. However, we need to repeat the exercise at lower levels of functionality in order to be able to form implications for product improvement in manufacturing. For this we draw out a simple tree structure clustering those more specific attributes which contribute to the three elements of capability, simplicity and aesthetics identified above. On the basis of this we can repeat the ex-ante and ex-post evaluation procedure to determine which product characteristics contribute most towards quality.

For example, under picture quality (our capability attribute), consumer research indicated that the quality of: the in-built flash, the lens exchange mechanism (if available), the lack of camera shake, the depth of field imaging and the quality of the lens were all contributory factors in determining the picture quality (Table 21.3). Other variables were identified as contributing to functional simplicity and aesthetic appeal, although in some cases, as with the single lens reflex system it could be argued as contributing to both simplicity and picture quality.

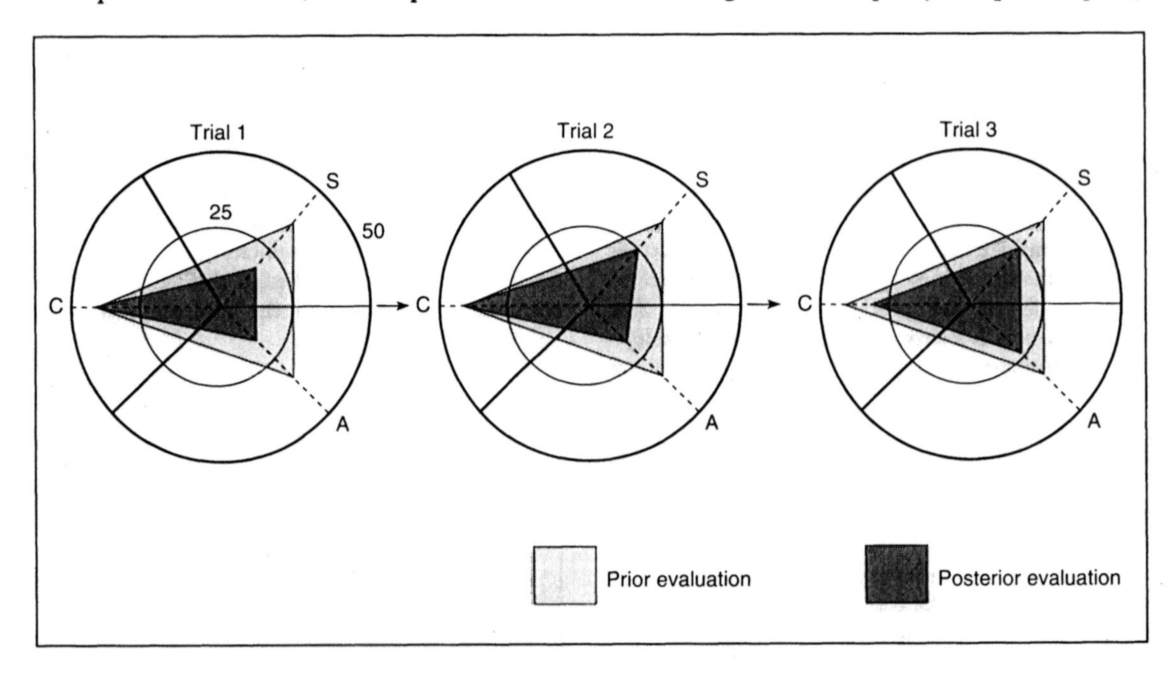

Figure 21.7 Quality evaluation maps.

Table 21.3

Primary quality attribute	Prior dist.	Attribute score	Posterior dist.	Secondary quality attribute	Prior dist.	Attribute score	Posterior dist.	Primary weight prior	Primary weight posterior
functional capability	40.00	10.00	40.00	In-built flash	10.00	4.00	4.00	4.00	1.60
				Lens exchange	10.00	4.00	4.00	4.00	1.60
				Lack of shake	25.00	10.00	25.00	10.00	10.00
				Depth of field	15.00	6.00	9.00	6.00	3.60
				Lens quality	40.00	10.00	40.00	16.00	16.00
						34.00	82.00		
				Unattributed		16.00	18.00		7.20
					100.00	50.00	100.00	40.00	40.00
functional simplicity	30.00	5.00	15.00	Auto rewind	5.00	8.00	4.00	1.50	1.20
				Auto-exposure	15.00	8.00	12.00	4.50	3.60
				Auto-focus	10.00	0.00	0.00	3.00	0.00
				Ease of film load	10.00	5.00	5.00	3.00	1.50
				Light weight	20.00	8.00	16.00	6.00	4.80
				SLR	20.00	0.00	0.00	6.00	0.00
				User display	5.00	5.00	2.50	1.50	0.75
				Viewfinder clarity	15.00	5.00	7.50	4.50	2.25
						39.00	47.00		
				Unattributed		1.00	3.00		0.90
					100.00	40.00	50.00	30.00	15.00
Aesthetic income	30.00	5.00	15.00	Black body	10.00	0.00	0.00	3.00	0.00
				Build quality	35.00	7.00	24.50	10.50	7.35
				Proportionality	15.00	4.00	6.00	4.50	1.80
				Sophistication	15.00	0.00	0.00	4.50	0.00
				Visual design	25.00	6.00	15.00	7.50	4.50
						17.00	45.50		
				Unattributed		8.00	4.50		1.35
					100.00	25.00	50.00	30.00	15.00

This problem often occurs in product quality evaluation and a decision should be made as to the principal function of the factor being considered. With the SLR capability, it would not necessarily contribute towards better pictures, but it certainly reduces complexity in use. For this reason it was deemed to be a simplifying factor.

For each of the three groups of secondary clusters, potential purchasers were asked to distribute 100 points as before. The same procedure was then adopted, in that given a particular camera, they were asked to score each variable out of ten. However, at the secondary level, and any further level if appropriate, the maximum number of points available must reflect their perception of the quality of that cluster of attributes taken as a whole. For functional simplicity, for example, there were eight secondary attributes chosen which would give a maximum of 80 points. Looking up the tree, we can see that this cluster of variables was only given a score of 5 out of 10, so only 50% of the 80 points, i.e. 40 points can be distributed amongst the eight variables. The resultant, ex-post distribution of scores can then be created by rescaling according to the prior distribution of scores. Thus, for auto-exposure, the prior of 15% is rated at 8 (out of 10) which gives a rescaled score of 12.

Note, that for each set of secondary variables, an element of score remains undistributed relative to the total specified for the cluster. Thus, the rescaled scores should total to 50% but a relatively modest (3%) element remains undistributed. Clearly, if this

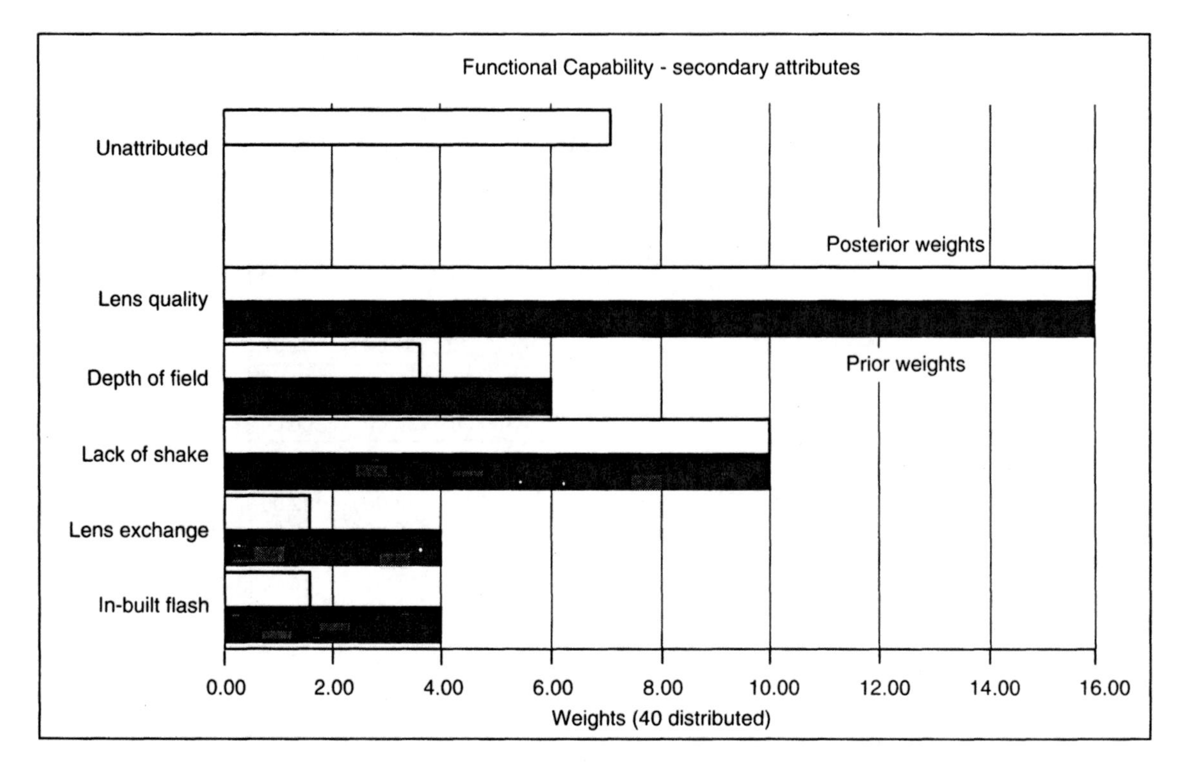

Figure 21.8 Functional capability – secondary attributes.

value was significant it may indicate that an important secondary quality variable has been missed.

Finally, we can now rescale the secondary prior and posteriors by the primary priors to scale the values onto a quality mapping. It is now very easy to see the perceived strengths and weaknesses of the particular product and the dimensions where product improvement could be considered.

In Figure 21.8 we have created a bar chart of the secondary variables associated with functional quality. The prior distribution placed lens quality, lack of shake and depth of field as the most important attributes with lens exchangeability and in-built flash tying for fourth position. Of these variables, depth of field, lens exchangeability and the functionality of the in-built flash are priority areas for improvement, whereas improvements in lens quality and the cameras smoothness in operation do not appear necessary at this stage.

You may like to consider the situation for simplicity and aesthetic income.

QUALITY AND LEARNING

Up to this point we have considered the evaluation of quality in isolation. We have given the concept more precise definition and through the Bayesian approach have developed a way of identifying routes for product improvement. In this section we will discuss the ways in which organisations can affect the contribution that they generate by combining learning with quality improvement. In order to do this effectively we need to consider how these two variables interact upon contribution given a set level of output. When we consider interactions we are forced to consider the system in question dynamically – that is, how the state of the system will *change* as the variables in question are allowed to change. In production we can identify three important contribution 'drivers':

- activity – the level of output chosen and which is related to contribution through all activity related costs;
- quality – the level of quality at which the product is manufactured and sold (including associated customer support);
- learning – the capability of the organisation to learn about market demand for its product and to feed back information from production and market research into product improvement.

We have discussed quality already and familiarised ourselves with the idea that a market will only reward a manufacturer for quality improvement as such once the quality moves beyond a minimum expectation level. To recall the point made earlier, quality expectations are formed (i) by the norms for equivalent products in the market and (ii) by minimum expectations of service.

Up to a certain point, product improvement will not make a significant impact upon consumers but, once that point is reached, consumers will re-evaluate that product as a superior product and be prepared to pay accordingly. If an organisation is learning from its market, then it will be able to adjust its production/price schedule accordingly and reap a higher level of contribution.

In Figure 21.9 we propose that at lower product quality levels the effect of changes will have a modest impact on contribution, largely through cost savings on lower levels of returns of faulty goods, lower after sales service and so on. However, there will not be a radical improvement in contribution until point B is reached at which point we expect that market buying behaviour will alter suddenly. With improvements in what the market perceives to be a low quality product there will be some resistance (represented by AB in Figure 21.9) to re-evaluating the product due to prejudice effects in the market place. The firm which has high learning efficiency should be able to reap the contribution from the market revaluation as soon as it occurs. Similarly, a producer may not suffer the full impact of quality deterioration beyond the market threshold if strong customer loyalty exists. However, once perceptions do change in the market the loss in contribution can be sudden and very significant for the firm.

If there is low organisational learning both at the market level and the production level, then the impact of quality upon contribution will be restricted to the savings in rework costs and service costs which the quality improvement will generate. The relationship of contribution to quality is likely to be smooth without the sudden discontinuities which can be experienced by the high learning firm (Figure 21.10).

The mathematical description of the dynamics of such a system is provided by Catastrophe Theory. Catastrophe Theory explains how a system state variable (in this case contribution) can change under the influence of two or more controlling variables. In the situation described above we have restricted our discussion to just two control variables and the mathematics predicts that the system states for the firm will not be smooth but will contain areas of instability. The two control variable system is described by the 'cusp catastrophe' model shown in Figure 21.11.

This model shows as the shaded surface the contribution which can be generated at a given level of output by all combinations of quality and learning. Viewing the model from the right we can see the folded plane shown as the edge in Figure 21.9 above for the high learning firm. Viewing the model from the left we can see the edge shown in Figure 21.10 for the low learning producer.

The shaded surface itself represents equilibrium states, i.e. the levels of contribution which will be

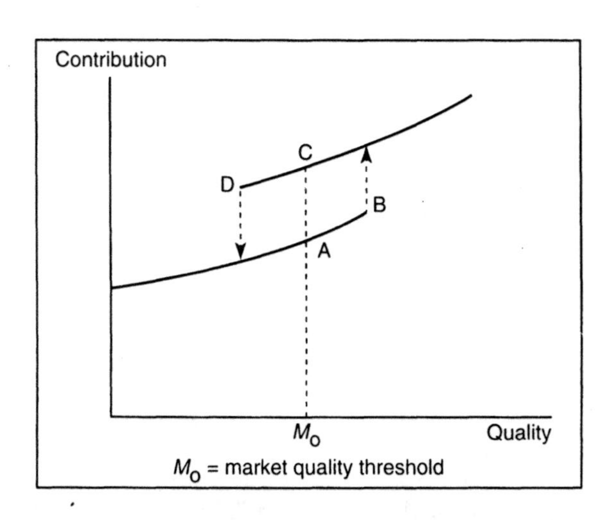

Figure 21.9 Quality influence on contribution for a high learning organisation.

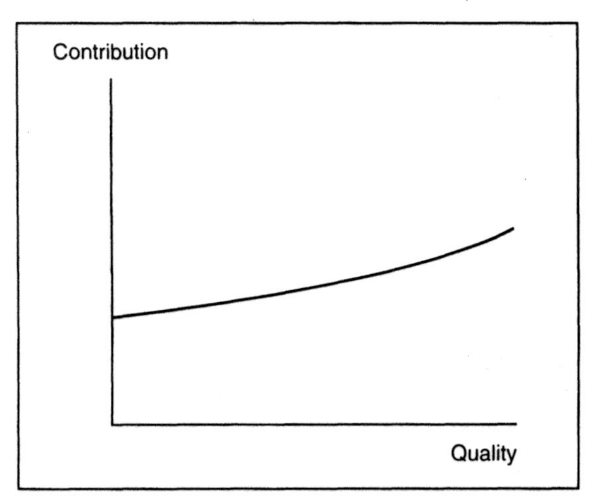

Figure 21.10 Quality influence on contribution for a low learning organisation.

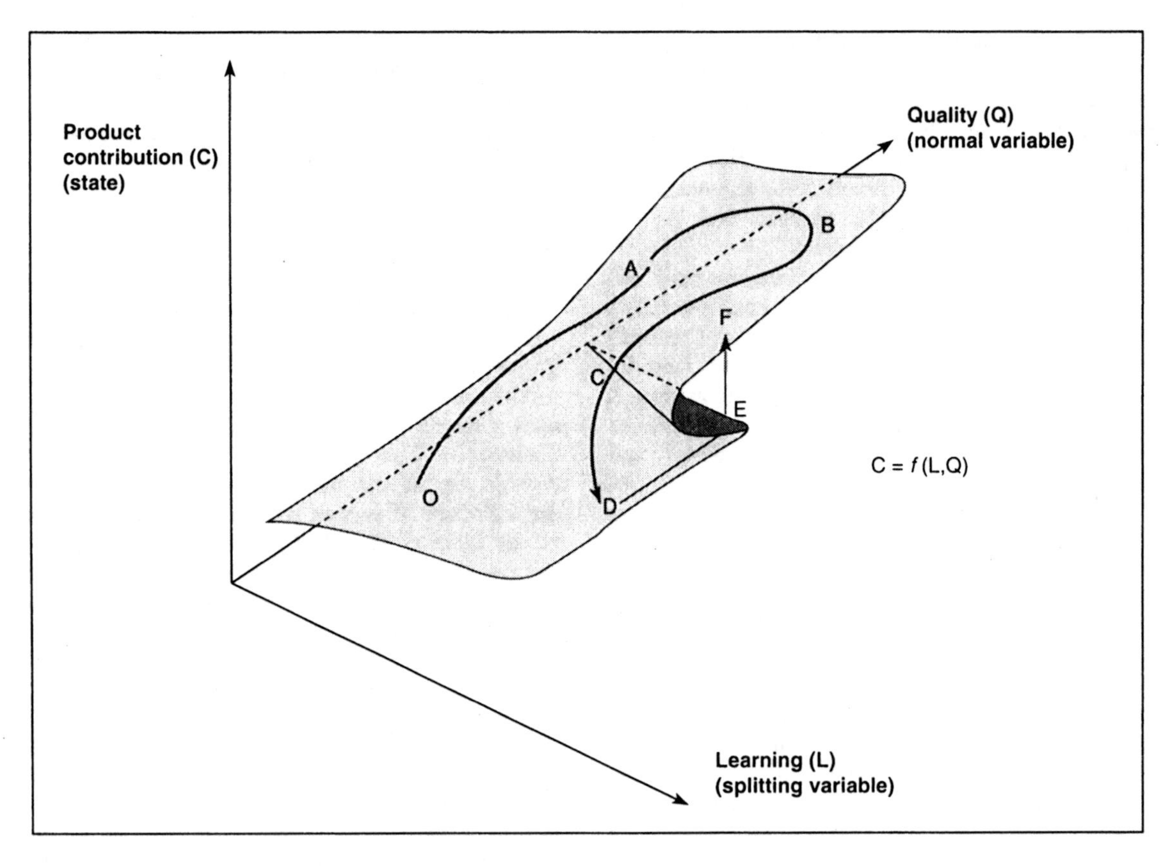

Figure 21.11 Interactivity of learning effects and quality.

generated by the firm given particular levels of quality and learning. In the language of Catastrophe Theory this surface is termed the 'catastrophe manifold' and its characteristic shape is implicit in any system where a single state variable is under the 'control' of two other variables.

To understand what the model is predicting, consider a firm producing a given level of output of a particular product at relatively low quality levels (O). The firm does not have particularly effective systems for monitoring market demand. It commences a quality improvement campaign and tracks up the surface to point A, gradually improving contribution as it does so. It then proceeds to develop its learning systems at both the market and the production level. The model predicts that this learning behaviour will take the firm to the high quality/high learning point B, where it is able to convert its quality image into higher prices for a given level of output and win quality-led improvements in production.

However, let us see what happens if the firm allows quality to slip towards point C. As it approaches the fold on the equilibrium surface it may not notice any sudden loss in contribution until it reaches point C itself. At that point there will be a sudden and dramatic loss in contribution as the market revises its beliefs about the quality of the firm's products relative to its competitors. It will find itself unable to earn the levels of contribution indicated by point C, but will plummet instantly to point D. The model then predicts that the firm will not be able to reinstate its position by a minor improvement in quality as fall C–D is irreversible. Rather it must achieve a substantial improvement in quality moving to point E before it can obtain the higher levels of contribution by the 'happy catastrophe' taking it to point F.

The power of the catastrophe theory model (apart from the mathematical rigour of its formulation) is its high descriptive power and the counter-intuitive implications which it generates. However, before discussing those implications it is worthwhile examining Figure 21.11 in more detail. First, 'learning', as we define it, is where an organisation can translate its experience of production and/or its market place into new designs, procedures and prices. Many businesses, for example, have always pursued rigorous statistical quality control methods but have never, or only haphazardly, translated their knowledge of failures into new designs or processes. Second, the contribution function for a non-learning organisation will be lower than that for a learning organisation at any given quality level, although the contribution function for such an organisation does have the possibilities of sudden changes.

It is this latter point which offers the most challenging problems for high learning, high quality organisations.

- Sudden changes in contribution may occur from relatively small changes in quality following quite long periods of effort in product improvement. However, in order to realise that contribution improvement, the organisation must couple careful external monitoring of the demand for its products and of market perception towards its products with its programme of quality improvement. Further, the most significant jumps will occur through improvements in functional quality, or functional simplicity or aesthetic value as opposed to improvements in formal quality.
- A firm which is losing its competitive edge relative to other suppliers in the market may be insured from the loss in its market position by the 'overhang effect'. However, at some point a relatively tiny change in either the firm's quality level or that of another competitor may bring a sudden and apparently disproportionate effect on the product's return and hence its contribution.
- A firm can always improve its contribution from production in a dynamic state by increasing its learning capability. This is most immediately profitable (in a contribution sense) in building effective and responsive market learning systems. Indeed, if a choice were placed before a firm, the model suggests that investment in learning may have more significant short-term benefits than engaging in speculative product improvement. This may seem obvious, but speculative product improvement, i.e. improvement generated by internal convictions rather than market knowledge, is the norm rather than the exception.

THE FINANCIAL IMPLICATIONS OF QUALITY IMPROVEMENT

In the last two sections we have explored the quality issue in some depth. In the last section we have suggested that quality improvement is unlikely to have a significant effect on a products contribution unless there is a high degree of organisational learning in place also. This presents us with something of a problem: valuing the benefits of either quality improvement or organisational learning are difficult enough if considered in isolation, but now we have to contend with the fact that they may be inextricably linked in determining a firm's contribution.

The financial benefits of quality improvement where organisation learning is in place can be summarised as follows:

- increased price per unit recovered under constant sales output, or increased sales under constant price, due to a demand curve shift induced by functional quality improvement;
- reduced variable cost per unit if wastage and reworking costs are built into variable costs, or a reduced fixed cost of production if wastage and reworking costs are held in that cost category (or a combination of both).

In order to assess the impact of quality upon the financial performance of the business it is necessary, over a series of different quality improvement programmes, to measure the direct changes in total organisational cost or revenue caused by movement along each of the three vectors in Figure 21.11 above.

From that diagram, cost studies should reveal a quality cost factor unique to each vector which can be applied to the current costs of production. This quality cost factor will have a fixed and quality variable component:

$$f_q = a_q - b_q q$$

where

a_q is the fixed cost of achieving a particular cost improvement;
b_q is the variable cost of improving quality as measured by changes in the quality score (q);
f_q is the quality cost factor.

Where a product is capable of continuous improvement, $a_q = 0$ but $b_q > 0$; however, where some quality improvement will entail some redesign, $a_q > 0$ but $b_q = 0$.

At this stage of the development of management accounting, few reliable methods have been developed which allow the evaluation of cost against quality changes to be performed. The procedure outlined above will only give approximate costs associated with programmes of either continuous improvement or radical improvement in particular products.

CONCLUSION

In this chapter we have explored the issue of quality and how it can be valued by the organisation. The main method developed here is a subjective Bayesian review technique which allows the firm to prioritise targets for quality improvement at the functional level. Then, using insights from Catastrophe Theory, we show how quality and learning are linked. In Chapter 24 we return to the problems of costing quality in production systems.

Part IV

Costing Resources and Products

Chapter 22

Overhead Accruals and Standard Costing

Level E

Contents

Summary

Cost accounting is the process within a firm where costs of production are analysed and prepared for decision-making or control purposes. Within the conventional cost-accounting framework, costs are defined as either 'direct' or 'indirect'. The former are costs which vary with the unit of activity; the latter are costs incurred because of pre-existing commitments which the accountant will seek to allocate on some basis or other to production units. In Chapter 6 we commented on the use of cost-based pricing procedures which involve the inclusion of some charge for the fixed resources of the firm – a fixed overhead allocation in other words. In this chapter we will examine some of the reasons which might explain why fixed costs are allocated to production processes by companies which in all other respects appear to conform to the axioms of economic rationality. We will then outline some of the techniques for allocating of fixed costs into production activities and 'absorbing' them into product unit costs. In this chapter we will consider three different ways of allocating cost to divisions: (i) as an overhead cost allocation, (ii) as a revenue tax on the division and (iii) as a profit tax on the division. We discover that only the latter avoids cost distortions and hence distortions in the perceived performance of divisions. Finally, we discuss the concept of a standard cost.

PURPOSE OF COST ACCOUNTING WITHIN THE FIRM

The principal objective of the cost-accounting function is to measure and record the costs of operating different processes and to compare those costs with the preset cost targets set by management. In this sense, cost accounting is a very important instrument of control within the firm. To serve their purpose, the costs which are collected do not have to be of any general value in the decision-making processes of the firm, although there are obvious benefits if they are. The major value of such costs lies in their role of monitoring the performance of the system being controlled and their ability to be consistently compared with the planned targets set by management.

The danger with cost accounting arises if managers come to believe that the cost data are automatically suited for general decision-making purposes. It may be that cost-accounting data (which are past data) can be converted to estimates of future costs which would be useful for decision-making purposes. But this is not the primary purpose of cost accounting, which is to monitor the cost behaviour of production and other systems in order that control decisions can be made.

Cost accounting is one part of the overall management accounting activity of the firm. Its primary function is one of providing data for the control decision, but it may have an additional purpose of providing 'off the peg' data which can be converted into information for other decision-making purposes at some later point in time. Within this context, cost accounting has become seen as a part of the more general activity of management accounting within firms.

COST ALLOCATION

As we saw in Chapter 17, many costs vary with output level in the short term. Nevertheless, there will also be costs which are committed and will not alter, no matter what level of output is produced, providing it is within the range of the firms current operating capacity. These costs are incurred as a result of a firm's long-run decision to produce. Such costs include:

- costs of financing (dividends and interest charges);
- salaries of administrative and supervisory staff;
- other head office expenditure;
- fixed charges of the production facility such as rent, rates and standing charges for utilities such as gas and electricity.

The term 'allocation' in costing refers to the allocation of prior committed costs to a production unit such as a division, department or production facility as a charge upon that unit's activity in a period. We have discussed the general issue of cost accrual in Chapter 6 where various bases for allocation were discussed. Once cost has been allocated to a production unit, those costs can then be absorbed into activity according to the allocation formula chosen.

The term 'absorption' refers to the process of absorbing allocated indirect costs into units of production in order to build a total product cost for inventory purposes.

EXAMPLE (i)

A company has two production units A and B which employ 120 staff between them. Production unit A has 50 staff on an average annual salary of £14 000 each and production unit B has 70 staff on an average annual salary of £14 800 each. The company's business costs are £3 500 000 per annum and it wishes to allocate business costs on a salary cost basis.

From Chapter 6 we know that the allocation formula is as follows:

$$\text{Fixed overheads allocated} = \frac{\text{total firm overhead}}{\text{total allocation units in firm}} \times \text{no. of units of allocation base}$$

Total labour cost = 50 × 14 000 + 70 × 14 800
= £1 736 00
Total overhead = £3 500 000
Allocation rate = 3 500 000/1 736 000
= £2.01613 per £ of salary

$$\text{Central overhead to A} = \frac{3\,500\,000}{1\,736\,000} \times (50 \times 14\,000)$$
$$= £1\,411\,290$$

$$\text{Central overhead to B} = \frac{350\,000}{1\,736\,000} \times (70 \times 14\,800)$$
$$= £2\,088\,710$$

EXAMPLE (ii)

The same company produces product x and product y in production unit B. Product x takes 2 hours of person time to produce each unit at £5.50 per hour and product y requires 3 hours at £6.00. The company plans to produce 500 units of x and 250 units of y.

Each unit of product x incurs a direct labour charge of 2 × £5.50 = £11.00 per unit

Each unit of product y incurs a direct labour charge of 3 × £6.00 = £18.00 per unit

The absorbed central overhead to product x is £2.01613 × £11.00 = £22.18 per unit

The absorbed central overhead to product y is £2.01613 × £18.00 = £36.29 per unit

In building up a product cost for x and y we would absorb central overheads at the rate specified above.

As we explained in Chapters 7 and 8, none of these costs are opportunity costs for the firm's short-run production decisions. However, many firms do attempt to relate fixed overheads to production through a variety of allocation procedures, and we need to understand why this is, given that the arbitrary allocation of fixed overheads can lead to defective decisions being made. The question which remains is whether, in a control context, the procedure can be justified. One argument in support of overhead allocation goes as follows. Senior management is largely responsible for the long-term decision making of the firm, while lower management is responsible for the tactical and operational decisions of selling, purchasing, production and so on. In the normal course of events, lower managers should only be accountable for the variables under their control and their performance against preset standards for those variables. However, senior management may well 'load' the performance criteria of lower management by adding some element of cost (the so-called fixed costs) into their operating budgets. In this way, the standards of performance for lower levels of management are raised to cover the costs which result from the consequences of senior management's decisions. It may well be that senior management will offer some additional compensation (in the form of increased salary, bonuses or even shares in the business) for the higher demands placed upon the performance of lower management.

The allocation of fixed overheads can be viewed, therefore, as the spreading of senior management costs throughout the organisation where they become part of the control criteria for lower management.

Another argument which is often put forward is that the allocation of fixed overheads is a very imperfect attempt to allocate the internal opportunity costs of scarce senior management time and scarce fixed resources (such as plant and equipment) to a firm's production activities. This argument is the same as that advanced in Chapter 20 in defence of fixed formula pricing, although we are now identifying the internal opportunity cost with the cost of senior managerial time and other fixed resources. The difficulty with this argument is that the very arbitrary allocation of fixed overheads is unlikely to lead to any better decisions than those made using unadjusted costs.

Fixed overheads are usually allocated on one of the following bases:

- The number of units of final production. This method assumes that volume of output justifies the total capacity of the firm in terms of its infrastructure of administration, marketing and other central resources.
- The number of labour hours employed in production. This method assumes that labour is the principal resource into production and that the amount of labour time devoted to production is proportionate to the total corporate commitment to that product.
- The number of machine hours employed in production. In this case, the presumption is that machine hours are the most important variable into production which may well be justifiable in high capital industries.
- The cost of materials employed in a particular process. This method is justified when materials cost is the principal component of total cost.
- The total wages allocated to a particular aspect of production. This basis of allocation is justified when wage costs are the principal cost of production. Many high technology companies employing relatively high cost labour allocate costs on this basis.
- The total revenue earned by a product. This converts the allocation mechanism into a form of taxation on the revenue of the product concerned.

EXAMPLE

Martin plc produces 16 000 units of Bolero for sale per month. Each Bolero sells for £5 per unit. The statistics for total factory production (of all products) and Bolero production are shown in Table 22.1. The total fixed overheads for the factory as a whole are £110 000.

The production of Bolero amounts to 16 000 units with a sales value of £80 000. An allocation of fixed overheads to Bolero production on the basis of sales value would be as follows:

Overhead charge to Bolero production

$$= £110\,000 \times \frac{80\,000}{725\,000}$$
$$= £12\,138$$
$$= £0.759 \text{ per unit produced}$$

This exercise can be conducted on a number of different bases (Table 22.2). As you can see each allocation base has produced a different charge per unit produced for fixed overheads which will, ultimately, lead to a different total unit cost. The basis of apportionment is purely arbitrary, although there may be some sense in the argument that apportionment should be on the basis of that aspect

Table 22.1

	Bolero production		Factory production	
Total production (units)	16 000			
Sales revenue (£)		80 000		725 000
Materials (usage (kg)	10 000		73 000	
Material cost per unit (£)		0.5		0.8
Labour usage (hours)	1 250		31 680	
Labour rate per hour		10.0		9.0
Machine hours	240		2 700	

Table 22.2

	Value of production	Materials usage	Materials value	Labour hours	Labour cost	Machine hours
Allocation ratio	80 000 / 725 000	10 000 / 73 000	5 000 / 58 400	1 250 / 31 680	12 500 / 285 120	240 / 2 700
Total fixed overheads (£)	110 000	110 000	110 000	110 000	110 000	110 000
Allocated overheads (£)	12 138	15 068	9 418	4 340	4 822	9 778
Charge (£) per unit produced	0.759	0.942	0.589	0.271	0.301	0.611

of production which most influences the level of fixed overheads. On this basis, rent and rates could perhaps be allocated according to the floor area used in production, while supervisors' wages, for example, could be allocated according to labour hours employed. However, no matter what allocation basis is chosen, the inclusion of fixed overheads into decision making can distort the relative costs and benefits of the various alternatives available.

THE PROBLEM OF COST DISTORTION

In order to demonstrate the problem of cost distortion in decision making, we tell the story of Farmer Joe.

Farmer Joe has a fixed-acreage farm with facilities to produce wheat, corn, chickens and pigs. To make our point, and to avoid confusion with other issues, we will assume that any labour not required for production can be laid off and that production facilities (including land) are not interchangeable in the short term.

Farmer Joe earns a net cash contribution as a result of his annual production, as shown in Table 22.3 (net cash contribution is calculated after the deduction of labour costs). The total anticipated fixed costs associated with running the farm and the farmhouse during the year are £7800.

Farmer Joe is reviewing his situation after he has been told by his 'financial adviser' that chicken production is not worthwhile, as it does not cover its fair proportion of fixed overheads. The total labour devoted to the farm is 3900 hours per annum. Therefore, the proportion of the total overheads attributable to chicken farming is:

Allocated overhead (chickens)

$$= £7800 \times 600/3900$$
$$= £1200$$

The same calculation for each product produces a profit and loss account for each (Table 22.4).

Farmer Joe wonders what would be the logical consequence of following his financial adviser's advice. If chicken production is stopped, the farm will still have to bear the full overheads of £7800,

Table 22.3

	Wheat	Corn	Chickens	Pigs
Net cash contribution	£5000	£2600	£1000	£2000
Labour hours required to produce	1500	900	600	900

Table 22.4

	Wheat	Corn	Chickens	Pigs
Net cash contribution	5 000	2 600	1 000	2 000
Allocated fixed costs	3 000	1 800	1 200	1 800
Net profit/(loss)	2 000	800	(200)	200

although on a reduced labour base of 3300 labour hours – assuming that the labour devoted to chicken production is laid off. We can now repeat the above calculations on the three remaining products (Table 22.5).

We have calculated the allocated fixed overheads to wheat production, for example, as follows:

Fixed overheads allocated to wheat production
= 1500/3300 × £7800
= £3545

On the basis of the revised net profit or loss figures, it would now appear that pig production is no longer worthwhile. Perhaps using the same argument as before, pig production should be stopped. But if pig production is stopped, what then?

This story does not have a happy ending!

The inclusion of fixed overheads into the decision has provided a performance target for each product. This has the result of deflecting attention from choosing the cash-maximising alternative (i.e. producing all products in the absence of any better alternatives) to deciding which is the least worthwhile of the four products if the resources needed for its production could be diverted to a better use.

Farmer Joe's problem clearly highlights the dangers of including fixed overheads as part of the cost of production in that it blurs the distinction between two types of decision making. First, the decision concerning production, where the allocation procedure may lead to the non-production of worthwhile products, and, second, the setting of performance targets, where it is intended to reflect, albeit inaccurately, the internal opportunity cost of managerial resources in the costing of individual processes.

OVERHEADS AS A TAX ON PRODUCTION

Many organisations operate on the basis of a number of business units which are accountable for their own performance. The role of central management in this context is to provide certain company-wide services and to establish and maintain the services of

Table 22.5

	Wheat	Corn	Pigs
Net cash contribution	5000	2600	2000
Allocated fixed costs	3545	2127	2127
Net profit/(loss)	1455	473	(127)

the business. In this case, central management will want to ensure:

- each production unit 'pays' central management for the services it provides;
- the central management levy becomes part of the control standard of each operating unit.

In many organisations in the public sector such as educational establishments, health service providers and other such public bodies, the problem arises as to how central management can fund its activities, given that the income of the organisation accrues at the operational level rather than the organisational level. In a business firm which is heavily divisionalised, and where those divisions are operationally independent, a similar problem can arise.

In this context, the charging of overheads is very similar to a taxation system. Taxation systems in companies can be:

- direct, i.e. based on revenue earned;
- indirect, i.e. based on costs expended.

Alternatively, the charge may be made on the direct consumption of central management services by the operating divisions. In Chapter 3 we discussed the role of the holding company in establishing an 'internal market' for certain resources. Such internal markets may be for:

- capital, which can be charged to divisions at the business's opportunity cost of capital;
- building space, which can be charged on a market equivalent rent for the space occupied;
- marketing, which can be charged on a direct basis for the costs of campaigns plus some revenue apportionment of total cost.

Where an external market for the resources is available to individual divisions and the holding company does not wish to prohibit the exploitation of those markets, the appropriate charge rate would be the external opportunity cost of the resource concerned. If the company does prohibit the use of viable external sources, and this creates artificial constraints on what a division can do then a shadow price for that resource will be created.

EXAMPLE

A large security systems manufacturer operated with five divisions, each responsible for its own, largely distinct market. The company permitted each division to borrow funds up to a maximum of £100 000 at market rates of interest. The other capital requirements of the group were allocated by the group company and each division was charged annual interest on its outstanding capital balances. Capital was regarded as an overdraft loan from the group and could be recalled at any time by the Group Financial Director. Divisions were charged differential rates above the ruling base rate in the market on individual drawings from the Group. One division concerned with the growing market of domestic security systems was required to pay 6% over base and, as a result, had minimised its capital requirements to the £100 000 per annum that could be drawn from the market. It had, on three occasions in the past five years breached the £100 000 ceiling to manage cost overruns on its investment projects.

The system described in the company case above is quite typical of the way many organisations manage their internal capital markets. It does, however, create difficulties.

- There is a great incentive for divisional management to 'dodge' the system either blatantly or by the use of leasing (to avoid capital expenditure).
- Where the group company exercises its power to vary the return it requires above ruling market rates this will tend to distort the attitude of divisional management away from capital and towards revenue spending.
- The creation of artificial constraints can create high shadow prices for the capital resources in question with the consequential distortion in decision making if these shadow prices are not recognised.

For a central tax system to be neutral in its impact upon divisional or departmental decision making, it should operate such that a decision which would be justifiable on contribution grounds would still be accepted with the taxation policy in place. If an organisation were to place a proportionate tax on revenue alone, this may make some products or projects which offer a positive cash contribution to the firm as a whole unworthwhile to the division responsible. However, a percentage tax on cash contribution will be neutral with respect to decision making from the company's point of view.

EXAMPLE

A company has three operating divisions: A, B and C. Each division reports a profit on its year's activities before recovery of central costs of £420 000.

The company is considering whether to recover its costs through:

- *an overhead charge based upon a labour cost recovery rate;*
- *a charge on revenue;*
- *a charge on contribution.*

The calculations are shown in Table 22.6.

The first three rows under each division show the revenue less divisional costs and the divisional profit obtained before recovery of central charges. The divisional costs do not include recovery of central charges at this stage. Each division is shown as making a profit, and the rates of profitability on revenue and the percentage of total profit generated by each division are shown in Table 22.7.

At the divisional level the ranking of profitability is C > A > B.

The three bases of recovery are as follows.

(i) Allocation of the central charge on the basis of labour cost:

$$\text{Allocation rate} = \frac{\text{total central charge to be allocated}}{\text{total divisional labour cost}}$$

$$= 420\,000/270\,000$$
$$= £1.556 \text{ per } £ \text{ labour cost}$$

This is then charged to each division on the basis of the labour costs of each division. We can then calculate the net profit per division/revenue and the proportion of total corporate profit contributed by each division (Table 22.8). Charging the central costs as an overhead alters the ranking of profitability in terms of their contribution of divisional net profit to the net profit of the business as a whole. The new ranking is C > B > A.

(ii) Allocation of central charge as a revenue-based tax on divisional performance (Table 22.9): the ranking of divisions in terms of their contribution to corporate profitability is C > A > B, with division B shown as a significant corporate loss maker. Indeed, senior management might fall into the Farmer Joe trap above and decide to close or sell off division B.

(iii) Allocation of central charge as a profit-based tax (Table 22.10): in this case the profitability ranking is the same as at the divisional level, i.e. C > A > B, and the proportions of divisional net profit/total corporate net profit after central cost recovery is identical to the proportions of divisional profit to the total before central cost recovery. Thus, this method of allocating central costs to divisions does not distort the perceived performance of divisions relative to the total and avoids the Farmer Joe trap.

Table 22.6

Central costs to be recovered		420 000			
	Division			Total	Percentage
	A	B	C		
Revenue	500 000	800 000	650 000	1 950 000	
Divisional costs	290 000	710 000	350 000	1 350 000	
Divisional profit	210 000	90 000	300 000	600 000	
Divisional labour costs	140 000	40 000	90 000	270 000	
Allocation rate	1.556	1.556	1.556	1.556	
Allocated overhead	217 778	62 222	140 000	420 000	
Profit or loss	(7 778)	27 778	160 000	180 000	
As a revenue tax	107 692	172 308	140 000	420 000	21.54
Profit or loss	102 308	(82 308)	160 000	180 000	
As a divisional profit tax	147 000	63 000	210 000	420 000	70.00
Profit or loss	63 000	27 000	90 000	180 000	

Table 22.7

	Division			Total
	A	B	C	
Profit/revenue	42.00	11.25	46.15	30.77
Divisional profit/total	35.00	15.00	50.00	100.00

Table 22.8

	Divisional			Total
	A	B	C	
Revenue	500 000	800 000	650 000	1 950 000
Divisional costs	(290 000)	(710 000)	(350 000)	(1 350 000)
Overhead recovery	(217 778)	(62 222)	(140 000)	(420 000)
Net profit	(7 778)	27 778	160 000	180 000
Net profit/revenue	(1.56)	3.47	24.62	9.23
Divisional net profit/total	(4.32)	15.43	88.89	100.00

Table 22.9

	Divisional			Total
	A	B	C	
Revenue	500 000	800 000	650 000	1 950 000
Divisional costs	(290 000)	(710 000)	(350 000)	(1 350 000)
Central charge	(107 692)	(172 308)	(140 000)	(420 000)
Net profit	(102 308)	82 308	160 000	180 000
Net profit/revenue	20.46	(10.29)	24.62	9.23
Divisional net profit/total	56.84	(45.73)	88.89	100.00

Table 22.10

	Divisional			Total
	A	B	C	
Revenue	500 000	800 000	650 000	1 950 000
Divisional costs	(290 000)	(710 000)	(350 000)	(1 350 000)
Central charge	(147 000)	(63 000)	(210 000)	(420 000)
Net profit	63 000	27 000	90 000	180 000
Net profit/revenue	12.60	3.38	13.85	9.23
Divisional net profit/total	35.00	15.00	50.00	100.00

In Chapter 24 we return to the problems of overhead allocation again and examine the techniques of activity-based costing and production flow costing, which attempt to produce a more rational basis for the allocation of indirect cost to production.

STANDARD COSTING

The standard cost of producing a product is an ex-ante estimate of the cost of producing a particular unit of product given specified operating conditions. It represents an 'ideal' in the sense that it is the cost which the firm's product designers believe a given product can be produced for under standardised production conditions. The notion of a standard is similar to the concept of a 'budgeted unit cost', although the latter may contain some anticipated differences from standard. Usually, where standard costing procedures are used, they are applied to:

- building a unit product cost for inventory purposes;
- creating budgeted product costs for subsequent periods.

The standard cost of a product consists of two components:

(i) standard direct costs such as the direct cost of materials, labour, energy costs and other costs which are expected to vary with output;
(ii) standard indirect costs which are the allocated fixed production and business costs absorbed into each unit of production. For this purpose, it is necessary to define a standard overhead absorption or recovery rate (the direct analogue of the allocation rate discussed above) for each class of overhead.

EXAMPLE

Division C produced a single product at a rate of 2000 units a year. The direct materials cost was dependent upon usage, and each unit required 5.5 kg of materials under standard operating conditions. Materials costs are £4.80/kg. The other direct costs were labour (3 hours per unit at £15.00 per hour), energy costs (£2.00 per unit) and variable overheads at £14.00 per unit. Divisional indirect costs are £175 200. The company policy is to charge central company overheads on the basis of labour cost at a standard allocation rates of £1.5556 per £ labour cost.

The total costs to production are shown in Table 22.11 with the standard unit cost alongside.

Note that the total anticipated production has been set at 2000 units and this is the basis upon

Table 22.11

	Total costs to production	Standard unit cost
Units of production	2 000	1
Direct costs		
Materials	52 800	26.40
Labour	90 000	45.00
Energy	4 000	2.00
Variable overheads	28 000	14.00
Total direct costs	174 800	87.40
Indirect costs		
Divisional overheads	175 200	87.60
Company overheads	140 000	70.00
Total cost/unit standard cost	490 000	245.00

which divisional overheads are allocated. Central overheads are absorbed using the rate of £1.5556 per £ labour cost. It is possible to see from this example that:

- if the division produces more than the planned 2000 units of output there will be an over-recovery of overheads (excluding variable overheads) into production costs;
- if the division produces less than the planned 2000 units of output there will be an under-recovery of overheads.

We will return to the problems of over- and under-recovery of overheads in standard costing systems when we look at budgeting and variance analysis in Chapters 25 and 26.

CONCLUSION

In this chapter we have returned to the problem of matching prior committed costs to activity and demonstrated the difficulties and dangers involved for decision making. We told the very important story of Farmer Joe, and showed how, with a little bit of ingenuity, his financial advisor put him out of business! We then turned to the problem, often associated with overhead allocation, of making fair and non-distortionary recoveries from services or production for the operation of the central management facility. We came to the conclusion that such production 'taxes' were most fairly collected by taxing divisional or departmental contribution, as this removed any distortionary effects from their decision making.

Chapter 23

Costing in Different Production Environments

Level M

Contents

Summary

In this chapter we examine the problems of costing in different production environments. In the first section we contrast the two extremes of job and continuous production, and point out the salient characteristics of each. We then proceed to an examination of job costing and show how a job cost card is assembled. Finally, we examine process costing and in particular the concept of the 'equivalent unit of production', which is invaluable in costing items of work in progress which may be incomplete at the end of the period of account.

PRODUCTION PROCESS DYNAMICS

Production dynamics fall along a spectrum of possibilities from single job to continuous production. Single job production is characterised by the unitary nature of production where control over all of the production variables is operated at the unit level. True job-based production would include:

- unit specification and design;
- procurement of inputs to specification;
- fabrication to design through one or more discrete production stages;
- quality and performance testing as a unit;
- delivery to customer.

A company operating in this type of production environment will need to concentrate its attention on efficient job scheduling, flexible design continuing through the production stage as well as at the start, the minimisation of process change time in switching mobile assets from use to use, and speedy delivery times from manufacturing to the customer. The essence of job-based production is that it is subject to 'demand pull', that is, the job is initiated by a customer order which triggers the sequence of activities outlined above. In recent years, the Japanese have been very successful in developing job-based production methods and utilising those methods in industries such as motor-cars and consumer electronics which had been dominated in the West by process manufacturing systems. The Japanese approach is characterised by the following.

- Job-based systems.
- A rigorous demand led approach where each stage in manufacturing is only activated by a demand order from a subsequent stage. The final stage of production is only activated by a customer order. This approach, which lies at the heart of 'just-in-time' production should lead to work in progress being minimised.
- An insistence on rapid change times in production, as less specific production assets than are typically found in the West are switched from job to job.
- The development of a learning and adaptive culture, where products are subject to incremental improvement on a continuous basis, and from

this an experimental approach to design which carries on throughout production.

As a result of these characteristics the emphasis on quality development has been at the functional as well as the formal level. The concept of 'fitness for purpose' is defined from the customer's rather than the producer's standpoint.

The Japanese approach has been to extend the boundaries of what can be successfully produced using job-based systems. However, job-based systems do have their limitations.

- The time to fulfil a discrete order is the total production time which with some products can be significant (e.g. fine chemicals and pharmaceuticals).
- Economies of scale and learning effects are won through production technique rather than through scale effects in production or large order discounting in procurement.

At the other end of the spectrum, continuous production is where there are no natural units of production and where variables are controlled at the process level. Electricity generation is a continuous production system in that there are no natural breakpoints in production. Similarly, many of the extractive and refining industries operate continuous systems.

The desirable features of a continuous production systems are as follows.

- The process can be refined towards greater and greater levels of operating efficiency.
- Economies can be generated by optimising the production system to the most efficient scale, given the capacity of the plant.
- The wait time for output is minimised, although final stock levels will be determined in the short run by variations in demand.

In between the two extremes, batch production can be used, where units are produced in sufficient quantities over a given period to cover anticipated demand. By its nature, batch production is supplier led, and holdings of final inventory will vary between batch size and zero, with the consequential stock holdings costs which such a level of inventory will entail. In Figure 23.1 we give some production examples and their positioning in the job–batch–continuous manufacturing spectrum. You will note that certain areas of the space defined by the production method and the degree of unit differentiation are forbidden. Clearly, for example, where there is a high degree of differentiation between products, continuous production is impossible.

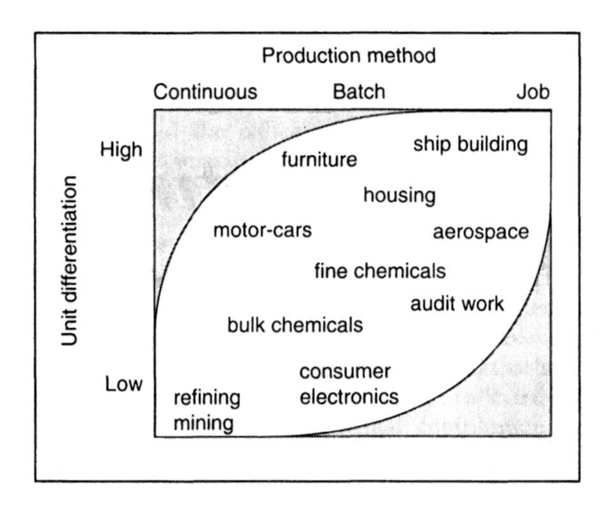

Figure 23.1 Production method versus the degree of unit differentiation.

TECHNIQUES OF COSTING DIFFERENT PRODUCTION SYSTEMS

All production systems can be described, at the highest level of generality, as processes for the conversion of inputs into outputs. For many decision situations this level of generality is all that is necessary, because we happen to be concerned with the overall characteristics of a system rather than with the precise detail of its operation. However, because cost accounting is concerned with monitoring detailed system performance it must match the complexities of the system concerned.

Two problems immediately arise:

- the identification of those aspects of production which attract specific costs;
- the time scale of any particular process.

In any production system there are certain physical positions where resources are applied to the system. Materials may be brought together or some labour or managerial activity may occur. For example, a car-body paint shop would be a point within a car production system where materials (car bodies, paint, pickling acid etc.) and other resources (labour scientific and managerial skills) are brought together as a production activity. Cost accountants call such a position a 'cost centre' because even though the activity does not attract revenue directly, it does attract costs which can be identified and recorded.

The planning of a firm's financial activities will include major cost items such as materials, various variable and fixed overheads, labour, scientific, tech-nical and managerial skills. These overall costs arise through the consolidation of individual elements of cost (the costs of specific items of materials, specific grades of labour etc.) which are incurred in the various cost centres within the firm. In Figure 23.2 we show, in outline, the consolidation of the various elements of cost into the overall cost of a particular process.

For example, one particular cost element may be the usage of electricity for the electrolytic coating of car bodies. The cost element is, therefore, the metered usage of electricity on that particular aspect of production. The cost centre concerned is the car-body paint shop and the basic cost classification is variable overheads (factory power).

The following factors can influence the selection of cost centres:

- the precision with which costs can be attributed to the process concerned;
- whether the costs attributable to a proposed cost centre can be controlled at that point in the production process;
- whether the costs collected through a proposed cost centre can be directly related to some aspect of the centre's performance.

With respect to the last point, the usage of electricity by a car-body paint shop could be related to the following aspects of performance.

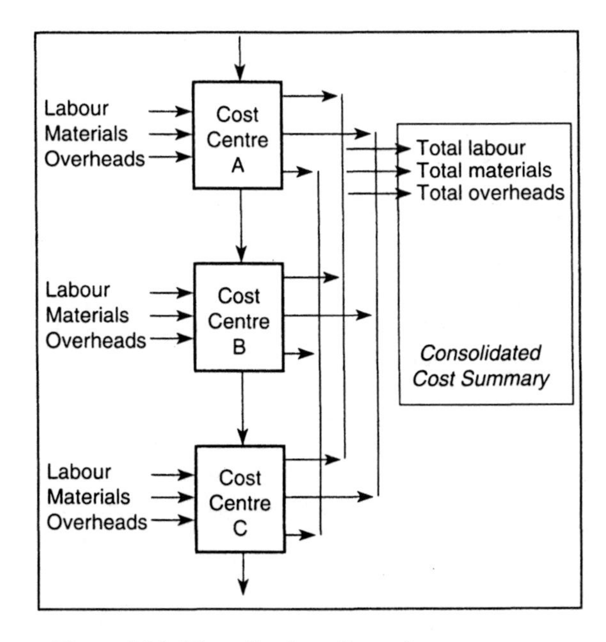

Figure 23.2 The collection of costs from cost centres.

- the throughput of car bodies (we would expect the usage of electricity to be directly related to the number of bodies treated);
- the thickness of the electrolytic deposit on the body parts treated (the required thickness will have been laid down in the production design specification);
- the quality of the cleaning and any other pretreatment which has been carried out on the car bodies;
- the quality of the steel, and hence the electrical conductivity, of the particular batch of bodies being treated.

Certain of the factors outlined above will be under the control of the operations staff working in the paint shop. Other factors, however, may be related to other parts of the production process or, indeed, as in the last factor mentioned, to the skill of the firm's purchasing department.

It is one of the cost accountant's tasks to form an opinion on the relationship between cost and cost centre and the degree to which variations in the costs concerned can be attributed to a given activity.

The second problem in costing production processes concerns the length of time over which production occurs. If the production time is longer than the time period over which control is to be exercised, then the system is essentially a continuous one. In this situation the production system must be 'notionally' stopped, so that the costs incurred in a particular period can be measured. If, on the other hand, production takes place over a shorter time period than that required for control purposes, then no such artificial stops are necessary. In the next section we will examine this problem in much more detail. We will look at the two opposite types of production system:

- job costing (discrete-time production processes);
- process costing (continuous time production processes).

JOB COSTING

Job costing, where it can be appropriately employed, is a relatively simple approach to costing in that the costing procedure itself can be matched to the actual physical process of production. However, job costing presents many more data handling, collation and control problems than process costing.

Job costing can be applied to a wide range of different production systems. For example:

- a car-repair shop;
- the production of custom-built furniture;
- a production run to print a book (like this one for example);
- a chemical produced on a batch process.

All of these processes can be regarded as discrete 'jobs', in that the time scale of the costing process has a definite beginning and end.

The core document in a job-costing system is the job card (or job sheet), one of which is assigned to each job or task performed by the particular production or service facility concerned. The job card records all cost elements charged to a particular job: materials withdrawn from stock, labour used, other services applied and, in many cases, a fixed charge for the use of the machinery and other fixed facilities. The job cards, once completed, can then be consolidated onto master job sheets which give the breakdown of different elements of cost applied to the particular aspect of production in a day.

In order to illustrate this type of costing we will describe the procedures which might be operated by a large car-repair shop.

When a motor-car is brought into a workshop, a set of multi-copy stationery is opened up. One part of this stationery eventually becomes the customer's invoice and another part acts as the job card. When the car comes to his or her workstation the mechanic will perform any diagnostic checks necessary and then proceed with the repairs and/or service. As the job proceeds the mechanic will withdraw from stores the necessary spare parts: plugs, oil, lubricants, points, etc. Each withdrawal from the stores entails two entries:

- A credit entry on a stock card showing the part withdrawn and any other details specified by the company's stock accounting system.
- A corresponding entry on the job card showing the item used on the job (this would form the corresponding debit entry).

Similarly, the engineer's time on the job would be shown by two entries: one on his or her daily (or weekly) time sheet and one on the job card for the particular repair or service. In Figure 23.3 we show the entries which would be made on the motor-repair job sheet.

Job-costing procedures, of necessity, revolve around the job card. In modern accounting systems the cost elements on the job card can be encoded and entered into a computerised cost analysis system, perhaps through a computer terminal located at the workstation concerned.

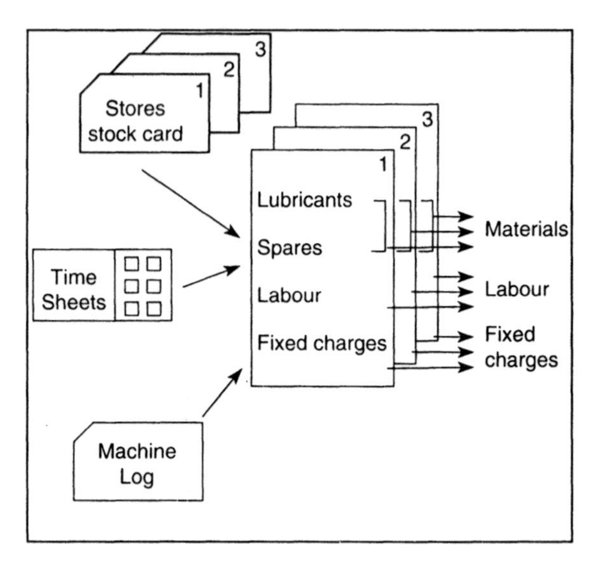

Figure 23.3 Consolidation of cost elements through a job card.

However, no matter how a card is actually entered up it must be intelligible and readily usable by the operator involved (such as the mechanic above). In addition, a good job card should disrupt the flow of work as little as possible and, indeed, should be designed, wherever possible, to enhance the production process. In our car-repair shop example an ideal job card might also include a checklist of the jobs to be performed, as well as clearly identifiable cost classifications.

PROCESS COSTING

Continuous production systems which do not have convenient breaks in their production runs present problems for the cost accountant in the assignment of costs. These problems arise because, at any point in time, a certain amount of production will still be in progress. For example, a motor-car production line will always contain a certain number of cars that are only partly completed.

A continuous production process will begin each period with a particular stock of work in progress. During the course of the production period, this initial stock of work in progress will be completed, followed by further units which will be both started and finished. In addition, at the end of the period there will be some units in production which have been started but remain uncompleted. The problem we have in establishing a cost per unit during the production period is that we can only identify the number of units fully completed. Some will be incomplete, although they will have consumed certain raw materials and other resources. It is the cost accountant's job to establish the cost of those units completed during the period and the cost incurred on uncompleted units remaining at the end.

EXAMPLE

Peteneras plc operates a continuous production process for the manufacture of one type of standard electronic component. Only four cost categories are involved (of course, in practice, there will be many more than this): materials, labour, power and other variable overheads. The cost of each month's production and the value of the work in progress are calculated for budgeting purposes. The components are produced on a continuous production line with monthly periods of account.

At the beginning of period 9, 15 units were in various stages of completion on the production line. On average, each unit had 80% of its materials in place, and 50% of the labour required to build each unit had been applied. In addition, 30% of the necessary power and 40% of the necessary variable overheads had been applied (on average) to each unit.

The opening work in progress had been valued at the end of the preceding period at:

Materials	*£600*
Labour	*£525*
Power	*£135*
Variable overheads	*£480*
	£1740

During the course of the period, 250 units were completed including the sets in progress at the beginning of the period. During period 9 the following costs were incurred:

Materials	*£13 475*
Labour	*£17 640*
Power	*£8 085*
Variable overheads	*£19 600*
	£58 800

At the end of the period, 20 units were in progress. Their average degree of completion was as follows:

Materials	*50%*
Labour	*30%*
Power	*25%*
Overheads	*10%*

In Figure 23.4 we show the degree of completion of each element of the production process.

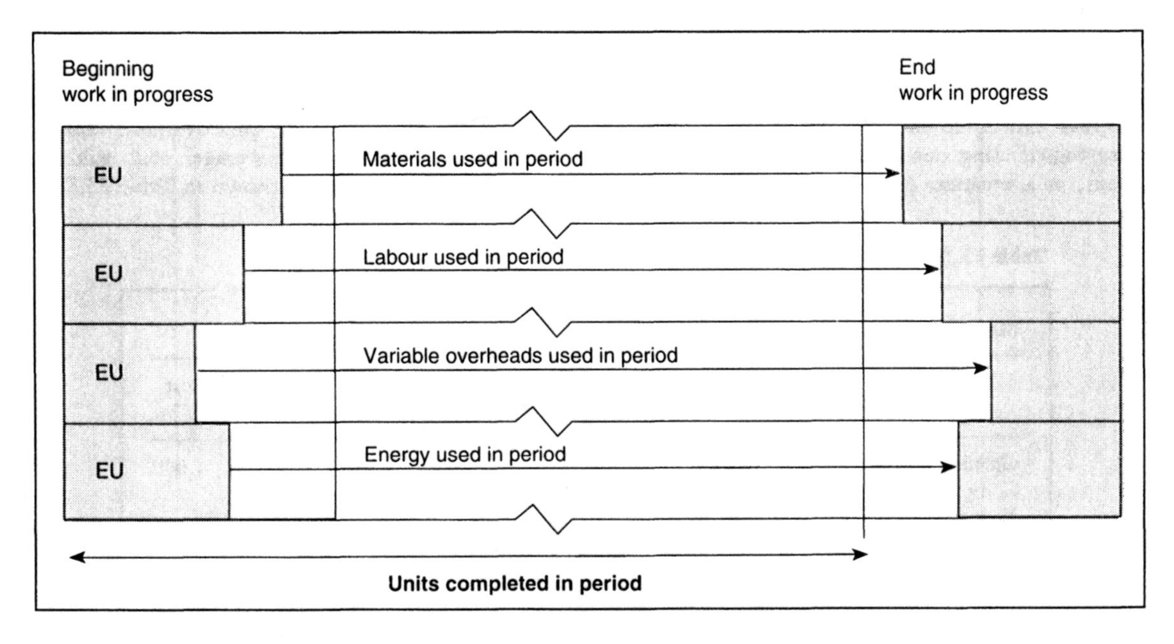

Figure 23.4 Degree of completion of production.

Taking materials as the first element of cost, the work in progress at the beginning of the period consisted of 15 units which were 80% complete as far as materials were concerned. This is equivalent to saying that these materials could have produced 12 (i.e. 0.8×15) complete units. For the purposes of this illustration we will assume that materials are homogeneous, although in practice materials would consist of different components. During the period of production, after finishing the work in progress, a further 235 units ($250 - 15$) were both started and completed in the period. In this, and indeed in any period, the work schedule is as follows.

- Complete the opening work in progress.
- Produce units which will be both started and completed within the period.
- Start the closing work in progress (WIP).

The final work in progress of 20 units is only 50% complete with respect to materials. This is equivalent to 10 fully completed units. The situation is summarised in Table 23.1.

Cost per equivalent unit produced =
£14 075/260 = £54.13

The equivalent unit of production is a very useful measure for partly finished products. The equivalent units produced in a period represent the theoretical number of complete units which could have been fully completed given the material resources used. The method of calculation employed above is known as the 'weighted average' method.

One objection can be raised to the way we have calculated the materials cost figure above. The materials tied up in the opening work in progress were valued using out-of-date materials costs. This means, in a situation of rising material prices, that the calculation of current period unit costs and the valuation of closing work in progress will be undervalued with respect to their current values. The materials cost per unit of the opening work in progress is given by:

$$\frac{\text{Cost of materials in opening WIP}}{\text{Equivalent units in progress}} = \frac{600}{12} = £50$$

The materials purchased during the period (£13 475) effectively completed the equivalent of 248 units giving a materials cost of £54.33 per unit (excluding, for the moment, the opening work in progress, which used prior period materials). The weighted-average valuation procedure, where the work in progress brought forward from the previous period is valued at the costs ruling in that period, implies that £50 is relevant for inclusion as part of the unit materials cost to be applied in the current period (period 9). On the other hand, it can be argued that the materials component of opening work in progress should be excluded when calculating the unit cost. A revised calculation procedure, excluding the value of the opening work in progress, will change the materials cost per unit charges from £54.13 (as above) to £54.33. This second method is referred to as the 'first in, first out' (FIFO) valuation method.

A summary is shown in Table 23.2.

We can repeat these calculations for the labour component of production. The only difference in this case is that the opening and closing work in progress are, respectively, 50% and 30% complete as far as their labour input is concerned. The calculation of the labour, power and overhead cost per unit using the weighted-average cost valuation procedure gives the figures shown in Table 23.3.

Table 23.1

Materials flow

	Equivalent complete units	Cost (£)
Opening work in progress (WIP) (15 × 0.8)	12	600
Completion of opening WIP (15 × 0.2)	3	
New units completed	235	
Closing WIP (20 × 0.5)	10	13 475
Total equivalent units	260	
Total material cost		14 075

Table 23.2

Materials flow

	Units	Weighted average cost (£)	Units	FIFO (£)
Opening work in progress	12	600		
Completion of opening WIP	3		3	
New units completed	235		235	
Closing WIP	10	13 475	10	13 475
Total equivalent units	260		248	
Total materials cost		14 075		13 475
Materials cost per equivalent unit		54.13		54.33

We can summarise these results into a final statement of unit cost:

Materials	£54.13
Labour	£70.97
Power	£32.24
Variable overheads	£79.68
	£237.01

If you have followed the details of our workings and have calculated the corresponding figures using the FIFO method we described before, you should be able to see how the difference between the methods has arisen, although you may be wondering why we bothered, given that the actual differences are so small. In most situations, what we have found is quite typical because:

- work in progress at the beginning of a period is usually quite small in relation to the month's total production;
- the specific price changes for individual resources are unlikely to be significant over the period of production.

However, on occasions, the difference between the two methods may be significant and the question arises as to which is the superior method of valuing work in progress. The more appropriate question, however, is 'significant for what?' If the aim of the costing procedure is simply to ensure adequate control of the resources devoted to production, then the answer to the question is that method which most simply relates cost figures to the resources being controlled. In most circumstances, because the weighted-average method relates costs to the normal flow of resources, it is probably the better of the two. However, if the firm concerned is seeking to use the costs obtained in other areas of decision making, such as pricing or output, then the answer to the question posed is neither; in such situations the opportunity cost of the resource concerned should be used. To restate a point we have made before, the information required for general decision making is quite different from that required for the purposes of control. Neither of the methods shown above uses current buying prices; nor do they necessarily reflect opportunity costs.

Once the schedule of unit cost has been calculated it is a reasonably straightforward matter to evaluate the total cost of the period's completed production, including the prior period's work in progress which is finished off. We will complete our calculations using the weighted-average method.

The cost of production during month 9 is as follows:

Materials cost (250 × £54.13)	£13 532.50
Labour cost (250 × £70.96)	£17 740.00
Power cost (250 × £32.24)	£8 060.00
Variable overheads (250 × £79.68)	£19 920.00
Total cost of production (Period 9)	£59 252.50

The valuation of work in progress is calculated in exactly the same way, except that instead of using the number of units produced (250), we use the

Table 23.3

	Units	Weighted average cost (£)
Labour cost		
Opening work in progress	7.50	525.00
Completion of opening WIP	7.50	
New units completed	235.00	
Closing WIP	6.00	17 640.00
Total equivalent units	256.00	
Total labour cost		18 165.00
Labour cost per equivalent unit		70.96
Power cost		
Opening work in progress	4.50	135.00
Completion of opening WIP	10.50	
New units completed	235.00	
Closing WIP	5.00	8 085.00
Total equivalent units	255.00	
Total power cost		8 220.00
Power cost per equivalent unit		32.24
Overheads		
Opening work in progress	6.00	480.00
Completion of opening WIP	9.00	
New units completed	235.00	
Closing WIP	2.00	19 600.00
Total equivalent units	252.00	
Total variable overheads		20 080.00
Overheads per equivalent units		79.68

number of equivalent units in progress at the end of the period.

The valuation of work in progress at the end of the period is:

Materials component (10 × £54.13)	£541.30
Labour component (6 × £70.96)	£425.76
Power component (5 × £32.24)	£161.20
Overhead component (2 × £79.68)	£159.36
Cost of work in progress	£1287.62

Process costing is useful in deriving a cost of work in progress and product unit costs over a period. It is especially valuable in those industries which utilise continuous production processes on a conveyor belt and where, at any instant in time, a number of units may be in process. For continuous chemical processes and other extractive industries it is largely irrelevant, as work in progress will be a constant 'priming stock' which will form part of the fixed cost of operating the plant.

CONCLUSION

In this chapter we have considered two traditional production costing techniques: job costing and process costing. A thorough understanding of these two methods gives an insight into most of the practical variations you are likely to encounter, as they are likely to be simple variants of one or other of these two methods. In the next chapter we turn our attention to what has become a major thrust in the development of management accounting – accounting for batch- or job-based production systems.

Chapter 24

Activity-Based and Product Flow Costing

Level G

Contents

Summary

In this chapter we continue our analysis of product costs from Chapters 22 and 23 and attempt to surmount the problems of creating unit costs by conventional allocation procedures. We describe two product costing techniques which seek to bring into the product cost some measure of the real organisational resources devoted to its manufacture. The first, called 'activity-based costing', defines a full product cost in terms of its direct cost plus a range of quality, change and logistical transactions required to bring the product to completion. The second method we develop is an extension of activity-based costing, which examines the types of interventions made in the creation of a product and how costs are associated with those interventions.

INTRODUCTION

Conventionally, indirect costs are accrued (or absorbed) into unit costs on the basis of resource consumption. However, where the indirect costs are unaffected by output then, as we have seen in Chapter 21, allocation problems can arise and distortions in decision making occur as a result. The fundamental difficulty here is that the accountant is attempting to convert period incurred business and production costs to output decision costs. In this chapter we explore two related methods of dealing with this problem. The first attempts to match quality and change transactions to product flows through a manufacturing process. The second matches on the basis of value-adding interventions in a manufacturing process.

Both of these methods attempt to estimate, in the unit costing process, the amount of organisational resource devoted to that product. In terms of the opportunity cost framework developed in Chapters 7 and 8, they provide closer approximations to the shadow price of the scarce organisational resources required to produce a product to a given level of quality and, in the case of product flow costing (PFC), in the most efficient way possible.

ACTIVITY-BASED COSTING

Disillusionment with conventional cost techniques in the 1970s and 1980s led a group of influential academics at Harvard and elsewhere to reconsider the fundamentals of cost allocation. They understood the problems of conventional overhead allocation methods and absorption costing techniques outlined in Chapter 22. They also pointed out that, over recent decades, the proportion of non-direct costs (what they referred to as the 'hidden factory') had risen as a proportion of total business costs, and that allocation of these costs by direct labour hours engaged in production was certainly not relevant now, even if it had been relevant in the 1930s. Allocating indirect costs according to labour hours also places an artificially high value on head count, and leads to the mistake that many managers make that reducing head count *per se* generates a concomitant reduction in fixed costs.

EXAMPLE

A motor manufacturer could trace its origins back to the 1920s when motor-car production had been largely manual with very low levels of automation. In the 1930s the business had introduced cost allocation system based upon labour hours in production and had created unit costs on that basis. This served the company well, or at least they did not appreciate the problems with such costing systems, until the late 1970s when the new generation of automotive plant and modern technology allowed them to become much more capital intensive. During the 1981 recession they saw their opportunity and began to shed labour and, indeed, during that period the direct workforce decreased to a third of its pre-recession size. In the late-1980s the company was taken over by a large multinational who put in place a programme of rapid retooling and modern production systems which served to reduce the labour force to one-tenth of its 1980 size. However, the company's full cost per labour hour had increased 15-fold. On the basis of this, senior management began to make a series of critical decisions:

- *further redundancies to reduce total operating costs (company senior management really believed that reducing labour allowed them to cut fixed overheads);*
- *the closure of some subcomponent and subassembly work in favour of buying in where the bid prices were compared with the 'full cost of manufacture' – a process which can best be described as 'vertical disintegration';*

As the process of concentration and increasing automation through robotics advanced, the point came where the whole production line was under the control of a small group of systems engineers and what the company referred to as 'goffers'. The production director, when looking at the full cost per employee, was reported as saying: 'Does this mean that if we get rid of our remaining staff we can get rid of all this cost or ought we to get rid of our accountants?'!

Activity-based costing (ABC) is based upon some very simple ideas.

- Costs are either direct (quantity related) or indirect. In the typical manufacturing firm indirect costs can form up to 90% of the total.
- Production consists of a multitude of activities which determine the shape and size of the 'hidden factory' and hence the burden of indirect cost.
- These production activities can be analysed into a series of fundamental 'cost drivers' which determine the amount of business cost committed. Sometimes the vocabulary of ABC is confused by reference to these cost-generating activities as 'cost transactions'. We will not use that terminology in this book.
- A metric is chosen for each cost driver which allows indirect cost to be accrued to production according to the level of activity undertaken in production utilising the source of the indirect cost concerned. So, for example, the activity of switching from one type of production to another within a flexible manufacturing system gives rise to a range of indirect costs. There will be indirect labour in transferring and resetting dyes, management and other support time in scheduling and planning such changes, record keeping and monitoring, associated maintenance costs and so forth. The number of machine changes could, therefore, become the chosen metric and an average change cost calculated which could be absorbed into unit costs according to the number of changes required to produce a unit of production.
- Activity-driven indirect costs can be absorbed to create costs by department, product line or units.

Two distinct approaches have arisen towards ABC:

- where only the relevant costs of production are absorbed into activities using appropriate metrics (an ABC contribution approach);
- where the full cost of the business is absorbed into each unit production according to the number of each class of activity engaged in producing that unit.

The originators of ABC have favoured the second approach and have promoted it as a technique for creating a full cost recovery system for manufac-turing which supersede's the classical system described in Chapter 22. Two principal cost drivers for manufacturing suggested by the originators of ABC are as follows.

- Logistical activities: these are the activities associated with moving resources from one place to another in order to get them into a position where manufacturing activities can be engaged; e.g. the costs incurred in procuring raw materials and transporting them into production would be a logistical transaction.
- Quality activities: these are the activities entailed in ensuring that the product is in conformity with what the customer demands. Design costs may be largely quality driven as well as the costs of the quality control department itself. A suitable metric could be the number of quality checks engaged in production.

We have described change activities earlier; these, along with logistics and quality, are said to be the three principal cost drivers in modern manufacturing.

Activity-based costing has gathered a considerable following in recent years, and a number of studies have been undertaken which make a compelling case for the benefits which can be gained by its implementation. We will defer a general critique of the approach until after we have discussed our own costing method which, whilst having some superficial similarities to ABC, does go considerably further in providing a means whereby management can analyse the amount of organisational resource devoted to a product, and in identifying where cost control can be most effectively targeted.

PRODUCT FLOW COSTING

At the philosophical level, production occurs as a series of human interventions into the physical ordering of certain resources at a particular place and at a particular time. For any given product there are many different ways of configuring its production and each way offers a different addition of value to the firm. The value maximising firm will seek out that configuration which generates maximum revenue at minimum cost.

Product flow costing relies upon the idea that a final product and its cost are derived from a series of physical resources (one of which is the originating or 'key' resource), a series of 'interventions' upon that key resource and the time cost of holding the partly formed product as work in progress. We use the term 'intervention' to describe an activity undertaken with the purpose of converting a given physical resource into a unit of final product in the hands of the customer.

An intervention is an action which can:

(i) transform the physical configuration of the resources (a value intervention, I_p);
(ii) transform the physical configuration of the fixed means of production (a change intervention, I_f);
(iii) change the physical location of a resource (a logistic intervention, I_l);
(iv) verify that the input resources, product or its subassemblies are in accordance with the design specification (a control intervention, I_c);
(v) add a contingent benefit to a product such as a warranty or service agreement. Because such interventions do not occur in the production sequence we refer to them as contingent interventions offering a default option to the customer (I_o) if the product should fail to achieve the benefits promised.

Interventions can be classified in two ways:

- Those which generate product value for the customer: interventions (i) and (v) are clearly of this type. In the first case they add value to a resource for the customer because they bring about the physical transformations which yield a final product in the configuration that the customer wishes to purchase. In the second case they can add value to the customer because they offer additional benefits through additional security in the use of the product.
- Those which offer no product value for the customer: interventions of the second type, (ii) and (iii), do not add value for the customer but serve to rearrange the configuration of the organisation and its fixed resources such that value enhancing transformations can be achieved within the process, or take the product from the firm's hands to a customer who is willing to pay its price. This latter activity will encompass transport, marketing and selling costs. Such interventions, which do not add to the value of a product, we term 'null interventions'.

Important note: although we can conceptually order interventions as either customer value adding or null, each class of intervention can be both. What we are referring to is the predominant characteristic of the interventions involved.

For example, control interventions (iv) are designed to ensure that the product at the stage it has reached is in conformity with its design and with the customer's specification. Such interventions can be value-adding to the customer if they serve to bring the product to the customer's specification of function. They will not be value-adding to the customer if they are designed to fulfil purely organisational needs.

The final class of cost which we build into the cost of the product is time costs. These costs are incurred as result of holding a product, as work in progress is designed to recover the opportunity cost of the money held as the product flow cost (PFC) at each stage in production. We use the simple continuous time discounting formula in Chapter 5 to estimate the time cost of work in progress.

In general, we can state (following Chapter 20) that customers will only reward the firm for the lower of:

(i) engaging in value enhancing activities to a given set of resources and for allowing them to avoid fabricating an identical product themselves;
(ii) the cost of purchasing an identical product elsewhere.

It is an important corollary of the product flow costing method that null interventions and time costs will not be rewarded by the market. In addition, business level costs which do not contribute to product level capability (such as marketing) must be taken from a firm's PFC contribution:

PFC contribution = sales revenue upon completion − PFC

Within PFC terminology, and referring back to the concept of a transaction discussed in Chapters 3 and 4, the series of null interventions and time costs required to create a product or one of its intermediate products generate the firm's 'transaction cost'. All product costs, whether null or value-adding to the customer are, of course, derived from the commitments which are engaged by the firm in order to acquire the resources or services entailed in fabricating that product.

The key resource comes into existence as soon as the commitment to procure that resource is made. From that point forward, costs accumulate on that key resource as decisions are made to take it through each subsequent stage on its path to becoming a final product. At each stage in the production process the opportunity cost to the firm will be the higher of:

(i) the realisable value of the partly formed product;

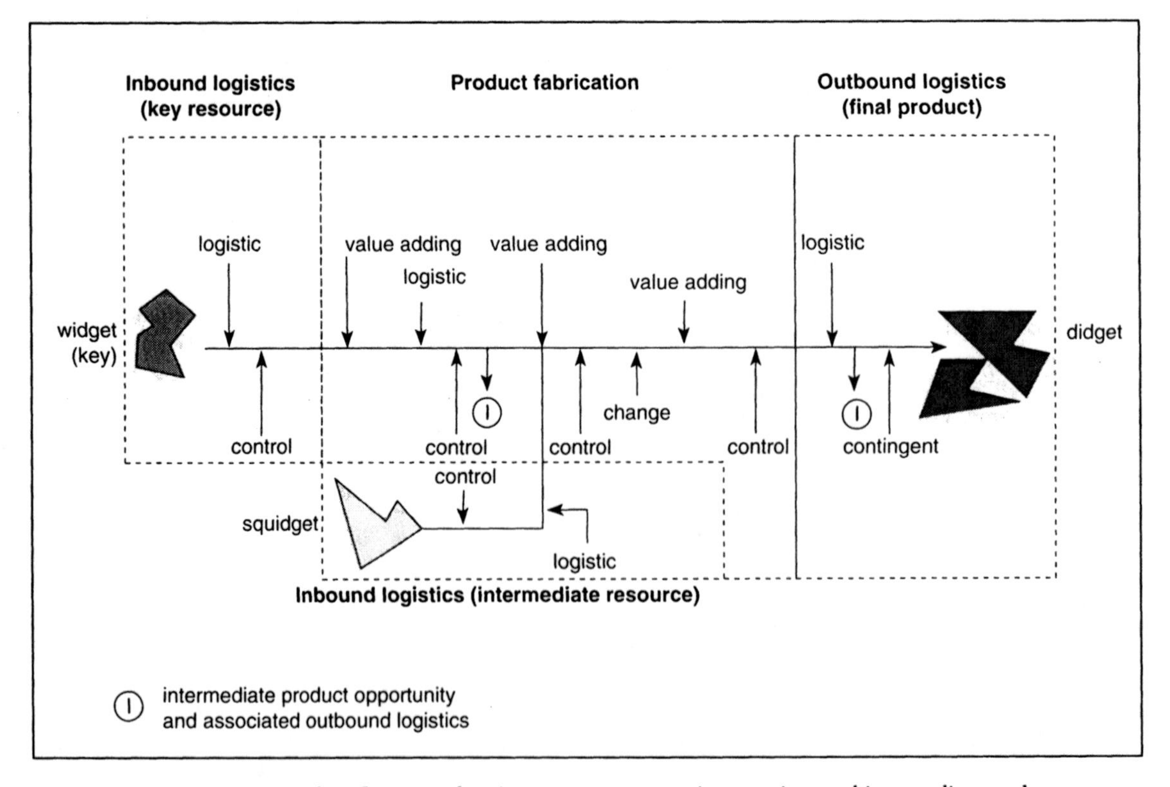

Figure 24.1 Product flow map showing stages, resources, interventions and intermediate market.

(ii) the cost of bringing an identical product to exactly the same point in production (this we will term the reinstatement or refabrication cost).

In Figure 24.1 we show a production sequence from a widget (and squidget) in the hands of the supplier to a didget in the hands of the customer. Along this sequence resource and intervention costs are absorbed *onto* the key resource (the didget) through three stages:

- inbound logistics, which includes procurement, shipping, quality control and order management;
- fabrication, where value-adding interventions are made on the key resource by either adding other resources or performing manufacturing operations, and null interventions are made to fixed plant and in quality checking;
- outbound logistics, where the product passes from final quality control to final stock holding, and from final stock holding to the customer.

You may like to piece together your own story of what is happening to the ubiquitous widget as it is transformed into a final product. However, you will notice the five types of intervention outlined above passing through the three stages of production.

THE PRODUCT FLOW COSTING STRATEGY

The PFC strategy described in Figure 24.2 is designed to provide a costing algorithm which will generate:

- an estimate of the full PFC cost of production, taking into account the real value of the resources and organisational capability required to generate a particular product (this PFC cost will be useful in determining minimum and maximum price ranges – see Chapter 20);
- a simple means of establishing the cost accretion to a product through its various stages;
- a simple control metric (the product tracking ratio) which will allow management to target areas for cost improvement and to value the benefit of quality changes to the product (see Chapter 21).

In order to create a full product flow cost, our analysis should proceed through the stages identified in Figure 24.2.

IDENTIFYING THE KEY RESOURCE

The choice of the key resource is determined by certain criteria, some of which are logical and others are a matter of convenience. The ultimate test, however, is the efficiency with which a given input resource yields a final product flow cost and generates the all important product tracking ratio. Suggested criteria are as follows.

- Which real input resource required into production is logically (in terms of the production sequence) procured first?
- Which resource is the production sequence designed around in terms of physical activities?
- Which resource has the highest procurement cost? This will only be significant where other resources entering the production sequence previously and including their subsequent interventions are of trivial cost compared with the cost of the resource concerned.

The concept of the key resource is fundamental to this approach to costing and care should be taken in establishing the prime candidate for this position. It is around the key resource that capability will be exercised and against which performance monitoring will occur.

DETERMINING THE PRODUCT FLOW SEQUENCE

The central ideas necessary to establish a product flow sequence are as follows.

- The product flow commences as soon as the commitment to procure the key resource is engaged (see below). The time costs associated with the procurement of the key resource and all subsequent physical resources required to fabricate the product are:

  (i) the time cost from commitment to engaging the fabrication stage;
  (ii) the time benefit between engaging the procurement commitment and its discharge (see Chapter 4).

- We separate out these two elements, as management would normally seek to minimise (i), but maximise (ii), commensurate with maintaining a high quality supplier relationship.
- The product flow ends at the point that the sale commitment is discharged by the customer with the product in his or her hands.

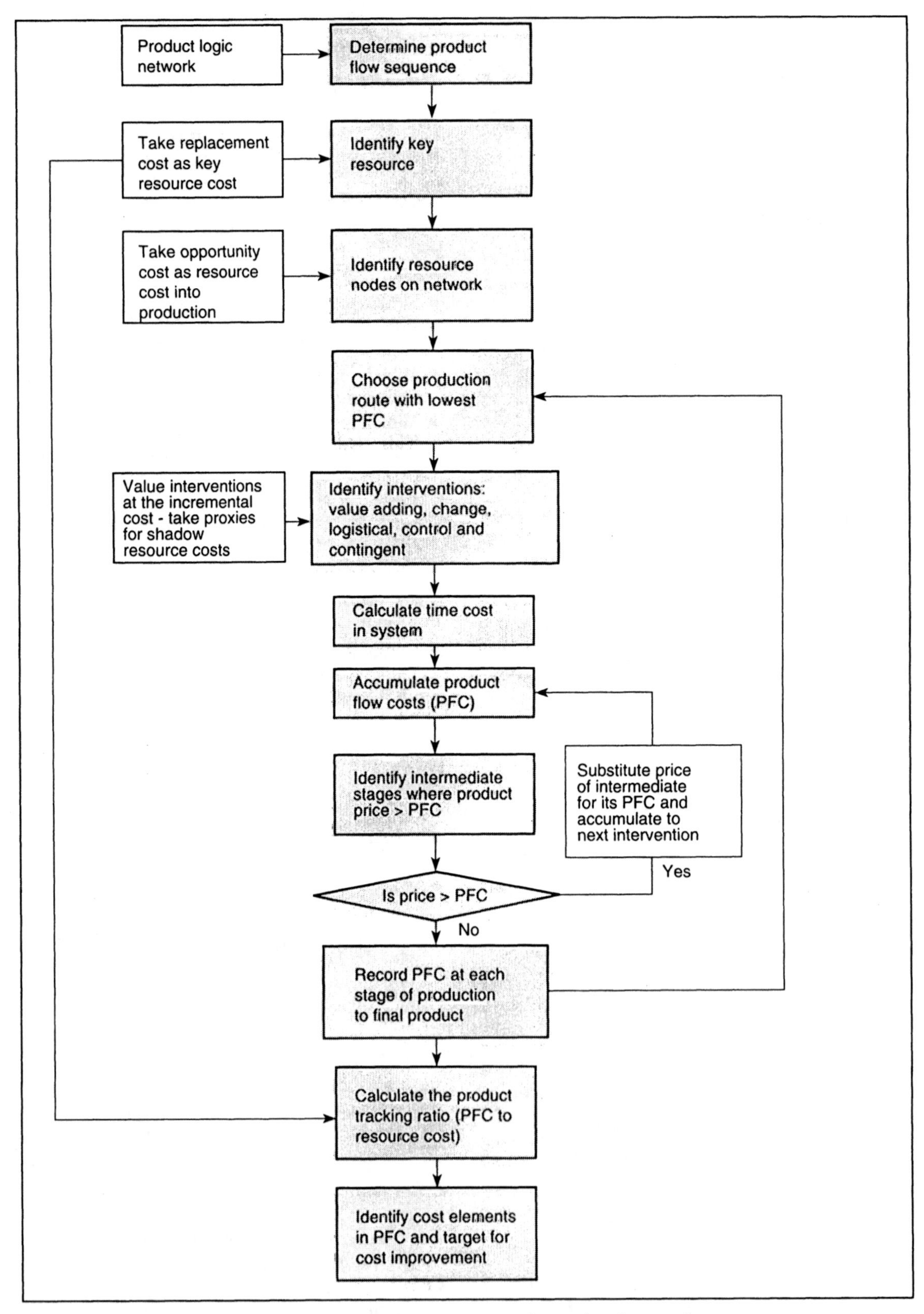

Figure 24.2 Cost development strategy for product flow costing.

The configuration of the product flow can only be determined for a product by product investigation and will include input from engineering, design, marketing, procurement and finance. In practice, many of these investigations will take on the form of a full scale 'value analysis' with the product cost agenda forming part of the brief for that analysis. A useful first step in such an analysis is the definition of an outline product logic network. A product logic network contains each of the input resources and intermediate product configurations linked by the interventions required to create them.

If, for example, three raw materials, A, B and C, are required to fabricate a final product (A + B + C) through an intermediate product stage consisting of any pair-wise combination of the three raw materials then three logical sequences are possible. It may well be that one or two of the intermediate combinations are logically forbidden in which case those possibilities would be excluded from the analysis. However, no sequence should be excluded from analysis on *a-priori* cost grounds but rather excluded as a result of the analysis.

In Figure 24.3 we show the three logical routes

Alternative Production Routes

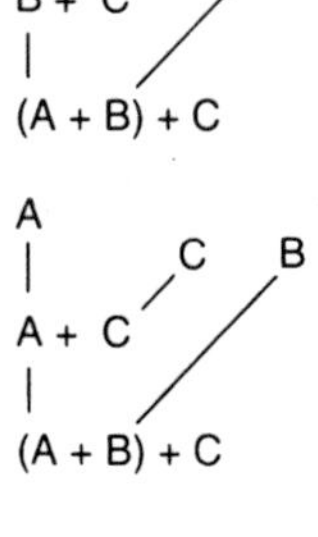

Route diagram		1	2	3	
					Resource Cost
	A	15	15	15	raw material A procurement
	B	25	25	25	raw material B procurement
	C	18	18	18	raw material C procurement
					Value adding intervention
	A + B	100			intermediate product fabrication
	B + C		105		intermediate product fabrication
	A + C			95	intermediate product fabrication
	A + B + C	75	75	75	final product fabrication
		233	238	228	
					Null interventions
A / B C / A + B / (A + B) + C	A > A + B	3			interventions A to A+B
	B > A + B	3			interventions B to A+B
	A + B > A + B + C	4			interventions A+B to A+B+C
	C > A + B + C	2			interventions C to A+B+C
B / C A / B + C / (A + B) + C	B > B + C		3		interventions B to B+C
	C > B + C		5		interventions C to B+C
	B + C > A + B + C		4		interventions B+C to A+B+C
	A > A + B + C		6		interventions A to A+B+C
A / C B / A + C / (A + B) + C	A > A + C			5	interventions A to A+C
	C > A + C			5	interventions C to A+C
	A + C > A + B + C			6	interventions A+C to A+B+C
	B > A + B + C			8	interventions B to A+B+C
		245	256	252	

Figure 24.3 Product logic networks for a three-resource, single-product flow.

for producing a final product and the associated fabrication costs for each option. The analysis indicates that the route of producing the final product by first combining A with B to form intermediate (A + B) and then combining with C leads to a lower overall product cost than the other alternatives. However, identifying and minimising the null costs of alternative 3 could well make that the preferred route for production.

In practice, the product logic network will need to be constructed and refined as the PFCs are collected and analysed. Again, in practical application it may be very difficult to establish a full specification of all possible routes to product completion and the interventions required to achieve them. In that situation a satisfactory solution may well be chosen as an interim solution and refined by incremental process improvement.

COSTING RESOURCES INTO THE PRODUCT FLOW

If in the production sequence, the realisable value of an intermediate product becomes greater than the refabrication cost then a product sale opportunity will arise. The sale of the intermediate product should be undertaken if the unit contribution turn-over (contribution per unit/sales revenue per unit) on the intermediate product is positive and the con-tribution turnover on the final product is negative given the realisable value of the intermediate product is taken as the input key factor cost into the subsequent stage of manufacturing. If, however, the contribution turnover on the final product is positive, using the realisable value of the intermediate product as the key factor cost, then both intermediate and final product should be produced and sold with priority going to the sale of the final product.

EXAMPLE

The cost of fabricating new motherboards for an established line of personal computers is shown in Table 24.1 with the costs of taking the motherboard through to final product. The sale price and contribution for each product is also given.

Notice in the above example, that as soon as a viable external market for the intermediate product arises, then the realisable value of that product becomes the key factor cost in the subsequent stage of manufacture towards final product (providing that the intermediate product can generate a positive PFC contribution). If the intermediate product does not offer a positive PFC contribution, then the accumulated PFC would be the key factor cost into the production of the final product.

Following this analysis, four possibilities for handling intermediate products arises where an external market exists for an intermediate product. We show these possibilities in Figure 24.4.

Table 24.1

Intermediate product costs	£	Final product costs	£
Component board	20	→ Motherboard	165
Additional electronics	38	Case	34
Interventions – value adding	18	Hard drives	60
Interventions – logistic	4	Minidisc drive	22
Interventions – change	24	Interventions – value	10
Interventions – control	8	Interventions – logistic	8
Time costs	6	Interventions – change	20
		Interventions – control	15
		Time costs	4
Total product flow cost	118		338
Sale price	165	Sale price	480
PFC contribution	47	PFC contribution	142
PFC contribution turnover (%)	28	PFC contribution turnover (%)	30

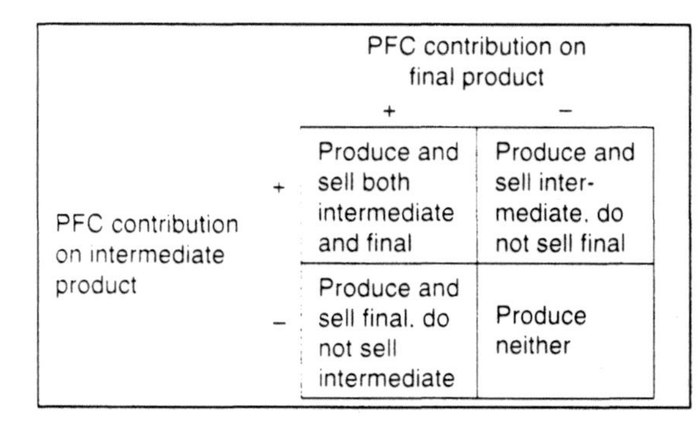

Figure 24.4 Decision matrix when an intermediate product market exists.

COSTING INTERVENTIONS INTO THE PRODUCT FLOW

As we discussed earlier, product flow costing recognises five classes of intervention, and it is through these interventions that the cost to the firm of applying its capability are accrued to the product. The general principle we apply in costing an intervention is that it should represent the full opportunity cost to the firm of making that intervention at the chosen stage in the production sequence. Each intervention absorbs capability in terms of the application of production resources, production labour, management time and so on. Further, applying that intervention will withdraw that capability from alternative use, and the firm will have to replace that capability from the external market on the margin.

In practice there are two ways of establishing the full cost of an intervention.

(i) The cash change to the organisation as a whole may be examined as a result of the decision to divert organisational capability to that product through the intervention. This will be the direct cash costs of the resources deployed (which will usually be the replacement cost of the resources concerned) plus the contribution lost on alternative activities if an element of redeployment is entailed. This procedure is exactly as we have described in Chapters 7 and 8.

(ii) Where a case-by-case analysis is not possible, and where it is believed that the firm is at, or close to, 100% capacity, we can average the total cost of establishing a given organisational capability and then allocate an estimate of the capability deployed to the product concerned. This method is similar to the procedure used in activity-based costing described above.

In order to construct reasonable proxies for opportunity costs, we must work on the assumption that the firm is at full capacity and that all of the resources which go to form its capability are divisible and replaceable. If either of these assumptions is violated, then the opportunity cost will not be the replacement cost of the marginal capability it consumes in unit production. In a situation of significant undercapacity, the product flow cost will fall towards the external opportunity cost of production (see Chapter 7). If, on the other hand the firm is extending itself significantly beyond capacity, then the full shadow costs associated with the production 'crowded' out will apply and the principles discussed in Chapter 8 become appropriate. Normally, as we will see later, these shadow costs will accrue as change costs associated with change interventions.

When a contingent commitment is engaged for after-sales service or warranty, that commitment can be treated and valued as a contingent intervention and valued as a contingent claim upon the firm (see Chapter 11 for the method of valuing such claims). The contingent intervention is always the last intervention to be applied and is always preceded by an intermediate sale opportunity as, presumably, the firm would be able to sell at a lower price but with the warranty or service agreement excluded.

In Figure 24.5 we show some of the principle cost heads which can be used to value an intervention of each type.

EXAMPLE

In a firm's production environment, the value-adding interventions were applied and incurred:

- *direct expenditures on energy, minor materials costs and some direct labour;*
- *indirect expenditures.*

For each indirect expenditure the company identified the most suitable allocation basis for accruing that cost to the intervention (the allocation basis should be dictated by the variable which is driving cost in each case):

- *skilled labour forming and setting products (an average hourly charge applied on a time basis to each intervention);*
- *machine turning and forming (the machine capacity in an operating period was determined*

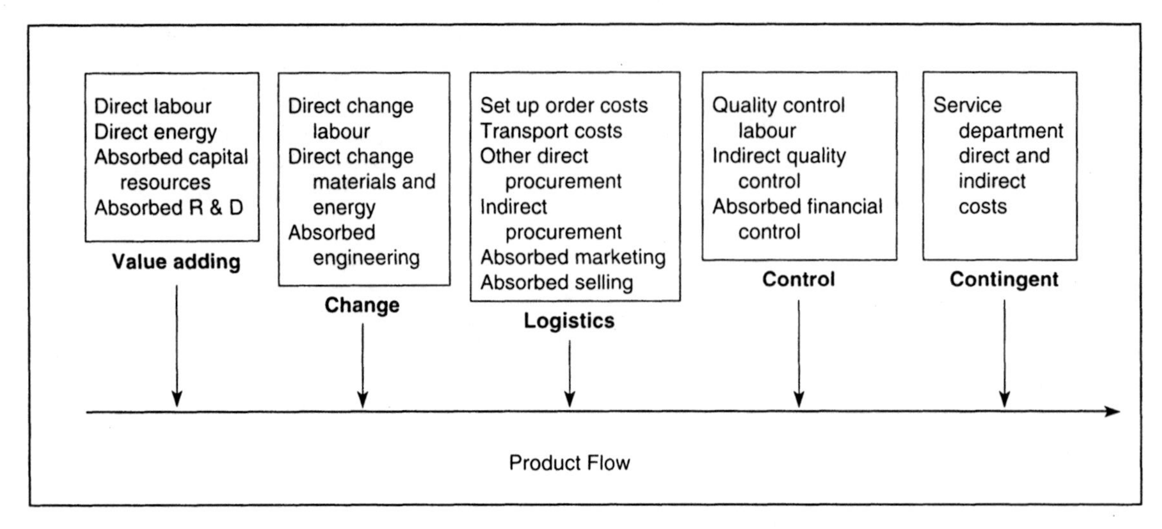

Figure 24.5 Cost elements assignable to interventions.

and the average cost of each intervention in the factory calculated);

- *production facilities and overheads (charged on the average time duration of each value-adding intervention).*

In order effectively to create an average intervention cost it is necessary to identify indirect cost allocation bases which most closely match the nature of the intervention being undertaken and the way in which the capability is being consumed. For many interventions the allocation is likely to be based on the time that a fixed capability is diverted into that activity. In this respect, PFC is very similar to the concepts behind activity-based costing described above, in that it is important in both activity-based costing and PFC to understand what characteristic of the activity or intervention is driving the consumption of the capability represented by the fixed resources.

EVALUATING THE TIME COSTS

In order to accumulate time costs within PFC it is necessary to determine the average time for a product to arrive at a given stage in production. For example, in Table 24.2 we show a four-intervention process on a key resource taking on average 78 days to pass from procurement to completion of sale. In addition, the company has a 30-day credit agreement with its suppliers. Using a cost of capital of 16% the time cost is calculated as

Time cost at intervention stage $N+1$

$$= \text{PFC}_N \times e^{(0.16 \times \text{days}/365)} - \text{PFC}_N$$

When the time cost of a benefit is taken we simply apply a negative sign to the cost of capital in the above equation.

EXAMPLE

A company deploys four production interventions to create the final product from a key resource. The company offers a 30-day credit period on its deliveries to its customers and takes a 30-day credit period from its own suppliers. A detailed production study shows the average number of days required to produce a unit of product and the intervention cost. In Table 24.2, using a 16% cost of capital we have calculated the time cost, the resultant PFC and the product tracking ratio.

In the analysis below we have calculated total cost statistics and the product tracking ratio which is taken as

Product tracking ratio

= PFC/Cost of the key resource

Examining the data above we see that the time cost accounts for 2.1% of the total PFC, whilst the

Table 24.2

Cost of capital 0.16

	Days	Resource cost	Intervention cost	Time cost	PFC	Product tracking ratio
Key		220.00			220.00	1.00
Credit period	30			−2.87	217.13	0.99
Intervention 1	15		23.00	1.45	241.58	1.10
Intervention 2	5		24.00	0.54	266.12	1.21
Intervention 3	18		45.00	2.13	313.25	1.42
Intervention 4	10		12.00	1.39	326.64	1.48
Completion	30			4.36	331.00	1.50
		220.00	104.00	7.00		
Percentage of total		65.89	31.15	2.10		

interventions costs 31.15%. In this situation, reduction of production time is not the key issue, but rather seeking to reduce the cost of intervention 3 could have a radical effect on overall cost.

MINIMISING THE PRODUCT FLOW COST

As we develop the full product flow cost, the manager is able to gain a clearer idea of how cost develops for a product as the firm expends its resources, and the effort in achieving the final outcome of placing the product into the customer's hands. The subtlety of PFC is that it focuses attention on those costs which add value to the product and those which do not. In the latter case, the company will seek the lowest cost commensurate with the efficient delivery of the intervention. Its opportunities for cost minimisation will occur whenever:

- there is a suboptimal sequence of production transactions required to generate the final product;
- there is misconfiguration of the fixed resources necessary for production;
- there are unnecessary organisational costs in engaging the economic transactions required to produce the intervention (we referred to this as misalignment costs in Chapter 3);
- there are excess time costs in the system.

Table 24.2 gives a series for the product tracking ratio as the product passes through the production system. It forces us to attend to certain stages in the production sequence where interventions are expensive on resource. Where the intervention is value adding, the cost may well be justified if the market appreciates the benefit delivered. Where a null intervention is involved, this indicates an important target for cost minimisation. 'Lean manufacturing' is the name given to that production philosophy which stresses the minimisation of change and logistical costs and where quality is designed into product.

COSTING JOINT PRODUCTS

A joint product occurs when a single production sequence creates an opportunity to sell two or more final products. In Figure 24.6 we show how the PFC for an intermediate product separates into two output product streams. The objective of joint product costing is to determine PFC1(final) and PFC2(final), given that we know only PFC1 (intermediate) plus PFC2(intermediate). There are a number of possible ways of achieving the division.

- Apportioning the intermediate PFC by final sales price of each product: this will bring each joint product into existence with a common PFC contribution ratio at that stage.
- Revaluing each joint product at the point of separation according to the resources and interventions required to create them in combination: this method can only work unambiguously if input resources can be uniquely assigned to each product.

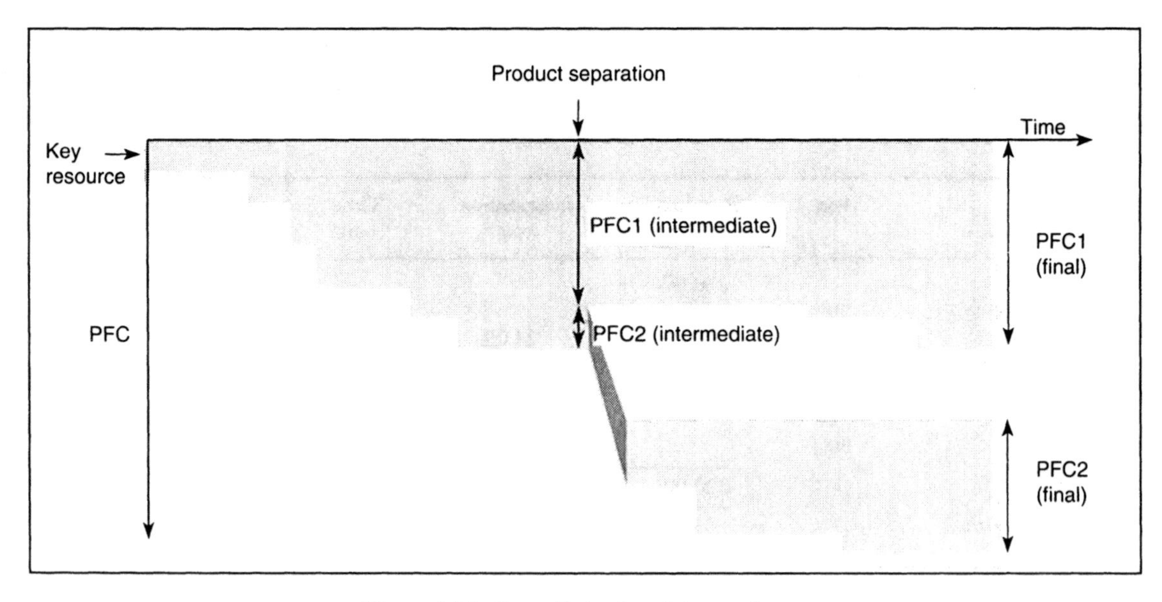

Figure 24.6 Cost splitting into joint products.

- Valuing each joint product at the point of separation according to the resources and interventions which would be required to create them as individual entities: this will only work in the rather special case where individual resources divert into particular joint products.
- Distributing by some physical value of the products concerned such as weight, or number of discrete components: this method rarely has any value significance but it does have the merit of being easily measured.
- Estimating by the net realisable value of each intermediate if an external market exists for each of the joint products at the point of separation: this method would yield the PFC directly in accordance with our algorithm for determining PFC described in Figure 24.2 above.

Given that net realisable sale values of the intermediate are not available, the first alternative is likely to lead to least distortion, providing that the null interventions required to finalise each product after splitting are in approximate parity. In the example in Table 24.3 we demonstrate the case where two products have different sales prices leading to the imputation of PFCs as shown.

Interventions which add value to the customer are likely to be directly rewarded by customers in the

Table 24.3

Total PFC at split 650.00	Value	Proportion
Sales price – product 1	1000.00	57.14
Sales price – product 2	750.00	42.86
Combined sales price	1750.00	100.00
PFC1 (intermediate) = 57.14% × 650 =	371.43	
PFC2 (intermediate) = 42.86% × 650 =	278.57	
	650.00	

selling price (thus not distorting the imputation of intermediate PFC), whilst this is not the case with null interventions which are unlikely to be rewarded in the price.

TRANSFER PRICING

In an opportunity cost of PFC environment, the cost of transferring products from one division of a business to another is relatively easy to determine for product costing purposes. In principle, if no external market exists for a transfer product, then the opportunity cost or the PFC at the point of transfer should form the transfer price to the new division. If an external sale market for the transferred product exists where the sale value is greater than cost, then both the principles of opportunity costs and the PFC algorithm require us to revalue the transferred product to its external sale price at that point.

This automatically gives a performance measure for the transferring division with the product tracking ratio and a base point for the receiving division if the transferred product is to become the key resource. If the received resource is to be added into an existing product flow for which a key resource has already been defined, then it simply becomes an added resource at its opportunity cost or PFC (which may be the realisable value).

If an intermediate market does not exist for the sale of the transfer product, but an alternative supply market exists at a cheaper buying-in price, then that buying-in price should become the PFC to the receiving division and the completion PFC to the transferring division.

COMPARISON OF ACTIVITY-BASED AND PRODUCT FLOW COSTING

Both costing methods attempt to focus attention on activities (or interventions as we call them in the case of PFC) in accruing business costs to production. ABC using full cost methods is a refinement of conventional overhead allocation methods, but with a more intelligent approach to the identification of allocation metrics. If the metrics are chosen carefully, ABC can give a measure of the cost of the organisational capability diverted into a particular production facility or individual through the application of the chosen cost drivers. Activity-based full cost is not, however, the opportunity cost of the product concerned, and this can lead to distortion in decision making. In addition, it does not automatically yield control or performance measures for specific products, nor does it allow management to target areas specifically for increasing cost efficiency.

Product flow costing is theoretically sound, but it does rely on very careful examination of production processes. It does, when implemented, yield a clear cost performance metric (the product tracking ratio) which can be used for management control and targeting for cost efficiency and savings. In achieving this the notion of the 'key resource' is critical, in that it provides the basis for accumulating costs along the product flow.

PFC maps the production process exactly and is suited to modern flexible manufacturing systems. However, it is a new technique, and much work still needs to be done to refine the methodology in practice. Nevertheless, it does accord with the principles of this book and is firmly rooted in the concept of opportunity cost.

CONCLUSION

In this chapter we have discussed two new ways of dealing with costing in advanced manufacturing systems. Activity-based costing has received considerable attention in recent years, although it does have deficiencies and it does not remedy the central problem of allocating non-attributable costs to production in an economically meaningful way. Product flow costing does partly correct these defects and it offers an important metric for monitoring production. We still have much work to do to give the opportunity accountant the best tools for the job in this area!

Part V

Controlling Financial Performance

Chapter 25

Budgeting

Level E

Contents

Summary

In this chapter we examine the general principles of budgeting: why organisations engage in budgeting at all, how the budgetary systems of accountability will vary with organisational structure and time and what different strategies for budget setting are available to management. In this chapter we outline six possible reasons why firms engage in the budgeting process and, in particular, we focus on the planning and control aspects of budgeting.

INTRODUCTION

Budgeting is an activity we all engage in some time or other – often because we have discovered that our cash outgoings have exceeded our cash income for some reason. Companies find themselves in exactly the same situation as the individual who is trying to manage his or her own personal affairs, except that the sums of money involved are usually much larger. We can identify six important purposes for budgeting in firms:

- as a method of planning the use of the firm's resources in the light of potential market opportunities;
- as a regular and systematic vehicle for the firm's forecasting activities (although these forecasts, allied with the planning aspect of budgeting, are likely to be self-fulfilling);
- as a means of controlling the activities of various groups within the firm;
- as a means of motivating individuals within the firm to achieve the performance levels agreed and set for them;
- as a means of communicating the wishes and aspirations of senior management to other interest groups within the firm;
- as a means of resolving conflicts of interest between the various groups within the firm.

Strategic thinking in any organisation is that process whereby management thinks about the integration of the organisational activities towards meaningful, goal orientated ends. The more turbulent the external market, technological or economic environment, the more searching will that process be as management seeks strategies for coping. The strategic thinking of management is realised in the various planning documents which management create, and this whole integration process is strongly supported by the budgeting procedures of the firm.

The role of budgeting within different firms will differ, depending upon the organisational needs of each. Each company will have different practices and procedures depending upon its own organisational characteristics. Therefore, very few general rules can be laid down concerning the practice of budgeting. Budgeting is not a simple technical skill which can be divorced from the context in which it is carried out. In Chapter 2 we developed a simple four-world model which does give us some clues as to the budgetary dynamics of organisations.

The four-world model, you may remember, consists of four levels, more or less in harmony with one another. In any particular organisation, at any given point in time, the locus of power and influence will lie at any one of these four levels. If it lies at the ethical level (usually the domain of senior management), then there will be a strong 'strategic' driver in the budgeting process of that organisation. If the actual power lies at another level, then that level may well become the budgetary driver for the organisation.

The model also points to the fact that entropy-induced costs (first-order misalignment costs) lie in the relationships between levels, and where entropy is high we would anticipate that management within levels will attempt to maintain and expand the degree of 'slack' within their budgets.

BUDGETS AND ORGANISATIONAL FORM

As we discussed in Chapter 3, organisations vary between close approximations to market systems with matrix type organisations through to formal, control-orientated line management systems. The problems posed for budgeting by these forms is to ensure that consolidation and accountability within the process follow the patterns of accountability within the management structure.

Within unitary (U) form organisations with formal hierarchies of control according to function, formal functionally based budgets, perhaps on a departmental basis, can be created where resources are planned and distributed according to the lines of managerial responsibility within the firm. With matrix type structures, managerial responsibility will be exercised through both the project (or programme) dimension and the functional dimension of the organisation. In such an environment, choices must be made as to how resources are distributed into one or other, or both, sides of the matrix (see Figure 25.1).

If an organisation operates internal pricing mechanisms to distribute resources throughout the organisation, then certain consequences for budgeting follow.

- It may be very difficult for senior management to fix a resource budget which is under the control of the internal market unless it is prepared to intervene in its internal market to ration supply. It would have to be prepared to do this, even though competing users may be able to justify their use of the resource concerned and are capable of paying the price.
- Management may not be able to predict resource usage within any one department or over the whole organisation with any degree of accuracy. In fact a budget within an internal market is more a forecast of the market out-turn than a plan of expected usage.
- The consumption of a resource subject to an

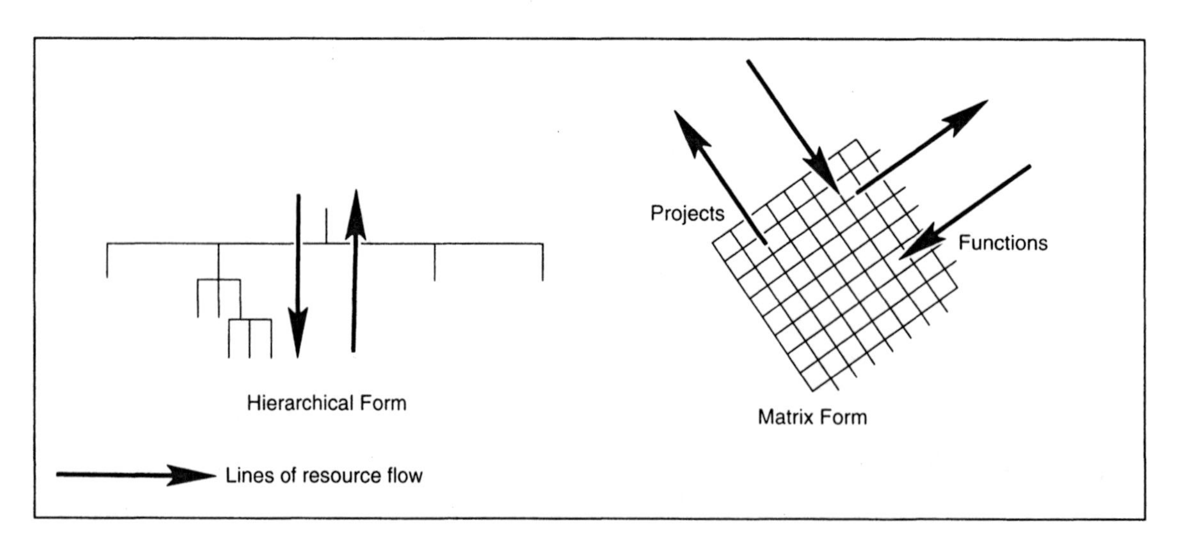

Figure 25.1 Resource flows within hierarchical and matrix organisations.

internal market will depend upon the way in which that resource is priced rather than the availability of that resource to the firm.

EXAMPLE

A university decided to charge building space to its departments using a rental which approximated to the going external market rate. The introduction of this rental was compensated by a reduction in the fixed overhead charge to departments levied as a fixed percentage of revenue. In the first year of operation little effect was noticed, but in the second year, departments began to contract their usage of space and began to release staff and teaching rooms back into the 'space' pool. This led to a drop in the total recovery (including the remaining fixed overheads from departments), and as a consequence the university increased its rental charge per square metre.

BUDGETING AND TIME SCALE

The time span of a budget is dictated by its purpose (Table 25.1). The long-range financial plans which a firm should construct when seeking new finance or justifying a new project will provide a context and a yardstick for all of its budgets of shorter time scale. Research into corporate distress and failure reveals that failure to set, and subsequently compare, performance against a financial plan is an important warning indicator of lack of proper financial control.

The annual budgeting exercise is an important activity for any business, as it links in with the directors' principal statements to their shareholders, namely the profit and loss and balance sheets. This budgeting activity can occupy the whole of the annual cycle of the business, with management engaged in negotiation and agreeing the various components of the new year budget and then reviewing actual performance as it is delivered by the various departments and groups within the firm. This annual budgetary process may lead to both quarterly and monthly budgets which in the latter case, will concentrate on commitments and cash movements rather than accrual accounts. Finally, within the range of days, larger firms will work to detailed treasury budgets, projecting the sources and usages of cash to the firm and embodying targets for extra return through the money markets for short-term funds.

SIX REASONS FOR BUDGETING

As we pointed out at the beginning of this chapter, there are six principal reasons why firms create budgets.

Planning

At each of the different levels within the firm, management faces the need to plan the resources under its control. Senior management, with its primary concern with strategic decision making will wish to ensure that the firm achieves its long-term targets. This will entail:

- planning the long-term aggregate cash resources of the firm;
- planning the deployment of physical resources to meet new market opportunities;
- planning to increase the welfare of the various groups who have an interest within the firm.

Of course, senior managers will also attempt to maximise their own interests as far as they can. In Chapter 1 we suggested that all of these different objectives can be distilled into the simple principle that managers, and senior managers especially, will

Table 25.1

Time period	Budget type
Greater than one year	Long-term financial plans
Within one year	Annual budgets for profit and loss, balance sheet and cash flow
Within one quarter	Quarterly budgets of profit and loss and balance sheet
Within one month	Monthly cash budgets and commitment accounts
Within the day, or days	Treasury budgets

work so as to maximise their decision-making discretion.

The planning activity at the lower levels of management will be determined by the degree of discretion which particular managers have over the types of decision they can make. However, the success of the budgeting exercise is largely dependent upon the degree of involvement of all levels of management in the planning process. A desirable feature of any budgeting system is the degree of consensus which it promotes throughout all levels of the firm. Unless all levels of management are involved in the planning process the formal budgets will be seen, by those who are not involved in their preparation, as a simple extension of senior management's authority. In the long run, imposed budgets are less effective than budgets agreed through negotiation and consensus.

The overall budgeting process is shown in Figure 25.2.

Forecasting

The planning aspect of the budgeting process is concerned with extending the control of management over as many variables in its decision-making process as possible. However, a number of decision variables will be outside the control of management at the point in time when the budgets are drawn up. We give two possible reasons why this may be so.

- The variables may be exogenous to the firm (i.e. determined by some group or agency outside the firm's control). Examples of such variables are: government interest rate policy, the future demand for the company's product (although this can be controlled to a limited extent through the firm's marketing activity), the level of inflation, nationally agreed wage claims which affect the company's labour force, exchange rate movements, the impact of new technology and so on.

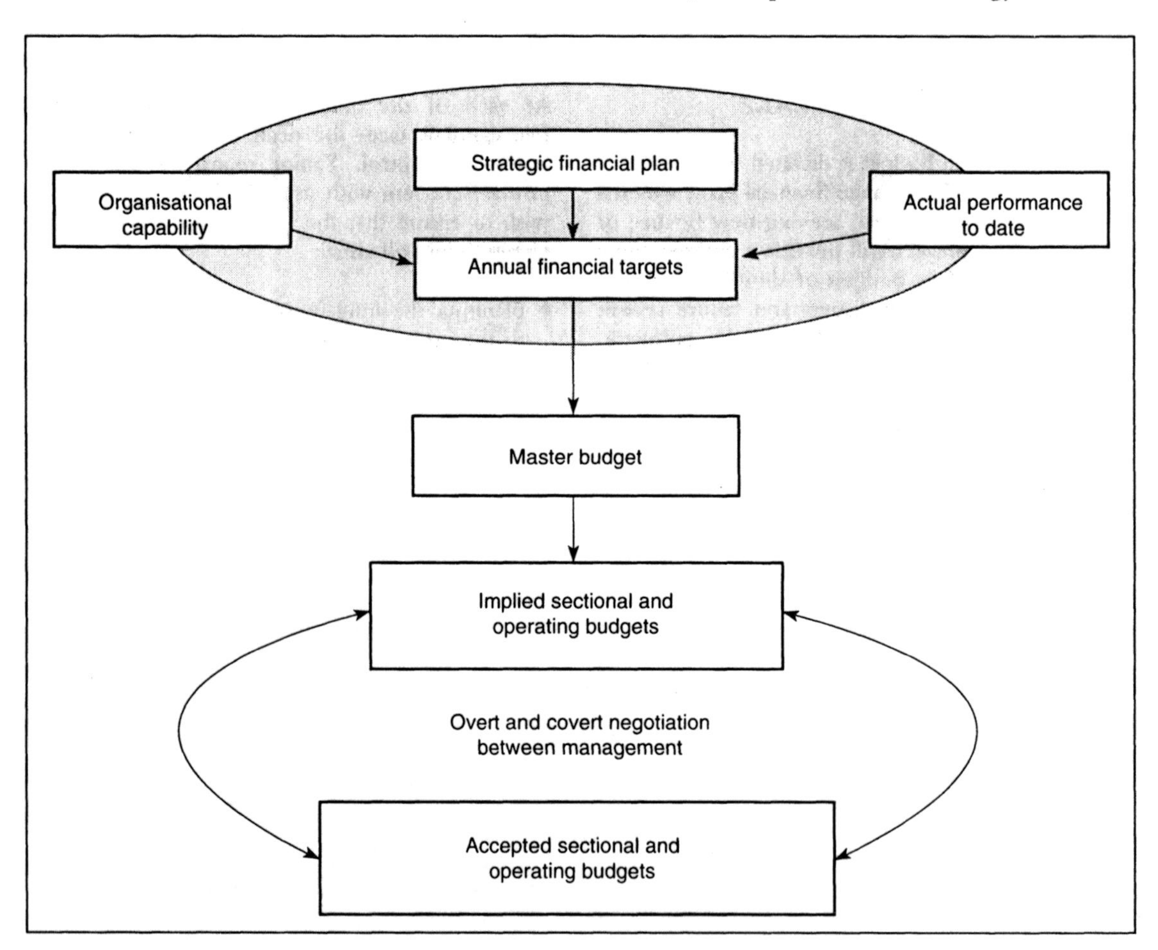

Figure 25.2 The overall budgeting process.

- The variables concerned are not expected to arise for a considerable period of time (the eventual sales level of a novel product still in the early stages of development).

In the first case, management will have to make forecasts or rely upon the forecasts of others when drawing up its budgets. The Treasury, for example, makes periodic forecasts of inflation and interest rates which are included in the national budgeting process. Similarly, many of the large stockbroking firms also prepare and publish forecasts of the macroeconomic variables which may be useful to an individual firm. For very long-range forecasting, management may have to resort to technological forecasting methods which can only give the order of magnitude for the second type of variable mentioned above.

Where management has some control over the variables in question, the process of forecasting merges into that of planning. In other words, the forecasts which management make become self-fulfilling, and this is most pronounced where there is only a short time difference between the budgeting process and the incidence of the variables in question.

Organisation control

Firm budgets are a very important instrument of managerial control. Once plans have been agreed and implemented, the need will arise to compare them with actual results as they occur. Differences (or variances) between actual and budgeted figures will guide management in:

- identifying areas where performance has been better or worse than anticipated and deciding what (if any) corrective action is appropriate;
- rewarding those individuals who have performed better than expected and punishing those who have failed to come up to expectations.

Deciding the necessary revisions to future plans and targets in the light of current actual results. An important technique of short-term control is called 'management by exception'. This technique entails identifying differences between actual and budgeted figures (variance analysis) and where these differences exceed certain preset bounds management will attempt to assign causes and take corrective action if appropriate. A crucial feature of any control system is the speed and reliability with which actual results can be collected evaluated and corrective action applied. We will discuss more general problems of control in Chapter 27.

Motivation

The idea of controlling performance through a firm's reward system is closely related to an understanding of how financial and non-financial rewards and punishments can motivate individuals. Indeed, one of the most important spin-offs from the budgeting procedure is its use for relating performance to motivation. A number of theories have been put forward to explain what motivates individuals to perform tasks to a specific standard.

Most of these theories revolve around the idea that men and women act so as to fulfil their 'needs'. One of the earliest theorists in the area of motivation through the satisfaction of personal needs was A. H. Maslow. Maslow's argument was as follows.

- Needs are the basis of the human drive to act.
- Human needs can be arranged in a hierarchy of relative prepotency (Figure 25.3). At the bottom of this hierarchy are the most basic needs for warmth, food and security. At higher levels we have the need to be loved (this even applies to accountants) rising at the highest level to the need for 'self-actualization' (the need to realise one's fullest potential). The lowest needs in this hierarchy will be satisfied first and if one of these lower needs is thwarted the individual concerned will switch attention to the satisfaction of that need at the expense of those above it.

Once a need has been satisfied, the individual will then shift attention toward satisfying needs at the next level in the hierarchy. Those individuals in whom a need has always been satisfied are best able to tolerate deprivation in the future.

Maslow's model has been criticised and developed since it was first formulated in 1943. However, what is interesting about the model, from the budgeting point of view, is that it suggests that financial rewards are unlikely to be successful motivators beyond a certain point. Money is most effective at satisfying lower needs. Higher needs, such as those concerned with self-esteem and self-actualisation, are often more effectively rewarded through rewards which enhance job satisfaction. There is much more to be learnt about the role of motivation and the effectiveness of rewards and punishments in achieving budget targets. What is certain is that a budgeting system cannot operate in isolation from its human context. It is the behavioural rather than the technical aspects of a

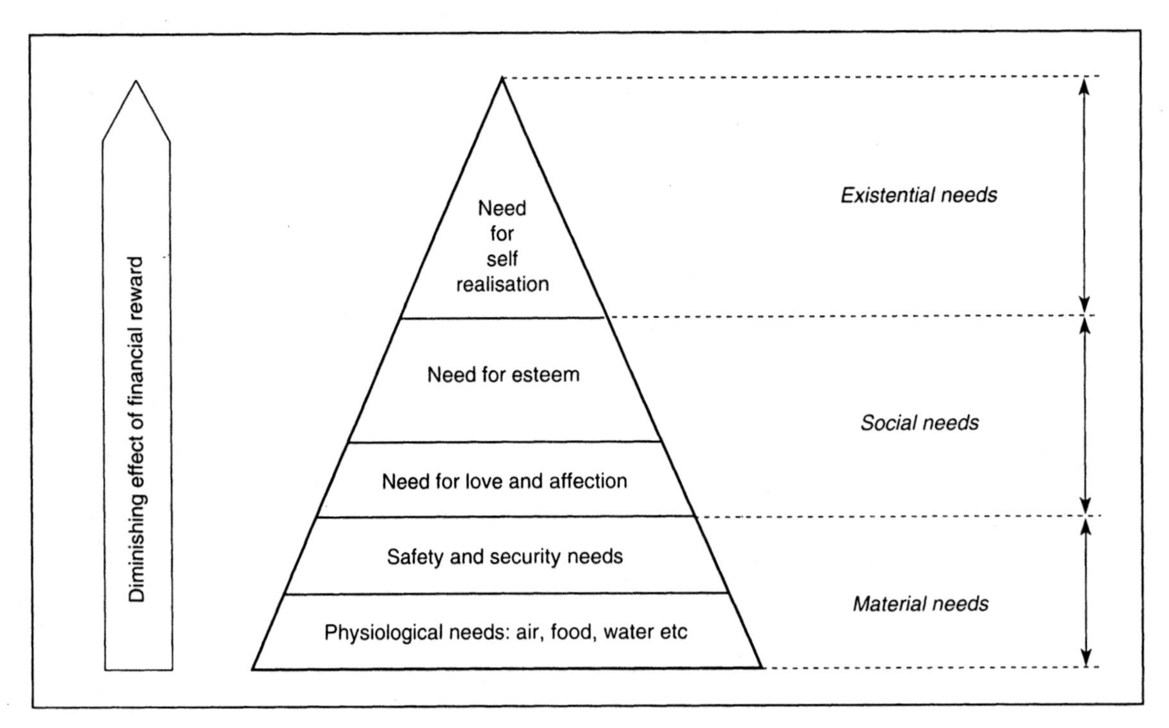

Figure 25.3 Maslow's hierarchy of needs.

budget which will govern its success as an integrative mechanism within the firm.

Authority of senior management

As the dominant power group within the organisation, senior management will see the budgeting process as one mechanism for establishing and maintaining its authority throughout the firm. Because senior managers, of all the groups within the firm, have the most discretion over the distribution of the firm's surplus they will form the dominant group in any negotiation procedure. In highly bureaucratic organisations with formal 'line' management systems the budgeting system will reflect the hierarchy of management within the firm. The responsibility for different levels of budgeting can be clearly related to the different levels of managerial responsibility in the line diagram shown in Figure 25.4.

At each stage going up through the organisation, the various budgets, reflecting the operating and tactical planning decisions made within the firm (sales, purchases, production, cash, labour, marketing etc.), are consolidated into a 'master budget'. The master budget is usually expressed in terms of the company's financial statements: budgeted profit and loss account, balance sheet and source and application of funds. These budgeted financial statements take the same form as the statements which, at the end of the accounting period, will be published and which form the principal vehicle for senior management accountability to the firm's shareholders and other external user groups. In a system such as we have outlined in Figure 25.4, the budgeting procedure is designed to reflect the aspirations of senior management and also reflect their performance.

In less formal organisations, the budgeting system should support the informal lines of communication within the firm and the shared nature of authority common in such organisations. The highly centralised authority associated with the formal, bureaucratic firm has high 'compliance' costs associated with enforcing senior management's will throughout the firm. In such organisations, senior management will have to spend considerable time ensuring that its wishes are properly complied with and that the firm's control systems are working effectively. In the less formal organisation these compliance costs will be much lower, but management must work much harder to integrate the overall activities of the various differentiated aspects of the firm.

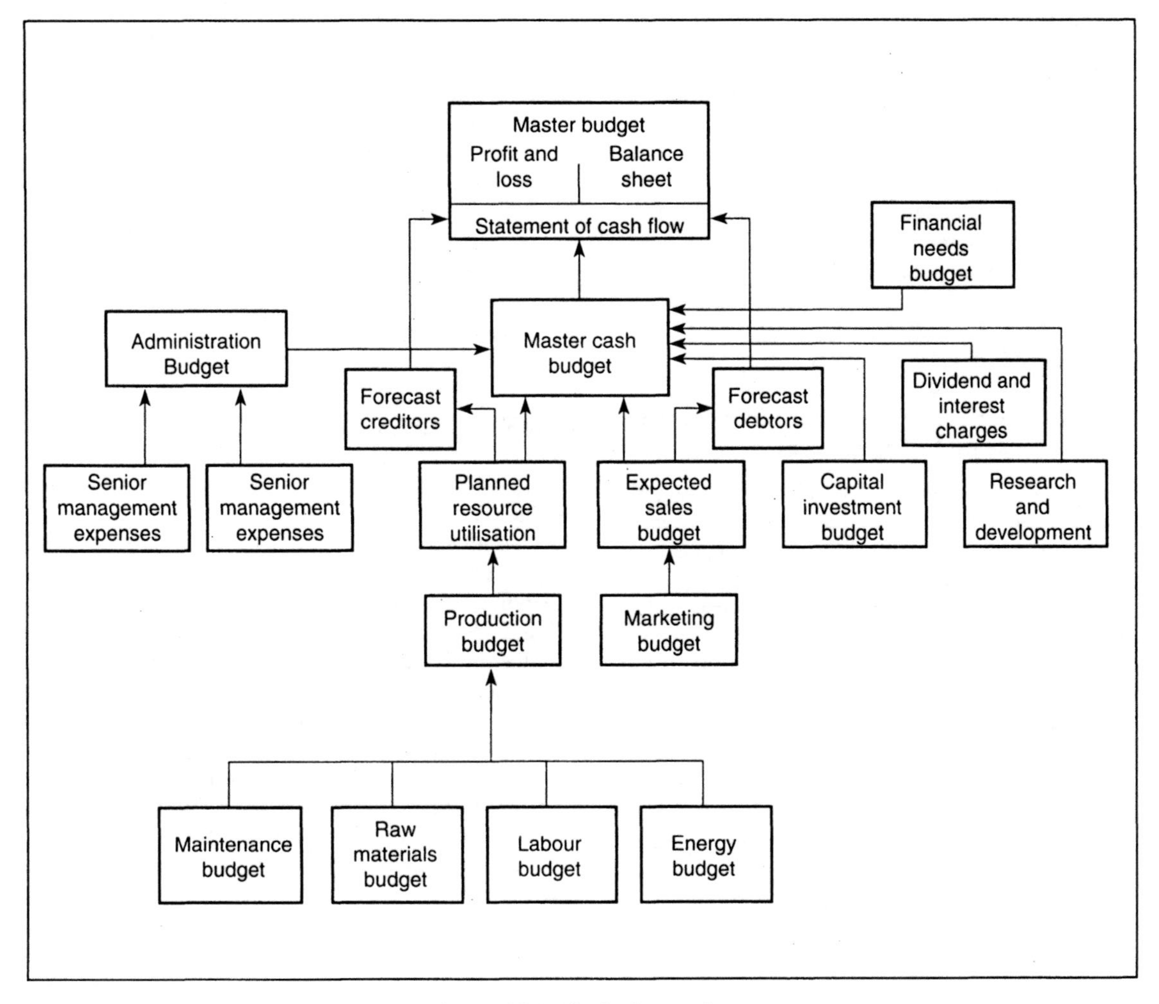

Figure 25.4 The budgetary flow.

Conflict resolution

In the first part of this book we painted a picture of the firm as a coalition of different groups with different interests and aspirations. The budgeting system can provide an important means for resolving the conflicts of interest which arise and producing the consensus necessary for the continued operation of the firm. A number of ways in which budgeting can help to resolve conflicts between various groups are indicated below.

- By providing a mechanism for negotiation (both overt and covert) between different groups within the firm: overt negotiation is normally conducted in the formal committees and other meetings set up to settle the budgets for the coming period. On the other hand, covert negotiation can occur in many different ways. For example, if a particular group within the firm (say a research and development department) realised that it was likely to underspend in a particular financial year, then we would expect a large amount of 'catch-up' spending as the financial year came to a close. Often this spending is done not so much because the group concerned needs the items purchased at that particular time, but rather to inform senior management that its budget should not be cut in future years.
- By the 'planned' creation of slack within the system so that incompatible aims can be satisfied without destructive internal competition between the various interest groups: indeed, at any point in time a large proportion of a firm's planned surplus will be devoted to allowing groups with incompatible aims to exist side by side.

By directing the attention of the organisation at different times to different aims: for example, within a production group one month's budget may be aimed toward enhancing the quality of materials produced. Another month's budget, on the other hand, could well be orientated toward cutting costs. Thus the budgeting system can, sequentially, focus attention upon two different aspects of production performance which are in conflict.

BUDGETING STRATEGIES

There are a number of budgeting strategies which have been deployed by organisations.

- Incremental budgeting: the new year budget is based upon the budget set for the previous period plus (or minus) some adjustment for changing prices or anticipated changes in activity. This method of budgeting is very popular, especially in those organisations who do not wish to disturb set patterns of working within their subsidiaries and departments.
- Zero-based budgeting: the planning of a department's resource for a given period commences on the presumption of a zero resource budget. The department is then required to produce a detailed top-down budget with priorities justifying its bid for resources. This form of budgeting has been adopted by a number of firms and public sector organisations with mixed results. It can be very threatening and time consuming if conducted on an annual basis, although a less frequent application of this approach (say triennial) with intervening years set using the incremental approach may be more productive. Its advantage is that it forces each department to review its activities, set goals and justify its claim on resources on a regular basis.
- Programme-based budgeting: the unit of budgeting activity is not conducted through fixed organisational units such as subsidiaries or departments but rather through programmes (for products, projects or campaigns). Military budgets, for example, are set in the UK with a programme element focusing on the deployment of resources to particular theatres of operation.
- Market test budgeting: service departments are required to bid for a continuation of its activities in competition with external suppliers. If they are successful in such a bid their submission will form their resource budget for the next period of operations. This method has become popular in the UK for many central and local government services, but it does generate considerable anxiety amongst staff and concerns that senior management are comparing like with like when evaluating bids.

LIFE CYCLE BUDGETING

With life cycle budgeting, cost and revenue flows over a whole product life cycle are projected and placed into a life cycle budgetary plan. As such, life cycle budgeting involves many of the financial planning and costing concepts discussed in Chapters 9 and 15 respectively. The problem with life cycle budgeting is that a multiproduct firm may well have a number of life cycles in operation, all of different durations and terminations. For this reason, life cycle budgeting can only operate as a performance measurement system for products alongside the normal periodic departmental or divisional budgets. Such 'parallel track' budgeting can provide useful control information providing that management is aware which of the alternative systems is the one against which their performance will be ultimately judged.

CONCLUSION

In this chapter we have examined the general issues of budgeting within organisations placing great emphasis on understanding the motivation for the budgeting exercise. We have identified a number of reasons why firms engage in budgeting, apart from the obvious and important ones of planning and control. In particular, we have focused on the role of budgeting as a 'stabilising' influence within the business, where various interest groups can argue out their cases for resources and be judged on their ultimate performance.

Chapter 26

Variance Analysis and Budgetary Control

Level M

Contents

Summary

Variance analysis is a technique for the analysis of differences between budgeted and actual costs. In this chapter we show how to calculate 'gross' variances – that is, differences between totals for profit, revenues and costs. From this gross variance analysis we commence to split up cost variances into price and usage effects; usage variances into activity and efficiency effects and, finally, efficiency variances into mix and yield effects for those production systems which warrant such a depth of analysis. With revenues we separate variances into a price and volume effect before analysing the influence of demand changes on our variance analysis. Finally, we discuss the nature of controllable and uncontrollable variances and how control limits can be set in practice.

THE PURPOSE OF VARIANCE ANALYSIS

The collection of actual production costs and revenues will inevitably yield discrepancies when compared with the preset budgeted costs and revenues. We call such discrepancies cost or revenue 'variances', and it is an important part of management's work to identify the reasons why such variances have occurred even when they are favourable. In this chapter we will discuss the simple numerical methods which are at the accountant's disposal for identifying variances.

Budgetary variances offer important control information to the manager as they report the differences between budgeted or standard costs and revenues and actual figures. Such variances, when used to manage a resource or revenue centre's performance, represent a form of positive feedback control in that favourable performance on revenue, say, will prompt management to revise budgetary revenue upwards in the next period and vice versa with costs (Figure 26.1).

We will consider variance analysis under the following headings:

- gross budgetary variances on total profit, revenue or costs;
  price and volume variances which consider variances at the level of unit price and volume of usage or sale;
- efficiency and activity variances which isolate from volume variances that component which is due to change in the activity level and that component which can be attributed to efficiency in the usage of resources;
- mix and yield variances which control the proportions and yield of combined resources entering into production;
- fixed overhead variances, which whilst having no economic significance, are commonly prepared by many firms;
- sales variances which examine the effects of known demand effects on budgeted output levels and prices.

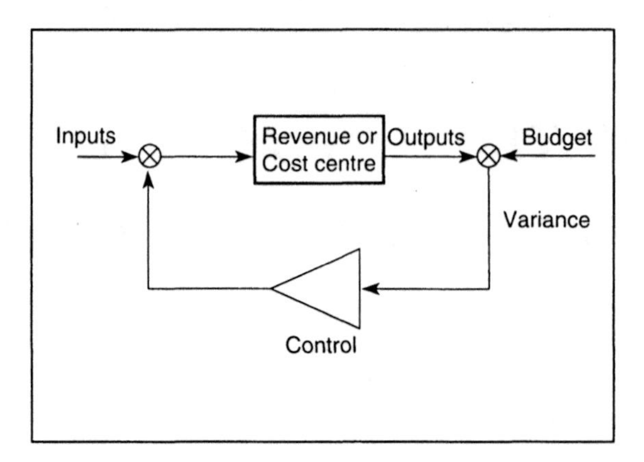

Figure 26.1 Simple budgetary feedback system.

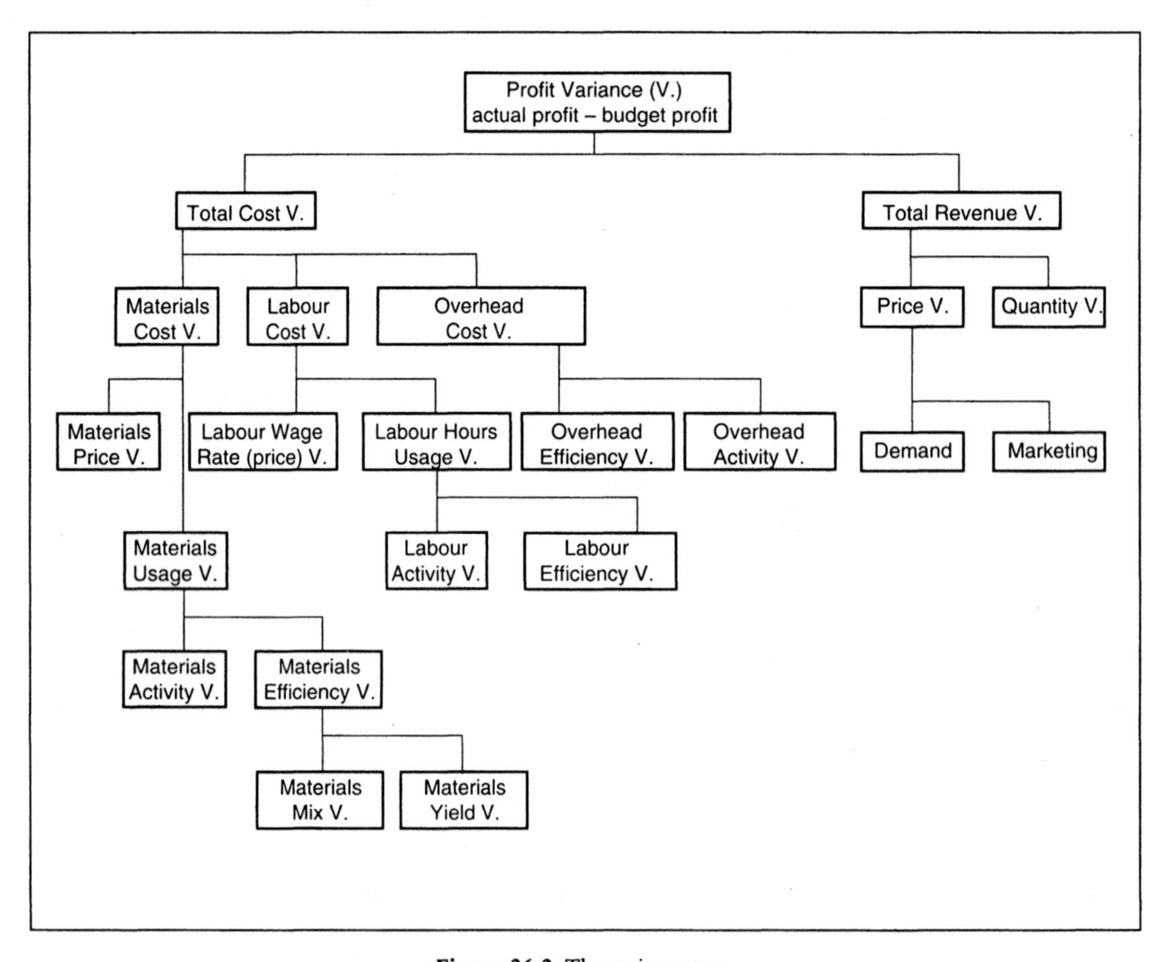

Figure 26.2 The variance tree.

In this chapter we will use the term 'budgeted cost' throughout even when referring to unit costs. It is important to bear in mind that many firms use (and textbooks refer to) the concept of a 'standard cost'. You may wish to refer back to Chapter 22 to revise the idea of a standard cost and how it relates to a budgeted cost. The mechanics of variance analysis are identical in both cases.

In Figure 26.2 we show the structure of the variance analysis technique described in this chapter. We take the fundamental equation

$$\text{Profit} = \text{Revenue} - \text{Cost}$$

which leads us to

Total profit variance
= Total revenue variance − Total cost variance

Total costs are defined as variable (direct materials and labour) and overheads. A third element of variable costs, namely variable overheads, can also be included. Under variable cost headings the unit cost (buying in price) variances and usage (or volume) variances are calculated. The volume variances can, as we shall see later, be attributed to variations in the level of actual output and to greater or lesser degrees of efficiency in the usage of resources.

You may find it helpful to refer to this tree as we discuss the methods of calculating variances under each heading.

GROSS VARIANCES

The variance between total budgeted profit and total actual profit is referred to as the 'gross profit variance'. Similarly, the difference between budgeted and actual total revenue and total costs is referred to as the gross revenue and gross cost variances respectively. In Table 26.1 we show the calculation of the gross variances on total profit, revenue and costs. Note that we use the convention that an adverse variance to the firm is labelled 'A' and a favourable variance 'F'. In practice, computer-generated cost systems use + or −; however, for learning purposes we find that the F–A system is easier, as the impact of the variance can easily be discerned by inspection, whereas the signs on cost and revenue variances mean different things.

PRICE AND VOLUME VARIANCES

We have already discussed the idea in Chapter 17 that the level of output chosen will directly influence revenue and cost. Total revenue is the product of price per unit and quantity and total cost is the product of cost per unit and quantity. Therefore, part of every variance between actual and budgeted total revenue or cost will be due to a change in the price or cost per unit, while the remainder will be due to a change in quantity sold or used.

EXAMPLE

The materials used in producing a particular product were budgeted to be 23 000 kg at £13.00 per kilogram. The actual usage was 27 000 kg at £14.00 per kilogram. It had been planned to produce 17 000 units of final product, although in the event 18 000 units were produced.

The variance between total budgeted and total actual material cost can be found as follows:

Actual materials cost (27 000 × £14.00)	£378 000
Budgeted materials cost (23 000 × £13.00)	£299 000
'Gross' materials cost variance	£79 000(A)

where (A) indicates that the variance is adverse in that actual cost exceeds budgeted cost.

Table 26.1

	Budget	Actual	Gross variance
Sales revenue	450 000.00	430 000.00	20 000.00 A
Total costs	300 000.00	295 000.00	5 000.00 F
Profit	150 000.00	135 000.00	15 000.00 A

The gross cost variance can be split into three components:

- a unit cost or 'price' variance caused by the change in the buying price per unit of the resource;
- a materials usage or 'volume' variance caused by the difference between the budgeted and the actual quantity used;
- a joint price/quantity variance which is, by convention, assigned to the price variance.

To illustrate how these three variances arise, we show, on a graph (Figure 26.3) the budgeted and actual unit costs and the budgeted and actual quantities of materials.

The total actual materials cost is given by the area of the larger rectangle, i.e. actual cost per unit times actual quantity (AP × AQ). The smaller rectangle gives the total budgeted cost, i.e. budgeted cost per unit times budgeted quantity (BP × BQ).

The total variance is given by the area of the border of the two rectangles, the horizontal portion (AP − BP) × BQ being the price variance; the vertical portion (AQ − BQ) × BP being the volume variance and the small corner portion (AP − BP) × (AQ − BQ) being the joint variance. Given the numbers in the example these three variances are:

Unit cost or price variance
= (AP − BP) × BQ
= (14.00 − 13.00) × 23 000
= £23 000(A)

Volume or usage variance
= (AQ − BQ) × BP
= (27 000 − 23 000) × 13.00
= £52 000(A)

Joint variance
= (AP − BP) × (AQ − BQ)
= (14.00 − 13.00) × (27 000 − 23 000)
= £4000(A)

Because the actual cost per unit of materials and the actual usages both exceed the budgeted values all three variances are adverse. Note again, when attempting to determine whether variances are adverse or favourable it is often easier to ignore the sign and to make the choice by inspection. With costs, actual figures in excess of budget give adverse variances, while the reverse is true for revenue items.

The sum of the three variances calculated above gives the 'gross' material variance of £79 000(A). Traditional variance analysis assigns the joint variance to the price variance. The reason for this is partly because prices are usually deemed to be outside management's control, whereas usages are not. Thus where there is some ambiguity, as is the

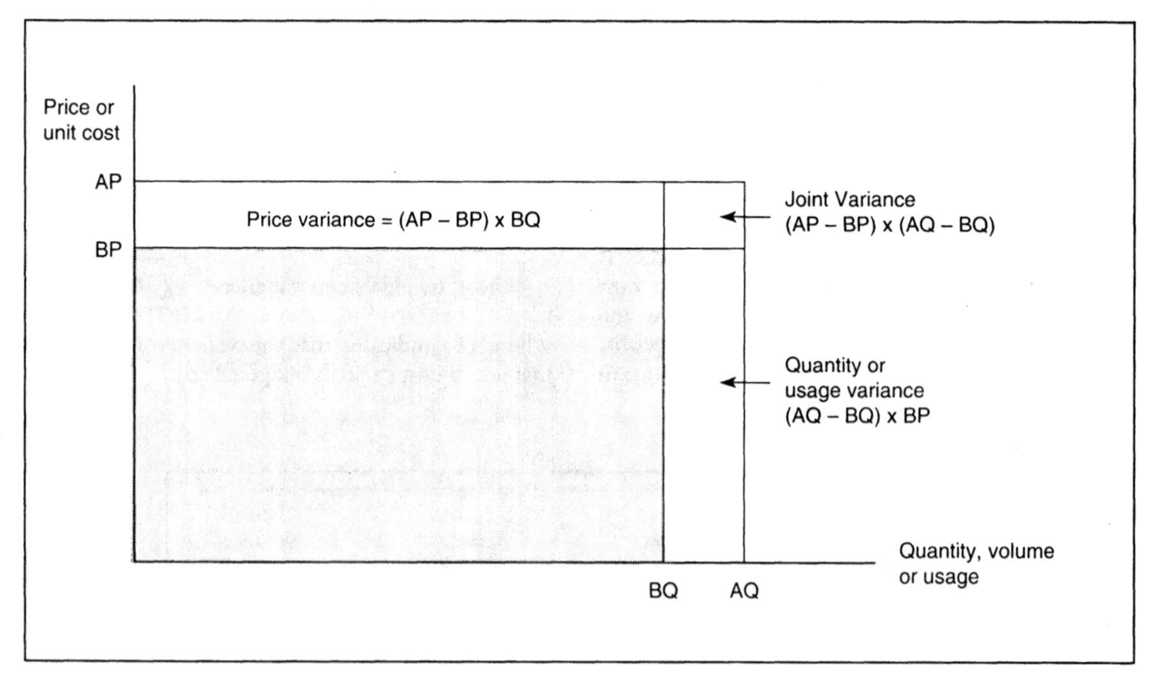

Figure 26.3 First level variances.

case with the joint variance, it is better to assign the variance to the non-controllable part. Following this convention the revised formulae for the price and volume variance are as follows:

Price variance (including joint variance)

$$= (AP - BP) \times AQ$$

$$\text{Volume variance} = (AQ - BQ) \times BP$$

These are two extremely important formulae in variance analysis.

The price variance now represents the entire area of the upper rectangle in Figure 26.3.

Using this revised price variance formula we obtain a variance of £27 000(A) as

$$(AP - BP) \times AQ = (14.00 - 13.00) \times 27\,000$$
$$= £27\,000(A)$$

An adverse price variance on materials indicates that any investigation should be directed toward the company's purchasing department. An adverse variance in the unit price for materials could arise for any number of reasons, including the following.

- A price increase has been imposed for materials of the same quality as those previously supplied.
- The purchasing department has taken a higher quality product which may well reveal itself in a favourable volume variance.
- The company may not have taken advantage of discounts for early payment.

The adverse quantity variance, on the other hand, directs attention toward the production department, although we are not yet in a position to say how much of the increase in material usage was due to the higher than expected output of final product and how much was due to changes in the efficiency of use of the material.

EFFICIENCY AND ACTIVITY VARIANCES

The original budget was set on the presupposition that 17 000 units of final product would be produced. However, an actual final output of 18 000 units was achieved. At this level of output we would have anticipated a materials usage (on budget) of 24 353 kg, calculated as follows:

Revised usage

$$= \text{original budgeted usage} \times \frac{\text{actual final output}}{\text{budgeted final output}}$$

$$= 23\,000 \times 18\,000/17\,000$$
$$= 24\,353 \text{ kg}$$

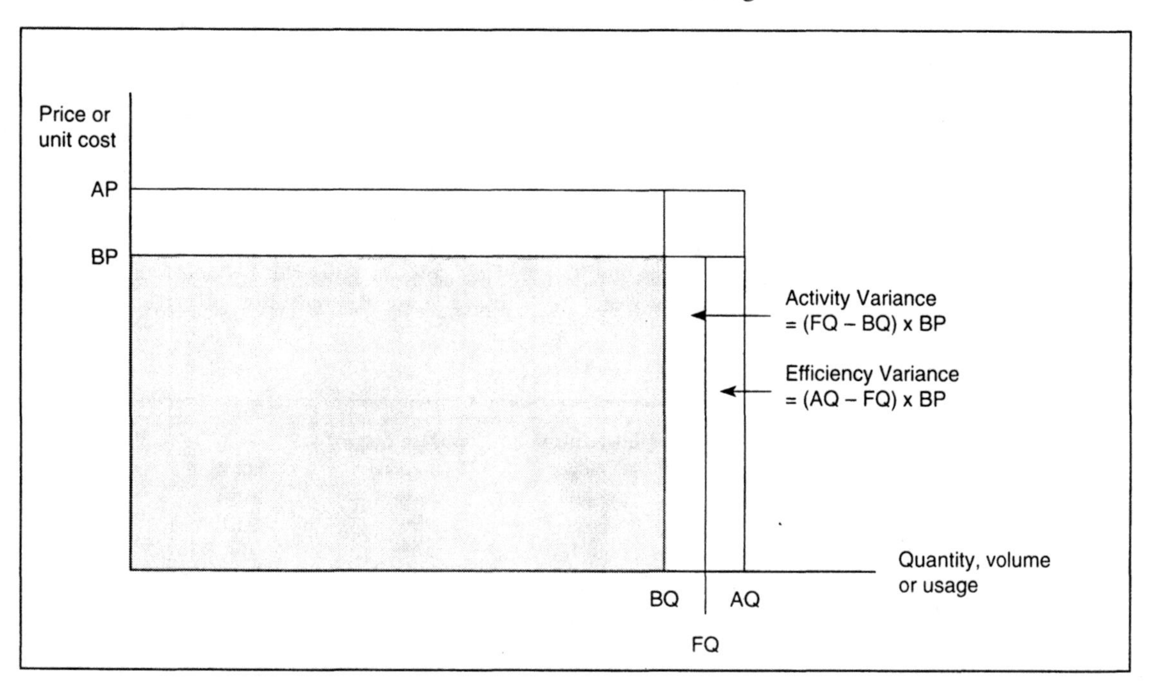

Figure 26.4 The analysis of quantity variances into activity and efficiency effects.

This revised usage is sometimes referred to as the 'flexed' usage or quantity (FQ). Note the usefulness here of the flexible budgeting concept discussed in Chapter 17. A flexible budget, especially when the basic budget is on computer, should be able to yield these flexed usages as soon as the actual output is known. In Figure 26.4 we show the analysis of the quantity or usage variance into its constituent activity and efficiency components using the flexed budget.

The original variance on materials usage,

Materials usage variance

$$= (AQ - BQ) \times BP$$
$$= (27\,000 - 23\,000) \times 13.00$$
$$= £52\,000 (A)$$

can now be separated into two components:

Variance due to inefficiency in materials use

$$= (AQ - FQ) \times BP$$
$$= (27\,000 - 24\,353) \times 13.00$$
$$= £34\,411 (A)$$

and

Variance due to higher level of activity

$$= (FQ - BQ) \times BP$$
$$= (24\,353 - 23\,000) \times 13.00$$
$$= £17\,589 (A)$$

where

Volume variance = activity variance + (in)efficiency variance

$$£52\,000 (A) = £17\,589 (A) + £34\,411 (A)$$

Clearly, the adverse activity variance is not the fault of the production department, but can be accounted for by the increase in overall production activity. However, the inefficiency variance may well be attributable to the production department, although the greater than anticipated usage of material may simply be due to an over-optimistic budget being set in the first instance.

MIX AND YIELD VARIANCES

When more than one material is used to produce a given product and the proportions of the materials can be altered by chance or by design then it is useful to identify the part of the (in)efficiency variance which has been caused by alterations in the mix of the two (or more) materials and the part which has been caused by differences in the efficiency with which each material is converted into final product (the individual material's yield variance).

Using the last example for one material, and introducing a second material into the analysis, we have the situation shown in Table 26.2. Our objective is to split the efficiency variance for each product produced into a part brought by variations in the mix of materials and a part brought about by poorer or better than expected material yields.

As we are working on components of the usage or volume variance everything is based on budget price per kilogram of the material concerned. To explain the method behind this calculation we will go through the above columns one by one.

(1) This column shows the technical specification for mixing materials into final product (now given). Three kilograms of materials in the specified mix will, under ideal conditions, yield one unit of final product.
(2) These are the budget unit prices of each material.
(3) This column gives the budgeted material usage based upon the specified mix from column 1

Table 26.2

Material	Specified usage per unit output (kg) (1)	Budget price per kilogram £ (2)	Budget usage at budget output (kg) (3)	Budget usage at actual output (kg) (4)	Actual usage (kg) (5)	Budget mix at actual usage (kg) (6)
A	1.353	13	23 000	24 353	27 000	26 609
B	1.647	8	28 000	29 647	32 000	32 391
	3.000		51 000	54 000	59 000	59 000

and the budgeted output of final product of 17 000 units (i.e. 1.353 × 17 000 = 23 000 and 1.647 × 17 000 = 28 000).

(4) At an actual output of 18 000 units we would expect a budgeted usage of materials:

A: 1.353 × 18 000 = 24 353 kg
B: 1.647 × 18 000 = 29 647 kg

The activity variance for each material can be calculated by deducting column (3) from column (4) and multiplying the resultant variance in usage by the budget price.

(5) This column gives the actual usage.

(6) This column gives the budgeted mix we would have expected on a total actual usage of the two materials of 59 000 kg:

Material A usage
= 1.353/3.000 × 59 000 = 26 609 kg
Material B usage
= 1.647/3.000 × 59 000 = 32 391 kg

The difference between actual usage and the budgeted mix (column (5) – column (6)) gives the mix variance when priced at the budgeted price. The remainder of the difference between the actual and budgeted usage at the actual output is the yield variance (column (6) – column (4)).

To summarise, the efficiency variance can be split into mix and yield variances as shown in Table 26.3.

The mix variance indicates the extent to which the technically specified mix has been met in production. With material A the mix variance is adverse, i.e. more material A was used than was anticipated given a total materials usage of 59 000 kg. With material B the reverse is true, as we would expect. The yield variance indicates the level of efficiency in production and immediately draws attention to the operating conditions under which production has been undertaken.

Mix and yield variances can be calculated on any joint, interdependent factors of production: different grades of labour, energy and materials, the number of labour and machine hours, respectively. The only constraint, when examining joint factors of production, is that the units of activity are comparable for the factors concerned. Material usages in kilograms can be compared with one another but labour (where the usage is in hours) and materials cannot.

OVERHEAD VARIANCES

Traditional variance analysis techniques assume that fixed overheads are included in the unit costing procedures and attempt to identify those parts of the overhead under- or over-absorption which can be attributed to variances in the allocation base. For example, if a particular class of fixed overhead has been apportioned on a labour-hour basis, then a greater usage of labour hours during a production period will lead to an over-allocation (or over-absorption) of overheads in the period.

Similarly, an under-absorption will occur if less labour hours are used than planned. However, the efficiency and activity variances on labour impart all the information we need to know concerning that factor of production. The fact that a particular fixed element has been included in the unit labour cost (which is what the allocation procedure is about) tells us nothing more about the long-term ability of production to cover overheads.

The more serious problem with fixed-overhead allocation is that it treats as variable a cost element which is fixed in the short run. Fixed-overhead allocation and fixed-overhead variances are only relevant if bonuses or other side payments made to lower level managers are related to the recovery of fixed overheads in production. Nevertheless, many firms do apply fixed-overhead allocation procedures

Table 26.3

Material	Efficiency variance (col. (5) – col. (4)) × budget price	= Mix variance (col. (5) – col. (6)) × budget price	+ Yield variance (col. (6) – col. (4)) × budget price
A	(27 000 – 24 353) × 13.00 = 34 411 (A)	(27 000 – 26 609) × 13.00 = 5083 (A)	(26 609 – 24 353) × 13.00 = 29 328 (A)
B	(32 000 – 29 647) × 8.00 = 18 824 (A)	(32 000 – 32 391) × 8.00 = 3128 (F)	(32 391 – 29 647) × 8.00 = 21 952 (A)

and then attempt to attribute variances to the over- or under-absorption which may occur.

EXAMPLE

Overheads are allocated at a rate of £5 per labour hour. The budgeted labour usage is 2100 hours, at a budgeted labour rate of £10 per hour. The actual labour usage was 2000 hours at an actual rate of £12 per hour. The actual production was 18 000 units compared with the budgeted production of 17 000 units.

Given the allocation rate of £5 per labour hour we can calculate the level of fixed overheads which management expects to recover from production as follows:

Total overheads to be absorbed
= £5 × 2100 = £10 500

Total wage-rate (price) variance
= (12.00 − 10.00) × 2000 = £4000 (A)

Labour-usage (volume) variance
= (2000 − 2100) × 10.00 = £1000 (F)

As fixed overheads are allocated on the usage of labour hours, we can easily see the level of under-absorption in the period:

Actual labour hours × budgeted absorption rate = 2000 × £5 =	£10 000
Budgeted labour hours × budgeted absorption rate = 2100 × £5 =	£10 500
Under-absorption of fixed overheads in the period =	£500

We could, if we wished, split this under-absorption into the part caused by changes in production activity (cf. activity variance) and the part caused by changes in the level of production efficiency (cf. the efficiency variance). To do this we first calculate the activity and efficiency variances on the budgeted labour hours and then apply the absorption rate to obtain the corresponding overhead variances.

Budgeted labour hours at actual (rather than budgeted) output (18 000/17 000 × 2100)	= 2224
Budgeted labour hours	= 2100
Activity variance in hours	= 124
Activity variance at the budgeted wage rate of £10 per hour	= £1240 (A)

Actual labour hours	= 2000
Budgeted labour hours at actual output	= 2224
Efficiency variance in hours	= 224
Efficiency variance at the budgeted wage rate of £10 per hour	= £2240 (F)

The overhead activity and the efficiency variances (in hours) can be derived using the overhead absorption rates:

Overhead activity variance (124 × £5.00)
= £620 (A)

Overhead efficiency variance (224 × £5.00)
= £1120 (F)

Therefore, the greater than expected efficiency in the use of labour has led to an under-absorption of overheads which has been partly offset by the increase in production activity.

SALES VARIANCES

As with materials, labour and other variable costs, total sales revenue variances can be split into volume and price effects. The formula to use are exactly the same as those we derived earlier for price and volume variances.

Price variance = (actual price − budget price) × actual quantity sold

Volume variance = (actual quantity − budget quantity) × budgeted price

Because sales revenue volume variance is determined by sales (or activity) level, it is impossible to split this variance in the way we did for materials and labour. However, it is possible to determine how much of the price variance can be attributed to suboptimal pricing, given a particular level of production and a known demand curve.

EXAMPLE

Given an actual level of production (which was all sold) of 18 000 units compared with a budgeted production and sales figure of 17 000 units, determine the element of price variance due to marketing (in)efficiency and the element due to market conditions. The actual and budgeted selling prices were £28 per unit and £30 per unit, respectively. The demand curve for the product was expected to be:

$$p = 40.5 - 0.00062 \times Q$$

where p is the price per unit sold and Q is the quantity demanded.

With an actual sales volume of 18 000 units we would anticipate a price of £29.34 per unit as

$$40.5 - 0.00062 \times 18\,000 = £29.34$$

Gross sales revenue variance

$$= (AP \times AQ) - (BP \times BQ)$$
$$= (28 \times 18\,000) - (30 \times 17\,000)$$
$$= £6000\,(A)$$

Price variance $= (AP - BP) \times AQ$

$$= (28 - 30) \times 18\,000$$
$$= £36\,000\,(A)$$

Sales volume variance

$$= (AQ - BQ) \times BP$$
$$= (18\,000 - 17\,000) \times 30$$
$$= £30\,000\,(F)$$

Note the reversal in the way we assign adverse and favourable to the variances we have calculated. In the case of revenue items, increases in price and volume are regarded as favourable to the firm, contrary to the situation with cost variances. The price variance,

$$\text{Price variance} = £36\,000\,(A)$$

can be split into two components:

Demand specific variance

$$= (£29.34 - £30) \times 18\,000$$
$$= £11\,880\,(A)$$

and

Marketing variance due to underpricing

$$= (£28 - £29.34) \times 18\,000$$
$$= £24\,120\,(A)$$

The interpretation of these variances is dependent upon the following assumptions.

- The original demand curve accurately represents prevailing demand conditions.
- There is no alteration in the position of the demand curve during the production period.
- The original price has been correctly set for the level of output planned.

Given these assumptions the marketing and demand variances can only, at best, indicate the possible causes of the overall sales revenue variance.

In practice, not all of these variances shown in Figure 26.2 can be calculated in all instances. Many firms which use standard costing procedures only extract price and volume variances and others adapt the concepts presented here to their own particular information structures and reporting systems. Do not be surprised, therefore, if you fail to meet the variance-analysis system described here in practice.

CONTROLLABLE AND NON-CONTROLLABLE VARIANCES

Variances of all types can be classified into two groups: controllable and non-controllable. Controllable variances are ones which come under direct management influence, for example:

- the usages of resources on processes;
- the level of production activity;
- the cost of labour and certain overheads.

Other costs are not directly controllable:

- suppliers' prices;
- the final market price of the product (which is subject to market influences).

The investigation of variances can be a very expensive process for management in terms of both time and the resources required to identify and explain their causes. 'Management by exception' is a name given to the process where, following the establishment of a range of acceptable variances, management only pursues those variances which lie outside the range. In practice, the magnitude of the range will depend upon the degree of control which management either wishes to have or feels that it can impose upon the system. It also depends upon the degree of slack which can be tolerated in the production or selling system. An effective management by exception system relies on periodic management reports which:

- provide a comparison between actual and budgeted figures and show the variances for each expenditure and revenue item reconciled to the variance of actual with budgeted profit or loss;
- flag those variances which exceed the ranges of acceptability specified by management.

Wherever possible the cost accountant should provide a commentary on the exceptional variances which have arisen during a period and give the

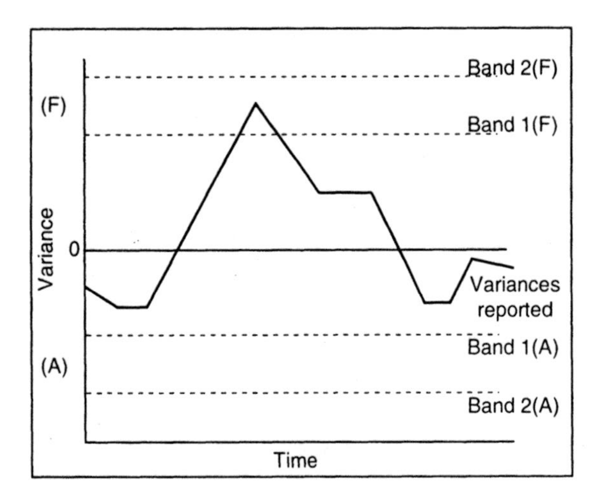

Figure 26.5 Exception limits.

results of any preliminary investigations which have been conducted to establish their causes.

SETTING CONTROL LIMITS

In practice, setting control limits entails that management should decide what level of variance will not be considered significant and therefore not be scrutinised, and what level should be reviewed with the level of management concerned. One particularly popular technique is to establish control bands around the budget (i.e. zero variance) against which reported variances can be monitored (Figure 26.5). These control bands (of which two are normally sufficient) can be established:

- arbitrarily by setting a percentage limit of (say) plus or minus 2% for band 1(F) and band 1(A) and (say) twice this level (i.e. 4%) for the second band;
- statistically using historical budgetary data. The first band can be set to capture one standard deviation from zero and the second band, two standard deviations of variances from zero. In the first case, we would expect approximately 68% of variances to lie within range, and in the second case we would expect approximately 95% of variances to lie within range.

In either case, the choice of band will be determined by the degree of control management wishes to exert on actual costs and revenues and, of course, it is quite possible to vary the criteria depending upon the perceived degree of control which budget holders have over the revenue and cost for which they are responsible.

CONCLUSION

In this chapter we have examined the methods of variance analysis as practised in a wide variety of companies across all sectors. Indeed, wherever an established budgetary system is in place, some version of what we have described here will also be in place. An important theme within our discussion is that variances of themselves do not pinpoint accountability; all they do is focus attention on the most likely problem areas for a business. In the next chapter we extend our discussion to the general problems of resource control within business.

Chapter 27

The Control of Short-Term Working Capital

Level M

Contents

Summary

In this chapter we consider a particular aspect of control, namely the control of short-term working capital. We will first examine the nature of control and why it can be regarded as a decision-making activity. We will then move on to an examination of the problems of controlling short-term working capital. In particular, we will outline some simple control theory and examine the role of control theory for the three important categories of working capital management: the control of debtor accounts, stocks and cash.

GENERAL PROBLEMS OF SHORT-TERM CONTROL

Many of the ideas that have shaped our understanding of the concept of control have come from other disciplines, notably electronics and communications. Over the years, management scientists have seen the relevance of the insights provided by electronics, communications and, especially, the theory of electronic control systems for the control of business organisations.

A control system is a structured decision system where managers use past and predicted data about a process to control its behaviour. The problems of control are an integral part of the decisions which managers take in order to operate their business. We will not, therefore, treat the problem of control as an isolated topic on its own, but as one aspect of the decision-making theme of this book.

The very idea of control presupposes that information concerning a system's performance will be acted upon and decisions made on the basis of any deviations from what was anticipated. Firms collect actual costs from their production processes and compare those costs with the budgets set up for that aspect of the firm's activity. The deviations of actual costs from budget provide management with some of the information it needs to make the control decisions necessary to keep the firm on its budgeted course.

Therefore, for our purposes, we can define control as:

> a process of reactive decision making, concerned with maintaining the performance of the firm or any of its component parts as close as possible to the targets set by management.

The type of control system shown in Figure 27.1 includes a closed 'feedback' loop where the system's actual and desired output (X_o and X_d, respectively) are compared and 'fed back' into the input stage in order to correct the system's performance. Such control may be automatic in that the error signal is used directly, perhaps through the intervention of some mechanical controller, to alter the level of input into the system.

An example of this would be a flow meter monitoring the rate at which a chemical flows into a

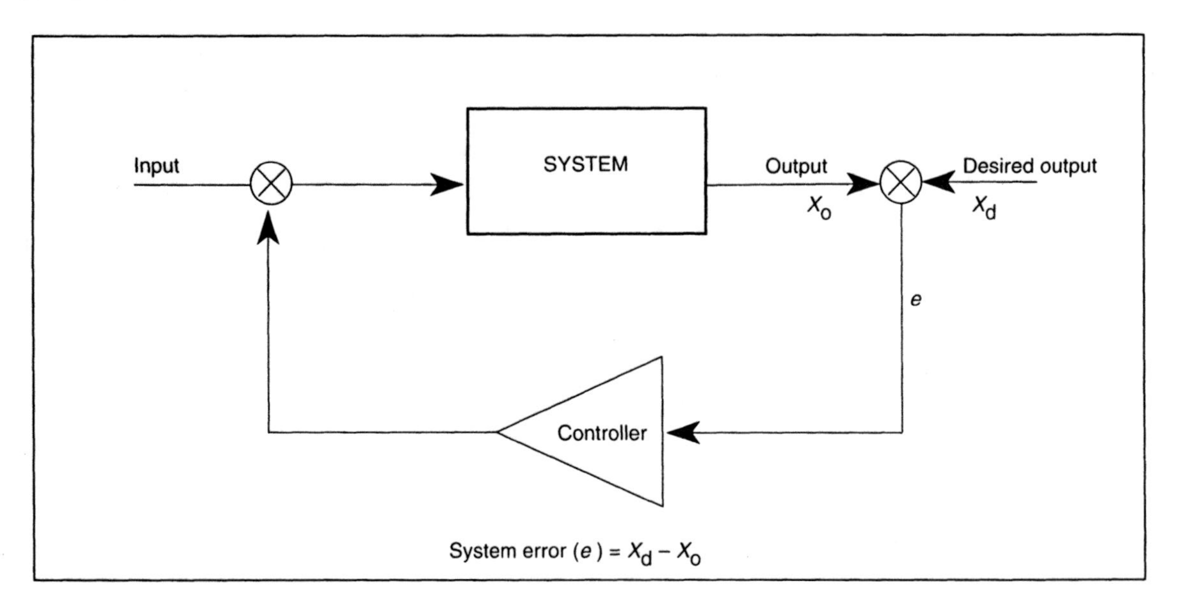

Figure 27.1 Feedback control.

reactor vessel. Deviations in flow rate from that set on the meter would cause a valve to open or shut as the case may be. In such a system, control is entirely automatic and does not rely on any human intervention in the system.

Alternatively, the control may be non-automatic, where disparities between actual and desired output are acted upon by some individual only if they exceed certain acceptable tolerances in system behaviour. For example, a driver operating the throttle of his or her car does not continuously monitor the speed of the vehicle in order to keep its speed exactly in line with what is intended. In this case, control is both intermittent and discretionary.

Control can also be positive or negative. With negative control, the control of the input variables is opposite to the sign of the system error on the output stage. For example, if management responded to over-high stock levels by cutting back on the rate of routine reordering this would be an example of negative feedback. With positive feedback, the control of the input variable is in the same direction as the sign of the error. So, for example, if revenue increased and management responded by increasing the advertising spend then we would have an example of positive feedback. Positive feedback can generate wide swings in the variable we are attempting to control. Negative feedback can dampen swings up to a certain point determined by the lags in the system. Beyond that point control may be lost and the system may suddenly change into chaotic patterns of behaviour. This topic has been discussed in terms of share price processes in Chapter 12.

VARIETIES OF CONTROL SYSTEMS

Both automatic and non-automatic control systems can be classified into three separate categories:

- feedback control;
- feedforward control;
- feedback/feedforward or 'hybridised' control.

Feedback control

We show a diagram of feedback control in Figure 27.1 where the error signal given by the differences between planned and actual output are fed back into the controller to produce changes in the inputs of the system. In Figure 27.2 we show how feedback can be used to control a stock system. The principal problem with feedback control arises because the control data (the error signal) are derived from the output stage and are, therefore, intrinsically out of date. The idea behind feedforward control is designed to surmount this problem.

Feedforward control

With feedforward control the inputs into a system are monitored in order to predict potential

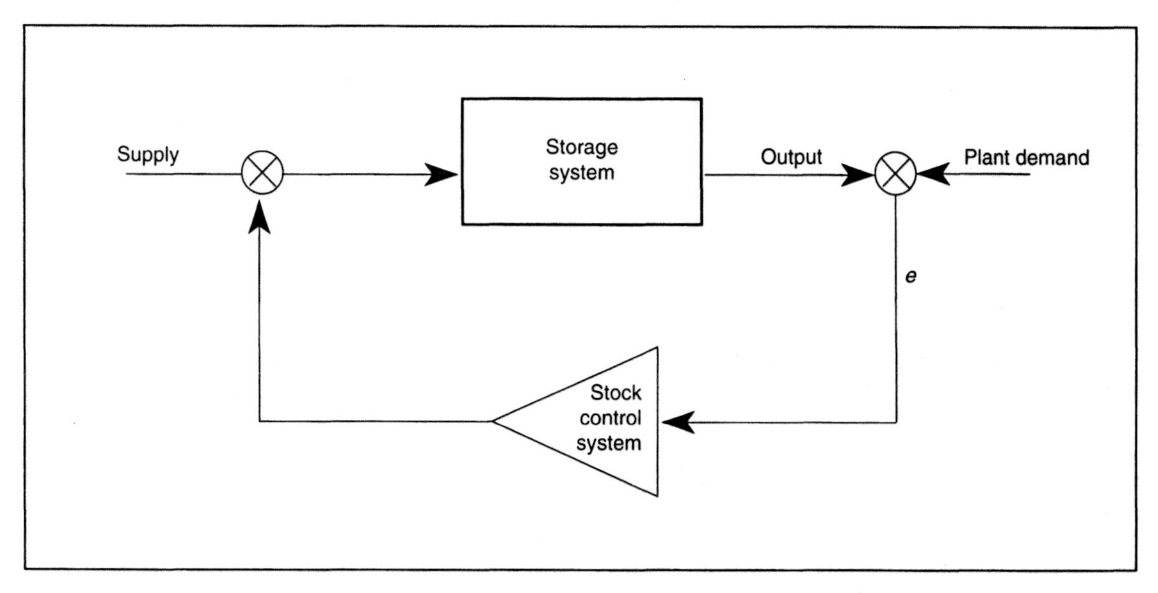

Figure 27.2 Feedback within a stock control system.

disturbances in its operating characteristics. If such disturbances can be successfully predicted then they can often be counteracted. The trick, of course, is to have reliable means of predicting the operating characteristics of the system concerned when input disturbances occur.

A feedforward stock control system linked to a production process would entail monitoring the quality of the raw material arrivals in order to predict variables such as rejection rates and yields on conversion of those raw materials into finished goods. These predictions of rejection rates and yields, allied with predictions of future plant demand, can give a greater degree of system control. In Figure 27.3 we show the structure of such a feedforward system.

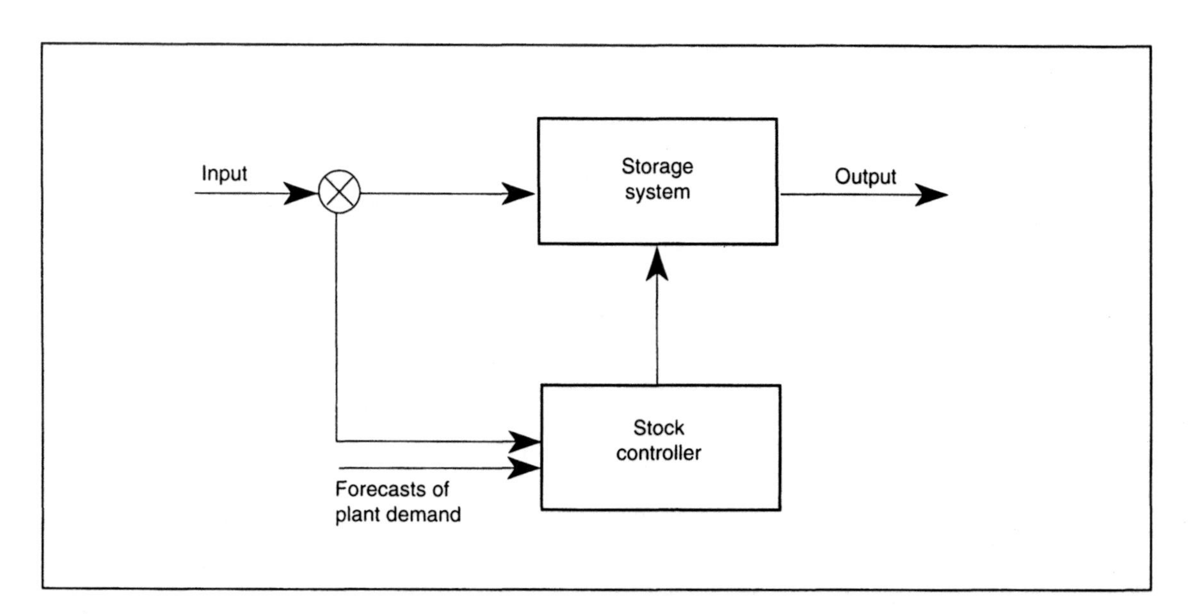

Figure 27.3 Feedforward in stock control.

Feedback/feedforward control

Feedback/feedforward control attempts to obtain the best aspects of both types of control system described above. In Figure 27.4 we show a stock-control system designed upon these lines. The feedback element compares the outflow of stock from the system with the actual production demand. Any discrepancies are fed back into either the input stage (thus changing the levels of new orders) or into the stock-handling system itself in order to speed up the rate at which orders from production are processed.

The feedforward element works in two ways. The first is by monitoring the quality of material stock as it is received from suppliers. These quality-control data can then be used to predict changes in production requirements caused by alterations in the raw material quality. Second, by predicting future production levels in order to match stock holdings with likely usages of the materials concerned.

A high degree of automation in the types of control system we have described can be very expensive. Indeed, fully automated stock-control ordering systems are still a rarity in industry. However, in many control situations the required response rate of the system under consideration is not fast enough to justify the cost of automation. The closer we get to the strategic levels of decision making within the firm, the less effective automation will, in any event, become.

In the remainder of this chapter we will consider three areas of tactical, short-term control. These are:

- the control of the firm's debtor balances through the use of credit-control techniques;
- the control of stocks through the use of simple, mathematical optimisation techniques;
- the control of cash flow.

We are, therefore, concerned with the control of the three main subdivisions of working capital which appear in the typical company balance sheet as 'current assets'.

When a company invests in current assets, such as debtors and stocks, it uses up cash. The use of this cash entails a cost to the firm in that it forgoes the opportunity of investing that cash in other ways and earning the returns which would result from those alternative investments. This forgone return is the opportunity cost of capital tied up in current assets. In principle, the way we calculate the opportunity cost of capital is much the same as for any other resources. This topic is discussed in Chapter 13.

CONTROL OF DEBTORS

Apart from the retail sector of the economy and the so-called illicit 'black economy', most selling by firms and by individuals is on credit. A credit sale means that the firm invoices its customers at the point of sale and requests payment within so many

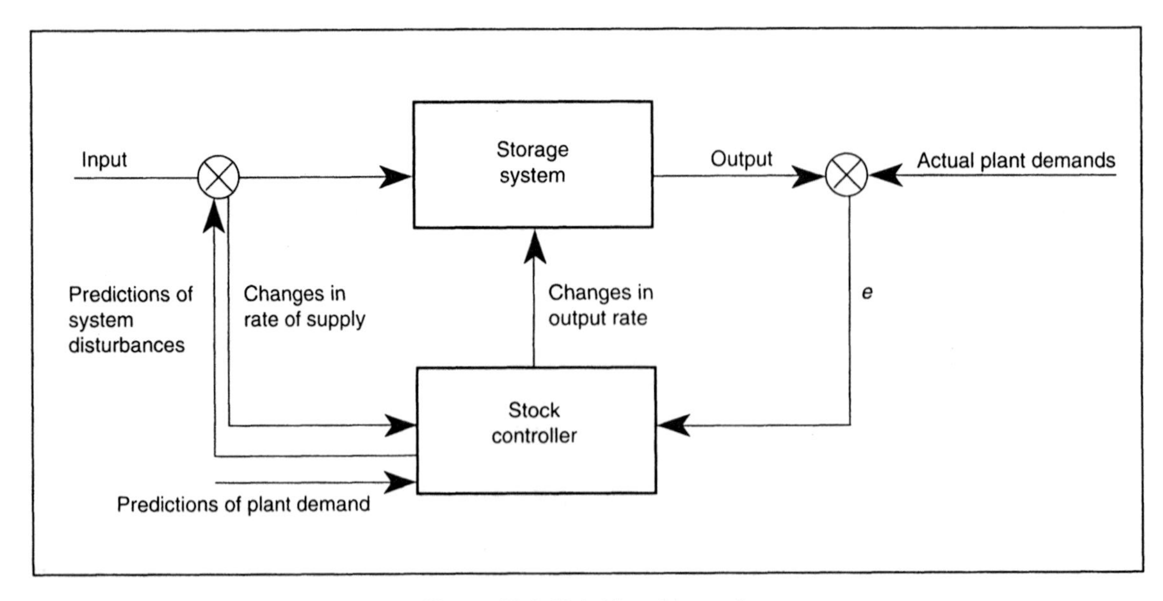

Figure 27.4 Hybrid stock control.

days or weeks of that time. The firm may offer a discount (usually expressed as a percentage of the sale price) for prompt payment, although some of its customers will still delay payment for as long as possible and, indeed, may not pay at all.

The rate at which debtors pay their bills can have a dramatic effect upon a firm's cash flow and hence its liquidity, as we have already discussed in Chapter 5. In that chapter we considered the problem of an adverse gap between debtor age and creditor age. The control of such an adverse credit gap entails:

- monitoring the time taken by customers to pay their debts (by means of a debtor 'ageing' analysis);
- the control of the level of debtors by
  (i) improved reminder and collection systems;
  (ii) offering discounts for early payment;
  (iii) improved credit control.

In Figure 27.5 we show the basic structure of a debt or control system.

Debtor ageing analysis

During the course of time a firm will gather a list of outstanding debts which will lengthen and contract over the firm's selling seasons. A simple test can be conducted on a firm's outstanding debts to determine their average age. Assuming a constant rate of sales during the year, the debtor turnover ratio (expressed in days) will give a rough-and-ready guide to the average age of debts. This ratio is calculated at a given time using the formula

Debtor turnover ratio

$$= \frac{\text{total outstanding debtors}}{\text{annual sales}} \times 365$$

This ratio gives the average age in days of a firm's debtors, although it cannot reveal the structure of the debtors' list. Similarly, the average time taken by the firm to pay its debts to its suppliers (its liabilities) can be estimated using the ratio

Creditor turnover ratio

$$= \frac{\text{total outstanding creditors}}{\text{annual purchases}} \times 365$$

Depending upon the business in which a firm is engaged some debtors' accounts may be very large, while others may be very small. Clearly, if the resources the firm can devote to retrieving its debts is limited, it will pay to attend to the large balances as a matter of priority while leaving the smaller accounts to some more automatic debtor-control system.

The first stage in analysing the structure of a firm's debtor listing is to create a cumulative ranking of the outstanding balances and to plot the resultant ranking against the number of individual debts held. A certain group of debts (group A in Figure 27.6)

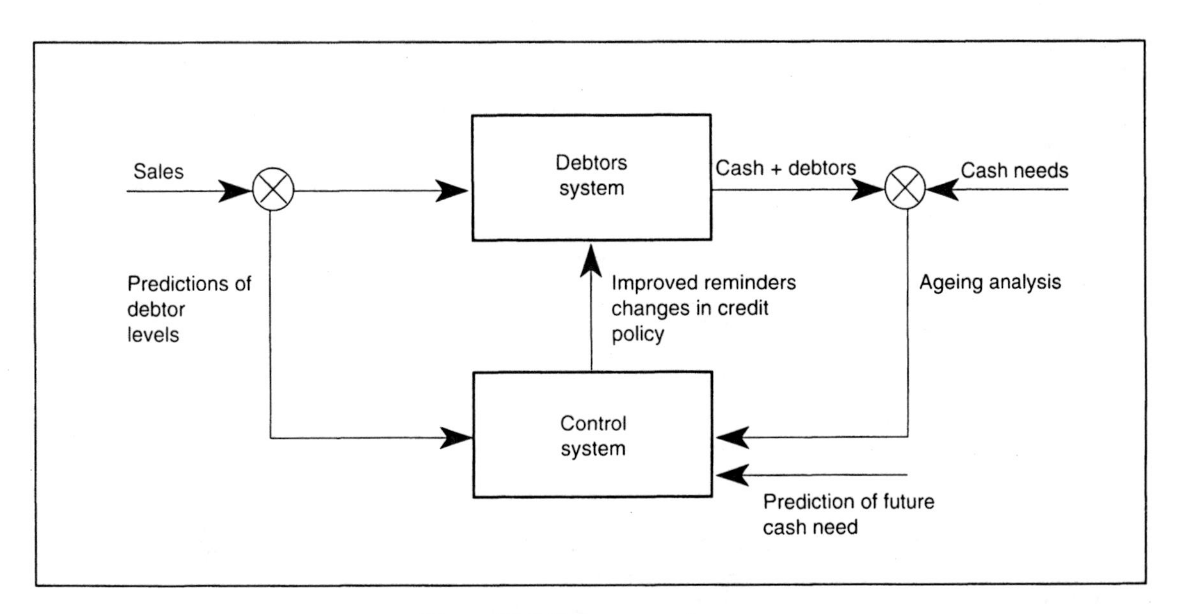

Figure 27.5 Debtor-control system.

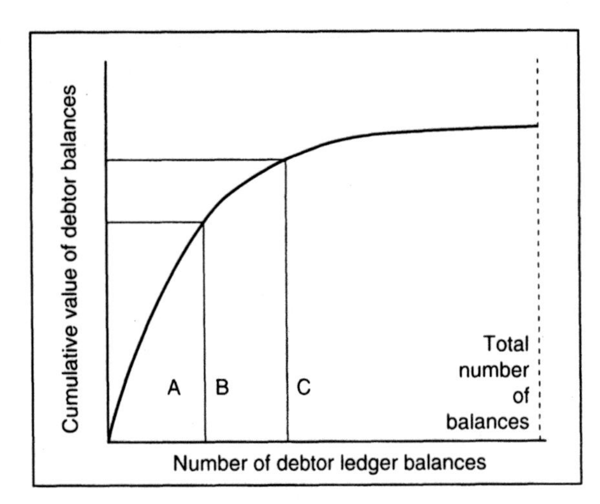

Figure 27.6 ABC analysis of debtor balances.

will account for the largest proportion of outstanding debts while being few in number. An intermediate group of balances (group B) will represent a large number of medium to small debts, while the final group (group C) will consist of a much larger number of very small accounts.

Group A debts involve the largest cash amounts and the firm may well consider it appropriate to devote every possible effort to recovering these debts as quickly as possible. The majority of these debts will have arisen for the simple reason that they are the balances on the accounts of the firm's largest customers. Some, however, may have arisen because the firm has continued to supply a customer with a poor payment record and a large outstanding balance has arisen as a result. Naturally, it should be this second class of debts which are the target of the firm's initial efforts.

The intermediate range of debts, while being important in the sense that the firm would not want them to default, are not of sufficient size to warrant a significant commitment of managerial time to their collection. The final range of debts will be for such trivial amounts that the cost of pursuing them may well be higher than the loss of interest resulting from the delay in their payment.

Once a listing of outstanding debtors in order of size has been compiled, the age of each outstanding debt can be analysed by month, week or even day, depending upon the nature of the business. Using the ABC analysis described above, the listing can be partitioned into three groups. In Table 27.1 below we show part of a simple debtor ageing analysis with the proportion of debt held (as a percentage) in each month to the total appended underneath.

Given the total sales figure for the year of (say) £1 778 000 the debtor turnover ratio would be

$$\text{Debtor turnover ratio} = \frac{243\,560}{1\,778\,000} \times 365$$
$$= 50 \text{ days}$$

The methods used to speed up the collection of debts vary from industry to industry. Indeed, in some cases firms sell their debts (just like any other assets) to financial institutions which specialise in this form of 'debt factoring' business. Other firms employ specialist debt-collection agencies who take over the problem of following up bad debts. The most common method for reducing the average age

Table 27.1

Account Code	Account Name	Total £	Dec. £	Nov. £	Oct. £	Sep. £	Aug. £
JU.006	Julio plc	15 360		12 100	500	2 760	
CA.001	Carlos plc	14 150	7 000				7 150
RA.010	Ramon Ltd	10 250			10 250		
JO.016	Joachim and Co.	9 000		9 000			
⋮	⋮	⋮	⋮	⋮	⋮	⋮	⋮
MA.004	Martin plc	25					25
BA.005	Barnabe, M	12					12
Total debts		243 560	112 837	51 147	44 815	15 831	18 938
Proportion (%)		100	46	21	18.4	6.5	8.1

of unpaid debtor accounts (apart from sending frequent reminders and statements or withdrawing credit facilities for delinquent customers) is by offering discounts for early payment. It is a fairly straightforward matter to evaluate the benefit (or loss) which will follows from a change in credit policy.

EXAMPLE

Mr Moron's credit sales currently stand at a constant value of £20 000 per month and are expected to stay at this level indefinitely. Mr Moron is considering introducing a 2.5% discount on the sale price of his goods for payment within one month. At the moment 25% of debtors pay within one month, 50% within two months and the remainder within three months. As a result of the change in credit policy, Mr Moron hopes that 80% will pay within the first month, 10% in the second month and the remainder in the third month. Mr Moron's opportunity cost of capital is 2% per month.

The first stage in the analysis of a credit policy change, such as that proposed by Mr Moron, is to analyse the change in cash flows from sales which will result. Obviously, in a steady-state situation, with no change in sales level and with no bad debts, the cash received each month will equal the monthly sales figure. In each month 25% of the cash received will relate to sales made three months before, 50% of the cash received will relate to sales made two months before and the remaining 25% comes from the previous month.

In the first month, operating the new policy, Mr Moron will receive outstanding debts of £5000 and £10 000, respectively, from sales made two and

Table 27.2

	Month numbers						
	0	1	2	3	4	5	6
	£	£	£	£	£	£	£
Original policy							
Cash receipts	20 000	20 000	20 000	20 000	20 000	20 000	
Revised policy:							
Receipts from							
month −3	5 000						
month −2	10 000	5 000					
month −1	5 000	10 000	5 000				
month 0		15 600	2 000	2 000			
month 1			15 600	2 000	2 000		
month 2				15 600	2 000	2 000	
month 3					15 600	2 000	2 000
month 4						15 600	2 000
month 5							15 600
	20 000	30 600	22 600	19 600	19 600	19 600	19 600
Change in cash flow	0	10 600	2 600	(400)	(400)	(400)	(400)
Discount factor		1.02	1.02^2			0.02	
Present values							
month 0	0						
month 1	10 392						
month 2	2 499						
			(20 000) / 1.02^2				
	(19 223)						
	(6 332)						

three months previously. In addition he will also receive 80% of the sales made in the previous month less the discount of 2.5%:

Receipts under the new policy in month (1)

$$t_1 = £20\,000 \times 0.8 \times 0.975 = £15\,600$$

In the second month of operation under the new policy Mr Moron will receive cash receipts of £5000 from three months previously (under the old policy), £2000 from two months previously (the first month under the new system) and £15 600 from the previous month (as calculated above). The pattern of cash flows will emerge as shown in Table 27.2.

As you can see, the disturbance caused by the change in credit policy occurs in the month following the change and disappears from the system two months later. In this case the net effect has been to produce two cash gains in t_1 and t_2 which are paid for by the cash loss thereafter of £400 per month.

The second stage in the analysis of this change in credit policy is to determine its net effect on Mr Moron's wealth using the discounting procedure discussed in Chapters 5 and 14. You will note that the perpetuity of £400 per annum which runs from t_3 is discounted in two stages. The perpetuity summation formula derived in Chapter 16 will bring the cash flows back to a 'present value' at t_2 (i.e. one year prior to the start of the perpetuity). This 'present value' at t_2 must then be brought to t_0 by discounting at the rate of 2% over the intervening two months.

The monthly rate of 2% gives

$$\begin{aligned}\text{Equivalent annual rate} &= (1 + i)^{12} \\ &= (1 + 0.02)^{12} \\ &= 26.8\%\end{aligned}$$

Even at this opportunity cost of capital the switch in credit policy is not worthwhile. Indeed, in practice the policy of offering general discounts can be a very expensive way of improving short-term liquidity.

CONTROL OF STOCKS

Figure 27.4 illustrated a combined feedback/feed-forward control system for either raw materials or finished stocks. As with debtor control, discussed in the previous section, a company attempting to control its stock may feel it appropriate to focus attention upon its most expensive lines, while keeping moderately large reserves of stocks of its cheaper items. For example, a television manufacturer may wish to optimise his or her holding of colour tubes, while keeping, at the same time, a very large stock of cabinet screws! As with the debtor analysis performed in the last section, an ABC analysis of stock can be an effective tool for identifying those items which require the highest degree of control (see Figure 27.7).

As can be seen from Figure 27.4 the control of stocks involves the following stages:

- predicting the future usages of stocks;
- monitoring the actual usages of stock;
- monitoring the actual cost of reordering stock;
- monitoring the time taken for stock to be delivered or produced (the supply or production 'lead time').

We will assume that an optimal stock policy will be one which minimises the overall cash cost of holding stock. Given a particular level of demand (from production for raw materials or from customers for finished stocks) the cost of holding stock will be a trade-off between two conflicting factors:

- the fixed cost of reordering;
- the opportunity cost of the capital invested in stock.

A certain fixed cost will be incurred each time stock is reordered. In the case of raw materials purchased from suppliers the reorder cost is the cost of placing the order plus any fixed transport costs which may be incurred. In the case of replenishing finished stocks from production, this fixed cost of reordering will be the set-up cost for the production

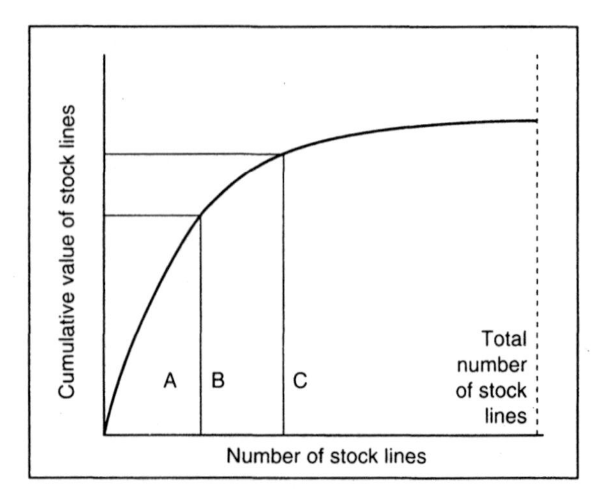

Figure 27.7 ABC analysis of stocks.

facility and any other fixed administrative charges which might be incurred. We will assume that the cost of warehouse space is fixed with respect to the range of stock levels which could be held.

The more often stock is reordered from suppliers or requisitioned from production, the greater will be the sum of the fixed reorder costs during a given period. On the other hand, the higher the average stock levels maintained by the firm, the less frequently stock must be reordered and, therefore, the lower will be the fixed reorder costs incurred during the period.

When a firm ties up its working capital in the form of stock, it forgoes the opportunity of using that capital in other ways. As a result, capital locked up in stock-holding has an opportunity cost associated with it, and the higher the average level of stock held, the higher this opportunity cost of capital will be.

In order to minimise overall annual stock holding costs, management can adopt one or both of the following strategies.

- Reduce the fixed cost of each reorder to the lowest possible level (which will permit lower average stock levels to be held with a consequent lowering of the opportunity cost of capital invested in stock).
- Given a particular fixed cost of each reorder, optimise the average level of stock holding so that the total cost of holding stock over a period (fixed reorder cost plus the opportunity cost of capital) is minimised.

The second strategy is subservient to the first in that, given the lowest possible reorder cost, the overall cost of stock-holding can then be minimised. Lower reorder costs mean that the firm can operate with a lower level of stocks (whether they be raw material or finished goods stocks) with more reorders during the particular period. Indeed, a logical extension of this would be that suppliers, for example, would be making many small deliveries during a day which were exactly matched to the firm's production requirements and that little or no raw-material stock need be held with the consequent avoidance of the cost of warehouse facilities and all of the other associated costs of holding stock.

Matching and optimising supply, production and deliveries requires a total production management philosophy which is only now being adopted by some UK and US firms. Japanese firms, on the other hand, deliberately follow a philosophy of carefully planned and designed total production systems. For example, Toyota (Japan) has only one hour's worth of back-up stocks, while Ford (USA) historically had three weeks. Small stock levels require efficient and predictable production systems while large stock levels can protect an inefficient and unpredictable production system from collapse.

The technique of minimising overall costs given a particular level of fixed reorder cost is reasonably straightforward. In Figure 27.8 we show a simplified diagram of how stocks vary through time.

The reorder quantity is the predetermined amount which a firm reorders whenever its stocks fall below a certain 'reorder level'. The lower the reorder quantity, the lower will be the average level of stock holding by the firm. To control stocks we need two items of information:

- the reorder quantity which minimises the cost of holding stock given a particular fixed cost of reordering and a given opportunity cost of capital;
- the reorder level which once passed indicates to the stock controller that fresh stock must be ordered. Stock must be reordered at the point where sufficient stock remains to sustain production (for raw materials) or satisfy customers (for finished stocks) over the time between order and delivery, which is normally termed the 'lead time'.

Setting reorder quantities and reorder levels

As noted above, the cost of holding stock consists of two elements: one which varies directly with, and one which varies directly against, the sizes of the batches ordered. Figure 27.9 shows the pattern of these two costs against batch size for a given period of time (we will assume a year although in some applications it may be a month, week or even day).

If the firm reorders a set amount (Q) of a particular stock line every time the recorded stock level falls below the reorder level then the average holding of stock (assuming an even rate of usage between deliveries) will be given by

$$\text{Average stock holding} = Q/2$$

Over the year the overall cost of holding this stock will be given by the following formula:

$$\text{Annual cost of holding stock} = iQV/2$$

where i is the opportunity cost of the capital tied up in stock (expressed as an interest rate) and V is the value per unit of stock. In this case stock should be valued at its replacement cost or current buying-in

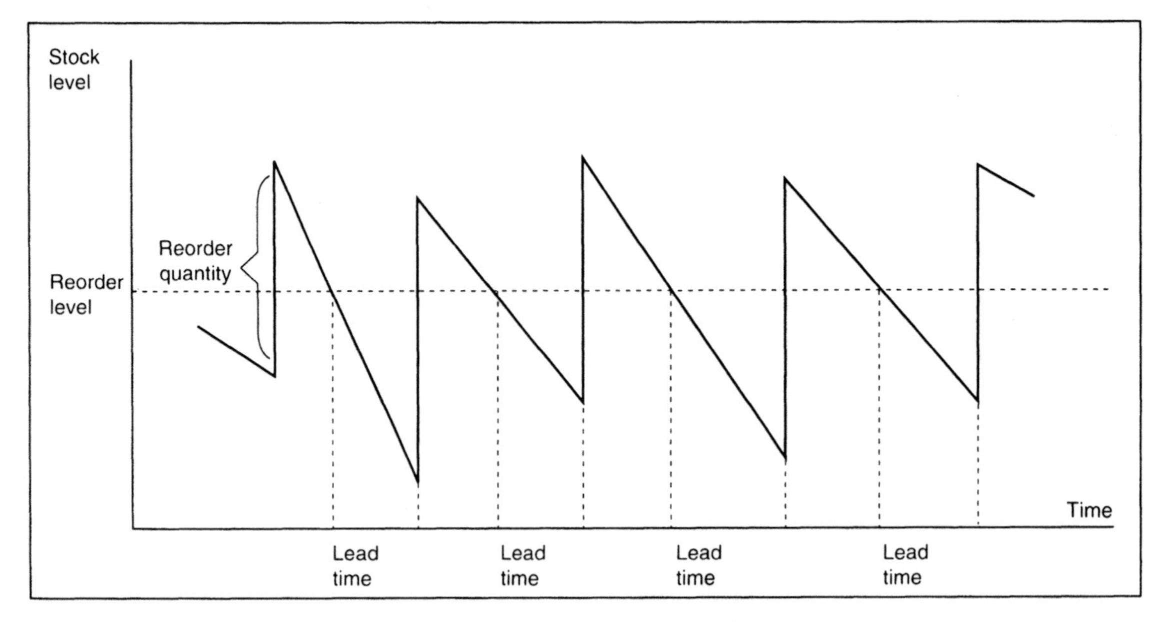

Figure 27.8 Stock movements through time.

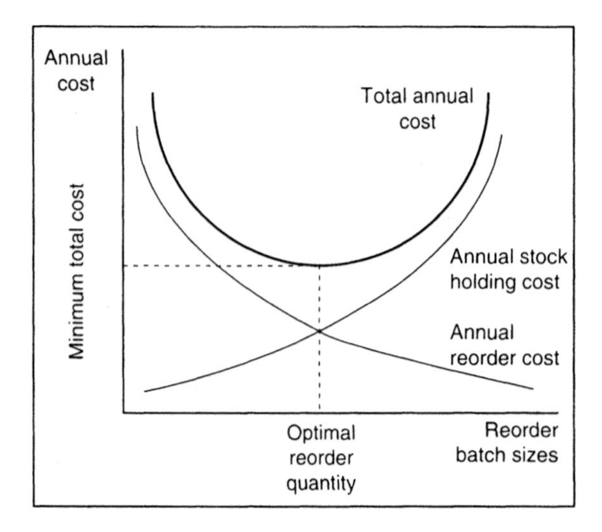

Figure 27.9 The cost of holding stock.

price plus any variable transport costs or other variable transaction costs incurred.

During the course of a year, if D is the annual usage or demand for the stock item then the number of reorders during the year will be given by

Number of reorders

$$= \frac{\text{annual usage of (or demand for) stock item}}{\text{reorder quantity}}$$

$$= D/Q$$

Now, if F is the fixed administrative cost incurred in setting up each order then

$$\text{Annual costs of reorder} = DF/Q$$

from these two formulae we obtain an equation for the total cost which is shown graphically in Figure 27.9.

$$\text{Total annual stock-holding cost} = iQV/2 + DF/Q$$

A formula for the minimum overall cost can be obtained by differentiating the above formula with respect to the reorder quantity (Q) and setting the resultant differential to zero:

$$\mathrm{d(TAC)/d}Q = iV/2 - DF/Q^2 = 0$$

where TAC is the total annual cost of holding stock.

By rearrangement of this formula we can find the reorder quantity which will give the minimum total annual cost of holding the stock line:

$$Q = \sqrt{(2DF/iV)}$$

EXAMPLE

Marchena's annual demand for a dangerous industrial chemical called olic acid is expected to be 16 000 kg in the coming year.

Each kilogram will cost £10 (including variable transport costs) and Marchena's opportunity cost of capital is 12% per annum. The fixed reorder cost is £200 per order and this includes a fixed handling charge by the carrier. The average lead time for delivery of stock is 18 days, and the firm has found that an average of an extra 10 days' supply is sufficient to cover the risk of stock-out. Marchena uses olic acid on a continuous production process.

The optimal order quantity for olic acid can be found by substituting the relevant data into the reorder quantity formula:

$$Q = \sqrt{(2 \times 16\,000 \times 200/0.12 \times 10)}$$
$$= 2309 \text{ kg (to the nearest kilogram)}$$

The reorder level is determined by two sorts of uncertainty:

- uncertainty in the length of the lead time (i.e. a delay by a supplier, for example, could lead to 'stockout');
- uncertainty in the usage of stock during the lead time period (i.e. excess usage could also lead to 'stockout').

The firm must decide, given the nature of its business, how much of this uncertainty it wishes to protect itself against when setting the reorder level. The reorder level will consist of two components:

- the level of remaining stock required to cover the expected lead time;
- the additional amount of stock required as a 'buffer' against running out of stock.

The lead-time demand can be calculated as follows:

Average lead-time demand
= (Annual demand × average lead-time (days))/365
= $DL/365$

Using the data in Marchena's example we can estimate the average lead-time demand as

$$\text{Average lead-time demand} = (16\,000 \times 18)/365$$
$$= 789 \text{ kg}$$

The buffer stock required is equivalent to 10 days' supply (management's assessment based upon historical evidence of delivery lead times). We can calculate this figure in exactly the same way as the average lead-time demand:

$$\text{buffer stock} = \frac{16\,000 \times 10}{365}$$
$$= 438 \text{ kg}$$

The reorder level (ROL) is equal to the sum of the average lead-time demand plus the buffer stock, i.e.

$$\text{ROL} = 789 + 438$$
$$= 1227 \text{ kg}$$

The reorder level specifies the level of stock at which the firm places its reorder quantity. In a continuous process such as that operated by Marchena, running out of stock could be disastrous. Equipment would have to be shut down, cleaned and reprimed when new stock becomes available – all of which could be very expensive. However, in other production situations a firm may be able to operate with lower buffer stocks and hence lower reorder levels, provided that some other process could take up the spare production capacity in the event of the necessary stocks running out.

The benefits of quantity discounts

Using the total annual stock-holding cost formula, given above, it is possible to calculate whether a quantity discount offered by a supplier is worthwhile. To do this we compare the total annual cost of holding the stock line without the discount against the total annual cost with the discount. We assume, for the first calculation, that the company uses the optimal reorder quantity as specified by the optimal reorder quantity formula; for the second calculation we use the reorder quantity required to earn the discount.

For example, Marchena's supplier is prepared to offer a 5% discount for all orders of 2750 kg or more. The total annual stock-holding cost formula was

$$\text{TAC} = (iQV)/2 + DF/Q$$

At the optimal reorder quantity of 2309 kg the total annual cost is given as

$$\text{TAC} = \frac{0.12 \times 2309 \times 10}{2} + \frac{16\,000 \times 200}{2309}$$
$$= £2771 \text{ per annum}$$

At the discounted order quantity of 2750 kg the total annual stock holding cost is given by

$$TAC = \frac{0.12 \times 2750 \times 9.5}{2} + \frac{16\,000 \times 200}{2750}$$
$$= £2731 \text{ per annum}$$

The effect of the discount is marginally favourable as it reduces the total annual cost by £40.

Two-bin stock-holding systems

The method of stock control outlined above lends itself quite naturally to a very simple, and effective, physical control system known as the 'two-bin system'. The stock is held in two containers or 'bins'; the first is filled to the reorder level and the second is filled with the remainder of the reorder quantity.

Withdrawals from stock are made from the second container, and as soon as it is emptied a new order is raised. Withdrawals are then made from the first, reserve container, until the new stock is delivered. Before the new delivery arrives the contents of the reserve container should be transferred to the second container (to avoid build-up of obsolete stock). When the new stock is delivered, the reserve container is filled first and any remainder then added to the old stock in the second container. With automatic feed containers such a dual container system as we have described may be too costly. If that is the case, the stock controllers will either have to take frequent measurements of stock level or fit some automatic level meter.

The valuation of stock

Raw-material stocks can be valued in one of two ways:

- on the basis of current market value;
- on the basis of the original cost of purchase.

For all normal decision-making purposes the first is the only relevant valuation basis if 'current market value' is the same as the opportunity cost of the stock item in use. We discussed the opportunity cost concept in detail in Chapters 7 and 8. However, in practice, stock is usually valued on the basis of one of several original-cost valuation methods. There can be some important reasons why this type of valuation basis is used, even though it is strictly irrelevant for decision-making purposes.

- The taxation authorities specify that stock should be valued using the original cost of purchase.
- The rate of turnover of certain stock may be so fast that there is no significant difference between the historical and the current market value of that stock.
- Historical cost is still the main basis for preparing accounts for external users.

A historical-cost valuation basis may be necessary for financial control purposes. If stock is valued at its original cost, it should be possible for the firm to reconcile its cash payments for raw materials during the year with the original cost of the stock used during the year and the difference between the opening and closing stock values.

The last point may be of considerable importance to a firm in determining stock wastages and losses and in keeping a check on cash movements.

We will discuss three bases for historical-cost stock valuation:

- first in first out (FIFO);
- last in first out (LIFO);
- average cost.

During the course of a firm's financial year its stock movements can be described as in Figure 27.10.

The FIFO system assumes that stock purchased first is used first leaving stock acquired last on hand at the end of the year. Note that this stock flow is only an assumption for stock-valuation purposes and need not necessarily coincide with physical stock flows.

EXAMPLE

Marchena plc purchased a chemical 'alpha-sludge' in six batches during the course of a year. The purchases and usages were as shown in Table 27.3. There was no stock of alpha-sludge at the beginning of the year; 3000 tons of the chemical were in stock at the end of the year.

Using a FIFO basis, the 8390 tons of stock which were used during the year would be valued as follows:

1800 tons at a price per ton of 4.50	8 100.00
2240 tons at a price per ton of 4.50	10 080.00
1000 tons at a price per ton of 4.60	4 600.00
3250 tons at a price per ton of 4.85	15 762.50
100 tons at a price per ton of 5.00	500.00
Total cost of used stock	39 042.50

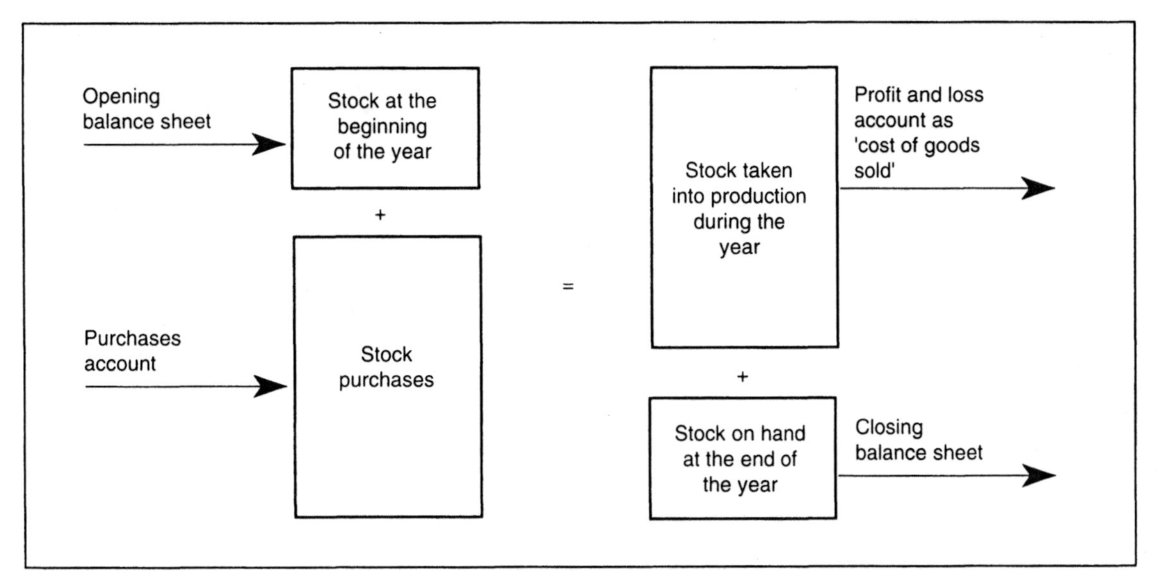

Figure 27.10 Stock movements in the financial accounts.

Table 27.3

	Purchases (tons)	Purchase price per ton (£)	Total cost (£)	Usage (tons)
1 Jan.	1 800	4.50	8 100	
16 Jan.				9 000
28 Feb.	2 240	4.50	10 080	
3 Mar.				20 000
30 Apr.	1 000	4.60	4 600	
27 Aug.	3 250	4.85	15 763	
29 Aug.				2 590
28 Sept.	1100	5.00	5 500	1 400
13 Oct.				
28 Dec.	2 000	5.25	10 500	
30 Dec.				1 500
	11 390		54 543	34 490

The remaining stock at the end of the year is valued as follows:

1000 tons at a price per ton of £5.00	£5 000.00
2000 tons at a price per ton of £5.25	£10 500.00
Total stock value at year end	£15 500.00 (FIFO)

The LIFO system assumes that stock used at any particular point in time is valued on the basis that it was the most recently purchased. In order to use the LIFO basis we need to know the pattern of usage of stock so that we can identify the most recent price applicable at the time of use. On a LIFO basis, therefore, we would value the stock used and the stock on hand at the end of the year, as shown below. Follow the numbers in Figure 27.11 through very carefully. Note that any usages in a given period are valued at the most recent price available.

Under the LIFO basis of stock valuation:

The value of stock used in the period	£40 442
The value of stock on hand at 31 December	£14 101
Total	£54 543

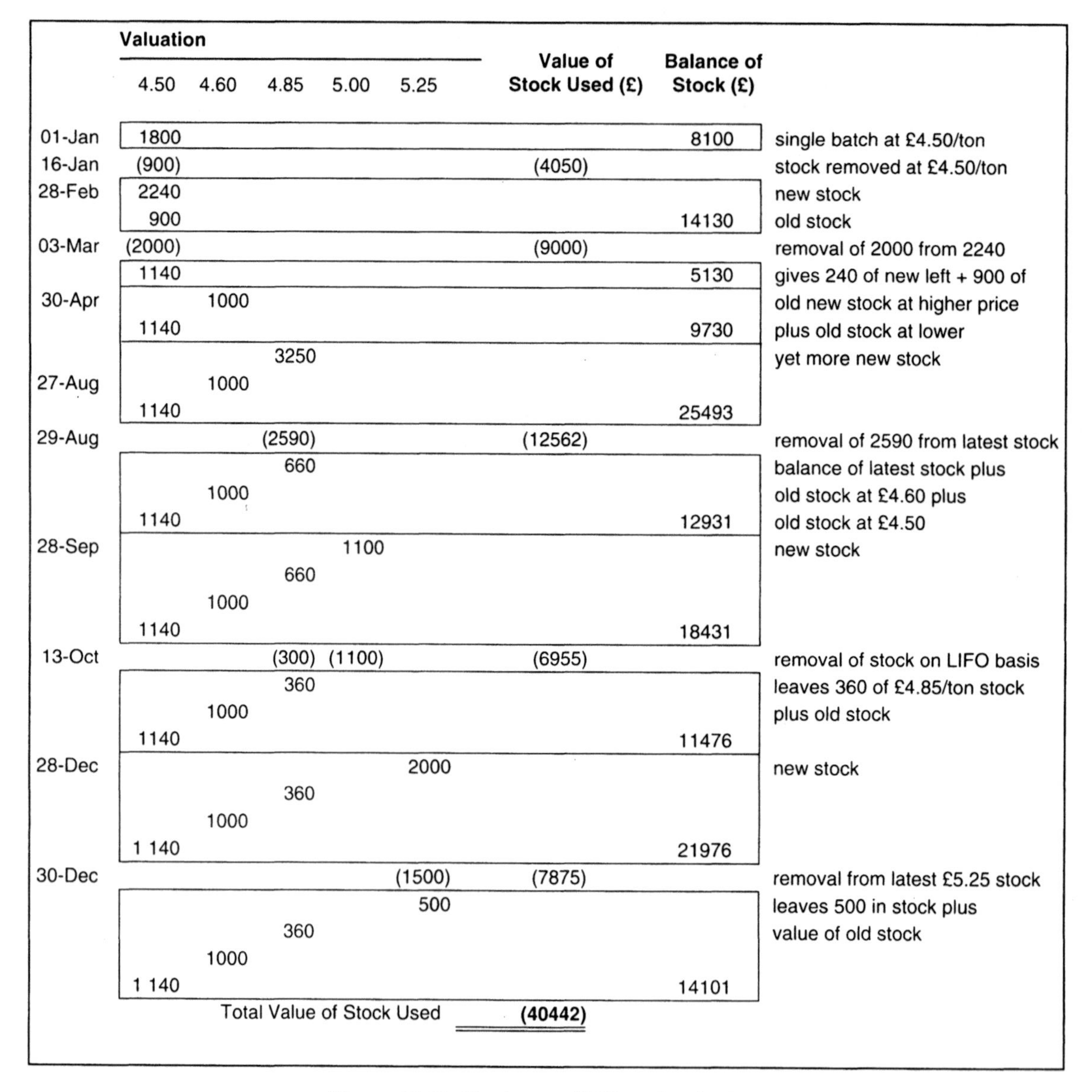

	Valuation 4.50	4.60	4.85	5.00	5.25	Value of Stock Used (£)	Balance of Stock (£)	
01-Jan	1800						8100	single batch at £4.50/ton
16-Jan	(900)					(4050)		stock removed at £4.50/ton
28-Feb	2240							new stock
	900						14130	old stock
03-Mar	(2000)					(9000)		removal of 2000 from 2240
	1140						5130	gives 240 of new left + 900 of
30-Apr		1000						old new stock at higher price
	1140						9730	plus old stock at lower
			3250					yet more new stock
27-Aug		1000						
	1140						25493	
29-Aug			(2590)			(12562)		removal of 2590 from latest stock
			660					balance of latest stock plus
		1000						old stock at £4.60 plus
	1140						12931	old stock at £4.50
28-Sep				1100				new stock
			660					
		1000						
	1140						18431	
13-Oct			(300)	(1100)		(6955)		removal of stock on LIFO basis
			360					leaves 360 of £4.85/ton stock
		1000						plus old stock
	1140						11476	
28-Dec					2000			new stock
			360					
		1000						
	1 140						21976	
30-Dec					(1500)	(7875)		removal from latest £5.25 stock
					500			leaves 500 in stock plus
			360					value of old stock
		1000						
	1 140						14101	
	Total Value of Stock Used					**(40442)**		

Figure 27.11 Marchena – LIFO stock valuation.

The difficulty with the LIFO method is that each usage must be valued according to the prices attaching to the latest arrivals. On 13th October, for example, stock of 1400 tons was used which was valued at £5 for for the first 110 tons (the latest arrival) and at £4.85 for the remaining 300 tons which was deemed to have arrived (for valuation purposes) on 27 August. Unlike the FIFO method, the use of the LIFO method entails keeping a precise account of the movements of stock in and out of the stock account and the prices at which purchases are made.

The average stock method prices stock withdrawals at the average cost of stock on hand prior to the withdrawal (Table 27.4). Purchases (i) are added to the balance of stock (iv) in tons and priced at their input price (ii) for addition to the stock value (vi). The average cost (v) is computed by dividing the stock value (vi) by the balance in tons. The average cost is then used to price withdrawals from stock as they occur.

We can now summarise these three valuation methods as shown in Table 27.5.

The FIFO system uses the most recent cost as its

Table 27.4

	Purchases (tons) (i)	Price (£) (ii)	Withdrawals (tons) (iii)	Balance (tons) (iv)	Average (£) (v)	Balance value (£) (vi)	Value of stock used (£) (vii)
01 Jan.	1800	4.50		1800	4.500	8 100	
16 Jan.			900	900	4.500	4 050	4 050
28 Feb.	2240	4.50		3140	4.500	14 130	
03 Mar.			2000	1140	4.500	5 130	9000
30 Apr.	1000	4.60		2140	4.547	9 730	
27 Aug.	3250	4.85		5390	4.730	25 493	
29 Aug.			2590	2800	4.730	13 243	12 250
28 Sept.	1100	5.00		3900	4.806	18 743	
13 Oct.			1400	2500	4.806	12 015	6 729
28 Dec.	2000	5.25		4500	5.003	22 515	
30 Dec.			1500	3000	5.003	15 010	7 505
			8390				35 483

Table 27.5

	FIFO (£)	LIFO (£)	Average cost (£)
Cost of stock as shown in the profit and loss account	39 043	40 442	39 534
Valuation of stock on hand as shown in the balance sheet	15 500	14 101	15 009
Total cost of purchased stock	54 543	54 543	54 543

valuation base for year-end stock, but out-of-date costs for the valuation of stock consumed during the year. In a situation of rising costs, therefore, the value of stock in the balance sheet will approximate current cost (because the most recent purchase prices of stock are used) while the cost of stock in the profit and loss account will be at a lower value. Because accounting profit is given as sales revenue less the cost of the resources used (including stock consumed in production) FIFO will tend to overstate that profit in a period of rising prices. Exactly the reverse holds for the LIFO system, which uses a closer approximation to current cost in computing the profit and loss account figures.

Of the three methods, LIFO charges the closest to the current cost in calculating profit but shows an undervalued closing stock figure in the balance sheet. The average-cost method combines the advantages and disadvantages of both FIFO and LIFO in that, in a situation of rising prices, it tends to overstate both accounting profit and understate the current value of stock held at the balance-sheet date. However, all three systems suffer from the disadvantage that the numbers they produce, while being objectively verifiable, have no economic significance, as all three involve the aggregation of costs acquired at different points in time.

CONTROL OF CASH

In most firms, cash is not held for its own sake, as an item of stock (banks are, of course, an important exception to this). For most firms, cash is a 'residual' of its operations and the amount held at any point in time will vary as trading activity varies. We have already described how the timing of payments from debtors and to creditors can strongly influence cash flow. Some other important influences upon cash flow are as follows:

- The seasonality of a firm's trading pattern: with most consumer goods peak demand comes in the pre-Christmas season; with travel services there is usually a peak in demand in early spring; in the energy supply industry demand is at its highest in the winter months. We would normally expect to find the peak in cash flows following behind the peak in demand. The actual lag between demand, sale and cash inflow will depend upon the firm's terms of trade.
- There may be seasonal elements in a firm's cash outflows which are quite independent of the cycle of demand. For example:

  (i) seasonal office and plant heating bills;
  (ii) fixed interest charges on debt capital;
  (iii) profit taxes which are paid to the Inland Revenue at the time specified by law;
  (iv) dividends to investors.

All of these items, and more, will form part of any cash budget. If the firm has high seasonality in its cash budget it may well benefit from diversification into areas of operation which will help to smooth its cash flows from one month to another. Consider the problems of a travel company specialising in summer sun holidays. Such a company would do well to diversify its business interests in the winter sports or winter sun market, although there may well be problems setting up in such a new market with different hotels, venues, etc. If successful, the winter sports business would produce cash flows which would 'countervary' with its primary specialisation. The overall effect will be, of course, to diversify away some of the variability associated with the single line of business.

In general, cash flows can be controlled by a mixture of the following methods:

- altering the incidence of payments, where management has some control over its timing (dividends and bonus payments are good examples of this);
- seeking the most favourable credit policies;
- optimising the holding of stocks and work in progress;
- making sure that cash does not lie idle for any length of time (it may be that short-term cash surpluses can be placed on deposit with a bank or in some other short-term investment);
- seeking diversification into new areas which complement the firm's existing pattern of cash flows.

CONCLUSION

In this chapter we have examined the issues of controlling the short-term resources of the firm through stock, debtors and cash. Through a careful examination of the problems of feedback and feedforward control we have identified certain common issues which affect all control problems. Our subsequent discussion has been concerned with the formal methods which are available for such control.

Part VI

Measuring and Interpreting Financial Performance

Chapter 28

Basic Financial Reporting Concepts

Level E

Contents

Summary

In this chapter we consider why cash accounts differ from commitment accounts and how the accruals concept leads to a generically different form of reporting statement. We then turn to the issues of stewardship and performance measurement and see how these management issues are resolved within financial accounting. Finally, we round off our discussion with an analysis of the difference between objective and subjective information and some other accounting concepts assumed by financial accountants as they go about their task. In this chapter we slip from the formal third person to the first person singular to emphasise the personal basis (and relevance of the ideas) presented here.

INTRODUCTION

It may be that this chapter is the first you are reading in this book. It is not unusual for managers to be preoccupied with financial accounts and to view them as the most important part of the accountant's black art. In order to give you a rapid insight into the fundamentals of financial reporting, this chapter draws upon some very simple domestic accounting insights to explain the issues involved in preparing cash, commitment and accrual accounts. In this chapter we introduce, using a very simple domestic example, the difference between cash, commitment and accrual accounts.

In Chapter 4 we introduced the idea that a commitment representing an agreement between two parties to transfer economic value was fundamental to the idea of strategic accounting. From that basis we showed that cash changes for the individual or firm resulted as a consequence of the completion of those commitments. In Chapter 6 we moved on to look at problems of measuring business performance and, in particular, the central role of the accrual concept in achieving that end. In our scheme of things an accounting system which recorded commitments would be the most fundamental with cash accounting forming a derivative of commitment accounting. Only when commitment and cash accounts have been prepared would the basis be made for the preparation of statements of period performance using the accruals concept.

In practice, most small and medium-sized businesses (and individuals) record cash transactions as their primary financial activity. From that, they proceed direct to statement of profit and loss and a balance sheet using the accruals principle. We will compromise between what we argue is the correct approach and show, using a familiar domestic example, how a cash account can be created, followed by an account of commitments. Finally, we demonstrate how a set of accrual accounts can be prepared from commitment and cash accounting data. To personalise the example we will consider a personal example of how I do (or should) keep my own domestic accounts.

CASH ACCOUNTS

The simplest way to understand cash accounts is to consider your own financial affairs. If you are a salaried employee, you will receive cash from salary payments and you will make a variety of cash payments during the course of (say) a month. For these purposes we will deem cash receipts and payments to be:

- direct cash receipts and payments in notes and coin;
- receipts and payments by cheque or standing order into, or from, your bank account;
- debit card transactions, resulting in direct credits or withdrawals to, or from, your bank account.

Credit card transactions are not deemed to be cash transactions. However, the settlement of a credit card account by cheque is a cash transaction.

In the statement shown in Table 28.1 we show a record of personal receipts and payments in a simple three-column cash book. In this account we show the cash balance brought forward from the previous month. To that is added a salary receipt, and then a series of cheque (ch) payments, standing orders (so) and debit (Switch) card (sw) are deducted giving a running balance on the account. Now if all cheques and other payments shown above are cleared by the bank, then the bank statement for June should show a balance of £675 at the end of the month. There will rarely be perfect congruence between a personal cash account and a bank statement because:

- cheques and payments made by debit card may not be presented to the bank by the recipient by the period end;
- cash receipts shown in the bank statement may not appear in the personal cash statement and vice versa (for a variety of reasons) by the period end.

A reconciliation may be required between a bank statement and a cash account at the end of the period:

Balance as per bank statement
less cheques drawn in cash book but not presented
credits shown in bank statement not entered in cash book*
plus credits shown in cash book not cleared into the bank statement
charges shown in bank statement not entered in cash book*
= the balance as per the cash book

However, in practice, once the reconciliation is complete the cash book should be adjusted for the items starred above.

Table 28.1 Domestic cash account.

	My Account as a Cash Book			June 19xx	
			Expenses	Income	Balance
1 Jun.	Cash balance brought forward	c		220	220
1 Jun.	Salary	ch		2000	2220
3 Jun.	Cash drawn	ch	40		2180
5 Jun.	GreenPeace	so	20		2160
5 Jun.	Insurance	so	110		2050
7 Jun.	Sainsbury's	sw	55		1995
10 Jun.	Poll Tax	so	27		1968
10 Jun.	Access	ch	330		1638
10 Jun.	Dillons	sw	25		1613
15 Jun.	Cash drawn	ch	40		1573
15 Jun.	Sainsbury's	sw	85		1488
22 Jun.	Cash drawn	ch	50		1438
22 Jun.	Sainsbury's	sw	78		1360
23 Jun.	Mortgage	so	485		875
29 Jun.	Sainsbury's	sw	100		775
29 Jun.	TV Licence	ch	100		675

UPGRADING TO A COMMITMENT ACCOUNTING SYSTEM

One of the great conveniences of modern life is plastic money. Access, Visa or other charge cards greatly simplify the problems of payments. However, in my experience, the principal problem with them is keeping track of expenditures and determining the magnitude of my commitments against my income. To solve this problem I use a 'commitment accounting system' for my domestic affairs, which includes on the payments side all of the expenditures I actually make, including all credit card transactions (Table 28.2).

Note, however, that I do not include the current period's cash payment to Access because that is not a commitment expenditure made in the current period, it is a cash expenditure incurred because of commitments I have made in the previous period.

In practice, I do not operate a full commitments system because I take the somewhat cautious approach of only counting income on a cash basis, but recognising expenditure on a commitment basis.

However, the principle of commitment accounts should be clear from this example – namely that the value changes on transactions are only deemed to occur when the contractual commitment to that transaction is made. We will explore the full application of this idea to corporate accounts in a later chapter.

ACCRUAL ACCOUNTS

The commitment accounting system described above is designed to show my financial position at any point in time. As an individual it offers me important information in that I can work out the amount of uncommitted income at any point in time and adjust my spending accordingly.

However, I might wish to estimate what my monthly surplus is if some of my lump sum expenditures were spread over the months in which I enjoyed the benefits of the transactions they represent (Table 28.3). In this example I have identified two items: the purchase of a suit and a TV licence as commitments in the month of June which will yield me benefits in the following months. For this reason I have only counted one-twelfth of the TV licence and one-sixth of the suit as costs for the period. I have assumed that I will wear the suit out progressively over 12 months and that my TV

Table 28.2 Domestic commitment account.

	My Account as Commitments		June 19xx		
			Expenses	Income	Balance
1 Jun.	Surplus brought forward			145	145
1 Jun.	Salary	ch		2000	2145
3 Jun.	Cash drawn	ch	40		2105
3 Jun.	Petrol	ac	22		2083
5 Jun.	GreenPeace	so	20		2063
5 Jun.	Insurance	so	110		1953
7 Jun.	Sainsbury's	sw	55		1898
10 Jun.	Poll Tax	so	27		1871
10 Jun.	Dillons	sw	25		1846
12 Jun.	Petrol	ac	23		1823
15 Jun.	Cash drawn	ch	40		1783
15 Jun.	Sainsbury's	sw	85		1698
16 Jun.	Restaurant	ac	35		1663
22 Jun.	Petrol	ac	22		1641
22 Jun.	Cash drawn	ch	50		1591
22 Jun.	Sainsbury's	sw	78		1513
23 Jun.	Mortgage	so	485		1028
24 Jun.	Petrol	ac	28		1000
28 Jun.	Suit Co.	ac	188		812
29 Jun.	Sainsbury's	sw	100		712
29 Jun.	TV Licence	ch	100		612

Table 28.3 Domestic accrual account

My Profit and Loss Account			June 19xx
Salary	actual		2000
less:			
Mortgage	actual	485	
Property maintenance	accrual	22	
Poll Tax	actual	27	
Insurance	accrual	9	
Food	actual	318	
Charitable giving	actual	20	
Car depreciation	accrual	36	
Petrol	actual	95	
Suit	accrual	31	
TV licence	accrual	8	
Misc. expenses	actual	130	
Books	actual	25	
Total expenses			1207
Monthly profit			793

watching is uniform over the 12 months of the year. I could be pedantic and say that because I watch little TV in the summer and a lot in the winter that the monthly charge for the licence should reflect that. Two new charges have appeared in the above account for costs which were neither discharged in cash or committed during the month: these were property maintenance and car depreciation. These costs had been incurred some time previously and were being depreciated equally over the period covered by the maintenance payment and the life of the car respectively.

Profit may be defined as the surplus earned on our committed income after all costs fairly attributable to the generation of that income have been deducted. In a domestic setting the concept of 'profit' has little meaning because the income I earn is not, by and large, determined by the expenditures I make. Rather, my expenditures are determined by the amount of income I earn. In a business setting, the concept of profit does have some meaning in that it provides some measure of the economic performance of the business in converting the resources it consumes into revenues.

The meaning of the accruals concept

In Chapter 6 we formally introduced the 'accruals' concept or 'matching' principle as it is sometimes referred to. In the last section we informally deployed the accruals concept in allocating costs to the month of June in my domestic accounts even though that cost was matched by neither a cash expenditure or a commitment. The accruals concept is, however, fundamental to the basis of accounting for performance measurement because it allows value flows to be used as an indicator of business efficiency.

There are three fundamental motives behind the preparation of accounts:

(i) the stewardship motive;
(ii) the performance measurement motive;
(iii) the performance prediction motive.

It is sometimes said that accounts are important in the valuation process, but for reasons we will see later, accounting estimates of value are a by-product of performance measurement.

'Stewardship' is an important function both within classical and modern management practice. Throughout history 'the steward' was seen as the custodian of the goods of the household and in both New and Old Testament writings stewards featured as individuals in whom trust was placed (and who frequently abused it). The contemporary emphasis on trust, quality and the contractual liabilities and responsibilities of agents places a premium on accurate, timely and verifiable information on the disposition of the stakeholders' assets. Accounting information for stewardship purposes is different in kind to that required for performance (valuation) or prediction purposes.

In managing my domestic affairs I need a system of measuring my liquidity from day to day. I could ask for a daily bank statement, but a much more efficient way of achieving the same level of surveillance of my domestic affairs is to create and maintain a simple cash book. I can easily pick up errors (both mine and the bank's) and keep an eye on my general patterns of expenditure. However, the ease with which I can make financial commitments on credit naturally leads me to a system of personal accounting where I can constantly monitor the level of my uncommitted income. This is more than adequate as a means of domestic accounting, as it offers me all the levels of control that I need over my financial affairs.

Cash-based and commitment accounting are characterised by:

(i) objectivity;
(ii) simplicity.

Because they offer a high degree of objectivity in measurement (and are thus efficient in picking up errors and discrepancies with the bank in my personal case), both methods are in practice simple to use. Simplicity is a great virtue in any information system, in that clear and precise information can be seen for what it is and its value for any given decision making environment determined.

Because cash accounts focus on a critical issue in my domestic management – my liquidity – they provide me with useful information which I can use to make judgements about the timing and sequencing of my cash receipts and payments. The simple cash account, operated side by side with a commitment account allows me to regulate my spending against a (relatively) fixed level of income.

For a business, cash and commitment accounts can perform exactly the same function in permitting the monitoring of the liquidity of the business and in allowing management to make sensible expenditure decisions. However, they do not allow us to form a clear judgement about the performance of management in converting resources in a given period into revenue. As we discussed in Chapter 6, this is the nub of the accruals concept. The accruals concept requires management to estimate the amount of resources consumed in a period in the process of earning revenue. The accruals concept allows us to create a 'profitability' measure from which the power of the business's cash engine can be determined.

Consider the situation where a business converts units of a single stock item into sales (Figure 28.1).

Each unit of materials costs £40 (throughout the year) and all units are sold at price of £80 per unit.

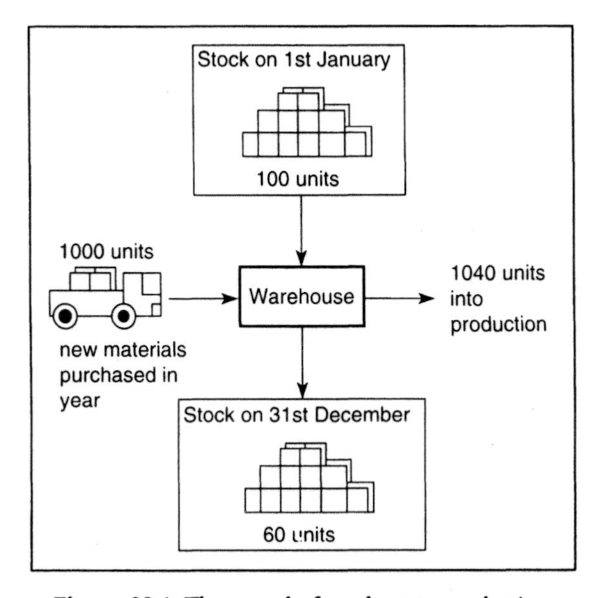

Figure 28.1 The accrual of purchases to production.

All units produced during the year in question are sold.

The cost of stock to production is therefore

$$(1000 + 100 - 60) \times £40 = £41\,600$$

We have accrued, as an expense against income, the cost of the stock which we believe has been consumed in production. The expenditure is 'matched' to the period in which it is used in earning income.

Clearly, in this case, the cost of the goods sold is easy to determine, and there is little room for argument about the application of the matching principle. However, not all resources are like stock (which can be physically matched against sales in a given period). Some, such as plant and equipment, are not smoothly used up in production throughout the years of their life, and judgements about the life of these assets will be subjective. In a later chapter we will explore the application of the accrual principle in much more detail, and consider how accounting judgements influence the measurement of business performance.

OBJECTIVE AND SUBJECTIVE JUDGEMENTS

We have used the terms 'objective' and 'subjective' somewhat freely in this chapter. Generally, we classify information as falling along a certainty–uncertainty spectrum (Figure 28.2).

Subjective information is high entropy information, in that there is considerable uncertainty concerning both its content and its interpretation. The accruals concept adds uncertainty to our interpretation of accounting information and, as we shall see in a later chapter, this has an impact upon the value of that information.

There is much argument amongst philosophers over whether information can ever be truly objective. In an accounting context, however, the problem is fairly easy to resolve: if two or more independent accountants, using an agreed convention for classifying revenues and expenditures, arrive at the same result from a given source of data, then the information so produced can be said to be objective. If, on the other hand, they are required to make judgements of interpretation and allocation, then the information will be subjective. Cash and commitment accounts tend towards the objective end of the spectrum, accrual accounting towards the subjective end.

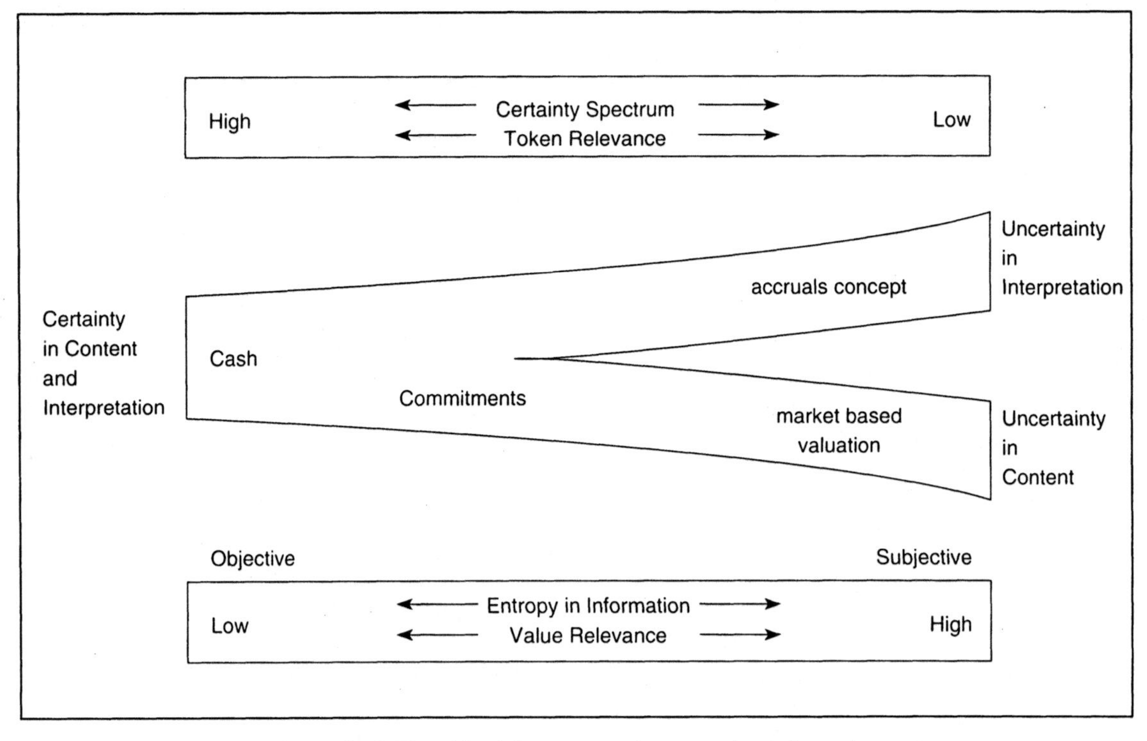

Figure 28.2 The objectivity spectrum in accounting information.

SOME EXAMPLES OF THE ACCRUALS CONCEPT IN FINANCIAL ACCOUNTING

Case 1. Depreciation

A company purchased a machine for £80 000 in 1989 which was expected to last 10 years before replacement. Its scrap value in 1999 should just equal the cost of dismantling and disposal.

Charge for expenditure in each year for the
machine = 80 000/10 = £8000

Assumptions:

- life expectancy is reasonable at 10 years;
- asset's value consumed equally over the life of the machine;
- price level is stable, i.e. £8000 of consumed asset value in 1999 is the same as £8000 of consumed asset value in 1989.

Case 2. Revenue accrual

A sailing school operates four-week courses for which it charges £600 per place. Seventy-five places were taken up and fees received at the beginning of the last week in July. The school's accounting year ends on 31 July.

Total revenue = 75 × £600 = £40 000

Revenue accruing to the old year
= £40 000/4 = £10 000

Revenue accruing to the new year
= £40 000 − £10 000 = £30 000

Assumption: the service, and the expenditure which the school incurs is spread evenly over the four years. Would your basis for accrual be different if you discovered that the boats used for training would only be paid for after the whole course had finished?

Case 3. Business rate

A company paid its annual charge for business rates on 30 April of £72 000. Its accounting year end falls on 31 July.

Accrual to old year for business rates paid on
30 April = 3/12 × 72 000 = £18 000

This accrual will be added to the accrued rates from the previous year to obtain the total rate for the year.

Assumption: the usage of local authority services is spread evenly throughout the trading year. This may be realistic if the business's pattern of trade is smooth throughout the year.

Case 4. Pre-acquisition profits

A company purchased an existing business on 1 July 19xx. At the end of the financial year on 31 December 19xx, the profits of the business acquired stood at £14 000.

Using the accruals principle, half of those profits (£7000) are added to the profit of the new enlarged company and half would be counted as part of the owner's capital acquired on 1 July.

Assumption: the profits of the acquired business were accumulated evenly throughout the accounting year.

SOME OTHER ACCOUNTING CONCEPTS

In practice, accountants abide by some other concepts or principles.

Prudence

Generally, accountants will make prudent or 'conservative' judgements when interpreting economic events. If a cost is likely to arise, then account-ants will 'recognise' it either as a direct charge against income, a provision or a contingent liability. Similarly, they take a somewhat sceptical view towards revenue, only recognising income when a commitment to receive it has been contracted.

Consistency

In the preparation of financial accounts, the accountant will endeavour to use the same conventions in preparing information in one period as used in previous periods. If a change is made, normally the impact of that change will be noted in the accounts. The rigorous application of this principle should, in theory at least, allow readers of accounts to determine the relative performance of a business as far as its individual costs and revenues are concerned. Unfortunately, although this principle is rarely overtly broken in published company accounts, it often requires forensic skills of analysis to understand the implications of the changes which are noted in the accounts.

Going concern

Generally, the accountant will assume that a business is a going concern when he or she prepares the accounts, unless there is clear reason for believing otherwise. Once there is a belief that the business may fail, the prudence principle takes over and the values of assets and stocks are written down to their immediate resale value and revenues discounted, unless there is clear evidence that they will actually be received.

CONCLUSION

You should now understand the difference between a simple cash account, a commitment account and accruals account. The cash account simply identifies value flows as occurring when the cash receipt or payment occurs. Commitment accounting identifies that value change as occurring when the commitment is received (for revenue) or made for expenditures. Accrual accounting takes away from the relatively certain world of cash flows or contractual commitments and into the world of matching expenditures against attributable revenues in a period. It is a world of assumptions and judgements – a world where the test of a cost is not its 'truth' but rather the 'fairness' with which it has been allocated.

The examples used in this chapter have been deliberately simple in order to offer you an intuitive understanding of the fundamental differences between these accounting systems. In the chapters which follow, we will explore the more substantial issues of business accounting and how accounting systems can be developed to solve the information needs of managers and other users.

Chapter 29

Commitment Accounts

Level E

Contents

Summary

In this chapter we will discuss how commitment accounts differ from cash accounts in practice. In particular we stress that commitment accounts are designed to show how much resource remains uncommitted at the end of a given financial period. To do this we concentrate on two important financial values: (i) the cleared position, which tells us what the cash level of the business would be if all receivables and payables were discharged at the year end; and (ii) given the net realisable value of all the organisational assets including the cleared position, what the level of uncommitted resource would be if all of the commitments of the business (including long-term loans) were discharged at the year end.

INTRODUCTION

A cash statement assumes that changes in economic value occur when cash changes occur. However, from Chapter 4, we know that value changes occur not when a cash change occurs, but rather when a legal commitment is engaged. This introduces the notion of 'receivables' and 'payables' into our accounting framework and leads to the concept of an outstanding 'list of balances' representing commitments outstanding not matched by cash receipts or payments. 'Commitment accounting' is the name of the system of accounting where value changes follow contractual commitments to sales or expenditures, rather than just the consequential cash flows.

Cash accounts have many virtues for management decision making, in that they focus attention upon the most critical financial aspects of any business, namely the strength of its cash engine and the proficiency of management in promoting and controlling the efficiency of that engine. However, it can be argued that external users of accounting information need more information than that provided by cash accounts. External users are not privy to the contractual information possessed by management in terms of sale and purchase agreements, nor are they aware, on the basis of cash accounts alone, of the receivables and payables which those agreements entail. It is this problem which commitment accounts are designed to surmount.

Commitment accounts are based upon a different principle to cash accounts. Cash accounts assume that value changes occur when cash is received or paid, commitment accounts assume that the value change occurs when the legal commitment to a purchase or sale is contracted. This principle of 'contracted commitments' super-sets the principle of 'cash completion' defined in Chapter 4.

Commitment accounts offer an objective statement of the financial position of a business and eliminate any discretion in the preparation of the information concerned, except in as far as commitments can be aggregated and classified under different headings. Indeed, unlike cash accounts and the opportunity cost principle discussed in earlier parts of this book, commitment accounts provide a straightforward rule for identifying when value changes occur, namely the point at which legally enforceable commitment is entered into. In this sense, the rules for determining who or what is the decision-making entity for accountability purposes is somewhat simplified.

Commitment accounts are not used for external reporting by such organisations as local authorities and grant-funded bodies for the following reasons.

- There is a mistaken view that accrual accounts can, through the profit measure, reflect the performance of all organisations.
- Commitment accounts are easy to understand and prepare, they minimise subjective interpretations of fact and, for this reason, do not lend themselves to manipulation (for good or bad ends), as do accrual accounts.
- The professional and other regulatory bodies have developed a huge (we use the word deliberately) body of law, standards and practices around accrual accounts to the point where a high degree of professional expertise is required to produce them to statutory standards. There is little professional interest in lobbying for a simpler approach to financial reporting.
- In the popular Western culture the profit and loss account has become the epitome of the business approach to public service organisations. In the UK, for example, there has been a tendency to appoint 'mature' business managers to the boards of public sector bodies. Their experience has usually been gathered through the interpretation of standard accrual accounts. There is also a confusion between operating public sector organisations as businesses and operating them in a business-like way.

Many organisations do use commitment accounts internally, especially in the public sector and education. For internal accountability purposes the issue of when a commitment is created can be more difficult especially where devolved organisational structures are involved. Intra-organisational transactions, both horizontally and vertically, may represent binding commitments on those parts of the organisation affected, but in the consolidation of intra-group accounts those commitments on internal transfers will disappear.

DIFFERENCES BETWEEN COMMITMENT AND CASH ACCOUNTS

Normal business practice recognises that a contractual commitment arises when a verbal agreement to purchase or to sell a service or a product is made, except in the case of land transfers, which must be evidenced in writing. When a business manager enters into a verbal agreement with a customer to supply a particular good for a stated price, a legally enforceable contract has been established. It is normal, however, for such verbal agreement to be evidenced by a purchase order or for the customer to offer an order number.

Few non-retail business transactions are made directly for cash, and as a result an 'outstanding' will be created:

- outstanding sales create 'debtor' balances (sometimes known as 'receivables');
- outstanding purchases create 'creditor' balances (sometimes known as 'payables').

Generally, an increase in debtor balances represents a loss of liquidity to the firm. whilst a decrease will increase liquidity. With creditors, the converse is true: an increase in creditor balances will increase liquidity, whilst a reduction will decrease liquidity. In Table 29.1, we show the case where a company, which is making constant monthly sales of £1000 per month, and in the second month were to either increase or decrease the average age for the recovery of its debtor balances by one month from its current credit period of two months. Its purchases are £500 per month and are paid for one month after receipt of the goods.

Changes in credit policy can have a significant impact upon the liquidity of a business and, as we see in Table 29.1, can change the cash stock of the business by the full value of its monthly sales. The cash accounts reveal the impact of these changes on the liquidity of the business but they give no indications of the future cash changes implicit in the contractual commitments the business has already made.

Some particular points to note are as follows.

(i) The surplus of £500 is not a measure of performance against sales in a given month. The value for purchases is the value of the contractual commitments entered into for the supply of materials in that period and is independent of whether or not those materials were actually used in production during that period.

Table 29.1 The impact of credit policy changes upon liquidity

	Credit terms extended by one month						Credit terms reduced by one month					
Month	1	2	3	4	5	6	1	2	3	4	5	6
Sales	1000	1000	1000	1000	1000	1000	1000	1000	1000	1000	1000	1000
Purchases	−500	−500	−500	−500	−500	−500	−500	−500	−500	−500	−500	−500
Surplus	500	500	500	500	500	500	500	500	500	500	500	500
Sales receipts												
Month −2	1000						1000					
Month −1		1000						1000				
Month 1			1000						1000			
Month 2					1000				1000			
Month 3						1000				1000		
Month 4											1000	
Month 5												1000
Purchase payments												
Month −1	−500						−500					
Month 1		−500						−500				
Month 2			−500						−500			
Month 3				−500						−500		
Month 4					−500						−500	
Month 5						−500						−500
Net monthly cash flow	500	500	500	−500	500	500	500	500	1500	500	500	500
Cash difference	0	0	0	−1000	0	0	0	0	1000	0	0	0

(ii) Commitment accounts are objective in the contractual sense, in that two or more independent accountants would be able to come to the same aggregate value for surplus and outstanding in any period, given a particular set of transactions upon which to work.

(iii) Commitment accounts introduce the concept of a 'cleared position', i.e. the total liquidity of the business if all receivables were recovered immediately and all payables paid off.

THE CONSTRUCTION OF COMMITMENT ACCOUNTS

Commitment accounts take a different form to the conventional profit and loss account and balance sheet described in the next chapter. Two documents are involved:

- a statement of financial commitments engaged in the period which lead to a figure for the cleared position (this cleared position is what the year end cash balance would be *if* all receivables were received and all payables paid at the year end);
- a statement of financial position which shows the net resource available to the business at the year end if all commitments were discharged.

EXAMPLE

Jackson Products had the outstandings shown in Table 29.2 at the beginning of a year (opening outstandings), showing net cash movements and outstanding payables and receivables.

In addition, Jackson had fixed assets with an estimated net realisable value of £125 000 and stocks, again valued at their net realisable value of £14 000. A long-term loan was outstanding of £55 000. The cash position of the business at the beginning of the year was £2300.

We have used the same categorisation of flows as introduced in Chapter 7, except that our analysis introduces those balances which are contractually outstanding at the beginning and end of the period of account. The data in the above table have followed the normal practical situation where cash data are extracted from a cash book and opening and closing commitments are extracted from other records. It would, however, be possible to achieve the same result by listing the contracted completion value of all commitments engaged within a 12-month period.

We can, from the above raw data, calculate the contractual commitments for sales which Jackson

Table 29.2

Statement of financial commitments in the year ended 31 December 19xx

	Opening outstandings	Cash	End of period: Payable	End of period: Receivable
Activity flows:				
Sales	(15 000)	120 000		20 000
Purchases	5 000	(89 000)	(4000)	
Production flows:				
Factory overheads	500	(18 000)	(1000)	
Business flows:				
Expenses	600	(15 000)	(1000)	
Sale of fixed assets				25 000
Financing flows:				
Interest paid	0	(5 400)	(500)	
	(8 900)	(7 400)	(6500)	45 000
Add: cash balance brought forward		2 300		
Cash balance at year end		(5 100)		
Year end commitments			(6500)	45 000
Net outstandings		38 500 ←		
Cleared position		33 400		

engaged in during the year. At the beginning of the year £15 000 was outstanding. Cash receipts from customers were £120 000 of which, therefore, £105 000 was due from sales contracted during the year. The receivables at the end of the year of £20 000 would also have been generated by sales during the year, giving total sales contracted of £125 000. In other words:

Contracted income = cash income
plus (minus) any increase (decrease) in receivables

Conversely, the payables outstanding at the beginning of the year against purchases was £5000. The cash payments to suppliers were £89 000 and therefore new purchases made during the year *and* paid for were £84 000. The purchases unpaid at the end of the year were £4000 and so the purchases contracted during the year were £88 000. In other words, as with contracted income:

Contracted expenditure = cash expenditure
plus (minus) any increase (decrease) in payables

At the end of the year, by virtue of the contracts he has entered into, Jackson is entitled to cash receipts of £45 000 but is liable for £6500 of payables he has not, as yet, discharged. The value of £38 500 represents the net outstandings – that is, the amount of cash receivable by the businesses all of its outstanding commitments are discharged. The cleared position is therefore:

Cash brought forward from previous year	£2 300
Less: net cash paid out during year	(7 400)
Cash balance on account at year end	(£5 100)
Add: net outstanding commitments	£38 500
Cleared position when all commitments discharged	£33 400

THE INTERPRETATION OF COMMITMENT ACCOUNTS

The analysis of commitments also leads us to some useful ratios for measuring the dynamic efficiency of the business.

(i) Dynamic ratio (unadjusted)

End of year outstandings/absolute cleared position
= 38 500/abs(33 400)
= +1.153

If the net outstandings are very small relative to the cleared position then this indicates that the business is leaving little net cash outstanding. Generally, a small dynamic ratio close to zero is desirable although a high receivables figure exactly matched by high payables could also be indicated. The sign of the dynamic ratio also indicates the net direction of the imminent cash flows clearing the current year's commitments. A negative sign warns of cash outflows necessary to clear commitments whilst a positive sign promises inflows and a consequential improvement of liquidity. The larger the value the more pronounced the expected effect.

In order to interpret more clearly what is going on further ratios are necessary.

(ii) Debtor age (unadjusted) in days

(Receivables/contracted sales income in period) × 365 = (20 000/125 000) × 365 = 58.4 days

With this ratio we have only taken into account sales on the activity account and have excluded the sale of the fixed asset. The justification for this is that the sale of the fixed asset would be counted as an extraordinary item and its inclusion would distort the average period for which sales income was normally uncollected. If it were included, the debtor age would increase to (45 000/150 000) × 365 =109.5 days, which may be a severe distortion of the typical debtor age if (say) this fixed asset sale had been contracted near to the end of the account with the cash due for collection within a short period.

(iii) Creditor age (unadjusted) in days

(Payables/contracted expenditures in period) × 365 = (6500/127 800) × 365 = 18.6 days

With this ratio we have taken into account all contracted expenditures and the payables against them. You may wish to check that the sum of the contracted expenditures does in fact equal £127 000.

(iv) Absolute credit gap (unadjusted) in days

Debtor age − creditor age = 58.4 − 18.6 days = +39.8 days

Alternatively this can be shown as follows.

(v) Relative credit gap

Debtor age/creditor age = 58.4/18.6 = +3.14

This is a crude measure of the degree of imbalance in the credit terms offered by Jackson Products to its customers compared with that offered by its suppliers. This gap is used by financial controllers and credit managers as a quick guide to financial balance. It can, however, be misleading in that a net position of zero days could be achieved by (say) 90 days credit given on a very high sales turnover with 90 days taken on a very small level of expenditures. In other words, a zero credit gap might not be a sensible objective for a company earning high value added on relatively small input costs.

(vi) Cash interest cover

Net cash flow in period before interest/cash interest paid in period = (7400 + 5400)/5400 = 2.37

This ratio measures the degree of immediate financial risk faced by a business in discharging its committed financing costs. In this case, Jackson Products has over twice the required level of necessary resource required to fund its interest commitment. Clearly, however, this ratio cannot reveal the full exposure to financial risk if a commitment to capital repayment is imminent. For that we need to turn to a statement of financial position.

THE STATEMENT OF FINANCIAL POSITION UNDER COMMITMENT ACCOUNTING

Table 29.3 gives a clear statement of the organisation's uncommitted resources at the date of account. This document, unlike the statement of financial commitments during the period, does contain estimates of value which will be a matter of opinion in the absence of the actual sale of the fixed assets and stock concerned. However, we can ascertain a security ratio against the long-term loans:

Security ratio

$$= \frac{\text{net resources available upon liquidation}}{\text{long-term loan}}$$

$$= 172\,400/55\,000$$

$$= +3.135$$

Table 29.3

Fixed assets valued at net realisable value		£125 000
Stocks valued at net realisable value		14 000
Cleared position:		
cash brought forward from prior period	£2 300	
cleared position for the year	31 100	
		33 400
Net resources		£172 400
less: long-term loan		55 000
Net uncommitted resources to the owner's account		£117 400

Any value for this ratio which is greater than unity would indicate that the loan is fully covered. In this case the business has up to three times the resources required to discharge all of its outstanding commitments.

Jackson's cash position would not appear to be healthy, with a negative balance on cash account of £7400 at the year end. However, the cleared position at the year end does indicate that the cash position of the business will soon be rectified (assuming that all commitments are properly discharged). In order to analyse the company's overall position, it is necessary to estimate how much the assets of the business would realise on liquidation at the year end. When these values are added to the cleared position, we are in a much better position to determine the company's ability to discharge any long-term liabilities and hence its margin of free resource (£117 400 in this case) which can be released to exploit further opportunities. Year-by-year analysis of the cleared position and its uncommitted resource will give a clear indication of the changing financial strength of the business.

CONCLUSION

In this chapter we have examined the mechanics of creating a commitment account for a business, and identified some measurement statistics which are useful in interpreting them. We have stressed the objective nature of commitment accounts, and suggested that they are most useful in situations where a business needs to know how much uncommitted resource it has available for the future.

Chapter 30

Accrual Accounts

Level M

Contents

*Accrual versus Cash and Commitment Accounts * The Preparation of Accrual Accounts * The Balance Sheet Equation Method * The Extended Trial Balance Method * Computer-Based Accounting Systems*

Summary

In the previous chapters of this book we have discussed how transactions can be analysed, first in terms of their cash implications for the business, and second in terms of the contractual commitments which they entail. However, the financial accounts which companies produce as part of their external accountability (the profit and loss account and balance sheet) invoke a further principle which introduces a considerable degree of subjectivity into the analysis of those accounts. This principle is known as the 'accruals' or 'matching' principle, and it depends upon the fair matching of costs and revenues to the period in which they are deemed to have been incurred. In this chapter we will explore the implications of the accruals concept and how it transforms the significance of the accounting information which is produced. Finally we will examine the other principles which accountants deploy in preparing financial accounting information.

ACCRUAL VERSUS CASH AND COMMITMENT ACCOUNTS

In previous chapters we have examined the central role of cash and its management within the business. We have argued that cash is an objectively measurable commodity and that economic events only have significance for a business if those events change the committed status of the business and, through that, the current or potential cash stocks of the organisation.

However, financial accounts are based upon a different concept to either commitment or cash accounts. Financial accountants would argue that cash accounts are not an adequate representation of the affairs of a business. They would say that cash changes may not map directly onto the economic events of a business and that neither cash- or commitment-based accounts offer a measure of performance in a given period.

Figure 30.1 shows the relationship between cash, commitment and accrual accounts. We can summarise this as follows.

- *Cash accounts*: value changes occur only when cash changes occur.
- *Commitment accounts*: value changes occur when legal commitments are made.
- *Accrual accounts*: value changes are matched to the accounting period in which either revenue is deemed to have been earned or the resources consumed in earning that revenue.

Cash accounts are the primary accounting records of a business and, as we have already seen, they can be objectively verified as statements of what has actually occurred through the business's cash records.

Commitment accounts are rarely produced in commercial operations. However, given that a company keeps good records of its commercial transactions, they too can be objectively verified, although there may be differences in judgement about the collectability of certain debts or the impact of certain liabilities.

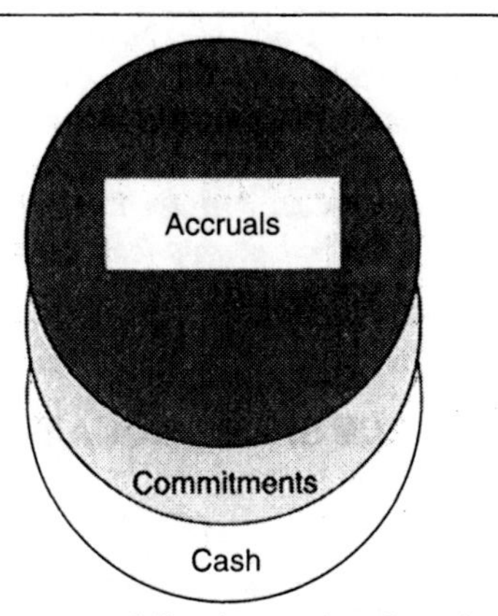

Note the net sum of all cash transations in a given year will equal the net sum of all contractual commitments engaged in that or during a prior period. The values within cash accounts and commitment accounts are simply 'time shifted'. Accrual accounts may contain value time shifts over a number of accounting periods (with, for example, the purchase of a machine and the subsequent charging of that expenditure as depreciation to subsequent periods). All we can say is that over the lifetime of a business (from incorporation to liquidation) the net sum of all transactions, whether on an accruals, commitment or cash basis, will equal one another.

Figure 30.1 The overlapping nature of cash, commitment and accrual accounts.

The transactions which any business may undertake result in a set of contractual commitments. These contractual commitments will result in a set of cash settlements by and with the business con-cerned (Table 30.1). For this reason, cash accounting is subordinate to commitment accounting. However:

- commitment accounting contains full information on contractual liabilities and claims, it does not fully reveal actual liquidity (cash changes);
- cash accounting reveals the liquidity of the business.

Table 30.1

Transactions ⟶	Commitments ⟶	Cash settlements ⟶	Accrued revenue and expenditure
Transaction lists	Contracted revenues and expenditures	Cash receipts and payments	Income account
List of assets	List of outstanding balances		List of unexpected balances (balance sheet)

The principle of accruals is designed to charge costs *fairly* to periods in which revenue is earned. When the auditor of a set of company accounts prepares a report on the veracity of a set of accounts, he or she will determine whether those accounts show a 'true and fair' view of the financial affairs of the business. The truthfulness refers to the quality of the recording of cash and commitments by the business. The 'fairness' relates to the matching of the value of resources consumed in any period to the revenues earned within that period.

It is important to understand the distinctions between the three bases of accounting outlined above, because it is in the application of the accruals or matching principle that the greatest opportunity for distortion occurs. The use of subjective judgement to serve the covert aims of management in presenting accounting information to external users is what we term 'creative accounting'.

The introduction of the accruals principle also forces us to think more carefully about the purposes for which financial accounting information is produced. However, before we do so we will examine, using some simple examples, how accountants produce accrual accounts, and the principles and conventions they employ to ensure that their judgemental processes are fair.

THE PREPARATION OF ACCRUAL ACCOUNTS

The preparation of accounts is, in principle, a straightforward process. It can be much more complex in practice. Here we will review two procedures: the first makes clear the mechanics of the procedure, but it is rather cumbersome to use in practical applications; the second, although intuitively less obvious, allows a much more complex set of accounts to be prepared.

EXAMPLE

Johnson Products, a small business, commences its accounting year on 1 January with an opening balance sheet showing a series of asset values outstanding, less the commitments incurred against those assets but which are unpaid at the commencement of the year's business (Table 30.2).

During the year, Johnson Products' transactions can be summarised as follows.

(i) Johnson purchased a further machine for £8000 for cash on 1 January 19xx. It is expected, like his other machinery, to have a four-year life.

(ii) He paid off all his opening liabilities for purchases and he then purchased, during the year, £85 000 of new stock on credit. At the end of the year £10 000 of stock was still left in his stores and £1250 of the purchases had not been paid for.

(iii) He converted some of his stock into finished goods which he sold for £170 000. He had £5500 of outstanding customer accounts at the end of the year. He had no finished goods stock in hand.

(iv) He paid £27 600 in rent, £5000 in Local Authority charges, and other expenses of £12 500. He paid his partner a salary of £14 700 – she was the only other person to work in the business during the year.

(v) He drew £8000 from his capital account for his own purposes. Annual interest of 8% was due on 31 December on a loan he had taken out the year before of £30 000.

THE BALANCE SHEET EQUATION METHOD

The balance sheet represents a series of assets (fixed and current) which have not been fully utilised in value at the end of the period. The matching principle has resulted in certain prior period expenditures on fixed assets and stock purchases, for example, only being partly attributed to those prior periods with certain of the expenditure remaining *unexpired*. At 1 January the assets of the business are matched by the claims upon those assets – the claims of short-term creditors (the current liabilities), the long-term creditors and the owners. This is a fundamental accounting identity. The value of the assets of any business must be exactly matched by the value of the claims upon that business, as a business cannot hold a claim against its own assets in its own right.

Table 30.2 Johnson Products – opening balance sheet

Johnson Products
Opening Balance Sheet as at 1 January 19xx

Fixed assets		58 000	Asset
Less accumulated depreciation		14 500	(Asset)
		43 500	
Current assets			
Stock	3 400		Asset
Debtors	9 900		Asset
Cash	1 500		Asset
	14 800		
Current liabilities			
Trade creditors	8 750		STC
Net current assets		6 050	
		49 550	
Long-term liabilities		30 000	LTC
		19 550	
Owner's equity		10 000	OE
Profit retained		9 550	OE
		19 550	

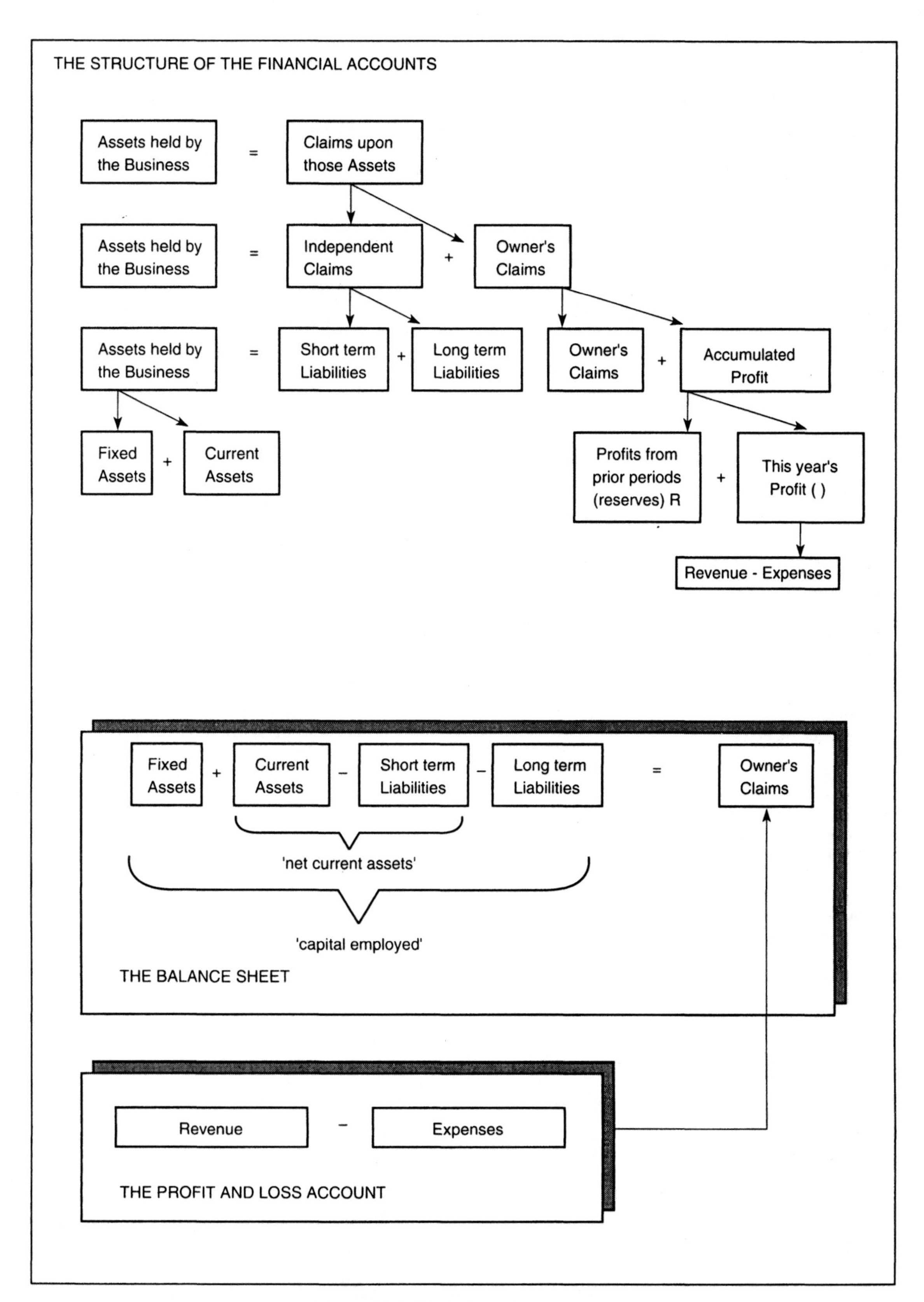

Figure 30.2 The balance sheet equation.

In Figure 30.2 we show how the value of the assets and claims of a business are broken down into the components of the balance sheet. Note that the ownership claim of the business will increase as profits are earned, and the profit and loss account is a secondary statement within the balance sheet equation. The profit and loss account shows how the revenue and expenditure transactions of the business lead to an increase in the owner's claim or capital during the year.

Conventional accounts show the balance sheet in 'net asset' format where the asset value is reduced by:

- depreciation on fixed assets;
- short-term independent claims;
- long-term independent claims;

to give a net asset value equal to the equity capital employed.

Our first step in analysing Johnson's transactions is to rearrange the opening balance sheet onto the balance sheet equation (Table 30.3) where:

Assets (A) = Short-term claims (STC)
+ Long-term claims (LTC)
+ Owner's equity (OE) to date
+ Profit for the year of revenue (R)
− Expenditures (E)

Table 30.3 Johnson Product's – balance sheet equation

	Assets =	STC	LTC	OE	R	(E)
Opening balance sheet:						
Fixed assets	58 000 FA					
Depreciation	(14 500) FA					
Stock	3 400 s					
Debtors	9 900 Db					
Cash	1 500 c					
Creditors		8 750				
Loan			30 000			
Capital				10 000		
Accumulated profit				9 550		
	58 300	8 750	30 000	19 550		
Transactions for the year						
Purchase of fixed asset	(8 000) c					
Purchase of fixed asset	8 000 FA					
Depreciation	(2 000) FA					2 000
Depreciation	(14 500) FA					14 500
Payment of creditors	(8 750) c	(8 750)				
Purchases on credit	85 000 s	85 000				
Payment for purchases	(83 750) c	(83 750)				
Opening stock into production	(3 400) s					3 400
Purchases to production	(85 000) s					85 000
Less: closing stock balance	10 000 s					(10 000)
Opening debtors recovered	(9 900) Db					
Into cash received	9 900 c					
Sales cash received	164 500 c				170 000	
Outstanding at year end	5 500 Db					
Rent	(27 600) c					27 600
Local Authority charges	(5 000) c					5 000
Other expenses	(12 500) c					12 500
Salary cost	(14 700) c					14 700
Drawing	(8 000) c			(8 000)		
Interest		2 400				2 400
	58 100	3 650	30 000	11 550	170 000	157 100
				12 900		12 900
		3 650	30 000	24 450	170 000	170 000
	58 100		58 100			

Certain of his transactions (such as the purchase of machinery, the purchase of stock and the receipt of cash from Johnson's debtors) represent exchanges between one type of asset and cash. Therefore, they only affect the asset column of the equation. Other transactions affect both sides of the equation.

The stock transaction appears somewhat cumbersome, although a moment's reflection will reveal the sense of what has occurred. At the beginning of the year £3400 of stock was held and we can assume (assuming a first in, first out approach) that this stock was transferred to production first and became an expense for the period. We know that £85 000 of stock was purchased during the year, but with £10 000 of stock being left on hand we can assume that only a net of £75 000 of this material can be charged as an expense.

Finally, we have assumed that the drawings made during the year are a withdrawal of part of Johnson's capital and not to be counted as an expenditure.

In order to create the year-end balance sheet, all that remains is to analyse the balance sheet equation back into the 'net asset' format required for presentation purposes (Table 30.4). Moving down the asset column, the fixed asset value is now £66 000 with £31 000 of accumulated depreciation, stock and debtors are easy to identify, although we need to cast the cash figure carefully to get the outstanding balance at the end of the year.

THE EXTENDED TRIAL BALANCE (ETB) METHOD

This is a practical system of preparing accounts, where the cash book forms the principle means of recording transactions throughout the year. The ETB is particularly useful when creating accounts for a small business where the number of transactions involved are too large for the balance sheet equation method to be useful. Like the balance sheet equation, the principles of this method of accounting are quite simple, although the ETB method follows more traditional methods of double entry book-keeping.

Stage 1

The opening balance sheet is laid out in the first of two columns headed 'debit' (Db) and 'credit' (Cr). Debits record assets owned or value received

Table 30.4 Johnson Products – balance sheet and profit and loss account

Johnson Products

Balance Sheet as at 31 December 19xx

Fixed assets		66 000
Less accumulated depreciation		(31 000)
		35 000
Current assets		
Stock	10 000	
Debtors	5 500	
Cash	7 600	
	23 100	
Current liabilities		
Trade creditors	3 650	
Net current assets		19 450
		54 450
Long-term liabilities		30 000
		24 450
Owner's equity		10 000
Less drawings		(8 000)
		2 000
Profit retained		22 450
		24 450

Johnson Products

Profit and Loss Account

for the year ended 31 December 19xx

Sales		170 000
Less:		
Opening stock	3 400	
Purchases	85 000	
Less closing stock	10 000	
Cost of goods sold		78 400
Gross Profit		91 600
Less:		
Salary	14 700	
Rent	27 600	
Local Authority charges	5 000	
Other expenses	12 500	
Depreciation for the year	16 500	
Interest	2 400	
		78 000
Net profit retained		12 900

whereas credits record commitments against those assets or value paid out. In Table 30.5 we show the opening balance sheet laid out in the first two columns of the table. The account names for the profit and loss account are listed under the balance sheet headings, but no profit and loss figures are shown in the first two columns. The list of account names for the balance sheet and profit and loss are called the 'nominal' accounts.

Stage 2

The current assets and liabilities in the opening balance sheet are 'cleared' to their respective nominal accounts. The opening debtor balance was due to sales in the previous year so the corresponding clearing entry in two new columns called 'reversal opening balances' is to credit the debtors row with £9900 and debit the sales row by an equivalent amount. The same procedure is followed for stock (to opening stock account) and outstanding liabilities (to purchases). The only current asset left untouched is cash. Given that each credit entry in these two columns is balanced by a debit entry and vice versa, then the two columns should balance.

Stage 3

The next two columns show the analysis of cash receipts and payments during the year in question. The cash row contains a debit entry of £174 400 and a corresponding credit entry of £174 400 for cash receipts in sales. The credit entry of £168 300 represents the total cash expenditure analysed as £8000 of drawings, £92 500 cash expenditure on the purchases account and so on. Again, if our arithmetic is correct, then the two cash columns should balance:

	Db	*Cr*
Cash (in balance sheet)	Total received	Total expenditure
Other asset or expenditure accounts	Expenditures in year	
Liability or income accounts		Receipts in year

Stage 4

The next two columns are the year-end analogue of the procedure conducted at the beginning of the year, where opening entries are created, except that with these two columns the closing balances on debtors and creditors are created. For example, £5500 on the sales account was a closing debtor balance and, similarly, £1250 of purchase commitments were unpaid at the end of the year. Again, these two columns should be self-balancing.

Stage 5

After our opening balances have been cleared, the cash entries made and the closing commitments recognised (the creation of the closing debtors and creditors), all that remains, before the final accounts are extended, is to make adjustments for the final stock left on hand at the end of the year and to enter any accruals or prepayments. The closing 'journal' is where these final adjustments are made and notice that we have used these columns to 'post' the depreciation charge from the profit and loss account to the balance sheet:

Db – debit depreciation in the profit and loss account;
Cr – credit accumulated depreciation in the balance sheet.

Stage 6

Extend the total net debit balances and net credit balance into two columns for the closing balance sheet and two columns for the profit and loss account. The balance on the profit and loss columns, when transferred to the balance sheet columns, will produce two pairs of balancing columns.

Stage 7

Create the final balance sheet and profit and loss account as in the balance sheet equation method.

The ETB method is a very simple, double-entry-based method, for creating a sophisticated manual accounting system around an analysed cash book. An accurate cash book analysed into various revenue and expenditure accounts is an important prerequisite for this system of accounts preparation. To understand how it works examine the sales row.

At the beginning of the year, Johnson Products was owed £9900 by customers on account of sales

Table 30.5 Johnson Products – extended trial balance

	Opening balance sheet		Reversal opening balance		Cash transactions		Closing balances		Closing journal		Closing balance sheet		Closing profit and loss	
Balance sheet accounts	Db	Cr	Db	Cr	Db	Cr	Db	Cr	Db	Cr	Db	Cr	Db	Cr
Fixed assets	58 000				8 000						66 000			
Accumulated depreciation		14 500								16 500		31 000		
Current assets														
Stock	3 400			3 400					10 000		10 000			
Debtors	9 900			9 900			5500				5 500			
Cash	1 500				174 400	168 300					7 600			
Current liabilities														
Trade creditors		8 750	8 750					1250				1 250		
Other creditors								2400				2 400		
Long-term liabilities		30 000										30 000		
Owner's equity		10 000										10 000		
Drawings					8 000						8 000			
Profit brought forward		9 550										9 550		
Profit for year												12 900 ↑		
Profit and loss accounts														
Sales			9 900			174 400		5500						170 000
Opening stock			3 400										3 400	
Purchases				8 750	92 500		1250						85 000	
Closing stock										10 000			(10 000)	
Salary					14 700								14 700	
Rent					27 600								27 600	
Local Authority charges					5 000								5 000	
Other expenses					12 500								12 500	
Depreciation for the year									16 500				16 500	
Interest							2400						2 400	
Profit retained													12 900	
	72 800	72 800	22 050	22 050	342 700	342 700	9150	9150	26 500	26 500	97 100	97 100	170 000	170 000

in the previous year. The cash receipts from customers of £174 400 were therefore attributable as:

- £9900 on account of the previous year;
- £164 500 on account of the current year.

There was also £5500 of sales on credit (creating the corresponding debtor balance in the balance sheet) and thus the final extended sales value was £164 500 + £5500, i.e. £170 000. Check through each of the other rows in the ETB to check that you can follow the logic implied by each sequence of numbers going to form the final accounts.

COMPUTER-BASED ACCOUNTING SYSTEMS

Although it is not our purpose to teach computer-based accounts in this book, some familiarity with the mechanics of account preparation using standard business accounting software is useful for the manager.

Most computer accounting packages are built around three fundamental data bases:

- a sales ledger, where goods sold are recorded in individual customer accounts and cash receipts from these customers are credited;
- a purchase ledger, where individual supplier accounts are recorded with purchase transactions and cash payments;
- a nominal ledger, which contains all of the accounts shown in the businesses profit and loss account and balance sheet (including the cash account).

Figure 30.3 shows a ledger structure found in many computerised systems.

The mechanics of the double-entry system are achieved through the use of nominal account codes and 'control accounts'. As a sale is entered into a

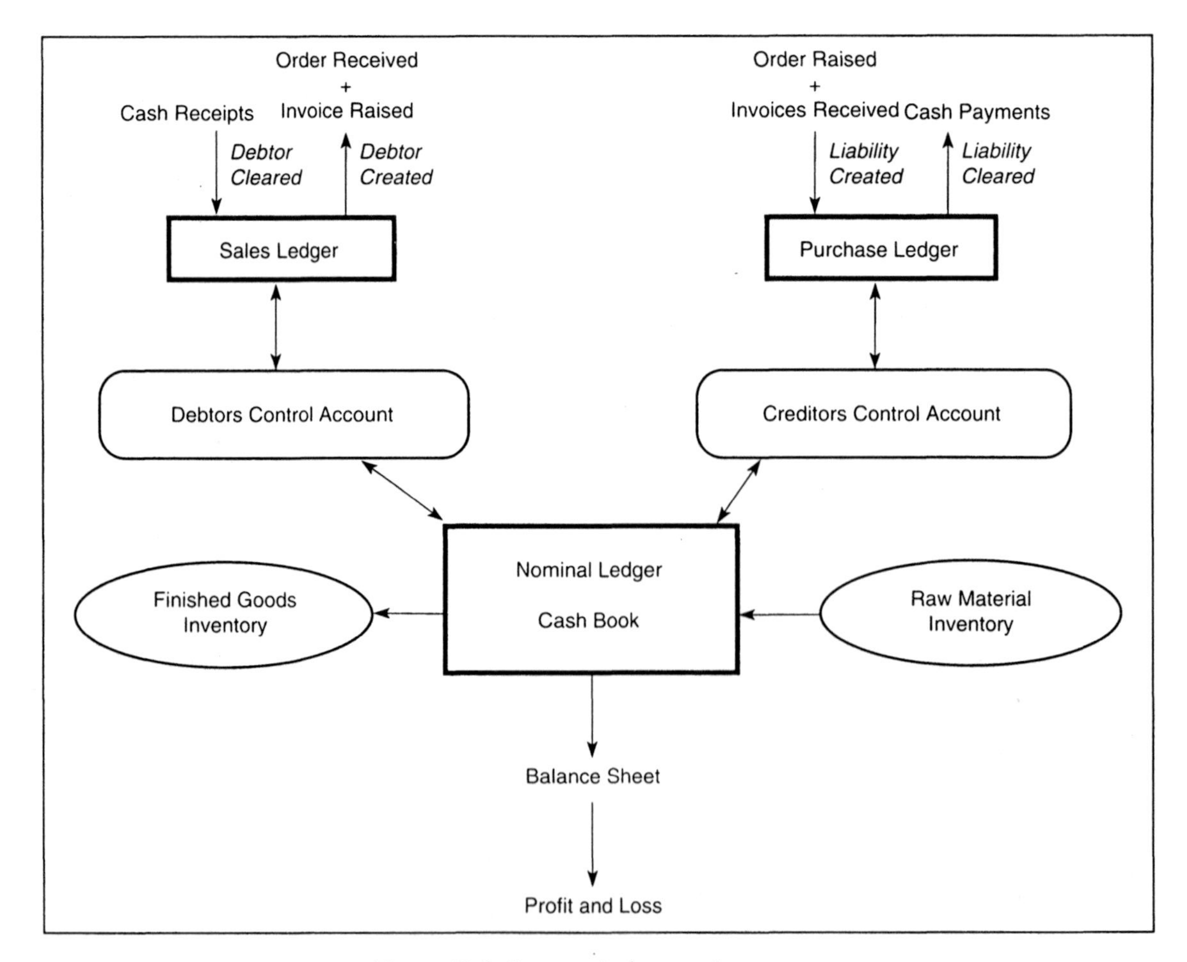

Figure 30.3 Computerised accounting systems.

particular customer's account in the sales ledger, the user will enter a code to identify the type of sale made (i.e. to provide a unique reference to a product sale account in the nominal ledger) which will be totalled with other product sales to create the total sales figure in the nominal list of balances. As cash is received from customers, the control account will pass the payment to the cash account in the nominal ledger. The balance between sales and cash receipts from customers is, of course, the outstanding debtor balance, which is shown as the 'debtor control' balance in the nominal ledger trial balance (Figure 30.4).

In setting up a computerised accounting system it is necessary to proceed through the following steps.

(i) Establish the structure of the accounts (here we assume a single business unit) and create the list of nominal accounts and codes. This list of nominal accounts would appear very similar to the list of account headings in our ETB in the previous section. Codes can be quite simple for a small business consisting of perhaps three or four numbers.

(ii) Nominate which of the accounts belong to the balance sheet and which belong to the profit and loss account.

(iii) Identify which nominal accounts are control accounts (in the balance sheet) of which at least two will appear – one for debtors and one for creditors.

(iv) Nominate default nominal accounts for placing uncoded expenditure and revenues.

(v) Set up the inventory account for input and output stocks (most packages have in-built systems to allow you to categorise the types of raw materials you typically receive and your main product headings for finished stocks).

(vi) Nominate a suspense account for undesignated transactions or for 'clearing balances' between one account and another.

(vii) Enter opening customer account balances into the sales ledger, supplier account balances in the purchase ledger and the opening balance sheet into the nominal ledger.

(viii) As you make sales, receive goods, make cash payments to suppliers or receive cash settlements from customers, enter these details into the respective accounts in the purchase or sales ledger. If your system has been correctly installed the program should 'post' these transactions to the relevant sales or purchase accounts in the nominal ledger, update the cash book and modify the stock records.

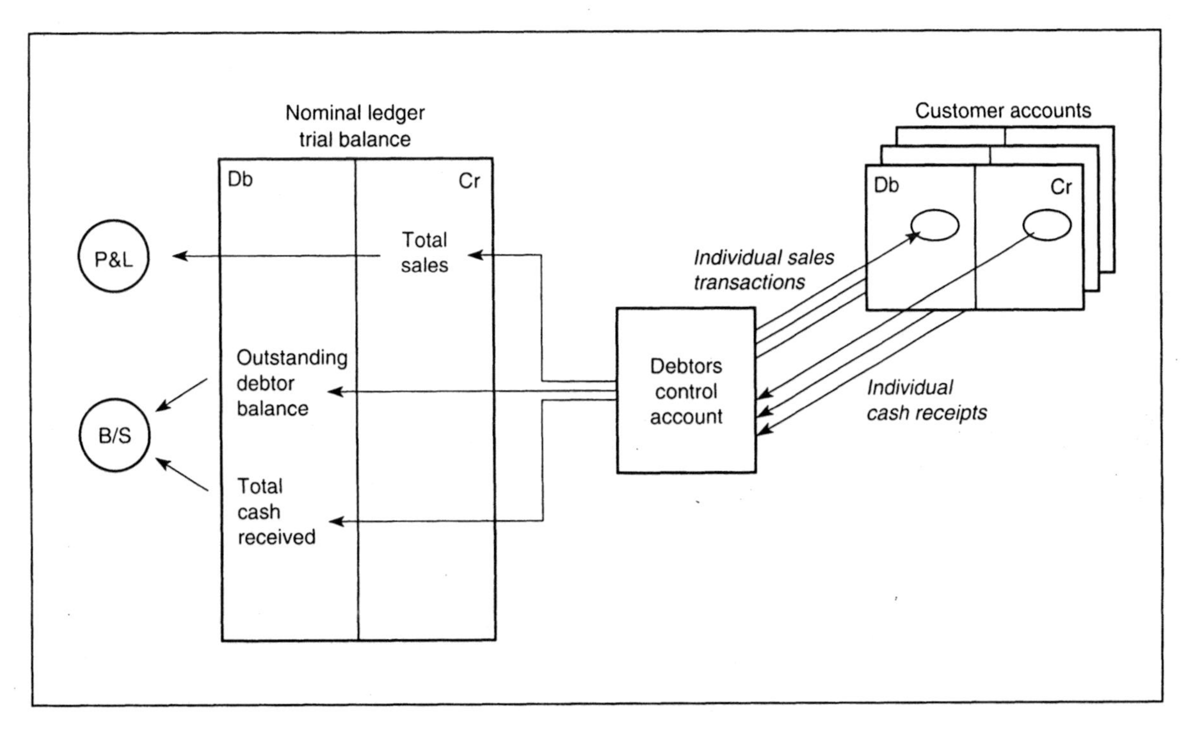

Figure 30.4 Nominal ledger trial balance.

Your program should have certain routines which allow you to make the appropriate adjustments for accruals, depreciation and prepayments. In addition, it should be able to generate a trial balance and sets of accounts on request.

Clearly, this is the barest outline of the mechanics of setting up computerised accounts. Most computerised accounting systems follow very similar procedures, although the more sophisticated packages will allow you to prepare budgets, raise invoices and order, manage the payroll and operate departmental, divisional or indeed holding company accounts with many subsidiaries. The constraint is rarely the software but rather the storage capacity of the computer system employed. For all but the largest companies most financial accounting systems can be comfortably handled by a single PC or networked group of PCs at relatively modest cost.

CONCLUSION

In this chapter we have discussed three methods for preparing accrual accounts. Each of these methods relies upon a system of double-entry transaction recording where the the dual nature of a transaction is recognised within the framework of a profit and loss account and balance sheet. We have briefly outlined how computerised accounting packages work although a specialist text should be consulted if you plan to implement such a system. In the next chapter we turn to our last topic – the interpretation of financial accounting reports.

Chapter 31

Interpreting Financial Reports

Level G

Contents

Summary

The detailed interpretation of accounting information forms a subject in its own right. Financial statement analysis, as the subject is often called, is usually undertaken from the point of view of the investor shareholder although, in practice, anyone who has an interest in the affairs of a company – its employees, customers, suppliers, bankers to mention just four possibilities – may have a need to understand and interpret the accounts as presented. In this chapter we examine three topics which are of importance in interpretation: the general methodology of interpretation of accounts, how accounting information can be manipulated and a range of tools for analysing financial information.

INTRODUCTION

Accounts are always produced from the perspective of some user (or more generally a group of users with common interests). Two questions can be posed immediately.

(i) Whose interests do these accounts serve?
(ii) What is my (the reader's) interests in this company's accounts?

Even if accounts were produced on a pure cash or commitments basis – which they are not in their published form – there would still be some subjectivity implicit in the allocation of expenditures to categories. When the accruals principle is introduced, an element of subjective judgement overlies the firm foundation represented by the actual commitments engaged in and their cash consequences. In addition, the layout of a conventional set of accounts focuses attention upon the profit surplus which legally belongs to the shareholders. It is a trivial jump then to view that profit figure as something which should be maximised, and the costs incurred before arriving at that profit measure as values which should be minimised.

Consider the two statements in Table 31.1.

Both statements are conveying the same information about values. In both cases £100 000 was earned as revenue, and in both cases exactly the same allocations of that sum were made. The difference is solely in the way in which the information is prioritised. In the first case, labour, lenders, government and shareholders are given equal status; in the second, labour and lenders' interest is deemed as a cost (which is an economic 'bad' and should, therefore, be minimised), taxation is a non-discretionary consequence of earning net profits of £21 000 and the value of £14 000 is the number by which performance is judged.

Table 31.1

Value-added statement	
Sales turnover	100 000
Less: cost of goods sold	50 000
	50 000
Labour stake	10 000
Depreciation	5 000
Management overheads	10 000
Interest payable	4 000
Taxation	7 000
Shareholder stake	14 000
Value Added	50 000

Profit statement		
Sales turnover		100 000
Less: cost of goods sold		50 000
Gross Profit		50 000
Less: labour cost	10 000	
depreciation	5 000	
overheads	10 000	
interest payable	4 000	
		29 000
Net profit before tax		21 000
Taxation		7 000
Net profit for distribution to ordinary shareholders		14 000

The conventional profit and loss account is a statement which, in layout as well as in content, reflects the primacy of ownership capital. In practical interpretation, the non-shareholder who has an interest in the reported information of the business may not see the profit and loss account as the most useful layout.

In Figure 31.1 we show six important variables which may be of interest to different groups: pre-tax profit, taxable profit, surplus for ordinary shareholders, ability to pay (as measured by accounting value added), ability to pay, liquidity and ability to deliver. Pre-tax profit and liquidity will be of importance to lenders, as their interest is a charge

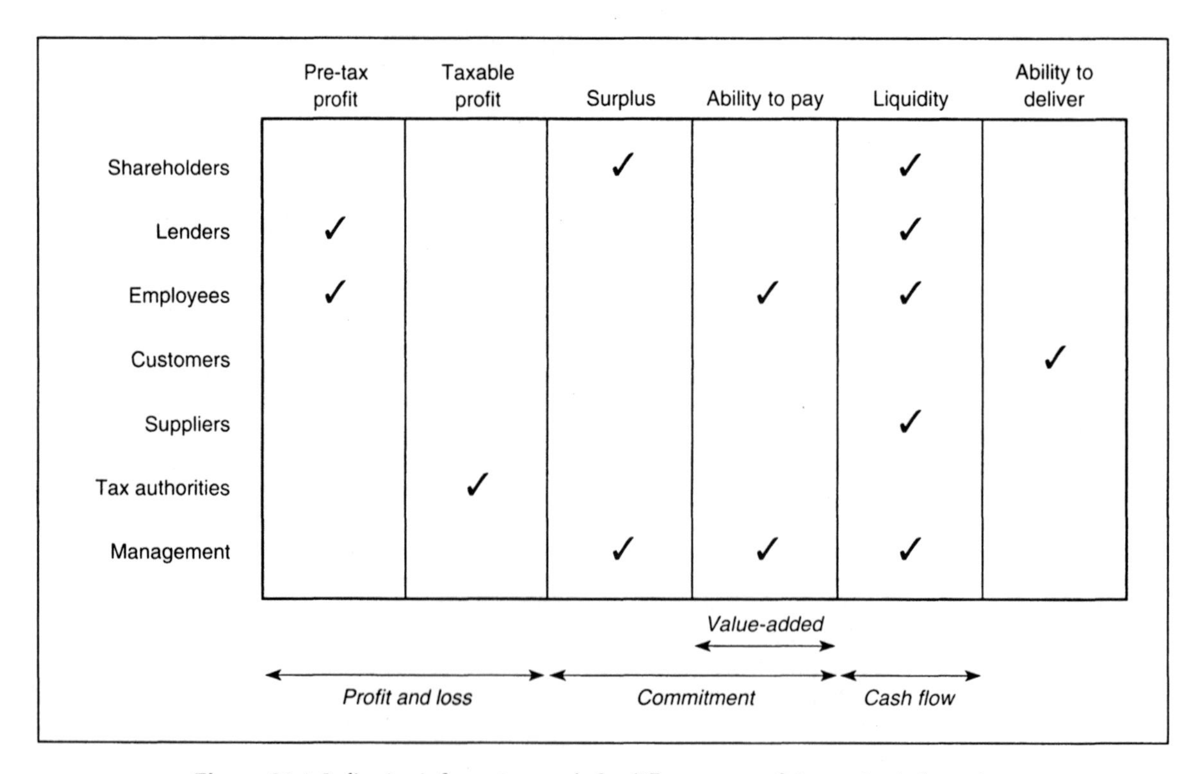

Figure 31.1 Indicative information needs for different users of accounting information.

Table 31.2

Earnings model	Dividend growth model	Capital asset pricing model	All models
Earnings	Dividends	Business risk	
Earnings growth	Dividend growth	Financial risk	
Earnings risk	Dividend risk	Bankruptcy risk	Liquidity

against profits before tax is assessed and, presumably they will be concerned to ensure that the business can repay at the due time.

Taxable profit is of interest to the tax authorities, whilst after-tax profit available for distribution (earnings) is presumably of primary interest to shareholders. The management of a business may also be interested in earnings if they are involved in some profit sharing or profit bonus scheme. Ability to pay as the amount of total resources available for distribution to all interest groups should be of interest to employees and management. Liquidity is of importance to suppliers and to management who have to satisfy the conflicting claims of different interest groups. Finally, ability to deliver goods on time and to the quality specified is of critical importance to customers.

Once the principal interest has been established in reading and interpreting accounts the next step is to establish your information needs. Figure 31.1 is a useful starting point, but more information will be needed for practical purposes. In order to identify the information needs you require you must first make specific the decision model you are using. For example, consider an investor who is considering acquiring a stake in the business. He or she will be concerned with those variables which are likely to affect the valuation of the company and its future prospects. We have considered the elements of a valuation model in Chapter 16. In such valuation models we can assume that the decision variables shown in Table 31.2 are of importance. In assessing many of these variables he or she would also be interested in:

- the competitive advantage enjoyed by the business in the market place (for sustaining and improving the quality of earnings growth);
- the efficiency of the business at converting its resources into surplus (these will be current as well as capital resources);
- the efficiency with which the resources of the business are managed.

These three points reduce back to the concept of measuring the efficiency of the business at generating cash for distribution both in a static and a dynamic sense.

Following from this, the interpreter/analyst should conduct a pre-evaluation of the business using what is available in the public domain to determine the strategic direction and quality of the business. This stage of analysis will help to frame a series of prior questions which subsequent, more detailed, analysis can attempt to answer.

Figure 31.2 summarises the stages described above.

THE STRATEGIC PRE-EVALUATION OF ACCOUNTS

Once a clear set of information needs have been established, the analyst should seek to determine the current competitive position of the business and to identify the strategic issues which it faces. The

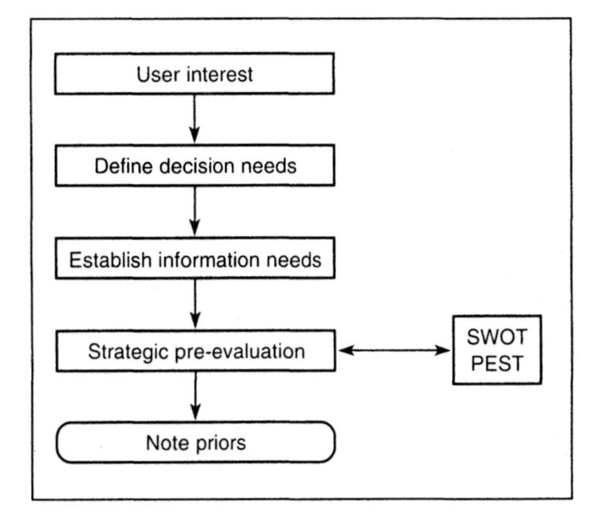

Figure 31.2 Elements of the preliminary stages of forming beliefs about a business's financial performance.

analysis of the business's strengths, weaknesses, opportunities and threats (SWOT) and its political economic, social and technological environment (PEST) should lead towards formulating the correct questions to ask.

The SWOT analysis (Figure 31.3) is a powerful tool for reflecting on a business's internal and external position. The following points are worthy of note.

- To be useful, each point about a company should be precise and correctly identified within its quadrant.
- Strengths and weaknesses are often the converse of one another. A strong liquid position may be a strength but it may also indicate underinvestment and poor management.
- Threats are said to be opportunities which are not matched against business strengths. The target of strategic policy is to bring about a conjunction of business strengths (core capability in our terms) with the opportunities available and to minimise the business's exposure to its weaknesses.
- Any series of four points materialising in the quadrants of the SWOT which can be linked indicate that a strategic issue is present. For example, a major defence contractor identified the following:

  (i) a strong cash position (strength);
  (ii) underinvestment in capital plant and equipment (weakness);
  (iii) strong demand for civil satellites for communications (opportunity);
  (iv) collapse of the defence requirements (threat).

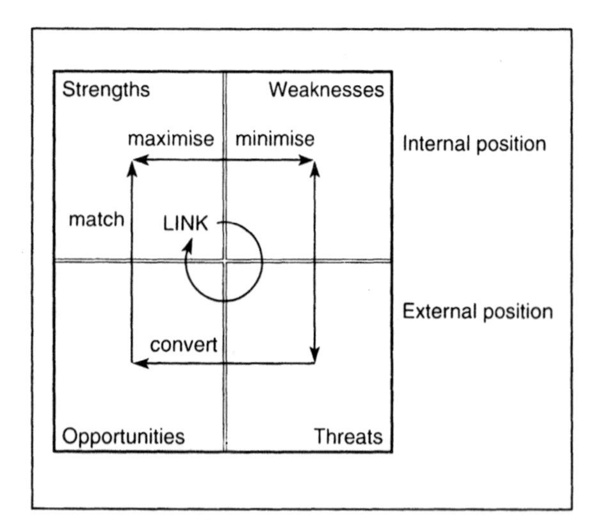

Figure 31.3 Elements of a SWOT analysis.

It is not difficult to see the strategic issue facing this company which concerns capital intensive diversification into civil markets using its healthy cash resources.

Once a thorough review of a business's competitive position has been undertaken, a series of questions can be posed which will form the context for a subsequent financial analysis.

CREATIVE ACCOUNTING

It is possible for a business to generate objective reports of its cash flows and commitments during the year. When analysing published financial accounts we are faced with the subjective 'overlay' of the operation of the accruals principle on top of what should be reliable cash and commitment figures. This overlay of subjectivity should be removed as far as possible. However, management can engineer its business to bring forward or delay commitments and cash payments to 'window dress' its performance during the year.

The first work to be done on any set of accounts is to correct any obvious distortions by:

- reversing or accounting for any variations in cash or commitments from what should be charged or received in the accounting period concerned;
- eliminating any distortions introduced by changes in the accruals principle.

Varying cash or commitments

Delaying or advancing commitments

If a sale or purchase contract is advanced or delayed relative to what would be the case in the normal course of business then management is said to be 'window dressing' the accounts.

In Table 31.3 we show the principal effects upon the profit and loss account of window-dressing activity. Generally, the only advantage of delaying a capital sale beyond the date of a balance sheet is to give a better position with respect to liquidity and the various ratios which measure performance against fixed assets. With revenue transactions, management can make modest changes to apparent profitability, although the position will correct as soon as the commitment is made early in the new financial year. This type of activity goes on with most businesses and is difficult to detect from published information. In some industries, such as

Table 31.3 Principal changes on accounts by window dressing (R=revenue, C=capital)

		Profit and loss account			Balance sheet				
		Revenue	Costs	Profit	Fixed assets	Current assets	Current liability	Long-term liability	Owner's equity
Advance sale	R	Increase		Increase		Increase			Increase
Delay sale	R	Decrease		Decrease		Decrease			Decrease
Advance purchase	R		Increase	Decrease			Increase		Decrease
Delay purchase	R		Decrease	Increase			Decrease		Increase
Advance sale	C				Decrease	Increase			
Delay sale	C				Increase	Decrease			
Advance purchase	C				Increase	Decrease			
Delay purchase	C				Decrease	Increase			

construction and defence, it can entail considerable variations from one account to another.

Withdrawing assets from the balance sheet

In this situation a company may appear to sell an asset, while still enjoying the benefit of that asset within the business. For example, the sale and lease-back of a fixed asset will have the effect of increasing the cash resources to the business through the consideration on the sale and in decreasing the fixed assets available. The cash may be used to increase current assets (as shown in Table 31.4) or decrease borrowings). The net effect on the profit and loss account may be minimal as depreciation is lost from that account but will be replaced by an increase on finance charges on the lease. So called 'finance leases' must be capitalised under the Accounting Standard (SSAP 21) and the lessor's account shown as a liability, whilst operating leases can be left undisclosed.

Off-balance sheet financing, as sale or lease-back is sometimes referred to, can be used to reduce borrowing and improve the apparent return on fixed assets employed in the business.

Adapting or changing the accruals principle

The greatest room for manœuvre in the preparation of financial reports comes through changes in the way in which the matching principle is applied. As we pointed out in Chapter 30, the accruals principle is a prerequisite for the measurement of accounting income. As we noted accounting income or 'profit' is based upon the need for a productive enterprise to measure the free surplus for owners resulting from a given level of business activity within a period.

EXAMPLE

Maxwell Demon commenced trading on 1 January as a consultant lecturer.

During the year his income was £66 000 although of that, £6000 was revenue from a teaching contract which started in October and was due to last six months. He had negotiated cash payment in advance. In order specifically to service that contract he had paid £3000 cash for books and materials in October. His other costs during the year

Table 31.4 The effect of the sale and lease-back of an operating lease.

	Profit and loss account			Balance sheet				
	Revenue	Costs	Profit	Fixed assets	Current assets	Current liability	Long-term liability	Owner's equity
Sale and lease of an asset		No change		Decrease	Increase			

totalled £24 000. His accountant believes that the £6000 should be accrued on a time basis, i.e.

Revenue (60 000 + 3000)		*63 000*
Other costs	*24 000*	
Accrued element of contract costs	*1 500*	
		25 500
Profit		*37 500*

However, suppose Maxwell Demon could argue that the bulk of the teaching hours fell in the first month of the contract. In that situation, a fair accrual would reflect the proportion of the £6000 which could be attributed to the year in question and the resultant proportion of cost which should be attributed to that revenue.

'Creative accounting' is the term which has been coined to describe the process of manipulating the accounting conventions employed through, usually, the accruals concept, but also through window dressing to achieve a particular level of profit or loss (Table 31.5).

We have already discussed in Chapters 6 and 30 how the accruals concept can be used to allocate costs or revenues to given periods and, as we pointed out, the concept of 'fairness' in this procedure will vary from time to time over different economic, market and technological conditions. In an influential British book *Accounting for Growth*, Smith (1992) discusses the principal ways in which accounts can be manipulated. He also asserts that: 'much of the apparent growth in profits which had occurred in the 1980s was the result of accounting sleight of hand rather than genuine economic growth' (p. 4). He analysed the accounting policies of a number of significant UK companies against a simple 'blob' index which is designed to highlight those who are using accounting procedures to manipulate reported profits.

Creative accounting is a skilful art, but the financier Jim Slater gives a useful tip for detecting significant abuse: 'when operating profit exceeds net cash inflow from operating assets, you know that creative accounting has certainly been at work' (Slater, 1993, p. 57). Similarly, it is fairly straightforward from a company's statement of its corporation tax payable to work out the profit which the Inland Revenue have deemed to be chargeable. If there is a material difference between that figure and the quoted taxable profit then it is reasonable to ask why.

ANALYSING FINANCIAL PERFORMANCE

To understand fully a business's performance, it is necessary for the analyst to proceed through a sequence of steps.

- Read the accounts thoroughly, cross-referencing and annotating all cross references to notes. This is a long job initially, but with practice it is possible to identify the main areas of concern.
- Undertake a comprehensive 'change analysis' over the year in question, recording the absolute and relative change as a percentage as well as the direction of change.
- Measure the power of the cash engine using simple financial performance ratios.
- Measure the cash dynamics of the business. We will demonstrate a powerful method for achieving this using what we refer to as the μ statistic.

Table 31.5 The effect of accounting policy changes on the accounts.

Policy change	Profit and loss account			Balance sheet					
	Revenue	Costs	Profit	Fixed assets	Current assets	Current liability	Long-term liability	Profit and loss	Other reserves
Increase depreciation charge		Inc	Dec	Dec				Dec	
Decrease depreciation charge		Dec	Inc	Inc				Inc	
Revalue up land and buildings	Inc		Inc	Inc				Inc	
or				Inc					Inc
Write off goodwill		Inc	Dec	Dec				Dec	
or				Dec					Dec
Write off R&D expenditure		Inc	Dec		Dec			Dec	
Capitalise R&D expenditure				Inc	Dec				
Write down closing stock value	Dec		Dec		Dec			Dec	

Table 31.6 The balance sheet for A Public Company plc

Balance sheet as at 31 December 19x1

		19x1 £	19x0 £
Fixed assets		6 760 000	6 700 000
Accumulated depreciation		3 970 000	3 900 000
		2 790 000	2 800 000
Current assets			
Stock	123 670		145 000
Debtors and prepayments	342 980		199 450
Cash in hand	89 876		103 400
	556 526		447 850
Less: current liabilities payables in one year			
Trade creditors	214 308		219 880
Tax and other	112 345		97 213
Accruals	43 400		40 876
	370 053		357 969
Net current assets		186 473	89 881
		2 976 473	2 889 881
Less: long-term liabilities		890 000	890 000
		2 086 473	1 999 881
Shareholders' funds			
Paid-up share capital on 600 000 £1 ordinary		1 200 000	1 200 000
Accumulated profit and loss		886 473	799 881
		2 086 473	1 999 881

Table 31.7 The profit and loss account for A Public Company plc

Profit and loss account for the year ended 31 December 19x1

	19x1 £	19x0 £
Turnover for the year	3 455 060	3 270 746
Less: cost of sales	2 253 718	2 134 281
Gross profit	1 201 342	1 136 465
Administrative expenses	890 560	875 920
Net profit before interest and tax	310 782	260 545
Interest	71 200	71 200
Net profit before tax	239 582	189 345
Taxation on ordinary activities	128 990	112 345
Net profit after tax	110 592	77 000
Dividends	24 000	22 000
Retained profit	86 592	55 000
Earnings per ordinary share	18.43p	12.83p

Table 31.8 Notes to the accounts of A Public Company plc

	19x1 £	19x0 £
Debtors and prepayments		
Trade debtors	291 980	148 950
Prepayments	51 000	50 500
	342 980	199 450
Stocks		
Raw materials	63 210	65 430
Work in progress	23 440	10 987
Finished stocks	37 020	68 583
	123 670	145 000

- Analyse the financial risk to which the business is exposed.

In our analysis (Tables 31.6 and 31.7) we examine figures from the accounts of A Public Company plc for the year ended 31 December 19x1. In the current assets and current liabilities there are accounts for prepayments and accruals. Examining the notes to the accounts we discover the situation shown in Table 31.8.

READING THE ACCOUNTS

Seasoned financial analysts and some accountants do become very adept at reading and interpreting financial accounts. Initially, it is easy to become swamped by detail but consistent and regular practice will produce dividends. The structure of a set of financial accounts is as follows:

- directors' report, which covers a statement of activities, a review of the businesses, items of significant financial note and statement of directors and other important interests;
- profit and loss account;
- balance sheet;
- statement of cash flow (this should be treated as a note to the rest of the accounts rather than as a primary financial statement);
- notes to the accounts, which will include a statement of accounting policies;
- the auditor's report, which will usually state that the accounts show a 'true and fair' view of the state of affairs of the company. It is worthy of note that very few of the major financial scandals are ever brought to light by the auditors.

CHANGE ANALYSIS

Using the accounts of A Public Company plc we:

(i) enter the profit and loss account figures into a trial balance format and calculate the absolute change between the two years (Table 31.9), identifying whether the change is favourable (f) to the business (an increase in revenue or a decrease in cost) or adverse (a) (a decrease in revenue or an increase in cost);
(ii) repeat for the balance sheet.

From such a change analysis it is possible to identify the main influences upon financial performance and relative improvements from year to year. A careful analysis of these changes compared with the results of the strategic review of the business should answer many of the questions posed by that review.

Given our approach that a business enterprise consumes cost in order to achieve revenue (or turnover) and profit, then it is appropriate to measure the change between the 19x0 and the 19x1, figures both as percentage changes across the year and as a percentage of turnover. In the case above, the most significant impact upon profitability was brought about by the increase in turnover (5.64%) and the increase in the cost of sales (5.60%) which taken with the leverage effect on net profit generated a very healthy improvement in the net profit after tax. However, the figures for percentage on turnover show that this is a very low margin business. With a net profit of just 3.20% on turnover we may begin to wonder just how powerful a cash engine the company actually has.

Table 31.9 Change analysis on profit and loss

	19x1		19x0				
	Dr	Cr	Dr	Cr	Change	%	19x1 turnover
Turnover for the year		3 455 060		3 270 746	184 313 f	5.64	100.00
Less: cost of sales	2 253 718		2 134 281		119 436 a	5.60	65.23
Gross profit		1 201 342		1 136 465	64 877 f	5.71	34.77
Administrative expenses	890 560		875 920		14 640 a	1.67	25.78
Net profit before interest and tax		310 782		260 545	50 237 f	19.28	8.99
Interest	71 200		71 200		0	0.00	2.06
Net profit before tax		239 582		189 345	50 237 f	26.53	6.93
Taxation on ordinary activities	128 990		112 345		16 645 a	14.82	3.73
Net profit after tax		110 592		77 000	33 592 f	43.63	3.20
Dividends	24 000		22 000		2 000 f	9.09	0.69
Retained profit		86 592		55 000	31 592 f	57.44	2.51
Earnings per ordinary share (pence)		21.50		18.72	2.77 f	14.82	

TESTING THE CASH DYNAMICS OF THE BUSINESS

The cash dynamics of a business focus on how effectively a business can convert the value generated by its operations into cash flows. In order to understand the cash dynamic performance of a company we proceed in three steps.

(i) Unadjusted liquidity analysis

Current assets are those which the company is holding with the intention of conversion into cash at the earliest opportunity. From the realisations of its current assets the company will pay the first trading calls on its cash reserves, namely its current liabilities.

In its 19x1 accounts our example company revealed the position shown in Table 31.10 with respect to its current assets and liabilities.

The first point to note is that the numbers presented are a mixture of cash-based figures, commitments and accruals. Our first task is to eliminate the latter from the analysis. It is rare, in a set of company accounts, to find sufficient information to do this completely. However, any level of correction will tend to improve the quality of the data from the cash analysis point of view.

From the notes to the accounts (Figure 31.8) we see that debtors and prepayments contain a prepayment element of £51 000 in 19x1 and £50 500 in

Table 31.10

	19x1	19x0
Current assets		
Stock	123 670	145 000
Debtors and prepayments	342 980	199 450
Cash in hand	89 876	103 400
	556 526	447 850
Less: current liabilities payable in one year		
Trade creditors	214 308	219 880
Tax and other	112 345	97 213
Accruals and deferred income	43 400	40 876
	370 053	357 969
Net current assets	186 473	89 881

19x0. The accounts do not tell us whether this represents a prepayment of manu-facturing expenses (in costs of goods sold) or administrative expenses. However, for a manufacturer it is rare for prepayments to relate to the former, and so it would only concern us if we had to age non-trade debtors which do not feature in these accounts. We can, therefore, safely remove prepayments from our statement of current assets and, as they will not feature in our ageing analysis, we need not correct any profit and loss values.

A similar argument applies to accruals under current liabilities and so we eliminate this value from the balance sheet.

Two ratios show the strength of the company's current position. First, the proportion of current assets to current liabilities (the current asset ratio) and second, the 'acid test' or 'liquidity' ratio. Both ratios should be calculated with accruals and prepayments eliminated.

Current asset ratio = (current assets − prepayments)/(current liabilities − accruals)

Thus,

Current asset ratio (19x1)
= (556 526 − 51 000)/(370 053 − 43 400)
= 1.548

Current asset ratio (19x0)
= (447 850 − 50 500)/(357 969 − 40 876)
= 1.253

This ratio shows a significant improvement in the ratio of current assets to liabilities, i.e. the value of assets due to be realised within 12 months exceeds the value of liabilities (claims upon the business within 12 months) by approximately 55%.

It is often argued that this ratio is too crude, in that it fails to recognise that in the case of a forced sale or liquidation, the business would not necessarily be able to realise its full stock value. This reflects the simple view that businesses fail because they cannot sell their products. If stocks are eliminated from the measure of current assets then:

Acid test ratio (19x1)
= (556 526 − 51 000 − 123 670)/(370 053 − 43 400) = 1.169

Acid test ratio (19xx)
= (447 850 − 50 500 − 145 000)/(357 969 − 40 876) = 0.796

This ratio suggests that the company has improved its liquidity significantly from a position where its liabilities were uncovered by short-term receivables and cash to a healthy safety margin of 17%. The conventional wisdom is that an acid test ratio close to one is ideal. For figures of less than one the company will have trouble paying its bills; for figures much greater than one the question becomes: why is the company holding so much cash and not using it within the business?

In practice neither of these ratios indicates the full position because the liquidity of a business is a function of the realisability of all its current assets including stocks and, indeed, many business failures are due to the failure of a significant customer or market segment rather than failure to sell stock. Before we can undertake such an analysis we need to age the current assets and current liabilities in the balance sheet.

(ii) Evaluation of the ages of current assets and current liabilities

The average ages of each asset type (in days) are calculated using the following formulae:

Debtor age
= (trade debtors/credit turnover) × 365

Stock age (raw materials)
= (raw material stocks/cost of goods sold) × 365

Stock age (finished goods)
= (finished goods stocks/turnover) × 365

Stock age (work in progress)

$$= \frac{\text{WIP}/0.5 \times (\text{turnover} + \text{cost of goods sold}) \times 365}{2}$$

and

Trade creditor age
= (trade creditors/cost of goods sold) × 365

Other creditors
= (other creditors/administrative expenses) × 365

Note that these formulae only give an approximate value for the average age of the year end balances. The age of the outstanding value for taxation is not deducible from the accounts, but year end liabilities are usually settled within nine months of the year end. We will take nine months as a reasonable guess, although this would be a matter for investigation if the sums involved appeared to be significant.

The age analysis in Table 31.11 shows that for

Table 31.11 Age analysis of current assets and liabilities but excluding taxation

Age analysis 19x1

	Trade debtors	Raw material stock	WIP	Finished stock	Creditors
	291 980	62 210	23 440	37 020	214 308
Turnover 3 455 060	30.8			3.9	
Cost of goods 2 253 718		10.2			34.7
Average 2 854 389			3.0		

Age analysis 19x0

	Trade debtors	Raw material stock	WIP	Finished stock	Creditors
	148 950	65 430	10 987	68 583	219 880
Turnover 3 270 746	16.6			7.7	
Cost of goods 2 134 281		11.2			37.6
Average 2 702 514			1.5		

19x1 the average debtor and creditor age are in reasonable parity with one another, although there appears to have been a large increase in the average debtor age since 19x0 which would be worthy of note and investigation.

(iii) Financial μ analysis

As we have mentioned before, the problem with much accounting information collected and distributed by an organisation is that it loses its 'value relevance' in favour of its 'token relevance' with the passage of time. In order to model the cash dynamics of the organisation we need to reinstate an element of value relevance in the numbers we use. To do this we invoke the concept of a liquidity factor which we will, henceforth, denote as μ. This factor is designed to evaluate the liquidity value of any given asset or liability and takes a value between zero and one.

The μ factor is designed to transform the value of an asset from its stated 'book value' to a realisable value in the normal course of business. In other words, the assumption is that the asset is being valued in terms of its current cash equivalent, given that the business is a going concern. It is not being valued in terms of a forced sale where the assets are liquidated by sale to the most immediate buyer.

If $\mu = 1$, then an asset is perfectly liquid, and in most businesses the only assets holding this value will be cash or near-cash deposits or instruments.

If $\mu = 0$, then an asset is perfectly illiquid, and in most businesses the only assets holding this value will be pure non-cash assets (such as goodwill) which cannot be realised. For the purpose of this, and future discussion, a liability is denoted as a negative asset and a business can be considered as a portfolio combination of assets and liabilities to give a net asset position.

The liquidity factor is a combination of two components:

- the probability (p_{i0}) that the asset (i) can be realised at the point of measurement, (t_0), where $1 \geq p_i \geq 0$;
- the time-based opportunity loss for holding that asset in its current state of liquidity.

Thus

$$\mu_{i0} = p_{i0} e^{-RT}$$

where:

- e is the exponential constant;
- R is the opportunity cost (as an annualised percentage rate (APR)) of cash associated with holding that asset over that period of time;
- T is the proportion of a year until that asset can be realised (expressed as a fraction of days);
- p_i is a probability factor which is dependent upon (i) the likelihood of realisation at the current book value for the asset concerned and (ii) the likelihood of non-realisation through default. As we shall discuss later when we examine the problem of process mechanics in production, p_i may be a combination of a series of probabilistic events.

For a given asset i with a book value B, at t_0 it will have a liquidated or realisable value (RV) as follows:

$$\begin{aligned} \mathrm{RV}_{i0} &= \mu_{i0} B_{i0} \\ &= (p_{i0} e^{-RT}) B_{i0} \end{aligned}$$

For a firm of n assets, the net realisable value of all its various assets and liabilities can be described by the equation

$$\mathrm{NRV}_0 = \sum_{1}^{n} \mu_{i0} B_{i0}$$

The opportunity cost of any decision to deploy one or more of these assets is the change in NRV_0 (to the firm as a whole) caused by that decision.

The 'μ factor' is a very simple concept to understand and in most situations it is simple to measure. The measurement of μ for an asset relies upon three factors.

(i) The anticipated age to the most likely recovery of the asset concerned (or the payment of the liability): this figure can usually be discovered by direct investigation (internally) or approximated from simple ratios (externally). The age to recovery of an asset forms the dynamic as opposed to the static saliency of the asset or liability concerned. Fixed assets have low dynamic saliency but high static saliency and vice-versa for current assets.

(ii) The probability that the asset will be realised at the stated book value: in most circumstances this will be a matter of management judgement based upon historical evidence. This is what is often referred to in the context of debtor balances as the 'quality' of the debtor balance. We will adopt this business terminology to relate to all assets and liabilities.

(iii) The opportunity cost of capital for the asset concerned: we offer a more thorough discussion of the opportunity cost of capital in Chapter 13, although for the moment we can define it in the following way:

Opportunity cost of capital equals the rate of return which the business concerned would have to offer the capital market to refund the business for the consumption of that capital in investment maintaining the gearing ratio constant (see Chapter 12 for a discussion of gearing).

The calculation of the μ value for A Public Company plc is shown in Table 31.12 for both years along with a corrected current asset ratio. We have assumed a cost of capital of 12% per annum for this company for the year in question.

Note the following.

- The ages have been rounded to the nearest day.
- We have estimated probabilities of recovery from general knowledge of the business. On average we expect for this trade (this would all have to be discovered in practice) that approximately 5% of raw materials are scrapped, 3% of work in progress is lost and 1% of finished stock is written off. The company also writes of 2% of its debtor balances each year.
- For cash, the probability of immediate and full conversion into cash is obviously certain, i.e. $p_{\text{cash}} = 1$ and thus $\mu_{\text{cash}} = 1$ also as:

$$\mu_{\text{cash}} = p_{\text{cash}} e^{-RT} = 1 \times e^{-0.12 \times 0/365} = 1$$

- For debtors (for example):

$$p_{\text{debtors}} = 0.98 \text{ (i.e. 2\% write-off)}$$

$$\mu_{\text{debtors}} = 0.98 e^{-(0.12 \times 31/365)} = 0.9701$$

- The corrected value is calculated as the product of and the book value of the assets:

Corrected debtors = 0.9701 × 291 980 = £283 253

Table 31.12 μ analysis with corrected current asset ratios for A Public Company plc

μ analysis for 19x1

	Cash	Trade debtors	Raw material stock	WIP	Finished stock	Creditors	Taxation
Balance sheet value	89 876	291 980	63 210	23 440	37 020	214 308	112 345
Age (days)	0	31	10	3	4	35	274
Probability of recovery or payment (estimated)	1	0.98	0.95	0.93	0.91	1	1
μ factor	1	0.9701	0.9468	0.9291	0.9088	0.9887	0.9139
Liquidated value	89 876	283 253	59 848	21 778	33 645	211 876	102 676
Corrected current asset ratio =		1.553			Power ratio = 1.0033		

μ analysis for 19x0

	Cash	Trade debtors	Raw material stock	WIP	Finished stock	Creditors	Taxation
Balance sheet value	103 400	148 950	65 430	10 987	68 583	219 880	97 213
Age (days)	0	17	11	1	8	38	274
Probability of recovery or payment (estimated)	1	0.98	0.95	0.93	0.91	1	1
μ factor	1	0.9747	0.9465	0.9295	0.9077	0.9877	0.9139
Liquidated value	103 400	145 175	61 930	10 213	62 254	217 178	88 846
Corrected current asset ratio =		1.251			Power ratio = 0.9987		

From this analysis we can establish that this business has a high safety margin on its adjusted current asset ratio:

Corrected current asset ratio = adjusted value of current assets/adjusted value of current liabilities

Thus, figures of 1.251 (19x0) and 1.553 (19x1) indicate substantially improved margins of safety as far as the company's liquidity is concerned.

In addition, we can calculate the business's power ratio. This ratio gives the weighted average value of the μ factor for current assets divided by the weighted average value of the μ factor for liabilities.

$$\text{Power ratio} = \Sigma w_{ia}\mu_{ia}/\Sigma w_{il}\mu_{il}$$

where:

w_{ia} is the weight of each current asset (book value of *i*th asset/book value of current assets);

w_{il} is the weight of each current liability (book value of ith liability/book value of current liabilities).

The power ratio is highly sensitive to changes in the dynamic management of a company's working capital.

- If the power ratio = 1, then there is an equal cash force in and out of the business.
- If the power ratio >1, then the force is towards the business (i.e. there is a greater inbound pressure on cash conversion of current assets than the outbound conversion on liabilities).
- If the power ratio <1, then the reverse is true.

With A Public Company plc the power ratio is close to unity which, given the high adjusted current asset ratio, represents a strong position on corporate liquidity. However, you should note that this analysis does rely on the identification of the appropriate figures in the accounts and reasonable judgements on the recoverability of current assets. Given these caveats, this method is a sophisticated technique for determining and monitoring the dynamical qualities of an organisation's cash management.

PERFORMANCE AND RISK ANALYSIS USING RATIOS

Two performance ratios

In Table 31.18 we have shown a range of percentages for the ratio of profit and loss figures to turnover. For A Public Company plc we can see that the business has a 35% gross profit margin (gross profit/turnover) and a 3.7% net profit margin (net profit/turnover). These simple ratios can be calculated on a year-by-year basis, and changes noted. As we have pointed out already, the net profit margin does indicate that the company is only taking a small percentage of its turnover to its bottom line, and in this case attention should be paid to the level of non-manufacturing costs within the business.

Another popular performance ratio is the return on capital employed. This measures the ability of the company to convert its total long-term capital resources into return for its long-term investors.

Return on capital employed

$$= \frac{\text{net profit after tax + interest payments to lenders}}{\text{net capital employed + long term borrowing}}$$

Return on capital employed(19x1)
= (110 592 + 71 200)/(2 086 473 + 890 000)
= 6.1%

Return on capital employed(19x0)
= (77 000 + 71 200)/(1 999 881 + 890 000)
= 5.1%

These ratios, whilst showing an improvement over the year, still represent a very modest return on invested capital and along with the profit/turnover ratio indicate that the business's cash engine is lacking in 'horsepower'. Clearly, such figures on their own would not be conclusive, but we might be forgiven for wondering why the investors are leaving their cash in this business rather than putting it into the bank!

Two risk ratios

The measurement of risk can be determined by two important ratios:

- gearing;
- cash flow/indebtedness.

The gearing ratio has already been discussed in Chapter 13. For A Public Company plc its book value gearing is

Gearing = long-term borrowing/
(net capital employed + long term borrowing)
= 890 000/(2 086 473 + 890 000)
= 29.9% (19x1)
= 890 000/(1 999 881 + 890 000)
= 30.8% (19x0)

This indicates that the company's gearing is improving slightly as the company improves its asset position through profitable operations and retentions. However, at approximately 30% the company would not appear to be overexposed to financial risk.

The cash flow to indebtedness ratio is recognised as very powerful in warning against impending financial failure. It does not have a specific name in the literature, so we have attributed it, in the table of key ratios (Appendix to this chapter) to the famous accounting academic William Beaver who discovered its significance as a predictor of corporate failure in a famous study he conducted in 1966. The Beaver failure ratio is calculated as follows:

Cash flow to indebtedness ratio

$$= \frac{\text{annual operating cash flow}}{\text{short- plus long-term borrowing}}$$

For A Public Company plc, only long-term borrowing is present, and we can estimate trading cash flow as profit plus depreciation for the year (the difference in the accumulated depreciation in the balance sheet):

Cash flow to indebtedness ratio (19x1)
= (110 592 + 70 000)/890 000 = 20.3%

This ratio indicates that the company could not easily repay its loans out of current operations and would have to resort to asset sales to redeem the loan *in extremis*. It is difficult, as with all ratios, to make judgements on the basis of one or even a pair of ratios. However, this ratio confirms our view of a company which is:

- earning very poor margins;
- of relatively low exposure to financial risk, but with a worrying inability to repay its long term indebtedness without asset sales;
- very tightly controlled financially.

If we believed that the trading position, from our strategic analysis, was likely to improve, then we would be confident in the ability of this company to recover its margins quickly. Remember, from Chapters 12 and 13, that gearing does lever up earnings in an upturn of trade.

Many more ratios are available to aid analysis, but with the tools presented in this chapter you should be able to gauge the real strength of a business as a cash engine and how management controls the cash resources at its disposal. In the Appendix to this chapter we provide a summary of the most useful ratios in accounts analysis and, in particular, those ratios which are 'key' to the analysis of business performance and risk.

CONCLUSION

In this concluding chapter, we have discussed the problems of understanding and interpreting financial accounting information. The most important requirement, for the managerial decision maker, is to be able to interpret the information content within accounts and to be able to do more than just understand what is on the surface, but rather what is hidden between the lines. For the opportunistic manager the job, to use a modern term, is to 'deconstruct' the meaning within the accounts. Published accounting information is not 'objective' nor is it 'reliable' – the best that can ever be said is that it is honest and fair. In this chapter, we have given you the tools to determine whether financial accounts fulfil this criterion.

APPENDIX. IMPORTANT RATIOS IN THE ANALYSIS OF ACCOUNTS

Measuring the power of the cash engine (statics)

Return on capital employed (ROCE)

$$= \frac{\text{profit after tax for shareholders + interest paid to long term borrowings}}{\text{shareholder capital employed + long term borrowings}}$$

Return on equity capital employed or return on investment (ROI)

$$= \frac{\text{profit after tax for shareholders}}{\text{shareholder capital employed}}$$

Two capital-based ratios

- Compare with equivalent businesses
- Compare over time for same business
- Compare with alternative uses of capital

Sales turnover

$$= \frac{\text{profit after tax for shareholders}}{\text{turnover (sales)}}$$

- Compare with equivalent businesses
- Compare over time for same business

Average asset age

$$= \frac{\text{Fixed assets (original cost)}}{\text{depreciation charge}}$$

- Relate to industry norms
- Relate to average expired life (accumulated depreciation/fixed assets at cost)

Measuring the financial risk of the business

Capital gearing

$$= \frac{\text{long-term borrowings}}{\text{shareholder capital employed + long term borrowing}}$$

Two ratios which measure the exposure of the business to bankruptcy risk through the level of long-term borrowing

- Compare with equivalent businesses
- Test for 'reasonable' level of risk

Dynamic ratios

Average debtor age (in days)

$$= \frac{\text{trade debtors}}{\text{credit turnover}} \times 365$$

Average creditor age (in days)

$$= \frac{\text{trade creditors}}{\text{purchases}} \times 365$$

These ratios are significant as a pair in that they measure the structural dynamics of the business's cash flow. Published accounts do not discriminate between credit and cash sales. Total turnover may be used instead as an approximation

Average stock holding period (in days)

$$= \frac{\text{raw materials stock}}{\text{cost of goods sold}} \times 365$$

More modern manufacturing methods can produce significant reduction in this ratio

Finished stock turnover ratio

$$= \frac{\text{turnover}}{\text{finished stock}}$$

The number of times the average finished stock level is sold (turned over) in the year concerned. This rate should show an increase year on year.

Ratio	Comment
Income gearing $= \frac{\text{interest paid on long term borrowing}}{\text{profit before tax} + \text{interest paid on long term borrowing}}$	
Beaver failure ratio $= \frac{\text{annual operating cash flow}}{\text{short- and long term-borrowing}}$	Powerful ratio in classifying distressed from non-distressed businesses • Look for sudden downturn in this ratio over time

Measuring the cash dynamics of the business

Ratio	Comment
Current ratio (current asset ratio) $= \frac{\text{current assets}}{\text{current liabilities}}$	A first-order ratio for determining a business's ability to cover short-term claims • Typically should be 1.0 or better
Acid test (liquidity) ratio $= \frac{\text{current assets} - \text{stocks}}{\text{current liabilities}}$	Assumes that in distress, stocks are the least liquid of the current assets • Depends on recoverability of debtors but should be 1.0 or better

Financial ratios

Ratio	Comment
Return on investment $= \frac{\text{profit after tax for distribution}}{\text{total equity including retained earnings}}$	Shareholder version of ROCE • Compare with industry norms • Compare over time
Price earnings ratio $= \frac{\text{price per share}}{\text{earnings per share}}$	Market measure of risk of business • Compare with industry norms
Dividend yield $= \frac{\text{dividend per share}}{\text{price per share}}$	• Compare with alternative investment sources. Does not reveal growth benefit of reinvestment
Dividend cover $= \frac{\text{earnings per share}}{\text{dividend per share}}$	Measures the reinvestment policy of the business. If <1, dividends are uncovered, >1 dividends covered
Earnings yield $= \frac{\text{earnings per share}}{\text{price per share}}$	• Compare with alternative investments but note part of yield is reinvested
Return (period) = period dividend yield (%) + (price change over period/opening price) × 100	Critical measure to compare with alternative investment opportunities

Part VII

Questions and Bibliography

Chapter 32

Questions in Strategic Accounting

Summary

In this we offer a range of questions for individual or group work. Many require a knowledge of one or more chapters and can be used on an individual basis, or by class teachers and facilitators for assignment work. For this reason the questions are not organised on a chapter-by-chapter basis. The questions are predominantly of a discussion type and are designed to focus thought and debate, as well as give the opportunity for further work and practice. These questions do not provide an exhaustive coverage of the issues dealt within the book, but should provide a basis for a sound technical understanding of the topics discussed.

1 Outline your objectives in purchasing this book. What criteria will you use for determining the success of this purchase?

2 List the principal financial decisions which you make during the course of every month. What information do you require in order to make those decisions? Analyse those financial decisions into those over which you have some discretion and those which are fixed commitments.

3 Outline the strategic accounting approach. How does it differ from management or financial accounting?

4 Distinguish between the long and short run in decision making. What personal financial decisions have you made which could be regarded as long run?

5 Distinguish between different levels of management and identify, in your own place of work or study, those individuals who occupy the levels of management you have specified. Outline the types of accounting information which you think those managers might require in the normal course of their work.

6 'Company law' is that part of the law which is concerned with the way companies are established and administer themselves. The law lays down the duties and responsibilities of the directors of a company and the rights and powers of company shareholders. Identify which Acts currently govern companies and which sections of those Acts specify the content and layout of company accounts.

7 There have been a number of different attempts to formulate overall objectives which both describe and prescribe the ways in which firms should behave. Some suggestions are as follows.

- Firms should work to maximise the profit which is distributable to their owners.
- Firms should act to maximise the market value of the firm's shares.
- The principal aim of a firm is to ensure its long-term survival.
- The principal aim of the firm is to maximise the its value added for all stakeholders.

To what extent do you think these objectives presume that shareholders are the most important group within a firm, and what reasons can you give to support that view?

8 What limits the power of management to do the following?

(i) Hire and fire employees
(ii) Influence the quality of supplies
(iii) Introduce new technology or products

With which groups must management negotiate in each case and to what extent are their interests likely to conflict?

9 What is meant by the following terms?

(i) Transaction
(ii) Commitment
(iii) Transactions cost

In what sense is it meaningful to talk about transactions cost minimisation as an objective of management?

10 At what stage of their life cycle would you place the following products and why?

(i) Video recorders
(ii) Asbestos
(iii) Electronic calculators
(iv) Jumbo jets
(v) This book

11 Perfect competition is an 'ideal' market type. The assumptions necessary for such a market to exist are:

- a large number of buyers and sellers of the commodity in question;
- a single ruling price which both buyers and sellers must take as given;
- no transaction costs or taxes which either buyers or sellers must pay in order to trade;
- no barriers of entry into the market (i.e. anyone who has a mind to set up as a producer of the commodity in question may do so without restriction).

Discuss the extent to which you agree with the following statements.

(i) Perfect competition defines an 'ideal case' against which reality can be compared.
(ii) The movement toward perfection in particular markets is regarded, in certain political senses, as desirable.
(iii) Perfect markets lead to an efficient allocation of resources within an economy with the minimum of political control.
(iv) Perfectly competitive markets are pure, self-regulating anarchies.

12 Discuss the meaning of the following terms:

(i) Organisation
(ii) Market
(iii) Organisational structure
(iv) Perfect competition

13 We can split input factors used by firms into four groups: capital, labour, managerial and technical skills and 'hard factors'. Suggest how these four inputs could be further subdivided for a motor-car manufacturer.

14 Discuss the different sorts of uncertainty which a manager might have to face in the sale of a new product. How does that uncertainty differ from the situation where a company is selling an established product?

15 Outline the differences between debt and equity capital. What does it mean to say that a loan is secured, and what sorts of security would an individual be able to offer to a bank in order to obtain a loan?

16 Discuss the influence which the structure of an organisation could have on the accounting carried on within it.

17 Lucia, Pena and Algericas have assets as shown in Table 32.1. Algericas has a bank deposit account in which he has invested £1000 per annum over the last five years. He has earned 10% per annum throughout the period. Pena expects to earn £6000 this year, although, at the moment, he has no further employment prospects beyond that time. Lucia, on the other hand, has just won a recording contract for five years which is worth £4000 per annum. Lucia feels that 10% per annum is the best rate he could get on either borrowing or lending. The value of £1 per annum invested for five years at 10% is £6.716. The present value of an annuity of 1 discounted over 5 years at 10% is £3.790. Which of the three has the greatest wealth?

Table 32.1

	Lucia (£)	Pena (£)	Algericas (£)
Cash in hand	200	100	10
House and chattels (resale value)	18 000	25 000	27 000

18 Define the concepts of capability, commitment, cash and control. Discuss their importance for the firm generally and for the accounting function more specifically.

19 To what extent do you think that the economist's concept of opportunity cost represents an absolute definition of the concept of cost? In what sense are Ryan's Second Law of Financial Management and the opportunity cost concept related?

20 The following materials are necessary for the production of a new chemical.

(A) Boro-grot: held in stock, but otherwise obsolete for other production.
(B) Boro-primo: on order from a supplier. The contract for delivery has been made at the price stated as the 'historical cost' below although the materials have not, as yet, been paid for. The original order was made in the belief that the company would be making another chemical altogether. However, for technical reasons the use of Boro-primo in the process was not feasible, and the company had planned to sell its stock of Boro-primo as soon as it was received from the supplier.
(C) Boro-secundo: none in stock, but currently available from suppliers.

The costs per kilogram of each of these raw materials are as shown in Table 32.2.

(i) State the relevant cost of each of the three raw materials in the production decision.
(ii) Define opportunity cost and classify, giving reasons, the main types of cost which are irrelevant for decision making purposes.

21 Seville Ltd manufactures scientific instruments. It is considering whether to manufacture a batch of oscilloscopes. The contract would last 12 weeks. A statement (Table 32.3) has been prepared on the basis that the contract should not be accepted. The following additional information is also available.

Materials. Material A was purchased two years previously at a cost of £750. If sold now it would realise £500. Alternatively, it could be adapted and used on another job as a substitute for material currently costing £800. It would cost £150 to make the necessary adaptation.

Material B was ordered six months ago when the price was £900. Since that time the original use for the material had disappeared, but Seville had planned to use the materials on the production of some laser-beam scanners. It would cost £100 to modify the materials for that use. The current buying price for material B is £1000; its selling price with modification would be £1200 and without modification £850. The supplier of material B has offered a 5% discount because of the delayed delivery although, under the terms of the original purchase agreement, delay would not be an excuse for Seville to rescind the contract.

Labour. The labour charge of £3500 includes £1000 in respect of a foreman's wages. Unlike the rest of the labour to be used on the contract the foreman will be employed whether or not the contract is accepted. However, if he does work on the contract the company will have to pay an extra £15 per week to take over his duties on other production. The remainder of the workforce earn half of their income by piecework payments, the other half is a basic payment.

Machinery. Two machines will have to be used on the contract. The first machine is already leased at £50 per week. This machine is currently being used in another department and, if it is used on the contract, a replacement machine will have to be leased at a revised rate of £60 per

Table 32.2

	Historical cost (£)	Replacement cost (£)	Realisable value (£)
Boro-grot	15	12	5
Boro-primo	32	35	26
Boro-secundo		17	13

Table 32.3

	£	£
Materials		
A: already in stock (original cost)	750	
B: ordered (original contract price)	900	
Total materials		1 650
Labour:		3 500
Machinery:		
Leased at £50 per week	2600	
Depreciation	2000	
Total machinery		4 600
General overheads		3 500
Design costs		2 400
TOTAL COST		15 650
Contract price offered		10 000
Surplus/loss on the contract		(5 650)

week. The second machine is due to be sold. If it is kept in use for the life of the contract its sale value will fall by £1200.

General overheads. These cover such items as rent and rates and other administrative overheads. These overheads are charged to contracts on the basis of £1 for every pound of direct labour cost. All of the general overheads will be paid, even if the contract is forgone.

Design costs. Some preliminary design costs have already been incurred which amount to £2400.

Table 32.4

	£	£
Materials		
A:		
B:		
Total materials		
Labour		
Foreman		
Others		
Total labour		
Machinery:		
Leased		
Owned		
Total machinery		
General overheads		
Design costs		
TOTAL OPPORTUNITY COST		
Contract price offered		10 000
Surplus/loss on the contract		

Fill in the revised statement of Table 32.4 to obtain the surplus or loss on the contract.

22 Phrygian and Co. produce metal containers. They have been approached by an instrument manufacturer who requires 10 000 boxes of set dimension with fancy clasps and letterings. Phrygian realise that in order to win the contract they must price very competitively. There are a number of other potential suppliers in the market. Phrygian's management accountant has identified the following facts,

Materials

0.001 gauge mild steel would be required. This material is no longer used on any other of the firm's production processes:

Requirement	8000 square feet
Stock held	5000 square feet
Original cost	£0.25 per square foot
Replacement cost	£0.75 per square foot
Scrap value	£0.45 per square foot

Labour requirements

- Machinists and cutters: 1000 labour hours. The firm has sufficient labour to meet the production requirements of this contract as well as the existing work although 500 hours overtime would have to be worked. The current wage rate is £4.00 per hour with overtime paid at time and a half. New staff could be employed for this contract and this would ensure that the contract would be completed in normal working time, although 1100 labour hours would be required as 100 hours would be used for training.

- Finishers: 1500 labour hours. Finishers belong to a highly skilled trade. They are paid £8 per hour (normal time) with double time paid for any overtime worked. Their current deployment means that half the hours required on the new job would have to be worked as overtime. In addition, a number of other jobs would have to be left undone. This will result in a loss of cash to the firm of £1800 in total, excluding the additional overtime which will have to be paid to this class of labour.

Incidental expenses

Clasps, letter punches and special tools	£600
Design costs (already incurred)	£550
Supervision of machinists during overtime	£1000
Variable overheads (with production)	£650
Fixed overheads charged per labour hour worked	£1.50

Cutting and welding equipment will also be used on this job. The depreciation chargeable to this job is £245. The use of this equipment is unlikely to effect its useful life.

(i) Evaluate the minimum, cash contributing price, for this contract.
(ii) What would be the contribution margin if a price of £2.00 per unit was obtained?

23 Consider and discuss the implications of the following two statements:

(i) When we discuss market behaviour of firms, we should talk about 'economic profit', which is total revenue less the full opportunity cost of production, where opportunity cost, in this case, includes the cost of the managerial and capital resources employed. In a perfect market no firm will earn positive economic profits because the mere existence of surplus profits will induce additional competitors to enter the market.
(ii) In reality, markets are not perfect, and firms employ many tactics to break the linkage between output and price. The commonest way of doing this is by the creation of stocks. If a firm attempts to sell all it produces immediately, it must take the market price dictated by its demand curve for that output level. However, with many products, the creation of stocks allows the firm to release its production onto the market when demand conditions are most favourable.

24 Construct a personal (or family) budget for yourself over the next month. Plan on the basis of cash inflows (wages or salary, grants etc.) and cash outflows under different expenditure headings (food, clothing, drink, entertainment etc.). Regard any permanent savings as an 'expenditure' to a deposit or other long-term savings account. Keep a record of all the cash receipts and expenditure you make during the month and then, at the end of the month, answer the following questions.

(i) What aim did you set yourself when drawing up your budget (making a cash surplus, breaking even, reducing your overdraft etc.)?
(ii) What information did you use to make your plans?
(iii) How carefully did you have to time your cash payments in order to avoid running into deficit?
(iv) Can you allocate causes to the differences between your planned and actual figures?
(v) Can you reconcile the figure on your bank statement and credit-card bills with your summary of actual receipts and payments?
(vi) How did you motivate yourself to keep within your budget?

25 Discuss the extent to which the distinction between the long and the short run is a distinction of convenience rather than a distinction of fact.

26 In the following situations, indicate whether the decisions to be taken should be considered long or short run, and specify any further information you would require in order to confirm your choice.

(i) A company is deciding the price at which to sell the maximum output of a particular plant. The plant is in continuous operation.
(ii) A pharmaceutical company is considering opening a new research centre into antiviral agents. Few such agents are available commercially.
(iii) A cosmetics manufacturer is considering the level of advertising which should be commissioned for its new range of male cosmetics. Male cosmetics usually have a product life of less than three years.

(iv) A football club is wondering whether to strengthen its defence by buying a South American international star of many years' experience.
(v) A motor-car manufacturer is drawing up its production budget for three versions of the same basic model line. Each version differs from the others in terms of engine size, quality of trim and extras. All three models are produced on the same production facility.
(vi) A firm of chartered accountants is deciding upon the maximum level of taxation work which the firm should undertake and the number of partners who should specialise in that aspect of the firm's work.

27 Outline the principal features of a personal budget for a single person with only one major source of income. The individual concerned holds both a current and deposit account at a bank, two credit cards and a building society share account which requires seven days' notice of withdrawal. The individual's monthly salary cheque is paid into the current account by monthly direct credit, and certain important monthly payments are made by standing orders and direct debits.

28 Determine the point price elasticity of demand at the following price–quantity points on the following demand curve:

$$p = 290 - 0.1\,Q$$

p (£)	Q (units)
290	0
190	1000
145	1450
115	1750

29 What does it mean if the demand curve has infinite elasticity along its entire length, i.e. the demand for the product is perfectly elastic?

30 Using the example in Chapter 18 of the text (Almeria), analysis of Almeria's old cost-accounting records reveals that the production costs for May and June were made up as shown in Table 32.5.
The same percentage increase for components applied in May and June as applied to the subsequent six months. There was no extraordinary increase in labour costs in May and June.

(i) Repeat the analysis of the production–cost–output relationship.

Table 32.5

	May (£)	June (£)
Component cost	26 117	14 990
Labour cost	36 364	20 450
Variable overhead	10 000	5 625
Fixed overhead	47 000	47 000
Total production cost	119 481	88 065
Output (units)	695	470

(ii) Then, using the additional two months' data for May and June, recalculate for Almeria's management (a) the correlation coefficient; (b) the coefficient of statistical determination.
(iii) Redraw the relationship between total production cost and output on a graph.

31 Sketch the following types of cost–output relationship and give at least one example of a typical cost for each.

(i) Fixed cost
(ii) Directly variable cost
(iii) Semivariable cost
(iv) Stepped fixed cost
(v) Stepped variable cost
(vi) Ratchet cost

32 A company faces a demand curve for one of its products which is of the form:

Price per unit = 300 − (0.1 × quantity demanded)

(i) Draw a table of (a) price, (b) quantity, (c) total revenue, (d) marginal revenue and (e) point elasticity of demand at intervals along the demand curve. Identify in your table the point at which total revenue is maximised.
(ii) Comment upon the relevance of a company's demand curve to its output decision.

33 Figure 32.1 shows a break-even graph for a coated paper production process. Identify the following items on the graph:

(i) Total-revenue function
(ii) Fixed cost
(iii) Directly variable cost
(iv) Semivariable cost
(v) Material cost with discounts
(vi) The points of break-even

Sketch a profigram on the break-even curve.

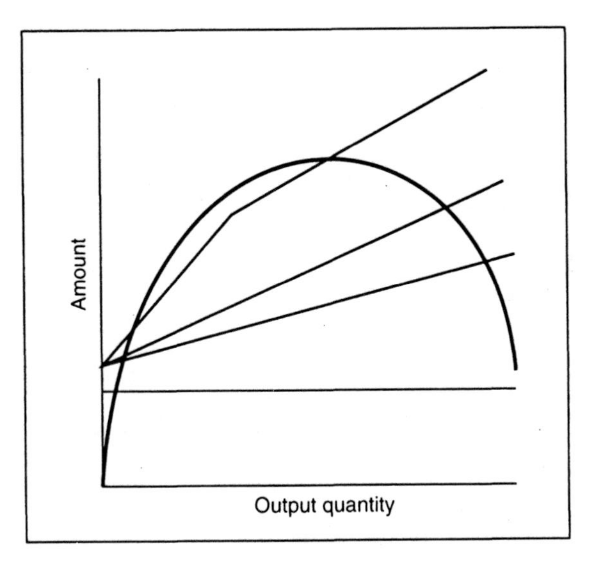

Figure 32.1

34 Records of catering costs have been kept for the last five years, along with the number of cooked meals provided in Upmarket University's refectory. The University Refectory Users Consultative Committee has asked you to estimate the total annual fixed costs and the average variable cost per meal provided (as at 1 January 19x6).

Wage rates for refectory staff were increased by 10% on 1 January 19x3 and a further 10% was made at the beginning of 19x6. The cost items marked with an asterisk have tended to increase in line with the Retail Price Index which has averaged 16% per annum over the period.

35 The Owen Steel works in Sussex produces steel strip on a continuous process. The molten steel is extruded through dies as it cools from red heat to a dull yellow colour. The steel is then pressed into shape and water quenched. It finally emerges from the process tempered to a light blue colour. This steel-die process can be operated at any level in the range 10 000–20 000 m of steel strip per production run. The variable and fixed costs are shown in Table 32.7.

A certain quantity of scrap steel is required to prime the process and this costs £8500 irrespective of output. The fixed costs of production apply over certain ranges (Table 32.8).

(i) Draw a break-even chart for the steel-making process outlined above and identify, within the specified range of output, both the points of break-even and the profit-maximising output.

(ii) Comment upon the assumptions implicit in break-even analysis and discuss the general usefulness of break-even analysis in output decision making.

(iii) Construct a flexible budget at 10 000 m output rising to 20 000 m in intervals of 2000 m.

36 A company in the mining industry has monitored its average annual productivity for a particular class of labour. The average pre-tax earnings per labour hour have also been collected for this class of labour. During the course of the latest round of wage negotiations, the employees' union has maintained that productivity is unrelated to earnings. Management believes otherwise. The relevant figures for the previous six years are shown in Table 32.9.

Table 32.6

	Year ended 31 December 19x1	19x2	19x3	19x4	19x5
Food* (£)	26 200	70 000	103 000	103 500	119 800
Wages (£)	35 400	82 000	139 000	140 000	162 900
Rent (£)	20 000	20 000	20 000	20 000	20 000
Sundry overheads* (£)	17 000	18 000	18 500	19 000	20 000
Depreciation of equipment (£)	5 000	5 000	5 000	5 000	5 000
Office salaries (£)	6 000	7 000	7 500	8 000	9 000
Heat, light etc. (£)	4 000	4 500	4 700	4 800	4 800
Sales revenue (£)	120 000	308 000	540 000	510 000	736 000
Meals sold	110 000	300 000	550 000	480 000	680 000

Table 32.7

	Per metre final product (£)
Iron ore	1.20
Scap iron	0.25
Energy	1.80
Labour	2.25

Table 32.8

Output (metres)	Fixed cost (£)
0– 4 999	10 000
5 000– 9 999	17 500
10 000–14 999	25 000
15 000–19 999	35 000
20 000–24 999	47 500

Table 32.9

Year to 31 Dec	Net earnings (£)	Average productivity per labour hour (tons)
19x1	800 500	16.2
19x2	910 100	16.4
19x3	922 000	17.3
19x4	977 000	17.4
19x5	1 050 000	17.7
19x6	1 100 000	17.7

Note the following points:

- Wages have kept pace with the annual rate of increase in the Retail Price Index, which has averaged 5% over the period.
- There was an additional increase of 5% over the Retail Price Index from 1 January 19x4.

(i) Advise the negotiators on the relationship between annual net earnings and average productivity per labour hour. Support your advice with any statistical techniques which you think appropriate.
(ii) Discuss the way in which labour costs could be expected to vary with output level.

37 If consumers act according to the rules of economic rationality, we would expect them to forget about the cost of a particular purchase once it had been made. However, in practice, most people find that the purchase of relatively expensive goods can lead to a state of internal conflict as they question whether they have used the money involved in a sensible way. Social psychologists argue that individuals seek means of reducing this internal conflict or 'dissonance'; hence the need for reinforcing advertising. In fact we can identify two phases of conflict: before and after a decision is made to purchase a particular product. First, in the phase of predecisional conflict, the consumer attempts to reconcile the conflicting claims upon his or her resources. Second, in the phase of postdecisional conflict – the cognitive dissonance referred to above – the individual attempts to subdue the feeling of 'maybe not having done the right thing'. This problem is often made worse because many consumption decisions involve 'hot cognitive processes', i.e. stressful decisions made under some sort of selling pressure.
Discuss the implications of this issue for:

(i) Pricing
(ii) Advertising
(iii) Marketing policy generally

38 The major clearing banks change their base rates in the light of economic events and in the light of one another's behaviour. In addition, they alter their charges on personal accounts in concert with one another. Gather any evidence that you can which supports this behaviour. Is there any bank which consistently appears to be a price leader?

39 Distinguish between the different types of product market which a firm may face and suggest the types of information the management accountant should produce in each market situation.

40 Discuss the extent to which the structure of a firm will influence its ability to make pricing decisions in different market contexts.

41 Alcala plc is about to launch a new product into the domestic 'do it yourself' market, and has just received a report from a team of marketing consultants it had commissioned to examine the problem of the product's price. They have established the following.

- Customers would be prepared to pay up to £450 for the first units made available by the firm.
- Subsequent sales would, on average, reduce the selling price by 1p for each unit sold.

These figures relate to monthly sales.
If the product was promoted once per annum at a time just prior to the peak selling Easter period, the firm's demand curve would shift as follows.

- The first unit sold in the month would fetch a price of £610.
- Subsequent sales would, on average, reduce the price by 0.85p for each unit sold.

Management requests you to consider the following requirements: the process should be operated at a level which, during the 'off season', will produce sufficient to maximise total revenue from sales and that the pre-Easter promotion campaign should offer a 20% discount on the year-round price for the month in which Easter falls.

(i) Draw up a full report for management on the implications of the consultant's advice concerning the market.
(ii) Determine, given management's requirements, the increase in revenue which would result from the Easter sales campaign.

42 You are given the following information concerning a particular product.

- The variable cost of production is £16.80 per unit.
- Each unit requires 0.5 labour hours and 0.1 machine hours in production.
- The total annual fixed costs attributable to the factory are £640 000. During the year, £150 000 labour hours and 30 000 machine hours were employed in the factory.
- The company has a target rate of return on capital employed of 15% per annum. The capital employed is £4 620 000.
- The factory's products are all physically similar to one another, although they have varying degrees of labour and machine inputs.

The product described above accounts for one-third of the units produced by the factory, uses 60 000 labour hours and 3960 machine hours in production.

(i) Calculate the price which will give the target rate of return when applied to the 'total' cost per unit produced on three overhead allocation bases.
(ii) Discuss the relative merits of the allocation bases you have used and comment upon the reasonableness of cost-based pricing procedures.

43 A friend of yours is considering setting up a factory/shop in a small, but developing new town. She is primarily interested in producing and selling women's clothing. The new town has been developed in a country area near a small village from which the new town has taken its name. The village is served by a fast train line to London, and it is anticipated that the town will attract some high-technology industry to the new science park being developed in the area. Over the next three years the population of the town is likely to expand to approximately 7500 households in owner-occupied properties. The average, disposable income of each household is expected to be 1.8 times the national average. Your friend would like to know the total sales, per annum, which her factory/shop could achieve, assuming no local competition.
What information would you need to obtain and how would you go about collecting that information in order to advise your friend?

44 Three years later, your friend (from Question 43) is doing very well. In broad outline your advice was soundly based, and as a result her business is prosperous and developing rapidly. However, she now has another problem: a chain of fashion shops has asked her to tender for the supply of a line of clothes which they will sell under their own brand label. The production would absorb 20% of her current capacity, which would mean an extension of her current production facilities in order to cover her current requirements. A condition of the contract would be that the buying firm would specify strict conditions on quality control and would hold the right to make unannounced factory inspections.
Your friend asks for both your general advice, and also for you to outline the procedure which she would have to follow in making a tender for the supply of the clothing.

45 Define the following terms:

(i) Internal opportunity cost
(ii) Dual price of a scarce resource

46 Answer the following.

(i) Why does the opportunity cost of a scarce resource include its market price even though, temporarily, a market for that resource does not exist?
(ii) What criterion is used to rank items of production when only a single scarce resource is in short supply?
(iii) What limits the applicability of dual prices as a means of assessing the merits of alterations to an existing production plan?

47 Torre produces seven products, each of which requires use of a raw material called anisrot. The contribution per unit, maximum annual demand and quantity of raw material required per unit of product are shown in Table 32.10.
Torre does not maintain stocks of either finished products or raw materials.

(i) Calculate the optimal annual production plan for Torre assuming:

- that anisrot is available in unlimited quantities at its market price of £6.25 per kilogram;
- that only 50 000 kg of anisrot are available per annum at the market price.

(ii) Calculate the maximum price which Torre would be prepared to pay for extra supplies of the raw material required on the assumption that only 50 000 kg are available at the price of £6.25 per kilogram.
(iii) Discuss the economic significance of your answers to (i) and (ii) above.

48 Describe using diagrams if necessary, and supply one example of each:

(i) Feedback control
(ii) Feedforward control
(iii) Hybrid control

49 Seville produces coated paper and is attempting to optimise its holding of its principal raw material, rolls of paper. Each roll is purchased at a price of £125 excluding variable freightage of £2 per roll. The fixed freightage for each order is £45 and Seville estimates that its fixed cost of ordering is £25 per order. Its annual usage of the paper is budgeted for the next year at 12 000 rolls although its usage could vary by 5% either way. Seville's cost of money is 12% per annum. Delivery from date of order is guaranteed at 10 days.

(i) Determine the reorder quantity on the basis that 12 000 rolls are required in the coming year.
(ii) Determine the reorder level, given that management wants to avoid the possibility of stock out.
(iii) Assuming an annual usage of 12 000 rolls, determine whether a discount of 2.5% on the invoiced cost (excluding freightage) would be worthwhile for orders in excess of 350 rolls.
(iv) Calculate the minimum acceptable discount for orders in excess of (a) 350 rolls and (b) 400 rolls.

50 Ruskin plc has implemented a programme for the reduction of its outstanding debtor balances and the time which they are outstanding. As a result of this they have also achieved a reduction in the amount of debt lost through defaults from 3% of receivables each year to 1.5%. The average outstanding period has been reduced from 45 to

Table 32.10

Product	Contribution per unit (£)	Maximum annual demand (units)	Quantity of anisrot per unit
A	2.40	6 000	2
B	1.60	2 000	2
C	4.20	2 500	5
D	5.00	10 000	10
E	2.20	7 000	1
F	6.00	6 500	3
G	1.50	7 700	1

30 days and the outstanding balance from £1.45m to £0.943m. The company has a cost of funds of 10%.

(i) Identify the total financial benefit to the company of this debtor reduction programme.
(ii) Calculate the benefit achieved through value reduction, timing and recovery effects.

51 For the success of firms, Oliver Williamson (1991), stated: 'I advance the argument that economising is more fundamental than strategising – or, put differently, that *economy is the best strategy* . . . Among other things, emphasis on economising restores manufacturing and merchandising to a place of importance within the business firm.'

(i) What do you believe Williamson means by the terms 'economising' and 'strategising' in this context?
(ii) Evaluate this statement with respect to your organisation seeking competitive advantage in the market place.

52 Define what is meant by the following terms:

(i) Call option
(ii) Put option
(iii) Hedge ratio

53 The premium on a 90-day call option in Atlee plc ordinary 25p shares is 34p per share. The current price of the stock is 245p per share and the exercise price is 250p per share. The expected variance of its distribution of continuous returns is 28%. The risk free rate of return is 6% per annum.

(i) Given the above data, is the quoted premium a fair reflection of the expected premium?
(ii) Discuss the extent to which the option pricing approach developed by Black and Scholes is applicable to the valuation of other corporate options.

54 A French manufacturer is contemplating entering the UK market as a vendor of holographic imaging systems for architectural practices. This is a new product opportunity and may well be extendable to related market areas. What sort of issues would you regard as important in devising a marketing and financial strategy for this product launch, and what problem areas would you foresee for the company entering the UK market?

55 The share price of Boddington plc is currently 282p per share and has varied between 299p and 189p over the last 12 months. The Company has offered modest real growth in dividends of 2.5% per annum and inflation currently stands at 4%. The cost of finance to Boddington, given its business risk, is estimated at 10.5% per annum. The dividend paid in the previous 12 months was 9.60p per share. Given these data, does the quoted share price fairly reflect the value of the share to an equity investor?

56 Martin plc is valuing its stock of 'sludge-nuts' at the end of June 19x5. There was no stock in hand at the beginning of the month. During the month the purchases and issues from stock shown in Table 31.11 were made.

(i) Determine the end-of-month stock value using (a) FIFO, (b) LIFO and (c) the average-stock method of valuation.
(ii) Comment upon the advantages and disadvantages of the three methods of valuing stock.

57 The monthly projections for a small electronics components manufacturer are as follows.
Sales revenue currently stands at £7800 per month and is expected to expand at 1% per month into the indefinite future. This is the average rate of expansion which the firm has enjoyed over the previous six months. The firm's debtors pay up as follows: one-third within one month, half within two months and the remainder within three months.
The company has enjoyed a gross profit margin of 25% on monthly sales over the past year and has tried to keep its inventory constant at a very low level. The company's suppliers require

Table 32.11

	Purchases (bags)	Purchase price per bag (£)	Issues (bags)
1 June	10	100	
4 June			5
7 June	20	110	
12 June			15
15 June	12	112	
22 June			8
24 June	10	116	
27 June			9

payment within one month. They can enforce this condition of trade because of the high demand for microelectronic components.
The company's management is considering a 1.5% discount on the invoiced value of goods if payment is received within one month. It believes that this will ensure that 50% of the firm's debtors pay within the month and that half the remainder will pay at the end of the second month and the rest at the end of the third month.
Assume all cash receipts and payments occur on the last day of the month and that the company's cost of capital is 0.8% per month.

(i) Create a projected cash budget for sales less purchases over the next six months, and show the effect on that cash budget if the change in credit policy is implemented.
(ii) Calculate whether the change in credit policy is worthwhile, given the firm's cost of capital.
(iii) Discuss the problems of maintaining liquidity in a situation of expanding trade.

58 Zambra plc wishes to prepare a budget for the production and sale of one of its products, the Mora, for the coming three years. Current financial statistics for Mora production are as follows.

Variable cost per Mora:	
Raw materials	£15.00
Labour	£10.00
Variable overheads	£5.00
Selling price per Mora	£55.00
Output quantity per annum	8000.00 Moras
Fixed overheads per annum	£45 000.00

Fixed overheads can only be avoided if production is discontinued. The expected rates of cost increases are:

Raw materials	10% per annum
Labour	15% per annum
Variable overheads	6% per annum
Fixed overheads	3% per annum

Zambra sells all of the Moras it can produce at the planned selling price. Because the Mora has an extremely short shelf life, no stocks are maintained.

(i) Draw up a projected budget for the next three years on the assumption that (a) output is held constant and (b) the current net profit margin (ratio of net profit to sales revenue) remains constant.
(ii) Outline the difficulties in controlling the cash resources of a firm and the ways in which they can be overcome.

59 Identify the cost centre in which you either work or study. If you are a student your department or scheme may be the cost centre in which you work. List the main costs which you think your cost centre is responsible for. Do the costs, as collected, give any information on the performance of your cost centre?

60 Design a job card for the construction of a pine, refectory-style table by a craftsman carpenter in a company specialising in custom-built pine furniture. Use your imagination!

61 Using the techniques of variance analysis on the actual and budget data presented in Table 32.12, extract a full set of information for a management report.
The relationship between price and quantity demanded is given by

$$p = 40.5 - 0.00062 \times Q$$

Management policy is to investigate all variances which differ from budget by more than 2%.

62 Briefly outline the meaning of the following cost-accounting terms:

(i) Cost centre
(ii) Overhead allocation
(iii) Weighted-average process costing
(iv) Job card
(v) Efficiency variance
(vi) Controllable and uncontrollable variances

63 Ramon Industrial (Chemicals) plc started up continuous production on its trinitrotoluene plant at the beginning of the month of January. The costs of production in the month of January were as follows:

Toluene (raw material)	£18 000
Nitric acid (raw material)	£6 500
Labour	£7 800
Energy costs	£6 600
Other variable production costs	£4 000
	£42 900

Of the final product, 10 000 kg were produced during the month and 1000 kg were still in progress. Mr Ken Tucky, the plant manager, believes that the state of completion of the work

Table 32.12

	Actual		Budget	
	Quantity	Price (cost per unit) (£)	Quantity	Price (cost per unit) (£)
Sales and production level	18 000 units	28.00	17 000 units	30.00
Material A	27 000 kg	14.00	23 000 kg	13.00
Material B	32 000 kg	13.00	28 000 kg	8.00
Labour – semiskilled	2 000 hours	12.00	2 100 hours	10.00
Labour – unskilled	600 hours	8.00	550 hours	8.00
Overheads (variable)		2.00		1.50
Overheads (fixed) (allocated on semi-skilled labour)		16.00 (per hour)		15.00 (per hour)

in progress is as follows:

Toluene	Complete
Nitric acid	Half-complete
Labour	Two-thirds complete
Energy	One-third complete
Other variable costs	Half complete

(i) Calculate the unit cost of trinitrotoluene during the month's production.
(ii) Value the work in progress at the end of the month.
(iii) Comment on the use of process costing in corporate decision making.

64 The budgeted and actual sales revenue and labour costs for a particular process are as follows:

Sales revenue:	
Actual price per unit	£65.00
Budgeted price per unit	£60.00
Actual quantity produced (tons)	12 000
Budgeted quantity produced	15 000
Labour costs:	
Actual labour rate per hour	£10.50
Budgeted labour rate per hour	£12.00
Actual labour hours employed in production	8400
Budgeted labour hours employed in production	8200

(i) Calculate the labour wage rate, the labour usage, the labour efficiency and the activity variances for the above process, and comment upon the figures you have produced.
(ii) Comment upon the usefulness of variance analysis as a technique of management control.

65 Lorca plc produces Garcias among other things. Lorca's manufacturing director believes that the production of Garicas is no longer viable, although, under pressure from the marketing director, she is prepared to conduct an investigation into this product's profitability. Toward this end the manufacturing director has decided to analyse the differences between actual and budgeted sales and production for Garcias for the year ended 31 December 19x2.
Financial figures, abstracted from the company's annual management reports, are shown in Table 32.13.
Stock levels were unchanged during the year. The fixed overheads are directly attributable to Garcia production, although they are only fixed over the range 6000–10 000 units.

(i) Prepare a statement showing the actual and budgeted profits for the year ended 31 December 19x2.
(ii) Calculate the price and efficiency variances for both labour and materials.
(iii) The company's master budget had specified sales of 9000 units. Calculate the variance which would appear to be attributable to the marketing function for the shortfall in sales volume.
(iv) What comments can you make about the figures you have prepared in (i) to (iii) above?

Table 32.13

	Actual	Flexible budget
Sales of Garcias (units)	7 000.00	7 000.00
Unit sales price (£)	24.00	24.00
Raw materials used (kg)	36 810.00	35 000.00
Cost per kilogram (£)	0.58	0.60
Labour hours employed	15 000.00	14 000.00
Cost per hour (£)	4.10	4.00
Fixed overheads (£)	88 500.00	85 400.00

66 Two materials are used in a chemical cracking operation. The output of final refined product, budgeted at 145 000 kg, was 8% down on budget. The usages (budgeted and actual) and the budgeted cost per unit of each material were as shown in Table 32.14.

(i) Draft a report for management identifying, as far as possible, the differences between actual and budgeted figures for the production period.
(ii) What do you understand by the term 'management by exception'?

67 Readings were taken from the distributions of weekly returns for a pair of securities.

(i) Draw the two distributions above on a sheet of graph paper using the same axes for both.
(ii) Calculate the mean, standard deviation and variance of the two distributions.
(iii) Determine which of the two distributions has the greatest standard deviation per unit of mean.
(iv) Define the concept of risk and uncertainty and outline how probability measures can assist in their measurement.

Security A		Security B	
Probability of return	Probability return	Probability of return	Percentage return
0.015	0.011	0.001	0.020
0.018	0.015	0.008	0.025
0.045	0.019	0.025	0.030
0.085	0.023	0.082	0.035
0.110	0.027	0.260	0.040
0.189	0.031	0.300	0.045
0.190	0.035	0.189	0.050
0.124	0.039	0.081	0.055
0.080	0.043	0.045	0.060
0.065	0.047	0.007	0.065
0.049	0.051	0.002	0.070
0.020	0.055		
0.010	0.059		

68 Outline the features which distinguish long-run decisions from short-run decisions. To what extent does this distinction represent reality, or an arbitrary classification for the purposes of analytical convenience?

69 Obtain the accounts of a large public company and identify its principal sources of finance. To what extent is it funded by equity capital or by debt capital? Has the firm raised any new finance during the previous year? If so, can you find any reasons why the money was required and why the firm chose to raise it in the way it did?

70 Explain what you understand by the following terms:

(i) The capital market
(ii) A security
(iii) The primary and secondary capital markets
(iv) Capital-market efficiency

71 Define the concept of the opportunity cost of capital. To what extent can the opportunity cost

Table 32.14

	Budget usage (kg)	Actual usage (kg)	Budget price (£)
Material A	90 000	87 000	24
Material B	65 000	65 000	38

of capital be likened to the opportunity cost of any other resource?

72 The minimum, average required rate of return for a firm's investors is estimated to be 12% per annum. Forty per cent of the market value of the firm's capital is attributable to the equity investors and the balance to debt holders. The equity investors require 4% more return than the debt holders. The firm wishes to finance a new project by a 10% increase in its debt capital.
Assume the following.

- The new issue will not disturb the market value of the firm's existing debt.
- The new debt will hold its market value at par.
- The market gearing ratio for the firm will rise to 0.65 following the new debt issue.
- There will be an increase in the premium which equity investors require over debt holders to 5%.

(i) On the assumption that the firm's overall cost of capital is constant through all levels of gearing, calculate the cost of equity, debt and the weighted-average cost of capital to the firm before and after the issue.
(ii) Explain the significance of all the assumptions outlined in this question.

73 Ventas has just heard about the capital asset pricing model and is extremely anxious to use the model in his portfolio management decision. He has found the following estimates of β for the following four companies:

Fama	1.35
Fisher	1.00
Jensen	0.00
Roll	0.51

The return on short-dated government stocks is 0.002% per month and the estimated market return is expected to be 0.01% per month.
Ventas believes he can predict the way the market will move in the near future and he generally tailors his investment strategy to anticipated market conditions.

(i) Plot the annual expected return for each security against its β value.
(ii) What will be the return on a portfolio of these four securities which bears 10% more risk than the market?
(iii) Which of the four securities would Ventas invest in if he expected: (a) a sudden rise in the market and (b) a sudden fall in the market.

74 The return on an all share indexed tracking fund is estimated to be 11% per annum with a standard deviation of returns of 85%. The rate of return on a risk-free investment is 6%. Calculate the distribution of funds for an investor who has £10 000 to invest, on the assumptions that (i) she wishes to bear only half the level of risk in the index and (ii) twice the level of risk than the index. She can also borrow at 6% per annum and she would like to know the expected level of return under each alternative.

75 What do you understand by the concepts of 'systematic' (or 'market') and 'unsystematic' risk? What effect does diversification have on these two types of risk?

76 Outline the assumptions necessary for net present value to measure the increase in wealth which accrues to an investor as a result of accepting an investment project.

77 Tonas Ltd produces Pacos in bulk. It is considering the installation of a new plant which would produce 10 000 Pacos per annum. The initial outlay would be £10 000, payable immediately. The plant is expected to have a life of three years and a zero scrap value at the end of that time. The following additional information is also available.

- The selling price per Paco is £1.50 during the first year, rising by 8% per annum thereafter.
- The labour cost on the new plant is £3500 for the first year, increasing at 15% thereafter.
- Other costs associated with the new plant are £7000 for the first year increasing at 20% per annum thereafter.
  The current inflation rate is 10% per annum. Tonas's opportunity cost of capital is 3% per annum in real terms.

(i) Evaluate the above project in both real and money terms.
(ii) Discuss the problems involved in handling inflation in project appraisal.

78 Melchor plc is considering two mutually exclusive projects, A and B (Table 32.15).
Melchor has a cost of capital of 10% per annum.

(i) Calculate the net present value and estimate the internal rate of return for each project and state (giving reasons) which one should be accepted.

Table 32.15

Project	t_0	t_1	t_2	t_3
Net cash flow A	(4 000)	3 000	2 000	2 000
Net cash flow B	(140 000)	70 000	30 000	80 000

(ii) Estimate, to the nearest month, the payback period for each project.

(iii) Comment upon the usefulness of the payback criterion in investment appraisal.

79 A chemical company is considering an investment in a short-term project to produce Burcolene, a wonder substance which fails to react with any known chemical. The production process is expected to operate for five years before the plant would become unsafe to use. The capital investment is £1.25 million in the first year and the net cash flows from the project would be £0.4 million per annum over the remaining five years of the project. At the end of the fifth year the plant would be dismantled and scrapped, the scrap proceeds just covering the dismantling costs incurred.

The company pays tax on its net cash flows (less tax allowances) at an average rate of 45% per annum. The company is allowed to deduct from its cash flows an allowance for the capital expenditure of one-fifth of the capital cost in each of the five years of the project's life. The tax payment is made one year after the liability for tax is incurred.

(i) Determine whether the above project is viable, assuming an opportunity cost of capital of 10% per annum.

(ii) Calculate the payback period and the discounted payback period for the above project.

(iii) Outline some of the difficulties which managers face in making long-term decisions.

80 Nueva plc is a company in the fashion industry faced with a short-term capital shortage. It is considering the projects shown in Table 31.16 for investment in 12 months (in £'000):
The capital available is limited to £2.0 million in the first year, after which funds will be freely available. Additional funds may be available in the first year at considerably higher rates of interest. Due to the nature of the industry, early market entry is vital and, consequently, investment in new projects cannot be delayed.

Assume the company's opportunity cost of capital is 10% per annum and that all projects are perfectly divisible.

(i) Calculate the net present value of each of the above projects and advise the company on their acceptability.

(ii) Determine which of the above projects should be accepted and the dual price of capital in year 1.

81 Three securities are reported to have the following average returns (capital gain plus dividend

Table 32.16

Project	t_0	t_1	t_2	t_3	t_4	t_5
A	(160)	(200)	450	150	(50)	
B	(50)	(550)		670	300	40
C	(2000)	1200	1700	300		
D	(1000)	(500)	1000	1000	1000	
E	(700)	(700)	100	1600		(50)
F	(3000)	4000				
G	(300)		500			

Table 32.17

	Average return (%)	Risk (%)
Security A	9.5	55
Security B	8.0	40
Security C	6.3	20

yield) and risk as measured by the standard deviation of returns.
The correlations of returns for the three securities are as follows:

A–B −0.95
A–C −0.25
B–C 0.89

(i) Calculate the risk and return of a portfolio consisting of equal proportions of each security.
(ii) Draw an efficient frontier using a range of combinations of the three securities (you may find a spreadsheet package useful here).

82 Plant has spent two years refining and developing a prototype navigational instrument which radically reduces the cost of hand-held ground positioning systems (GPS). This product is likely to undercut significantly the existing market which is just developing, following the launch of the final satellites to form a whole-Earth space link. Plant has taken out a series of patents securing the technology in his product, both in the UK and abroad. Further, the technology is much more reliable than that which is currently available and it can be operated off a single nickel cadmium power cell.

Plant has been in discussion with a national chain of ship chandlers who believe that they can sell 2200 units per annum of the standard model through their own catalogues at a price of £225 per unit. A large component of their sales would be made during the first three months of the year and at the Southampton Boat Show in September. The remainder would be sold equally throughout the year. The chandler would require a 30% return with a full replacement guarantee and 60 days' credit.

Plant believes that he can sell a further 600 units of a more advanced unit by mail order and at the London and Southampton Shows at a price of £275. His sales projections for the first full year of trading are shown in Table 32.18.

His materials cost is expected to be 35% of the final selling price. In addition, the business would require a stock 'float' of £4000 to be purchased in the first month of trading. Plant has negotiated 30 days' credit, on average, with his suppliers. Both the standard and advanced model have high reliability after soak testing, and only one in 400 is likely to require complete replacement. This level of replacement could be achieved within their labour capacity.

Plant's partner has helped in the development of the product and would be employed within the new business as its marketing manager. Four other employees would be necessary: three on production and one as an office manager and secretary. The production salaries, including a salary for Plant himself and employer's taxes would be:

Production employees	
one senior	£24 000 per annum
two juniors (each)	£14 500 per annum
Plant	£18 000 per annum

His partner would take a salary of £18 000 per annum and the office manager's salary would be £14 000 per annum.

Plant is well advanced in discussion with the landlords of a new science and business park attached to his old university. He has an option on a 200 square metre unit, ready partitioned at a rent of £150 per square metre including maintenance and common services. The rent would

Table 32.18

	Jan.	Feb.	Mar.	Apr.	May	Jun.	Jul.	Aug.	Sep.	Oct.	Nov.	Dec.
Chandler's sales (standard)	500	500	500	50	50	50	50	50	300	50	50	50
Own sales (advanced features)	200	20	20	20	20	20	20	20	200	20	20	20

be payable a quarter in advance. He plans to take up a 25-year lease with a five-year reversion clause from December prior to production and deliveries commencing in January. The business rates for the unit would be £4800 per annum, payable from January and quarterly in arrears.

The capital equipment would cost £280 000, including final fitting out of the premises, and some initial advertising and brochure costs would be required totalling £15 000. The capital equipment and fittings should last five years. The cost of tools and consumables would be £1400 per month, electricity and heating £600 per month and office costs a further £1200 per month (including mailing and telephone). Plant plans to produce to expected monthly demand and, during the slack parts of the year, divert efforts to product improvement and product development. Ongoing advertising will cost £1400 per month for an advertisement in the principal sailing magazines, and the cost of fitting out his Boat Show stand in January would be £3000, with £600 expenditure for the pitch each January and September subsequently.

Plant and his partner would be able to put capital of £50 000 into the project. They expect sales to grow by an average of 3% per annum and inflation on their costs can be assumed to be approximately 4% per annum. They believe that this rate can be passed into prices but no more would be sustainable without significant loss of demand to producers of the cheaper old technology.

(i) Given the above data, prepare as comprehensive a financial plan as you can, including any summarising statements of profit and loss and balance sheets as you think appropriate.
(ii) Determine the maximum financial need for this business.

83 Arabian Nights & Co. Ltd commenced their year's operations with the balance sheet shown in Table 32.19.

During the year the business engaged in the following transactions.

- New plant was purchased for £8000 and depreciation provided at one-tenth of the original cost of the asset.
- Sales of £176 000 were made, of which £16 000 were still outstanding at the end of the year. No bad debts were incurred in the year.

Table 32.19

Fixed assets		86 000
Less depreciation		20 000
		66 000
Current assets		
Stock	13 000	
Debtors	27 600	
Cash in hand	4 200	
	44 800	
Liabilities falling due within one year:		
trade creditors	37 600	
		7 200
		73 200
Long-term liabilities		50 000
		23 200
Equity capital – ordinary shares		10 000
Profit retained		13 200
		23 200

- Purchases of £65 600 were made during the year, and the outstanding payables were £31 200 at the end of the year. There was £8790 of stock on hand at the end of the year.
- Other expenses of £71 000 were incurred during the year.
- A dividend of 15p per £1 share was declared and paid during the year.
- Corporation Tax was provided at 40% of net profit, excluding depreciation but including a writing-down allowance of 25% on fixed assets purchased during the year. No allowances were available against the company's other assets.

(i) Prepare a profit and loss account and balance sheet for Arabian Nights for the year.
(ii) Calculate ratios to measure liquidity, business performance and financial risk.

84 Obtain the accounts of a large public limited company in the manufacturing sector. Prepare a full report on its financial performance and prospects using those accounts and any other information which may be available.

85 The data for NERC plc on 14 July for its Call and Put options are shown in Table 32.20.

Using the data, explain the significance of each item of data and the relationship between them.

Table 32.20

		Calls			Puts		
Option		Jul.	Oct.	Jan.	Jul.	Oct.	Jan.
NERC plc	420	13	30.5	39	7	19.5	27.5
(*425)	460	1.5	13	22	36.5	43.5	50

Table 32.21

	19x1	19x0
Sales	1 500 000	1 454 000
Cost of goods sold	788 000	780 300
Trade debtors	85 500	132 500
Trade creditors	68 560	111 000
Cash	46 550	22 760

Table 32.22

Sales	1 450 000	Fixed assets	3 200 000
Cost of goods sold			
Gross profit			
		Stock	18 760
Administrative expenses	88 000	Debtors	
Depreciation		Cash	11 540
Interest			
Audit fee	18 000		
Directors' emoluments	34 500	Short-term liabilities	
Gross profit before tax		Long-term liabilities	1 560 000
Corporation Tax			
Net profit after tax		Share capital	800 000
Dividend paid		Retained earnings	
Profit retained			

Draw a profit diagram for each option and determine if any profit opportunities exist using combinations of these various options.

86 Taking the accounts of a Times Top 100 company, prepare a thorough analysis of the latest published accounts from the point of view of:

(i) A shareholder
(ii) A major supplier
(iii) A prospective employee

In each case describe the main areas of risk to which each class of stakeholder is exposed, and the variables which are likely to dominate in their decision models.

87 An abstract from a service company's accounts reveals the information shown in Table 32.21. Assuming the company's cost of short term finance is 8% per annum, determine the debtor and creditor age and the value of debtors and creditors, adjusted for liquidity. The company has been forced to write off 5% of its outstanding debtors each year.

88 The information from a set of company accounts is shown in Table 32.22. Complete the accounts using the supplementary information provided.

- The gross profit margin for the business is 45%.
- The average age of the fixed assets is 3.5 years.
- The average depreciation period is 10 years.
- The average debtor age is 14 days. All sales are on credit.
- The acid test ratio is 0.95.
- The long-term liabilities bear interest at 7% (gross).
- A provision for Corporation Tax should be made at 40% of gross profit.
- The cover ratio on dividends is 200%.

89 For the above business, calculate its gearing ratio (capital and earnings), its return on capital employed and on equity, its current asset and acid test ratios.

Bibliography

Summary

We offer here a series of additional readings which will help you develop the subject of strategic accounting further. The readings are organised in alphabetical order and represent a first 'reference' library for you in this subject area.

Arnold, J., and Scapens, R.W., The British contribution to opportunity cost theory, in Bromwich, M., and Hopwood, A. (eds), *Essays in British Accounting Research*, Pitman, 1981

One of an excellent set of articles examining a long tradition of management accounting research in the UK.

Ashton, D., Agency theory and contracts of employment, in Ashton, D., Hopper, T. and Scapens, R.W. (eds), *Issues in Management Accounting*, Prentice Hall International, Englewood Cliffs, 1991

Ashton, D., Hopper, T. and Scapens, R.W. (eds), *Issues in Management Accounting*, Prentice Hall International, Englewood Cliffs, 1991

Chapters 1 and 2 discuss the modern history of management accounting in a contextual way.

Bhide, A., Bootstrap finance – the art of start-ups, *Harvard Business Review*, **70** (6), 109–117, 1992

This article gives an interesting insight into the problems of starting and sustaining a business without substantial initial financial support. It also advocates a strongly opportunistic approach to management.

Black, F. and Scholes, M., The pricing of options and corporate liabilities, *Journal of Political Economy*, **81**, 673–654, 1973

This is *the* article on option pricing. The easy bits are at the beginning and the end. The middle relies upon the solution of partial differential equations.

Brearley, R. and Myers, S.C., *Principles of Corporate Finance*, 4th edition, McGraw-Hill, 1991

This would be our choice for a follow-on text from this one in the area of finance. It is a clear and readable exposition of the subject which imparts a fully professional level of expertise in the subject.

Carsberg, B. and Hope, A., *Business Investment Decisions under Inflation*, The Institute of Chartered Accountants, 1976

An influential empirical study, somewhat dated now, which examined the investment appraisal practices of 100 top UK firms. What is surprising is how many got it wrong.

Clarke, R. and McGuiness, T. (eds), *The Economics of the Firm*, Blackwell, 1987

An excellent review of the agency and transactions cost economics approaches to the firm.

Coase, R.M., The Nature of the Firm, *Economica*, **4**, 386–405, 1937

Cooper, D., A social and organisational view of management accounting, in Bromwich, M. and Hopwood, A. (eds), *Essays in British Accounting Research*, Pitman, 1981

Cooper, R. and Kaplan, R.S., *The Design of Cost Management Systems – text, cases and readings*. Prentice Hall International, 1991

A comprehensive reference work to the issues in costing within manufacturing systems, with some excellent case material on activity-based costing.

Gordon, M., *The Investment, Financing and Valuation of the Corporation*, Irwin, 1962

This book develops the dividend growth model for the valuation of equities.

Kay, J., *Foundations of Corporate Success*, Oxford University Press, Oxford, 1993

A scholar's view of why firm's succeed, with a wealth of case histories and anecdotes to support a rigorous analysis of the economics of firms. Chapter 13 is an excellent review of the valuation of competitive advantage and the role of accounting in that process.

Parker, R.H., History of accounting for decisions, in Arnold, J., Carsberg, B. and Scapens, R. (eds), *Topics in Management Accounting*, Phillip Allan, 1980

A brief discussion of the background to the decision-orientated approach to accounting which is a precursor to the strategic accounting approach.

Porter, M.E., Towards a dynamic theory of strategy, *Strategic Management Journal*, **12**, 95–117, 1991

A very effective summary of Porter's theoretical developments in strategy including his 'five forces' and 'value chain model' – indeed, the 'bluffers guide' to Porter.

Pratt, J.W. and Zeckhauser, R.J., *Principal and Agents – the structure of business*, Harvard Business School Press, 1991

An excellent survey of the agency literature. In particular, the reading by R. C. Clark, (Agency costs versus fiduciary issues, pp. 55–80) explains the critical role of directors within organisations.

Ryan, R.J., Scapens, R.W. and Theobald, M., *Research Methods and Methodology in Finance and Accounting*, Academic Press, London, 1992

This book gives a brief review of some of the philosophical issues in financial theory, as well as three chapters on the history and development of thought in financial accounting, managerial accounting and finance.

Slater, J., *The Zulu Principle*, Orion, 1993

An interesting, non-theoretical approach to investment, with some sensible advice on the interpretation of company accounts by one of the masters of investment.

Smith, Jr, C.W., *The Modern Theory of Corporate Finance*, 2nd edition, McGraw-Hill, 1990

An excellent set of readings in corporate finance which, along with Brearley and Myers, gives an excellent coverage of the subject. This book also contains a seminal article by M. C. Jensen, and W. H. Meckling (The theory of the firm, managerial behaviour, agency costs and ownership structure, pp. 82–137) on agency theory.

Smith, T., *Accounting for Growth*, Century Publishing, 1992

The 'book they tried to ban'. A professional financial analyst with UBS Phillips and Drew writing in a very clear and persuasive way about the manipulative practices of some major British firms in preparing their financial reports.

Stacey, R.D., *Strategic Management and Organisational Dynamics*, Pitman, 1993

An excellent strategy textbook which supplements this text very well.

Stancill, J.M., When is there cash in cash flow? *Harvard Business Review*, May–June, 1986 (reprinted in *Getting Numbers You can Trust – the new accounting*, A Harvard Business Review Paperback Harvard Business School Press, 1991, pp. 87–94.

Tomkins, C., *Corporate Resource Allocation*, Blackwell, 1991

One of the most successful recent attempts to integrate accounting and financial thinking into a strategic framework.

Williamson, O.E., Strategising, economising and economic organisation, *Strategic Management Journal*, **12**, 75–94, 1991

A superb but difficult article encapsulating Williamson's approach to strategy.

Yoshikawa, T., Innes, J., Mitchell, F. and Tanaka, M., *Contemporary Cost Management*, Chapman and Hall, 1993

Not particularly contemporary, but does explore a range of cost accounting issues in a manufacturing context.

Index